Tort Law
for Paralegals

Tort Law
for Paralegals

George E. Guay, III

Robert Cummins, Esq.

Prentice Hall

Boston   Columbus   Indianapolis   New York   San Francisco   Upper Saddle River
Amsterdam   Cape Town   Dubai   London   Madrid   Milan   Munich   Paris   Montreal   Toronto
Delhi   Mexico City   Sao Paulo   Sydney   Hong Kong   Seoul   Singapore   Taipei   Tokyo

Editor in Chief: Vernon Anthony
Senior Acquisitions Editor: Gary Bauer
Editorial Assistant: Megan Heintz
Director of Marketing: David Gesell
Marketing Manager: Leigh Ann Sims
Marketing Assistant: Les Roberta
Senior Managing Editor: JoEllen Gohr
Project Manager: Christina Taylor
Senior Operations Supervisor: Pat Tonneman
Art Director: Diane Ernsberger
Manager, Rights and Permissions, Image Resource Center: Zina Arabia

Image Permission Coordinator: Angelique Sharps
Cover Art: Royalty Free/Corbis/Jupiter Images; Studio DL/Art Life Images; Dream Pictures/Blend Images/Jupiter Images
Full-Service Project Management: Elm Street Publishing Services
Composition: Integra Software Services Pvt. Ltd.
Printer/Binder: Edwards Brothers, Inc.
Cover Printer: Coral Graphics
Text Font: Goudy

Credits and acknowledgments borrowed from other sources and reproduced, with permission, in this textbook appear on appropriate page within text.

Photo Credits: Chapter 1: Brand X Pictures; Chapter 2: Corbis; Chapter 3: Getty Images; Chapter 4: Corbis; Chapter 5: Brand X Pictures; Chapter 6: Brand X Pictures; Chapter 7: Superstock; Chapter 8: Superstock; Chapter 9: Getty Images; Chapter 10: Superstock; Chapter 11: Corbis; Chapter 12: Brand X Pictures; Chapter 13: Superstock; Chapter 14: Corbis.

Library of Congress Cataloging-in-Publication Data
Guay, George E., III.
Tort law for paralegals / George E. Guay, III. — 1st ed.
  p. cm.
Includes bibliographical references and index.
ISBN 0-13-500055-6 (alk. paper)
1. Torts—United States.   2. Legal assistants—United States.   I. Title.
KF1250.G83 2010
346.7303—dc22   2008051649

Prentice Hall
is an imprint of

www.pearsonhighered.com

10 9 8 7 6 5 4 3 2
ISBN-10:   0-13-500055-6
ISBN-13: 978-0-13-500055-7

PREFACE

When teaching a class in tort law, I've often told students that many law firms regard tort law as "meat and potatoes," the kind of steady work that can sustain a law practice. For example, given our mobile society, automobile accidents occur frequently. Because an accident can result in injuries, the injured party will often need help to recover the expenses involved in treating the injury, such as medical expenses and for pain and suffering. That's when the injured party may need the help of a lawyer who can then rely on an educated paralegal to best serve the interests of the client.

Tort law focuses on the losses incurred by an injured party. A lawyer helping that injured party may rely on an educated paralegal to:

- gather information in an interview or through correspondence;
- prepare memos for lawyers to understand the state of the law about a particular tort;
- draft legal documents, such as the complaint or motions; and
- manage the pre-trial activities prior to trial or settlement.

To serve a legal practice effectively, a paralegal has to know more than just the definition of a tort. The paralegal needs to understand how to apply that definition. If the defendant files a motion to dismiss, will the paralegal know what information to gather so as to defeat that motion? What about an opponent's filing of a summary judgment, which assumes that if all the facts as alleged are true, the client has failed to make a claim as a matter of law? Knowing tort law means that a paralegal can appreciate the litigation process.

The paralegal needs to be able to recognize what facts are needed and, most importantly, how those facts can support the claim. Studying the components of torts enables a paralegal to recognize what information matters, the facts that will make it possible to serve the client's interest.

This text goes beyond developing an understanding about the components of torts. Paralegals need to show why certain facts, when applied to the law, lead to a particular outcome. The hypothetical problems in each chapter will challenge the reader to identify relevant facts so as to determine a particular result under the law. In this way, you will see how a problem in tort law is resolved in "the real world." And that means being well prepared to get paid to do such work.

■ ORGANIZATION

In these fourteen chapters, readers will develop a practical understanding of tort law. Chapter 1 provides an overview of tort law, signaling what readers can expect in the text. Then in Chapter 2, readers will learn how a claim may be resolved through use of the legal process, from initial client contact, to filing suit, to addressing pretrial activities like the filing of motions to dismiss or for summary judgment, to trial, and on to appeal. Also, readers will discover that litigation is the exception, not the rule; most matters get resolved through settlement or the use of a noncourt-based problem-solving approach like mediation or arbitration.

In Chapters 3 through 5, readers will study the tort of negligence. Readers will see what comprises this tort (perhaps the most common tort), consider issues of proof, and anticipate what defenses exist that may partly or completely negate a defendant's liability. Chapter 6 deals with premises liability, on establishing a landholder's liability in negligence for someone who has slipped and fallen on the property. Chapter 7 leads readers in an exploration of intentional torts, which are quite distinct from the tort of negligence. Readers will learn about critical issues regarding intentional torts, such as what needs to be shown in court to prove that the tort occurred and why a society, through the availability of defenses, would excuse otherwise tortious conduct. Chapter 8 focuses on misrepresentation, interference with economic relations, and other business-related torts.

The concept of nuisance, public and private, serves as the focus of Chapter 9. In Chapter 10, readers will explore defenses, involving circumstances where liability would be excused, as a matter of law. Chapter 11 emphasizes privilege and immunity as circumstances where society has, as a matter of policy, decided to excuse liability. Strict liability is the focus of Chapter 12. In Chapter 13, readers learn about product liability, which can involve all legal theories for recovery in negligence, strict liability, as an intentional tort, and even contract law. Chapter 14 considers liability of someone who has designated another to serve that person's interests, when liability has arisen.

Chapter Features

Each chapter opens with a short quote that sets the tone for examining that chapter's subject matter. Chapter topics at the beginning of every chapter outline the topics considered under the broader scope of the chapter. Every course includes objectives, so the chapter objectives describe the goals for readers after a careful examination of each chapter's content.

Every chapter has Cases in Point, which explore a legal concept within the context of an actual case. These cases give readers a sense of how people, in many kinds of situations, suffer injury. Not only do courts continue to determine whether the plaintiff should recover damages; also they, continue to use case law as a means of shaping tort law to address new problems.

Regular commentary in every chapter comes from a trio of treatises. *The Restatement (Second) of Torts* reflects the work of scholars at the American Legal Institute, whose mission has been to create documents that encompass the best understanding of the law, also known as, "black letter" law. *The Restatement (Second) of Torts* has undergone some revision. Most significantly, the topic of product liability has become new *Restatement of Product Liability*, an area of intense tort litigation over the past few decades.

Hornbooks are standard references used by practitioners. (They are called hornbooks because to make the covers, animal horn was softened in water so that it unfolded and was wrapped around the text; other types of coverings wear out too quickly because of the frequent use of these references.) *Prosser & Keaton on Torts* is a standard in the field, although it has not been revised since 1984. Its true successor is *Dobbs on Torts*, which was updated in 2007.

Each chapter ends with key terms, a summary, and concept review questions designed to provide readers with a recap of the material presented in the chapter. Thereafter follows a series of critical thinking applications, which are hypothetical problems readers can use to apply what they've learned in the chapter. Finally, readers will find a skill-building application that provides an opportunity to engage in a "hands-on" analysis of a problem set that relates to the material presented in the chapter.

The text ends with materials that can assist a reader in gaining a better understanding of tort law: a glossary, table of cases, table of references to the *Restatements*, and an index.

Readers should come away from this text with an appreciation of the fundamental principles and concepts of tort law. Readers will find that the text provides them with guidance and insight about a dynamic area of the law, one that has always played a critical role attempting to create and sustain an ordered society.

■ STUDENT RESOURCES

Companion Website

Students can access a wealth of study aids at www.prenhall.com/Guay. The online Companion Website includes the following: chapter learning objectives, test-prep quizzes for each chapter with immediate feedback, web exercises for each chapter, and online resource links to additional websites.

■ INSTRUCTOR RESOURCES

To access supplementary materials online, instructors need to request an instructor access code. Go to **www.pearsonhighered.com/irc,** where you can register for an instructor access code. Within 48 hours of registering you will receive a confirming e-mail including an instructor access code. Once you have received your code, locate your text in the online catalog and click on the Instructor Resources button on the left side of the catalog product page. Select a supplement and a log in page will appear. Once you have logged in, you can access instructor material for all Prentice Hall textbooks.

Instructor's Manual

The instructor's manual, written by George Guay, contains sample syllabi, chapter outline and summary, answers to end of chapter exercises, and teaching notes.

Test Generator

The Test Generator allows you to generate quizzes and tests composed on questions from the Test Item File, modify them, and add your own.

PowerPoint Lecture Presentation

The PowerPoint Lecture Presentation package provides screens outlining key concepts discussed in each chapter.

CourseConnect Online Tort Law Course

Looking for robust online course content to reinforce and enhance your student learning? We have the solution: CourseConnect! CourseConnect courses contain customizable modules of content mapped to major learning outcomes. Each learning object contains interactive tutorials, rich media, discussion questions, MP3 downloadable lectures, assessments, and interactive activities that address different learning styles. CourseConnect Courses follow a consistent 21-step instructional design process, yet each course is developed individually by instructional designers and instructors who have taught the course online. Test questions, created by assessment professionals, were developed at all levels of Blooms Taxonomy. When you buy a CourseConnect course, you purchase a complete package that provides you with detailed documentation you can use for your accreditation reviews. CourseConnect courses can be delivered in any commercial platform such as **WebCT, BlackBoard, Angel, Moodle,** or **e-College** platforms. For more information contact your representative or call 800-635-1579.

■ ACKNOWLEDGMENTS

This textbook builds on the scholarly work of Professor Robert Cummins, Esq. His views regarding tort law have served as means of continuing a discussion about the nature of tort law, in the context of a class. From his work, this book flows.

I wish to thank the reviewers of the manuscript for their insights and comments that helped refine the presentation, including:

Nashiba Boyd, Central Carolina Technical College

Cathy Underwood, Pulaski Technical College

Elaine S. Lerner, Kaplan University

Heidi K. Koeneman, Ivy Tech Community College

Lisa Newcity, Roger Williams University

Jennifer Jenkins, South College

Prentice Hall earns my gratitude for providing me with the opportunity to satisfy a passion for writing about the law. My editor, Gary Bauer, provided the guidance necessary for seeing this project to fruition, ably assisted by Kevin Happell, Katie Rowland and Megan Heintz. My thanks to them and all at Prentice Hall who can make a group project like writing a text seem like an individual effort; they made a manuscript into a text. Nothing would have happened without them.

I would also want to acknowledge the "binding forces" in my private universe—Anne, Jane, Octavia, and Ramona—without whom I'd have no chance at all for completing this kind of project.

George Guay

CONTENTS

CHAPTER 3

The Tort of Negligence   81

CHAPTER 4

Proof of Negligence   119

CHAPTER 8

Misrepresentation, Interference with Economic Relations, and Other Business-Related Torts   289

The law can ask no better justification than the deepest instincts of man.

—*Justice Oliver Wendell Holmes*

Foundations of Tort Law | CHAPTER 1

A study of the law of torts begins with a definition of the term *tort*, along with an appreciation of the history of tort law and an understanding of its place in American jurisprudence. To fully understand the tort concept, the paralegal student must understand the categories of tort law and have a fundamental knowledge of its sources.

CHAPTER TOPICS

1. Tort Defined
2. History
3. Evolution
4. Purpose
5. Categories

OBJECTIVES

After completing this chapter, you will be able to:

1. Define the basic concept of tort law.
2. Discuss the history of torts.
3. Understand the sources of tort law.
4. Summarize the purposes behind the law of torts.
5. List the various categories of tort law.

■ TORT DEFINED

The term *tort* refers to a violation of a civil rule of conduct causing injury to another. Thus, a **tort** is a civil wrong resulting in injury to the person or property of another. It is any civil wrong that infringes on an individual's private rights (see box below).

WHAT IS A TORT?

A tort is conduct that amounts to a legal wrong and that causes harm for which courts will impose civil liability.

The essence of tort is the defendant's potential for civil liability to the victim for harmful wrongdoing and, correspondingly, the victim's potential for compensation or other relief.

Dobbs, *The Law of Torts* §1 (2000)

The term originates from the Latin term *torquere*, meaning "to twist." The twisting is the bending of the rules of proper human behavior resulting in harm to another person.

An individual's private rights are the enjoyment of one's property and the maintenance of one's physical well-being. The infringement may be through an act or omission, or as the result of careless behavior. The intentional or unintentional behavior that results in harm to another is called **tortious conduct,** or conduct that is harmful to another's individual rights.

The parties to a tort action consist of the **plaintiff,** the party to a lawsuit that commences the action, and the **defendant,** the party in a lawsuit against whom an action has been brought. The plaintiff in a tort action is the party that has sustained an injury to person or property. The defendant to a tort action is the wrongdoer, the party responsible for tortious conduct.

The wrongdoer, the person whose behavior resulted in injury to another, is referred to as the **tortfeasor.** The "feasor" part of the term comes from the Latin *facere* meaning "to make or do." Thus, the term refers to one who does a tort. The following case considers the concept of the tortfeasor. Here, the court has to determine whether the plaintiff has set forth a claim so strong, that as a matter of law, the defendant should be found liable (see Case in Point 1-1).

CASE IN POINT 1-1

Ross v. Allstate Insurance Co.

40 Va. Cir. 537 (1996)

[...]

Plaintiff Barbara Ross was a passenger in an automobile that was involved in an accident on December 19, 1993. As a result, Plaintiff sustained serious physical injuries. Among other expenses, Plaintiff had approximately $70,000 in emergency medical expenses. The car in which Plaintiff was riding was struck from the rear by a car driven by Kevin Dawson. At the time of the accident, Dawson was insured under an automobile liability insurance policy with Defendant, Allstate.

In April of 1995, Allstate paid Plaintiff the limits of the liability portion of the policy. In exchange, Plaintiff executed a "Release of All Claims." This release did not include any claim Plaintiff might make under the "Supplemental Payments" portion of the policy for the emergency medical expenses attributed to this accident. The pertinent part of the policy states that Allstate will pay for:

(c) expenses incurred by the insured for such immediate medical and surgical relief to others as shall be imperative at the time of an automobile accident insured hereunder and not due to war [emphasis added](sic).

Plaintiff made a claim under this provision, and Allstate refused payment. She now sues under this "Supplemental Payments" provision.

Allstate has moved for summary judgment on the ground that this provision does not cover claims by third parties (as opposed to insureds).

Analysis

The premise of the defense is that this provision does not cover claims made by the Plaintiff but is limited to reimbursement to the tortfeasor/insured for expenses incurred by him. Allstate points to the phrase "incurred by the insured." Kevin Dawson was the insured. Allstate argues that Mr. Dawson incurred no emergency medical expenses to aid others and it would only be his out-of-pocket expenses that could be reimbursed under this provision. To support this position, Allstate cites cases from other jurisdictions interpreting identical or similar provisions in other policies which conclude that Plaintiff cannot recover. (citations omitted)

[...]

The cases cited by Allstate support its position. Some of those cases were based on policies containing similar or identical language to the one in dispute here. They are persuasive on the issue of whether this provision was designed and intended to cover claims such as this one. However, they do not deal with the argument raised in this case; namely, that the insured incurred the expenses by assuming liability for the accident.

Since no Virginia cases have been found addressing the policy language in dispute or the argument advanced by Plaintiff, this Court will now turn its attention to the interpretation of this language.

[...]

As stated above, the basic argument advanced by Plaintiff is that when the insured became liable for the accident, he incurred the emergency medical expenses of parties injured in the accident. The question for the Court to answer, then, is what exactly does an individual "incur" when he or she becomes liable in an accident.

The basis for imposing liability upon a person in a situation such as this is found in that body of law known as tort. A person who negligently causes an accident, thereby becoming liable, is said to be a tortfeasor. A tort is a "private or civil wrong or injury...for which the court will provide a remedy in the form of an action for damages." (citation omitted). Therefore, when a person is found liable for a tort, whether through a jury verdict or a settlement, his or her liability is in the form of damages.

Damages are "pecuniary compensation or indemnity, which may be recovered in the courts by any person who has suffered loss, detriment, or injury, whether to his person, property, or rights, through the unlawful act or omission of another." (citation omitted). Compensation is "[t]hat which is necessary to restore an injured party to his former position." (citation omitted). Indemnity is "[r]eimbursement...the compensation given to make a person whole from a loss already sustained." (citation omitted). Therefore, when a person is liable for a tortious act, he or she must pay damages in the amount necessary to make the injured party whole.

The liability incurred by the tortfeasor, Dawson, was not to pay Plaintiff's medical bills, but to make her whole. If Plaintiff had incurred medical bills, she still would have had a cause of action against Dawson. By incurring the liability for the accident, Dawson does not incur liability for Plaintiff's medical bills. Had Plaintiff not paid the bills herself, the doctors would have no cause of action against Dawson directly. Dawson's liability is to reimburse Plaintiff for her injuries. Damages may be calculated, in part, by adding together medical bills, but Dawson is not liable to pay those medical bills directly.

Conclusion

Plaintiff is correct that the term "incurred" includes the legal obligation to pay a debt as well as the actual payment of a debt. However, the debt Dawson became legally obligated to pay here is not the emergency medical expenses charged by the doctors, but the damages suffered by the Plaintiff. Dawson's liability insurance policy has a limit as to these kinds of damages, and that limit has been reached. As such, Plaintiff has no further recourse under this policy. The provision in question does not afford Plaintiff the remedy beyond the policy limits of $25,000. Summary Judgment is awarded to Allstate Insurance Company.

In trying to resolve the issue here, the court looked at prior court decisions as well as to the "plain meaning" of the insurance coverage. The defendant Dawson, who drove the car that hit the car in which the plaintiff Ross was a passenger, had his insurance company pay up to the limits on his automobile insurance policy. Once Ross had signed a release of claims, she then had no legal basis for seeking payment for emergency medical expenses.

Legal scholars have attempted for centuries to define the term *tort*. Most efforts at defining the term describe what a tort is *not*. A tort has been defined as something that is "not a contract" and as something that is "not a crime." Contracts are agreements that parties have formed that are enforceable at law. A crime is considered an offense against the public, while a tort is considered an offense against an individual. An understanding of what a tort *is not* is of some value in appreciating its nature, but paralegal students are best served by understanding what a tort *is*.

Civil versus Criminal Legal Proceedings

While a civil action in tort seeks to hold a defendant liable for injuries to a plaintiff, a criminal action seeks to hold a defendant liable for breaching the orderliness of society. While a crime might have an identifiable victim, an act is criminal because of the way that it can contribute to a perception about safety. People who don't feel safe find their attentions drawn away from working at a job and maintaining a family, activities possible when there is order, which would give rise to a stable society (see box below).

TORT AND CRIME

The relationship between tort law and criminal law is largely explained by their respective purposes. The purpose of criminal punishment is primarily to vindicate the state's interests in deterring crime and imposing justice. The purpose of tort liability is in no way inconsistent, but its emphasis is different. It is primarily to vindicate the individual victim and the victim's rights and secondarily to confirm and reinforce public standards of behavior.

Dobbs, *The Law of Torts* §2 (2000)

So if a bar patron is fighting and takes a beer mug, swings and breaks it in the face of someone who just happened to be sitting there, that person may sue the patron individual in civil law for **damages** as compensation for any injuries sustained. Local law enforcement will want to get involved when the bar patron feels that it is acceptable to use beer mugs as weapons.

Civil and criminal law differ besides who suffers because of a defendant's actions. Only in a criminal action may a defendant be sentenced to prison. And since that is so grave a penalty, the amount of proof—or evidence—needed to gain a conviction is more than what's needed to establish liability under a civil action. Table 1-1 lays out the ways in which these legal actions materially differ.

Table 1-1 Differences between Actions in Civil Law and in Criminal Law

	Civil law	Criminal law
Burden of Proof	Preponderance of the evidence	Beyond a reasonable doubt
Penalty	Damages	Imprisonment, community-based supervised release; fines
Parties	Individual (most commonly), government	Government only

History of Tort Law

An understanding of the evolution of the law of torts begins with an appreciation of the role of natural law. A natural law is a fundamental legal principle that is essential to an ordered social existence. Natural law forms the rules that dictate socially unacceptable human behavior. The English common law was founded on principles dictated by natural law. As the social order evolved from agrarian to urban and from regional to national, legal principles were adapted accordingly.

Tort law originated in the **English common law.** Common law developed through the decisions of the courts of England over many centuries. It served as the foundation of many principles and rules under the legal philosophy, or jurisprudence, in America today (see box below).

ORIGINS OF TORT LAW

The early common law was based upon decisions by judges developed gradually in England after the Norman Conquest. Local lords or the courts they controlled decided some cases, but the medieval English King as the chief feudal lord claimed the right to decide cases involving property rights and the "King's peace."

Dobbs, *The Law of Torts* §14 (2000)

Tort law preceded criminal law in permitting vengeance by individuals for personal wrongs. Personal revenge was later replaced by a system of monetary compensation, becoming the first recovery of damages for tort (see box on next page).

AIMS OF TORT LAW

Tort law is at least partly rights-based. That is, it is at least partly based on ideals of corrective justice, ideals of righting wrongs, or (somewhat relatedly) ideals about accountability or personal responsibility for harm-causing conduct.

Dobbs, *The Law of Torts* §9 (2000)

Courts and writers almost always recognize that another aim of tort law is to deter certain kinds of conduct by imposing liability when that conduct causes harm. The idea of deterrence is not so much that an individual, having been held liable for a tort, would thereafter conduct himself better. It is rather the idea that all persons, recognizing potential tort liability, would tend to avoid conduct that could lead to tort liability.

Dobbs, *The Law of Torts* §11 (2000)

In his learned treatise on the law of torts, Professor Keeton acknowledges that the principle underlying the evolution of tort law is the concept of socially responsible conduct (see box below).

PROSSER AND KEETON ON TORTS, SOCIAL RESPONSIBILITY

So far as there is one central idea, it would seem that it is that liability must be based upon conduct which is socially unreasonable. The common thread woven into all torts is the idea of unreasonable interference with the interest of others.

W. Page Keeton et al., *Prosser & Keeton on the Law of Torts* at 6 (5th ed., 1984)

The law of torts is rooted specifically in the thirteenth-century concept of **trespass.** At that time trespass was considered any serious breach of the King's peace by act of force or violence that resulted in injury to person or property. The modern version of trespass now most often narrowly deals with interfering with an owner's use of property.

To obtain redress for such a breach, the victim petitioned the King's court through a formal process by submitting a **writ.** Writs are still used in many of our modern systems of civil procedure as a form of petition to a court (see box below).

WRITS

The writs were stylized documents or forms containing certain words that remained more or less the same from case to case. Lawyers and judges naturally called these writs by a short name based on that commonly used language. Certain early writs, all in Latin, asserted a claim that defendant had transgressed by force and violence. An English word for "transgress" was *trespass,* as these writs were called writs of trespass. The trespass writ developed several subject forms.

Dobbs, *The Law of Torts* §14 (2000)

Two writs were available to the victim of a breach of the King's peace. The writ of trespass existed for a breach of the King's peace by a direct and forceful act causing injury to the victim's person or property. The writ of trespass evolved into the contemporary body of law involving intentional torts (discussed in Chapter 5). The writ of **trespass on the case** existed for a breach of the King's peace in the form of a wrongful act indirectly causing an injury. Trespass on the case was the forerunner of our modern concept of negligence, where redress is sought on the basis of fault (See Chapter 3). The redress provided by the King's court was in the form of monetary damages compensating the victim for the loss or injury and punishing the wrongdoer (see Case in Point 1-2).

CASE IN POINT 1-2

Mueller v. Brunn

105 Wis.2d 171 (1982)

...The plaintiffs, Albert R. Mueller and Delores J. Mueller, his wife, hereinafter plaintiffs, have petitioned for review of a decision of the court of appeals which reversed an order of the trial court and directed that the plaintiffs' action against the Town of Vernon be dismissed. We reverse the court of appeals.

The plaintiffs, who are property owners in Waukesha county, commenced an action alleging that Donald B. Brunn and Marion F. Brunn, his wife, the vendors of the property purchased by plaintiffs, made material misrepresentations because they stated that they had no knowledge of any defects in respect to the adequacy and quality of the well, while, in fact, plaintiffs allege, the sellers had notice of salt contamination prior to the execution of the real estate contract...

...Trespass on the case is the ancestor of the present day action for negligence where problems of legal and factual cause arise.

In this case, the Muellers did have a basis in tort law, for misrepresentation, against the Brunns regarding their awareness of contamination of a well. Therefore, their lawsuit to recover damages could proceed.

Recovery for injury to an individual's person and property turned from the ancient writs toward a system of recovery based upon the dual concepts of intentional torts and negligence. These concepts allowed compensation for many more wrongs than had been contemplated by the ancient writs. As we will see in subsequent chapters, the nature of recovery for tort continues to change and expand along with our modern society (see Case in Point 1-3).

CASE IN POINT 1-3

Waller v. First Savings & Trust Co.

103 Fla. 1025 (1931)

The facts upon which this suit is based, as disclosed by the allegations of the declaration, are most unusual, and, so far as we know, unprecedented in this state.

The declaration alleges that on April 24, 1930, the plaintiff and his wife were residing in a dwelling in Hillsborough county, owned by the plaintiff, and that on said date one John Hodasz, for whose estate the defendant had been appointed administrator, intentionally injured and damaged said dwelling house by placing a bomb, or other high explosive, underneath or near to said residence, and had willfully and intentionally caused the same to be exploded, with the intention of injuring and damaging the plaintiff, and that such explosion did damage the plaintiff's dwelling house to the amount of $3,000. The declaration further alleges that, in addition to injuring said dwelling house, the said Hodasz caused plaintiff to suffer other pecuniary damage and loss, in that the explosion inflicted very serious injuries upon the plaintiff's wife, necessitating the amputation of her left leg between the ankle and the knee, seriously injuring her right leg and causing the loss of sight in one eye, and injuring her right arm and hand so that she cannot use them, and so maiming her that she will be practically an invalid the balance of her life, rendering it impossible for her to perform the duties of a wife, and thereby depriving plaintiff of her companionship and services, and making it necessary that he have some one with her at all times to wait upon her. That plaintiff was forced to expend $800 for hospital bills for the treatment of his wife, and that he will be required to expend other large sums for her care and treatment in the future. The declaration further alleges that after the commission of said wrongful act, the said John Hodasz died, and that the First Savings and Trust Company of Tampa, a corporation, was duly appointed administrator of his estate and duly qualified, and is now acting as such administrator. The action was brought against said corporation as administrator of the estate of John Hodasz, and claimed damages in the sum of $50,000 [...]

The theory of the English common law is that a tort action is to be regarded as punitive in character, while under the intendment of the Declaration of Rights contained in the Florida Constitution, there is recognized and preserved in organic language a legal remedy for tortious wrongs, with a provision that the courts shall always be open to afford that remedy to the person wronged, the effect of which is to change the nature of tort actions as recognized in our legal system, from that of an action almost wholly punitive, to one largely remedial, in character.

While there seemed to be no question of fact that Hodasz had set off a bomb that injured the Wallers, the court recognized that the Wallers had a right under the state constitution to seek compensation for their injuries. The fact of the language in the state constitution, allowing for suit to gain compensation for damages, meant that actions in tort no longer focused only on punishing defendants and discouraging others from engaging in this unacceptable conduct but allowed for a recovery in damages.

The paralegal student must understand how the common-law roots of tort law continue to influence contemporary court decisions. Common law remains as the single most significant source of today's tort law. These principles of common-law tort are modified in many instances by courts and legislatures to meet the demands of a complex technological society. While the law needs to keep pace with the values of society by constantly redefining acceptable social conduct, common law continues as the foundation for a modern system of tort recovery. When courts recognized the need at common law for an action in tort for battery (defined as 'an uncontested touching'), those courts did not likely anticipate how battery may occur all the time during business hours on a subway system and more importantly, that people would accept crowding as just part of the opportunity to take public transportation to get to work.

Sources of Tort Law

Constitutions

A **constitution** is the highest law of a jurisdiction. It establishes the form for the organization of government and provides for the rights and privileges of the citizens it protects. The United States Constitution is the written instrument that forms our Union and establishes the fundamental law of the United States. Each state has its own constitution to provide for the organization of the state government and protect the individual rights and freedoms of the state's citizens. The individual rights guaranteed by the U.S. Constitution or any of the state constitutions are the very rights that tort law seeks to protect. A right that originates in a constitution and protection in the law of torts is called a **constitutional tort.** For example, § 1983 of Title 43 of the United States Code provides a civil tort action remedy for any person who has been deprived of his or her individual rights as set forth in the U.S. Constitution and its Amendments (see box below).

---

42 U.S.C. § 1983

§ 1983. Civil action for deprivation of rights

Every person who, under color of any statute, ordinance, regulation, custom, or usage, of any State or Territory or the District of Columbia, subjects, or causes to be subjected, any citizen of the United States or other person within the jurisdiction thereof to the deprivation of any rights, privileges, or immunities secured by the Constitution and laws, shall be liable to the party injured in an action at law, suit in equity, or other proper proceeding for redress.

The federal statute provides a cause of action for any citizen of this country for any deprivation of rights guaranteed by the U.S. Constitution. So if someone is the target of injury because of ethnicity, religion, sex or race, a federal law exists to provide for recovery when that person has been deprived of the use of rights provided in the U.S. Constitution.

Statutes

A **statute** is a formal written act of a legislative body that creates a law. Enactments of the U.S. Congress form the body of federal statutes found in the United States Code. The legislative acts of the individual states can be found in each state's statutes. Acts of Congress and the state legislatures must comply with the principles established by their respective constitutions. Federal law and individual state statutes express principles of tort law. An example of this can be seen in the modification of the tort principle of sovereign immunity (discussed in Chapter 11). While the U.S. government cannot be sued without its permission according to the principle of governmental immunity, the Federal Tort Claims Act enacted in 1946 established certain conditions under which the federal government may be sued for tort.

Today, the United States Congress and the legislatures of the individual states have enacted many statutes that either embody the common law or modify it to meet contemporary needs.

Since the landmark ruling of Chief Justice John Marshall in the case of *Marbury v. Madison,* 5 U.S. (1 Cranch) 137 (1803), the Federal courts have exercised the power of **judicial review.** Judicial review is the power of a court to review legislative enactments to determine their validity. It enables courts to interpret the meaning of statutes dealing with the law of torts in light of common law principles superimposed upon the realities of our modern society.

Case Law

Case law is made up of court decisions issued by appellate courts reviewing the decisions of lower courts. Also referred to as the **common law**—to distinguish it from statutory law—it is made up of the court decisions that form the principles and rules of proper behavior relating to the government and its citizens. As applied to the law of torts, case law also contributes to those principles or rules that apply to actions for redress of civil wrongs resulting in injury to an individual's person or property.

■ CATEGORIES OF TORTS

Tort law provides a civil remedy for injuries. The remedy is in the form of a **cause of action,** which is the legal right of the injured party to bring a lawsuit against the wrongdoer. The goal of tort law is to assign financial responsibility, referred to as **liability,** to the tortfeasor for tortious conduct that has resulted in injury to an individual's property or person.

The plaintiff may be able to secure a remedy for tortious conduct by alleging that the defendant caused an injury (by acting or by failing to act) due to:

- **Negligence** (the defendant owed a duty of care towards the plaintiff, failed to live up to that obligation, and that failure caused an injury to the plaintiff);
- **Strict liability** (where, as a matter of social policy, all that matters is whether the defendant engaged in the activity that caused injury to the plaintiff); and
- Committing an **intentional tort** (where the defendant sought to injure the plaintiff).

Table 1-2 lists the categories into which the body of tort law is divided.

Table 1-2 Categories of Torts	
Category	**Examples of causes of action**
Negligence	• Negligence • Negligence *per se*
Strict liability	• Unsafe products • Abnormally dangerous activities
Intentional Torts	• Assault and battery • Infliction of emotional distress • Fraud and misrepresentation • Trespass to land and chattels • Invasion of privacy • Intereference with adventageous business relationships

■ PURPOSE OF TORT LAW

In the latter half of the twentieth century a rapid expansion occurred in the law of torts. That expansion has led to criticism of tort law in light of its intended purpose, and that criticism has led to the replacement of some time-honored tort principles by whole systems of recovery based upon injury compensation without regard to fault (see box below).

An analysis of the aims of tort law is necessary to understand its foundations, to appreciate its evolution, and to recognize its shortcomings. Tort law has relied traditionally and primarily on remedies at law, such as compensatory damages, but has increasingly look to remedies in equity, such as the issuance of an injunction, as a societal response to tortuous conduct. A professional sports athlete may claim that a serious physical injury prevents the completion of a contract but will face a court order forbidding the athlete from playing elsewhere if there is a sudden, "miraculous" recovery from that injury.

Compensation

The theory of compensating a tort victim for loss involves the award of money as payment or reparation by the defendant for injury to the plaintiff or the plaintiff's property. Since the defendant caused the injury, the defendant will become liable, as a matter of law, to remedy the effects of the injury. Money paid by the defendant to compensate a victim of tortious conduct is called **compensatory damages.** (This topic is discussed in greater detail in Chapter 3.) Money cannot provide a remedy that literally "makes the victim whole," returning the victim to a state of being before the occurrence of the tort. So, a capitalist society uses damages as a way of recognizing the victim's specific loss and of coming up with a suitable remedy for loss. For example, if the driver of an automobile strikes a pedestrian, the driver-defendant will be responsible for the hospital expenses incurred by the pedestrian to get treatment for injuries that arose as a result of the defendant's actions. The defendant may also have to pay for the pedestrian's pain and suffering experienced while recovering from the injuries. Finally, the defendant may need to pay damages to the pedestrian for whatever permanent loss the pedestrian sustained, for example, the loss of the ability to earn a particular livelihood because of the injuries caused by the defendant's tortious conduct.

Regardless of the justification for holding a defendant liable in damages, society has provided a mechanism for managing the payment of damage awards. By purchasing insurance and making regular premium payments, a policyholder can gain protection himself in the event of an accident that involves a huge damage claim. In a world where damages at tort could total millions of dollars, a business insurance policy with a $250 monthly premium seems like a sensible way to manage the risk of having to pay damages.

When a commercial business is found liable and is assessed damages, the cost of paying those damages is passed on to the consumer by increasing the prices for goods or services. Since consumers benefit from the business's commercial activity, the cost of the award of damages is spread out among all consumers who benefited from that specific commercial activity. So, for example, the price of a new automobile may rise by $100 to cover the manufacturer's costs arising out of tort suits for negligent product design.

Deterrence

In rare instances, the law might allow a judge to impose (or exemplary) **damages.** These are above the amount used to compensate the plaintiff and usually are assessed due to a defendant's willful and malicious conduct. A court might impose these, especially when a business is a defendant, to compel that business to change its business practices. Theoretically, the number of tortious acts will decrease if such activity carries a heavy economic burden because the risk of such sanctions will deter the specific defendant and other potential tortfeasors.

Using damages to deter future tortuous conduct might not actually work. Actions in negligence involve a failure to act responsibly rather than a calculated effort to cause harm to plaintiff. Few tortfeasors may expect to face legal action involving the imposition of economic sanctions like having to pay damages. Some defendants might not realize that a connection exists between imposing a sanction and the wrongful conduct. The imposition of these economic sanctions may occur so far in time from the occurrence of the injury that a defendant may not associate the damages with having caused a tortuous injury. Furthermore, the availability of insurance may alter people's perceptions such that the threat of sanctions does not seem to impose as a great a financial burden as it might.

Courts are reluctant to impose punitive damages, however, as judges might not have enough of the kind of information that would justify the imposition of such damages. More commonly, punitive damages are expressly provided for in some statutes but only under certain specific circumstances. Even then, there may be an upper limit to what a court may assess as punitive damages.

◼ FINDING TOOLS

Legal research in tort law involves the use of both primary and secondary authority. Access to those authorities can be facilitated by the use of **research resources.** Finding tools are legal research aids to locate primary and secondary sources of the law.

Authorities

Constitutions, statutes, and case law provide the resources within which modern tort law can be found. For legal research into the law of torts, these resources are considered **primary authority,** meaning that they are statements *of* the law.

Primary authority is distinguished from **secondary authority.** Secondary authority consists of statements *about* the law. Secondary authorities present an explanation, analysis, or criticism of the law and often provide insight regarding trends. Therefore, the paralegal student can find the body of the law of torts located in primary authorities and obtain an explanation and critique of the law from secondary sources.

Primary Authority

Court Reporters

Case law is found in the court reports of the various federal and state jurisdictions. **Court reporters** are published volumes of case law, and can be found in multivolume sets containing the written opinions of the appellate courts within a jurisdiction.

For example, the *Federal Reporter* (Fed.), the *Federal Reporter,* Second Edition (Fed. 2d), and the *Federal Reporter,* Third Edition (Fed. 3d) contain all of the written opinions of the United States Circuit Courts of Appeal.

An example of a court reporter at the state level can be found in the Michigan Reports, which contain all of the case law decided by the Michigan Supreme Court.

Codes

Codes are compilations of statutes. Some states might not use the term 'codes' but will have some kind of compilation of statutes. Paralegals should explore the designation used in their jurisdiction of practice.

Secondary Authorities

Legal Treatises

A valuable research tool for the paralegal student is the legal **treatise.** A treatise provides an exposition on an area of the law in greater depth than that offered by encyclopedias or periodicals. It serves to organize the vast body of case law into chapters and sections arranged for ease of study. *Prosser and Keeton on the Law of Torts* is considered a **hornbook,** which is a treatise used by law students to study well-settled principles found in landmark cases. Reference to it occurs frequently in this text, as it does to its successor, *Dobbs on the Law of Torts*.

None of these treatises have the binding force of law unless a jurisdiction or court has specifically accepted that language as being law in that jurisdiction. So, a court may quote from a treatise and might adopt the logic of the quoted material, thereby investing it with the binding power of law.

Law Reviews

Law reviews, published by various law schools throughout the country, can also be used to research specific areas of tort law.

Restatements of Law

The American Legal Institute has published a series of books containing summaries of the law, known as **Restatements,** on many legal topics. The most comprehensive Restatement about tort law is the *Restatement (Second) of Torts*. A partial update of that series of volumes has begun, so some provisions now come from the *Restatement (Third) of Torts*. Given the rise in tort litigation regarding products, a new Restatement, on Product Liability, goes beyond what the *Restatement (Second) of Torts* said on the topic it is called the *Restatement (Third) of Torts: Product Liability*. Again, none of these treatises—such as the Restatements—have the binding force of law unless a jurisdiction or court has specifically accepted that language as being law in that jurisdiction.

The resources containing primary and secondary authority along with their finding tools are partly summarized in the list provided in Table 1-3.

Table 1-3 Tort Law Research		
PRIMARY AUTHORITY		
	<u>FEDERAL CASE LAW</u>	
		United States Reports
		Supreme Court Reporter
		United States Law Weekly
		Federal Reporter 3d
		Federal Supplement 2d
	<u>STATE CASE LAW</u>	
		North Western Reporter
		North Eastern Reporter
		South Eastern Reporter
		Southern Reporter
		Pacific Reporter
		State Reporters
	<u>FEDERAL STATUTES</u>	
		United State Code
		United State Code Annotated
		United State Code Service
		Code of Federal Regulations
	<u>STATE STATUTES</u>	
		State Codes
		Codes of State Regulation
SECONDARY AUTHORITY		
	<u>ENCYCLOPEDIAS</u>	
		American Jurisprudence 2d
		Corpus Juris Secundum
	<u>LAW REPORTS</u>	
		American Law Reports
	<u>TREATISES</u>	
		Prosser and Keaton on *the Law of Torts*

		Dobbs on *the Law of Torts*
		American Jurisprudence Trials
		American Jurisprudence Proof of Facts
	<u>LAW REVIEWS</u>	
		Western New England Law Review

Table 1-3 continued

While this list is not intended to be comprehensive, it provides the paralegal student with an overview of the basic resources for researching the law of torts.

KEY TERMS

Case law   12

Cause of action   12

Codes   15

Common law   12

Compensatory damages   13

Constitution   11

Constitutional tort   11

Court reporters   15

Damages   14

Defendant   4

English common law   7

Hornbook   15

Intentional tort   12

Judicial review   11

Law reviews   15

Liability   12

Negligence   12

Plaintiff   4

Primary authority   14

Research resources   14

Restatements   15

Secondary authority   15

Statute   11

Strict liability   12

Treatise   15

Trespass   8

Trespass on the case   9

Tort   4

Tortfeasor   4

Tortious conduct   4

Writ   8

SUMMARY

Tort law deals with civil litigation as a means of resolving injuries sustained by an individual to either person or property. As commerce helped to transform Western Europe's societies from agrarian to industrial, new methods at law developed to resolve injuries that would inevitably arise in a dynamic society. So, courts and legislature recognized the need for new types of tort. Actions in tort law now exist where a defendant intentionally injured a plaintiff, where injury arose because of a breach of duty of care or where a defendant simply engaged in certain conduct.

CONCEPT REVIEW QUESTIONS

1. Define a *tort*.
2. What are the private rights of an individual that the law of torts seeks to protect?
3. Define *tortious conduct*.
4. What is a tortfeasor?
5. Discuss the origins of the law of torts.
6. What is the distinction between the writ of trespass and the writ of trespass on the case?
7. What role has judicial review played in the development of tort law?
8. List the primary sources of tort law.
9. List the three principal aims of the law of torts.
10. What are the three broad categories of tort law?

CRITICAL THINKING APPLICATIONS

1. A driver is operating an automobile within the legal rules of the road. Suffering a heart attack, the driver loses control of the car and hits a pedestrian. The pedestrian sues the driver for negligence, claiming that the defendant's failure to meet the care of duty when driving an automobile was breached and that such a breach caused the pedestrian's injuries. What are the chances of the pedestrian winning, at a civil trial, to recover damages for the injuries that arose out of this accident? Does your answer change if this is the driver's second heart attack?
2. A walker comes along a pair of dogs who are fighting. Hoping to stop either animal from injuring the other, the walker picks up a heavy stick and swings it at the dogs, to scare them apart. As the walker swings the stick, the stick hits a jogger in the face. The jogger sues the walker for negligence. Will the jogger win at a civil trial? Does your answer change if the walker knew someone was approaching but hadn't checked to see who was approaching or how quickly the person was approaching?
3. The owner of a plant uses a toxic gas to refine metal that is critical in the operation of jet aircraft. The owner checks all valves and seals in the gas canisters once a month, even though federal law requires such safety inspections only once every three months. Despite these inspections, a seal fails and toxic gas leaks out, sickening a family that lives near the plant and killing the family dog. Even though the owner checks all safety features more frequently than required by law, is the owner liable for damages to the family for the death of the dog? Why or why not? Does your answer change if the house was built before or after the construction of the plant? Why or why not?
4. A law enforcement officer has parked a law-enforcement vehicle in the breakdown lane of a highway, to aid a stranded motorist. The officer has left on all emergency lights. The driver of another vehicle suddenly loses power and the vehicle slowly drifts into the breakdown lane and into the law-enforcement vehicle. The driver sues the law-enforcement officer's employer, on the grounds that the law-enforcement officer breached a duty of care by parking in the breakdown lane. The officer's employer, a governmental agency, files a motion for summary judgment, which assumes that

even if all the facts are true, the employer still won't be liable as a matter of law. Will that motion be granted? Why or why not? Does your answer change if the employer filed a motion to dismiss for failure to state a claim? Why or why not?

5. A fire has broken out at a home. The fire department responds. The owner of the house watches as the firefighters use a crane to reach to the second floor so as to rescue the family pet. While pulling the cat out of the house, the firefighter cannot hold onto the cat and the animal falls two stories. The homeowner, watching the rescue of the beloved pet, has a heart attack when the firefighter loses hold of the cat. If the homeowner sues the fire department for the negligence of its firefighter, and the fire department files a motion to dismiss, will the court grant the department's request because the homeowner has failed to allege a claim that would support the issuance of damages for the medical expenses that homeowner incurred as a result of the heart attack? Why or why not?

6. A victim was injured after being hit by a drunk driver. Going to the local law library, the victim asks the law librarian for a book that explains what he should do to file suit against the drunk driver, in a cause of action for negligence. The librarian accidentally provides the victim with a text that contains old and out-of-date laws. The victim sees that a suit for negligence has to be filed within six months of the injury. But since the publication of that text, the legislature has changed the law so that a suit for negligence must be filed within a year. This change has been made public and is contained in a text that contains the current law. Based upon the out-of-date text, the victim does not file suit because more than six months have passed since the time of injury. A year later, the victim talks with a lawyer and discovers that a suit could have been filed within a year, but that it's now too late for him to file suit. The victim wants to sue the librarian for being negligent in erroneously providing an out-of-date text regarding the law. Will the victim win in a lawsuit for damages?

7. An automobile manufacturer knows that if there's an accident with its new car, there's a risk of an explosion because of the lack of padding around the gas tank. Encasing the tank with padding would add $200 to the price of the car. The manufacturer determines that the likelihood of an explosion at an accident occurring because of the lack happening was one in 500,000. The manufacturer makes the car without the padding and sells it. Three years after the first models have rolled out, an accident happens with one of the cars where there is an explosion because the gas tank was hit, killing the driver. The family of the driver sues the manufacturer. During pre-trial discovery, they learn of the manufacturer's study about the cost of the padding and the risk of an explosion. The court rules that the manufacturer was at least negligent in designing the vehicle and awards damages. The lawyer for the family asks that the court assess punitive damages against the automobile manufacturer. What is the likelihood, based upon the information provided, that the court will impose punitive damages against the automobile manufacturer?

8. Property owners live adjacent to an old warehouse. They learned that the property had been sold during the previous week. They did not know that the new owners moved black explosive powder, in 55-gallon drums, into the warehouse because the new owners were about to start to manufacturer fireworks to be sold. The new owners had received all appropriate permits to operate such a business out of the warehouse. One night, a fire

breaks out and eventually gets to the drums containing the black powder. The resulting explosion shakes the adjacent house and breaks all the windows. The property owners sue to recover damages. The new owners claim that since they had complied with the law, they should not be liable in damages, so they ask the court to dismiss this civil suit. How will the court likely rule on this request?

SKILL-BUILDING APPLICATION

Ali stood in front of the law librarian, who was seated at a plain desk, head in hands, studying a book under the light of a gooseneck lamp. "Can you help me?" Ali asked. The law librarian looked up and smiled. "What help do you need?" Ali cast a glance towards the bookshelves behind the law librarian's desk, which were filled to their top shelves. "I'm trying to figure out something about the law."

"Okay," the librarian said. "What about the law?"

"I'm trying to figure out whether I should see a lawyer." Ali said. "Maybe the answer is in one of these books."

The law librarian nodded. "Can you be more precise?"

"I was at the ferry port, and had delayed getting off the ferry because I'd been trying to make one of those big 'life decisions.' By the time I'd gotten off, I was alone and the terminal was empty. Heading up a ramp, I was stopped by a man who said that he was a police officer. He didn't look at all like an officer because he was in street clothes. When I stopped, he flipped out an ID and showed it to me, although I hadn't gotten a good look at it."

"This guy wanted to know why I was the last one off. And I felt like telling him that it was none of his business. But he stood between me and the door and if I started to move to one side, so did he. He asked for ID and I wanted to challenge him, but it looked easier just to give in and show him my driver's license. The guy looked at it, gave it back to me, and then stood aside. When I got outside of the terminal, I discover that I've just missed a bus, and had to wait an hour and a half until the next one came."

"So, what I want to know is whether I've got a lawsuit and whether I should see a lawyer. Can you tell me if I should?"

"No." The librarian said. "That's something you and the lawyer you might hire would want to talk about. But you're welcome to do research to see whether you have a lawsuit."

To find out whether there has been the kind of conduct that rises to the level of being a tort, what types of books would you recommend that Ali look at? Why? What books would you not recommend that Ali look at?

Has Ali undergone the kind of experience that will make it plausible to file a claim in tort law against the police officer? Why not, based solely upon what you've read in this chapter?

A Matter of Ethics

Take the scenario above. Now have the librarian go to the stacks and pull out those law books that could provide the answer of there was a law suit. Is this the unauthorized practice of law? Under the American Bar Association's

Model Rules of Professional Conduct, the unauthorized practice of the law is designed to protect the interests of those who end up experiencing grave consequences from relying on the legal advice of a non–lawyer. Do the questions, here, indicate a need to protect the person asking the questions from being mislead about the issues of law?

Law, says the judge as he looks down his nose,
Speaking clearly and most severely,
Law is as I've told you before,
Law is as you know I suppose,
Law is but let me explain it once more,
Law is the Law

—*W. H. Auden, 1939*

Litigating a Cause of Action in Tort Law | CHAPTER 2

Every jurisdiction has rules of civil procedure, rulings that apply in every civil proceeding. Working chronologically, this chapter examines basic concepts associated with any kind of civil trial.

CHAPTER TOPICS

1. Introduction
2. Preliminary Matters
3. The Complaint
4. Service of Process
5. The Answer, Joinder (Counterclaims, Crossclaims), and Class Actions
6. Motions
7. Discovery
8. Trial
9. Judgment
10. Execution
11. Appeals

OBJECTIVES

After completing this chapter, you will be able to:

1. Identify alternative methods to resolve a dispute without resorting to litigation.

2. Expound upon why no proceeding can commence without personal jurisdiction, subject matter jurisdiction, and proper venue.

3. Describe features common to a complaint, the document filed to commence litigation.

4. Recognize how service of process plays a critical role in the commencement of litigation.

5. Appreciate the significance and role played when a party files a motion before the court.

6. Account for the role of discovery, and of the types of discovery.

7. Expound upon those steps needed to conduct and to conclude a trial.

8. Understand the right of appeal, as of right and at the discretion of an appeals court.

■ THE CIVIL LITIGATION PROCESS

Civil litigation involves the use of the courts to resolve a problem of law. The idea of a lawsuit as a means of "making the plaintiff whole" presumes that compensatory damages will approximately offset the injury that plaintiff has sustained.

Through civil litigation, an injured plaintiff seeks compensation from a defendant. Each suit follows a process that starts with filing a complaint, gathering information, going to trial, then arriving at a judgment, with the losing party having the option to appeal. Paralegals should know what each step involves so as to develop an understanding of how a case might end up resolved through the use of the courts.

■ PRELIMINARY MATTERS

Settlement and Alternative Dispute Resolution (ADR)

Few disputes about the law go to court. Filing suit can involve a slow, expensive process to achieve a result that may please neither party. So parties may avoid a trial by settling their dispute, arriving at terms that suit both of their interests.

Besides negotiating a settlement, the parties have several methods for avoiding a trial to solve their dispute. **Alternative dispute resolution (ADR)** involves methods for resolving problems of law without going to trial.

Mediation

With **mediation,** an unbiased third party helps the disputing parties to arrive at a result that best serves each of party's interests. Mediation hopes to achieve a "win-win" for the disputants where a legal proceeding may result in "win-lose."

Mediators help the parties to understand their interests and collaborate with them so that the disputing parties arrive at a mutually agreeable resolution. Mediators need not be lawyers nor must they undergo any certification process to work as a mediator. They may undergo training, under the tutelage of an experienced mediator, to develop the skills needed to facilitate resolution.

By casting the dispute in terms of interests rather than positions, the mediator hopes that the parties can then discover how to meet their interests without necessarily causing a loss by an opponent. When a mediator has helped to create an agreement that the parties accept, the parties may have a greater incentive to uphold the agreement because it gives them what they want.

Lawyers may participate in the process of creating an agreement that satisfies both sides but may prove unnecessary, which helps to keep down costs. Mediation avoids the use of a jury. In mediation, more information may be available to the parties that might otherwise be excluded if offered at trial.

Arbitration

In this type of dispute resolution, an unbiased third party called an **arbitrator** resolves the problem for the parties. Much like a judge at trial, an arbitrator looks to develop a clear understanding of the facts to arrive at a resolution that seems just.

Parties may use binding arbitration, where they enter into an agreement to abide by whatever the arbitrator determines. Often with binding arbitration, the parties give up their rights to pursue resolution of the dispute in a court or a right to appeal the arbitrator's solution. If they agree to use nonbinding arbitration, that may give them a sense of the strength of each side's arguments, which may then spur the parties to settle the matter.

Since arbitrators resolve the dispute, they might operate much like a judge would during a trial. Like mediators, arbitrators do not have to undergo formal training or licensing. They could be paralegals, lawyers or retired judges.

And also like mediation, arbitration may achieve a better resolution for the parties because the formal procedures of a trial do not apply. The arbitrator can play a more dynamic role in solving the problem by asking for information from the parties, and does not have to deal with a jury. This means the parties can get a less costly solution in a shorter period of time than what a trial would require.

Mini-trials

The parties may choose to resolve their dispute through a **mini-trial,** which has some of the characteristics of a trial. With the emphasis on producing a speedy outcome, mini-trials could allow for the use of a jury, could hear testimony, or could allow for some of the pre-trial discovery process (see below). The parties can choose any configuration of a trial that would help them come quickly to a resolution at a lower cost than if they went to a full trial. They may have a judge, if allowed under the law, or a retired judge oversee the proceedings.

In some jurisdictions, courts may require parties to go through a mini-trial before having a full trial. Judges could encourage this practice as a way of giving the disputants a sense of a likely outcome, which could spur them on to negotiating a settlement.

Private Trials

The parties could seek the help of a third party who would act like a judge during a trial; that third-party might even be a retired judge. The result of a **private trial** will not have the force of a full trial because it won't be conducted in a court, using court personnel. Here, too, the proceeding may give the parties a sense of what to expect if the dispute goes before a sitting judge, where the results would be binding on the parties and creates precedent.

A variation on this concept could include hiring people to serve in the same capacity as jurors during a full legal proceeding. While the parties may not accept whatever verdict this jury-like group of people produces, it may give them a better idea of an outcome at trial.

Jurisdiction

Before a court can resolve the parties' dispute, it needs to establish that it has jurisdiction. **Jurisdiction** involves the power to reach a solution that courts in that state will respect as valid and legitimate. Jurisdiction involves two critical questions, whether the parties have found the proper place to resolve the problem—**personal jurisdiction**—and whether this particular court has the authority to resolve this kind of dispute—**subject matter jurisdiction.**

Personal Jurisdiction

The critical issue with personal jurisdiction involves determining whether this is the correct court and legal system to resolve the dispute. For example, the place where an automobile accident occurs would have personal jurisdiction, since the problem started there.

Yet complexities can arise that impair a court's ability to determine whether it has jurisdiction. For example, what if the driver lives in another state and the car's owner in a third state, and the company that provides insurance coverage in a fourth state? Courts generally look at the nature of the connections, or contacts, that any one place has to the problem. They will look at whether the parties have had meaningful contact with the place where the trial court operates. Having the plaintiff and defendant live in the same state could be enough to establish a court's personal jurisdiction over their problem. Often, a court in the state where the accident occurred would have jurisdiction. If a court does not have personal jurisdiction, no other court will honor the decision; they will not enforce any judgment that arises out of such a proceeding.

Subject Matter Jurisdiction

Some states have found it helpful to create courts that specialize in resolving certain types of disputes; this involves subject matter jurisdiction. The state will create such courts to "siphon" these types of cases away from courts that would otherwise handle this and many other problems.

A court that helps resolve issues of property ownership might be called a land court. One that reviews the wishes of a person, after death, regarding the distribution of property would be a probate court. By having these specialized courts deal only with those problems, judges can develop a sophisticated understanding of this particular topic.

Courts that handle only one kind of legal dispute have limited jurisdiction to resolve just that type of problem. A court of general jurisdiction may handle any kind of criminal case one day, and then any kind of civil case the next. These courts will provide a forum to resolve disputes that don't require the development of special, narrow, and tailored courts like those of limited jurisdiction. So states may have courts of limited jurisdiction to deal with narrow, specialized areas of the law and courts of general jurisdictions, where parties with all other types of disputes can have a judge resolve a problem.

Venue

Once the parties have established that a court has personal and subject matter jurisdiction over their problem, the selection of the **venue**, or actual physical location of the trial, arises. A problem of law that receives regular coverage in the media may end up influencing the citizenry and running the risk that people have made up their minds before the trial, making it questionable whether the defendant can get a fair trial in that community.

If the dispute has attracted extensive media attention in one community, it may make sense to move the trial to another venue—for example, a court building 100 miles away—to a community where the people have not been exposed to the media coverage and thus might be more likely to listen to evidence presented at trial with an open mind. A change in venue improves the chances of getting a fair trial.

The following case illustrates how a case might have issues regarding personal jurisdiction, subject matter jurisdiction, or venue (see Case in Point 2-1). [Note: a *pro se* litigant does not have a lawyer to handle the case in court.]

 # CASE IN POINT 2-1

Greer v. Del Mar Fairgrounds
1999 U.S. Dist. 12429 (E.D. Mich. July 31, 1999)

Plaintiff William Greer, acting *pro se*, claims that in March 1998, he filed an application to display his business at the Del Mar Fairgrounds which is located in the 22nd District in southern California. Plaintiff claims that Defendant Nancy Strauss, a concession coordinator, and Defendant Dori Whitesell led him to believe that his application was complete. Plaintiff claims that he later found out that his application required a picture of his booth and his product in order to be complete although he was told by Ms. Whitesell that "everything is alright." Plaintiff alleges that he was told that calling back to check on his application could lead to his application being denied. When Plaintiff received a letter of regret from the Del Mar Fairgrounds, he went to the main office and spoke with Defendant Donna Ruhm, Commercial Manager. Ms. Ruhm allegedly informed Plaintiff that his application was incomplete because it was completed incorrectly and contained no picture of his booth. Plaintiff claims that Ms. Ruhm stated she would talk to Mr. Fennell, the CEO. When she returned, Ms. Ruhm allegedly asked Plaintiff if he would take an outside booth. Plaintiff claims he shook hands with Ms. Ruhm to consummate the deal. When Plaintiff delivered his display, a water machine, Defendant Strauss refused delivery, stating that Plaintiff had no contract with Del Mar Fairgrounds. Plaintiff seeks one million dollars for pain and suffering, gross incompetence, defamation of character, court costs and attorney fees.

Defendants now bring this Motion to Dismiss. [footnote omitted] Defendants argue that this Court lacks subject matter and personal jurisdiction and that this is an improper and inconvenient venue.

[...]

1. General Personal Jurisdiction

The law of the state of this forum, Michigan, provides that a court may exercise general personal jurisdiction over a non-resident corporate defendant as follows:

The existence of any of the following relationships between a corporation and the state shall constitute a sufficient basis of jurisdiction to enable the courts of record of this state to exercise general personal jurisdiction over the corporation and to enable such courts to render personal judgments against the corporation.

1. Incorporation under the laws of this state.
2. Consent, to the extent authorized by the consent and subject to the limitations provided in section 745.
3. The carrying on of a continuous and systematic part of its general business within the state. Mich. Comp. Laws Ann. § 600.711.

Michigan provides that a court may exercise general personal jurisdiction over an individual defendant as follows:

The existence of any of the following relationships between an individual and the state shall constitute a sufficient basis of jurisdiction to enable the courts of record of this state to exercise general personal jurisdiction over the individual or his representative and to enable such courts to render personal judgments against the individual or representative.

[...]

Due process requires "continuous and systematic" contacts with the forum state.

It is unclear whether Defendant Del Mar Fairground would be considered a corporate entity or an individual. In any event, neither the Michigan long arm statutes, nor due process would allow Plaintiff's claims to be brought in Michigan. Defendants Ruhm, Strauss, Whitesell, and Fennell have all filed affidavits which state than none of them were in Michigan or domiciled in Michigan at the time process was served, nor have they consented to the jurisdiction of this Court. (citation omitted) Plaintiff did not dispute this at oral arguments. Defendants made a limited appearance for the purposes of filing this motion and expressly reserved all other rights including the right to contest jurisdiction. Defendant Fennell also attests that the 22nd District Agricultural Association has no contacts with or business interests in the state of Michigan. (citation omitted) Plaintiff also did not dispute this at oral arguments and accordingly has failed to meet his burden of establishing general personal jurisdiction.

2. Limited Personal Jurisdiction

Michigan's corporate limited personal jurisdiction statute provides:

The existence of any of the following relationships between a corporation or its agent and the state shall constitute a sufficient basis of jurisdiction to enable the courts of record of this state to exercise limited personal jurisdiction over such corporation and to enable such courts to render personal judgments against such corporation arising out of the act or acts which create any of the following relationships:

1. The transaction of any business within the state.
2. The doing or causing any act to be done, or consequences to occur, in the state resulting in an action for tort....

Mich. Comp. Laws Ann. § 600.715(1)–(2).

The following provision applies to individual defendants,

The existence of any of the following relationship between an individual or his agent and the state shall constitute a sufficient basis of jurisdiction to enable a court of record of this state to exercise limited personal jurisdiction over the individual and to enable the court to render personal judgments against the individual or his representative arising out of an act which creates any of the following relationships:

1. The transaction of any business within the state.
2. The doing or causing an act to be done, or consequences to occur, in the state resulting in an action for tort.
3. The ownership, use, or possession of real or tangible personal property situated within the state.
4. Contracting to insure a person, property, or risk located within this state at the time of contracting.
5. Entering into a contract for services to be rendered or for materials to be furnished in the state by the defendant.
6. Acting as a director, manager, trustee, or other officer of a corporation incorporated under the laws of, or having its principal place of business within this state.
7. Maintaining a domicile in this state while subject to a marital or family relationship which is the basis of the claim for divorce, alimony, separate maintenance, property settlement, child support, or child custody.

Mich. Comp. Laws Ann. § 600.705.

Defendants attest in their affidavits that none of them has any of these seven relationships with the state of Michigan. (citation omitted) Defendants argue, that even if any of the relationships existed, Plaintiff's claims do not "arise out of" these contacts with Michigan. Again, Defendant Fennell attests that the 22nd District Agricultural Association has no contacts with or business interests in the state of Michigan. (citation omitted)

In order to satisfy due process, a defendant must have minimum ties with Michigan so as not to offend "traditional notions of fair play and substantial justice." (citation omitted) The Sixth Circuit has set forth a three-prong test to determine whether a district court may, consistent with due process, exercise limited personal jurisdiction:

First, the defendant must purposefully avail himself of the privilege of acting in the forum state or causing a consequence in the forum state. Second, the cause of action must arise from the defendant's activities there. Finally, the acts of the defendant or consequences caused by the defendant must have a substantial enough connection with the forum state to make the exercise of jurisdiction over the defendant reasonable.

[...] The Supreme Court has held, "In judging minimum contacts, a court properly focuses on the relationship among the defendant, the forum, and the litigation." (citation omitted) Defendants have not purposefully availed themselves of the privilege of acting in Michigan, nor have they caused a consequence in the forum state. None of the Defendants own Michigan property or businesses. Defendant Ruhm and Whitesell have never been to Michigan. Defendant Strauss was only in Michigan briefly around 1979 when she was an (sic) flight attendant, and Defendant Fennell was only in Michigan in the early to mid-1980s when he came for a business trip with a former employer. Defendants made no contacts with Michigan on behalf of the 22nd District Agricultural Association or Del Mar Fairgrounds. (citation omitted)

Under the second and third prong [...], Plaintiff must establish that the cause of action arose from Defendants' contacts with Michigan, and that these acts or consequences have a substantial enough connection to Michigan to make the exercise of personal jurisdiction reasonable. "An action will be deemed not to have arisen from the defendants' contacts with the forum state only when they are unrelated to the operative facts of the controversy." (citation omitted) Defendants lack contacts with the forum state as set forth above. In addition, Plaintiff completed his application in California, the decision to deny his application was made in California, the letter of regret was sent from California to Plaintiff's California business address. (citation omitted) All the Defendants, and presumably all the witnesses, except Plaintiff, live in California. California law would more than likely be applicable, and Michigan has no interest in this litigation. The only reference to the state of Michigan in Plaintiff's Complaint is Plaintiff's current address in Taylor, Michigan. Defendants could not have reasonably anticipated being hailed into a Michigan court, and it would be unreasonable for this Court to require them to litigate this case here. Plaintiff can seek relief in California. (citation omitted)

Plaintiff has failed to meet his burden of showing that Defendants have sufficient contacts with Michigan so as not to offend "traditional notions of fair play and substantial justice." Defendants could not have reasonably anticipated being hailed into a Michigan court. It would violate due process to exercise limited personal jurisdiction over Defendants, and as explained above, there is no general personal jurisdiction. The case must be dismissed under Rule 12(b)(2) of the Federal Rules of Civil Procedure.

[...]

IV. INCONVENIENT VENUE

Defendants argue that even if venue is proper, the case should be transferred to California. [...]

To grant a transfer of venue, a district court must find the following: "(1) the action could have been brought in the transferee district court; (2) a transfer serves the interest of justice; and (3) transfer is in the convenience of the witnesses and parties." (citation omitted) In deciding the motion, "the court must consider the following factors: (1) the convenience of the parties; (2) the convenience of the witnesses; (3) the relative ease of access to sources of proof; (4) the availability of process to compel attendance of unwilling witnesses; (5) the cost of obtaining willing witnesses; (6) the practical problems associated with trying the case most expeditiously and inexpensively; and (7) the interest of justice." (citation omitted) District courts have broader discretion to transfer than was previously allowed under the doctrine of forum non conveniens. (citation omitted) However, "District courts should give deference to a plaintiff's choice of venue. When a defendant moves to change the forum, he must overcome the presumption that the plaintiff has chosen the proper forum." (citation omitted)

This case could have been brought in California. All of the Defendants and all of the witnesses, except Plaintiff, reside in California. The interests of justice and the convenience of the witnesses and parties would be better served if the case were brought in California. It would be inconvenient for Defendants and their witnesses to try this case in Michigan, although it would also be inconvenient for Plaintiff to try the case in California. The harms which allegedly occurred were suffered in California, and accordingly California law would most likely apply. Considering all of these factors, the interests of justice would not be served by trying this case in Michigan.

V. SUBJECT MATTER JURISDICTION

Defendants claim that this Court lacks subject matter jurisdiction over Plaintiff's claims, and the case should be dismissed pursuant to Rule 12(b)(1) of the Federal Rules of Civil Procedure. Del Mar Fairgrounds is owned by the state of California. (citation omitted) Pursuant to the California Tort Claims Act, any party filing a claim against the state of California must first file a formal claim with the State Board of Control. (citation omitted) Only after the State Board of Control denies the claim can the party file a court action. (citation omitted)

Defendants claim that because the California Tort Claims Act is jurisdiction, this Court lacks subject matter jurisdiction over Plaintiff's claims. Additionally, Defendants argue that because Plaintiff has failed to file a claim with the California State Board of Control, he has failed to exhaust his administrative remedies. Because this Court concludes that it does not have personal jurisdiction over Defendants and that Michigan is an improper and inconvenient venue, the Court leaves the issues of subject matter jurisdiction and exhaustion of administrative remedies to be determined by the appropriate court.

[...]

IT IS ORDERED that this case is hereby DISMISSED.

With no meaningful connection between Michigan and the defendants, outside of the plaintiff coming from that state and all other contacts originating in California, the court dismissed the case for lack of jurisdiction and improper venue.

Rules of Procedure

The steps involved in litigation remain constant no matter where in a state a party lives. Refinements have arisen over time, such as steps involved in electronic document discovery, but the process of litigation has remained unchanged for some time. The structure common to all civil proceedings involves **rules of procedure.** Whether modeled on the **Federal Rules of Civil Procedure (Fed. R. Civ. P.)** or on state common law, proceedings follow an established course, no matter the nature of the problem (see box below).

SELECT PROVISIONS OF THE FEDERAL RULES OF CIVIL PROCEDURE

Part II. COMMENCEMENT OF ACTION; SERVICE OF PROCESS, PLEADINGS, MOTIONS, AND ORDERS

  3. Commencing an Action
  4. Summons
  5. Serving and Filing Pleadings and Other Papers

Part III. PLEADINGS AND MOTIONS

  7. Pleadings Allowed; Form of Motions and Other Papers
  8. General Rules of Pleading
  9. Pleading Special Matters
10. Form of Pleadings

U.S.C.S. Fed Rules Civ Proc R 1 et. Seq.

For the sake of convenience, this examination of the rules of procedure will track the Fed. R. Civ. P. Since many states and the federal government rely upon the Fed. R. Civ. P. to conduct civil litigation, most paralegals will encounter these rules in their home state. For those in states that have not adopted the format of the Fed. R. Civ. P. perhaps in favor of procedures developed under common law, the terms may differ but all seek to have civil trials proceed in a consistent, predictable fashion, leading to a just resolution of a problem of law.

■ THE COMPLAINT

A plaintiff initiates legal proceedings by filing a **complaint.** This legal document must contain certain essential pieces of information.

The caption, at the top of the page, describes the court's personal and subject matter jurisdiction. A defendant may dispute whether the court actually has personal or subject matter jurisdiction, but the caption at least contains the plaintiff's view about what kind of court in what jurisdiction has authority to resolve the dispute.

The plaintiff files the complaint, so the plaintiff has the problem that it hopes a court will solve. Also named is the defendant, whom the plaintiff claims caused the problem and should be held responsible for the consequences, often in the form of money designed to compensate the plaintiff for the damages the plaintiff sustained.

A plaintiff may not have all the information about the nature of a problem and/or the parties involved, and would need to file a suit as a way of getting the information. So long as the complaint contains enough information to identify the nature of the problem, the parties, and the remedy that a court should provide, it should provide enough notice to defendant to understand that plaintiff has a problem at law.

In the body of the complaint, the plaintiff needs to identify who the plaintiff is, and where the plaintiff resides or does business. Then, the complaint must identify the defendant and where that party resides. Some disputes may involve more than one party, one defendant, or one problem of law. Each must be identified in the complaint.

The complaint should then provide information about the date, time, and location where the dispute arose. While a plaintiff may not know all of this precisely, the more definite the information, the better the quality of notice of the problem that a defendant and a court will have. After having filed suit, the plaintiff will be able to gather more information, especially from the defendant, to produce a more accurate sense of the problem.

The complaint should describe the cause of action: the problem of law that the plaintiff has asked the court to resolve at trial. While the plaintiff might indicate that a defendant's negligence produced the plaintiff's damages, a better written complaint would describe the elements of this action in tort. To win a cause of action in tort law arising out of negligence, the plaintiff must show, by a preponderance of evidence, that the defendant owed a duty of care to the plaintiff, that the defendant failed to uphold that duty, and that this failure led to the plaintiff suffering injury. To win a cause of action in tort law arising out of interference with an advantageous business relationship, the plaintiff will need to show, by a preponderance of evidence, that a business relationship existed, that the defendant chose to interfere with that relationship, the nature of the interference, and the damages the plaintiff suffered because of this interference.

The following case illustrates how a plaintiff failed to set out the elements of a claim in tort for malicious prosecution so that the claim was dismissed (see Case in Point 2-2).

CASE IN POINT 2-2

Broad-Bussel Family LP v. Bayou Group LLC (In re Bayou Hedge Funds Inv. Litig.)

472 F. Supp. 2d 528 (S.D.N.Y. 2007)

[...]

The moving defendants are a law firm (hereinafter referred to as FR&O) and one of its partners, who at unspecified times performed unspecified legal services for unspecified entities among the Bayou Group hedge funds. Plaintiffs have asserted a total of five claims against FR&O and its partner Steven Oppenheim:

The complaint alleges the following non-conclusory facts against FR&O:

FR&O was a "close associate" of Bayou and Bayou's principals, Samuel Israel and Daniel Marino. (P 4)

Bayou Management LLC, Bayou Advisors, LLC and Bayou Equities LLC allegedly maintained one of two "principal offices" at FR&O's law firm address, 488 Madison Avenue. (P 19).

FR&O is a limited liability partnership engaged in the practice of law. It served as counsel for "Bayou" during "all or some" of the Class Period, performing unspecified services at unspecified times.

Steven Oppenheim is a partner in FR&O and is also a certified public accountant. Prior to practicing law at FR&O, Oppenheim was the managing partner of Spicer & Oppenheim, an accounting firm that dissolved in or around December 1990. Thereafter, he joined the accounting firm of Grant Thornton, which served as Bayou's auditor until in or about 1998. However, Oppenheim left Grant Thornton in 1991 to join FR&O, which is not an accounting firm. (P 37) As legal counsel for Bayou, FR&O and Oppenheim provided (unspecified) counsel and advice to the Bayou Defendants in planning, forming and operating the Bayou Hedge Funds, and the Firm was privy to (unspecified) non-public information and documents concerning the true structure, operations and finances of the Bayou Hedge Funds. (P 38)

Oppenheim knew or ignored various (unspecified) aspects of the fraud and other misconduct that was being committed by the Bayou Defendants. (Id)

[...]

Standards on a Motion to Dismiss

Rule 12(b)(6) of the Federal Rules of Civil Procedure provides for dismissal of a complaint that fails to state a claim upon which relief can be granted. The standard of review on a motion to dismiss is heavily weighted in favor of the plaintiff. The Court is required to read a complaint generously, drawing all reasonable inferences from the complaint's allegations. (citation omitted) "In ruling on a motion to dismiss for failure to state a claim upon which relief may be granted, the court is required to accept the material facts alleged in the complaint as true." (citation omitted) The Court must deny the motion "unless it appears beyond doubt that the plaintiff can prove no set of facts in support of his claim which would entitle him to relief." (citation omitted)

The Negligence Claim Must Be Dismissed

The predicate for a claim in negligence is the running of a duty from the defendant to the plaintiff. [...] [T]he question of whether a duty exists is a question of law for the court, and only if the court concludes that a duty exists will it be necessary to reach the question of breach. (citation omitted)

[...] [A]n attorney's duty runs to his client and (ordinarily) not to third parties. (citation omitted) Because the existence of a legal duty is a prerequisite to any claim for the negligent performance of an attorney's duty, a party cannot generally sue someone else's attorney for negligence. (citation omitted) The only exception to this

> rule is where an attorney performs a specific act for the intended benefit of a non-client (example: paying off a mortgage on behalf of a non-client). (citation omitted)
>
> Plaintiffs are clients of the Hennessee Group who invested in Bayou funds. The complaint in this case fails to allege any facts from which one could fairly infer that FR&O had any duty to the plaintiffs. Their status as investors or limited partner shareholders in the Bayou entities does not create the necessary attorney-client relationship with FR&O. (citation omitted) The complaint is also devoid of a single factual allegation tending to show that FR&O undertook any action for the intended benefit of plaintiffs. Accordingly, the negligence claim against FR&O [...] is dismissed with prejudice.
>
> [...]
>
> To be completely candid, the complaint, fairly read, does not allege that Bayou and its principals were negligent—rather, it alleges that they perpetrated a massive fraud with full knowledge that they were doing so. Israel's and Marino's guilty pleas admit as much. No reasonable trier of fact could conclude from the allegations of the Amended Complaint that Bayou's investors were harmed through Bayou's negligence!
>
> [...]
>
> The complaint is dismissed as to defendants Faust Rabbach & Oppenheim LLP and Steven Oppenheim.

Since the plaintiffs failed to include statements in the complaint that described how the defendant engaged in the tort of malicious prosecution, the court dismissed the claim. Worse, since the plaintiffs chose a particular legal option to review the prior dismissal, they have lost the option of refilling the claim.

A plaintiff must include a request of what action the court should take to resolve the dispute of law. So a plaintiff might include an **ad damnum clause,** which sets forth the specific damages award the plaintiff seeks from the court. A plaintiff might also ask for damages to deal with specific expenses, such as medical expenses or loss of income because the defendant's actions interfered with the plaintiff's ability to make a living. Other expenses could include the payment of the filing fees to initiate the lawsuit as well as the fees incurred by the plaintiff's lawyer in bringing the problem of law to a resolution that serves the plaintiff's interests.

Most jurisdictions require that a plaintiff provide a signature to establish clearly that the plaintiff wants a court to resolve the dispute. Plaintiffs may often have a lawyer prepare the complaint; in that case, the lawyer will need to sign the complaint and provide useful information such as the address and telephone number of the lawyer's firm.

Some jurisdictions might require additional evidence of the plaintiff's intention to start a lawsuit. It might require the completion of an attestation clause. In a paragraph, a disinterested third party must state, under oath, that the plaintiff signed the complaint free of any outside influence.

Once the plaintiff files the complaint with the court, the clerk or other judicial official charged with overseeing the paperwork involved in a legal dispute will issue a case number, the permanent designation for this particular dispute of law. Most courts require that a plaintiff pay a fee to start the lawsuit, although in some instances a court might waive the fee, such as when a plaintiff lacks the requisite funds.

The clerk may also determine, at the time of filing, what track the case should follow. As a method for managing the flow of complaints, courts have created tracks for the cases, which can indicate what timetable the parties must follow in having the dispute proceed to trial. A complaint with multiple disputes at issue, multiple parties, or multiple claims may want to put the case on a slower track, since the number of issues and/or parties will each need sufficient time to follow the proceedings to resolution.

■ SERVICE OF PROCESS

For a lawsuit to go forward properly, the plaintiff has to ensure that the defendant is properly notified of the initiation of the suit; this involves **service of process.** Service of process involves a third party's delivering the complaint and a summons to the defendant. A **summons** is a court document that informs the defendant that, with the initiation of this lawsuit, the defendant needs to file a response—an **answer**—at the court by a particular date. The process server will fill out a form indicating that service has been made to the defendant or to an adult who could reasonably be expected to pass the complaint and summons along to the defendant.

The plaintiff may not have an opportunity to get personal service, perhaps because the defendant's precise location is not known or when a defendant deliberately avoids service of process. If the plaintiff can convince a judge that personal service of process cannot take place, the court might permit alternative service of process, such as by having notice presented in a newspaper for a certain number of days. The preferred method of notifying the defendant, however, involves personal service.

■ THE ANSWER, COUNTERCLAIMS, AND CROSS-CLAIMS

The Answer

Once the defendant has received service of process, the defendant has to file an answer with the court where the plaintiff initiated the lawsuit. While the time that the defendant will have to file the answer may vary by state, many states require the defendant to file within twenty days of service. If the defendant fails to file an answer, the plaintiff could then move the court to issue a judgment in the plaintiff's favor. While courts will issue such judgments, courts may nullify that judgment if a defendant files an explanation for the delay and then enters an answer, so that resolution of the dispute involves the facts of the case and not because of the defendant's failure to comply with the court's procedures (see Fed. R. Civ. P. Rule 4).

In an answer, the defendant files a response to the information contained in the complaint. This often means that the defendant denies the validity of the plaintiff's description of the facts. The defendant then says that, because the facts happened differently from what the plaintiff has alleged, the court should enter a judgment in favor of the defendant. That answer may include a request for the court to order the plaintiff to pay the defendant's legal expenses incurred in responding to the complaint.

Counterclaims

To use court resources effectively and spare all parties the costs of filing multiple suits to resolve other disputes involving the parties, a defendant will be encouraged to file a **counterclaim** (see FED. R. CIV. P. Rule 13). In a counterclaim, the defendant alleges that the plaintiff has caused a dispute that only a court could resolve. Having the court hear all problems of law involving the parties means that a resolution can free the courts to deal with the problems of other cases.

Cross-claims

The defendant may also file a **cross-claim.** In a cross-claim, the defendant wants to bring in a third party to the proceeding. Perhaps the defendant claims that this third party actually caused the problem so that if the defendant loses at trial, the defendant can then pass liability to the third party. For example, in an auto accident, the defendant might have driven the car that hit the plaintiff. However, the defendant could sue a third party, for example, the mechanic who negligently repaired the brakes of the defendant's automobile, because the mechanic's actions actually created liability for the damages the plaintiff incurred (see Fed. R. Civ. P. Rule 13).

Joinder

The plaintiff and defendant may have other disputes of law. To conserve judicial resources by addressing all disputes between the parties, the court may permit that other actions be combined into one action. This is **joinder** (see Fed. R. Civ. P. Rules 18-21). Joinder may also lead to adding other parties to the original complaint.

Interpleader

If a person fears facing liability to a number of parties but does not know for certain who those parties are, under Fed. R. Civ. P. Rule 22, that person can join—**interplead**—those parties so that the court has the opportunity to determine who might stand first in line to recover.

Class Action Suits

A plaintiff might have a claim similar to that of many others; for example, people who bought a defectively designed infant car seat and whose children suffered injuries when the product failed to work properly. As a practical matter, a **class action suit** might combine the interests of all plaintiffs who had purchased the product (see Fed. R. Civ. P. Rule 22). This can mean a reduction in the overall number of cases filed, so that if 1,000 people purchased the car seat, one legal action—the class action suit—that settles all of their claims will result in a more efficient use of judicial resources. A plaintiff can file a class action suit only with the court's permission. To receive permission to go forward with the suit, the plaintiff needs to show that:

- The number of people with claims is so large that joinder and other methods of bringing in parties would prove impractical;
- These similarly situated people will have issues of fact or law common to all;
- The points plaintiff raises in the complaint represent commonly what others in the class would allege if they filed separately; and
- Plaintiff will do a good job of representing the interests of these similarly situated people.

Plaintiffs often may file a class action suit for product liability, because the defendant may have sold a defective product nationwide or over a span of years.

The following case, based upon the tort of invasion of privacy, shows how difficult it is to maintain a class action suit (see Case in Point 2-3).

CASE IN POINT 2-3

Castro v. NYT TV

370 N.J. Super. 282 (App.Div., 2004)

This appeal involves the maintainability as a class action of a complaint asserting tort claims for invasion of privacy by an unreasonable intrusion upon the seclusion of another and by giving unreasonable publicity to another's private life.

The two putative class representatives, Michael Castro and Julio Costa, were admitted to the emergency room at Jersey Shore Medical Center in July 2001. Castro had a severe stab wound to his abdomen inflicted by his girlfriend and Costa had a serious hand injury caused by catching his hand in a cement mixer. While plaintiffs were in the emergency room, they were videotaped by defendants NYT Television, The New York Times Company and Discovery Communications (referred to collectively as "NYT"), with the permission of defendants Jersey Shore Medical Center and Meridian Health System (referred to collectively as "Jersey Shore"), for a television show called "Trauma: Life in the ER," which was shown on The Learning Channel.

Plaintiffs signed forms consenting to this videotaping. However, Castro alleges that his consent was given in exchange for NYT's agreement that no information concerning the circumstances of his stabbing would be broadcast and that the footage would be used solely for medical training purposes, and that NYT violated those conditions. Costa, whose native language is Portuguese, alleges that he did not understand the consent form because he cannot read English and no one explained or translated the form for him. He also alleges that he believed the persons who did the videotaping were working for the hospital, not a television show. Some of the videotape footage of both Castro and Costa was broadcast in one of the "Trauma: Life in the ER" television shows. Plaintiffs' complaint asserted liability on the basis of numerous legal theories. However, we concluded in a prior interlocutory appeal that various counts of the complaint failed to state a cause of action. (citation omitted) (citation omitted) As a result of that decision, plaintiffs' only remaining claims are for invasion of privacy by an unreasonable intrusion upon the seclusion of another, invasion of privacy by giving unreasonable publicity to another's private life, and common law fraud. (citation omitted)

Plaintiffs' complaint sought certification of a class of plaintiffs consisting of "all persons wherever situated who, at any time from January 1, 1998 to present, while patients at any hospital in the United States (footnote two) were filmed in connection with the production of the television show, 'Trauma: Life in the ER.'" Plaintiffs' counsel also filed individual actions, containing allegations nearly identical to the complaint in this action, on behalf of eight other patients who were videotaped in the Jersey Shore emergency room. [Footnote 2] (citation omitted)

The trial court granted plaintiffs' motion with respect to every patient videotaped or observed at Jersey Shore, but denied certification of a nationwide class consisting of every patient videotaped or observed in any hospital in the United States. The order granting class certification contains the following description of the class:

All persons wherever situated who, at any time from June 26, 2001 through July 27, 2001, while patients at the Jersey Shore Medical Center, had their confidential medical procedures, treatment or information disclosed to and/or observed by persons on behalf of NYT Television; the New York Times Company or Discovery Communications, Inc. in connection with the production of a television show called "Trauma: Life in the ER."

We granted defendants' motions for leave to appeal the order certifying this class and plaintiffs' cross-motion for leave to appeal the order denying the part of their motion that sought certification of a nationwide class. We now consolidate NYT's and Jersey Shore's appeals. On appeal, defendants argue that the trial court erred in certifying any class at all because issues common to the putative class do not predominate over issues affecting only individual members, and a class action would not be superior to an individual action for the fair and efficient adjudication of the controversy. In the alternative, defendants argue that even if the court properly granted class certification, it erred in expanding the class to include patients who were observed but not videotaped by the NYT film crew because the claims of such patients are barred by the statute of limitations.

We conclude that the trial court erred in granting class certification because issues common to the class do not predominate over individual issues. This conclusion makes it unnecessary to address defendants' alternative argument. Because the trial court erred in certifying any class at all, it follows a fortiori that the court properly denied certification of a nationwide class.

I

Plaintiffs moved for class certification under Rule 4:32-1(b)(3).

[...]

Rule 4:32-1(b)(3) provides in pertinent part:

An action may be maintained as a class action if the prerequisites of paragraph (a) are satisfied, and in addition: ... the court finds that the questions of law or fact common to the members of the class predominate over any questions affecting only individual members, and that a class action is superior to other available methods for the fair and efficient adjudication of the controversy.

[...]

Consequently, we [...] consider whether plaintiffs have established the requirements of Rule 4:32-1(b)(3) that class issues must predominate over individual issues and that a class action provides a superior method for adjudication of plaintiffs' claims.

To determine whether a proposed class action satisfies the requirement of "predominance," a trial court must first identify "the relevant factual and legal issues" in the case. (citation omitted).

[...]

The requirement of Rule 4:32-1(b)(3) that common issues of law or fact must predominate over any issues affecting only individual members of the class is "far more demanding" than Rule 4:32-1(a)(2)'s requirement that there be questions of law or fact common to the class. (citation omitted).

In this case, plaintiffs assert causes of action for invasion of privacy by an unreasonable intrusion upon the seclusion of another and invasion of privacy by giving unreasonable publicity to another's private life [footnote omitted], and defendants' primary defense is that plaintiffs and every other alleged class member who was shown on "Trauma: Life in the ER" consented to the videotaping and broadcasting. A review of the proofs required to establish plaintiffs' invasion of privacy claims and defendants' consent defense demonstrates that this is not a case in which class issues predominate over individual issues.

II

The elements of invasion of privacy by unreasonable intrusion upon seclusion [...] are delineated in the Second Restatement of Torts:

One who intentionally intrudes, physically or otherwise, upon the solitude or seclusion of another or his private affairs or concerns, is subject to liability to the other for invasion of his privacy, if the intrusion would be highly offensive to a reasonable person. (citation omitted) To establish liability for this tort, a plaintiff must show that "the interference with the plaintiff's seclusion is a substantial one, of a kind that would be highly offensive to the ordinary reasonable man, as the result of conduct to which the reasonable man would strongly object." (citation omitted)

Although the record of the videotaping conducted by NYT at Jersey Shore is limited to the footage actually broadcast, it is evident from this footage that the circumstances of the videotaping of individual patients varied greatly. Some of the videotaping was conducted in public areas of the hospital, such as the waiting room or hallways, while other videotaping was conducted in private areas, such as operating or patient rooms. Some of the videotaping consisted of interviews of patients lying in bed, while other footage was of patients who were unconscious or semiconscious or of doctors performing surgery.

Therefore, a trier of fact could find that the videotaping of some patients at Jersey Shore would not support imposition of liability for invasion of privacy by unreasonable intrusion upon seclusion, either because the videotaping did not involve any "intru[sion] … upon the solitude or seclusion of [the patients] or [their] private affairs or concerns" or because "the intrusion would [not] be highly offensive to a reasonable person." (citation omitted) On the other hand, a trier of fact could find that NYT's videotaping of other patients satisfied all the elements of this cause of action. […] Thus, the determination of defendants' liability for this tort will necessarily turn on the particular circumstances of the videotaping of each individual plaintiff, including the nature of the area where the videotaping was conducted, the appearance of the plaintiff during the videotaping, what medical procedure, if any, was being performed, and whether the plaintiff objected to or welcomed the videotaping. Moreover, the amount of damages to be awarded to any plaintiff whose right to seclusion was unreasonably intruded upon would depend on evidence of those same individual circumstances.

Consequently, even though all the claims of invasion of privacy by an unreasonable intrusion upon seclusion are based upon what the trial court characterized as a "common thread of facts"–NYT's videotaping of patients in the Jersey Shore emergency room–the proof of those claims will rest on evidence of the individual circumstances surrounding the videotaping of each patient rather than factual circumstances common to all putative class members.

III

Plaintiffs' claim of invasion of privacy by giving unreasonable publicity to another's private life also depends upon the circumstances of the broadcasting of footage of each individual plaintiff. The elements of this cause of action […] are delineated in the Second Restatement of Torts: One who gives publicity to a matter concerning the private life of another is subject to liability to the other for invasion of his [or her] privacy, if the matter publicized is of a kind that (a) would be highly offensive to a reasonable person, and (b) is not of legitimate concern to the public. (citation omitted)

Initially, we note that this cause of action may be asserted only by those plaintiffs who were actually shown on one of the two "Trauma: Life in the ER" television shows based on the filming at Jersey Shore. As explained in the comments to this section of the Restatement: "Publicity," as … used in this Section … means that the matter is made public[] by communicating it to the public at large, or to so many persons that the matter must be regarded as substantially certain to become one of public knowledge … .

Thus it is not an invasion of the right of privacy, within the rule stated in this Section, to communicate a fact concerning the plaintiff's private life to a single person or even to a small group of persons. (citation omitted)

Thus, claims for invasion of privacy by giving unreasonable publicity to the private life of another may not be predicated on the fact that the small group of people who filmed and edited the television show may have learned information concerning plaintiffs' private lives.

One element of this cause of action that any patient who was shown on "Trauma: Life in the ER" would be required to prove is that the information broadcast on the television show was in fact "private." However, the putative class representatives, as well as one plaintiff who brought an individual action, may have difficulty proving this element because stories concerning the incidents that resulted in their admittance to Jersey Shore were published in local newspapers. Consequently, the trial of these plaintiffs' claims of invasion of privacy by giving unreasonable publicity to their private lives will involve individual determinations of whether the information about their lives revealed in the television show was actually private even though it had been previously revealed in newspaper articles. (citation omitted)

Moreover, the alleged "private facts" about each patient revealed in the television show varied greatly. For example, putative class representative Costa was not named or interviewed in the episode in which he appeared and in fact is barely identifiable, while putative class representative Castro was identified by name, shown talking to the camera, and most significantly, the narrator indicated that Castro's injuries were caused by his wife stabbing him. Thus, the determination whether the dissemination of information concerning plaintiffs' alleged private lives "would be highly offensive to a reasonable person," which is another element of this cause of action (citation omitted) also would have to be made on a case-by-case basis. Therefore, the proof of this cause of action will turn on the factual circumstances of the broadcasting of each individual plaintiff and is not suitable for presentation in a class action.

IV

Every patient who was shown on "Trauma: Life in the ER" signed a written consent to the videotaping and broadcasting. If those consents were valid, they presumably would provide a complete defense to the claims of the plaintiffs who signed them. (citation omitted). However, plaintiffs allege that their consents were invalid for varying reasons. Castro testified at his deposition that NYT representatives agreed, as a condition of his consent, that the circumstances of his stabbing, which was a domestic violence incident, would not be publicized and that the videotape footage of him would be used for medical training purposes, both of which conditions NYT violated. Costa, whose native language is Portuguese, testified that he did not understand the consent form because he does not read English, and no one translated or explained the form to him. Several plaintiffs in the individual actions testified that they did not have the capacity to consent to the videotaping because they were heavily medicated when they signed the forms. Another plaintiff testified that an NYT representative stated that an unnamed "sponsor" would pay his medical bills if he consented to the videotaping and broadcasting. Therefore, the determination of the validity of the patients' consents does not involve a common question of law or fact, but will instead require the presentation of proofs relating to the individual circumstances of each plaintiff's execution of the consent form. (citation omitted)

Although there probably were some patients in the Jersey Shore emergency room who were videotaped but did not sign consent forms, plaintiffs have not identified any such patients. Furthermore, even as to patients who did not sign written consent forms, NYT may be able to show that they gave oral consent or implied consent by their conduct. Whatever the form of consent, however, the parties would have to present individualized proofs regarding the circumstances of that alleged consent.

In sum, the claims of each of the putative class members depends primarily on proofs that cannot be presented on a group basis. Therefore, the trial court erred in concluding that questions of law and fact common to the class predominate over questions affecting only individual members.

V

Because plaintiffs failed to establish the predominance of class issues over individual issues, there is no need to address the additional requirement that a party seeking class certification under Rule 4:32-1(b)(3) establish that a class action provides a method of adjudication of the putative class members' claims that is superior to individual actions. (citation omitted) However, if this requirement had to be addressed, we would conclude that plaintiffs failed to show the superiority of a class action for substantially the same reasons plaintiffs failed to show that issues common to members of the class predominate over issues affecting only individual members. Accordingly, the denial of certification of a nationwide class is affirmed. The certification of a class of patients who were videotaped or observed by NYT while at Jersey Shore is reversed, and the case is remanded to the trial court.

FOOTNOTES

2 The parties indicate that such videotaping was conducted in 35 hospitals located in 22 states.

At the conclusion of discovery, plaintiffs moved for class certification. In this motion, plaintiffs sought to expand the proposed class to include not only every patient who was videotaped for "Trauma: Life in the ER" in any hospital anywhere in the country but also every patient who had been "observed" by any of the NYT film crews while videotaping for this television show.

Since plaintiffs could not show that they shared sufficient interests, in common, with all other potential plaintiffs, the appeals court agreed to the decertification of this class in this class action suit.

Pre-trial Conferences

Parties to a dispute sometimes meet before a trial with the judge assigned to the case. Such a **pre-trial conference** (Fed. R. Civ. P. Rule 16) often involves a review of the schedule for the case, which had been established when plaintiff filed the complaint. Judges may use these meetings as an opportunity for the parties to settle a claim. If the parties can resolve the dispute before trial, that will end further involvement by the courts. Parties sometimes settle because they have more control over the final resolution, which could get lost if the matter ended up going to trial. Often, parties settle their dispute because of the high cost associated with continuing the litigation. Whatever the reasons, a judge can heartily encourage the parties to take action instead of, after a full trial, have the judge resolve the dispute.

■ MOTIONS

During legal proceedings, a party may ask a judge to rule on a particular aspect of the trial. When a party asks the court to act, that party files a **motion** with the court. The plaintiff can file a motion before the trial, during the trial, and after the entry of a judgment.

For example, a party may ask the judge to dismiss the case because of a defect in the complaint. Or a party may ask the judge to direct an opponent to produce requested documents that contain information that could help resolve the problem of law. Granting a pre-trial motion could resolve the dispute and eliminate the need for a trial.

Pre-trial Motions

Motion to Dismiss | Demurr

Early in the proceedings, counsel for the defendant may file a **motion to dismiss** the complaint filed by the plaintiff. This falls under Rule 12, in those jurisdictions that follow the Fed. R. Civ. P. While the defendant could ask the court to dismiss the suit because the court lacked jurisdiction or because of improper venue, the most common request is a Rule 12(b)(6) motion, motion to dismiss for failure to state a claim.

What defense counsel is saying in this motion is that, taking into consideration only what the plaintiff says in the complaint, the plaintiff has failed to allege in sufficient detail that a wrong has occurred and that the defendant should be liable for the damages incurred. Since plaintiff's counsel will likely check to see that the elements (components of the civil wrong) have been properly set out in the complaint, courts rarely grant this motion.

For example, filing suit for negligence, plaintiff's counsel has to allege duty, breach of duty, causation, and damages (see Chapter 3). Fail to include any of these elements, and the defendant will prevail since plaintiff's counsel has left out some allegations that will prove critical at trial for plaintiff to establish a claim for damages.

The following case describes a situation in which the plaintiff could not identify a specific law that had been violated by the defendants, so the court could find no basis for assessing the claim (see Case in Point 2-4). (Again, the plaintiff here is *pro se*, which mean that the plaintiff is acting without the assistance of legal counsel.)

 ## CASE IN POINT 2-4

Nzongda v. The United States

77 Fed. Cl. 64 (2007)

[…]

The Court has carefully reviewed Plaintiff's Complaint, and discerns the following allegations against the Defendants, identified in the Complaint as the Metropolitan Police Department ("MPD"), the Federal Bureau of Investigation ("FBI"), and the United States Capitol Police ("USCP"):

1. That Defendants have failed to prevent unidentified private individuals from stalking Plaintiff;
2. That Defendants have conspired with private individuals to deny Plaintiff certain "Public Benefits," including financial assistance and medical treatment, to which she claims entitlement;
3. That Defendants have failed to protect Plaintiff from becoming the victim of ridicule, theft, and invasion of privacy; and
4. That Defendants have failed to prevent the commission of racial discrimination against Plaintiff.

The Court initially notes that it holds the pleadings of *pro se* Plaintiffs "to a lesser standard than those drafted by lawyers when determining whether the complaint should be dismissed for failure to state a claim[.]" (citation omitted) The Court has no duty, however, "to create a claim which [Plaintiff] has not spelled out in [her] pleading[.]" Id. (citation omitted)

In order to invoke this Court's jurisdiction, a plaintiff must present an allegation that falls within the category of claims identified in The Tucker Act. The Tucker Act provides: The United States Court of Federal Claims shall have jurisdiction to render judgment upon any claim against the United States founded either upon the Constitution, or any Act of Congress or any regulation of an executive department, or upon any express or implied contract with the United States, or for liquidated or unliquidated damages in cases not sounding in tort (citation omitted).

Additionally, plaintiffs in this Court must identify a separate "money-mandating" statute that requires the government to pay the plaintiff for the injury alleged. In other words, the plaintiff "must also demonstrate that the source of law relied upon 'can fairly be interpreted as mandating compensation by the federal government for the damages sustained.'" (citation omitted)

Having reviewed Plaintiff's Complaint against the requirements of The Tucker Act and the cases cited above, the Court is unable to discern any claims for which the Court may grant relief to Plaintiff. In their essence, Plaintiff's claims assert that Defendants have (1) failed to perform their official duties with respect to Plaintiff; (2) negligently performed their official duties with respect to Plaintiff; and (3) conspired with private individuals against Plaintiff. These allegations do not support a cause of action under the Tucker Act. As the Court noted in Cottrell v. United States:

The court does not have jurisdiction over claims that defendant engaged in negligent, fraudulent, or other wrongful conduct when discharging its official duties. It does not have jurisdiction over harassment claims, or breach of duty claims, or claims involving tortious interference with contractual relationships[.] Even where the claim is framed under non-tort law, the "court lacks jurisdiction if the essence of the claim lies in tort." Finally, the Court of Federal Claims lacks jurisdiction over conspiracy claims because these, too, sound in tort. (citations omitted).

Conclusion

For the reasons stated above, [...] Plaintiff's Complaint is DISMISSED with prejudice. [...] The Clerk of the Court shall enter judgment consistent with this opinion, and shall not accept future filings from Plaintiff without an order by a judge of this court approving the filing.
[...]

Since the plaintiff could not cite the law upon which to base a claim, the plaintiff had no valid legal basis for filing a claim.

If a court grants a Rule 12(b)(6) motion, it likely won't do so 'with prejudice'. If a court grants a motion to dismiss with prejudice, the plaintiff is now prohibited from refiling that claim, even if some defect in the pleadings has now been fixed. By granting the motion without prejudice, the court hopes that plaintiff's counsel, now aware of the defect, will file a complaint with all the components needed to make out a cause of action in tort. In the previous case, since no basis at law existed for this claim, the court could see no basis for allowing a refiling of an action with no valid statute on point.

Filing this motion means that, until the hearing on the motion, scheduled for within 30 days of the filing, all court activity involving the suit halts. That means if defense counsel filed the motion before filing an answer, the defendant doesn't have to file until after the motion is ruled on. From a defendant's perspective, this may mean delaying the overall progress of the lawsuit and thereby create opportunities for settlement.

Motion for Judgment on the Pleadings

When plaintiff's counsel files a **motion for judgment on the pleadings,** the lawyer is asking that the court grant the plaintiff a judgment because what is set forth in the complaint and in the answer is sufficient for the plaintiff to win (see Fed. R. Civ. P. Rule 12). Courts rarely grant this motion since the plaintiff needs to offer only enough information in the complaint to provide sufficient notice to the defendant that suit has commenced. If the defendant admits to liability in the answer, a court might grant the motion. But it might hesitate to do so since neither side has yet offered any evidence to the court outside of the pleadings.

Motion for a Summary Judgment

When a party files a **motion for summary judgment,** according to Fed. R. Civ. P. Rule 56, that party is saying that, assuming certain facts are true, it is entitled to a judgment as a matter of law. Neither party may have gathered much information at this point in the legal process, although the discovery process (see below) may have yielded some facts.

The moving party asks the court for judgment and supports the request with an affidavit. An affidavit contains statements of fact and is signed by the person who alleges the facts are true. The person who made the statements in the affidavit faces the risk of perjury charges if that person has lied in the affidavit. The affidavit may have supporting exhibits, such as a medical report or photographs.

In the following case, the court had to determine that, accepting all facts as true, the plaintiff had no basis at law to be able to prevail in the lawsuit (see Case in Point 2-5).

CASE IN POINT 2-5

Wood v. Fineberg Management, Inc.
24 Mass. L. Rep. 140 (Mass. Super. Ct. 2008)

[...]

At approximately 7:00 a.m. on December 8, 2003, Ms. Wood entered the building at 150 Royall Street in Canton, MA, where she worked for a company called Equiserve. After presenting her pass to posted security guards, Ms. Wood made her way across the lobby where she slipped on accumulated water on the floor and fell, injuring herself. While unable to see the water at the time she crossed the lobby, Ms. Wood saw a watery footprint as she lay on the floor. At the time Ms. Wood fell, there were no mats on the ground or warning signs posted. The night before, approximately eight inches of snow had fallen.

At the time of the incident, Equiserve was a tenant in the premises, which was owned by Blue Hills Park, LLC and managed by Fineberg. Equiserve hired Apollo as an independent contractor to provide security services on the premises and Fineberg hired Janitronics to provide cleaning services in the building.

DISCUSSION

I. Standard of Review

Summary judgment is appropriate when the summary judgment record shows "there is no genuine issue as to any material fact and that the moving party is entitled to judgment as a matter of law." (citation omitted) A fact is "material" if it would affect the outcome of the suit. (citation omitted) A dispute is "genuine" where a reasonable finder of fact could return a verdict for the non-moving party. (citation omitted) The moving party bears the initial burden of demonstrating the absence of a triable issue and that the summary judgment record entitles it to judgment as a matter of law. (citation omitted) The moving party may satisfy its burden by submitting affirmative evidence that negates an essential element of the opposing party's case or by demonstrating that the non-moving party has no reasonable expectation of proving an essential element of his case at trial. (citation omitted)

In reviewing a motion for summary judgment, the court views the evidence in the light most favorable to the non-moving party and draws all reasonable inferences in her favor. (citation omitted) If the moving party has carried its burden, and the plaintiff has not responded with specific facts to establish a genuine, triable issue, the court grants the motion for summary judgment. (citation omitted)

II. Apollo's Motion

Apollo argues it did not owe a duty to Ms. Wood to protect her from, or warn her of, accumulated water on the lobby floor. "To recover for negligence, a plaintiff must show 'the existence of an act or omission in violation of a ... duty owed to the plaintiff[s] by the defendant.'" (citation omitted) [...] While every actor has a duty to exercise reasonable care to avoid physical harm to others, (citation omitted) generally, a person has no legal duty to prevent the harmful consequences of a condition or situation he or she did not create. (citation omitted) [...]

Here, the duty to clean and/or warn did not rest with Apollo. Apollo's contractual duties were limited to "security services." The evidence shows these duties consisted primarily of monitoring people entering the building, but could also include such security procedures as revolving patrol. Apollo's duties, however, did not extend to caring for the floors of the lobby. The evidence is that a day porter, employed by Janitronics but leased to Fineberg, was on call to perform janitorial services throughout the work day. At the direction of Fineberg, the day porter's job was to mop the lobby floor, put up caution signs, and put down mats when the lobby floor was wet due to cleaning or inclement weather.

Furthermore, Apollo did not control the area in question. There is no evidence that Apollo had control over the lobby apart from their security duties. Apollo was an independent contractor hired to provide security services. It was not a tenant in the building. It also did not have authority or supervisory capacity over the lobby, and was not in a position to direct the day porter in his work; the day porter took his directions from Fineberg. Consequently, Apollo did not owe Ms. Wood a duty to protect her from, or warn her about, the water on the lobby floor by virtue of its responsibilities as a security service. (citation omitted)

Nevertheless, Ms. Wood argues Apollo assumed the duty to maintain the safety of the lobby. Her argument is based on deposition testimony indicating Apollo could have requested the day porter to put out mats or warning signs. (citation omitted) Because Apollo could have made this request, Ms. Wood continues, it assumed a duty to maintain the safety of the lobby. Where a duty has been voluntarily assumed, it must be carried out with due care. (citation omitted) "If a person voluntarily assumes a duty or undertakes to render services to another that should have been seen as necessary for her protection, that person may be liable for harm caused because of the negligent performance of his undertaking." (citation omitted)

Contrary to Ms. Wood's argument, this court finds Apollo did not assume a duty to maintain a clean and water-free lobby floor. Here, Apollo's role in alerting others the floor may be slippery was akin to a switchboard operator's; if someone alerted Apollo of the existence of a problem in the lobby, it would contact the day porter and inform him of the situation, which then became his responsibility. [footnote omitted] In fact, this was the general scheme set up by

> Equiserve, as any problem encountered in the building would be routed to Apollo, who would then alert the appropriate party.
>
> Alerting the party whose job it is to respond to a particular problem is not tantamount to assuming a duty to respond to the problem itself. Here, Apollo did not volunteer its services to inspect or mop the floor or to set up warning signs or mats. As discussed above, these tasks were the job of the day porter. While it is the case that Apollo would call the day porter if it observed a problem, there is no evidence Apollo either observed the wet floor or was informed of the slippery floor prior to Ms. Wood's fall, and thus, was not on notice to call the day porter. As a result, Apollo did not assume a duty in this instance. (citation omitted) [...]
>
> It is hereby ORDERED that Apollo's Motion for Summary Judgment is ALLOWED.

Since no duty existed between plaintiff and defendant, the plaintiff could not possibly win on a claim of negligence against the defendant, so the court granted the motion for summary judgment under Rule 56.

Courts may not often grant this motion since the presence of any questions of fact will mean that only through further discovery and potentially, trial, will they be resolved. Still, this is another opportunity, as with the motion to dismiss, for the court to evaluate a claim so as to winnow out those that clearly do not require additional judicial resources to arrive at a resolution of the dispute.

Motion to Compel Discovery

A **motion to compel discovery** involves finding all information, before trial, that could prove relevant and material to resolving the question of law. Different types of discovery exist, as noted in the following.

Under the Fed. R. Civ. P., each request for each type of discovery comes with a deadline by which the party or witness has to provide the information; often it is for 30 days. Failure to do so can mean that the party requesting the discovery may move for a court order to compel the party with the information to provide it. In extreme instances, when a party with information chooses not to comply with that court order, the court might cite that party for the crime of contempt of court. Or, among other options available under Fed. R. Civ. P. Rule 37, a court may choose to end the case in the favor of the party who is seeking the information.

Motions during the Trial

Several opportunities could arise during a trial for filing motions.

Motion in Limine

Among the motions that a lawyer can file during a trial, counsel for either party might file for a **motion *in limine*.** By making this motion, counsel is asking for the court to determine whether certain information should be allowed to be used as evidence. This motion usually requires the court to hear arguments presented by counsel, but out of earshot from the jury. Otherwise, if the jury heard the lawyers argue the issue and the judge decides not to admit the information, the jurors would still know of the information, even though it had not been accepted into evidence.

Motion for Directed Verdict

A **motion for directed verdict** can be made during trial. Once the plaintiff has presented the case in chief—that is, the plaintiff has shown, by a preponderance of evidence, all elements needed for a court to issue a damages award—the defendant can file for a motion for directed verdict (see Fed. R. Civ. P. Rule 50). This motion effectively says that even if all the evidence plaintiff has provided turns out to be valid, plaintiff has somehow failed to present enough evidence on one of the elements of the tort.

Counsel for a defendant has an ethical obligation to file for a directed verdict, regardless of the likelihood of success. Lawyers have an obligation to represent their client's interests zealously, for example, through cross-examination of witnesses. But as with the motion to dismiss for failure to state a claim, the court might not grant the motion because it is obvious that the plaintiff has met the burden of proof on all of the elements of the tort claim.

A judge ruling on such a motion may face a dilemma. If he or she grants the motion, the losing party appeals, and the appeals court reverses the decision, the entire trial must be restarted. But if the judge holds off on issuing a ruling and lets the defendant present a defense, and sends the case to the jury, the judge can minimize repercussions. The jury could find for the defendant, so that the issue on appeal would be the jury's decision and not the judge's ruling on the motion for a directed verdict. If the jury does not find for the defendant and the judge disagrees because he or she feels the plaintiff didn't provide enough evidence, the plaintiff could file an **appeal**. If the appeals court reverses on appeal, the trial judge can reinstate the jury's verdict instead of having to conduct a new trial. So judges may have a tendency not to rule on a motion for directed verdict. Instead, by having the case go to the jury, the judge increases the chance that even a reversal, on appeal, of its decision won't result in the need for a new trial.

Post-trial Motions

Motion for Judgment Notwithstanding the Verdict

When the jury has completed its deliberations, it will issue a verdict. If the jury has concluded that liability exists but the judge does not believe the plaintiff met the burden of showing, by a preponderance of evidence, each element of the claim, then the judge may reject that conclusion if counsel has filed a **motion for judgment notwithstanding the verdict** (see Fed. R. Civ. P. Rule 50).

For example, if the plaintiff is suing the defendant for injuries that arose when pajamas that should have been treated with a flame retardant were not treated, and during the trial the pajamas somehow caught on fire, any verdict for the plaintiff would have to be thrown out. That's because the risk existed that the jury, having witnessed the accident in court, was reacting to it and not to the evidence.

Motion for Additur or Remitter

Even if a court accepts a jury's verdict, a party may make a **motion for additur** or a **motion for remitter,** that is, move to increase or decrease the amount of damages imposed by the jury. Among the reasons for granting such a motion, the court may rule to change the amount since the jury had not given full enough consideration to all the facts, or if it emphasized some facts over others (see Fed. R. Civ. P. Rule 59).

Motion for a New Trial

Counsel for the losing party has an ethical obligation to make a **motion for a new trial.** The lawyer might talk about an error made in a ruling, improperly admitted evidence, or because the result was altered by an outside event (see Fed. R. Civ. P. Rule 59).

For example, assume that a trial started on Friday, September 7, 2001 regarding a passenger's claim against an airline for losing the passenger's luggage. The attacks with the jet airliners on Tuesday, September 11, 2001 would dramatically affect any jury's perspective on the specific case. That would call into question any verdict of the jury, since the jurors might be reacting to the events of September 11 and not to the evidence presented at trial.

■ DISCOVERY

The American legal system, with an interest in achieving a just outcome, seeks a verdict based on the facts. During the pre-trial process called **discovery,** the parties may gather information that will help the court—if there is a trial—to resolve the issue of law faster. This is "wide open" discovery, so that parties must disclose all facts within a party's control, absent any exceptions.

Exceptions

Exceptions to the discovery process arise in two situations, where the **privilege** of non-disclosure exists and under the **"work product" doctrine.**

Privilege

Certain information might not be disclosed if that information arises out of privileged communication. The legal system recognizes that a benefit may accrue if people who receive information do not have to fear getting a court order to disclose this information at trial. For example, a jurisdiction might make privileged communications between an individual and that person's religious or spiritual leader so as to gain spiritual comfort. Or, under the attorney-client privilege, having all discussions exempt from disclosure means that the lawyer can get all necessary information and can answer all questions of law that a client might have. Some jurisdictions might have a spouse's privilege, since having that privilege means that in this venerable social institution, married partners may speak freely with one another. For more on the concept of privilege, see Chapter 11.

"Work Product" Doctrine

Discovery cannot include information about how the lawyer handles the case for the client. The lawyer needs to have the freedom to consider all possible strategies that will benefit a client and might feel inhibited if an opposing party could learn of them simply through discovery. In the following landmark ruling by the U.S. Supreme Court, the majority looked into the purpose of pre-trial discovery, especially Rule 26(b)(3), which protected a lawyer's "work product"—the pre-trial strategizing that a lawyer does for and with a client—from disclosure (see Case in Point 2-6).

Read on More on this.

🏛 CASE IN POINT 2-6

Hickman v. Taylor

329 U.S. 495 (1947)

This case presents an important problem under the Federal Rules of Civil Procedure (citation omitted) as to the extent to which a party may inquire into oral and written statements of witnesses, or other information, secured by an adverse party's counsel in the course of preparation for possible litigation after a claim has arisen. Examination into a person's files and records, including those resulting from the professional activities of an attorney, must be judged with care. It is not without reason that various safeguards have been established to preclude unwarranted excursions into the privacy of a man's work. At the same time, public policy supports reasonable and necessary inquiries. Properly to balance these competing interests is a delicate and difficult task.

On February 7, 1943, the tug 'J. M. Taylor' sank while engaged in helping to tow a car float of the Baltimore & Ohio Railroad across the Delaware River at Philadelphia. The accident was apparently unusual in nature, the cause of it still being unknown. Five of the nine crew members were drowned. Three days later the tug owners and the underwriters employed a law firm, of which respondent Fortenbaugh is a member, to defend them against potential suits by representatives of the deceased crew members and to sue the railroad for damages to the tug.

A public hearing was held on March 4, 1943, before the United States Steamboat Inspectors, at which the four survivors were examined. This testimony was recorded and made available to all interested parties. Shortly thereafter, Fortenbaugh privately interviewed the survivors and took statements from them with an eye toward the anticipated litigation; the survivors signed these statements on March 29. Fortenbaugh also interviewed other persons believed to have some information relating to the accident and in some cases he made memoranda of what they told him. At the time when Fortenbaugh secured the statements of the survivors, representatives of two of the deceased crew members had been in communication with him. Ultimately claims were presented by representatives of all five of the deceased; four of the claims, however, were settled without litigation. The fifth claimant, petitioner herein, brought suit in a federal court […] on November 26, 1943, naming as defendants the two tug owners, individually and as partners, and the railroad.

One year later, petitioner filed 39 interrogatories directed to the tug owners. The 38th interrogatory read: "State whether any statements of the members of the crews of the Tugs 'J. M. Taylor' and 'Philadelphia' or of any other vessel were taken in connection with the towing of the car float and the sinking of the Tug 'John M. Taylor.'

Attach hereto exact copies of all such statements if in writing, and if oral, set forth in detail the exact provisions of any such oral statements or reports."

Supplemental interrogatories asked whether any oral or written statements, records, reports or other memoranda had been made concerning any matter relative to the towing operation, the sinking of the tug, the salvaging and repair of the tug, and the death of the deceased. If the answer was in the affirmative, the tug owners were then requested to set forth the nature of all such records, reports, statements or other memoranda.

The tug owners, through Fortenbaugh, answered all of the interrogatories except No. 38 and the supplemental ones just described. While admitting that statements of the survivors had been taken, they declined to summarize or set forth the contents. They did so on the ground that such requests called 'for privileged matter obtained in preparation for litigation' and constituted 'an attempt to obtain indirectly counsel's private files.' It was claimed that answering these requests 'would involve practically turning over not only the complete files, but also the telephone records and, almost, the thoughts of counsel.'

In connection with the hearing on these objections, Fortenbaugh made a written statement and gave an informal oral deposition explaining the circumstances under which he had taken the statements. But he was not expressly asked in the deposition to produce the statements. The District Court for the Eastern District of Pennsylvania, sitting en banc, held that the requested matters were not privileged. (citation omitted) The court then decreed that the tug owners and Fortenbaugh, as counsel and agent for the tug owners forthwith

"Answer Plaintiff's 38th interrogatory and supplemental interrogatories; produce all written statements of witnesses obtained by Mr. Fortenbaugh, as counsel and agent for Defendants; state in substance any fact concerning this case which Defendants learned through oral statements made by witnesses to Mr. Fortenbaugh whether or not included in his private memoranda and produce Mr. Fortenbaugh's memoranda containing statements of fact by witnesses or to submit these memoranda to the Court for determination of those portions which should be revealed to Plaintiff." Upon their refusal, the court adjudged them in contempt and ordered them imprisoned until they complied. The Third Circuit Court of Appeals, also sitting en banc, reversed the judgment of the District Court. (citation omitted). It held that the information here sought was part of the 'work product of the lawyer' and hence privileged from discovery under the Federal Rules of Civil Procedure. The importance of the problem, which has engendered a great divergence of views among district courts, led us to grant certiorari. (citation omitted).

The pre-trial deposition-discovery mechanism established by Rules 26 to 37 is one of the most significant innovations of the Federal Rules of Civil Procedure. Under the prior federal practice, the pre-trial functions of notice-giving issue-formulation and fact-revelation were performed primarily and inadequately by the pleadings. [Footnote omitted] Inquiry into the issues and the facts before trial was narrowly confined and was often cumbersome in method. [Footnote omitted] The new rules, however, restrict the pleadings to the task of general notice-giving and invest the deposition-discovery process with a vital role in the preparation for trial. The various instruments of discovery now serve (1) as a device, along with the pretrial hearing under Rule 16, to narrow and clarify the basic issues between the parties, and (2) as a device for ascertaining the facts, or information as to the existence or whereabouts of facts, relative to those issues. Thus civil trials in the federal courts no longer need be carried on in the dark. The way is now clear, consistent with recognized privileges, for the parties to obtain the fullest possible knowledge of the issues and facts before trial. [Footnote omitted]

[...]

The deposition-discovery rules create integrated procedural devices. And the basic question at stake is whether any of those devices may be used to inquire into materials collected by an adverse party's counsel in the course of preparation for possible litigation. The fact that the petitioner may have used the wrong method does not destroy the main thrust of his attempt. Nor does it relieve us of the responsibility of dealing with the problem raised by that attempt. It would be inconsistent with the liberal atmosphere surrounding these rules to insist that petitioner now go through the empty formality of pursuing the right procedural device only to reestablish precisely the same basic problem now confronting us. We do not mean to say, however, that there may not be situations in which the failure to proceed in accordance with a specific rule would be important or decisive. But in the present circumstances, for the purposes of this decision, the procedural irregularity is not material. Having noted the proper procedure, we may accordingly turn our attention to the substance of the underlying problem.

In urging that he has a right to inquire into the materials secured and prepared by Fortenbaugh, petitioner emphasizes that the deposition-discovery portions of the Federal Rules of Civil Procedure are designed to enable the parties to discover the true facts and to compel their disclosure wherever they may be found. It is said that inquiry may be made under these rules, epitomized by Rule 26, as to any relevant matter which is not privileged; and since the discovery provisions are to be applied as broadly and liberally as possible, the privilege limitation must be restricted to its narrowest bounds. On the premise that the attorney-client privilege is the one involved in this case, petitioner argues that it must be strictly confined to confidential communications made by a client to his attorney. And since the materials here in issue were secured by Fortenbaugh from third persons rather than from his clients, the tug owners, the conclusion is reached that these materials are proper subjects for discovery under Rule 26. As additional support for this result, petitioner claims that to prohibit discovery under these circumstances would give a corporate defendant a tremendous advantage in a suit by an individual plaintiff. Thus in a suit by an injured employee against a railroad or in a suit by an insured person against an insurance company the corporate defendant could pull a dark veil of secrecy over all the pertinent facts it can collect after the claim arises merely on the assertion that such facts were gathered by its large staff of attorneys and claim agents. At the same time, the individual plaintiff, who often has direct knowledge of the matter in issue and has no counsel until some time after his claim arises could be compelled to disclose all the intimate details of his case. By endowing with immunity from disclosure all that a lawyer discovers in the course of his duties, it is said, the rights of individual litigants in such cases are drained of vitality and the lawsuit becomes more of a battle of deception than a search for truth.

But framing the problem in terms of assisting individual plaintiffs in their suits against corporate defendants is unsatisfactory. Discovery concededly may work to the disadvantage as well as to the advantage of individual plaintiffs. Discovery, in other words, is not a one-way proposition. It is available in all types of cases at the behest of any party, individual or corporate, plaintiff or defendant. The problem thus far transcends the situation confronting this petitioner. And we must view that problem in light of the limitless situations where the particular kind of discovery sought by petitioner might be used.

We agree, of course, that the deposition-discovery rules are to be accorded a broad and liberal treatment. No longer can the time-honored cry of 'fishing expedition' serve to preclude a party from inquiring into the facts underlying his opponent's case. [Footnote omitted] Mutual knowledge of all the relevant facts gathered by both parties is essential to proper litigation. To that end, either party may compel the other to disgorge whatever facts he has in his possession. The deposition-discovery procedure simply advances the stage at which the disclosure can be compelled from the time of trial to the period preceding it, thus reducing the possibility of surprise. But discovery, like all matters of procedure, has ultimate and necessary boundaries. As indicated by Rules 30(b) and (d) and 31(d), limitations inevitably arise when it can be shown that the examination is being conducted in bad faith or in such a manner as to annoy, embarrass or oppress the person subject to the inquiry. And as Rule 26(b) provides, further limitations come into existence when the inquiry touches upon the irrelevant or encroaches upon the recognized domains of privilege.

We also agree that the memoranda, statements and mental impressions in issue in this case fall outside the scope of the attorney-client privilege and hence are not protected from discovery on that basis. It is unnecessary here to delineate the content and scope of that privilege as recognized in the federal courts. For present purposes, it suffices to note that the protective cloak of this privilege does not extend to information, which an attorney secures from a witness while acting for his client in anticipation of litigation. Nor does this privilege concern the memoranda, briefs, communications and other writings prepared by counsel for his own use in prosecuting his client's case; and it is equally unrelated to writings which reflect an attorney's mental impressions, conclusions, opinions or legal theories.

But the impropriety of invoking that privilege does not provide an answer to the problem before us. Petitioner has made more than an ordinary request for relevant, non-privileged facts in the possession of his adversaries or their counsel. He has sought discovery as of right of oral and written statements of witnesses whose identity is well known and whose availability to petitioner appears unimpaired. He has sought production of these matters after making the most searching inquiries of his opponents as to the circumstances surrounding the fatal accident, which inquiries were sworn to have been answered to the best of their information and belief. Interrogatories were directed toward all the events prior to, during and subsequent to the sinking of the tug. Full and honest answers to such broad inquiries would necessarily have included all pertinent information gleaned by Fortenbaugh through his interviews with the witnesses. Petitioner makes no suggestion, and we cannot assume, that the tug owners or Fortenbaugh were incomplete or dishonest in the framing of their answers. In addition, petitioner was free to examine the public testimony of the witnesses taken before the United States Steamboat Inspectors. We are thus dealing with an attempt to secure the production of written statements and mental impressions contained in the files and the mind of the attorney Fortenbaugh without any showing of necessity or any indication or claim that denial of such production would unduly prejudice the preparation of petitioner's case or cause him any hardship or injustice. For aught that appears, the essence of what petitioner seeks either has been revealed to him already through the interrogatories or is readily available to him direct from the witnesses for the asking.

The District Court, after hearing objections to petitioner's request, commanded Fortenbaugh to produce all written statements of witnesses and to state in substance any facts learned through oral statements of witnesses to him. Fortenbaugh was to submit any memoranda he had made of the oral statements so that the court might determine what portions should be revealed to petitioner. All of this was ordered without any showing by petitioner, or any requirement that he make a proper showing, of the necessity for the production of any of this material or any demonstration that denial of production would cause hardship or injustice. The court simply ordered production on the theory that the facts sought were material and were not privileged as constituting attorney-client communications.

In our opinion, neither Rule 26 nor any other rule dealing with discovery contemplates production under such circumstances. That is not because the subject matter is privileged or irrelevant, as those concepts are used in these rules. [Footnote omitted] Here is simply an attempt, without purported necessity or justification, to secure written statements, private memoranda and personal recollections prepared or formed by an adverse party's counsel in the course of his legal duties. As such, it falls outside the arena of discovery and contravenes the public policy underlying the orderly prosecution and defense of legal claims. Not even the most liberal of discovery theories can justify unwarranted inquiries into the files and the mental impressions of an attorney.

Historically, a lawyer is an officer of the court and is bound to work for the advancement of justice while faithfully protecting the rightful interests of his clients. In performing his various duties, however, it is essential that a lawyer work with a certain degree of privacy, free from unnecessary intrusion by opposing parties and their counsel. Proper preparation of a client's case demands that he assemble information, sift what he considers to be the relevant from the irrelevant facts, prepare his legal theories and plan his strategy without undue and needless interference. That is the historical and the necessary way in which lawyers act within the framework of our system of jurisprudence to promote justice and to protect their clients' interests. This work is reflected, of course, in interviews, statements, memoranda, correspondence, briefs, mental impressions, personal beliefs, and countless other tangible and intangible ways—aptly though roughly termed by the Circuit Court of Appeals in this case (citation omitted) as the "Work product of the lawyer." Were such materials open to opposing counsel on mere demand, much of what is now put down in writing would remain unwritten. An attorney's thoughts, heretofore inviolate, would not be his own. Inefficiency, unfairness and sharp practices would inevitably develop in the giving of legal advice and in the preparation of cases for trial. The effect on the legal profession would be demoralizing. And the interests of the clients and the cause of justice would be poorly served.

We do not mean to say that all written materials obtained or prepared by an adversary's counsel with an eye toward litigation are necessarily free from discovery in all cases. Where relevant and non-privileged facts remain hidden in an attorney's file and where production of those facts is essential to the preparation of one's case, discovery may properly be had. Such written statements and documents might, under certain circumstances, be admissible in evidence or give clues as to the existence or location of relevant facts. Or they might be useful for purposes of impeachment or corroboration. And production might be justified where the witnesses are no longer available or can be reached only with difficulty. Were production of written statements and documents to be precluded under such circumstances, the liberal ideals of the deposition-discovery portions of the Federal Rules of Civil Procedure would be stripped of much of their meaning. But the general policy against invading the privacy of an attorney's course of preparation is so well recognized and so essential to an orderly working of our system of legal procedure that a burden rests on the one who would invade that privacy to establish adequate reasons to justify production through a subpoena or court order. That burden, we believe, is necessarily implicit in the rules as now constituted. [Footnote omitted.]

Rule 30(b), as presently written, gives the trial judge the requisite discretion to make a judgment as to whether discovery should be allowed as to written statements secured from witnesses. But in the instant case there was no room for that discretion to operate in favor of the petitioner. No attempt was made to establish any reason why Fortenbaugh should be forced to produce the written statements. There was only a naked, general demand for these materials as of right and a finding by the District Court that no recognizable privilege was involved. That was insufficient to justify discovery under these circumstances and the court should have sustained the refusal of the tug owners and Fortenbaugh to produce.

But as to oral statements made by witnesses to Fortenbaugh, whether presently in the form of his mental impressions or memoranda, we do not believe that any showing of necessity can be made under the circumstances of this case so as to justify production. Under ordinary conditions, forcing an attorney to repeat or write out all that witnesses have told him and to deliver the account to his adversary gives rise to grave dangers of inaccuracy and untrustworthiness. No legitimate purpose is served by such production. The practice forces the attorney to testify as to what he remembers or what he saw fit to write down regarding witnesses' remarks. Such testimony could not qualify as evidence; and to use it for impeachment or corroborative purposes would make the attorney much less an officer of the court and much more an ordinary witness. The standards of the profession would thereby suffer.

Denial of production of this nature does not mean that any material, non-privileged facts can be hidden from the petitioner in this case. He need not be unduly hindered in the preparation of his case, in the discovery of facts or in his anticipation of his opponents' position. Searching interrogatories directed to Fortenbaugh and the tug owners, production of written documents and statements upon a proper showing and direct interviews with the witnesses themselves all serve to reveal the facts in Fortenbaugh's possession to the fullest possible extent consistent with public policy. Petitioner's counsel frankly admits that he wants the oral statements only to help prepare himself to examine witnesses and to make sure that he has overlooked nothing. That is insufficient under the circumstances to permit him an exception to the policy underlying the privacy of Fortenbaugh's professional activities. If there should be a rare situation justifying production of these matters, petitioner's case is not of that type.

We fully appreciate the wide-spread controversy among the members of the legal profession over the problem raised by this case. [Footnote omitted.] It is a problem that rests on what has been one of the most hazy frontiers of the discovery

> process. But until some rule or statute definitely prescribes otherwise, we are not justified in permitting discovery in a situation of this nature as a matter of unqualified right. When Rule 26 and the other discovery rules were adopted, this Court and the members of the bar in general certainly did not believe or contemplate that all the files and mental processes of lawyers were thereby opened to the free scrutiny of their adversaries. And we refuse to interpret the rules at this time so as to reach so harsh and unwarranted a result.
>
> We therefore affirm the judgment of the Circuit Court of Appeals.

So, the Court's ruling merely acknowledged the importance of preserving for lawyers the ability to consider strategy related to the representation of a client.

The court in USW v. Ivaco, Inc., 2003 U.S. Dist. 10008 (N. D. Ga. 2003), noted that the essence of this case had been codified in Rule 26(b)(3).

General Duty to Disclose

Fed. R. Civ. P. Rule 26 describes the general principles related to the concept of discovery. Besides talking about the role that discovery plays in litigation, this rule describes a general principle about discovery, about the need to have access to any information that can help to resolve the question of law that underlies the parties' dispute. Subsequent rules define specific ways of uncovering this information. But Fed. R. Civ. P. 26 reflects the broader policy of getting to all the information, so that if it comes to a trial, the proceedings can unfold smoothly since everyone will know about the facts associated with the dispute.

Depositions

A **deposition** involves asking someone a series of open-ended questions, with the hope of finding information that would merit further exploration. Depositions are often conducted in the law office of a party, with no judge presiding, only lawyers for the parties. The lawyers will question the deponent—the person being deposed. The deponent needs to respond to all questions provided. Depositions can be lengthy, as the lawyer for the party who has sought this deposition might explore different topics relating to the case.

Objections

During the deposition, if opposing counsel objects about the nature or scope of the questions, the proceeding continues, with the objection being noted in the transcript that is generated during any deposition. Unlike a trial, an objection here will not stop the proceeding, since no judge is present to offer a ruling on the objection. Recording the objection preserves the option of challenging the use of the facts contained in that answer if counsel wishes to introduce those facts into evidence at trial.

Use at Trial

In some rare instances, statements made during a deposition might be admitted, at trial, as testimony. This happens if the deponent no longer has the option to answer a subpoena to testify at a trial. Courts allow for the use of a deposition transcript under extremely limited circumstances since the deposition took place without the presence of the judge and opposing counsel did not have the opportunity to get a ruling upon raising an objection (see Fed. R. Civ. P. Rules 27-32).

Interrogatories

A party poses written questions, or **interrogatories,** to an opponent; Fed. R. Civ. P. Rule 33 limits those to 25. These can be used only with an opponent and not with someone who would only be a witness at trial. These questions can include any topic that could be discovered under other rules or the broader provisions of Rule 26.

The recipient can object to the nature of the questions and so, the parties may need to go before a judge to determine if valid grounds exist to support the objection.

Production of Documents

A party can ask for **production of documents**—that is, a copy of any kind of writing relating to the dispute in the possession of an opponent (see Fed. R. Civ. P. 34). Documents secured through discovery may be used as exhibits at trial. As with other forms of discovery, a party may object to the request for production and so, require a court to rule on the appropriateness of the request.

If a party cannot provide copies to an opponent, the opponent has to arrange for a reasonable time and place to allow the party requesting the documents to inspect them.

Production of Electronically Stored Information

A party may request access to or copies of electronically stored information; this might include e-mail, word processing files, or other forms of information stored electronically (see Fed. R. Civ. P. Rule 34).

This rule applies to information kept in the normal course of business. Unless the party requesting this information asks that it be provided in a particular format, such as a compressed file, the party with the file may provide it in a format commonly used by the party that possess the information. The party with the information does not have to produce the information in multiple formats.

In the following case, the court considered the nature of electronically stored information, the obligations of the parties to preserver that evidence, and the need to produce this information, in electronic format, when requested (see Case in Point 2-7). (The plaintiffs sued a group of agencies and officials in Baltimore, referred to below as the Local Defendants, as well as the federal government; this excerpt deals only with the Local Defendants.)

CASE IN POINT 2-7

Thompson v. United States Department Of Housing And Urban Development

219 F.R.D. 93 (D. Md. 2003)

[...]

A background of the discovery and motions practice in this case is necessary. Plaintiffs served a series of Rule 34 document production requests on the Local Defendants in 1995, 1998, and 2000. Despite some confusion by Local Defendants regarding whether e-mail records were sought in these requests, this court ruled that the requests for production clearly sought electronic records, including e-mail. [...]

When the Local Defendants failed fully to produce e-mail records after the Court ruled that they were discoverable, the Plaintiffs filed a motion seeking sanctions [...] [under] Rule 37(b) (2) [...] that the Local Defendants could not call as witnesses at trial former or present employees of HABC or the City of Baltimore unless they were able to demonstrate by a preponderance of evidence that there were no e-mail records generated or received by the witness that were responsive to the Plaintiffs' Rule 34 requests or, if such records did exist, that they had been produced to the Plaintiffs by a certain date. [...]

Intertwined with this issue also was Plaintiffs' contention that sanctions were appropriate for the unexpected discovery by the Local Defendants of approximately 80,000 e-mail records responsive to Plaintiffs' Rule 34 requests. The discovery of these records, and therefore their production, was long after the discovery cutoff for fact discovery, and long after the deadlines imposed [...]

A. Discoverability of Electronic Records.

[...] The starting place is the discoverability of electronic records under the Federal Rules of Civil Procedure [...] Rule 34(a) defines the word "documents" broadly, and the commentary to the 1970 changes to the Federal Rules of Civil Procedure makes it clear that a request to produce documents or records includes electronically stored information. [...] Courts similarly have held that e-mail and other electronically stored information is subject to the disclosure requirements of Rule 26(a)(1), as well as discovery by a Rule 34 document production request. (citation omitted)

Courts also have recognized, however, that requests to discover electronically stored information do not have the same impact on the receiving party as do those requests for "hard copy" records. For example, the scope of what is included in the phrase "electronic records" can be enormous, encompassing voice mail, e-mail, deleted e-mail, data files, program files, back-up files, archival tapes, temporary files, system history files, web site information in textual, graphical or audio format, web site files, cache files, "cookies" and other electronically stored information. (citation omitted) According to one study, "93% of all information generated during 1999 was generated in digital form, on computers. Only 7% of information originated in other media, such as paper." (citation omitted) Obviously, the burden and cost associated with searching for all electronic records responsive to a broadly-worded Rule 34 document request can be substantial. [...]

Additionally, since "deleting" electronic records does not actually result in their instantaneous erasure, but rather simply designates the file as "not used," thereby enabling the computer to write over it, (citation omitted) courts have ruled that Rule 34 requests seeking "deleted" electronic records are permissible. [...] Thus, searching for deleted electronic records can be particularly time consuming and expensive given the number of storage locations that may have to be checked(e.g., desk-top computers, laptops, PDA's, employee home computers, back-up and archival data, and systems files, for instance), coupled with the possible need to use special search methods to locate deleted files.

Because of the possible burden and expense associated with broad discovery of electronic records, courts have acknowledged the need to employ the Rule 26(b)(2) cost-benefit balancing factors to determine just how much discovery of electronic records is appropriate in any given case, and which party should bear the cost associated with the production—the requesting party or the producing party. In this regard, it is clear that, ordinarily, the presumption is that the producing party should bear the cost of responding to properly initiated discovery requests. (citations omitted)

However, given the minimal threshold requirements of Rule 26(b)(1) for the discoverability of information (a requesting party is entitled to seek discovery of non-privileged information "relevant" to the claims and defenses raised in the pleadings), and the potentially enormous task of searching for all relevant and unprivileged electronic records, courts have attempted to fashion reasonable limits that will serve the legitimate needs of the requesting party for information, without unfair burden or expense to the producing party. The precise formulas used have varied.

[...]

In addition to the tests fashioned by these courts, it also can be argued with some force that the Rule 26(b)(2) balancing factors are all that is needed to allow a court to reach a fair result when considering the scope of discovery of electronic records. Rule 26(b)(2) requires a court [...] to evaluate the costs and benefits associated with a potentially burdensome discovery request. The rule identifies the following factors to be considered: whether the discovery sought is unreasonably cumulative or duplicative; whether the information sought is obtainable from some other more convenient, less burdensome or inexpensive source; whether the party seeking the information already has had adequate opportunity to obtain the information; and whether the burden or expense of the proposed discovery outweighs its likely benefit, taking into consideration the following: the needs of the case, the amount in controversy, the resources of the parties, the importance of the issues at stake in the litigation and of the discovery sought to the resolution of the issues.

Regardless of which test is used, the most important ingredient for the analytical process to produce a fair result is a particularization of the facts to support any challenge to discovery of electronic records. Conclusory or factually unsupported assertions by counsel that the discovery of electronic materials should be denied because of burden or expense can be expected to fail.

[...]

The rationale for this requirement is obvious. Under Rules 26(b)(2)and 26(c), a court is provided abundant resources to tailor discovery requests to avoid unfair burden or expense and yet assure fair disclosure of important information. The options available are limited only by the court's own imagination and the quality and quantity of the factual information provided by the parties to be used by the court in evaluating the Rule 26(b)(2) factors. [...]

[...]

B. The Duty to Preserve Electronic Records.

The Local Defendants also argued that they should not be sanctioned for having destroyed or otherwise failed to preserve electronic records during the pendency of this case, asserting that the Plaintiffs had a duty to seek a preservation order from the court, which they failed to do. The Local Defendants reasoned that, despite the Plaintiffs' serial Rule 34 requests clearly seeking electronic records, they were justified in deleting or failing to maintain the e-mail records of departing HABC and City of Baltimore housing officials whose employment ended during the pendency of this suit because the Plaintiffs failed to seek an order from the court directing the preservation of the electronic records. (citation omitted) This argument is without merit.

[...]

Among the electronic records subject to the "litigation hold" are those generated or maintained by the "key players" in the case (citation omitted). [...] Clearly, in this case, former HABC Commissioner Daniel Henson and former HABC employee Estella Alexander would qualify as "key players" whose e-mail records should have been preserved by the Local Defendants, regardless of whether the Plaintiffs asked for a preservation order or not. The same is true for those of Lyle Schumann, the current deputy to the HABC Commissioner.

C. Spoilation of Evidence and the Adverse Inference Instruction.

The failure to preserve electronic or other records, once the duty to do so has been triggered, raises the issue of spoliation of evidence and its consequences. "Spoliation refers to the destruction or material alteration of evidence or the failure to preserve property for another's use as evidence in pending or reasonably foreseeable litigation... . The right to impose sanctions for spoliation arises from a court's inherent power to control the judicial process and litigation, but the power is limited to that necessary to redress conduct 'which abuses the judicial process.'" (citation omitted)

[...]

As this court noted [...] the Local Defendants took many positions regarding the existence or non-existence of e-mail. Initially, the Local Defendants claimed that the e-mail records sought by the Plaintiffs did not exist because they had been deleted or otherwise were unavailable; at the same time, they contended that some e-mail records had been located and had been produced. Subsequently, and as trial was rapidly approaching, however, the Local Defendants acknowledged that an estimated 80,000 e-mail records of former HABC personnel had been located, contradicting their prior representations to the Plaintiffs and the court regarding the non-existence of most of these records and the completeness of the prior production of the limited e-mail records that had been found (citation omitted). Because of these contradictory assertions, and for other reasons [...] the court concluded that the Local Defendants had violated the earlier orders of this court to produce electronic records, and that Rule 37(b) sanctions were justified because the noncompliance by the Local Defendants was not substantially justified and also was prejudicial to the Plaintiffs. (citation omitted)

[...]

D. Sanctions.

Once a court makes the threshold determination under Rule 37(b) that a party has failed to obey a prior discovery order issued by it, then it must determine what sanctions are warranted. Rule 37(b)(2) provides a non-exclusive list of possible sanctions, [footnote omitted] which include ordering that certain facts be taken as established at trial; that the disobedient party may not oppose adverse claims or support its own defenses at trial; that pleadings may be stricken, the action dismissed, or a default judgment issued against the disobedient party; and that an order treating the failure to obey the prior order as a contempt of court be issued. As can be seen, the potential remedies may be draconian, to the point of being case determinative.

[...]

First, the Plaintiffs certainly were surprised by the Local Defendants' announcement, long after the discovery cutoff deadline, that it had discovered 80,000 e-mail records from past and present HABC and City personnel. Indeed, counsel for the Local Defendants herself was surprised, not to mention chagrined, by this discovery, having repeatedly told Plaintiffs and the court that e-mail records either did not exist or already had been produced. Second, given the enormous volume of e-mail records involved, the fact that discovery had been closed for months, (thereby preventing the Plaintiffs from having the opportunity to use the e-mail records during deposition of the fact witnesses), and that the trial was set to begin on December 1, 2003, there was no effective way to cure the surprise. [footnote 9] Similarly, given the sheer number of e-mail records—80,000—allowing them to be used by the Local Defendants, or even to permit the testimony of the witnesses who drafted the e-mails and/or received them, would have the potential for disrupting the trial substantially. Plaintiffs could be expected to request a continuance in the case to review the e-mails and to determine how they affected the possible testimony of the authors and recipients. Issues undoubtedly would arise regarding whether the fact witnesses of the Local Defendants refreshed their recollection based on the e-mails. Dealing with these issues alone would have had a substantially disruptive effect on the trial.

[...]

Fourth, because the e-mail records were produced so late, and Plaintiffs had no opportunity to review them, digest them, and assess their impact on the case, it is not possible to determine their importance with certainty. Nonetheless, given the volume of e-mails, the importance of their authors and recipients as potential fact witnesses, and comparing them to the substantive content of e-mails that were in fact produced during discovery, it is reasonable to conclude that the

80,000 e-mail records related to important issues in the case. [footnote omitted] Finally, as the court noted in its September 16, 2003, order, no explanation was given by the Local Defendants as to why the 80,000 e-mails were not produced earlier. (citation omitted) Indeed, an August 25, 2003, letter from counsel for the Local Defendants to the court advising it of the discovery of the 80,000 e-mail records five days earlier is devoid of any explanation regarding when the e-mails were discovered or why they were not earlier discovered. Similarly, the February 25, 2003, deposition of Amy Wilkinson, the self-described conduit between counsel for the Local Defendants and the Local Defendants themselves regarding responses to Plaintiffs Rule 34 requests indicates that no specific request ever was made to those searching for responsive records to look for e-mail records. (citation omitted) Thus, the court was entirely in the dark about the circumstances relating to the discovery of the 80,000 e-mail records, and why they had not earlier been discovered. Accordingly […] the court clearly was within its sound discretion to impose Rule 37(b)(2) sanctions against the Local Defendants for their violations of the court's earlier orders regarding the discovery of e-mail records.

[…]

Because the September 16, 2003, letter order placed the burden squarely on the Local Defendants to demonstrate compliance with the deadlines stated therein, their failure to do so means that they were unable to meet the foundational showing imposed in the court's order, and, therefore, by its terms, Henson, Alexander and Lyle would not be permitted to testify.

As noted during the hearing on this motion and from a review of the pretrial order, Henson, Alexander and Schumann were important witnesses to the Local Defendants. Indeed, it would not be an exaggeration to say that the former Commissioner, Daniel Henson, was one of the most important fact witnesses in the litigation. For the court to adhere to the September 16, 2003, letter order and totally preclude testimony by these three witnesses during the Local Defendants' case would deprive them of the opportunity to defend themselves in such a significant way, that it could prove fatal to their ability to prove their defenses. Against the somewhat murky factual backdrop of the dispute regarding the production of e-mail records, the court was not willing to do so.

Accordingly, the Rule 37(b)(2) sanctions were modified by: (1) precluding the Local Defendants from introducing into evidence in their case any of the 80,000 e-mail records that were "discovered" during the last minute; (2) ordering that counsel for the Local Defendants were forbidden to use any of these e-mail records to prepare any of their witnesses for testimony at trial, and that at trial counsel for the Local Defendants were forbidden from attempting to refresh the recollection of any of their witnesses by using any of the 80,000 undisclosed e-mail records; (3) ordering that the Plaintiffs were permitted to use any of the 80,000 e-mail records during their case and in cross-examining any of the Local Defendants witnesses, (4) ordering that, if the Plaintiffs incurred any additional expense and attorney's fees in connection with reviewing the 80,000 records and analyzing them for possible use at trial, this could be recovered from the Local Defendants upon further motion to the court; and finally (5) ordering that if, at trial, the evidence revealed additional information regarding the non-production of the e-mail records to clear up the many uncertainties that existed as of the resolution of this issue, that the Plaintiffs were free to make a motion to the court that the failure to produce e-mail records as ordered by this court constituted a contempt of court, under Rule 37(b)(2)(D).

Additionally, from the factual record before me, the court readily concluded that the Local Defendants were under a duty to preserve e-mail records at least as early as the date this lawsuit was filed and that they failed to comply with that duty. Further, from the samples of e-mail records that were submitted as exhibits during motions practice on this issue, it is clear that the e-mail records that were not produced were relevant to the Plaintiffs claims and that the failure to produce the e-mail records as ordered was done with, at a minimum, a negligent state of mind. [...]

FOOTNOTES

9 It must be remembered that this case was filed in January 1995 and has been aggressively litigated for nearly nine years. It involves allegations of purposeful discrimination by the defendants in connection with the operation of public housing in Baltimore, spanning three quarters of a century. The docket sheet reflects more than 550 entries and is in excess of seventy pages in length. A bench trial date of December 1, 2003, was specially set with trial scheduled to take a full month. Further, the court gave unambiguous signals to counsel that the trial date would not be postponed. Thus, the disclosure of 80,000 e-mail records approximately ninety days before trial in a case of this magnitude, and long after all fact discovery was over, constituted a surprise that could not have been cured without postponing the trial date and reopening discovery.

The court makes clear why these e-mails had to be produced, in terms of their potential impact on the proceedings. More importantly, the court made clear that a failure to produce these items, which were completely in the control of the Local Defendants, should preclude their use by the Local Defendants, at trial.

Site Visit

This rule also allows for parties to visit an opponent's real estate for an inspection, if that property lies at the center of the dispute or relates in some material manner to the dispute.

Physical and Mental Examinations

When a party's state of mind or physical well-being plays a significant role in the dispute, an opponent may request that party undergo a physical and/or mental examination. The requesting party has to arrange for this to take place at a reasonable time, place and manner. The expert who evaluates the party must generate a report about that expert's findings and provide a copy of that to the opposing party (see Fed. R. Civ. P. 35).

Request for Admissions

Either party may make a **request for admission**—that is, ask an opponent, in writing, for admissions regarding facts in the case (see Fed. R. Civ. P. Rule 36). For example, a request might ask a plaintiff whether a previous medical condition left the plaintiff with a permanent disability or might ask whether defendant was the owner and operator of a vehicle at the time of an auto accident. The responding party can admit to the validity of a request, deny its validity, or claim not to be able to admit or deny the validity of the statement.

Sanctions

A party that fails to respond to a request for discovery, whether deliberate or inadvertent, may need to answer to a court for such a failure (see Fed. R. Civ. P. Rule 37). If the court finds insufficient justification exists to account for this failure, the court has a range of potential consequences known as **sanctions** that it can employ:

- The court could issue a specific order compelling discovery. Disobedience of this specific court order can result in a criminal finding of contempt of court, which could lead to the payment of fines or even imprisonment, in very rare circumstances.
- The court could impose a fine on the non-complying party.
- The court could impose a payment of fees to the party requesting the discovery for legal expenses that party has incurred.
- In some instances, the court could issue a judgment in favor of the party making the request for discovery, if it seems that the opposing party will not or cannot produce the information requested.

The following case describes a situation where defendant's uncooperativeness resulted in the court ruling that the plaintiff was entitled to a judgment (see Case in Point 2-8).

 # CASE IN POINT 2-8

National Front Page, LLC v. State Ex Rel. Pryor
350 Ark. 286 (2002)

This case calls into question a circuit court's authority under Ark. R. Civ. P. 37(d)(2002) to issue sanctions, including a default judgment, based on a party's failure to timely respond to discovery requests. The appellants, National Front Page, LLC, and Curtis E. Venn, individually and as owner and operator of National Front Page (hereinafter referred to as "NFP"), contend that the circuit court abused its discretion in granting default judgment after they not only failed to respond to interrogatories and requests for production, but also after they (a) failed to appear at the hearing on the State's motion to compel discovery and (b) refused to appear on the date set for trial. We disagree and affirm.

On April 13, 1999, the Attorney General for the State of Arkansas filed suit against NFP alleging violation of the Arkansas Deceptive Trade Practices Act, the Arkansas Telemarketer Registration Act, and common law fraud in connection with NFP's practice of soliciting businesses to purchase advertising for sports-related activity calendars. On February 4, 2000, the State served NFP with interrogatories and requests for production of documents. When NFP failed to respond to the State's discovery requests by March 16, the State sent a letter to NFP's attorney in which it expressed a willingness to consider settlement if specified disclosures and admissions were made. The State then filed a motion to compel discovery [...] pursuant to Ark. R. Civ. P. 37(a)(2) (2002). During June, July, and August 2000, NFP filed its own requests for discovery, and the State responded to those requests. Meanwhile, NFP had not yet responded to the State's discovery requests.

A hearing on the State's motion to compel discovery was set originally for July 18, 2000, but NFP requested and obtained a postponement. The hearing was rescheduled for August 29, 2000, with the trial being set for November 20-21, 2000. Because of a conflict with another hearing scheduled in a separate action pending in Missouri, NFP requested a second postponement that was granted, and the circuit court rescheduled the hearing on discovery for September 29, 2000. Once again, the hearing was postponed a third time at NFP's request until three days before the scheduled trial date. Shortly before the November 17 hearing date, NFP conferred with the Attorney General's office about securing a continuance. Although both parties requested a continuance, the circuit court denied the request and notified them by letter dated November 15, 2000, that the hearing would still be held on November 17, followed by the trial previously scheduled to begin on November 20. On the same day that the trial court sent the above written notice to the parties, NFP faxed the following message to the court and the Attorney General's office: "The attorney I hired has backed out on me and I will not face the big bad boys without attorney representation on Friday 17th or Monday 20th." NFP did not appear at the November 17 hearing on the State's motion to compel, whereupon the State made an oral motion for default judgment pursuant to Rule 37(d) of the Arkansas Rules of Civil Procedure.

The circuit court granted the State's motion and entered default judgment against NFP on November 22, 2000. In striking NFP's original answer and entering a judgment by default pursuant to Ark. R. Civ. P. 37(b)(2)(C) and 37(d), the court noted that NFP had failed to respond to any of the State's discovery requests, that NFP's counsel had been allowed to withdraw in June [footnote omitted.], that the motion-to-compel hearing had been postponed three times at NFP's request, and that NFP had advised the court it would not appear at the hearing on November 17, 2000, or at the trial on November 20-21, 2000. The default judgment enjoined NFP from engaging in certain business activities in Arkansas and set a hearing on March 8, 2001, to determine the amount of restitution, civil penalties, and attorney's fees and costs. NFP then filed a *pro se* notice of intent to appeal on December 22, 2000. Later, after retaining counsel, NFP moved to set aside the default judgment.

After the March 8, 2001 hearing, the circuit court entered its final judgment and permanent injunction on April 3, 2001. The circuit court (1) denied NFP's motion to set aside the default judgment; (2) permanently enjoined NFP from doing business of any kind in Arkansas; (3) ordered restitution in the amount of $2,497.45; (4) awarded $14,000 in attorneys fees; and (5) assessed civil penalties totaling $26,000 that would be reduced to $5,000, provided NFP paid restitution within ten days. NFP filed a notice of appeal on April 30, 2001.

On appeal, NFP contends it had a justifiable excuse for failing to appear at the motion-to-compel hearing because it did not have counsel and mistakenly thought that the November hearing and trial would be postponed. [...]

II. Authority to Issue Rule 37(d) Sanctions

The first question is whether the circuit court had the authority to issue sanctions, including default judgment, under Rule 37(d) of the Arkansas Rules of Civil Procedure. [...]

Rule 37 provides two methods of imposing sanctions. First, sanctions may be imposed for failure to comply with an order compelling discovery. Ark. R. Civ. P. 37(b). Second, sanctions may be imposed for failure to respond to interrogatories or other discovery requests. Ark. R. Civ. P. 37(d). Sanctions issued under Rule 37(d) do not require an order compelling production as a prerequisite.

Indeed, this court has upheld Rule 37(d) sanctions without an order to compel production where a defendant has failed to answer interrogatories or otherwise failed comply with discovery. [...]

Thus, we hold that the circuit court had the authority to issue sanctions, including default judgment, without an order compelling discovery. The only question remaining is whether, under the facts of the instant case, the circuit court abused its discretion.

III. Discretion to Issue Rule 37(d) Sanctions

On November 17, 2000, the circuit court was faced with the following situation: NFP had refused to answer the State's discovery requests even after it had been advised by counsel that NFP's failure to respond to discovery could result in severe sanctions, including the striking of its answer. In an attempt to obtain discovery, the State had filed a motion for order compelling discovery. The circuit court allowed NFP to postpone the motion-to-compel hearing three times, with the fourth hearing date set for November 17—only three days before trial was scheduled to begin on November 20.

Over nine months passed between the service of the interrogatories and requests for production of documents on February 2 and the hearing on November 17; yet, the State was faced with trying the case in three days without NFP having complied with a single discovery request. NFP had been informed in April by its attorney that he intended to ask the court for permission to withdraw as attorney of record in the case. The circuit court granted the attorney's petition to be relieved on June 26, 2000.

According to the record, another attorney conveyed a settlement offer to the Arkansas Attorney General by letter dated June 28, 2000; however, NFP proceeded *pro se* between June and November 2000. The only other indication in the record of NFP retaining counsel is a letter from yet another attorney dated November 7, 2000, that informed the circuit court he would not be representing NFP. As previously noted, NFP advised the circuit court by fax on November 15 that it would not appear for either the November 17 hearing or the November 20-21 trial. At the November 17 hearing, NFP did not appear in person or by counsel.

Thus, the circuit court was faced with a defendant that refused to answer any requests for discovery, that failed, after three postponements, to appear at a hearing on a motion to compel discovery three days before trial, and that stated it would not appear for trial. Under these facts, we cannot say that the circuit court abused its discretion in granting the State's motion for default judgment. The trial court was in a superior position to judge the actions and motives of the parties, and we will not second guess the circuit court in the instant case. (citation omitted).

NFP contends that it would have been unfair to face the "big bad boys" without counsel. However, a party's failure to retain counsel is not sufficient, by itself, to defeat a default judgment. (citation omitted). NFP also contends that it was unfair to proceed after he informed the circuit court that he would not attend the hearing or trial on the dates scheduled, and especially after NFP and the State had agreed to a continuance. "[I]t is crucial to our judicial system that trial courts retain the discretion to control their dockets." (citation omitted). [...]

Because the trial court controls its docket, parties do not have the power to change a hearing date set by the court.

Finally, NFP argues that a default judgment was too harsh a sanction in this case. We disagree. The finality or severity of the sanctions imposed by the trial court is of no consequence because Rule 37 specifically provides for dismissal of the action in the case of a flagrant failure to comply with discovery. (citation omitted).

Rule 37(d) of the Arkansas Rules of Civil Procedure authorizes a circuit court to impose sanctions, including default judgment, for noncompliance with the rules of discovery without first issuing an order compelling discovery. Under the circumstances of this case, we cannot say that the circuit court abused its discretion in granting default judgment in favor of the State.

Affirmed.

Mindful of the risks that a trial court could abuse its exercise of discretion, the appeals court nonetheless found that a valid basis existed for imposing sanctions according Rule 37.

■ TRIAL

Rules of Evidence

Information that, if presented during the trial, can help resolve a dispute is known as **evidence.** A judge uses **rules of evidence** to evaluate information that could help produce a resolution of the problem at trial. Consider these select provisions of the Federal Rules of Evidence (F. R.E.) (see box on next page).

SELECT PROVISIONS OF THE FEDERAL RULES OF EVIDENCE

ARTICLE IV. RELEVANCY AND ITS LIMITS

Rule 401. Definition of "Relevant Evidence"
Rule 402. Relevant Evidence Generally Admissible; Irrelevant Evidence Inadmissible
Rule 403. Exclusion of Relevant Evidence on Grounds of Prejudice, Confusion, or Waste of Time
[...]
Rule 412. Sex Offense Cases; Relevance of Alleged Victim's Past Sexual Behavior or Alleged Sexual Predisposition
[...]

ARTICLE VI. WITNESSES

Rule 601. General Rule of Competency
Rule 602. Lack of Personal Knowledge
Rule 607. Who May Impeach
Rule 608. Evidence of Character and Conduct of Witness
Rule 609. Impeachment by Evidence of Conviction of Crime
[...]
Rule 613. Prior Statements of Witnesses
Rule 615. Exclusion of Witnesses

ARTICLE VII. OPINIONS AND EXPERT TESTIMONY

Rule 701. Opinion Testimony by Lay Witnesses
Rule 702. Testimony by Experts
[...]
Rule 705. Disclosure of Facts or Data Underlying Expert Opinion
Rule 706. Court Appointed Experts

ARTICLE VIII. HEARSAY

Rule 801. Definitions
Rule 802. Hearsay Rule
Rule 803. Hearsay Exceptions; Availability of Declarant Immaterial
Rule 804. Hearsay Exceptions; Declarant Unavailable
Rule 805. Hearsay Within Hearsay
Rule 806. Attacking and Supporting Credibility of Declarant
Rule 807. Residual Exception

ARTICLE X. CONTENTS OF WRITINGS, RECORDINGS, AND PHOTOGRAPHS

Rule 1001. Definitions
Rule 1002. Requirement of Original
Rule 1003. Admissibility of Duplicates
[...]

Application

The judge examines information presented as evidence to determine whether it relates to the problem of law. If so, then the judge needs to find that this information will help a party to resolve some material aspect or issue of the case. For example, in a case arising out of an automobile accident, the color of the cars might apply to this case but would not necessarily help resolve whether the accident occurred. The fact that the accident occurred on the day of an election likely would not apply to the case.

Examples of Issues

Rules of evidence can deal with different issues regarding information. They might set out the steps involved in showing that a witness's testimony cannot be trusted, perhaps because the witness had said one thing during a deposition but said the opposite when testifying at the trial.

These rules can help a court decide whether a statement not made in the court room can be deemed sufficiently trustworthy to be admitted into evidence; this involves hearsay. So, while the dates carved on a headstone are hearsay—a statement made out of the court, where the stone carver has not been asked to testify—information on headstones can be trusted because the custom in this country is to record accurate information on them.

All Courts Have Rules of Evidence

Many jurisdictions have adopted the format and numbering of the Federal Rules of Evidence, although they might not adopt all the provisions of that version. Some jurisdictions may still rely upon common law rules of evidence, so paralegals should take care to determine what type of rules of evidence a jurisdiction uses.

Jury Selection

Before the official start of the trial, the parties might choose people who will serve as jurors. Jurors will have received a summons to serve as jurors.

Voir dire

At the court, people will face questioning to determine whether each could serve as a juror during the specific trial. The process of questioning a group of prospective jurors (known as the *venire*) is called **voir dire** (see Fed. R. Civ. P. Rule 47).

The questions focus on whether prospective jurors have a predisposition towards one party or the other even before evidence is produced in open court. For example, a juror might have read in the newspaper that the plaintiff had filed suit against the defendant. If so, questions put to this prospective juror focus on whether that knowledge has predisposed the individual to draw a conclusion about the outcome of the case, even though the trial has not started. Those questions can also focus on whether a juror has formed an opinion regarding a particular kind of case. A prospective juror who suffered injury in a car crash might feel one way or the other about the issue at trial, due to this experience and not due to the evidence accepted at trial.

Challenges

Lawyers for the parties may file a **challenge**—that is, they may ask the court, based upon the questions and answers received during voir dire, to excuse a prospective juror from the case.

For Cause. When filing a challenge for cause, the lawyer tells the court that because of personal experience or what the juror has heard elsewhere, that person lacks the ability to serve as an unbiased juror. Lawyers may make as many challenges for cause of prospective jurors as they wish, but would need to be able to convince the judge why this person should not serve on the jury.

Peremptory Challenges. Lawyers may also ask the court to excuse a prospective juror for no apparent reason at all; this involves filing a peremptory challenge. Most jurisdictions limit the number of peremptory challenges that a party can make.

Some in the legal field believe that people of certain backgrounds may decide questions of law one way or the other. So, lawyers might want to have prospective jurors with college degrees serve on a case where the amount of damages could involve large numbers and that people who have earned a college degree will be able to evaluate the appropriateness of those figures, upon a finding that the defendant was liable. Whether this is true or not remains an open question.

Courts will not allow for the use of peremptory challenges if a party seeks to remove prospective jurors based upon the perception how a prospective jurors' gender, race, or religion would lead to a particular outcome. For example, in a divorce proceeding, counsel for the wife cannot use peremptories to exclude all men; that, of course, also applies to counsel for the husband.

In the following case, the court looked at how both sides used their peremptories to discriminate against the race of prospective jurors (see Case in Point 2-9).

 # CASE IN POINT 2-9

Maloney v. Washington

690 F. Supp. 687 (N.D. Ill. 1988)

[...]

Shortly after Mayor Washington was elected in November 1983 and his subsequent appointment of Fred Rice as Superintendent of the Chicago Police Department, the plaintiffs were removed from the exempt ranks and reassigned to positions within the department consistent with their career service ranks. All four claim that such action constituted a racially and politically motivated demotion. In essence, the four white officers claim discrimination by the newly elected black administration of the City of Chicago—a claim hotly contested by the defendants.

[...]

Plaintiffs claim they were removed from the exempt ranks by Superintendent Rice with the advice and consent of Mayor Harold Washington because they are white and because they had supported the candidacy of Jane Byrne in the 1983 Democratic mayoral primary. Given the nature of their case, plaintiffs have apparently concluded that they would prefer to have their case tried by members of their own race. During the selection of the first jury in February, the plaintiffs used all four of their peremptory challenges against blacks. It is the court's recollection that no blacks were accepted on the first jury until the plaintiffs had exhausted all of their challenges. The defendants, meanwhile, appeared intent on seating as many black jurors as possible and, accordingly, aimed all four of their peremptory challenges at whites. Because the venire contained a substantial number of both black and white citizens, neither side was successful in excluding members of the opposite race and the final jury (including alternates) contained five whites and five blacks. The court was concerned about the mandate of the Supreme Court in Batson v. Kentucky (citation omitted) throughout the selection of the first jury, but proceeded to trial given the parties' respective lack of success in excluding members of a particular race from the panel. (footnote omitted.)

Prior to beginning the retrial, this court advised counsel for both sides that the holding in Batson would be applied during the selection of the second jury and that the plaintiffs would be required to justify their use of peremptory challenges against blacks and the defendants their use of peremptories against whites. Despite the court's admonition, the plaintiffs exercised three of their peremptory challenges against blacks, and the city exercised their four peremptory challenges exclusively against whites. The plaintiffs allowed only one black prospective juror to survive its challenges. The group ultimately selected consisted of five whites and one black. (footnote omitted.) (The three individuals chosen as alternates were also white.) This court has refused to empanel this jury.

[...]

In Batson, the United States Supreme Court held that the use of peremptory challenges by a prosecutor to exclude members of the black race from a jury in a criminal case deprived both the black defendant and the excluded jurors of equal protection of law. In so holding, the Supreme Court stated that:

The harm from discriminatory jury selection extends beyond that inflicted on the defendant and the excluded juror to touch the entire community. Selection procedures that purposefully exclude black persons from juries undermines public confidence in the fairness of our system of justice. Discrimination within the judicial system is most pernicious "because it is a stimulant to that race prejudice which is an impediment to securing to [black citizens] that equal justice which the law aims to secure to all others." (Citations omitted.)

Thus, the Supreme Court concluded that the Equal Protection Clause forbids a prosecutor to challenge potential jurors solely on account of their race or on the assumption that black jurors as a group will be unable to impartially consider the state's case against a black defendant.

We recognize, as we must, that the Supreme Court's decision in Batson was necessarily limited to the facts before it—the discriminatory use of peremptories by a prosecutor against a black defendant in a criminal case. The case before this court is arguably different. First, it is a civil rather than a criminal case, and second, the use of peremptories to exclude black citizens was undertaken by private plaintiffs, not a governmental entity. In Batson, the Supreme Court expressed no view on whether its prohibition against the use of peremptory challenges based on race extended to defense counsel. (citation omitted.) For the reasons set forth below, we now conclude that the rationale of Batson applies with equal force to all litigants.

Peremptory challenges are by definition arbitrary and until Batson had, as a practical matter, been left to the discretion of the trial lawyer. But as noted by the Supreme Court, they permit "those to discriminate who are of a mind to discriminate." (citation omitted.) Accordingly, the Supreme Court found constitutionally impermissible a prosecutor's use of peremptory challenges when that use is designed to practice racial discrimination. The Court's finding rested on the Equal Protection Clause of the Fourteenth Amendment, which applies equally to criminal and civil cases. (citation omitted.)

Discrimination deprives both a party and the prospective juror of equal protection of law. [...]. Jury service is both a responsibility and privilege of all citizens. Discrimination in the selection of jurors in a United States District Court is anathema to a court sworn to uphold the Constitution. [...] We conclude that the Equal Protection Clause and Batson make the use of racially motivated peremptory challenges in civil cases constitutionally impermissible.

While it is true that equal protection guarantees are limited to governmental actions, we find that the private plaintiffs' attempted use of the powers of a federal court implicates the Equal Protection Clause. [...]

Here the plaintiffs seek to secure rights guaranteed to them under federal law by invoking the jurisdiction of the United States District Court. We will not permit our power under Article III of the Constitution to be used to sanction such discriminatory conduct. [...] White plaintiffs who seek redress for alleged discriminatory practices by black city officials cannot be themselves permitted to discriminate against prospective black jurors who are fully qualified to decide this controversy.

We now turn to the question of whether the plaintiffs indeed exercised their peremptory challenges in a systematic effort to exclude members of the black race. In doing so, we consider the use of peremptory challenges in the selection of both juries in this case. Given the plaintiffs' use of challenges in the first trial (all four directed at blacks) and the three (out of the three utilized) peremptories against blacks in the selection of the second jury, we asked plaintiffs' counsel to justify the latter strikes on non-racial grounds. We find plaintiffs' counsel has failed to do so. We will discuss each black prospective juror excused by the plaintiff at the second trial individually.

Black Prospective Juror No. 1 was excused by the plaintiff because she worked for the Urban League of Chicago. Plaintiffs suggested that such employment would indicate that this prospective juror was interested in helping minorities and was therefore partial to blacks. Plaintiffs' challenge was made despite the fact that this prospective juror testified that she believe the work of the Urban League was to help all disadvantaged people regardless of race and despite the fact that she indicated that she could be color blind in deciding the case. We found the prospective juror to be completely unbiased, yet acknowledged that plaintiffs may have had a good faith basis for challenging this prospective juror based on her affiliation with the Urban League.

Black Prospective Juror No. 2 was excused by the plaintiffs on the grounds that she had been a temporary employee of the Chicago Police Department for six months several years earlier. Plaintiffs suggested a possibility that her supervisor might be a witness for the plaintiffs. We find this attempted justification specious. Since police officers are involved on both sides of this litigation, that Prospective Juror No. 2 formerly worked for the police department in itself means nothing. She testified she had never heard of the "supervisor" and nothing suggests that this supervisor had any relevant testimony in this trial. We found this juror to be without any bias after substantial questioning by both the court and the parties.

Black Prospective Juror No. 3 was excused by plaintiffs on the grounds she had "lied" about having any prior trouble with the law. On her questionnaire, she indicated she had no prior arrests. During questioning by the court, however, she volunteered that she had been arrested for disorderly conduct during a dispute in the street and later fined $25. Though plaintiffs cited this discrepancy as their reason for challenging this juror, we find this justification to be pretextual; plaintiffs had accepted several white jurors who had similarly been mistaken about answers in the questionnaire and who had likewise amended those answers under questioning by the court. Again, Prospective Juror No. 3 had demonstrated a complete absence of bias under careful scrutiny.

In sum, we find that at least two of plaintiffs' three peremptories at the second trial were used to exclude members of the black race solely because of their race. Moreover, plaintiffs permitted only one prospective black juror to survive their use of peremptories in the two selection processes combined, and they never used a peremptory challenge in either trial to strike a prospective white juror from the panel of six which would decide the case. We find that the plaintiffs have ignored this court's admonition that racial discrimination in the jury selection process will not be tolerated.

In reaching our conclusion, we are not troubled by the fact that the plaintiffs did permit one black prospective juror to survive the second selection process. [...]

However, merely because two blacks were seated on the jury is not sufficient to prevent or defeat the establishment of a prima facie case of racial discrimination. The affirmative racial exclusion of available black jurors by the State which results in only one or two blacks being seated on the jury is no less evil and no less constitutionally prohibited than the same procedure which results in the total exclusion of blacks. No available black person should be excluded either singularly or systematically from being a juror solely because he or she is black.

> The defendants fare only slightly better. All of their peremptory challenges were used against whites in both trials. However, they did permit some whites to survive their strikes—probably because it was impossible, given the composition of the second venire (35 whites, 13 blacks, 1 Hispanic), to strike all of the white people. We further find the attempted justifications for the defendants' use of their peremptories to be less than satisfactory.
>
> For these reasons, we concluded that racial discrimination permeated the jury selection process. Because plaintiffs had actually been successful, on the whole, in excluding black people from service, we refused to empanel the jury. We also found that because both sides had twice used their challenges almost exclusively along racial lines—the second time in violation of the court's clear admonition—their right to make peremptory challenges has been lost. Therefore, we have decided to eliminate the use of peremptory challenges in the next selection of the jury. We have done so as a sanction because we believe both sides have consistently ignored the court's orders to select a jury without considering race, and because it will be the most effective means of ensuring an unbiased jury selection process.

Given the unacceptable conduct of the parties, who tried to use peremptories on the basis of race, the court ruled that in a retrial, neither side could make any peremptory challenges.

Alternates

If a jurisdiction provides plaintiff with the option of a jury trial, with twelve jurors, the trial court might actually select sixteen people from the *venire* to serve as jurors. These four additional jurors are **alternates** who could replace one of the twelve needed to issue a valid verdict, if one of the twelve could not complete the trial. Having these alternate jurors available can minimize the possibility of having to repeat the trial if one of the twelve jurors cannot serve through the entire proceeding.

Judges typically do not identify who will serve as alternates, since that might negatively affect the degree of attention those alternates direct towards the evidence. While the judge might dismiss those four once the case has gone to the jury, the judge might have them remain nearby in case a jury member cannot complete deliberations to arrive at a verdict.

Presentation of the Case

Since the plaintiff has filed suit, the lawyer for the plaintiff will start off the case.

Opening, Closing Statements

Each party, through that party's lawyer, can present an **opening statement** to the court (and to the jury, if a party has requested that a jury serve to evaluate questions of fact). In the opening statement, the lawyer provides the jurors with a preview of the case. Besides describing the nature of the problem, the lawyer tells the juror what that party will show in court.

For example, in the opening statement of a plaintiff's counsel, the lawyer could say that the case involved an automobile accident that occurred when the defendant's car hit the plaintiff. The lawyer can then say that this constitutes the tort of negligence, and that during the trial, the lawyer will show through presentation of the evidence that the defendant owed the plaintiff a duty of care, the defendant breached that duty, that the result produced injury, and that the injury led to the plaintiff seeking damages.

Next, the attorney for the defendant would make an opening statement, telling the jury that the plaintiff has gotten the specific facts wrong. Even if the facts were true, the lawyer for the defendant could talk about how the plaintiff still won't be able to make out a valid claim by a preponderance of the evidence or that the defendant has a defense that negates any claim of liability that the plaintiff might establish by presenting evidence at trial. So the defense counsel could say that even if the plaintiff can provide evidence sufficient to make out a claim for the tort of battery, the defendant should escape liability because he or she acted in self-defense, under the belief that using force could avoid greater injury.

After all parties have presented all of their evidence, the lawyer for each party can make a **closing statement.** The plaintiff's counsel goes first, since the plaintiff has the obligation to provide, by a preponderance of the evidence, the validity of each element of the tort.

The defense counsel could then, in a closing statement, explain how the plaintiff failed to provide enough evidence on each component of the claim in tort or how the defendant had a defense that excused any liability. To do that, the defense counsel might point out the inconsistencies in a witness's statements or how the defendant could show that he or she correctly believed that the use of force was not a battery but self-defense, intended to avoid greater harm.

Plaintiff's Presentation of the Case in Chief

Because the plaintiff has filed the complaint, the plaintiff goes first. The plaintiff's lawyer has to show, by a preponderance of the evidence, that the defendant has committed a tort. To do that, the lawyer might ask for the testimony of an eyewitness, who could describe what happened. The lawyer could introduce into evidence the accident report filed by the plaintiff, to support the plaintiff's interpretation of the facts.

In every instance, the defense counsel will have the opportunity to test the validity of the evidence. That could mean that the defendant's attorney cross-examines the eyewitness about the accuracy of that witness's testimony or if the eyewitness was wearing glasses whether that person needed corrective lenses to see accurately.

In some instances, the defense counsel may ask to question a witness on a point raised by the defense counsel during cross examination only; this is called *redirect*. Then, the defendant's lawyer can question the witness about statements made during redirect; that is called *recross*. So, the eyewitness might have claimed that the defendant was driving the car that struck the plaintiff. On cross-examination, the defendant's attorney could ask whether the witness wore glasses and whether the witness wore them at the time of the accident. The plaintiff's lawyer, on redirect, could get the eyewitness to testify about how wearing or not wearing the glasses did not affect the validity of that eyewitness's testimony while on recross, the defense counsel might ask the witness whether the witness was sure that, wearing glasses or not, the witness could see the details that the witness testified about earlier in the questioning.

Presentation of Case by the Defendant

After the plaintiff has presented all the evidence needed to establish the validity of the plaintiff's claim—"the plaintiff rests"—the defendant can now move for a directed verdict. If the court denies that request or will not rule on the request at that time, the defendant could offer no case for the defense, as the burden is completely on the plaintiff's part to provide evidence sufficient to establish the claim, by a preponderance of the evidence.

Or the defendant could present a defense. This also could involve putting into evidence statements of witnesses or showing that information contained in a document helps to establish that the defendant should not suffer liability for plaintiff's injury.

Counsel for the plaintiff will also have the opportunity to test the validity of the evidence presented by the defense counsel during this portion of the trial, through cross-examination, for example, or by showing that two versions of a document exist, and that the jurors might not want to trust the information contained in either document. After having presented all information relating to the defendant's view of the events, the defendant can then rest.

Jury Instructions

Once the parties have presented all evidence about that party's side of the dispute, the judge provides **jury instructions**—that is, the judge prepares the jury to deliberate upon the case and return a verdict. Jurors are selected because of the practical experience and insights that each has developed and not for any knowledge of the law. For that reason, judge tells the jury what concepts of law it need to apply when evaluating the evidence.

Jury instructions include statements about the law. A judge's instructions could include statements referring to the plaintiff's burden of proof: the obligation to make out each of the elements of the claim, by a preponderance of the evidence. That statement could also include an explanation that "preponderance of the evidence" is not a fixed concept but means "more likely than not." The court then might say that on the evidence, the jury has to find the plaintiff's evidence merely more credible than the defendant's evidence or arguments.

Jury instructions would include the definition of the tort. For example, an instruction could explain that the tort of negligence involves duty, breach of duty, a causal link between the breach and the damages, and damages.

Although the jury likely will have heard of the law during the trial—as both parties will focus on the elements of the tort and what defenses may relieve the defendant of liability—the judge provides an unbiased definition of what the jury needs to know about law or trial procedures.

Jury Deliberations

Having seen the parties present each side of the dispute in open court and having received the statements of law, the jury needs to apply the law to the facts. By way of metaphor, the jurors function like a computer, where the law is equivalent to the software needed to accomplish the task of arriving at a verdict, and the facts make up the data that the jury needs to process.

Often, a jury will return a **general verdict.** They will determine whether the plaintiff has proven the claim; the verdict, then, is to hold the defendant "liable" (a "guilty" verdict). If the plaintiff fails to establish this or the defendant has raised a defense or cast enough doubt about the validity of evidence, a jury could return a "not liable" verdict (a "not guilty" verdict).

In some instances, usually with very elaborate or complicated cases, a judge may ask the jury to return a **special verdict** requiring the jury to respond to questions posed by the judge. If the jury found that the jury had no duty, then it was to return a verdict of "not liable." In a class action suit, for example, the judge might first ask if the representative of the class has shown that the defendant had a duty of care. If it did find duty, the jury may need to determine whether the defendant has breached that duty. With a special verdict, the judge uses the questionnaire as a way of helping the jury focus on discrete aspects of the case, so that they can establish liability overall based upon their conclusions provided to all the questions.

The following case offers an exploration of the difference between these verdicts to help to pinpoint liability. Here, the plaintiff filed suit against his employer and a third party, and his employer separately sued the third party for indemnification, seeking to recover whatever damages it had to pay (see Case in Point 2-10).

 # CASE IN POINT 2-10

Dessauer v. Memorial General Hospital
96 N.M. 92 (N.M. Ct. App. 1981)

The personal representative of the Estate of Dessauer sought damages for wrongful death on the basis of negligence in administering a dosage of medication. The defendants were the Hospital (Memorial General Hospital) and the Nurse (Bourque), who was an employee of the Hospital. The Hospital and the Nurse filed third-party complaints against the Doctor (Malleis). The third-party claims alleged the Doctor was negligent in his care and treatment of Dessauer, and was negligent in his supervision of the Nurse. The third-party claims sought either contribution or indemnity from the Doctor. Among the defenses to the third-party complaints was the contention that negligence of each of the third-party plaintiffs was the sole cause of Dessauer's death. The Estate's suit against the Hospital and the Nurse was settled for $ 225,000.00, and a joint tortfeasor release was executed. The third-party contribution and indemnity claims were tried, and the jury's answers to interrogatories were to the effect that neither of the third-party plaintiffs should recover against the Doctor. The Hospital and the Nurse appeal. [...]

[...]

General Verdict

Because the issues being tried involved contribution and indemnity claims of two parties, the trial court was of the view that the best procedure would be by interrogatories which, when answered, would amount to a special verdict. Accordingly, no "general verdict" in the traditional sense was submitted to the jury.

Following are the pertinent interrogatories, and the answers thereto:
INTERROGATORY NO. 1: Was Dr. Ronald J. Malleis negligent? Answer—No.
[....]
INTERROGATORY NO. 3: Was Glorious Bourque negligent? Answer—Yes.
INTERROGATORY NO. 4: If the answer to Interrogatory No. 3 is "yes," was the negligence a proximate cause of the death of Wiley J. Dessauer? Answer—Yes.
INTERROGATORY NO. 5. If the answers to Interrogatories Nos. 3 and 4 are "yes," was Memorial General Hospital negligent apart from the negligence of Glorious Bourque? Answer—Yes.
INTERROGATORY NO. 6: If the answer to Interrogatory No. 5 is "yes," was the hospital's negligence a proximate cause of the death of Wiley J. Dessauer? Answer—Yes.

The Hospital and the Nurse do not claim that the above answers were improper under the evidence. Nor do they claim that the answers would not have disposed of the case if there had been a general verdict. The contention is that the answers have no legal effect because there was no general verdict.

The Hospital and the Nurse rely on R.Civ.Proc. 49, which reads:
In civil cases, the court shall at the request of either party, in addition to the general verdict, direct the jury to find upon particular questions of fact, to be stated in writing by the party requesting the same. When the special finding of facts is inconsistent with the general verdict, the former shall control the latter, and the court shall give judgment accordingly.
[...]

Rule of Civ.Proc. 49 refers to a general verdict and "special findings," also known as special interrogatories. A third category is the special verdict, which the trial court utilized in this case. The United States Supreme Court [...] distinguished between general verdicts and special verdicts as follows:

Now a general verdict embodies both the law and the facts. The jury, taking the law as given by the court, apply that law to the facts as they find them to be and express their conclusions in the verdict .... Beyond this, it was not infrequent to ask from the jury a special rather than a general verdict, that is, instead of a verdict for or against the plaintiff or defendant embodying in a single declaration the whole conclusion of the trial, one which found specially upon the various facts in issue, leaving to the court the subsequent duty of determining upon such facts the relief which the law awarded to the respective parties.

The distinction between a special verdict, and special interrogatories with a general verdict, is [...]

A special verdict is in lieu of a general verdict, and its design is to exhibit all the legitimate facts and leave the legal conclusions entirely to the court. Findings of fact in answer to interrogatories do not dispense with the general verdict. A special verdict covers all the issues in the case, while an answer to a special interrogatory may respond to but a single inquiry pertaining merely to one issue essential to the general verdict. (citation omitted)

If a jury finds on special questions of fact in answer to interrogatories, without a general verdict, the finding is of no force, and the court cannot give to the special finding any weight unless they are sufficiently numerous and explicit to leave nothing for the court to do but to determine questions of law. If they affirmatively show the existence of every fact necessary to entitle plaintiff to a recovery and the nonexistence of every defense presented under the issues, or if they show as a matter of law that a valid defense has been established by the evidence, they may then constitute a special verdict.

[...]

Careful consideration has been given the contention of the defendant that what was done here amounted to a submission on a special verdict, and that such is not prohibited under our rules, but our rule 49 is too limited to allow such construction. Reversible error was committed by the action taken in this case over the objection of the claimant as he was entitled to a general verdict as a matter of right when he asked for it. Such action must be held to have been prejudicial, and this in the face of the negative answer to interrogatory No. 2, supra.

[...] Because there was no traditional general verdict [...], the question is whether the jury's answers were the equivalent of a general verdict. We particularly consider the answer to Interrogatory No. 1. If that answer was, in fact, the equivalent of a general verdict, the absence of a verdict form labeled "General Verdict" does not matter. (citation omitted).

The Hospital and the Nurse requested that three "General Verdict" forms be submitted to the jury. The first would have awarded $225,000.00 to the Hospital and the Nurse on a theory of indemnity. The second would have awarded $112,500.00 to the Hospital and the Nurse on a theory of contribution. As we point out in discussing the issue involving vicarious liability, the claims of the Hospital and the Nurse must be distinguished. Because the verdict forms failed to make that distinction, they were properly refused.

The third general verdict form submitted by the Hospital and the Nurse provided: "We find that the Defendant [Doctor] was free from any negligence ...." The answer to Interrogatory No. 1 said the same thing. This verdict form went on to state: "Plaintiffs are not entitled to recover any sum." Such is the legal effect of the jury's answer; not being negligent, the Doctor was not liable for either contribution or indemnity as an alleged tortfeasor. [...]

Because the jury's answer was determinative of the right of the Hospital and the Nurse to recover damages from the Doctor as an alleged tortfeasor, that answer is the equivalent of, and is to be given effect as, a general verdict. (citation omitted) [...]

Although the foregoing disposes of this point, we recommend to the Supreme Court a change in R.Civ.Proc. 49 to permit special verdicts. [...]

■ JUDGMENT

Once the judge has received the verdict, the judge then can enter a **judgment** about the claim (see Fed. R. Civ. P. Rules 54, 58). As noted earlier, if asked, a court may determine that it should not uphold the verdict, and should enter a judgment different from what the jury thought should be the outcome for the case. A court may also hear a motion to increase or decrease the amount of damages that the jury would award if it has determined that the defendant is liable for the plaintiff's injuries.

■ EXECUTION

After the court has formally entered a judgment on behalf of the plaintiff, the court may then issue an **execution** (see Fed. R. Civ. P. Rule 69). This is a court order that allows the plaintiff to demand, payment for the damages set forth in the judgment. (The court won't need to do that if the judgment was in favor of the defendant.) The plaintiff could lawfully seize enough of the defendant's assets to pay off the judgment. Often, however, the defendant will readily satisfy the judgment by making payment directly to the plaintiff so that the plaintiff will not need to get an execution.

■ APPEALS

The American legal system recognizes the fallibility of human nature. The party that lost the lawsuit will always have the option to appeal the trial court's decision.

An appeal operates differently from a trial. Where a trial involved taking the testimony of witnesses and could have had a jury resolve questions of fact, the hearing on appeals focuses only on the actions of the trial court at trial. Instead of retrying the case, the appellate court will look to see whether the trial court made mistakes during the trial. For example, the trial court judge might have determined that certain information should be entered into evidence, but on appeal, the appellate court might have disagreed with the trial court judge.

Appellate Review

Mandatory

A critical component of the legal process allows for independent review of a trial court's actions and rulings. Because this is regarded as quite important to the trial process, jurisdictions will designate appeals courts where the losing party in a trial can expect, as a matter of right, to file an appeal to this court. No one has to file an appeal, but if a party does want to do so, then there will be an appeals court available to hear the appeal.

The Process Involved in an Appeal

Appellate review often involves a panel of judges (with an odd number of judges, like three or nine, to reduce the chance that the judges might deadlock). On appeal, the parties—through their lawyers—may have twenty or thirty minutes to present their arguments to the panel of judges. This is known as *oral argument*.

Often, the panel of judges will question the lawyers. They might aim to develop a better understanding of the legal arguments or the judges might want to establish the limits of an argument that a lawyer has made during the oral presentation or in the appellate brief.

Appellate Court Briefs

The lawyers will have had to file briefs in support of their arguments. Those briefs address the issues that have been raised on appeal by making reference to that law that supports their argument. Appellate courts impose strict requirements about the length of the brief and what's to be included in the brief, such as a table of the cases that counsel presents in support of the legal arguments that counsel makes in the brief and in oral argument.

As an appendix, the lawyers include a copy of the transcript generated from the trial.

Rulings by an Appellate Court

An appellate court could determine that the trial court acted properly, so it issues a ruling affirming the trial judge's actions.

However, disagreement does not automatically mean that the party who has filed the appeal has won. The panel of judges might conclude that the trial judge made a "harmless error," one not so significant as to justify overturning the judgment.

The panel might find that error did occur during the trial and **reverse** the judgment of the trial court. In this case, the appellate court would explain its ruling and include instructions on how the trial court should now proceed. Then, the appellate court could return the case to the trial court, to make a ruling consistent with that panel's understanding of the law.

That ruling could include retrying the case. The appellate court could decide that the error so significantly undermined the case that retrying the case would change nothing and so would not return the case to the trial court for further action but would dismiss the case. An appellate court could reverse in part and affirm in part, indicating where the error arose and what the trial court did correctly.

Discretionary

The legal system of a jurisdiction might provide additional appellate review. That court system could also allow for further review, but not automatically. Instead, further appellate review might arise when the party who lost on the first round of an appeal argues that the appellate court made a mistake. Depending on a jurisdiction's laws, the party who lost on appeal may have only the possibility of additional appellate review. This is called *discretionary review*. Another appellate court might grant a request for further appellate review, for example, as a way of reconciling different appellate results that arose over time in the jurisdiction.

For example, the trial court of general jurisdiction in the federal jurisdiction is the U.S. District Court. The losing party in a civil action will have a right to appeal that decision by presenting the appeal to the Circuit Court of Appeals. In the great majority of civil cases, the federal legal system does not mandate further appellate review, beyond review by the Circuit Courts of Appeal. But the circuit courts deal only with appeals of trial court decisions in a particular region. A party who loses at trial in U.S. District Court in Boston has a right of appeal to the First Circuit Court of Appeal while the losing party of a U.S. District Court trial held in San Francisco has a right of appeal to the Ninth Circuit Court of Appeals. Yet the appellate courts might not agree on how to evaluate and resolve a question of law on appeal. The First Circuit Court of Appeals might affirm the U.S. District Court's ruling, which had found that the defendant did owe a duty of care to the plaintiff, in a claim for negligence arising out of the manufacture of a product. The Ninth Circuit Court of Appeals, however, might reverse a U.S. District Court's ruling, having determined that the defendant did not owe plaintiff a duty of care in a claim for negligence arising out of the manufacture of a product.

Given these different determinations on a similar issue of law, the U.S. Supreme Court might decide to grant a request for further appellate review. That court might have decided that it needed to reconcile the different rulings of the First and Ninth Circuits, choosing to favor one over the other or to clarify the issue for further review. The U.S. Supreme Court did not necessarily have to take a case for appellate review as an opportunity to reconcile the verdicts but it could. If the U.S. Supreme Court declined to hear the case, the ruling of each Circuit Court of Appeal would stand as valid.

KEY TERMS

SUMMARY

Parties with a dispute may use a number of strategies to solve their disagreement. Alternative dispute resolution (ADR) involves such activities like arbitration or mediation, which can produce a settlement without having to prepare for the expense of litigation.

Litigation involves filing a claim in court to resolve a dispute as a matter of law. Before a court can review the claim, it has to have authority over the parties involved and the problem of law. The court needs to be authorized to handle this kind of claim and to be located where the parties can get a trial before an unbiased jury.

The plaintiff—the party that initiates the lawsuit—files a complaint against a defendant, whom the plaintiff claims is liable in damages for injuries caused by the defendant. The defendant responds with an answer, and the parties may add additional parties and claims, so that a court can resolve all disputes.

With litigation started, the parties now uncover information that can help to resolve the issue of law, through the process of discovery. This includes the gathering of oral and written information as well as visits to sites or medical examinations, among other things.

At any point in the proceedings, a party might request that the court take action by filing a motion. For example, a motion to compel discovery would mean ordering a noncompliant party to turn over the requested information.

Periodically before trial, the parties will meet to address at least the possibility of resolving the matter without going to trial; courts favor settlements since the parties retain control and more likely reach a result that pleases both sides.

During the trial, the plaintiff has an obligation to present sufficient information—evidence—to make a claim valid enough to merit an award of damages. The plaintiff can produce evidence through the introduction of documents or the testimony of witnesses, among the many options used to generate evidence. The defendant will have the opportunity to test the validity of the evidence; with a witness, this can involve cross-examination. The defendant need not present a defense but may also use documents and testimony to support the assertion that the plaintiff does not have a valid claim.

Often, members of the community, as a jury, have to evaluate all the evidence to determine what facts seem most likely to describe what happened with those who have the dispute. If they find a plaintiff's arguments more believable, the jury might then issue an award of damages—money offered in compensation to "make the plaintiff whole," even though money may only offset the effects of an injury.

The losing party may file an appeal, a request for review by another court, to determine whether the trial court judge acted properly when ruling on motions or other procedures related to the litigation. The appeals court can uphold the judgment, reject it, or return it to the trial court, with instructions on how to proceed properly to resolve the legal dispute.

CONCEPT REVIEW QUESTIONS

1. What are rules of civil procedure?
2. Identify and explain the types of jurisdiction needed by a court before it can hear a complaint.
3. What is a complaint?
4. Explain what a class action suit is.

5. What is a party asking for when filing a motion for summary judgment?
6. What is discovery?
7. Explain the difference between depositions and interrogatories.
8. What are sanctions that a court can impose when a party fails to comply with a request for discovery?
9. What's the difference between a challenge for cause and a peremptory challenge?
10. What kind of evidence is testimony?
11. Explain the difference between a verdict and a judgment.
12. What difference exists between an appeal as a matter of right and a discretionary appeal?

CRITICAL THINKING APPLICATIONS

1. During voir dire for a civil trial, questions to a prospective juror reveal that this person has seen every episode of the television series *Law and Order*, including all of the spin-off shows. If one of the lawyers files a challenge for cause to dismiss the prospective juror, how will the judge likely rule? Why?

2. An insurance company is hoping to recover some of the money stolen by a former bank teller. The former teller escaped prosecution while serving in the military. The insurance company's lawyer believes that the former teller/soldier had sent e-mails describing where to find the money. No other copies of these e-mails exist. The lawyer for the insurance company files a motion for the e-mail service provider to turn over the e-mails. How will the judge likely rule on that request for discovery? Why?

3. An auto accident happens in New York. The driver of the car lived in New Hampshire. The owner of the car lived in Tennessee and had registered the car there. The owner's insurance company was based in Arizona. Evaluate the possibility that each state might have personal jurisdiction and be sure to offer an opinion about the likelihood that a court in fact will find personal jurisdiction sufficiently strong enough to hear a claim for injuries resulting from the accident.

4. A plaintiff's child suffered injuries when the child had discovered and played with a hidden pair of lawn darts. (The child threw the plastic darts in the air to see if they would land in a target on the ground; the darts have heavy metal points on one end. The plaintiff had bought the darts before the product was taken off the market by the manufacturer because of the high incidence of injuries even when the product was used properly.) The plaintiff sues the store where the darts were purchased twelve years earlier. The store files a motion to dismiss for failure to state a claim because the statute of limitations for filing an action in tort is three years. Explain the most likely ruling that the court would make and why the court ruled that way.

5. Consider the previous fact pattern. The plaintiff had bought the darts when it was still possible to buy them. The plaintiff's child is injured when using the darts twelve years later. The plaintiff sues the store where the darts were sold; in this jurisdiction, there is no statute of limitations. The store wants to add the manufacturer as a party to this case. What rule, under the Federal Rules of Civil Procedure, would most easily allow for this to happen?

6. After an auto accident, the two drivers exchange registration papers. The registration for the car that caused the accident indicates the car is owned by John Washington. In suing the driver of the car that caused the accident, the lawyer for the party names John Washington as a defendant. After serving the complaint and a summons at the address given for John Washington, John

Washington's lawyer comes to court to file a motion to dismiss. Two men named John Washington live at the address on the registration. Will the court grant John Washington's motion to dismiss? Why?

7. A homeowner sues an insurance company, claiming that the company failed to honor the terms of its insurance contract because the homeowner's house burned down and the fire department reported that the fire occurred under "mysterious circumstances." That night, the local television stations broadcast a story about a fire that leveled a city block of homes and small businesses. Two days later, the jury returns a verdict for the homeowner. The lawyer for the insurance company immediately files a motion for a new trial on the grounds that the jurors had been influenced by the news reports of the fire from a few nights earlier. What will the judge likely rule? Why?

8. Using the previous fact pattern, the homeowner files requests for discovery to the insurance company for any documents that relate to the insurance company's internal policy or policies about settling claims. The lawyer for the insurance company opposes the motion. When the homeowner requests the court to compel the insurance company to provide these documents, the lawyer for the insurance company says that the policies are part of the "work product" used to defend against the lawsuit and so, should be privileged against discovery. Will the court issue an order to compel discovery for the production of these documents? Why or why not?

SKILL-BUILDING APPLICATION

If the Lion's Den was the hottest place to be seen in town, the Pride Room was the hottest spot in the bar. An L-shaped room, only a few, select people could be admitted to this space. A small room adjacent to the Pride Room contained the electrical service, accessible only from a separate entrance. Although the service had been recently upgraded to handle the greater demand for power in the Den—it had been an old "townie" bar for years up until a change in ownership—most of the wiring in the club had not been upgraded. One Friday night, a fire broke out when wiring behind the bar in the Pride Room shorted out. It killed everyone in the Pride Room as well as half the patrons in the Den itself. A fire-fighter suffered from third-degree burns and inhaled toxic fumes.

Families of the victims file a class action suit against the owner of the Lion's Den, King of the Jungle, LLC. The plaintiffs brought a separate suit against the power company, which had provided the upgraded electrical service. They also separately sued the prior owners, Frank and Joe Beekly. Finally, the plaintiffs also separately sued the manufacturer of the wiring, All Aluminum Wiring, for failing to identify the type of wiring or its gauge on the grounds that if had the power company known of this, it would not have provided the service upgrade.

King of the Jungle, LLC objected to the request for class certification.

During the trial, a juror sought out a spool of wire identical to that used in the Lion's Den. That juror then tested the wire to see how much power it could handle; it clearly could not carry the power coming through the upgraded service.

The jury returned a verdict against all of the defendants for joint and several liability. All of the defendants filed a motion for the court to set aside the jury's verdict. The court denied that motion and entered a judgment for the plaintiffs.

The defendants wish to appeal. Given the facts contained here, identify all issues that the defendants will raise on appeal. Then explain how the appeals court should rule on these motions.

There is occasions and causes why and
wherefore in all things.
  —*William Shakespeare*, Henry V

The Tort of Negligence | CHAPTER 3

The tort of negligence involves a failure to fulfill a duty that causes injury to another. It is the most common basis for lawsuits in the United States today. Rather than focusing on the intent of the defendant, negligence depends upon whether the defendant acted reasonably. While a defendant has to engage in acceptable conduct, that kind of conduct depends on the specific circumstances. So, the trier of fact has to assess all factors to determine if the defendant has engaged in unacceptable conduct. This chapter will introduce the elements of a cause of action for negligence and will explore what each element involves. At trial, the fundamental question is: Given a duty of care, did defendant's failure to act reasonably under the circumstances cause plaintiff's injuries?

CHAPTER TOPICS

1. Negligence Explained
2. Elements of Negligence
3. Duty of Reasonable Care
4. Breach of Duty of Reasonable Care
5. Proximate Cause
6. Damages

OBJECTIVES

After completing this chapter, you will be able to:

1. Define the tort of negligence.
2. Understand the duty of reasonable care, the reasonable person standard, and the sources of the duty.
3. Discuss the concept of a breach of the duty of reasonable care.
4. Understand the concepts related to the requirement of proximate cause.
5. Profile the issue of damages in a tort action.

■ NEGLIGENCE EXPLAINED

Accidents will happen. Could that have been avoided? Did the defendant breach a duty to act reasonably? Did that breach result in injury to the plaintiff? A cause of action for the tort of negligence depends upon the defendant having a duty, failing to uphold that duty so that plaintiff suffered an injury.

The tort of negligence differs from the generally used definition of negligence. To recover for injuries, the plaintiff has to establish—by a preponderance of the evidence—four elements to prevail in a lawsuit for negligence. Miss any one element, and the plaintiff cannot recover. The defendant still may have acted negligently but if that can't be proven in court, the plaintiff will not recover damages for his or her injury.

Many torts depend upon the intent of the defendant to injure the plaintiff. Negligence does not consider the defendant's state of mind. Rather, it looks to see if the defendant has a duty to act with care. So, the tort of negligence emphasizes the need for people to act reasonably in society. For example, Christian takes aim, swings and hits Peter; since Christian intended to injure Peter, Christian will be held liable for the torts of assault and battery. But if Christian trips over his own feet and knocks Peter over, Christian will be held liable for the tort of negligence because while Christian did not intend to harm Peter, he did breach a duty of care to walk safely.

Negligence arose out of the common law, which is made up of court decisions that considered whether a defendant had an obligation to act with greater care. Today, common law can also draw more broadly on the scholarly works that examine the finer points of the law. So, in 1923 a group of prominent American judges, lawyers, and legal scholars founded the American Law Institute (ALI), with the goal to produce a clear and concise statement of all common law. The stated goal of the ALI was to issue Restatements of law, scholarly publications intended to clarify uncertainty and complexity of the law. No Restatement has the force of law unless a court quotes or a legislature incorporates language from the Restatement to incorporate it into the law. That might happen because Restatements present scholarly statements about what the law should be. The paralegal researcher should be familiar with the *Restatement* as a well-respected secondary authority.

In its *Restatement (Second) of Torts*, the American Law Institute defines negligence as a standard of conduct (see box below).

NEGLIGENCE

Negligence is conduct which falls below the standard established by law for the protection of others against unreasonable risk of harm.

Restatement (Second) of Torts §282 (1965)

By focusing on the conduct rather than the intent of the defendant, the tort of negligence reflects society's desire to protect people from the unreasonable conduct of careless individuals. Professor Keeton states that the law must look not to the mind of the defendant, but to the demands that society places on the conduct of people (see box on next page).

STANDARD OF CONDUCT

The standard of conduct imposed by the law is an external one, based upon what society demands generally of its members, rather than upon the actor's personal morality or individual sense of right and wrong. A failure to conform to the standard is negligence, therefore, even if it is due to clumsiness, stupidity, forgetfulness, an excitable temperament, or even sheer ignorance. An honest blunder, or a mistaken belief that no damage will result, may absolve the actor from moral blame, but the harm to others is still as great, and the actor's individual standards must give way in this area of the law to those of the public. In other words, society may require of a person not to be awkward or a fool.

W. Page Keeton et al., *Prosser & Keeton on the Law of Torts* §31 at 169 (5th ed. 1984)

■ ELEMENTS OF NEGLIGENCE

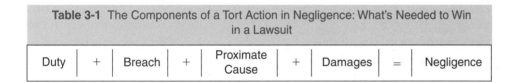

Table 3-1 The Components of a Tort Action in Negligence: What's Needed to Win in a Lawsuit

Duty	+	Breach	+	Proximate Cause	+	Damages	=	Negligence

The tort of negligence consists of four components, or elements. In court, the plaintiff has to prove, by a preponderance of the evidence, the following **elements:**

- The defendant had a duty to act reasonably
- The defendant failed to fulfill that obligation
- That this breach of duty caused the plaintiff's injuries
- The plaintiff suffered injuries

Looking at these elements from the perspective of a trial, the plaintiff will provide to the fact-finder answers to these questions:

- Did the defendant owe a duty of reasonable care to the plaintiff?
- Did the defendant breach the duty of reasonable care?
- Was the defendant's breach the proximate cause of the plaintiff's injury?
- Did the plaintiff suffer damages?

The law will not hold a defendant liable for every injury to the plaintiff but only for those injuries that are directly related to a breach of a duty.

■ DUTY OF REASONABLE CARE

The first element required to prove negligence lies in the answer to the question: Did the defendant owe a **duty of reasonable care** to the plaintiff? Society defines the duty of reasonable care as a standard of conduct expected of everyone. An action in negligence looks specifically to the duty of care owed by the defendant to the plaintiff. Under the law, a **duty** is an obligation requiring an individual to do or refrain from doing something to protect others from harm.

Black's Law Dictionary offers this definition for a duty:

DUTY

A legal obligation that is owed or due to another and that needs to be satisfied; an obligation for which somebody else has a corresponding right.

Black's Law Dictionary (8th ed. 2004)

It requires that individuals drive their automobiles, operate their water craft, maintain their equipment, and otherwise act to avoid the risk of harm to others. For example, Terrence has had four beers in the past hour and operates his boat so as to create a wake that capsizes Elmer's small boat. While Terrence did not intend to cause Elmer harm, Terrence breached a duty of care to operate his boat safely.

Whether a duty exists is a question for the court to decide; whether facts show a breach of that duty is reserved for the fact-finder, a role often played by a jury. The court must make its determination based on the question: Did the defendant owe an obligation to the plaintiff to act or not to act in a certain manner? In the previous example, Terrence owed Elmer a duty of care when operating his boat so as not to cause injury to other boaters.

The duty of reasonable care is best understood if examined in light of the following categories:

- Reasonable person standard
- Scope of the duty
- Source of the duty
- An act or omission
- Foreseeability

An examination of each category will help the paralegal student understand the concept of the duty of reasonable care.

Reasonable Person Standard

Society has created a legal standard to measure the conduct of a community's members. That standard arises out of the actions of a "reasonable" person. No such person actually exists, but courts have found it useful to imagine a person who could exemplify the abstract ideal of a 'typical' adult in our society the duty of reasonable care. This imaginary person forms the basis for the **reasonable person standard.** This standard (formerly called the *reasonable man standard*) compares the conduct of an individual to that of an imaginary person under the same or similar circumstances in avoiding harm to another. The *Restatement (Second) of Torts* defines the reasonable person standard in similar terms (see box below).

CONDUCT OF A REASONABLE MAN: THE STANDARD

Unless the actor is a child, the standard of conduct to which he must conform to avoid being negligent is that of a reasonable man under like circumstances.

Restatement (Second) of Torts §283 (1965)

Professor Dobbs' formulation clarifies what this conduct involves:

CARE EXERCISED BY A REASONABLE AND PRUDENT PERSON

"The duty owed by all people generally—the standard of care—is the duty to exercise the care that would be exercised by a reasonable and prudent person under the same or similar circumstances to avoid or minimize risks of harm to others." [footnotes omitted]

Dobbs, *The Law of Torts* §117, (2000)

Under the reasonable person standard, an individual conducts himself or herself as an imaginary reasonable person would to avoid or prevent injury to another. Similarly, Professor Keeton states that the reasonable person is an ideal individual embodying all the proper qualities absent some human shortcomings (see box below).

REASONABLE PERSON STANDARD

The actor is required to do what such an ideal individual would be supposed to do in his place. A model of all proper qualities, with only those human shortcomings and weaknesses which the community will tolerate on the occasion, "this excellent but odious character stands like a monument in our Courts of Justice, vainly appealing to his fellow-citizens to order their lives after his own example."

W. Page Keeton et al., *Prosser & Keeton on the Law of Torts* §32 at 174 (5th ed. 1984)

The question of the application of the standard of the reasonable person is one for the trier of fact, usually the jury, to decide. The jury must answer this question: Under the same or similar circumstances, would a reasonable person act as this individual did? The jury must recognize that the unpredictability of human behavior dictates a certain amount of latitude in defining this imaginary person. The reasonableness of the individual's conduct must be measured in light of certain characteristics:

- Physical attributes
- Mental condition
- Age
- Knowledge, skill, and intelligence

Thus, the reasonableness of the conduct depends upon the circumstances of the situation and certain individual traits. Professor Dobbs offers a more nuanced set of criteria for what a "reasonable person" needed to have done (see box below).

ESTABLISHING WHAT A REASONABLE PERSON WOULD DO

When we ask about the judge, we find that the standard is not wholly objective. The reasonable person whose standards the defendant must meet is said to have these attributes:

1. normal intelligence;
2. normal perception, memory, and at least a minimum of standard knowledge;

continued

> 3. all the additional intelligence, skill, or knowledge actually possessed by the individual actor; and
> 4. the physical attributes of the actor himself
>
> [footnotes omitted]
>
> Dobbs, *The Law of Torts* §118, (2000)

Physical Attributes

The general rule is that the reasonable person has the same physical attributes as the defendant.

A physically incapacitated defendant cannot be held to a standard of conduct that would be impossible for him or her to meet. For instance, a deaf individual is entitled to have allowance made for his or her disability. Thus, the deaf person cannot be held to a standard that would require him or her to hear an approaching locomotive. The applicable criterion in that case requires that the person take the precautions that an ordinary reasonable deaf person would under the same circumstances (see Case in Point 3-1).

CASE IN POINT 3-1

Jakubiec v. Hasty

337 Mich. 205 (1953)

Plaintiff Theresa Jakubiec was 18 years of age at the time of her injury. Her father, Joseph Jakubiec, as her next friend, instituted an action for her damages and a separate action for medical expenses and the loss of her services. These actions were combined and tried before a jury.

Defendants Arthur L. Hasty, the owner of the taxicab which struck Miss Jakubiec, and John P. Nugent, his employee driver, have appealed from judgments entered upon the jury's verdicts in the personal injury case of $6,500, and in the medical expense and loss of service case of $1,000.

It is admitted that the taxicab struck the plaintiff while she was crossing Michigan Avenue in the city of Detroit on August 4, 1948, at 3:40 p.m. She was walking from the northwest curb of the intersection of Brooklyn Avenue to the east-bound streetcar safety zone on Michigan. The day was rainy and the pavement was wet.

Plaintiff is deaf and mute and was examined through an interpreter. On the day of the accident she was employed at the Banner Laundry on Brooklyn Avenue, a few blocks north of Michigan, from which place she walked southerly down the west side of Brooklyn to the northwest corner of the intersection. Michigan Avenue runs almost due east and west, while Brooklyn runs about 30 degrees west of north. She testified she looked both ways, saw a truck and car coming from the east at a distance of about 300 feet, about a block away. A streetcar was approaching from the west at the same time, also about a block distant.

Plaintiff testified that the truck passed her at about 30 miles per hour and the car that followed it was moving at about the same speed. She then started across Michigan to the east-bound safety zone. When she reached the west-bound streetcar tracks, defendant's taxicab, also going west, suddenly appeared and struck her. She said she first saw the approaching taxicab when 20 feet away in the center of the street near the west-bound rails.

[....]

Another witness for the defense was Claude D. McKim, who was the motorman of the east-bound streetcar that was involved in the accident. He testified that he saw a woman run in front of a Checker cab. In answer to the question: 'Have you any estimate of the speed of the cab?' He answered: 'No, just the usual rate of speed, around twenty-five miles an hour.' Upon objection, the court ruled: 'The answer after the word no will be stricken.' He stated that the woman did not look when she left the curb. A Checker Cab Company employee testified that he but that he could not be found. Neither defendant testified at the trial. Plaintiff testified that the truck passed her at about 30 miles per hour and the car that followed it was moving at about the same speed. She then started across Michigan to the east-bound safety zone. When she reached the west-bound streetcar tracks, defendant's taxicab, also going west, suddenly appeared and struck her. She said she first saw the approaching taxicab when 20 feet away in the center of the street near the west-bound rails....

Another witness for the defense was Claude D. McKim, who was the motorman of the east-bound streetcar that was involved in the accident. He testified that he saw a woman run in front of a Checker cab. In answer to the question: 'Have you any estimate of the speed of the cab?' He answered: 'No, just the usual rate of speed, around twenty-five miles an hour.' Upon objection, the court ruled: 'The answer after the word no will be stricken.' McKim said that the woman left the curb at a point about 10 feet west of the west end of the safety zone; that when he first saw the taxicab it was about 15 feet away and swerving to its left after straddling the north west-bound rail. He stated that the woman did not look when she left the curb. A Checker Cab Company employee testified that he made a search for Hasty's driver, Nugent, but that he could not be found. Neither defendant testified at the trial.

The jury, in announcing its verdicts, assessed the amounts in each case against Hasty. The trial judge informed the jury that Hasty, the owner, could not be held liable unless it was found that the driver, Nugent, was guilty of negligence. After some colloquy between the court and the jury, and an indication that some of its members wanted to further discuss the matter, the jury again retired. Verdicts against both defendants were thereafter returned.

The first question in the case is whether plaintiff was guilty of contributory negligence as a matter of law. Defendants claim that the accident occurred about 50 feet west of the westerly line of Brooklyn Avenue. Their police witness said the body was lying about 20 feet west of the crosswalk. McKim testified that the woman did not look when she left the curb and that she ran directly in front of the taxicab. Plaintiff testified that she could not see the taxicab because of the large passing truck. The speed of the taxicab is a matter of dispute. In view of the conflicting testimony a question of fact was raised for the jury as to plaintiff's contributory negligence....

We are urged to grant a new trial because of the court's refusal to instruct the jury in accordance with defendants' requests Nos. 8 and 9, which read: "The plaintiff is a deaf mute. The fact that plaintiff is a deaf mute, and has not full use of all of her senses, is a fact which she, herself, must take into consideration in essaying to cross a thoroughfare.

"You must decide this case wholly on the evidence presented to you, and keep your minds and hearts free of any question of sympathy or prejudice."

The first request, which is in conformity with that suggested in Covert v. Randall, supra, might well have been given.

The court in its charge did not specifically instruct the jury that sympathy should not enter into their deliberations or that a deaf-mute is not excused from using the standards of care that an ordinarily prudent person would exercise under similar circumstances, as was charged in the Covert case. However, there is no showing that the jury's verdicts were unjust or that they were reached as the result of undue sympathy for the plaintiff. They should not be set aside on this ground. (citation omitted)....

The judgments are affirmed, with costs to appellees.

Mental Condition

If the defendant claims an impairment existed at the time the tort was committed, a court will hold a defendant to an objective standard of reasonableness regardless of his or her mental health. This contrasts with the law governing the physical attributes of an imaginary reasonable person; courts are not as tolerant concerning a defendant's mental condition. For a minor mental deficiency, bad judgment, or an excitable temperament, the law will hold the defendant to a standard of reasonable conduct. For the defendant to allege that he or she did the best that he or she knew how is never a defense to an action in negligence.

In the case of more serious mental disorders, the courts also hold the individual to a standard of reasonable conduct regardless of whether the defendant could achieve such a standard, as a Florida court noted (see Case in Point 3-2).

 ## CASE IN POINT 3-2

Jolley v. Powell

299 So.2d 647 (Fla. Dist. Ct. App. 2d Dist. 1974)

The alleged facts underlying the question are that on October 28, 1972, the defendant James Powell shot and killed Karen Ann Jolley under most bizarre circumstances. He was acquitted of homicide "by reason of insanity" in a subsequent prosecution. This action followed.

At the outset, we restrict the scope of the question. We do so because, while Florida has not answered the precise question, the general rule in jurisdictions which have considered it make a distinction between insanity as a defense to an unintentional tort and as a defense to those torts requiring a specific state of mind which defendant may be incapable of forming. These latter would include, for example, actions based on deceit, malice or defamation. Therefore, since this action is based on a "wrongful act" or "negligence," as circumscribed by Florida's wrongful death act, we limit the scope of the question as relating to unintentional tort actions and answer the question in the negative.

It is surely not unusual in tort law nor indeed is it unfair that persons may be held responsible for failing to live up to a standard which, as a matter of fact, they cannot meet. As Justice Holmes observed:

The standards of the law are standards of general application… It does not attempt to see men as God sees them, for more than one sufficient reason…[the awkward man's] slips are no less troublesome to his neighbors than if they sprang from guilty neglect.

And who would deny that the victim of a nuisance may have it abated regardless of the intent of the offending party?

So liability without subjective fault, under some circumstances, is one price men pay for membership in society. The sane and the insane, the awkward and the coordinated are equally liable for their acts or omissions. In such cases we do not decide fault, rather we determine upon whom our society imposes the burden of redress for a given injury. As Holmes implied in his "awkward man" parable, a principle at least co-equal with that of the fault principle in the law of torts is that the innocent victim should have redress….

In addition to the foregoing reasoning, we are also of the view that practical considerations in the administration of justice militate against unnecessarily injecting all of the confusion and potential for false claims inherent in the unsatisfactory tests of insanity in criminal cases into civil actions. We therefor reiterate, when the predicate for a wrongful death action is unintentional tort the standard against which such tort is measured is the objective, "reasonable man standard" and the subjective state of mind of the tortfeasor is irrelevant.

In passing, we point out that we do not mean to say here that insanity would not be a defense to a claim for punitive damages. Our rationale would seem to suggest that such a defense would indeed be available in such cases. We need not decide the point now, however, since punitive damages are not sought herein.

So, the law requires severely disturbed or psychotic individuals to conform to general standards of conduct and renders them responsible for any harm caused. The *Restatement (Second) of Torts* provides that a mental illness does not relieve the actor from responsibility (see box below).

MENTAL DEFICIENCY

Unless the actor is a child, his insanity or other mental deficiency does not relieve the actor from liability for conduct which does not conform to the standard of a reasonable man under like circumstances.

Restatement (Second) of Torts §283 (1965)

The following case talks about the nature of *Restatement (Second) of Torts* §283 B, and why it should not apply even after determining that a person with a mental deficiency should be held liable (see Case in Point 3-3).

CASE IN POINT 3-3

Creasy v. Rusk

730 N.E.2d 659 (Ind. 2000)

[...]

On May 16, 1995, Creasy and another certified nursing assistant, Linda Davis, were working through their routine of putting Rusk and other residents to bed. Creasy knew that Rusk had been "very agitated and combative that evening." (citation omitted) By Creasy's account:

[Davis] was helping me put Mr. Rusk to bed. She was holding his wrists to keep him from hitting us and I was trying to get his legs to put him to bed. He was hitting and kicking wildly. During this time, he kicked me several times in my left knee and hip area. My lower back popped and I yelled out with pain from my lower back and left knee.

(citation omitted)

Creasy filed a civil negligence suit against Rusk, seeking monetary damages for the injuries she suffered as a result of Rusk's conduct.

[...]

In many, if not most, jurisdictions, the general duty of care imposed on adults with mental disabilities is the same as that for adults without mental disabilities. (citation omitted) Adults with mental disabilities are held to the same standard of care as that of a reasonable person under the same circumstances without regard to the alleged tortfeasor's capacity to control or understand the consequences of his or her actions.

[...]

Consistent with recognizing a rule that holds a child to a standard of care proportionate to his or her capacity [...] Judge Kirsch observed that Indiana has also indicated a willingness to consider the mental capacity of an adult with mental disabilities when determining negligence liability, (citation omitted). [...] Judge Kirsch reasons that these cases either rely on or adopt the authority which calls for special consideration in applying the reasonable person standard under extenuating circumstances where a person "'unable to apprehend apparent danger and to avoid exposure to it cannot be said to be guilty of negligence.'" (citation omitted). Based on this authority, the Court of Appeals held that the rule in Indiana is "that a person's mental capacity, whether that person is a child or an adult, must be factored [into] the determination of whether a legal duty exists." (citation omitted).

[...]

As briefly noted ... the generally accepted rule in jurisdictions other than Indiana is that mental disability does not excuse a person from liability for "conduct which does not conform to the standard of a reasonable man under like circumstances." [footnote omitted] (citation omitted) People with mental disabilities are commonly held liable for their intentional and negligent torts. No allowance is made for lack of intelligence, ignorance, excitability, or proneness to accident. (citation omitted).

Legal scholars and authorities recognize that it is "impossible to ascribe either the volition implicit in an intentional tort, the departure from the standard of a 'reasonable' person which defines an act of ordinary negligence, or indeed any concept of 'fault' at all to one who ... is by definition unable to control his [or her] own actions through any exercise of reason." (citation omitted) Rather, the Restatement rule holding people with mental disabilities liable for their torts was founded upon public policy considerations.

The public policy reasons most often cited for holding individuals with mental disabilities to a standard of reasonable care in negligence claims include the following.

1. Allocates losses between two innocent parties to the one who caused or occasioned the loss. (citation omitted). Under this rationale, the one who experienced the loss or injury as a result of the conduct of a person with a mental disability is presumed not to have assumed risks or to have been contributorily negligent with respect to the cause of the injury. This policy is also intended to protect even negligent third parties from bearing excessive liabilities. (citation omitted).

2. Provides incentive to those responsible for people with disabilities and interested in their estates to prevent harm and "restrain" those who are potentially dangerous. (citation omitted).

3. Removes inducements for alleged tortfeasors to fake a mental disability in order to escape liability. (citation omitted) The Restatement mentions the ease with which mental disability can be feigned as one possible basis for this policy concern. (citation omitted)

4. Avoids administrative problems involved in courts and juries attempting to identify and assess the significance of an actor's disability. (citation omitted). As a practical matter, it is arguably too difficult to account for or draw any "satisfactory line between mental deficiency and those variations of temperament, intellect, and emotional balance." (citation omitted)

5. Forces persons with disabilities to pay for the damage they do if they "are to live in the world." (citation omitted) The Restatement adds that it is better that the assets, if any, of the one with the mental deficiency be used "to compensate innocent victims than that [the assets] remain in their hands." (citation omitted) A discussion draft for the Restatement (Third) of Torts rephrases this policy rationale and concludes: "If a person is suffering from a mental disorder so serious as to make it likely that the person will engage in substandard conduct that threatens the safety of others, there can be doubts as to whether this person should be allowed to engage in the normal range of

society's activities; given these doubts, there is nothing especially harsh in at least holding the person responsible for the harms the person may cause by substandard conduct." (citation omitted) [footnote omitted]

[...]

In balancing the considerations presented in the foregoing analysis, we reject the Court of Appeals's approach and adopt the Restatement rule. We hold that a person with mental disabilities is generally held to the same standard of care as that of a reasonable person under the same circumstances without regard to the alleged tortfeasor's capacity to control or understand the consequences of his or her actions.

[...]

Rusk was entitled to…judgment because public policy and the nature of the relationship between Rusk, Creasy, and the nursing home preclude holding that Rusk owed a duty of care to Creasy under these factual circumstances.

Similarly, voluntary intoxication and drug use do not change the fact of holding the defendant fully responsible for his or her actions. The drunk or drugged person is held to the same standard as a reasonable person who is sober.

Age

When determining what a reasonable person would do, a court will make allowances for individuals of advanced age or when considered to be a minor, at law. The trier of fact compares the individual with a reasonable person of similar age and infirmity under the same or similar circumstances. After having lit a cigarette, a sixteen-year-old tosses aside a lit match. If a fire starts, that sixteen-year-old's conduct will be compared to that of a reasonable sixteen-year-old.

Courts regard a child (often called a minor) as a person incapable of exercising the level of prudence of a reasonable adult. The law does not require children to meet the adult physical standards or match their ability to form mature decisions. Professor Keeton provides his observation of the law regarding the standard to be applied to children (see box below).

APPLYING THE STANDARD TO CHILDREN

The standard which is ordinarily applied, and which is customarily given to the jury, is to measure the child's conduct against what would be reasonable to expect of a 'child of like age, intelligence and experience.' There is something of an individual standard: capacity of the particular child to appreciate the risk and form a reasonable judgment must be taken into account.

W. Page Keeton et al., *Prosser & Keeton on the Law of Torts* §32 at 179 (5th ed. 1984)

The law will not hold a child responsible for his or her actions below a specified minimum age; this will vary by state, but a common minimum age for responsibility is set at seven. Above that age, the standard is that of a child of similar age and discretion, and is applied up to the age of majority, when the person is then held to an adult standard. As an example, a child of five may not be held responsible for his or her actions, but at age ten, he or she will be held to a standard of conduct of a reasonable ten-year-old. According to Professor Dobbs, beyond the age of majority, the individual is held to the objective reasonable person standard used with adults (see box on next page).

> ### CHILDREN
>
> "A minor, even an older one, is not required to conduct himself as a reasonable adult or even as a reasonable child of similar age. The minor is instead required to conduct himself only with the care of a minor of his own age, intelligence, and experience in similar circumstances..." [footnotes omitted]
>
> Dobbs, *The Law of Torts* §124 (2000)

The court in *Creasy*, Case in Point 3-4, explains why the *Restatement (Second) of Torts* §283A contains the same rule for children as was used for adults with a mental deficiency in *Restatement (Second) of Torts* §283B.

 ## CASE IN POINT 3-4

Creasy v. Rusk

730 N.E.2d 659 (Ind. 2000)

[...]

With respect to children, Indiana has incorporated the essence of the Restatement standard for determining the liability of children for their alleged tortious acts. The Restatement standard of conduct for a child is "that of a reasonable person of like age, intelligence, and experience under like circumstances." (citation omitted) (hereinafter, "Restatement rule"). Indiana reformulates the Restatement rule into a three-tiered analysis:

Children under the age of 7 years are conclusively presumed to be incapable of being contributorily negligent, from 7 to 14 a rebuttable presumption exists they may be guilty thereof, and over 14, absent special circumstances, they are chargeable with exercising the standard of care of an adult.

[...] In the age seven to fourteen category, Indiana applies the Restatement standard and ascertains whether the child exercised the care under the circumstances of a child of like age, knowledge, judgment, and experience. (citation omitted)

So, a six-year-old who takes the family car on a jaunt around the block will not be held liable for the injuries that result when the six-year-old rear-ends a police cruiser.

Knowledge, Skill, and Intelligence

An individual has to know that his or her act involves a risk of causing harm to hold that individual liable in negligence for that the action. Courts have frequently wrestled with making a determination about just *what* the defendant is required to know. **Knowledge** is defined as an awareness or understanding gained through experience or study. An individual cannot be presumed to know everything, and the law does not require such an impossibility. But the reasonable person standard does require a certain minimum level of knowledge and understanding necessary to survive. For instance, a reasonable person is aware that an object that is dropped will fall, that fire burns most things, and that water offers a potential for drowning. The *Restatement (Second) of Torts* suggests the reasonable person standard for recognizing the existence of risk (see box on next page).

RECOGNIZING EXISTENCE OF RISK

The actor is required to recognize that his conduct involves a risk of causing an invasion of another's interest if a reasonable man would do so while exercising

a. such attention, perception of the circumstances, memory, knowledge of other pertinent matters, intelligence, and judgment as a reasonable man would have; and

b. such superior attention, perception, memory, knowledge, intelligence, and judgment as the actor himself has.

Restatement (Second) of Torts §289 (1965)

The following case provides a practical analysis about an awareness of whether a risk exists (see Case in Point 3-5).

CASE IN POINT 3-5

Poplar v. Bourjois, Inc.

272 A.D. 74 (N.Y. App. Div. 1947)

Defendant Bourjois, Inc., appeals from a judgment establishing its liability in negligence for the loss of a finger by plaintiff Myrtle B. Poplar. She pricked her finger on the point of a metal star, which decorated a box of cosmetics that her husband had given to her, which he had bought at a retail store in Maryland. It became infected with hemolytic streptococcus, usually a fatal germ, which her doctor said would have been fatal in this instance except for sulfanilamide, but she recovered after a critical illness. Appellant is a manufacturer of perfumery and cosmetics. It purchased the box with the metal star on it from the impleaded defendant-respondent Lorscheider Schang Co., Inc., filled it with its own products, and sold it to the retailer which in turn sold to Mr. Poplar.

The verdicts against appellant must be set aside and the complaint dismissed since the gangrenous infection and ensuing amputation of Mrs. Poplar's finger was, as matter of law, so extraordinary and unpredictable a result from the otherwise trivial puncturing of her skin as to be a type of danger that would not ordinarily be foreseen. The metal star was innocent enough in itself. It became dangerous due to the intervention of another agency (poisonous bacteria) whose presence was unexpected and extraordinary. Although to uphold a cause of action it is not necessary to be able to prophesy the extent of the damages, which will flow from a negligent act (citation omitted) or the particular method by which they will be sustained (citation omitted), nevertheless the quality of the act as negligent or otherwise depends upon whether the injurious consequences resulting from it constitute a risk which a reasonably careful and prudent person would ordinarily have anticipated and guarded against (citation omitted). It would doubtless make a difference if the negligence charged were likely to result in substantial bodily injury of which infection becomes a concomitant, as where infection complicates a compound fracture of the arm sustained by being thrown negligently from a street car (citation omitted). Here, however, appellant cannot be held to answer for failing to anticipate a situation which did not involve elements of danger except from the remote chance that the streptococcus germ might be present where plaintiff's finger was pricked and get into her blood stream. In *MacPherson* v. *Buick Motor Co.* (217 N.Y. 382, 389) the court said: "If the nature of a thing is such that it is reasonably certain to place life and limb in peril when negligently made, it is then a thing of danger. Its nature gives warning of the consequences to be expected. * * * There must be knowledge of a danger, not merely possible, but probable." This may be said to mark the boundary of the legal doctrine outlined and developed in the *MacPherson* case, on which the recoveries below depend. Plaintiff testified that she nicked the middle finger of her right hand on the point of the star, that it did not seem serious at the time. Her doctor testified that "it was an unusual result for a small injury like that." Appellant's records show that 10,217 boxes of the same type were distributed to dealers without untoward result during the same Christmas season, and several million since they were first put on the market in 1929. As stated in *Cullem v. Renken Dairy Co.* (citation omitted) where plaintiff's thumb became seriously infected by a sharp projection on a milk bottle which had been delivered after a routine inspection: "In delivering a bottle of milk that may have some slight defect, the defendant, having exercised ordinary and reasonable care, may not be charged with negligence where some unusual result occurs that cannot be reasonably anticipated and foreseen or is not within the 'ordinary prevision, the range of probable expectation.' (citation omitted) It cannot be reasonably expected to recognize the existence of such risk. (citation omitted)" A contrary determination would result in opening the door to liability in negligence cases for the consequences of infection in all sorts of minor cuts and abrasions sustained in the ordinary course of life.

[...]

The judgment in favor of plaintiffs and against defendant Bourjois, Inc., should be reversed upon the law.

[...]

Most individuals who have led a normal life have absorbed information about such mundane matters as the weather, animals, machinery, electricity, sharp objects, and basic human behavior. A reasonable person will be presumed to possess such knowledge. By the same token, he or she will not be expected to know those things that are beyond daily experience. With society's rapid changes, individuals possess knowledge today that would not have been required of them 25 or 50 years ago. The lack of knowledge tolerated yesterday forms the basis of liability for negligence tomorrow.

Just as the reasonable person standard requires minimum levels of knowledge for an individual, it also demands that an individual possessing superior knowledge or intelligence must act accordingly. Experts and professionals such as doctors, lawyers, dentists, and accountants are required to possess a certain minimum level of knowledge and ability beyond the exercise of reasonable care. So long as these people acquire the training and/or certification needed to work in a particular field, they will be held to a higher standard than those who have not received such knowledge or training. So, at the scene of an automobile accident, an EMT who does not intubate a person experiencing difficulty breathing will be held liable if that person dies, since EMTs are trained to recognize when intubation is necessary.

Professional negligence is known as malpractice.

Act or Omission

The existence of a duty of reasonable care depends upon whether the defendant acted or failed to act as a reasonable person. Conduct forming the basis of an action for negligence may be either an *act* or an *omission*. An **act** within the meaning of the law is the process of doing something. To provide the basis of an action for negligence, the act must be a duty required of a reasonable person under the same or similar circumstances. An act of misconduct is called **misfeasance,** and may form the basis of liability for negligence if the act results in harm to another and fails to meet the reasonable person standard.

An **omission** is the failure to do something. A failure to act is termed **nonfeasance,** and forms the basis of an action for negligence if a reasonable person would not have failed to act under similar circumstances. An action in negligence may arise where the nonfeasance of the defendant injured the plaintiff. The key to understanding whether a court will impose liability for either misfeasance or nonfeasance lies in an application of the reasonable person standard. So, if a reasonable person would have acted or refrained from acting, the defendant will be held to that standard. In the following case, a court explains the difference between the two, much to the chagrin of the plaintiff (see Case in Point 3-6).

CASE IN POINT 3-6

Minch v. Department of The California Highway Patrol
140 Cal. App. 4th 895 2006 140 Cal. App. 4th

While plaintiff Troy Minch, a tow truck operator, was working at the scene of a traffic accident, a passing motorist lost control of his vehicle and hit plaintiff. Severely harmed, plaintiff brought a personal injury action against the California Highway Patrol (CHP), alleging that CHP officers at the scene were negligent in "failing to properly monitor and/or regulate traffic within the vicinity of the [accident scene]." Finding the officers had no duty of care as to plaintiff, the trial court entered summary judgment in favor of the CHP. Plaintiff appeals.

We agree with the trial court. As we will explain, undisputed evidence demonstrates the CHP officers did not have a duty of care toward plaintiff because they did not create or increase the risk of harm that led to plaintiff's injuries, and the circumstances did not establish a special relationship between the officers and plaintiff such that the officers would have had a duty to protect him. We also reject his claim that the provisions of the CHP Officer Safety Manual establish the officers owed plaintiff a duty in tort. Although the manual would be admissible evidence on the question of breach of duty, if a duty of care existed, the manual was not formally adopted as a regulation. Thus, it does not have the force of law and its provisions do not establish a duty of care on the part of CHP officers. Accordingly, we shall affirm the judgment.

[...]

On January 12, 2003, the driver of a Volkswagen Jetta was involved in a single-car accident on San Benito Avenue in Tehama County. San Benito Avenue is a two-lane road with a double yellow line in the center and solid white fog lines separating the traffic lanes from the shoulder. To the north of the accident site, the road is straight such that southbound traffic would have a clear view of the site. To the south of the accident site, the road curves such that northbound traffic would be coming around a curve shortly before the accident site.

The accident occurred around midday. It had been cloudy and raining, and the road was wet. CHP Officer Tim Larios and his supervisor, Acting Sergeant Vincent Zambrana, responded to the scene. They observed the Jetta upside down in a ditch next to the southbound lane of the road. Larios advised CHP dispatch that a tow truck was needed.

Plaintiff, an employee of J & L Towing, was notified by his employer to respond to the scene. At the scene, the CHP officers did not give directions to plaintiff regarding the extraction of the Jetta from the ditch; rather, plaintiff relied on his own knowledge and experience. While he worked, plaintiff turned on the overhead amber beacons, flashing emergency lights, and Reyes slowed down when he saw Officer Larios signal him to do so. Garcia, apparently inattentive, did not immediately slow down. When he noticed the brake lights on Reyes's truck, he hit his brakes hard, causing the wheels to lock, and turned to the left. The truck slid out of control. Larios yelled a warning to plaintiff, who nonetheless was hit by Garcia's truck, which slid across the road, struck the tow truck, knocked plaintiff to the ground, and came to rest against the Jetta. Plaintiff suffered severe personal injuries when he was struck.

[...]

Turning to the facts of this case, some clarification is necessary. In his brief, plaintiff frequently refers to the process of extracting the Jetta from the ditch. For example, he states that while extracting the Jetta, he was required to position the tow truck within the lane of travel and was required to walk within the lanes of travel to retrieve tools and equipment, and to operate the tow truck controls. He asserts that while a tow truck driver is within a lane of travel to extract a vehicle, the CHP is required to use its best efforts to keep the area and the driver safe from oncoming traffic.

The record establishes that while plaintiff extracted the Jetta, the CHP officers placed a patrol vehicle with flashing lights within the southbound lane about 20 to 30 feet north of the tow truck. The officers directed traffic, with one officer standing along the southbound lane to the north of the tow truck and another officer standing along the northbound lane to the south of the tow truck.

The officers successfully protected plaintiff as he extracted the Jetta. Plaintiff was not injured during that process. Rather, his injury occurred after he had extracted the Jetta and while he had parked the tow truck, with the Jetta in tow, for business purposes. The officers did not require that plaintiff remain at the scene, and they did not tell him where to park after he extracted the Jetta. Thus, negligence, if any, in the manner in which the officers directed traffic during the extraction process did not result in the harm that occurred and cannot serve as the basis for recovery in tort. (citation omitted)

Plaintiff asserts that shortly after his arrival with the tow truck, Sergeant Zambrana departed, leaving only Officer Larios. Plaintiff later argues: "Just like in *Mann, supra,* after summoning the tow truck, Sergeant Zambrana left the scene without warning, and with him left any warning lights that may have been on in his vehicle." In fact, the record establishes that Zambrana stayed at the scene throughout the extraction process. After the Jetta was extracted and plaintiff had parked on the shoulder of the road, the officers walked to a position behind the Jetta and then Zambrana left. Plaintiff was fully aware when Zambrana left.

Plaintiff repeatedly claims he was injured while preparing the Jetta for transport. However, in his deposition, plaintiff was clear that the injury occurred after the Jetta was in tow and while he was walking to the cab of the truck to get his receipt book for business purposes.

[...] Under the circumstances presented, we agree with the trial court that the CHP officers did not owe a duty of care in tort to plaintiff. They did not create the risk of harm. After plaintiff extracted the Jetta, they did not direct him to stay at the scene or tell him where to park. They did not lock the passenger door of the tow truck, thus compelling plaintiff to walk on the traffic side of the truck. Plaintiff was not in a position of dependency on the officers, and they did not say anything to indicate that they would guarantee his safety. Plaintiff could not have detrimentally relied upon the officers' conduct when he walked toward the cab of the truck to retrieve his receipt book; at that time, he was fully aware that Sergeant Zambrana had departed and, by plaintiff's testimony, Officer Larios was behind the Jetta talking to the owner.

[...]

According to plaintiff, the CHP and the trial court confused the issues of misfeasance and nonfeasance. [...] Simply put, misfeasance occurs when the defendant's affirmative actions create a risk of harm to the plaintiff; nonfeasance involves the failure to save the plaintiff from a peril that was not of the defendant's making. (citation omitted) All persons are ordinarily obligated to exercise due care in their own actions so as not to create an unreasonable risk of injury to others. (citation omitted) This standard applies to instances of misfeasance.

Nonfeasance requires a special relationship obligating the defendant to act to protect the plaintiff. (citation omitted)

[...]

Plaintiff asserts that his lawsuit is based upon the CHP's misfeasance, not nonfeasance. However, he has not identified specific conduct by which the officers created a risk of peril. Rather, plaintiff's action is based on the generic claim that the officers did not adequately protect him from the risk of harm. [...]

In this case, the trial court said in reaching its decision: "Plaintiff has failed to establish, either through witnesses or expert testimony, that the officers did anything wrong." Plaintiff asserts that whether the officers did anything wrong is a matter that goes to breach of duty, and that it was error for the court to make such a finding in resolving the question of duty.

There is some overlap in the factors that a court considers in determining the existence of a duty and those the trier of fact will consider in determining whether a duty was breached. (citation omitted) Here, the court's observation that plaintiff did not show the officers did anything wrong reflects that plaintiff's claim is based upon a general failure to protect, rather than affirmative conduct creating a risk of harm—i.e., nonfeasance rather than misfeasance. The trial court did not err in making that observation. [footnote omitted.]

DISPOSITION

The judgment is affirmed.

Although the parable of the Good Samaritan, of a person spontaneously coming to the aid of another, speaks to aspirations about human behavior, almost all states do not require its citizens to come to the aid of another.

Source of Duty

A person may have a duty to act, according to common law, or when imposed under statute, in the states and the federal legal systems. Statutes may change or eliminate a duty imposed under common law.

Case Law

The common law of this country, embodied in its case law, forms the primary source for authority establishing the duty of reasonable care. Appellate court decisions have established the guidelines for negligent conduct. At trial, the trier of fact uses those guidelines to determine whether defendant's conduct conformed to those standards. The appellate courts decide the reasonableness of conduct for the community. Juries determine whether the defendant has met those standards.

The criteria established by the courts constantly change as communities demands change. So, the courts continue to scrutinize what constitutes the duty of reasonable care as society evolves. This process helps to minimize inflexibility in the application of the duty of reasonable care.

Statutory Law

Congressional and legislative enactments may also impose or alter the duty of reasonable care. Statutes can protect the individual from certain harm just as the common law mandated that defendants exercise ordinary care. Some statutes establish a fixed standard to be met under certain specified circumstances. For instance, statutes addressing product warranties, medical consent, and limitations of actions represent situations where a legislature has abrogated common law principles and established new standards of conduct. Worker's compensation laws and federal tort claim actions are other areas where there has been legislative modification of common law negligence principles. For example, a statute may impose a higher duty of care on licensed professionals who provide a service, in recognition of the additional training and certification that these individuals had assumed voluntarily.

■ BREACH OF THE DUTY OF REASONABLE CARE

If a defendant owes a duty of reasonable care, breach of that duty due to a failure to exercise reasonable care may support an action for negligence. The second element, as Professor Dobbs notes, required to maintain a tort action for negligence lies in the question: Did the defendant breach the duty of reasonable care (see box below)?

DUTY TO ACT

Unless the defendant has assumed a duty to act, or stands in a special relationship to the plaintiff, defendants are not liable in tort for a pure failure to act for the plaintiff's benefit. The fact that the defendant foresees harm to a particular individual from his failure to act does not change the general rule.

Dobbs, *The Law of Torts* §314, (2000)

A **breach** is a failure to perform a legal obligation or duty. A violation of the duty of reasonable care, such as acting unreasonably, constitutes a breach of the duty. Breach of duty occurs if the defendant fails to perform a duty that would be expected of a reasonable person.

As seen in the discussion of the duty of reasonable care, negligence requires more than a mere state of mind of the defendant; it is conduct that falls below a standard established by law.

Therefore, the trier of fact must focus on the conduct of the defendant rather than his or her state of mind. An individual will not be held liable for thinking negligently, but will be held liable for conduct that is unreasonable. A mere failure to exercise due care is insufficient to constitute a breach of the duty. According to Professor Keeton, the breach must be more than a failure to consider another (see box on next page).

> ### BREACH OF DUTY
> The almost universal use of the phrase "due care" to describe conduct which is not negligent should not obscure the fact that the essence of negligence is not necessarily the absence of solicitude for those who may be adversely affected by one's actions but is instead behavior which should be recognized as involving unreasonable danger to others.
>
> W. Page Keeton et al., *Prosser & Keeton on the Law of Torts* §31 at 169 (5th ed. 1984)

■ PROXIMATE CAUSE

The third element needed to bring a valid action in tort for negligence involves proximate cause. Was the defendant's breach the proximate cause of the plaintiff's injury?

Proximate cause simply means that the defendant's conduct caused an injury to a forseeable plaintiff. Looking for proximate cause means asking whether a link exists between the defendant's breach of a duty of care and the plaintiff's injury.

The term **cause** means something (an act or omission) that produces an effect, a result, or a consequence. The term **proximate** means something (an act or omission) that is closely related in space, time, or logical order. A combination of the two definitions results in a definition of proximate cause as a closely related act or omission by the defendant that produces an injury to the plaintiff. Later in this chapter, the case of *Plasgraf* offers an opportunity to explore this concept in greater detail.

Proximate cause is frequently called *legal cause*. It refers to a conclusion by the trier of fact that the plaintiff's injuries are a natural and probable consequence of the conduct of the defendant. A defendant cannot be found liable for negligence without a cause that is proximate to the harm.

Causation

Proximate cause looks at what the law requires to hold a defendant liable for the damages that arise out of the injury.

Cause in Fact

In order for a defendant to be liable to an injured plaintiff, the trier of fact must decide that the conduct of the defendant has caused the harm. **Cause in fact** means the defendant's conduct was the cause of the plaintiff's injury. It is the simplest and most direct way to look at causation of injury, and refers to all things that lead to the eventual injury. To illustrate cause in fact, assume that Arthur threw a banana peel on the sidewalk in front of his home. When Samantha rode by on her bicycle and struck the hazard with her front tire, she fell to the ground, injuring herself. Arthur's conduct in throwing the banana peel on the sidewalk was the cause in fact of Samantha's fall and injury.

Cause at Law: The "but-for" Rule

The trier of fact must conclude not only that the defendant's conduct was a cause in fact, but also that it was the legal cause of the injury; this is legal causation. One test used by courts to establish legal causation is called the **but-for rule.** The but-for rule states that if the harm would not have occurred without (but for) the conduct of the defendant, then the defendant is liable. Professor Keeton also refers to this as the *sine qua non* rule (see box on next page).

ABOUT THE "BUT-FOR" RULE

From such cases many courts have derived a rule, commonly known as the "but-for" or "sine qua non" rule, which may be stated as follows: The defendant's conduct is a cause of the event if the event would not have occurred but for that conduct; conversely, the defendant's conduct is not a cause of the event, if the event would have occurred without it.

W. Page Keeton et al., *Prosser & Keeton on the Law of Torts* §41 at 266 (5th ed. 1984)

In the illustration above, but for the fact that Arthur threw his banana peel on the sidewalk, Samantha would not have been injured. The application of the but-for rule makes Arthur's conduct the proximate cause of Samantha's injury. The trier of fact could conclude that his conduct was the legal cause of the injury, according to Professor Dobbs (see box below).

ANOTHER PERSPECTIVE ON DEFENDANTS AND THE "BUT-FOR" RULE

"Under the but-for test, the defendant's conduct is a cause in fact of the plaintiff's harm if, but-for the defendant's conduct, that harm would not have occurred." [Footnote omitted]

Dobbs, *The Law of Torts* §168, (2000)

The but-for rule works well to define legal cause with one cause involved in the equation but *only* when there is one causative factor. If more than one cause led to the plaintiff's injury, either one of which would have been sufficient to result in harm, another test is required.

Substantial Factor Rule

A more widely accepted rule used to determine proximate cause is the **substantial factor rule.** It states that proximate cause exists if the defendant's conduct was a substantial factor in bringing about the plaintiff's injury. In determining if the cause was a substantial factor in the production of the plaintiff's injury, the trier of fact must conclude that a reasonable person would regard it as a cause. The trier of fact may find that the defendant's conduct was a substantial factor if it was a material element in bringing about the injury. The *Restatement (Second) of Torts* provides the generally accepted rule for legal causation (see box below).

WHAT CONSTITUTES LEGAL CAUSE

The actor's negligent conduct is a legal cause of harm to another if

a. his conduct is a substantial factor in bringing about the harm, and
b. there is no rule of law relieving the actor from liability because of the manner in which his negligence has resulted in the harm.

Restatement (Second) of Torts §431 (1965)

Conversely, the defendant's conduct would not be a substantial factor if the harm would have occurred anyway. Consider a situation wherein Clarence takes his friend Walter fishing on a large body of water in his canoe. Clarence has not provided a life jacket for Walter. In a storm so heavy that a life jacket would have been of no value, Walter falls overboard and drowns. Certainly, Clarence's conduct in failing to provide a life jacket for Walter is negligent. But the storm was the substantial factor in the drowning, not the lack of a life jacket. Here, the trier of fact is faced with two causes: a failure to provide a life jacket, and a violent storm. The trier of fact must choose which of the causes was a substantial factor in Walter's death. A reasonable person would conclude that the storm was the substantial factor in the death.

Scope of Liability

A determination of legal responsibility for harm to the plaintiff only starts with a finding that the defendant's conduct was one of the causes of the injury. To find a defendant legally responsible for an injury, the defendant's conduct must have been the proximate cause of the harm to the plaintiff, under the "substantial factor" or but-for rule. A finding of proximate cause will support a finding of liability for the injury (see Table 3-2).

Table 3-2 Components of Proximate Cause					
Proximate Cause	=	(cause in fact)	+	Foreseeable

Liability is legal responsibility for the harm caused to another. The trier of fact must conclude that the defendant's conduct was not merely *a* cause of the injury to the plaintiff, but must conclude that it was *the* proximate cause of the harm. The confusion over the use of this term has been the subject of much debate by legal scholars, as noted by Professor Keeton (see box below).

PROXIMATE CAUSE

The term "proximate cause" is applied by the courts to those more or less undefined considerations which limit liability even where the fact of causation is clearly established. The word "proximate" is a legacy of Lord Chancellor Bacon, who in his time committed other sins. The word means nothing more than near or immediate; and when it was first taken up by the courts it had connotations of proximity in time and space which have long since disappeared. It is an unfortunate word, which places an entirely wrong emphasis upon the factor of physical or mechanical closeness. For this reason "legal cause" or perhaps even "responsible cause" would be a more appropriate term. There is, however, no present prospect that long ingrained practice will ever be altered by the substitution of either.

W. Page Keeton et al., *Prosser & Keeton on the Law of Torts* §42 at 273 (5th ed. 1984)

Then, contrast that observation with what Professor Dobbs offers for the purpose of having rules about proximate causation (see box on next page).

> ### PURPOSE OF PROXIMATE CAUSE RULES
>
> "Proximate cause rules are among those rules that seek to determine the appropriate scope of a negligent defendant's liability [Footnote omitted]. The central goal of the proximate cause requirement is to limit defendant's liability to the kinds of harms he risked by his conduct. Judicial decisions about proximate cause rules thus attempt to discern whether, in the particular case before the court, the harm that resulted from the defendant's negligence is so clearly outside the risks he created that it would be unjust or at least impractical to impose liability. The proximate cause issue, in spite of the terminology, is not about causation at all but about the appropriate scope of responsibility. [Footnote omitted]
>
> Dobbs, *The Law of Torts* §180 (2000)

Foreseeability or Unforeseeability

To find proximate cause, the trier of fact must conclude that a reasonable person would have anticipated the injury to others resulting from his or her conduct. If a reasonable person could have anticipated the harm, then the harm was foreseeable. **Foreseeability** is a reasonable anticipation that harm will occur from an act or omission.

Consider foreseeability by looking at those causes that are beyond the scope of foreseeability, which means that they are viewed as to their **unforeseeability.** Courts frequently view liability in terms of the unforeseeability of harm as opposed to its foreseeability. Unforeseeability occurs when a reasonable person could not conclude that an injury would occur from an act or omission. If the defendant could not reasonably foresee harm from his or her conduct, i.e., harm is clearly unforeseeable to a reasonable person, then no liability exists.

A better appreciation of the concept of proximate cause or legal cause can arise if the paralegal student considers it in terms of foreseeability or unforeseeability. The case of *Bogle v. Duke Power Company* explores the issues of duty and causation by looking at what happens when a metal ladder comes into contact with a visibly obvious power line (see Case in Point 3-7).

CASE IN POINT 3-7

Bogle v. Duke Power Company

27 N.C. App. 318 (1975)

This is an action for wrongful death instituted by Corina B. Bogle, administratrix of the estate of her son, Roy D. Bogle, Jr.

Plaintiff's complaint is summarized in pertinent part as follows:

On 17 May 1971 defendant, through transmission lines which it maintained, transmitted electric power to the Glen Alpine Grammar School in Glen Alpine, N. C., as well as to other communities in the surrounding area, and was well acquainted with the dangers incident to the transmission of electric energy. Defendant failed to exercise due care toward plaintiff's intestate by continuing to utilize transmission lines situated in such proximity to said school that it knew, or should have known, presented a hazard to maintenance men working in and around the school building; in failing to adequately insulate, inspect, repair and maintain said transmission lines; and in failing to provide warning signs alerting the public to the presence of a dangerous electrical hazard. The death of plaintiff's intestate was the direct and proximate result of negligent acts and omissions of defendant.

In its answer, defendant denied any negligence and pled the negligence of plaintiff's intestate as a proximate cause of the accident.

Extensive discovery was utilized by both parties. This included answers to interrogatories, depositions from E. D. Wortman, manager of defendant's operations in the Morganton area, Frank Corpening, the line foreman under whose supervision damage to the transmission line was repaired, as well as the affidavit of George M. Mode, the carpenter who plaintiff's intestate was employed to assist.

Defendant moved for summary judgment and materials submitted at the hearing established the following:

On 17 May 1971 plaintiff's intestate and Mode, employees of the Burke County Public School System, were called to the Glen Alpine Grammar School to check for leaks in the roof and to clean out some guttering. In the course of their work, they used a twenty-eight foot aluminum extension ladder to gain access to the roof. When they had finished clearing the gutters, intestate started to take down the ladder. Mode told intestate to wait until he could help and warned intestate about defendant's transmission line. The line was located some twenty-one feet from the building, suspended from a pole at a height of twenty-two feet, and had been so situated since before the line's acquition from another power company some thirty-five years earlier. Weather stripping on the line had become cracked and peeled away, leaving the copper line exposed. Intestate ignored Mode's warnings and tried to take the ladder down by himself. As he pulled the ladder away from the building it fell against the transmission line, showering the area with sparks. Intestate then attempted to push the ladder off the wire; the ladder momentarily broke contact with the ground, causing the full charge of 7200 volts to pass through intestate's body. The line burned through where it came in contact with the ladder and snapped, throwing intestate to the ground. Despite efforts to revive him, he was pronounced dead shortly thereafter.

We hold that the trial court properly granted defendant's motion for summary judgment.

[...]

In an action for wrongful death predicated on negligence, summary judgment for defendant is correct where the evidence fails to establish negligence on the part of defendant, establishes contributory negligence on the part of the decedent, or determines that the alleged negligent conduct complained of was not the proximate cause of the injury.

(citation omitted).

Negligence is the failure to exercise that degree of care for the safety of others that a reasonable prudent person would exercise under the same circumstances. (citation omitted). To be actionable the conduct complained of must be the proximate cause of the injury. (citation omitted). An essential element of causation is foreseeability, that which a person of ordinary prudence would reasonably have foreseen as the probable consequence of his acts. A person is not required to foresee all results but only those consequences, which are reasonable. (citation omitted).

Electric companies are required to exercise reasonable care in the construction and maintenance of their lines when positioned where they are likely to come in contact with the public. Here, defendant insulated its transmission line by height and isolation in accordance with existing regulations. (citation omitted). It equipped its poles and lines with fuses and circuit breakers designed to alleviate the risk of an uncontrolled discharge of electricity. We hold that defendant exercised reasonable care in the operation of its transmission lines near the

Glen Alpine Grammar School and was not in breach of any duty of care toward plaintiff's intestate.

Defendant's conduct in allowing the line to remain near the school where plaintiff contends defendant knew or should have known it posed a hazard to maintenance personnel, was not the proximate cause of death to plaintiff's intestate. The law requires only the exercise of reasonable care to provide for those eventualities, which a reasonable prudent person would have foreseen under the circumstances. It would have been beyond the parameters of reasonable foreseeability to require defendant to construct and insulate its transmission line so as to withstand the impact of a heavy metal extension ladder. It is unreasonable to call on the defendant to foresee that plaintiff's intestate would ignore the warning of his supervisor and cause a metal ladder to fall against the line, setting in motion a series of events resulting in his death.

Furthermore, we think summary judgment was proper because of intestate's contributory negligence. The materials presented at the hearing established that intestate, in attempting by himself to remove the ladder from the building after being warned of the power line, and attempting to remove the ladder from the line, failed to use ordinary care for his own safety and that such want of due care was at least one of the proximate causes of his death. (citation omitted). "The law imposes upon a person *sui juris* the duty to use ordinary care to protect himself from injury, and the degree of such care should be commensurate with the danger to be avoided."

For the reasons stated, the judgment allowing defendant's motion for summary judgment and dismissing plaintiff's action is Affirmed.

The risk of injury in this case was reasonably foreseeable: make contact with the power line, and get injured. A breach of duty of care in maintaining that power line would have been the proximate cause of an injury if there was accidental contact with the power line. In this case, however, Bogle could see clearly that there was a power line and, he failed to exercise ordinary care in getting off the ladder.

The question for the trier of fact does not depend on whether the defendant actually foresaw the injury, but on whether it was reasonable to have foreseen it. The *Restatement (Second) of Torts* supports the principle that if the conduct was a substantial factor, and a reasonable person would conclude foreseeability, then proximate cause exists (see box below).

FORESEEABILITY OF HARM

1. If the actor's conduct is a substantial factor in bringing about harm to another, the fact that the actor neither foresaw nor should have foreseen the extent of the harm or the manner in which it occurred does not prevent him from being liable.
2. The actor's conduct may be held not to be a legal cause of harm to another where after the event and looking back from the harm to the actor's negligent conduct, it appears to the court highly extraordinary that it should have brought about the harm.

Restatement (Second) of Torts §435 (1965)

Foreseeable Plaintiffs: The *Palsgraf* Case

In 1928 the New York Court of Appeals issued a decision in what became the most significant tort case regarding proximate causation. This famous case is *Palsgraf v. Long Island Railroad Co.*, 248 N.Y. 339, 162 N.E. 99 (1928). Justice Cardozo wrote the opinion for the majority. He held that there is no liability to a plaintiff that is not foreseeable. The principle of proximate cause was forsaken for the principle of a foreseeable plaintiff. The focus shifted from the foreseeability of the consequences to the foreseeability of the plaintiff.

The facts are these: Mrs. Palsgraf, the plaintiff, was standing on a platform of the defendant, Long Island Railroad. As a train stopped at the station, two men ran forward to board it. One of the men was carrying a package and jumped aboard the railroad car unsteadily. While two guards on the train tried to assist him, the package dropped to the tracks. Although there was nothing in its appearance to give notice of its contents, the package in fact contained fireworks, which exploded when the package fell. The shock of the explosion caused a set of scales at the other end of the platform to fall and strike Mrs. Palsgraf.

Judge Cardozo held that the defendant railroad was not liable to plaintiff Palsgraf for negligence. He found that negligence must be based upon the foreseeability of harm to the plaintiff. While the conduct of the employees of the defendant railroad may have been negligent toward someone else, it was not a foreseeable risk to the plaintiff (see Case in Point 3-8).

CASE IN POINT 3-8

Palsgraf v. Long Island R. Co.
248 N.Y. 339 N.E. 99 (1928)

CARDOZO, C. J.

Plaintiff was standing on a platform of defendant's railroad after buying a ticket to go to Rockaway Beach. A train stopped at the station, bound for another place. Two men ran forward to catch it. One of the men reached the platform of the car without mishap, though the train was already moving. The other man, carrying a package, jumped aboard the car, but seemed unsteady as if about to fall. A guard on the car, who had held the door open, reached forward to help him in, and another guard on the platform pushed him from behind. In this act, the package was dislodged, and fell upon the rails. It was a package of small size, about fifteen inches long, and was covered by a newspaper. In fact it contained fireworks, but there was nothing in its appearance to give notice of its contents. The fireworks when they fell exploded. The shock of the explosion threw down some scales at the other end of the platform many feet away. The scales struck the plaintiff, causing injuries for which she sues.

The conduct of the defendant's guard, if wrong in its relation to the holder of the package, was not a wrong in its relation to the plaintiff, standing far away. Relative to her it was not negligence at all. Nothing in the situation gave notice that the falling package had in it the potency of peril to persons thus removed. Negligence is not actionable unless it involves the invasion of a legally protected interest, the violation of a right. Proof of negligence in the air, so to speak, will not do... "Negligence is the absence of care, according to the circumstances."... (Citations omitted.) The plaintiff, as she stood upon the platform of the station, might claim to be protected against intentional invasion of her bodily security. Such invasion is not charged.... These, from the point of view of the law, were the bounds of her immunity, with perhaps some rare exceptions, survivors for the most part of ancient forms of liability, where conduct is held to be at the peril of the actor.... If no hazard was apparent to the eye of ordinary vigilance, an act innocent and harmless, it happened to be a wrong, though apparently not one involving the risk of bodily insecurity, with reference to someone else. "In every instance, before negligence can be predicated of a given act, back of the act must be sought and found a duty to the individual complaining, the observance of which would have averted or avoided the injury." (Citations omitted.) "The ideas of negligence and duty are strictly correlative." The plaintiff sues in her own right for a wrong personal to her, and not as the vicarious beneficiary of a breach of duty to another. A different conclusion will involve us, and swiftly too, in a maze of contradictions. A guard stumbles over a package, which has been left upon a platform. It seems to be a bundle of newspapers. It turns out to be a can of dynamite. To the eye of ordinary vigilance, the bundle is abandoned waste, which may be kicked or trod on with impunity. Is a passenger at the other end of the platform protected by the law against the unsuspected hazard concealed beneath the waste? If not, is the result to be any different, so far as the distant passenger is concerned, when the guard stumbles over a valise which a truckman or a porter has left upon the walk? The passenger far away, if the victim of a wrong at all, has a cause of action, not derivative, but original and primary. His claim to be protected against invasion of his bodily security is neither greater nor less because the act resulting in the invasion is a wrong to another far removed. In this case, the rights that are said to have been violated, are not even of the same order. The man was not injured in his person nor even put in danger. The purpose of the act, as well as its effect, was to make his person safe. If there was a wrong to him at all, which may very well be doubted, it was a wrong to a property interest only, the safety of his package. Out of this wrong to property, which threatened injury to nothing else, there has passed, we are told, to the plaintiff by derivation or succession a right of action for the invasion of an interest of another order, the right to bodily security. The diversity of interests emphasizes the futility of the effort to build the plaintiff's right upon the basis of a wrong to someone else. The gain is one of emphasis, for a like result would follow if the interests were the same.

Even then, the orbit of the danger as disclosed to the eye of reasonable vigilance would be the orbit of the duty. One who jostles one's neighbor in a crowd does not invade the rights of others standing at the outer fringe when the unintended contact casts a bomb upon the ground. The wrongdoer as to them is the man who carries the bomb, not the one who explodes it without suspicion of the danger. Life will have to be made over, and human nature transformed, before prevision so extravagant can be accepted as the norm of conduct, the customary standard to which behavior must conform....

The law of causation, remote or proximate, is thus foreign to the case before us. The question of liability is always anterior to the question of the measure of the consequences that go with liability. If there is no tort to be redressed, there is no occasion to consider what damage might be recovered if there were a finding of a tort. We may assume, without deciding, that negligence, not at large or in the abstract, but in relation to the plaintiff, would entail liability for any and all consequences, however novel or extraordinary. (Citations omitted.) There is room for argument that a distinction is to be drawn according to the diversity of interests invaded by the act, as where conduct negligent in that it threatens an insignificant invasion of an interest in property results in an unforeseeable invasion of interest of another order, as, e.g., one of bodily security. Perhaps other distinctions may be necessary. We do not go into the question now. The consequences to be followed must first be rooted in a wrong.

The judgment of the Appellate Division and that of the Trial Term should be reversed, and the complaint dismissed, with costs in all courts.

The *Palsgraf* case has been cited many times to support the principle that when an injury to an individual cannot be anticipated, negligence does not exist. In other words, if there was no foreseeable plaintiff, there cannot be an action for negligence. An action for negligence may be maintained only when the plaintiff is within an obvious area of danger. Thus, a defendant owes a duty of reasonable care only to the foreseeable plaintiff. While the ruling in the *Palsgraf* case has received widespread acceptance in the tort law of most states, a lack of certainty as to what is foreseeable and what is unforeseeable has resulted in court decisions that seem to contradict this ruling. The paralegal student must carefully research the law of his or her individual state for specific precedents.

Intervening Causes

A principle in the law of causation exists that is similar to proximate cause, yet it serves to relieve a defendant from responsibility. That principle states that a negligent defendant is relieved from liability by an **intervening cause.** An intervening cause is the act of a third person or some other force that produces injury to the plaintiff *after* the negligent act of the defendant. The intervening cause relieves the defendant from liability even though the defendant's negligence was a substantial factor in bringing about the injury. For example, Drew is driving and hits a car driven by Enid. Enid's injuries are serious enough that Enid needs to be brought to a hospital immediately. On the way to the hospital, Jason is randomly shooting at people from a building's parapet. One bullet hits the ambulance and kills Enid. Drew will not be held liable for Enid's death.

The *Restatement (Second) of Torts* calls an intervening cause a *superseding cause*, and takes the position that it relieves the defendant from liability (see box below).

SUPERSEDING CAUSE

A superseding cause is an act of a third person or other force which by its intervention prevents the actor from being liable for harm to another which his antecedent negligence is a substantial factor in bringing about.

Restatement (Second) of Torts §440 (1965)

Given an unlimited number of intervening causes, the courts apply the element of foreseeability to the intervening event. Professor Dobbs takes the position that the superseding event must be foreseeable to alleviate the defendant's liability (see box below).

INTERVENING CAUSE

"In the intervening cause cases, the defendant negligently creates risks of harm, but the immediate trigger of harm is another person or a force of nature. That by itself presents no impediment to relief. If the first actor negligent creates a risk of harm and the second actor negligently triggers the risk, both actors are tortfeasors, both are cause in fact of the harm, and both are commonly held liable to the plaintiff under the rules of joint and several liability or comparative fault shares. " [Footnote omitted]

Dobbs, *The Law of Torts* §186, (2000)

Just as the courts have diluted the rule in the *Palsgraf* case, their uneven treatment of the intervening cause principle has weakened that rule as well. For specific situations, the paralegal student must research the law of his or her particular jurisdiction.

■ DAMAGES

The fourth essential element in an action for negligence focuses on the plaintiff's injury: Did the plaintiff suffer damages? In an action for negligence, the plaintiff must suffer actual harm to person or property for any recovery. **Damages** consist of the recovery of money to compensate for loss or harm as a result of an unlawful act or wrong by another. In all tort actions for negligence, damages is money awarded to the plaintiff for injury resulting from the tortious conduct of another. Damages in a tort action are always monetary in nature, but the type of recovery may vary in its function.

Types of Damages

The form of damages awarded will depend on both the tort and the actual loss or injury. Three major types of damages that may be awarded for the tort of negligence include:

Compensatory Damages

The form of damages most frequently awarded in negligence actions, **compensatory damages,** are intended to compensate the plaintiff for actual loss or injury. Compensatory damages are meant to "make the victim whole," to return the plaintiff to that state of being before the defendant's negligence caused injury. Of course, compensatory damages can never actually return plaintiff to such a state of being. Compensatory damages include medical expenses, property damage, lost wages, permanent loss of bodily function, and pain and suffering.

Punitive Damages

A court will occasionally award **punitive damages** for intentional torts or gross negligence to punish the defendant. These look to discourage similar conduct by the defendant in the future. They are sometimes called *exemplary damages* or *treble damages*.

Nominal Damages

Nominal damages are awarded when the plaintiff has sustained no actual loss or injury, but has suffered a symbolic loss. They may be awarded in intentional tort cases and in those involving strict liability (see Table 3-3).

Table 3-3 Categorization of Damages and What They are Intended to Remedy	
Past injury	**Anticipated injury**
• compensatory damages	• punitive damages
• nominal damages	

Damages in a Particular Jurisdiction

A paralegal student must consult the law of that individual's state to determine what damages will be allowed. Tort reform legislation in many states has altered the amounts of damages available under common law that may be awarded in particular types of tort cases, for example, medical malpractice. Such statutes may also have placed a limitation on the amount of damages that can be awarded for pain and suffering. For example, one state may limit the amount of compensatory damages available for medical malpractice to $10 million dollars. The paralegal student must review the statutes of his or her state on the question of damages allowed in tort actions.

Loss of Consortium   *Skip*

One distinct type of damage available in some tort cases seeks to compensate the spouse of the injured party for the loss of love, companionship, services, affection, and sexual relations. This form of damages is referred to as a claim for **loss of consortium.** If one's spouse sustains injury at the hands of a defendant and that injury results in an inability to perform all that is customarily expected within the marital relationship, the uninjured spouse has also suffered a loss. While such a loss may be beyond any precise determination of monetary damage, the trier of fact will make a subjective evaluation of the loss, an evaluation that is difficult and often based upon emotion rather than fact.

While the claim for loss of consortium under the old common law was available only to husbands, the U.S. Supreme Court eliminated that gender bias in 1950 in *Hitaffer v. Argonne Co.* In virtually every jurisdiction, wives may now claim a loss of consortium for injuries to their husbands. Similarly, parents may claim a loss of consortium for injuries to children based upon a loss of society, companionship, and affection. Nigel, having consumed so much liquor as to impair his ability to drive, gets behind the steering wheeling and starts to drive, and strikes and kills Nell. Among other actions in tort, Nell's parents can seek damages for loss of consortium since they will no longer enjoy the company of their young daughter.

The following case talks about the nature of damages for loss of consortium (see Case in Point 3-9).

CASE IN POINT 3-9

Gorman v. McMahon

792 So. 2d 307 (Miss. Ct. App. 2001)

[...]

Charles and his wife, Louise, were married on May 26, 1984. This was the second marriage for Charles and the sixth marriage for Louise. In 1987, due to problems in their marriage, Louise moved out of their marital home and did not return for approximately three weeks. Louise again left the marital home in 1991 and, this time, did not return for roughly three months. Louise claims that she returned to the marital home on both occasions only because Charles had promised her that he would be "different." However, in September 1993, Louise was unhappy in their marriage and once more left Charles. Louise asked Charles for a divorce, although the parties dispute whether she did so in August or September of 1993. Louise made it very clear that she had no intention of again reconciling with Charles. Among the things which Louise cited as her reasons for asking Charles

Skip

for a divorce were an unsatisfactory sex life, her claims that Charles practiced regular insurance fraud and the fact that she and Charles had no type of social life or loving relationship any longer. Louise stated that because of these things, she no longer had affection or respect for Charles and could not continue in the marriage.

P #4. On the other hand, Charles disputed these reasons given by Louise and insists that his marriage to Louise was indeed affectionate and that the two of them enjoyed socializing with friends on many occasions. Charles also denied that his sex life with Louise was suffering and he stated that the two of them went out together on occasions and even took a few trips together, one of which was a trip to Las Vegas shortly before their final separation in 1993. Charles even called witnesses at trial who testified that Charles and Louise appeared to be a very loving and affectionate couple. However, it is Louise's assertion that she had been unhappy in the marriage for some time before she left for good in 1993, and she stated that she did not feel affection for Charles as she had in the beginning of their marriage.

P #5. While still married to Charles, Louise began a romantic relationship with Gorman, a physician who had treated Louise's daughter for injuries she had previously sustained in a car accident. Louise and Gorman had an admitted sexual relationship with one another, and Gorman had rented an apartment for the two of them to meet for their encounters. Charles also alleges that Gorman bought Louise extravagant gifts while Charles and Louise were still married and that Gorman would make obscene gestures at him whenever the two men would cross paths. Charles also cites that only nine months after their divorce was final, Louise and Gorman adopted a child together, something that Charles and Louise were never able to do for financial reasons. Charles asserts that Gorman won Louise over with his money and luxurious lifestyle and that he simply could not compete for Louise's affections any longer.

P #6. Louise testified at trial that she, in fact, initiated the relationship with Gorman. Gorman and Louise both stated that Gorman was not receptive to her alleged advances at first and that Gorman even attempted to talk Louise into going back to Charles to try to make their marriage work. Louise asserts that she pursued the relationship with Gorman because she felt as if she had no husband and because she felt that she and Charles had no relationship anymore. Gorman denies Charles's allegations that he alienated Louise's affections and claims that he did absolutely nothing to interfere with Charles and Louise's marriage. Rather, it is Gorman's contention that Louise alone brought about any relations in which Gorman and Louise had engaged themselves. Further, Louise claims that Gorman could not have alienated her affections from her husband because, at the time that she began to pursue Gorman, she no longer had any affections or love for Charles.

P #7. A key point at trial involved the proper measure of damages for the tort of alienation of affection. Charles claims that he suffered from depression and that his work suffered because of Louise's affair and, as a result, his income decreased. Over the objection of Gorman, the trial court allowed Charles to put forth evidence of this emotional and mental distress and the related loss of wages, as well as proof of related medical bills, divorce costs, fees for private investigators, attorneys (sic) fees and the like. Gorman alleges that this was error on the part of the trial court because this evidence was not proper in an alienation of affection case. Gorman also alleges that two jurors were improperly struck "for cause" during voir dire. Further, Gorman claims to be aggrieved because it is his contention that Charles's counsel presented inflammatory arguments before the jury in his closing statement, intending to outrage the jury and divert their attention from the applicable law in this case. Gorman claims that these errors caused him to experience an unfair trial and caused the jury to wrongly find against him. Although

Gorman has never denied his affair with Louise while she was still married to Charles, he asserts that he is not responsible for Louise's loss of affection for Charles because he did not initiate their relationship and because, as Louise testified, the marriage was essentially over when his affair with Louise began.

P #8. Citing his innocence and these errors on the part of the trial court, Gorman asks this Court to relieve him of the damages which the trial court ordered that he pay to Charles.

[...]

Keeping in line with our standard of review, we find that we cannot reverse on this issue. We find that the limited situations in which this Court would be justified in overturning a jury verdict do not apply here. Gorman argues that he did not initiate the romantic relationship that he had with Louise and therefore contends that he is not responsible for the breakdown in her marriage with Charles. Gorman charges that Charles did not meet his burden of proving the elements of the tort of alienation of affection, which, under Mississippi law, include the following: (1) wrongful conduct of the defendant; (2) loss of affection or consortium; (3) causal connection between such conduct and loss. (citation omitted) For Charles to succeed in his action for alienation of affection against Gorman, Charles has the burden of proving that there was a direct interference on Gorman's part sufficient enough to satisfy the jury that the alienation of Louise's affections was caused by Gorman. (citation omitted) Further, Charles must prove that Gorman's interference damaged his marriage to Louise. (citation omitted)

P #13. The jury in this case was evidently convinced that, were it not for Gorman, Charles could have attempted to save his marriage to Louise, as he had done before. We are convinced from the evidence in the record that, although Louise claims to have lost all affection for Charles before her affair with Gorman began, Charles was oblivious to how miserable Louise claimed to be. Furthermore, we take note of the fact that Louise is currently still in a relationship with Gorman and that the two of them have adopted a child together. It stands to reason therefore that Louise would protect the interests of Gorman in this action against him. Quite clearly, Gorman and Louise would like to move on with their new life together and their new child without the hassle of a lawsuit. Gorman argues that Louise had left Charles twice before in 1987 and 1991 and that this is evidence that she was unhappy in her marriage and had lost affection and love for Charles. We do not agree. We cannot ignore the fact that Louise did return to the marriage on both of those occasions and it is our opinion that the evidence of Louise's deliberate and voluntary reconciliations with Charles after these two short separations would tend to indicate that Louise wanted her marriage with Charles to work, contrary to her recent claims.

P #14. We have thoroughly reviewed the record in this case and the briefs of both parties in this case. Louise and Gorman both attempt repeatedly to convince this Court that Louise started the relationship with Gorman by seducing him. Louise and Gorman also both testified that Gorman made numerous efforts to persuade Louise to try to make her marriage to Charles work and that, it was only after her ceaseless, persistent advances toward him that he finally gave in to her and began an extra-marital affair. We find that this is of no relevance. The facts indicate to this Court that Gorman entered the picture and his actions served to transfer any affections that Louise harbored for Charles to Gorman. We also take note of the fact that Gorman presented Louise with very extravagant gifts, things that Charles could not afford to buy for her and, in our opinion, it would stand to reason that these gifts strengthened the lure and attraction that Louise had toward Gorman and eventually induced her into finally leaving Charles and asking him for a divorce. Even though Gorman did not initiate the relationship with Louise, the evidence shows that he certainly did interfere with what Charles thought was a healthy marriage.

P #15. We find that any reasonable juror could have reached a decision in favor of Charles because the evidence shows that Charles proved: (1) Gorman's wrongful conduct in having an affair with the woman to which Charles was still married; (2) Charles lost Louise's affections, including loss of companionship, society, love and comfort, all of which are elements of the loss of consortium. (citation omitted) and (3) there was a causal connection between the affair had by Gorman and Louise and the loss of consortium suffered by Charles, no matter that Gorman did not "initiate" the relationship. As it is sometimes said, "it takes two to tango" and Gorman was evidently half of the affair which, in our opinion, ultimately caused Louise to leave Charles for good. Gorman has not shown that, without the affair he and Louise were carrying on, Louise would have still left Charles and asked him for a divorce. It is clear from the record that in the past when Louise had left Charles for whatever reason, she always went back to him. It is undoubtedly speculation that leads Gorman to argue that she would not have done the same here absent the affair and the luxuries lavished upon her by Gorman. Interestingly and, in our opinion, worth noting, it is also shown in the record of this case that Louise did not ask Charles for a divorce until after Gorman separated from his own wife. Even if Louise did launch this affair all on her own, we are convinced that this information alone does not prove that she had already lost all affection and love for Charles. In fact, the jury, who watched and listened to the testimony of Louise personally, was likewise not convinced.

P #16. The facts show that Charles was still Louise's husband at the time her affair with Gorman began, something that both Louise and Gorman appear to ignore in this matter. She continued to live in the marital household with Charles as his wife during the early stages of her extra-marital affair with Gorman, continuing all of her spousal activities including doing Charles's laundry, taking care of Charles, cooking for Charles and paying half of the marital bills, to name a few. We are not convinced that Louise had, at this time, lost all feelings for the man to whom she was still married and continuing to attend to so readily.

P #17. We conclude that the jury's verdict in favor of Charles was not against the overwhelming weight of the evidence and that any reasonable juror could have found in favor of Charles in his alienation of affection claim. Furthermore, we believe that Charles proved the elements of alienation of affection and loss of consortium entitling him to compensation for such losses. On this issue, we affirm.

2. Whether the trial court improperly admitted evidence on the issue of damages which do not properly constitute damages for the loss of consortium thereby unfairly prejudicing the defendant?

P #18. Gorman argues that Charles should not have been allowed to present evidence of his medical expenses, attorneys fees and fees for private investigators because these are not elements of damages to be considered in a loss of consortium case. Gorman argues also that Charles should not have been allowed to argue for punitive damages in such an action. Gorman cites error on the part of the trial judge in allowing the jury to hear such evidence and asks us to reverse. First, we note that there is no Mississippi case law providing that punitive or any other type of damages are completely prohibited in an alienation of affection or loss of consortium action. Secondly, we have observed from the record that, through testimony and other evidence, Charles has sufficiently shown that these damages can be readily connected to this instant action against Gorman. Charles explicitly argues, and seems to prove, that he suffered both physical and psychological problems caused by his reaction to Louise's affair with Gorman and Louise and Charles's looming divorce because of that affair. As well, Charles has shown that he hired private investigators to observe Gorman and Louise after learning of their affair to verify that it was indeed taking place. We find that Charles has additionally shown that the divorce was ultimately caused by Louise's shifting affections from Charles to Gorman and therefore, we see no reason why Charles should not recover the attorneys' fees he incurred in the divorce action. It certainly appears that, but for the extramarital affair between Louise and Gorman, the divorce may very well not have ensued.

[...]

P #20. Consortium does not consist alone of intangible mental and emotional elements, but may include services performed by [one spouse] for [the other spouse] which have monetary value." (citation omitted) Charles not only lost the love and affection of Louise to Gorman, but he lost her services such as cooking his meals, cleaning their home, taking care of most all of Charles's needs, paying half of the household bills, all services that Louise regularly performed for Charles. Furthermore, the evidence shows that Louise did all of these things for Charles on a daily basis without ever complaining to Charles that she was unhappy, therefore keeping him oblivious to her "misery." As such, these were all services which Charles had come to expect from Louise as a part of their marriage and may be calculated into Charles's monetary award for his loss.

P #21. This Court is unable to find any authority that would prohibit Charles from recovering for additional losses caused by the alienation of Louise's affections by Gorman. Gorman has failed to show this Court that recoverable damages in an alienation of affection case are limited to damages for loss of consortium alone. [...]

We find that this opens the door for allowing certain other types of damages to be argued in an alienation of affection case. Here, Charles testified that he suffered from depression and physical problems, leading to medical expenses and loss of income, due to his discovery of Louise's affair with Gorman. Additionally, Charles submitted expenses for private investigators and fees for his divorce attorney, both also a result of the illicit affair had by Louise and Gorman.

P #22. We find that Charles was entitled to present evidence of these types of damages because the evidence in the record shows that these losses by Charles were caused directly by the alienation of Louise's affections by Gorman. Therefore, this evidence goes directly to the issue of causation, the third prong of proof in alienation of affection actions. [...]

[...] We are convinced that there was nothing to prohibit the trial court from hearing evidence of such damages.

P #23. Because we do not now know, nor will we ever know, how the jury arrived at such a verdict of $50,000 in favor of Charles, we cannot render a decision on whether the verdict itself was appropriate. We are not in possession of any information which would show us what evidence the jury took into consideration when coming up with such a figure. Inasmuch as we are not equipped with a means of probing into the jurors' heads, we cannot say that the $50,000 award in favor of Charles is out of line with the evidence presented to them because we do not know their reasoning for such a verdict. (citation omitted) What we do know is that, had their reasoning included these expenses submitted by Charles, it would not have been improper. [...]

Therefore, this issue is dismissed for lack of merit.

Avoidable Consequences

If the plaintiff has sustained an injury, the doctrine of **avoidable consequences** mandates that he or she must take reasonable steps to prevent any further injury. The doctrine provides an effective limitation on damages for which the defendant may be responsible. The plaintiff's potential recovery can be reduced by the amount of damage brought on by his or her own subsequent conduct. The doctrine of avoidable consequences is also sometimes called a failure to mitigate damages.

For example, consider a plaintiff who fails to seek medical attention. The conduct of the plaintiff has added to the damage from the original injury.

The defendant is not to be held responsible for damages after the initial injury when the plaintiff subsequently fails to seek reasonable medical attention.

This principle is different from the principle of contributory negligence, which serves as a total bar to any claim for damages by the plaintiff. Contributory negligence is considered in detail in Chapter 5.

Collateral Source Rule

Under the **collateral source rule,** a defendant may not benefit from the fact that the plaintiff has received compensation for his or her injuries from some other source. When calculating the damages that a defendant may be responsible for, the fact that the injured plaintiff receives money from a source independent of the defendant will not reduce the defendant's liability.

For example, many individuals carry medical insurance or can receive medical benefits for injuries. These are known as collateral sources, and do not serve to reduce the amount of damages for which the defendant is responsible even though a double recovery for the plaintiff may result. To prevent the possibility of double recovery, many collateral source providers require the plaintiff to transfer the plaintiff's right to recovery from the defendant in exchange for having made payment to the plaintiff (see box below).

THE COLLATERAL SOURCE RULE

"In many instances, the collateral source rule only operates to preserve the sub-rogation rights of an insurer. To the extent an insurer pays the plaintiff under an insurance policy, the insurer acquires the plaintiff's rights to sue."

Dobbs, *The Law of Torts* §380 (2000)

Reprinted with permission from Thomson West. All rights reserved.

Although the parable of the Good Samaritan, of a person spontaneously coming to the aid of another, speaks to aspirations about human behavior, almost all states do not require its citizens to come to the aid of another. This arrangement is called *subrogation.* So, if Bad Dog Insurance Agency pays its insured for pain and suffering that arose when the insured was hit in an automobile accident, Bad Dog Insurance will acquire its right to sue the driver of the car that caused the action, to the same degree that its insured might have recovered, had the insured filed suit instead of filing a claim with Bad Dog Insurance.

KEY TERMS

SUMMARY

An action in tort for negligence depends on society's expectation that individuals have a duty to avoid creating an undue risk of harm to others. Negligence occurs when the individual's conduct falls below his or her duty to avoid creating the risk of injury. An action for negligence arises when the duty has been breached, proximately causing damages to the person harmed. The legal concepts of duty, reasonable person, breach of duty of reasonable care, proximate cause, and damages are all issues with which the paralegal student must be familiar. By mastering these concepts, the paralegal student will have the capacity to understand better other, ancillary issues—such as the source of the duty and reasons for limiting damages—that are central to determining whether a valid tort action in negligence exists.

CONCEPT REVIEW QUESTIONS

1. Provide a definition of negligence.
2. List the four elements that are essential to maintain an action for negligence.
3. What is the duty of reasonable care?
4. Describe the reasonable person standard.
5. What does the reasonable person standard require of an individual with superior knowledge and training?
6. Discuss the distinction between misfeasance and nonfeasance.
7. What constitutes a breach of the duty of reasonable care?
8. List the two forms of cause in fact.
9. What is proximate cause?
10. What are the three principal forms of damages?

CRITICAL THINKING APPLICATIONS

1. A school district has hired people to serve as monitors on the school buses. One afternoon, a bus monitor overheard a pair of teenagers plotting to get guns. The monitor made no mention of overhearing this, even though the teenagers had a history of behavioral problems. Two days later, the teenagers stood at a busy intersection, with guns drawn. Before police arrived and re-established order, one of the teens had shot a motorist in the head, causing permanent damage. The motorist sued the monitors for negligently failing to notify law enforcement of the threats. Lawyers for the monitor file a motion for summary judgment on the grounds that the claim fails to establish that the monitors' negligence was the proximate cause of motorist's injuries. Will the court grant the request for summary judgment, assuming that all facts are true? Why or why not?
2. Firefighters are called to a pond, to rescue a dog that has fallen through thin ice. The dog's owner watches anxiously as the firefighters inch towards the dog. The ice starts to break and the firefighters can't get close enough before the dog drowns. The dog's owner sues the fire department on the grounds that its

negligence in rescuing the dog led to the dog's death and the dog's owner is liable in damages for the loss of the family pet. Did the fire department breach of duty of care when it failed to rescue the family dog? Why or why not?

3. During recess, a second-grade student accidentally hits a classmate in the head. Six months later, the classmate who was hit begins to have seizures. The classmate's parents sue the second-grade student's parents for negligence and the school department for negligence. What, if any, damages will the school system be liable for the classmate's injuries?

4. A homeowner's child is playing with a neighborhood friend in the homeowner's back yard. The playmates discover one of the homeowner's golf balls, which has been lying outdoors during the winter. The neighborhood friend throws the golf ball into the air. It lands on the roof of a passing car. Is the homeowner liable for damages because he failed to properly supervise the children? Why or why not? Does your answer change if it turns out that the neighborhood kid knew that there was a car approaching?

5. A farm worker has stopped driving a farmer's tractor to fill the vehicle up with gas. The farm worker goes to a five-gallon metal gas tank and opens it. The tank is ten years old and the threads to the tank's nozzle are worn down. In removing the loose nozzle to fill the gas tank from a larger gas storage tank on the farm, the farm worker accidentally causes a spark, which causes the five-gallon tank to explode, injuring the farm worker. If this happens in a state where the farm worker cannot file a claim for recovery under the state's worker's compensation statute, will the farmer be liable for the medical expenses incurred by the farm worker? Does your answer change if it turns out that three years ago, the state forbade the sale of metal five-gallon gas tanks and allowed, from that day forward, the sale of only plastic five-gallon gas tanks?

6. A car owner has just settled into the driver's seat of a car when the owner hears an alarm go off at a nearby bank. Looking in the driver's side mirror, the owner sees a masked individual running out of the bank with a canvas bag that has the bank's name on its side. The bag seems to be bulging but from the way that the individual is running, the bag likely contains bills and not coins. The individual runs towards owner's car. As the individual just passes by the owner's car, the owner panics and throws open the driver's side door. The fleeing individual hits the door and is knocked down. The individual suffers a broken nose upon hitting the door, and a concussion upon impact with the ground. While facing charges for bank robbery, the fleeing individual sues the car owner for the damages and medical expenses incurred to repair the broken nose and to treat the concussion. Will the car's owner be found liable? Does your answer change if it turns out that the owner had no idea that there was an individual fleeing from the bank, with a bag of cash in hand, and opens the car door at the moment the robber runs by the car?

7. The child of the owner of a snowmobile is pulling a neighborhood friend by a rope attached to the snowmobile. As the child turns the snowmobile to turn around again to take the friend, who is on skis, up a snow-covered field, the rope breaks. The friend is whipped into a tree that borders the field. Is the owner of the snowmobile liable to the friend for damages that include at least the medical expenses the friend has incurred because of abrupt contact with the tree? Why or why not? Does your answer change if the rope had been attached to the rear of the snowmobile two months earlier by the owner of the snowmobile? Two years earlier?

8. The modern term for the concept called a mental breakdown is called a psychotic break. When a person is suffering from such a break, that person does not have the same experiences of reality that others do. A bicycle rider is enjoying a pleasant ride on a bike path on a sunny fall day. The rider suffers a psychotic break that lasts for only a few minutes but during that time, the rider loses control of the bike and hits a pair of marathon runners who are in training. Will the rider be found to have negligently operated the bicycle so as to cause the marathoners' injuries? Why or why not? Does your answer change if this is the second time that the rider has experienced such a break and has dutifully been taking prescription medicines that reduce the likelihood of such occurrences in the future?

SKILL-BUILDING APPLICATION

On August 11, 2000, employees of Ajax—Cruz and DeSousa—were providing construction services in the city of Fisherton in response to a work order from BigPhone. Dennison, BigPhone's employee, drew up plans for the work to be done as per the work order. At the worksite was a construction backhoe. Cruz and DeSousa needed to unload a manhole cover from the bed of a flatbed truck. The flatbed truck also contained a pallet of cement blocks that needed to be repositioned so the manhole cover could be chained for removal using the backhoe's bucket. Cruz did not have a license to operate a backhoe. He used the backhoe's bucket to move the pallet and accidentally struck and killed DeSousa. The state's Chief Medical Examiner established the cause of death to be blunt head and chest trauma caused by the backhoe's bucket striking DeSousa.

O'Leary, BigPhone's contract work inspector (who was at that site every day), was present to make sure Ajax performed the work described in the work order. He submitted daily progress reports to BigPhone. O'Leary could order the work stopped such as for safety concerns. He also had to see that the work followed BigPhone's work-site practices as well as all federal, state, and local laws. O'Leary specifically obtained a work permit from the City of Fisherton to do the work on the date of the incident.

The facts of the case present a unique opportunity for an analysis of the negligence issues presented. Review the case and provide your summary of these issues:

A. Duty
B. Reasonable care
C. Causation
D. Damages

To hear patiently, to weigh deliberately and
dispassionately, and to decide to impartially; these
are the chief duties of a Judge.

—*Albert Pike (1809–1891)*

Proof of Negligence

A tort action for negligence presents unique legal issues of proof. Is there any liability if the accident was unavoidable? Are there situations in which the defendant's negligence was so obvious that liability is automatic? How far must a plaintiff go to prove the defendant's negligence? Who is responsible when there is more than one defendant-tortfeasor? In a death resulting from negligence, who is the plaintiff? These questions have provided legal scholars with ample opportunity for disagreement and debate for many years. A thorough knowledge of tort law requires that the paralegal student be familiar with the legal issues involved in the proof of a negligence case. This chapter presents an analysis of the legal issues specific to proving an action for negligence. The chapter on tort litigation addresses investigation, information gathering, discovery, and trial of a negligence case.

CHAPTER TOPICS

1. Issues Common to All Litigation
2. Questions of Fact, Opinion, and Questions of Law
3. Evidence
4. Burden of Proof
5. Presumptions
6. *Prima Facie* Case
7. Issues Common to Actions in Negligence
8. Unavoidable Accidents
9. Acts of God
10. Degrees of Negligence
11. Willful, Wanton, and Reckless Conduct
12. Negligence *Per Se*
13. *Res Ipsa Loquitur*
14. Joint Tortfeasors' Liability
15. Survival Actions and Wrongful Death

OBJECTIVES

After completing this chapter, you will be able to:

1. Analyze the processes used to resolve questions of law and of fact.
2. Evaluate the burden of proof in a negligence case.
3. Discuss the significance of unavoidable accidents in an attempt to prove negligence.
4. Distinguish between the degrees of negligence.
5. Understand and apply the doctrine of *res ipsa loquitur*.
6. Profile joint tortfeasors' liability.
7. Summarize the principles of wrongful death and the survival of actions.

■ ISSUES COMMON TO ALL LITIGATION

Questions of Fact, Opinion, and Questions of Law

Function of Court and Jury

Under the United States system of jurisprudence, the existence of negligence depends upon the jury's decision about a question of fact or facts and upon the judge's decision about a question of law or laws. So, courts decide questions of law and juries decide questions of fact. The following questions have to be answered during a trial:

- Questions of Law
    - Is there a duty—the imposition of a legal obligation on one person for the benefit of another?
    - What is the general standard of conduct? (Once the court has found that a duty exists, the general standard of conduct is imposed, that of a reasonable person under the same or similar circumstances.)
- Questions of Fact
    - Is the evidence sufficient? Have facts been proven that give rise to the existence of a duty, a breach thereof, and resulting damages?
    - What is the weight of the evidence and the conclusions to be drawn from it?
    - What is the particular standard of conduct? What would a reasonable person have done under the circumstances?

Courts may be asked to serve as a finder of facts; however, the preferred option is that if reasonable minds may differ as to the conclusion to be drawn from a weighing of the facts, then the matter is best left to the jury.

Resolving Questions of Fact

Questions concerning the law applicable to those facts are the judge's sole province. The jury, as the trier of fact in a negligence case, decides **questions of fact** based upon what information has been admitted into evidence. If one witness testifies that an object was black and another witness testifies that the object is white, the jury has to decide which testimony to believe or whether to believe any testimony.

Facts and Opinions

It is sometimes difficult for the student to draw a distinction between a fact and an opinion. A **fact** is the existence of an actual occurrence or event as determined by the evidence presented. An **opinion** is what a person thinks or believes as a conclusion drawn from facts. It is an inference from facts, but is not a fact in and of itself. The jury may consider opinion evidence only from expert witnesses, after they have reviewed only observable phenomena (see Table 4-1).

Table 4-1 Differences between Facts and Opinions

Facts	Opinions
• Witness's testimony as to what happened, who was involved, and other details about the underlying issue of the case	• Testimony of expert witness (based upon training, experience and evidence)
• Believability assessed by the finder of fact	• Witness comments based upon experience
	• In both instances, believability assessed by the finder of fact

Consider a situation in which the plaintiff in a tort action must prove that the defendant was angry at the time of the injury. The defendant's anger can be established by an expert witness qualified to render an opinion concerning human behavior. That opinion would represent the expert's inferences drawn from certain facts, e.g., facial tension, redness, sweating, verbal statements, and related behavior. These observable phenomena, like defendant's appearance, are the facts, while the conclusion of anger would be the expert's opinion.

Evidence

Evidence aids in establishing the validity or invalidity of an issue of fact at trial. Such evidence may come through testimony of witnesses' testimony or presentation of exhibits, documents, and physical objects. The trier of fact, after a review of the evidence, must then draw valid inferences and make decisions.

Rules of Evidence

The **rules of evidence** govern the presentation of facts to be used at trial. Federal court rules are contained in the *Federal Rules of Evidence* found in Title 28 of the United States Code. Most states have modeled their respective rules of evidence after the *Federal Rules* (see Table 4-2).

Table 4-2 Comparison of Rule 609, Rule of Evidence (Impeachment by Evidence of Conviction of Crime), Federal and the State of New Hampshire

Federal Rules of Evidence, **Rule 609**	New Hampshire Rules of Evidence, **Rule 609**
a. General rule. For the purpose of attacking the character for truthfulness of a witness, (1) evidence that a witness other than an accused has been convicted of a crime shall be admitted, subject to Rule 403, if the crime was punishable by death or imprisonment in excess of one year under the law under which the witness was convicted, and evidence that an accused has been convicted of such a crime shall be admitted if the court determines that the probative value of admitting this evidence outweighs its prejudicial effect to the accused; and (2) evidence that any witness has been convicted of a crime shall be admitted regardless of the punishment, if it readily can be determined that establishing the elements of the crime required proof or admission of an act of dishonesty or false statement by the witness.	a. General rule. For the purpose of attacking the credibility of a witness, evidence that the witness has been convicted of a crime shall be admitted if elicited from the witness or established by public record during cross-examination but only if the crime (1) was punishable by death or imprisonment in excess of one year under the law under which he or she was convicted, and the court determines that the probative value of admitting this evidence outweighs its prejudicial effect to the defendant, or (2) involved dishonesty or false statement, regardless of the punishment.
b. Time limit. Evidence of a conviction under this rule is not admissible if a period of more than ten years has elapsed since the date of the conviction or of the release of the witness from the confinement imposed for that conviction, whichever is the later date, unless the court determines, in the	b. Time limit. Evidence of a conviction under this rule is not admissible if a period of more than ten years has elapsed since the date of the conviction or of the release of the witness from the confinement imposed for that conviction, whichever is the later date, unless the court determines,
	(continued)

Table 4-2 continued	
Federal Rules of Evidence, **Rule 609**	**New Hampshire Rules of Evidence, Rule 609**
interests of justice, that the probative value of the conviction supported by specific facts and circumstances substantially outweighs its prejudicial effect. However, evidence of a conviction more than ten years old as calculated herein, is not admissible unless the proponent gives to the adverse party sufficient advance written notice of intent to use such evidence to provide the adverse party with a fair opportunity to contest the use of such evidence.	in the interests of justice, that the probative value of the conviction supported by specific facts and circumstances substantially outweighs its prejudicial effect. However, evidence of a conviction more than ten years old as calculated herein, is not admissible unless the proponent gives to the adverse party sufficient advance written notice of intent to use such evidence to provide the adverse party with a fair opportunity to contest the use of such evidence.
c. Effect of pardon, annulment, or certificate of rehabilitation. Evidence of a conviction is not admissible under this rule if (1) the conviction has been the subject of a pardon, annulment, certificate of rehabilitation, or other equivalent procedure based on a finding of the rehabilitation of the person convicted, and that person has not been convicted of a subsequent crime which was punishable by death or imprisonment in excess of one year, or (2) the conviction has been the subject of a pardon, annulment, or other equivalent procedure based on a finding of innocence.	c. Effect of annulment, or certificate of rehabilitation. Evidence of a conviction is not admissible under this rule if the conviction has been the subject of an annulment, certificate or rehabilitation, or other equivalent procedure.
d. Juvenile adjudications. Evidence of juvenile adjudications is generally not admissible under this rule. The court may, however, in a criminal case allow evidence of a juvenile adjudication of a witness other than the accused if conviction of the offense would be admissible to attack the credibility of an adult and the court is satisfied that admission in evidence is necessary for a fair determination of the issue of guilt or innocence.	d. Juvenile adjudications. Evidence of juvenile adjudications is generally not admissible under this rule. The court may, however, in a criminal case allow evidence of a juvenile adjudication of a witness other than the accused if conviction of the offense would be admissible to attack the credibility of an adult and the court is satisfied that admission in evidence is necessary for a fair determination of the issue of guilt or innocence.
e. Pendency of appeal. The pendency of an appeal therefrom does not render evidence of a conviction inadmissible. Evidence of the pendency of an appeal is admissible.	e. Pendency of appeal. The pendency of an appeal therefrom does not render evidence of a conviction inadmissible. Evidence of the pendency of an appeal is admissible.

The fundamental principles of evidence common to all statutory codes of evidence include:

- Evidence that is not relevant to the case cannot be used.
- With certain exceptions, hearsay evidence cannot be used.
- Opinion testimony can be used only from expert witnesses.
- The content of most writing cannot differ from oral testimony to be admissible.
- Privileged communications cannot be used.
- Evidence must comply with the formal rules of court.

The paralegal student should be aware that these rules are primarily designed to prevent the jury from hearing evidence that traditionally has been found to be unreliable. The function of the trier of fact is best served by reliance on evidence that is competent as opposed to reliance on facts that are not trustworthy.

A full understanding of the concepts contained in these basic principles goes well beyond the scope of this text. Treatises on evidence, such as *the Restatement of Law or the, Model Rules of Evidence*, go into much greater detail regarding answers to questions about relevancy of evidence, hearsay testimony, the parol evidence rule, and privileged communications, among other issues.

Preponderance of the Evidence

Once the rules of evidence have determined the type and quantity of evidence the jury may consider, the jury weighs that evidence to form a conclusion as to the existence of a fact. As noted in Chapter 1, in a criminal case, the guilt of the defendant must be proven beyond a reasonable doubt. In civil actions for tort, the standard of proof is less stringent, requiring that the existence of a fact be proven by a **preponderance of the evidence.** This is a conclusion that a fact is more probable than not, more true than untrue, more likely than not (see Table 4-3).

Table 4-3 Differences between Actions in Civil Law and Criminal Law		
	Civil Law	**Criminal Law**
Burden of Proof	Preponderance of the evidence	Beyond a reasonable doubt
Penalty	Damages	Imprisonment, community-based supervised release; fines
Parties	Individual (most commonly), government	Government only

A jury must apply the standard of the reasonable person to determine the credibility of witnesses, resolve conflicting testimony, and find if there was proximate causation. A jury will use this standard to determine the value of damages once it sees that, by a preponderance of the evidence, the defendant is liable.

Burden of Proof

The plaintiff can establish liability under a theory of negligence if the plaintiff has met the **burden of proof** (see box below).

BURDEN OF PROOF

...the burden of proof that the tortious conduct of the defendant has caused the harm to the plaintiff is upon the plaintiff.

Restatement (Second) of Torts §433 B (1965)

To meet that burden, the plaintiff has to show, by a preponderance of the evidence, the defendant's liability. A preponderance of the evidence involves measurement: did the plaintiff show, through the use of evidence, that the defendant was more likely than not to be liable due to negligence?

The burden of proof sometimes is called the *burden of persuasion and the risk of non-persuasion*, because the plaintiff has the obligation to persuade the jury or judge that the defendant was liable. If the plaintiff has failed to provide enough evidence to meet the obligation of the burden of proof, then the defendant wins automatically and so, would not need to present any defense.

Presumptions

A **presumption** is an assumption about the law made in all litigation; this assumption can be disproved on a case-by-case basis. For instance, in a negligence action, a frequent presumption is that a person is presumed to possess normal mental faculties and reasoning powers. So the defendant will be presumed to possess the ability to make reasonable decisions. But if the defendant's attorney can show that the defendant has suffered a serious brain injury that impairs that ability to reason, then the presumption has been disproved; it has been rebutted. Once the defense presents persuasive rebuttal evidence, the presumption ceases to exist.

Presumptions are used to facilitate litigation. For example, instead of the plaintiff having to show that the defendant possesses the ability to make reasonable decisions (which would be a time-consuming process and prove to be true in the great number of cases), the defendant is presumed to have that ability.

Many other presumptions may arise in the course of litigation. For example, a defendant is presumed not liable under a theory of evidence unless the plaintiff can rebut the presumption by providing evidence that it is more likely than not that the defendant is liable. Paralegal students should carefully consult the laws of their state to identify those presumptions currently used in that jurisdiction's courts.

Prima Facie Case

The plaintiff has set forth a ***prima facie*** case for the defendant's liability due to negligence action when the plaintiff has shown, by a preponderance of the evidence, that the defendant had a duty of care and breached that duty, which proximately caused injury to plaintiff. Having done this, the burden of proof shifts to the defendant to rebut the plaintiff's case. The defendant might do this by establishing that he or she, by a preponderance of the evidence, has a valid defense at law that negates liability. Failing to do this results in a verdict for the plaintiff.

Consider the intertwining of these legal concepts (see Case in Point 4-1).

 # CASE IN POINT 4-1

Anesthesiology Critical Care & Pain Management Consultants, P.A., v. Kretzer

802 So. 2d 346 (Fla. Dist. Ct. App. 4th Dist. 2001)

[...]

Plaintiffs-appellees, Kathleen Kretzer, as parent and natural guardian of Amanda J. Kretzer, a minor, filed suit against appellant and The Edward and Lucille Kimmel Outpatient Surgical Center Limited Partnership (hereinafter "the Kimmel Center") seeking to recover damages arising from an injury the minor allegedly sustained as a result of medical care and treatment rendered by their respective employees. Specifically, appellees claimed that the minor developed temporomandibular joint dysfunction after appellant's employees administered anesthesia to her during sinus surgery and employees of the Kimmel Center monitored her recovery from the anesthesia.

Prior to the trial's commencement, the trial judge, pursuant to a motion *in limine*, ruled that appellees were entitled to a *Valcin* rebuttable presumption of negligence against appellant and the Kimmel Center. Both defendants repeatedly voiced their opposition to the *Valcin* presumption, but their objections were repeatedly overruled before and during the trial. During both the opening and closing statements to the jury, appellees emphasized the *Valcin* presumption of negligence.

[...]

The jury returned a verdict in favor of appellees and against appellant and the Kimmel Center, finding the Kimmel Center to be 80% liable for appellees' injuries and appellant to be 20% liable. In accordance with the verdict, the trial court entered a final judgment in favor of appellees and against appellant, in addition to entering a cost judgment against appellant. This appeal ensued.

The *Valcin* Presumption

In *Public Health Trust of Dade County v. Valcin*, 507 So. 2d 596 (Fla. 1987), the plaintiff's ability to proceed in her medical malpractice action against a hospital was hindered because the hospital could not produce the records of her surgical procedure. Without the production of those records, her expert was unable to give an opinion as to the hospital's negligence. The supreme court held that this problem could be solved through the use of rebuttable presumptions that could either shift the burden of producing evidence or the burden of proof. The court noted that "rebuttable presumptions which shift the burden of proof are 'expressions of social policy,' rather than mere procedural devices employed 'to facilitate the determination of the particular action.'" (citation omitted).

The *Valcin* doctrine, as it is now called, is applied when, through the defendant's negligence, essential records are missing or inadequate, and such absence or inadequacy hinders the plaintiff's ability to establish a *prima facie* case. (citation omitted) In those instances, a rebuttable presumption of negligence is placed on the defendant. *See id.* Once the defendant introduces evidence tending to disprove the presumed fact, the jury then decides whether the evidence introduced is sufficient to meet the burden of proving that the presumed fact did not exist. (citation omitted) The doctrine is applicable to those cases in which either primary or secondary evidence is lost, destroyed, or not maintained. [...]

The *Valcin* presumption is limited in its application. The supreme court cautioned, "The presumption, shifting the burden of producing the evidence, is given life only to equalize the parties' respective positions in regard to the evidence and to allow the plaintiff to proceed." [...] In the present case, appellant contends that the trial court improperly applied the *Valcin* presumption because the only records allegedly missing related to a time period *after* the injury allegedly occurred. Further, even if the records were insufficient in regard to the care and treatment rendered by appellant's employees, they would have had no causal relationship to the procedure employed, and in no way hindered appellees' ability to establish a *prima facie* case.

In support of its claims, appellant presented the testimony of the board-certified registered nurse anesthetist who administered the minor's anesthesia. Though she had no independent recollection of the procedure, she testified that based upon her review of the surgical notes there were no problems. Had there been any, she would have noted them. She further testified that the minor's extubation was conducted without any trauma or stress, and that it was simple and uneventful. Appellant also presented the testimony of the anesthesiologist. He, too, testified that the intubation was straightforward, routine, and without any trauma.

A board-certified anesthesiologist testified as an expert for appellant. He opined, after reviewing the operative chart, that there was no evidence of any trauma or temporomandibular joint injury during the surgery or before the minor was delivered to post-operative care. He further stated that the attending operative anesthesia personnel adequately charted the procedure and did not depart from the operative standard of care.

On the other hand, appellees assert that the operative records were inadequate because they failed to contain any information concerning the alleged injury. Appellees contend that the records, when taken as a whole, demonstrate an interesting failure to report anything adverse to appellant. Unlike appellant, appellees failed to present any evidence, expert or otherwise, to the court to support these claims.

The trial court nevertheless applied the *Valcin* presumption against both the Kimmel Center and appellant. It apparently concluded that the operative *and* postoperative notes were deficient because they failed to indicate any trauma to the minor.

After a careful review of the record, we note that the only evidence demonstrating a failure to adequately maintain records relates to the *post-operative* notes. The post-operative notes were the Kimmel Center's responsibility and were not appellant's responsibility. Further, the record in this case is completely devoid of any evidence, implied or otherwise, that supports appellees' characterization that appellant was engaged in "fraudulent record keeping" and "a concerted effort to 'sanitize' the chart." Therefore, the trial court should not have applied the presumption against appellant.

In *Valcin*, the Florida Supreme Court further held that a presumption of negligence should not apply in situations such as the present case, where the alleged insufficient record does not bear on the issues at trial. The court stated, "[A] plaintiff must first establish to the satisfaction of the court that the absence of the records hinders his ability to establish a prima facie case." (citation omitted) The court continued:

We stress this point in order to avoid the potential problems involved in confusing the absence of the records with the true issues at trial. Negligence in failing to make or maintain medical records does not necessarily bear at all on the question of whether the medical procedure involved has been conducted negligently.

(citation omitted)

As this court and the other district courts have held, where a party seeking to apply *Valcin* does not show that the alleged missing records hindered its ability to establish a defense or a *prima facie* case, a *Valcin* instruction and presumption are reversible error.

[…]

The evidence adduced at trial in this case failed to support the imposition of a *Valcin* presumption against appellant. Appellant was only responsible for the minor during the operation and there was no evidence presented that appellant failed to keep adequate records or injured the minor in any way. Lastly, the alleged failure to make a record or maintain an adequate record had no relation to the negligent act alleged by appellees. For these reasons, we conclude that the trial court abused its discretion in applying a *Valcin* presumption against appellant.

[…]

Absent the *Valcin* presumption, appellant correctly notes that appellees failed to prove the first two elements. They did not present any expert testimony that appellant's treatment fell below the appropriate standard of care. […] Appellant is also correct that, without the presumption, appellees failed to prove the third element, causation. […] Because appellees failed to prove the essential elements of their claim, a […] verdict should have been entered in appellant's favor.

Appellees contend that if the court reverses on the *Valcin* issue, then it should not remand for entry of a [...] verdict. Instead, the court should remand with instructions to permit them an opportunity to prove a *prima facie* case without the *Valcin* presumption. They claim that they never proved a *prima facie* case at the initial trial because of their reliance on the two-year-old *Valcin* presumption order. Appellant replies that appellees also knew for two years that appellant was challenging the *Valcin* presumption and appellees had every opportunity to present a *prima facie* case the first time around.

[...]

[H]ere, appellees knew that appellant was challenging the *Valcin* presumption every step of the way, yet made no attempt to prove a *prima facie* case absent the presumption. Appellees' "failure to buttress [their] position because of confidence in the strength of that position is always indulged in at [their] own risk." (citation omitted) This argument rings even more true in this case where the presumption was rebuttable. Appellees thus had an even greater incentive to introduce evidence that appellant breached the applicable standard of care and caused the minor's injuries.

Appellees urge this court to analogize this situation to one where a summary judgment on liability is reversed and the plaintiff is permitted to introduce evidence of liability anew. However, this case is distinguishable from that scenario. First, the summary judgment on liability may be reversed because genuine issues of fact exist that require a trial and the introduction of evidence. Second, the *Valcin* presumption was rebuttable, not absolute like a determination of liability, and provided more of an incentive to fully present the case the first time. Finally, the *Valcin* court specifically rejected conclusive presumptions, which would have been more analogous to a summary judgment on liability, as a violation of due process. (citation omitted) [...]

Accordingly, we respectfully decline to accept appellees' invitation to remand with instructions to permit them another opportunity to prove a *prima facie* case without the *Valcin* presumption.

The final judgment and cost judgment in favor of appellees are hereby reversed, and this cause is remanded for entry of a [...] verdict in favor of appellant. [...]

At trial, the plaintiff's family failed to provide sufficient evidence on all elements of the claim to win. Instead, it said that the law presumed that since the hospital failed to turn over the records, it had something to hide and that what it was hiding was evidence of liability. The trial and appellate courts disagreed. While the presumption was that hospital had something to hide because it failed to produce the records, the plaintiff still had an obligation (in this specific case, the *Valcin* presumption) to show there was evidence on each element sufficient to prove the claim.

■ ISSUES COMMONLY FOUND ONLY IN CLAIMS OF NEGLIGENCE

Unavoidable Accident

That an accident has happened does not prove negligence as a matter of law. The plaintiff has to prove that the injury was proximately caused by the breach of a duty by the defendant. As discussed in Chapter 3, an essential element of proximate cause is the requirement that the injury to the plaintiff must have been clearly foreseeable. It follows that if the plaintiff could not have foreseen the occurrence of the accident nor could have prevented its occurrence by the exercise of reasonable care, there can be no proximate cause.

The doctrine of **unavoidable accident** states that an accident is unavoidable if it was not proximately caused by the act or omission of the plaintiff. This doctrine arises out of the practical necessity of having to draw a line at some point, of limiting the responsibility for human behavior. The law does not hold that every human act or omission is done at peril of facing exposure for liability. The limitation exists to prevent a defendant from being held liable for a mere accident, the result of which was clearly unforeseeable. For example, in case of *Palsgraf* (see Chapter 3), from the previous chapter, a subway conductor pushes a rider into a crowded subway car. The rider loses grip of a package in a brown paper bag, which contains fireworks that go off on impact. The shock of the explosion rattles the subway platform, so that a large scale tips over on top of Mrs. Palsgraf. The court there noted that the likelihood of an explosion going off on a wooden subway strong enough to topple a scale onto Mrs. Palsgraf, was unforeseeable.

Some courts and juries have shown a degree of certain skepticism towards an action in negligence due to an unavoidable accident, while others can accept the possibility under certain circumstances (see Case in Point 4-2).

CASE IN POINT 4-2

Bed, Bath & Beyond, Inc. v. Urista
211 S.W.3d 753 (Tex. 2006)

[...]

While shopping at a Bed, Bath & Beyond, Inc. ("BBB") store, Rafael Urista claims he was hit on the head and knocked unconscious by plastic trash cans that fell from a twelve-foot-high shelf. According to Urista's wife, a BBB employee on a ladder in the adjacent aisle on the other side of the shelf was attempting to retrieve merchandise with a broom when the trash cans fell. Although the BBB employee was not called to testify at trial, Urista's wife stated that the employee came around the aisle and observed the scene before returning to assist his customer. After learning of the incident, the BBB store manager approached the Uristas and completed an accident report. At that time, Urista declined the manager's offer of assistance and did not report being knocked unconscious or that he had been injured. The Uristas resumed shopping before leaving the store. Five weeks later, Urista sued BBB claiming that the trash can incident caused him severe back injuries. The BBB store manager conceded during his testimony at trial that the employee working on the other side of the shelf probably caused the trash cans to fall, but he believed the employee had been acting in a safe manner when the incident occurred.

[...]

The trial court submitted the case to the jury in a broad-form charge. The liability question asked: "Did the negligence, if any, of Bed, Bath, and Beyond, Inc. proximately cause the occurrence in question?" Over Urista's objection, the trial court also included two inferential rebuttal instructions in the charge, including this "unavoidable accident" instruction: "An occurrence may be an 'unavoidable accident,' that is, an event not proximately caused by the negligence of any party to it." In its brief, BBB conceded that this instruction should not have been submitted. In a ten-to-two verdict, the jury answered "NO" to the liability question and thus did not reach the conditionally submitted damages question. In accordance with the verdict, the trial court rendered a take-nothing judgment in favor of BBB.

In a divided opinion, the First Court of Appeals held on rehearing that the trial court erred when it submitted the unavoidable accident instruction and that it was likely, although not conclusively established, that the erroneous instruction formed the sole basis for the jury's negative answer to the liability question. (citation omitted) The court concluded that the erroneous instruction "probably was reversible error that prevented Urista from presenting his [appeal]." (citation omitted) The court accordingly reversed the trial court's judgment and remanded the case for a new trial. (citation omitted) The court declined to reach Urista's remaining issues, including whether the jury's failure to find negligence was against the great weight and preponderance of the evidence.

Unavoidable accident is not an alternative theory of liability but is "an inferential rebuttal issue that requires plaintiffs to prove the nonexistence of an affirmative defense," (citation omitted) or "seeks to disprove the existence of an essential element submitted in another issue," (citation omitted). In this case, the unavoidable accident instruction was given in reference to the causation element of the plaintiff's negligence claim. When, as here, the broad-form questions submitted a single liability theory (negligence) to the jury, [...] we apply traditional harmless error analysis and consider whether the instruction "probably caused the rendition of an improper judgment." (citation omitted)

[...]

"A review of the record in this case reveals at least two reasons why we cannot conclude that the unavoidable accident instruction probably resulted in an improper judgment. First [...] the inclusion of an improper unavoidable accident instruction is ordinarily harmless and indeed can serve an explanatory role: The standard broad-form question is structured such that the jury is not asked whether any particular person was negligent, but whether "the negligence, if any," of particular persons proximately caused an occurrence. There is at least a potential implication in this phraseology that the occurrence was caused by someone's negligence. We see no harm in explaining to the jury through an inferential rebuttal instruction that no such implication is intended. (citation omitted). The truth is, sometimes accidents are no one's fault, and an unavoidable accident instruction, like the one in this case, simply explains to the jury that they are not required to find someone at fault. In this instance, the jury was reminded that it could consider the possibility that the trashcans fell for reasons other than someone's negligence. That kind of a jury instruction does not by itself amount to harmful error. (citation omitted) Second, it is reasonable to conclude that Urista failed to carry his burden of proof.

According to this court of appeal, the trial case made no critical error by allowing BBB to argue at trial that the tumbling of the plastic trashcans was an "unavoidable accident." "Unavoidable accident" were appropriate to argue if there were several arguments presented about why the defendant was liable. Here, there was just an argument of liability based on negligence. Here, 'unavoidable accident' turned out only to focus on an element of the claim; since it was meant only as an explanation, including mention of it did not materially affect the outcome of the trial. This court of appeal concluded that the mistake of allowing the jury to consider "unavoidable accident" did not materially affect the jury's determination that BBB was not liable, so the trial court's ruling was reinstated.

Act of God

Closely related to the concept of an unavoidable accident is the legal principle of an act of God. An **act of God** is a sudden, unexpected, and extraordinary demonstration of the force of nature from which humans cannot protect themselves. When harm results from an act of God, there is no liability for negligence.

For example, consider the issue of a common carrier's liability for the safekeeping of goods placed in its possession (a common carrier, like a bus, train, or airplane, makes itself available for public use). If the goods are destroyed through an act of God, such as a flash flood that washes out a road or railroad tracks, and does not in any way arise through the negligence of the bus, train, or truck, the common carrier will not be liable for negligence. Professor Keeton supports this view (see box below).

UNFORESEEABLE CAUSES

If the defendant can foresee neither any danger of direct injury, nor any risk from an intervening cause, the defendant is simply not negligent. Negligence cannot be predicated solely upon a failure to anticipate that extraordinary and unprecedented rainfall will flood the streets, that a pedestrian will slip and fall upon an apparently safe highway, that the wind will blow a door latch against the eye of a boy, or that a ribbon held across a street to stop a wedding procession will cause one carriage to run into another. But once the defendant's negligence is established, because injury of some kind was to be anticipated, intervening causes which could not reasonably be foreseen, and which are no normal part of the risk created, may bring about results of an entirely different kind.

W. Page Keeton et al., *Prosser & Keeton on the Law of Torts* §44 at 311-312 (5th ed. 1984)

The application of this rule precludes any recovery for injuries caused by extreme weather conditions. No one is liable for an injury proximately caused by an act of God, which is an injury due directly and exclusively to natural causes, without human intervention, that could not have been prevented by the exercise of reasonable care and foresight (see Table 4-4).

Table 4-4 What Is Considered an Act of God?

Act of God	Not an Act of God
• Flash flood caused by an earthquake • Force 5 hurricane • Volcanic eruption where there had been no volcanic activity in 10,000 years	• Flooding of oceanfront property • Car accident caused by sudden downpour • Ice damaging the hull of a vessel moored in the Arctic Sea

Extreme weather conditions such as excessive rains and floods have long been considered acts of God (see Case in Point 4-3).

CASE IN POINT 4-3

Joseph Resnick Co., Inc. v. Nippon Yusen Kaisha
39 Misc. 2d 513 (N.Y. Civ. Ct. 1963)

This is an action by an importer against both a steamship line and a pier operator to recover $1,594.54 for flood damage to a shipment of 100 cartons of cabana sets, purchased by plaintiff and shipped from Hong Kong to New York aboard defendant's steamship. The vessel arrived in New York on or about February 12, 1960, and the cargo was discharged into the hands of defendant pier operator. The cargo was eventually delivered to plaintiff in a damaged condition.

Defendant steamship cross-claims over against defendant pier operator, claiming that its control over the property ceased six days before damage was sustained. Both defendants, however, unite in the common defense that an unprecedented flood on the night of February 18, 1960 caused the damage.

Against defendant steamship, plaintiff's complaint alleges liability both as a common carrier and as a bailee. Against defendant pier operator, plaintiff alleges liability only as a bailee. Liability as a common carrier transcends liability as a bailee. A common carrier can be excused only by an "act of God" or by the act of a public enemy. All that plaintiff needs to prove is damage in the hands of the carrier. A bailee, however, must be proven negligent (citation omitted).

To excuse a carrier, and a fortiori a bailee, from liability, the defendant must prove that the damage was caused by an "act of God" (citation omitted)

"Any misadventure or casualty is said to be caused by the 'act of God' when it happens by the direct, immediate, and exclusive operation of the forces of nature, uncontrolled or uninfluenced by the power of man and without human intervention, and is of such a character that it could not have been prevented or escaped from by any amount of foresight or prudence, or by any reasonable degree of care or diligence, or by the aid of any appliances which the situation of the party might reasonably require him to use." (citation omitted)

However, in order for this defense to be effective, it must be shown that the "act of God" was the sole and exclusive cause of the casualty and that there is no admixture of human agency (citation omitted). In order to determine whether or not there has been an admixture of human agency, this basic question must be resolved: Did defendant's negligence place the goods in such a position as to be vulnerable to damage? Or, stated in another way, could the effects of the storm or force of nature have been reasonably avoided by the defendant?

[...]

There is no question but that this flood was of itself an "act of God." Testimony showed that the flood occurred somewhat after midnight of the night of February 17, 1960. At 5:00 p.m. of the same day the United States Weather Bureau forecast predicted tides of only two feet above normal, a forecast which in and of itself would not have imposed a duty or placed an obligation upon the defendants to alter their normal course of operations. There was nothing contained in this official weather forecast to put the defendants on notice that the tides would rise in fact to more than five feet above normal, nor could they have reasonably foreseen this unseasonable occurrence from any of the surrounding circumstances. According to tide records kept by the United States Army Corps of Engineers and introduced at the trial, only two tides since 1893, a period of 67 years, have ever reached the height and proportions of the tide of February 18, 1960. One occurred in November of 1950 and the second in November of 1953. Both tides were the result of hurricanes and both were in the Fall, the traditional season for high tides. In addition, and considered by the court, was the fact that both previous tides had happened years before the defendant pier operator leased the premises in 1957. It would be manifestly unjust to charge a party with lack of foresight under such circumstances.

Further, to attribute liability to the defendant pier owner for not avoiding the effects of the resulting flood, in effect, would be to penalize him by making him pay a premium for the lack of superhuman qualities, in failing to envision a sudden high tide, out of season, without experience with any prior one, and without adequate notice thereof.

So far, this court has applied the traditional common-law principle embodied in the tried if not tired phrase "act of God." In this nuclear age, man's unlimited capabilities and scientific advancement have brought him to the very threshold of other planets. His newly harnessed nuclear power causes atmospheric reactions as yet unresolved and unpredicted, next to which his ability to create rain by the use of dry ice seems almost primitive. Is it not time to relieve Nature of even the formal blame for many acts which now seem to be within the scope of man's prowess? Perhaps the term "act of God" should be replaced by a concept which reflects the possibility of human causality as well as that of the Divine. In determining liability in a situation like the present, what is more important than the identification or nomenclature of the unknown cause is the answer to the question of whether there was any intervention or foreseeability or control on the part of defendant. If there is a negative answer to

> this question, then the result simply must be *damnum fatale,* in that the damage to plaintiff's goods must be borne by him and not by the carrier or bailee in whose custody the goods had been entrusted.
>
> The court then holds that the damage to plaintiff's goods was caused by an act over which neither defendant had the slightest control and whose effects could not have been reasonably foreseen nor avoided.
>
> Accordingly, this court awards judgment for defendant Nippon Yusen Kaisha [...]

A flood of this intensity was so rare that the trial court correctly concluded that it was an "act of God." Since such a flood happened so rarely, the defendant shipping company could not have taken measures to avoid damages. Thus, the defendant was not liable for the damages to the plaintiff's goods.

However, when an act of God combines with the negligence of the defendant to produce harm or injury, the defendant is liable for the damage. The theory is that the injury would not have occurred *but for* the defendant's negligence, which creates an element of foreseeability upon which to base a finding of liability.

For instance, if a common carrier delivered the goods to the wrong recipient, and in so doing placed the goods in the path of a sudden and unexpected force of nature, e.g., a tornado, the carrier would still be liable. The act of God would not preclude the defendant's liability for negligence.

In modern times, where the common carrier could easily purchase insurance, Professor Dobbs wonders whether the concept of an "act of God" should remain in tort law (see box below).

ACT OF GOD

"Forces of nature play a role in many negligence cases. Unforeseeable natural forces are still sometimes called acts of God. [fo] Courts often speak of natural forces as if special rules are needed in those cases, but with the exception of certain statutory claims and a few common law cases now of little significance, the decisions comport with the general rules of negligence and proximate cause. It is thus entirely possible to drop terms like 'act of God' altogether.

Dobbs, *The Law of Torts* §191 (2000)

Degrees of Negligence

A now-obsolete viewpoint in the law of negligence once imposed differing standards of conduct for different defendants or situations. The old law held that the greater the risk, the greater the care required by the defendant. It recognized three distinct degrees of negligence (see Table 4-5).

Table 4-5 Degrees of Negligence	
Type of Negligence	**Breach of Duty of Care**
Slight	The failure to use great care; still used in cases of common carrier liability;
Ordinary	The failure to use ordinary care; and
Gross	The failure to use slight care, falling short of willful and wanton disregard.

For example, under the old law, a package delivery service might be liable for slight negligence for not loading safely onto the delivery vehicle a package prominently labeled "Fragile—handle with care!" That same delivery service would be liable for ordinary negligence if the driver of the delivery vehicle was speeding and got into an accident. Finally, the driver might be liable for gross negligence if the driver was driving while under the influence of alcohol and drove so recklessly as to cause an accident. Attempts to apply degrees of care to all negligence cases resulted in confusion and lack of uniformity in court decisions.

One Standard

The difficulty in classifying conduct and care drove courts to seek a single standard by which negligence could be measured. The current view in most jurisdictions is that there are no degrees of negligence, but merely one standard of care which is the same thing as ordinary negligence (see Case in Point 4-4).

 # CASE IN POINT 4-4

Massey v. Scripter

401 Mich.385 (1977)

On July 24, 1972, the plaintiffs, Lester and Wanda Massey, were riding their newly purchased tandem bicycle in an easterly direction on the shoulder of the westbound lane of Holmes Road in Ypsilanti Township, Washtenaw County, so that they were riding against the traffic. Mr. Massey was on the tandem's front seat and Mrs. Massey on the tandem's rear seat. As they approached the intersection of Ridge and Holmes Roads, Lester Massey pulled out onto Holmes Road to avoid chuckholes in the road shoulder.

A pickup truck driven by the defendant, Daniel Scripter, was legally stopped at the stop sign on southbound Ridge Road, waiting for traffic to clear on Holmes Road. As the truck started moving to enter the intersection, the tandem bicycle reached the intersection and passed slowly in front of the pickup truck. Defendant testified that as soon as he saw the bicycle he slammed on his brakes. Although the truck was traveling at a maximum speed of six miles per hour, according to a witness's testimony, an impact occurred causing both plaintiffs to sustain injuries requiring medical treatment.

The plaintiffs sued to recover for the personal injuries sustained in the accident and a jury returned a verdict of no cause of action. The plaintiffs appealed, claiming three errors in the trial court's instructions to the jury, and a fourth error in the trial judge's exclusion of testimony concerning the safety aspects of riding bicycles against the traffic. The Court of Appeals affirmed the trial court as to all four issues. This Court granted leave on November 1, 1976.

[...]

Under Michigan law, while the standard of conduct required may differ depending upon the activity one is involved in, the standard of care required does not change. The standard of care required of a party is always that which a reasonably careful person would do or would refrain from doing under the circumstances....

One standard of care, that care which a reasonably prudent person would use under similar circumstances, is mandated in view of the medley of circumstances that may be presented to the trier of fact. While legal scholars and law school professors may use language intimating varying degrees of care, when charging a jury but a single standard of care is permissible.

[...]

In a legal opinion addressed to bench and bar it is not inappropriate to speak in terms of degrees of care and caution, as a form of legal shorthand; but when a jury of laymen is charged on the common law of negligence, the charge must be cast only in terms which a jury will understand impose a standard measured by that which a reasonably prudent man would regard as reasonably required by the specific factual circumstances of the case....

Therefore, we hold that the trial judge erred in instructing the jury that if plaintiffs' operation of their bicycle violated the Michigan statute, they would be required to use greater care than if they had kept the bicycle as near to the right side of the road as practicable. Viewing the instructions as a whole, this charge stands out as clear judicial usurpation of the jury's function. The necessity of greater or lesser care under the given circumstances is a question for the trier of fact. The Court of Appeals decision is reversed and this case is remanded to the trial court for a new trial.

As the court stated in *Massey*, the trier of fact should be charged with deciding whether the degree of care appropriate under the circumstances. To impose degrees of care as a matter of law would only serve to infringe on the duty of the trier of fact, requiring the trier of fact to see whether the facts justified the imposition of a particular standard of care rather than to see whether there was a breach of a reasonable standard of care.

Willful, Wanton, and Reckless Conduct

Modern negligence theory provides for a category of conduct that exists somewhere between ordinary negligence and purely intentional harm: **willful, wanton, and reckless conduct.** The three terms are used interchangeably and almost invariably describe a form of highly unreasonable behavior that goes far beyond ordinary negligence. Running a stop sign might lead to an automobile accident, usually a cause of action in negligence. Drinking and driving and running stop signs will likely rise to the level of willful, wanton, and reckless conduct so that those injured by such conduct could win at trial under a theory based on a theory of gross negligence, which might result in a higher award in damages.

The courts have treated this behavior as aggravated negligence or, in some cases, gross negligence. Professor Dobbs offers a current perspective (see box below).

RECKLESS, WILLFUL, OR WANTON MISCONDUCT

"The defendant is guilty of reckless, willful, or wanton misconduct only if he was conscious of the risk or had specific reason to know about it [footnote omitted] and proceeded without concern for the safety of others. [footnote omitted] The defendant does not intentionally harm another, but he intentionally or consciously runs a very serious risk with no good reason to do so. He is guilty of 'conscious indifference' as the courts say. Although reckless, willful, or wanton misconduct is not the same as intentional harm, in extreme cases courts may treat wanton misconduct more like an intentional tort than like negligence. [footnote omitted]"

Dobbs, *The Law of Torts* §147 (2000)

Professor Keeton states the essence of this principle (see box below).

WILLFUL, WANTON, AND RECKLESS CONDUCT

Lying between intent to do harm, which, as we have seen, includes proceeding with knowledge that the harm is substantially certain to occur, and the mere unreasonable risk of harm to another involved in ordinary negligence, there is a penumbra of what has been called "quasi-intent." To this area the words "willful," "wanton," or "reckless" are customarily applied; and sometimes, in a single sentence, all three. Although efforts have been made to distinguish them, in practice such distinctions have consistently been ignored, and the three terms have been treated as meaning the same thing, or at least as coming out at the same legal exit. They have been grouped together as an aggravated form of negligence, differing in quality rather than in degree from ordinary lack of care.

W. Page Keeton et al., *Prosser & Keeton on the Law of Torts* §34 at 212 (5th ed. 1984)

The difference between reckless conduct and negligence lies in the amount of risk (see Table 4-6).

Table 4-6 Difference in Amount of Risk between Negligent and Reckless Conduct	
Negligence	Ordinary amount of risk
Recklessness	Very high amount of risk

It requires that the defendant's behavior involve a risk substantially greater in amount than that necessary to make the conduct negligent (see box below).

RECKLESS DISREGARD

The actor's conduct is in reckless disregard of the safety of another if he does an act or intentionally fails to do an act which it is his duty to the other to do, knowing or having reason to know of facts which would lead a reasonable man to realize, not only that his conduct creates an unreasonable risk of physical harm to another, but also that such risk is substantially greater than that which is necessary to make his conduct negligent.

Restatement (Second) of Torts §500 (1965)

The trier of fact determines whether conduct is willful, wanton, and reckless. The jury decides whether there has been a failure to exercise due care, and whether there was a great probability harm would result from the lack of care. The presence of the second element in this test allo____ ____illful, wanton, and reckless conduct (see Table 4-7).

The following case elaborates upon this point (see Case in Point 4-5).

Table 4-7 Difference in Probability of Harm between Negligence and Reckless Conduct	
Negligence	Probability of harm
Willful, Wanton, Reckless Conduct	Probability of great harm

CASE IN POINT 4-5

Matkovich v. Penn Central Transportation Company Supreme Court of Ohio

69 Ohio St.2d 210 (1982)

In this case, the jury found that Penn Central and Jennings were guilty of wanton misconduct. However, the Court of Appeals reversed. Therefore, we must determine whether the jury could have reasonably concluded, based on the evidence, that wanton misconduct existed. We will consider the conduct of appellees separately—first Penn Central, then Jennings.

The test for determining wanton misconduct was defined in *Hawkins v. Ivy* (citation omitted). As stated by the Court of Appeals in the instant case, *Hawkins* created a two-part test for wanton misconduct. First, there is a failure to exercise any care whatsoever by those who owe a duty of care to the appellant. Secondly, this failure occurs under circumstances in which there is great probability that harm will result from the lack of care. The first prong of the test requires that we determine the duty appellees owed appellant, and also the extent of care exercised by appellees. Then, we must consider the nature of the hazard created by the circumstances. [...]

Penn Central contends that the train in the crossing is, in itself, actual notice and an adequate warning. Because the train extended across the road, Penn Central argues that the train preempted the crossing and ordinary care did not require any additional warnings. Furthermore, it argues that the crossing was not exceptionally hazardous and no extra-statutory warnings were required. [...]

The concept of a train serving as notice may have been reasonable decades ago when this standard was formulated. However, we must determine whether the train constituted actual notice of the hazard under the circumstances in this case. The train itself had no reflective tape, and the record reflects that the jury could have reasonably found that no warning devices were used by the railroad at the crossing. Considering the darkness of the night and of the train and the normal rate of speed of today's motor vehicles, appellant may not have had sufficient time to stop and avoid the collision after it became evident to him that the train blocked the road ahead. Therefore, we conclude that the train may not have been perceived at a sufficient distance to serve as notice. Penn Central had a duty to exercise ordinary care to protect the public safety and in this case that duty required giving additional warning of the presence of the train.

The infrequent use of the tracks is another reason for our conclusion that the railroad had an affirmative duty to warn of the train's presence. The record indicates that the tracks were a spur line and seldom used. [...] In the instant case, appellant lived in the area and was well aware of the crossing, but he also was cognizant that the tracks were rarely used. Penn Central should have foreseen that motorists would not expect a train to be in the crossing because it was an unusual occurrence. Therefore, ordinary care would dictate that Penn Central should have taken some affirmative precautions to warn of the hazard. The Court of Appeals concluded that there was no crossbuck sign, which the railroad is statutorily required to erect at the track, and no other device or signal to warn of the actual presence of the train in the crossing. Penn Central created the hazard by placing the train in the crossing; however, it did nothing to warn motorists of the hazard, even though any of [several] warning devices could have been easily used. This lack of care at the crossing was more than simple negligence.

Wanton misconduct is a jury question. On these facts, the jury could have reasonably concluded that Penn Central disregarded the safety of motorists and failed to exercise any care whatsoever to motorists. [...]

The second prong of the *Hawkins* test is that the failure to exercise care occurs under circumstances in which there is a great probability that harm will result. In its previous decisions, this court has recognized that "almost every railroad grade crossing involves a substantial risk of danger to those using the highway over such crossing." [...] Clearly, the dark train on a seldom used crossing at night creates a hazard and there is a great probability of collisions and injuries when no precautions are taken to warn of its presence. [...]

Although we recognize the needs of railroads to preempt crossings to carry on their business, the primary consideration should be the public's safety, especially when the track is an infrequently used spur line. The cost is minimal, in terms of dollars and time, for a railroad to warn with flares, fuses, reflective tape and lanterns. In comparison, the probability of accidents occurring and the gravity of harm are both great. A railroad has a responsibility to exercise ordinary care to prevent accidents, a potential it creates when a train is in a crossing. A jury could have concluded, based on these circumstances, that a great probability of harm could result from the lack of care exercised. Therefore, the second prong of the *Hawkins* test for wanton misconduct is satisfied.

Since the train company could have easily and inexpensively implemented safety procedures that would have warned motorists of the train's arrival, failure to take such measures amounted to willful, wanton, and reckless conduct.

The behavior of the defendant in a willful, wanton, and reckless situation takes two different forms. One is an act and the other is a failure to act (see Table 4-8). Either one is sufficient to impose liability, and in either case the recklessness must be unreasonable and something more than ordinary negligence.

Table 4-8 Contrasting Malfeasance and Nonfeasance

Deliberately acting with willful, wanton, and reckless disregard	Malfeasance
Failing to act so as to be equivalent of acting with willful, wanton, and reckless disregard	Nonfeasance

The nature of the behavior goes well beyond ordinary negligence yet does not equal intentional conduct. The drunk driver who ignores stop signs likely did not mean to cause an accident but did operate the motor vehicle while drunk, which increases the risk of the occurrence of an injury.

Guest Passenger *Statutes*

A few states have statutes under which the distinction between negligence and reckless conduct takes on f   ance. Such statutes impose liability for harm done to a guest in   nly when the driver's conduct is in reckless disregard of the guest's safety. This statute, called a **guest passenger statute** or automobile guest statute, provides that the driver of an automobile is liable to a gratuitous guest (as opposed to a paying customer) only for gross negligence or aggravated misconduct. For example, in a state that has a guest passenger statute, a passenger involved in an automobile accident could not recover for damages. Only if the driver operated the car with such a degree of recklessness—for example, driving drunk and through red lights and stop signs—would the passenger be able to recover.

Many states at one time had guest passenger statutes on their books, but found the statutes presented too many varying issues to be enforceable and had to be repealed. Several of these statutes have been held unconstitutional as a violation of the Equal Protection Clause, since the state where the accident happened could have more to do with whether an injured passenger could recover would matter more than the conduct of the driver. Paralegal students must consult their state's statutes and case law to determine the status of any such statutes.

Negligence *Per Se*

In some circumstances, state legislatures have defined a standard of conduct for a reasonable person applicable to all people. Any deviation from that standard of conduct by a defendant is presumed by statute to be negligent. Proof of negligence in such a case is met by showing that the statute has been violated. Violation of a statutory standard of conduct is termed **negligence *per se.*** In an action for negligence, once the plaintiff has shown that the defendant's conduct was in violation of a statutory standard of conduct, the defendant's negligence is presumed. For example, suppose a state's statutes require that drivers act with reasonable care. If a driver causes an accident that injures a passenger and is cited for violating this statute, the driver is liable for negligence *per se.*

Consider the concept from the perspective of case law (see Case in Point 4-6).

CASE IN POINT 4-6

Greenwald v. Hooe

2006 Mich. App. 3651 (Mich. Ct. App. Dec. 19, 2006).

Plaintiffs appeal as of right from a circuit court judgment denying their motion to vacate an arbitration award. We affirm. [...]

Plaintiffs argue that the arbitration award should be vacated because it contravenes controlling principles of law by failing to apply the assured clear distance statute, (citation omitted)

[...]

The Supreme Court has held that violation of the assured clear distance statute (citation omitted) constitutes "negligence *per se.*" (citation omitted) "Negligence *per se*" does not denote strict liability. (citation omitted) Rather, "the rule is that evidence of violation of a penal statute creates a rebuttable presumption of negligence." (citation omitted) The assured clear distance statute must be reasonably construed and is subject to qualification (citation omitted). For example, the statute is inapplicable "when a collision is shown to have occurred as the result of a sudden emergency not of the defendants' own making." (citation omitted)

Plaintiffs have failed to demonstrate that the decision of the majority of the arbitrators was in contravention of controlling principles of law. [...]

> They have not shown that the arbitration decision was affected by an error of law that led to a wrong conclusion.
>
> [...]
>
> Affirmed.

The fact that the defendant violated a law supported a claim of negligence *per se*. Yet the presumption of liability as negligence *per se* could be overturned if the defendant presented evidence that suggested otherwise. Since there was sufficient evidence that a sudden emergency had developed so that the defendant would be relieved of liability under the statute, the plaintiff was not entitled to a recovery based on a theory of negligence *per se*.

Persons to Be Protected by Statute

The burden of proving negligence has been met merely by establishing the statutory violation, as Professor Dobbs notes (see box below).

NEGLIGENCE *PER SE*

That rule holds that an adult's violation of statute is negligence in itself if it caused harm of the kind the statute was intended to avoid and to a person within the class of persons the statute was intended to protect.

Dobbs, *The Law of Torts* §134 (2000)

A recovery under a theory of negligence *per se* requires that the plaintiff be a part of a class of individuals the legislature sought to protect when it enacted the statute. For instance, if a state statute prohibits the sale of fireworks to minors, the legislature clearly intends to protect the class of minors from the fireworks. Should a minor be injured through the use of fireworks that were purchased in violation of the statute, he or she would be able to maintain an action based upon a theory of negligence *per se* (see box below).

INTERPRETING NEGLIGENCE *PER SE*

Once the statute is determined to be applicable—which is to say, once it is interpreted as designed to protect the class of persons, in which the plaintiff is included, against the risk of the type of harm which has in fact occurred as a result of its violation—and once its breach has been established, probably a majority of the courts hold that the issue of negligence is thereupon conclusively determined, in the absence of sufficient excuse, and that the court must so direct the jury. The standard of conduct is taken over by the court from that fixed by the legislature, and "jurors have no dispensing power by which to relax it," except insofar as the court may recognize the possibility of a valid excuse in a tort action for damages for disobedience of a criminal law.

W. Page Keeton et al., *Prosser & Keeton on the Law of Torts* §36 at 229-230 (5th ed. 1984)

If the injured plaintiff in this case was not a part of the protected class, such as an adult who was not involved in the purchase of the fireworks, the theory of negligence *per se* would be unavailable.

Defenses

A number of defenses are open to the defendant in an action based upon a theory of negligence *per se*. Chapter 4 addresses the traditional defenses available in any negligence action, many of which may be available in such a case. Examples of defenses available include contributory negligence and assumption of the risk.

Res Ipsa Loquitur

In the law of negligence, a unique doctrine of proof may be available to assist the plaintiff in establishing the negligence of the defendant. Normally, the mere occurrence of an injury will not give rise to an inference that it was due to negligence on the part of the defendant. Yet the doctrine of **res ipsa loquitur** provides an exception, permitting an inference of negligence under only certain circumstances.

The term *res ipsa loquitur* literally means "the thing speaks for itself," and represents a fusion of the concept of circumstantial evidence (which indirectly proves the existence of a fact) with the plaintiff's burden of proof. When the instrumentality that caused the injury is under the defendant's control and when in the ordinary course of things the injury would not have occurred if the defendant used proper care, there is an inference that the injury arose from the defendant's lack of care.

Some consider that the concept of *res ipsa loquitur* arose from the comments of Baron Pollock made in the English case, *Byrne v. Boadle,* in 1863. There, a barrel of flour rolled from a warehouse window and struck a pedestrian. Baron Pollock argued that it was a reasonable conclusion from the unusual circumstances of the accident that the defendant was at fault, since the injury would not have occurred if the defendant had used proper care when storing the keg of flour.

Conditions for Imposition of This Doctrine

Most jurisdictions require that the following conditions are necessary to the application of the doctrine:

- The event must be of the type that would ordinarily not occur without the defendant's negligence; in the light of ordinary experience, there must have been negligence on someone's part.
- The accident must be caused by some instrumentality in the exclusive control of the defendant. The purpose of this requirement is to link the defendant with the presumed negligent act.
- The accident must not be due to any contribution on the part of the plaintiff; otherwise, such contribution would be considered a valid defense.

Table 4-9 Examples of Cases Involving Liability under the Doctrine of *Res Ipsa Loquitur*		
	Liability	**No Liability**
Event wouldn't normally occur without the defendant's negligence.	• X-ray therapy causing burn to the plaintiff's neck and head • Small-engine aircraft crashes, where weather was good and there was sufficient fuel for an extended flight	• Water heater burst on a floor above the floor occupied by tenants • Placement of a freight elevator control box allowed for accidental activation of the elevator when unloading furniture

Defendant had to have exclusive control over the circumstances.	• Chair in a class at a private art school • Surgical instruments left in the patient during a surgery	• Chair collapsed in the waiting area in the airport • Cleaning companies alternated in daily cleaning of offices
Plaintiff cannot have contributed in any way to the occurrence of the event.	• Operating a motor boat at high speeds on a lake when there were swimmers in the water • Eating of a fish sandwich causes the chipping of a plaintiff's tooth after having bitten on something "hard" in the sandwich	• Delay in receiving medical care resulted in death at an emergency room • Use of a boat battery to start an automobile

Courts continue to evaluate the concept to determine when it is appropriate to apply the doctrine (see Case in Point 4-7).

 # CASE IN POINT 4-7

Hake v. George Wiedemann Brewing Co.
23 Ohio St.2d 65 (1970)

The question presented is whether the trial court erred in refusing to apply the rule of *res ipsa loquitur* at the close of plaintiff's case.

It is well established by earlier decisions of this court that *res ipsa loquitur* is a rule of evidence which permits the trier of fact to infer negligence on the part of the defendant from the circumstances surrounding the injury to plaintiff. [...]

To warrant application of the rule a plaintiff must adduce evidence in support of two conclusions: (1) That the instrumentality causing the injury was, at the time of the injury, or at the time of the creation of the condition causing the injury, under the exclusive management and control of the defendant; and (2) that the injury occurred under such circumstances that in the ordinary course of events it would not have occurred if ordinary care had been observed. [...] Whether sufficient evidence has been adduced at trial to warrant application of the rule is a question of law to be determined initially by the trial court, subject to review upon appeal. It is prejudicial error for the trial court to direct a verdict for defendant at the close of plaintiff's evidence where the evidence presented warrants the application of the rule. [...]

In the instant case, plaintiff presented two witnesses who testified that, on October 11, 1962, they saw a beer keg roll off and fall from an exterior second-story stairway platform at premises owned by the Cincinnati Gas & Electric Company. They also saw plaintiff in a contracted position underneath the platform immediately thereafter, and the beer keg lying on the ground nearby. One of those witnesses saw two Wiedemann employees descend the staircase shortly after the barrel rolled off the platform, and both that witness and plaintiff testified that they saw the two Wiedemann employees at the bottom of the staircase shortly thereafter. Plaintiff testified that he was hit by a metal beer keg as he walked out a doorway and underneath the platform. There was extensive testimony with respect to the seriousness of plaintiff's injury. Defendant admitted ownership of the metal beer keg and the presence of its employees on the premises who were there for the purpose of removing several empty beer kegs from the second story, which kegs were left from a gas company employees' party the night before. However, no witness actually saw the keg being handled by a Wiedemann employee, and defendant argues that proof of this fact is critical to plaintiff's case.

In other words, defendant insists that plaintiff should be required to show exclusive management and control by the defendant of the particular beer keg which struck plaintiff during the period immediately prior to the time plaintiff was struck in order to warrant application of the rule of *res ipsa loquitur* to this case. Plaintiff argues that no such showing is necessary since defense counsel admitted the fact of exclusive management and control during his opening statement to the jury.

During his opening statement counsel for the defense revealed:

The evidence will disclose that Mr. Griese and his helper were up on the second floor of the party room at the Cincinnati Gas & Electric Company, where they, the gas company employees, had apparently had a party, and had had some beer. The (sic) went to get the empty beer barrel. The evidence will disclose that accidentally Mr. Griese in some manner stubbed his toe, and he accidentally let the thing slip. He didn't toss it, and he didn't kick it. The evidence will show that it accidentally slipped out of his hands and came down.

We agree with plaintiff that defense counsel's opening statement constitutes a judicial admission sufficient to establish exclusive management and control on the part of the defendant at the time of the occurrence of the injury to plaintiff.

This being so, does the evidence adduced by plaintiff lead to the conclusion that the injury occurred under such circumstances that in the ordinary course of events it would not have occurred if ordinary care had been observed? We believe that it does.

[...]

We are convinced that the rule of *res ipsa loquitur* applies in the instant case and that the trial court erred in directing a verdict for the defendant at the close of plaintiff's evidence. Therefore, the judgment of the Court of Appeals, affirming the judgment of the trial court, should be, and hereby is, reversed.

The plaintiff could not show clearly who caused the beer keg to roll out of the property to hit him. The theory of *res ipsa loquitur* applied to create liability for the defendant because the plaintiff had no other way of showing who had control of the keg and because the defendant was in the best possible position to have determined how this had happened.

Statutory Modification of the Doctrine

While these are the traditional elements of *res ipsa loquitur*, individual states have substantially modified the doctrine. For instance, many courts have added a requirement that the doctrine cannot be applied unless the evidence of the true explanation of the accident is more accessible to the defendant than to the plaintiff. For example physicians in a surgical facility have a better idea about accounting for the presence of surgical instruments than the patient would. Other jurisdictions have taken the position that the doctrine exists to shift the burden of proof to the defendant that the defendant acted appropriately. This is another instance where the paralegal student should consult individual state case law to determine the status of the doctrine.

Joint Tortfeasors' Liability

Not all harm as a result of negligence involves merely one defendant. In many situations an injured party has a claim against multiple defendants. The term for the liability of two or more persons together is **joint liability**. While a defendant cannot be held liable in tort for an injury that he or she did not cause, liability for injury does attach to each defendant involved in the injury to the plaintiff. If two or more defendants were negligent, whether they acted in concert or alone, and each was the cause of a single harm to the plaintiff, both are liable to that plaintiff (see box below).

> ### GROUNDS FOR IMPOSING JOINT AND SEVERAL LIABILITY: VICARIOUS LIABILITY
>
> "One group of grounds for imposing joint and several liability are related to vicarious responsibility. The employer is jointly and severally liable along with his employee for torts committed by the employee within the scope of employment. Similar, partners and joint enterprisers are vicariously liable for the torts of each other committed within the scope of the partnership or enterprise. Finally, persons who act in concert, pursuant to a common plan or design, to commit a crime or tort are true joint tortfeasors; each is liable for harm done by the others involved, though he himself has committed no direct harm. In all these case, joint and several liability is imposed vicariously."
>
> Dobbs, *The Law of Torts* §170 (2000)

Concerted Action

Under criminal law, when two or more people intend to cause a felony, those defendants could be found guilty of conspiracy. The defendants, then, have engaged in a joint enterprise or have acted to advance some common design or goal. When there was a common design and joint enterprise involved in the act, it was found that the act of one was the act of all. Therefore, each individual was liable for the damage done.

Imputing responsible to one defendant because of the actions of another, when these people acted in a joint enterprise or under a common design, applies under civil law to actions in tort law.

Two negligent defendants will rarely be liable for concerted action because of the lack of intent. While they may be liable for one or more intentional torts, concerted action is not frequently found in negligence cases.

Joint and Several Liability

A defendant is liable for the entire harm sustained by the plaintiff even if only his or her negligence combined with that of another defendant to produce the ultimate injury. If the acts or omissions of two or more individuals, acting simultaneously or in sequence, were the proximate cause of the injury to the plaintiff, they are both liable for the entire result. This is called **joint and several liability.** Each defendant is individually liable for the full extent of the harm proximately caused to the plaintiff.

For example, assume that Winston was a passenger in an automobile driven by Carlisle, which collided with a truck driven by Morton. Both Carlisle and Morton were negligent in their driving and the negligence of both contributed to the collision. As a result of the collision, Winston sustained serious injuries. The theory of joint and several liability would find both drivers, Carlisle and Morton, individually or jointly, liable to Winston for the full extent of the injury.

Contribution and Indemnity

A common issue facing joint tortfeasors in a negligence action is the sharing of the payment of any award to the plaintiff. Most states have statutory provisions for **contribution** among joint tortfeasors. The principle of contribution allows a defendant against whom a judgment has been entered to recoup a proportionate share of the judgment from any other tortfeasors who contributed to the injury. That multiple defendants will be liable for the award in damages will increase the likelihood that plaintiff will get full satisfaction of the award in damages (see Case in Point 4-8).

CASE IN POINT 4-8

Ambriz v. Kress

148 Cal. App. 3d 963 (Cal. App. 2d Dist. 1983)

How should damages be apportioned among joint tortfeasors? [...]

Here, we ponder a variation on this theme. Is it ever proper for a plaintiff, along with other solvent defendants, to share in the shortfall caused by an insolvent defendant? We too, are prepared to squarely answer the question. Yes...and no. [...]

This appeal is from a judgment for contribution that arose out of a cross-complaint for partial equitable indemnification against Annie Marie Ambriz, one of three plaintiffs in the initial action for negligence. That lawsuit concerned an accident which took place on October 20, 1974. Mrs. Ambriz was the driver. With her was her son Patlan. Her husband Jesus Ambriz observed the immediate aftermath of the accident which had occurred in front of the Ambriz residence. His cause of action was for emotional distress and loss of consortium. Other parties to the action were defendant and cross-complainant Larry Lynn McDowell who filed a cross-complaint for partial equitable indemnification against Mrs. Ambriz and defendant Kerry A. Kress.

The jury awarded damages to the three plaintiffs as follows: Mrs. Ambriz, $300,060; Patlan, $81,000; and Mr. Ambriz, $22,670. The jury apportioned responsibility among the parties by assessing percentages of comparative negligence as follows: Mrs. Ambriz, 20 percent; Kress, 70 percent; McDowell, 10 percent.

Kress carried minimum 15/30 financial liability insurance, but prior to trial his insurance carrier was in receivership. Mrs. Ambriz's insurer then paid $30,000 under the provision for uninsured motorist coverage for which it received a reimbursement of $15,000 from the California Insurance Guarantee Association. McDowell ultimately paid a total sum of $317,071.87 to the Ambriz plaintiffs on April 16, 1979. This sum included various cost bills but was $30,000 short because McDowell claimed a credit for the uninsured motorist proceeds. The trial court denied McDowell's motion to compel full satisfaction of judgment. This ruling was affirmed on appeal on May 27, 1980. On July 17, 1980, plaintiffs filed a full satisfaction of judgment.

On April 3, 1981, McDowell and his insurer, United Pacific/Reliance Insurance Company (hereinafter referred to collectively as McDowell) filed a motion for contribution against Mrs. Ambriz. He argued that since she was 20 percent negligent and McDowell was only 10 percent negligent, their proportionate responsibility for the 70 percent shortfall caused by the insolvency of Kress, vis-à-vis, plaintiffs Patlan and Mr. Ambriz, should be borne in a ratio of two to one. Therefore, he argued that in computing the percent of responsibility chargeable to Mrs. Ambriz for damages suffered by Patlan and Mr. Ambriz, she should be liable for two-thirds of the Kress deficit, plus her 20 percent of contributory negligence. The combined total to be borne by Mrs. Ambriz under McDowell's theory is $ 65,478.67, which equals 63 percent of the total damages awarded to Patlan and Mr. Ambriz. The trial court rendered judgment for contribution in the amounts requested by defendant McDowell.

[...]

In *Li*, our Supreme Court replaced the complete defense of contributory negligence with "pure" comparative negligence, "the fundamental purpose of which shall be to assign responsibility and liability for damage in direct proportion to the amount of negligence of each of the parties." (citation omitted) In *American Motorcycle Assn. v. Superior Court* (citation omitted), the Supreme Court held that *Li* did not signal the abandonment of joint and several liability of concurrent tortfeasors.

The court pointed out that even though it might be possible to assign percentages of relative culpability among negligent defendants, that does not suggest that each defendant's negligence is not a proximate cause of the entire indivisible injury to a plaintiff. The court reasoned that a plaintiff's recovery should only be diminished in proportion to his degree of fault for the accident. He should not, however, be forced to bear a portion of the loss of a financially insolvent defendant because "a plaintiff's negligence relates only to a failure to use due care for his own protection, while a defendant's negligence relates to a lack of due care for the safety of others." (citation omitted)

Mrs. Ambriz argues that the trial court is disregarding the principle enunciated in *American Motorcycle* that a plaintiff's recovery should not be reduced by an amount greater than the percentage of his or her own contributory negligence. What she fails to realize, however, is that her award is not diminished beyond her 20 percent share of the negligence. Her status entitles her to this award. Her status, however, vis-à-vis co-plaintiffs Patlan and Mr. Ambriz, is a different matter. In that role, she is not a plaintiff, but a cross-defendant.

[…] We note […] that *American Motorcycle* permits partial indemnity among concurrent tortfeasors on a comparative fault basis. "In *American Motorcycle* joint and several liability principles are cojoined with the concept of liability governed by proportionate fault to which is added the right of equitable contribution. These premises, so constellated, give form and outline for the next logical extension and application of these rules. An insolvent defendant's shortfall should be shared proportionately by the solvent defendants as though the insolvent or absent person had originally not participated." (citation omitted)

[…] This reasoning should apply to all defendants, including any cross-defendant who, fortuitously, happens to be a plaintiff. This approach satisfies the majority opinion in *American Motorcycle* by respecting the principle that a plaintiff is entitled to relief for indivisible injuries suffered as the result of the combined negligence of joint tortfeasors. It also addresses some of the concerns expressed in the dissent in *American Motorcycle* which decried the foisting of large percentages of fault onto a marginally negligent defendant.

The view of the landscape in the case at bench depends on one's perspective. Just as in the Escher lithograph, "Waterfall," water appears to flow uphill or downhill, depending upon how one looks at the lithograph at a particular moment, so here, Mrs. Ambriz is a plaintiff from one perspective, but she is also a cross-defendant from another. That she can be both is neither inconsistent nor paradoxical. She is a cross-defendant vis-à-vis her coplaintiffs, and must bear the burden of a shortfall caused by the insolvency of another defendant in direct proportion to her respective degree of culpability. (citation omitted) She is no less a cross-defendant merely because she is also a plaintiff. In many cases a litigant is a plaintiff only because he or she was the first to file a complaint. A defendant with a valid cross-complaint could just as easily have been the plaintiff. In the race to the courthouse a defendant should not be penalized because traffic was greater at his end of town.

Mrs. Ambriz contends that McDowell is barred from contribution because the cross-complaint was framed in terms of equitable indemnity. When the court in *American Motorcycle Assn. v. Superior Court,* (citation omitted) examined contribution and indemnity, it concluded that "the dichotomy between the two concepts is more formalistic than substantive." What McDowell seeks is partial indemnification or contribution among the solvent tortfeasors. The court in *American Motorcycle* concluded that in light of the principles enunciated in *Li*, equitable indemnity should be modified to permit partial indemnity among concurrent tortfeasors on a comparative fault basis.

Appellant further contends that the judgment for contribution is null and void because it purports to be in favor of a cross-complainant (United Pacific/Reliance Insurance Companies) and against the insurer of the cross-defendant, neither of whom were parties to the action. Further, she contends it is unenforceable because it orders payment of indefinite amounts which might arise from future litigation. The judgment specifically provides for recovery from Mrs. Ambriz. The judgment is not invalid because it correctly states that the insurer is liable for the insured's judgment, subject to the terms and limitations of the policy of insurance. (citation omitted) The provision in the judgment that refers to the possibility of additional recovery from Mrs. Ambriz's insurer for a "bad faith" failure to settle the contribution claim is not a judgment on a case yet to be tried. Mrs. Ambriz assigned to McDowell an inchoate claim for bad faith on the part of her insurer. (citation omitted) The judgment merely states that the assignment takes effect if in some future case it is determined that Mrs. Ambriz's insurer acted in bad faith. (citation omitted)

We further reject Mrs. Ambriz's contention that the judgment for contribution releases her from all liability.

[...] The judgment only acknowledges that McDowell agrees to limit his recovery to those sums he may recover from Mrs. Ambriz's insurance carrier. Such an arrangement between McDowell and Mrs. Ambriz is acceptable and legitimate under the law. (citation omitted)

[...]

The trial court properly apportioned costs in its judgment of contribution so that McDowell only received that portion attributable to Mrs. Ambriz's share of the costs of Patlan and Mr. Ambriz, a total of $616.31.

The judgment is affirmed.

Here, the court recognized that the recovery owed to the plaintiff could not be paid among all deemed responsible for damages. The plaintiff had also been found partially liable. When one of the parties to payment of the damages award could not pay, the plaintiff had to accept responsibility for a percentage of the shortfall proportional to the degree of liability. The court concluded that this apportionment recognized the degree to which the plaintiff was responsible for damages; if there was a shortfall, the plaintiff would proportionately lose an amount from the damages awarded.

Related to this concept is the principle of **indemnification,** which calls for a full reimbursement of the party paying a judgment to the plaintiff. Indemnification differs from contribution in that it involves reimbursement for the *entire* amount of the award instead of a proportionate *share* of the award. Indemnification can arise in situations involving the concept of vicarious liability (see vicariously liability, Chapter 14), where an employer would reimburse an employee for paying damages from an accident that occurred while the employee was working, and is often a matter of contract between parties.

Survival Actions and Wrongful Death

The English common law contained three principles that materially affected the ability to maintain an action for negligence involving a death. Those rules provided the following:

- A defendant's death terminated the right of the plaintiff to proceed.
- The plaintiff's death before any recovery terminated the cause of action.
- Relatives of a deceased plaintiff-victim of a tort had no cause of action for loss of support and affection.

The principles terminating the right of recovery with the death of either the plaintiff or the defendant often produced great hardship upon survivors. States sought to minimize this grave outcome by enacting **wrongful death statutes** (see box below).

WRONGFUL DEATH STATUTES

Wrongful death statutes create a new action in favor of certain beneficiaries who suffer from another's death as a result of a tort.

Dobbs, *The Law of Torts* §294 (2000)

These laws work to overcome the effects of a tragedy that appears to threaten the entire integrity of the family as a unit (see Case in Point 4-9).

CASE IN POINT 4-9

Ly v. State of Louisiana

633 So. 2d 197 (La.App. 1 Cir. 1993)

This suit arises out of a vehicular collision which resulted in the deaths of Phat Duong and his wife, Ha Xu Ly. Plaintiffs herein are Hung Chi "Tim" Ly, the major son of the decedents, and [...] the decedents' minor children, Oanh Duong, Nga Duong, Chau Duong, Quy Duong, and John Duong. [...]

The accident occurred on August 14, 1990, at approximately 5:10 a.m., on Interstate 10 in Baton Rouge, Louisiana. This portion of I-10 is a three-lane interstate with a one percent upgrade or incline. At the time of the accident, it was dark outside, but this section of I-10 was lit by continuous street lights. The posted maximum speed limit on the portion of I-10 involved in this accident is fifty-five miles per hour. Decedents' 1983 Chevrolet Malibu was stalled in the eastbound center lane of travel. It was later determined that the Duong vehicle had a faulty ignition coil which, when moved or vibrated slightly, could cause the car to stall. Decedents had purchased this vehicle about one week prior to the accident and were not aware of the defect.

Louisiana State Trooper Glynn Delatte was on duty at the time of the collision. He had begun a twelve-hour shift at 6:30 p.m. on the evening of August 13, 1990. At approximately 5:00 a.m. on August 14, 1990, as he neared the end of his shift, Trooper Delatte was driving to the east bank of the Mississippi River in his 1989 Chevrolet Caprice trooper's vehicle, headed either to the troop headquarters or his home. As he traveled eastbound on I-10, Delatte moved into the center lane of travel behind a vehicle driven by Ronnie Andrus.

According to Trooper Delatte, he was traveling a distance of approximately 100 feet or eight or nine car lengths behind the Andrus vehicle when he observed the Andrus vehicle swerve to the right. Delatte testified that his immediate reaction was to focus on what the Andrus vehicle was doing. Delatte stated he then saw an object in his lane of travel and immediately swerved to the left. After moving his vehicle to the left, he applied his brakes and began to skid approximately thirty-nine feet from the decedents' vehicle. The front right half of Delatte's vehicle eventually collided with the rear left half of the Duong vehicle. The parties stipulated that Trooper Delatte was driving at a rate of speed in excess of the legal maximum allowed at this portion of the interstate.

Delatte's vehicle veered to the left after colliding with decedents' vehicle, striking and riding up onto the left retaining wall of I-10. His vehicle traveled 162 feet on the retaining wall before coming to rest. Delatte suffered only minor injuries.

After the initial impact, the decedents' vehicle was propelled into the right retaining wall. At some point after the initial collision, the Duong vehicle burst into flames and was completely consumed. Ha Xu Ly was seated in the driver's seat at the time of the collision, and was pronounced dead at the scene. At the time of the impact, her husband, Phat Duong, was not in the car.

Duong had been standing on the driver's side of the Duong vehicle, and was thrown approximately 149 feet as a result of the collision. Duong suffered a traumatic amputation of one of his legs and underwent numerous surgeries in the two weeks following the accident. However, on the fourteenth day after the collision, Phat Duong died while hospitalized in the Intensive Care Unit at Baton Rouge General Hospital.

On October 16, 1990, suit was filed by Hung Chi "Tim" Ly, individually (as the major child of the decedents) and as representative of the estate of decedents, and City National Bank of Baton Rouge, as tutor of the decedents' five minor children, against Delatte and his employer, the State Police. [...]

After a four-day bench trial of the principal demand, the trial court concluded that both the decedents and Trooper Delatte were negligent and apportioned fault at two-thirds to the decedents and one-third to Trooper Delatte. The court also awarded several categories of damages to the plaintiffs. The court awarded $200,000.00 for the survival action of Phat Duong, consisting of $150,000.00 for pain and suffering, $25,000.00 for loss of love, affection and consortium for the death of his wife, and $25,000.00 for loss of future income. The court also awarded plaintiffs $55,645.70 for medical expenses incurred by Phat Duong prior to his death. The court awarded $125,000.00 for the survival action of Ha Xu Ly, consisting of $50,000.00 for pain and suffering prior to death, and $75,000.00 for loss of future income. The court further awarded $325,000.00 to plaintiff, Hung Chi "Tim" Ly, consisting of $225,000.00 for loss of love and affection from his mother, and $100,000.00 for loss of love and affection from his father; $525,000.00 for each of the five minor children, consisting of $300,000.00 for each child for loss of love and affection from their mother, and $225,000.00 for each child for loss of love and affection from their father. These damages totaled $3,330,645.70, for which defendants were held liable for one-third.

Defendants also challenge as excessive the awards for the loss of love and affection of their parents. "Tim," who was nineteen years old at the time of trial, was awarded $100,000.00 for the loss of his father and $225,000.00 for the loss of his mother. The five minor children, Oanh (who was thirteen years old at the time of trial); Nga, (eleven years old); Chau, (ten years old); Quy, (seven years old); and John, (four years old), were each awarded $225,000.00 for the loss of their father and $300,000.00 for the loss of their mother.

The facts of this case are especially tragic. The Duong family immigrated to the United States approximately four to five years before the accident. Only the youngest child, John, was born in the United States. Phat did not speak English, and Ha spoke very limited English. The evidence adduced at trial indicates that the family was very close-knit, undoubtedly due to the fact that they were of a different culture and had no relatives living in this state. The children are now being raised by an American couple.

Brandt Hardy, a therapist, had been counseling the children and opined that the children's loss is compounded by the fact that both parents died within a two-week span, and by the type of accident involved. Moreover, the tragedy and loss are exacerbated because the children are of a different culture.

We agree with the trial court that "the loss when you lose both parents should be greater per parent because when you have lost one parent, at least you have somebody else to sympathize and get through your grief with." Moreover, because the children are of a different culture, their feeling of separation was established at trial as being pronounced. While these awards may be on the high side, after considering the trauma sustained by these children as a result of the double loss they suffered in this single disaster, and considering their particular circumstances, we cannot conclude that the trial court abused its much discretion in making these awards.

[...]

We conclude that each child could have brought suit separately for their wrongful death actions, thereby entitling each to a separate legal cap. Each party's demand for enforcement of a legal right is regarded as a separate action which may be cumulated in a single suit where there is a community of interest, each action is within the jurisdiction of the court and in the proper venue, and all actions are mutually consistent and employ the same form of procedure. (citation omitted) The mere fact that all actions were brought together should not serve to penalize plaintiffs. Each child has a separate cause of action against defendants as a result of the child's loss of his or her parents.

[...]

This assignment of error lacks merit.

[...]

AFFIRMED.

While the law in Louisiana caps damages that parties can recover when suing the state, each injured party could receive damages to that cap. It did not matter that each lawsuit by each surviving child for the death of their parents arose out of the same accident. Each suffered, each had a separate claim, and each claim was subject to the cap. The cap would not apply, then, to the children's claims as if they had filed one suit, as a group.

Today, most jurisdictions have also enacted **survival statutes** that allow for the survival of a negligence action after the death of the plaintiff. These statutes are compensatory in nature for the loss of the decedent's support and affection.

Both types of statutes vary greatly as to the torts covered and the parties affected. The paralegal student must carefully review applicable state statutes to determine the extent of coverage.

KEY TERMS

SUMMARY

The issues related to the proof of a claim for negligence arise once the necessary elements exist: duty, breach, proximate cause, and damages. Yet, proof preponderance of the evidence, on each element, depends upon applying the rules of evidence that govern the presentation of the information a trier of fact needs to determine whether liability has arisen. While the standard of the ordinary reasonable person remains unchanged as the fundamental fact to be proven by competent evidence, every injury will not necessarily result in a valid action for negligence. Issues may exist, such as whether a statute changes the standard of care, the function of the court as opposed to the jury, the doctrine of *res ipsa loquitur*, the issues related to multiple tortfeasors, and the survivability of actions involving a death. Only after a court reviews each of these issues can a defendant then present evidence on the availability of potential defenses.

CONCEPT REVIEW QUESTIONS

1. What is legal proof?
2. Discuss the distinction between fact and opinion.
3. Distinguish the standard of proof in a civil case from that in a criminal case.
4. What is the doctrine of unavoidable accident?
5. Discuss the degree of negligence that must be proven by a preponderance of the evidence in an action for negligence.
6. What are the functions of the court and the jury in an action for negligence?
7. Define *res ipsa loquitur*.
8. What is the principle underlying joint and several liability?
9. Discuss the distinction between contribution and indemnification.
10. What is the purpose of a wrongful death statute?

CRITICAL THINKING APPLICATIONS

1. A driver is operating an automobile within the legal rules of the road. Suffering a heart attack, the driver loses control of the car and hits a pedestrian. The pedestrian sues the driver for negligence, claiming the defendant's failure to meet the care of duty when driving an automobile was breached and that such a breach caused the pedestrian's injuries. During trial, the driver

claims that he should pay no damages because the heart attack was an act of God. Do you agree with that argument? Does your answer change if this is the driver's second heart attack?

2. Jonni and Bob engage in an impromptu race on an interstate highway. Remaining abreast of one another while driving between 95 and 100 mph, they come over a hill to see that there's a car in Jonni's path, operating at the speed limit. Jonni jams on the brakes but loses control of his car and rams the car in his lane. Bob sees this and is able to slow down, then stop his car without hitting either of the two cars. Bob calls for medical help and for the police. The victims in the car that Jonni hit sue Jonni for damages. They also sue Bob, who files a motion to dismiss on the grounds that since he did not hit their automobile, he should not be liable for damages. How will a court likely rule?

3. A truck driver is operating a brand-new eighteen-wheel tractor-trailer rig at a lawful speed on an interstate highway. The spare tire under the rig breaks free, bounces, then caroms into a nearby subcompact car which was also moving at a lawful rate of speed. The driver of the subcompact car sues the truck driver, the truck driver's employer, and the owner of the leased eighteen-wheel rig for negligence in securing the spare tire properly. At trial, evidence is introduced that the cradle holding the spare tire showed no signs of damage or wear. The truck driver testified that chains had been wrapped around the spare tire to hold it even tighter to the cradle. After the lawyer for the car driver has presented all the evidence used to support the car driver's case, counsel for defendant moved for dismissal on the grounds that the plaintiff had failed to show sufficient evidence that the defendants breached a duty of care. Would you expect the court to grant this motion? Why or why not?

4. During a bar fight, a defendant smashes a victim in the face. Between the testimony of the bartender and evidence that indicates that the victim had been hit in the face by someone else and the bits of glass found on the victim's clothing, the defendant is convicted of assault and battery. The victim now civilly sues for damages. What are the victim's chances for winning in a civil trial? Why?

5. A farmer's silo is filled with a fall harvest of produce. A tornado strikes, knocking the silo onto a car parked beside the farmhouse; the owner of the car was interested in buying fresh milk. There is no historical record that tornadoes occur in that part of the state. The driver sues. The farmer files a claim with his insurance company under a general liability policy, to pay for the cost of replacing the car. The insurance company refuses to pay on the grounds that since this kind of storm has never happened before, it should not have to make payment under the insurance policy. The driver sues the farmer and the farmer joins the insurance company in the suit, to pay for the damages. Is the farmer liable for damages to the car's driver due to a cause of action in negligence?

6. A Thanksgiving Day parade float, covered with paper flowers, is being towed back to its garage in accordance with local traffic laws. Suddenly, the power goes out on a set of traffic lights. The power shortage knocked out a neon sign that indicates, when it's blinking, that there were traffic lights around a sharp corner. The driver of a car, who is unfamiliar with the area, sees the sign but notes that it is not blinking. Coming around the corner, the driver hits the tail-end of the float; sparks fly and the float is

suddenly engulfed in flames. The owner of the float sues the driver who replies that the accident was unavoidable and that he should not be held liable. What's the likelihood of a court's dismissing the civil suit against the driver of the car?

7. For the first time in 100 years, hurricane-force winds blow through a coastal community. High power transmission lines are buffeted until they fall. The sputtering wires sets off a brush fire that destroys five acres of land, including one house. The house's owners sue the power company. Would you recommend to the power company that they claim an act of God relieves them of liability? Whether you would or not, explain to the power company whether the occurrence of these unusually strong winds frees it from liability.

8. Jamal, a co-owner of a small hotel, oversees the maintenance of the hotel while Inga, the other co-owner, makes sure that accounts are maintained and bills are paid. Having received complaints from guests that the water doesn't get hot enough when the guests are taking a shower, Jamal contacts Fremont, a plumber who has done work for the hotel. Fremont looks to discover that the water heater is rated as safe up to 3000 watts; the current heating coil draws 2500 watts. Fremont removes the old coil and installs one that draws 3000 watts. Two days later, the water heater explodes, causing a fire. One guest is killed from inhaling smoke from the fire. The guest's survivors sue the hotel under a theory of *res ipsa loquitur*. Jamal and Inga file a motion to dismiss on the grounds that it is not they but the manufacturer of the water heater who is the proper party to sue. Do you think the court will grant the motion? Why or why not?

SKILL-BUILDING APPLICATION

On the morning of April 3, 2000, a thunderstorm occurred near Lake Saorbannes in Union County, Minn. At 6 a.m., an intense lightning strike from the storm destroyed the electrical transformer serving the lake home of Joe and Sara Hanks, causing a fire that destroyed their home. E-nergy, Inc. ("E-nergy") owned and maintained a transformer and lightning arrester on a pole 90 feet from the plaintiffs' home. The lightning arrester (also known as a surge arrester), bolted to the transformer, diverts high voltage surges into the ground.

All agreed that the specific surge suppressor was the appropriate protection when lightning struck (about twice a year) and when there were surges along the distribution lines. Lightning arresters can fail because of missing internal parts (some can erode over time as a result of numerous strikes), design flaws, or poor ground connections. This particular transformer had been installed in 1996. An E-nergy engineering manual states notes that very high current strikes or a strike directly to the lightning arrester could destroy the transformer. E-nergy never received complaints about it or requests for repairs. E-nergy employees had received instructions to inspect equipment visually when performing their regular duties; there were no specific instructions to inspect the transformers.

On April 8, E-nergy employees visited the Hanks home and found that the bottom of the transformer's steel tank had been blown out, damage so severe that it was rarely seen. No damage; of the transformer showed that the lightning arrester apparently sustained no damage; E-nergy didn't keep the lightning arrester after its worker installed a new transformer when the Hanks house was rebuilt. E-nergy's investigator, who was on the scene, made no effort to preserve the lightning arrester.

Do the Hankses have a cause of action? Why or why not? What difficulties seem likely, based upon what's mentioned in this chapter, for the Hankses if they do have a cause of action?

No man's error becomes his own Law; nor
obliges him to persist in it.

—*Thomas Hobbes*, Leviathan *(1650)*

Defenses to Negligence | CHAPTER 5

The plaintiff has the burden of proving—by a preponderance of the evidence—duty, breach of duty, causation, and damages. Yet the mere negligence of the defendant may prove insufficient for the plaintiff to win the case. The defendant can offer a legal defense that diminishes or prevents recovery by the plaintiff. If the plaintiff contributes to the eventual injury, any damages award may be reduced according to the degree the plaintiff contributed to the injury and, in some instances, may entirely defeat the plaintiff's claim. Previous chapters focused on the plaintiff's actions in creating an action for negligence. This chapter addresses defenses at law available to a defendant as well as when a plaintiff's acts or omissions may reduce or eliminate any award for damages.

CHAPTER TOPICS

1. Contributory Negligence
2. Comparative Negligence
3. Assumption of Risk

OBJECTIVES

After completing this chapter, you will be able to:

1. Understand the defense of contributory negligence.

2. Evaluate the concept of last clear chance as a negligence defense.

3. Discuss comparative negligence as a defense to a negligence action.

4. Distinguish assumption of risk from the other negligence defenses.

Defendant may face liability for breaching a duty of care to a foreseeable victim. Society recognizes that if the victim had a role in producing the injury, that victim may not receive all damages. Sometimes, the plaintiff's actions may alter or negate an award in damages.

■ CONTRIBUTORY NEGLIGENCE

The plaintiff's conduct may provide a partial or complete defense to an action for negligence so that if the plaintiff fails to act to protect herself or himself, the defendant may have a defense.

Contributory negligence focuses on the plaintiff's acts or omissions and imposes a duty to care for one's own safety. The *Restatement (Second) of Torts* defines contributory negligence precisely (see box below):

CONTRIBUTORY NEGLIGENCE DEFINED

Contributory negligence is conduct on the part of the plaintiff which falls below the standard to which he should conform for his own protection, and which is a legally contributing cause co-operating with the negligence of the defendant in bringing about the plaintiff's harm.

Restatement (Second) of Torts §463 (1965)

Application of this defense focuses on the issue of whether the plaintiff's conduct conformed to that of an ordinarily reasonable person under the same or similar circumstances. A person walking around a burning building, while firefighters battle the blaze, cannot expect to sue the building's owners successfully for having tripped over a fire hose.

Bar to Action

A defense of contributory negligence, as a complete **bar to action** by the plaintiff, ends the plaintiff's claim. Once a plaintiff has provided, by a preponderance of the evidence, each element of a claim for negligence (and so, establishes a *prima facie* case), the defendant's successful presentation of evidence of the plaintiff's contributory negligence may defeat the plaintiff's case. Consider the use of the defense in the case of *Brown v. Piggly-Wiggly* (see Case in Point 5-1).

 CASE IN POINT 5-1

Brown v. Piggly-Wiggly Stores
454 So.2d 1370 (Ala. 1984)

The plaintiff, Frank C. Brown, appeals from a summary judgment entered against him in favor of Piggly-Wiggly Stores and Kenny Poffenbarger in a personal injury suit. We affirm.

The facts are as follows: On February 10, 1983, Brown went shopping at the Piggly-Wiggly store located in Citronelle, Alabama. After purchasing his groceries and placing them in his pickup truck, Brown proceeded to return his shopping cart to the area designated for cart returns. Enroute, Brown bumped a motorcycle which had been parked on the sidewalk approximately thirty-two feet from the store entrance. The motorcycle fell on Brown and broke his leg.

The motorcycle was owned by one of the defendants, Kenny Poffenbarger, who was employed by the Piggly-Wiggly store as a second assistant manager. The store's manager, Craig McLendon, had authorized Poffenbarger to park his motorcycle on the sidewalk in front of the store.

Brown filed suit [...] alleging that Poffenbarger, with Piggly-Wiggly's authorization, had negligently parked his vehicle so as to create an unsafe and dangerous condition which caused Brown's injury. [...]

The second issue raised by Brown concerns whether the trial court properly entered summary judgment in favor of Piggly-Wiggly and Poffenbarger. Our review must consider whether the moving parties have shown that there is no genuine issue of material fact and that they are entitled to a judgment as a matter of law [...] After reviewing the record in its entirety, we conclude that the defendants have met their burden.

Under the laws of Alabama, a plaintiff cannot recover in a negligence suit where plaintiff's own negligence is shown to have proximately contributed to his damage, notwithstanding a showing of negligence on the part of the defendant. Of course, this principle applies only where contributory negligence has been raised as an affirmative defense....

In order to prove contributory negligence, the defendant must show that the party charged: (1) had knowledge of the condition; (2) had an appreciation of the danger under the surrounding circumstances; and (3) failed to exercise reasonable care, by placing himself in the way of danger....

The question of contributory negligence is normally one for the jury. However, where the facts are such that all reasonable men must reach the same conclusion, contributory negligence may be found as a matter of law.... This is such a case.

By all accounts, the motorcycle in question was in plain view, both from within and without the store. It was parked approximately two feet from the store front on a sidewalk which was nine feet wide. Brown had already walked past the vehicle once, moments before the accident. By his own admission, the motorcycle fell on him only after he had bumped it. The record is devoid of any evidence indicating that Brown bumped the motorcycle for any reason other than his own inattention. We find that reasonable men could reach no other conclusion than that: (1) Brown knew the motorcycle was parked by the wall; (2) Brown appreciated the danger inherent in a two-wheeled vehicle resting on a kickstand, specifically, that it may fall if disturbed; and (3) Brown nevertheless put himself in the way of the danger by carelessly bumping the motorcycle. Therefore [...] we hold that Brown's injuries were the proximate result of his failure to exercise reasonable care when he bumped a parked motorcycle. It follows that there was no genuine issue as to a material fact and summary judgment was properly entered against Brown.... Accordingly, the judgment of the trial court is due to be, and it is hereby, affirmed.

Since the plaintiff in this case knew about the motorcycle, he was precluded from recovery of damages suffered because he could have avoided having the motorcycle fall on him.

Or consider that one evening Larissa bicycles without lights into a busy intersection and fails to stop at the red stop sign. She is struck and injured by an automobile driven by Dusty. Dusty had been driving his automobile without lights on and at an excessive rate of speed. A court may find that Dusty was negligent in the operation of his automobile, but may bar any recovery by Larissa because of her negligence in bicycling at night without lights and failing to stop when required. In such a case, Larissa would recover nothing from Dusty.

Courts justify application of this policy primarily when allowing the plaintiff to recover damages that would be unwarranted or even unconscionable. The paralegal student must research local law to determine whether a particular jurisdiction still provides for a court's use of this doctrine.

Distinguished from Negligence

Negligence involves a duty toward another person, while contributory negligence involves the conduct of the plaintiff creating an undue risk of harm to self. As Professor Keeton points out, it is unfortunate that contributory negligence uses the term *negligence* at all. A more accurate phrasing would be to refer to the defense as *contributory fault*:

CONTRIBUTORY FAULT

Negligence as it is commonly understood is conduct which creates an undue risk of harm to others. Contributory negligence is conduct which involves an undue risk of harm to the actor himself. Negligence requires a duty, an obligation of conduct to another person. Contributory negligence involves no duty, unless we are to be so ingenious as to say that the plaintiff is under an obligation to protect the defendant against liability for the consequences of the plaintiff's own negligence.

W. Page Keeton et al., *Prosser & Keeton on the Law of Torts* §65 at 453 (5th ed. 1984)

Yet, contributory negligence continues to be measured in exactly the same terms as ordinary negligence, since application of the doctrine looks equally at the negligence of either the defendant or the plaintiff. In the example above, Dusty still has a duty of care to operate the car legally and safely no matter what Larissa does. It would seem more likely that Dusty has a greater duty to act with care since negligence driving the car could produce greater injury.

Role of Causation

To win a cause of action in negligence, the plaintiff has to show that the defendant's breach of a duty of care proximately caused the plaintiff's injuries. Applying the doctrine of contributory negligence would mean that any action by the plaintiff that contributed to proximately causing the injury would mean the plaintiff should not receive any recovery. It might seem that any contribution, no matter how slight, would bar the plaintiff's action. Most courts, however, avoid applying this doctrine strictly by ruling that the plaintiff's contributory negligence had to be a substantial factor in causing the injury. That way, courts can avoid denying recovery even when a plaintiff's actions contributed, only slightly, like five percent, to causing the negligence.

Further, the injury to the plaintiff must have been clearly foreseeable for the defense of contributory negligence to operate, according to the principles of the doctrine of proximate cause discussed in Chapter 3. In the *Palsgraf* case, the court ruled that Mrs. Palsgraf was not a foreseeable plaintiff when the train worker pushed a passenger into a crowded train, and the package of fireworks that the passenger carried in a brown paper package fell so that the fireworks went off, shook the subway platform, and caused a scale to fall on Mrs. Palsgraf.

Consider the facts of *Garreans* in applying the principles of proximate cause, where twelve-year-old boys dropped lit firecrackers into a drum of flammable liquid (Case in Point 5-2).

CASE IN POINT 5-2

Garreans v. City of Omaha

216 Neb. 487 (1984)

This is an action under the Nebraska Political Subdivisions Tort Claims Act against the City of Omaha, Nebraska, to recover damages for the injuries sustained by the plaintiffs, John Garreans, Jr. and Vince Hartline, in an explosion which occurred at N.P. Dodge Park on July 5, 1980, while the plaintiffs were visiting with their grandparents, Ray and Evelyn Stoops, at the park. The petition included a second cause of action for the medical expenses incurred by the parents of the plaintiffs as a result of the explosion. At the time of the accident both plaintiffs were 12 years of age. The action was brought by their fathers as the next friends of the plaintiffs. The defendant has raised no issue in this court concerning joinder.

The evidence shows that on July 3, 1980, Ray and Evelyn Stoops entered N.P. Dodge Park in Omaha, Nebraska, with their camper, intending to camp in the park over the 3-day holiday. Evelyn Stoops paid a $10.50 fee at the concessionaire's office for the use of camper pad No. 25 for the 3-day period. Electrical service was provided at that pad. While they were setting up camp, the Stoopses noticed a black, 55-gallon drum nearby. The black drum was in addition to a trash barrel at the pad, which was a 55-gallon drum from which the top had been removed. Trash barrels, which consisted of 55-gallon drums from which the tops or lids had been removed, were distributed throughout the park, including the camping area. These drums were painted various colors and were labeled "TRASH" on the side.

Printing or lettering on the side of the black drum indicated that it had contained an antifreeze compound. A red or orange label, approximately 4 inches square, was affixed to the top of the drum. The label bore the legend "Flammable Liquid" printed below a representation of a fire or flames.

The lid or top of the black drum was intact, and the drum was closed except for a small opening, approximately 1 inch in diameter, from which a plug had been removed. There is no evidence that the city placed the black drum in the park, and a search of city records showed that the city had not purchased the black drum. The plaintiffs contended that the city was negligent in failing to remove the drum from the park.

On July 5, 1980, the plaintiffs entered the park to visit with their grandparents at camper pad No. 25. In accordance with park policy, no admission fee was charged them. Both boys had been given firecrackers by their fathers. The boys used a cigarette lighter to light the firecrackers, and used the black drum as a shelf for their activities. The explosion occurred when they dropped a lighted firecracker into the black drum through the 1-inch hole in the lid. The drum exploded, spraying flammable liquid on the boys. John received severe burns on his lower extremities. Vince suffered injuries to his nose and arm, and was also burned.

The trial court found that the city had failed to properly supervise the area around camper pad No. 25; had failed to observe, inspect, and remove the 55-gallon drum; had failed to warn the public of the dangerous nature of the drum; was guilty of willful negligence; and that the plaintiffs were not contributorily negligent.

[...]

An actor is contributorily negligent if he breaches the duty imposed upon him by law to protect himself from injury; if his actions concur and cooperate with actionable negligence of the defendant; and if his actions contribute to his injuries as a proximate cause [...] A child is required to exercise that degree of care which a person of that age would naturally and ordinarily use in the same situation under the same circumstances [...]

Although we have concluded that no "willful or malicious" negligence existed on the part of the city, we believe the evidence in this case shows that the plaintiffs were contributorily negligent sufficient to bar their recovery as a matter of law. The finding of the trial court to the contrary was clearly wrong.

The use of firecrackers in the city of Omaha and within the park was prohibited by ordinance, as well as by park regulation. The plaintiffs had been warned by their parents that fireworks were dangerous and that they should be careful when using them. The plaintiffs testified that they were aware of the danger involved in using fireworks. The degree of care required increases when an actor is dealing with a dangerous activity such as exploding firecrackers. Despite these warnings, the evidence is that the plaintiffs were lighting firecrackers above the opening in the drum and dropping lighted firecrackers into the drum.

Although there is conflicting testimony with regard to whether the boys noticed the "flammable" marking on the drum, the label was plainly visible, and the plaintiffs testified that they understood what the term "flammable" meant. In the exercise of proper care the boys should have seen the warning label on the top of the drum upon which they were lighting firecrackers. Moreover, they should have known that dropping lighted firecrackers into the drum created an unreasonable risk of explosion.

The judgment of the district court is reversed and the cause remanded with directions to dismiss the petition.

Since the boys knew the drum contained a flammable liquid, they are precluded from recovery for injuries sustained when they dropped firecrackers in that drum.

Avoidable Consequences

The doctrine of avoidable consequences (see Chapter 3) is closely related to the issue of contributory negligence. This rule of law denies recovery for any damages that could have been averted by the plaintiff's exercise of reasonable conduct. The principle behind the doctrine of avoidable consequences is that the plaintiff must take proper care to protect his or her own interests. It can occur when an injured plaintiff who would reasonably require medical attention fails to obtain proper medical treatment. Any consequences attributable to the failure to obtain medical care could not form the basis of a claim for damages.

However, the doctrine of contributory negligence applies to acts or omissions *before* the injury, while the doctrine of avoidable consequences applies *after* any injury.

The court in the following case offers some insight (see Case in Point 5-3).

CASE IN POINT 5-3

Portman v. Clementina Company
147 Cal. App. 2d 651 (Cal. App. 1st Dist. 1957)

[...] The complaint alleges that the defendants, without procuring permission from the city and county of San Francisco, as required by city ordinances, dumped rock and dirt on Shafter Avenue, San Francisco, an unaccepted public street; that this interfered with the drainage customarily afforded by said street, with the result that plaintiff's premises were flooded and plaintiff was thereby damaged.

[...]

A general description of the area follows. Shafter Avenue runs east and west. The eleven hundred block is bounded on the east by Griffith Street and on the west by Hawes Street, both running north and south. The next street south of and running parallel to Shafter is Thomas Avenue. The dimensions of this block are 400 feet (on Shafter and Thomas) by 200 feet (on Griffith and Hawes). Larkin owned the entire block with the exception of a parcel having a frontage on Shafter of 87 1/2 feet and a depth of 100 feet. The building in which plaintiff conducted his business was on the westerly part of this parcel and had a frontage of 30 feet. One O'Neill conducted a general contracting business in a building on the easterly part of the same parcel. The distance from the easterly side of O'Neill's building to Griffith Street was 200 feet.

Plaintiff had been in possession of the premises occupied by him since 1946 or 1947. During the fall of 1951, Larkin directed Devincenzi and Clementina to dump fill on his property. Prior to this, surface water ran down Shafter Avenue from the west toward the east. There was a shallow ditch about one or two feet deep and about three or four feet wide running along the southerly side of Shafter Avenue, commencing at a point a few feet east of the O'Neill property and extending easterly to Griffith Street. This ditch helped to carry off the surface water. For the purpose of improving the access to the Larkin property, Devincenzi, with Larkin's knowledge and consent, also dumped fill on Shafter Avenue, thereby filling up the ditch and raising the grade of the street. As the result, when heavy rains fell on December 1, 1951, and thereafter, the surface waters backed up and flooded plaintiff's premises. The jury estimated his damages at $10,000.

[...]

The last point made by Larkin is that the judgment should be set aside under the so-called rule of 'avoidable consequences.' He argues that plaintiff could have easily avoided the flooding by taking steps to prevent it. Just how this could have been done is not clear but Larkin suggests that, inasmuch as O'Neill (who was on higher ground) put in a pump and a drain at a cost of only $150, plaintiff could have done something of the sort. Without passing upon the propriety of instructing on contributory negligence, it is a sufficient answer to this contention to point out that the jury was instructed that the plaintiff could not recover if he did not exercise reasonable care to avoid the damage to himself. The jury by its verdict found, by necessary implication, that plaintiff did exercise such reasonable care and this finding is amply supported by the record. It is true that there is a distinction between contributory negligence and avoidable consequences. Contributory negligence usually refers to conduct at and before the time of injury and avoidable consequences to conduct after the injury. However, under the facts of this case the concept would be the same as a practical matter because the first flood was the one which did the damage.

Larkin has also called attention to a number of instructions which he contends are conflicting and which must have confused the jury. We do not agree. It is true that the charge was a long one and undoubtedly could have been streamlined. But in essence this is a very simple case. The jury was correctly instructed on the fundamental issues and what plaintiff was required to prove in order to recover. We do not feel impelled to discuss each and every instruction and compare it with the others in order to justify our conclusion that the jury was not misled or confused. The verdict against Larkin was eminently fair and, to say the least, was not a miscarriage of justice either in the broad sense or in the sense of whether Larkin received a trial in accordance with the rules of law pertaining thereto.

[...]

Although the plaintiff could have eliminated any damages by having installed a pump, that would not prevent the plaintiff from recovery. The flooding happened after the defendant had dumped fill into a drainage canal, so the plaintiff could not clearly foresee that flooding would occur and cause damages to the plaintiff's property.

Knowledge of Peril

The doctrine of contributory negligence requires that the plaintiff should have known of the danger to which he or she was exposed, and failed to prevent injury. Conversely, the plaintiff will not be barred from by the doctrine of contributory negligence if he or she had no knowledge of the danger and could not anticipate the hazard that caused the injury. A plaintiff who dives into a swimming pool when the defendant pool owner has put in ten times the chlorine that is reasonably used to keep a pool clean will not be subject to the defense of contributory negligence of any burns suffered. Knowledge on the plaintiff's part is required to maintain a defense when filing a claim for damages because of contributory negligence.

When a sudden emergency denies a plaintiff the opportunity to evaluate the peril, the law will not strictly apply the ordinary reasonable person standard. Most jurisdictions will not apply the doctrine of contributory negligence if the plaintiff has no time for deliberation and so, failed to take the safest course of action. The courts will first consider the defendant's control of the circumstances before considering the plaintiff's contributory negligence (see Case in Point 5-4).

 CASE IN POINT 5-4

Evans v. General Explosives Company
293 Mo. 364 (1922)

This is an action for personal injuries received by plaintiff while in the employ of the defendant. [...]

The defendant is an incorporated company engaged in the manufacture of explosives at Carl Junction, Jasper County. The plaintiff, at the time he was injured, was a boy between seventeen and eighteen years of age and was working at a power wringer, which, as designated by defendant, is a centrifugal extractor for wringing clothes, but is used by the defendant in wringing the water from cotton in preparing the same for use in the manufacture of powder. It is described as a heavyload, high-speed machine, which, when in operation, is under great strain. It consists of a basket and an outside shell. The latter, with its legs and bearing base, is one solid casting, which, when installed, is bolted to the floor. The basket is intended to revolve inside of the shell; it has a cast iron bottom, with perforated brass mesh on its sides; inside of same there is a screen of about one hundred mesh to the inch, to retain the cotton and at the same time permit the forcing out of the water. When the machine is in operation, the basket makes from nine hundred to fourteen hundred revolutions per minute, with an average surface speed of seven thousand feet per minute. There were no knives or cogs in the wringer. When the pulp, consisting of cotton and water, was put into the basket, it was a mushy substance, which was completely dried after from two to four minutes operation of the wringer. There was a cover for the basket intended as a safeguard, but it was not in use when the plaintiff was hurt. The accident occurred July 3, 1919. Prior to that date plaintiff and one Woods had been performing general work around the plant for defendant, but had not been employed at the wringer; those who had been thus employed had quit. On the morning of the injury, as plaintiff testifies, he and Woods, after engaging in other work for about an hour, were directed by defendant's superintendent to operate the wringer. This is denied by the latter, but plaintiff's testimony in regard thereto was corroborated and the jury gave it credence rather than the statement of the superintendent. Thus directed, Woods and the plaintiff began to operate the wringer. When it was started by plaintiff, it commenced to wobble and he used his fingers to steady it. The heat of the basket, caused by its rapid revolutions, burned his fingers; and he picked up a chisel and in the effort to use it to steady the basket, the suction caused by its rapid revolution jerked his right arm entirely off of his body at the shoulder.

[...]

Finally, the contention is made that the demurrer should have been sustained on account of the use of the chisel by the plaintiff in steadying the operation of the wringer; that the defendant could not know that the plaintiff would use it for that purpose at the time he was injured, and that it should not be held liable for what it did not know and could not expect. The testimony shows that the defendant's superintendent saw those who had operated the wringer before the plaintiff, use the chisel for the same purpose it was used by him, and that it was so used by them every time they ran out a batch of cotton. In the exercise of ordinary care, the defendant, as represented by its superintendent, may be reasonably presumed to have known not only that the employees were likely to use the chisel, but that they were using it. This presumption, however, need not be invoked in the face of the fact that the superintendent had actual knowledge of the manner in which the chisel was used. A boy of the age of plaintiff, finding that the revolving basket burned his fingers as he attempted to steady it, would instinctively use anything at hand rather than his fingers. The superintendent's knowledge of the use that was being made of the chisel made it incumbent on him, if the use was dangerous, to warn the plaintiff of same. The plaintiff, not having been warned, in merely following the example set by others in the use of the chisel, was not guilty of such negligence as to preclude the submission of his case to the jury.

[...]

A plaintiff's knowledge of peril will not be sufficient to defeat his right of recovery unless the defective condition of the machinery is of so glaring a nature as to threaten immediate danger. (citation omitted)

[...]

Where the danger is concealed and is known to the employer but not to the employee, it is the duty of the former to notify the latter of its existence. A failure in this regard constitutes negligence as a matter of law. (citation omitted) [...] [O]nly one thing excuses a master from the duty to warn and instruct a young and inexperienced servant as to the hazards usually not comprehended by the inexperienced, and that the exception is found in cases wherein the person applying for employment holds himself out as capable of being able to perform the work with its attendant danger and as having a knowledge and comprehension of same. It is further held [...] that where the servant says nothing about his experience and the master knows nothing in regard thereto, if the servant is ignorant and inexperienced, there arises a duty to warn him of danger not obvious to one without experience. The defendant was not authorized in assuming that the plaintiff was experienced. There is no evidence that he held himself out as such. He was a school boy, working during vacation, and it was the duty of the defendant in putting him at the wringer to have warned him of the source from which danger might come in the operation of same, and the information given should be so explicit as to have enabled him to avoid injury. (citation omitted)

[...]

Finding no error authorizing a reversal, the judgment of the trial court is affirmed. [...]

While the plaintiff had used a chisel to steady the wringer as it spun the wet load of cotton, the plaintiff had not used the wringer before. More importantly, the defendant had seen the chisel used this way before and did nothing to install a permanent fix that would have steadied the wringer during operation.

Momentary Forgetfulness

Any individual may have a moment of temporary forgetfulness that may place him or her in a position of peril. Forgetfulness is not considered contributory negligence unless it constitutes a failure to exercise due care. Assume that defendant, a business owner, has neglected to remove a thin layer of ice that has formed on the sidewalk in front of defendant's business. If plaintiff is walking along that sidewalk, in front of defendant's business, and stops to greet another person, but resumes walking and slips and falls, defendant will not avoid liability because plaintiff had momentarily forgotten about the ice on the sidewalk. The doctrine of momentary forgetfulness states that forgetfulness is one factor in determining the plaintiff's contribution to the negligence.

The trier of fact must decide whether the plaintiff's own peril was due to mere momentary forgetfulness or to a breach of his or her own duty to avoid peril. The standard to be applied is that of the ordinary reasonable person. Consider the contributory negligence of the professional exterminator who fell down stairs that he had traversed on many occasions (see Case in Point 5-5).

CASE IN POINT 5-5

Hundt v. LaCrosse Grain Co., Inc.
446 N.E.2d 327 (Ind. 1983)

This case began when Everett Hundt, a professional exterminator, filed a complaint for damages as a result of a fall down the basement stairs in the office building of LaCrosse Grain Company in LaCrosse, Indiana....

The underlying facts of this action are not in dispute. Mr. Hundt and his son went to LaCrosse Grain Company on March 9, 1976, to do pest control work which involved spreading a chemical on rafters in a storage shed to discourage birds from being present and damaging the grain. After finishing this work, Hundt and his son went into the office building to wash up. Mr. Hundt had done pest extermination work for LaCrosse since 1955, and was thoroughly familiar with the office building and its facilities. On this occasion, Hundt entered the back door of the office building and then mistakenly opened the door leading to the basement rather than the washroom door. He stepped through the doorway and fell down the basement stairs through his own momentum. It was uncontradicted that the basement door was closed, the hallway was well lighted, and there were signs above two doors indicating the men's and ladies' washrooms. It was also uncontradicted that the basement door opened inward, there was no landing inside the door, and there was no handrail or bracing device beside the stairs. Hundt acknowledged at the trial that he knew where both the washroom and the basement were located and had been in these areas about 100 times during the twenty years he had visited the LaCrosse buildings. He also admitted that he was familiar with the fact that the basement door opened inward while the washroom door opened outward, and that the basement stairway had no landing or handrails. He also testified that he had never entered the building from the rear door before, but had previously always entered from the front....

This Court has consistently held that the basis for contributory negligence is conduct on the part of the plaintiff which falls below the standard to which he should conform for his own protection and safety. Lack of reasonable care that an ordinary man would exercise in like or similar circumstances is the factor upon which the presence or absence of negligence depends.... Further, it must be shown that the plaintiff's negligent act was a proximate cause of his injury and that he was actually aware of or should have appreciated the risks involved....

Accordingly, Indiana courts have found contributory negligence as a matter of law in cases in which the voluntary conduct of the plaintiff exposed him to imminent and obvious dangers which a reasonable man exercising due care for his own safety would have avoided....

Here, the fact is undisputed that the door to the stairway was closed, thus guarding that area.... Hundt was an adult and did not have any disability or limitation of perception. The hallway area where the basement and washroom doors were located was well lighted and the washroom doors were clearly marked. Hundt had been in the building and in both the washroom and basement on numerous prior occasions. He acknowledged that he was familiar with the fact that the basement door opened inward while the washroom door opened outward. In this case, the plaintiff was thoroughly familiar with the hallway area of the building and with the types of rooms and areas that were protected by the closed doors. The only conclusion which can be drawn from the facts in this case is that Hundt was disregarding an obviously known and appreciated danger by opening the closed door in such a manner as to preclude any opportunity to observe what was on the other side.

We find that the undisputed evidence establishes that Hundt was guilty of contributory negligence which was the proximate cause of his injury. Such negligence is contributory negligence as a matter of law under the circumstances of this case and for this reason the verdict of the jury is contrary to law.

The plaintiff claimed to have momentarily forgotten about the location of the stairs down which he fell. But the court did not accept that excuse because he had passed by them too often.

The doctrine of momentary forgetfulness gives the trier of fact the option to place the plaintiff's conduct in perspective within the test of reasonable care. It mitigates the harsh, "all or nothing" aspect of the contributory negligence principle.

Last Clear Chance

A mitigation of the doctrine of contributory negligence is found in the doctrine of **last clear chance.** This doctrine allows a plaintiff in a negligence action to recover regardless of his or her own negligence if the defendant had the last clear chance to avoid the injury. It has been called the *discovered peril doctrine* because it refers to a situation wherein the defendant had the last opportunity to discover the plaintiff's peril and avoid injury through reasonable care. A bartender throwing out a highly intoxicated patron into a cold winter's night would be liable if that patron passed out and died because of exposure to the cold.

This doctrine counteracts the defense of contributory negligence by providing the plaintiff with a response to that defense. Professor Dobbs concurs:

THE LAST CLEAR CHANCE DOCTRINE

A complicated exception to the contributory negligence defense was called the last clear chance doctrine. In these cases the plaintiff negligently put herself in danger from which she could not escape. The defendant then negligently caused harm to the helpless plaintiff. The salient fact was that the plaintiff could do nothing to save herself once she had put herself in danger, but that the defendant could have avoided injury by ordinary care. In such case, the plaintiff's earlier contributory negligence would be no bar.

Dobbs, *The Law of Torts* §200 (2000)

The doctrine arose in England in 1842 with the case of *Davies v. Mann*. In that case, the defendant's carriage struck an animal left tied in the highway by the plaintiff. The court found that the plaintiff could recover notwithstanding his own negligent act of leaving of the animal tied in the street. The defendant, by exercising reasonable care, could have avoided striking the animal. While the doctrine provides justice in some cases, the net result has been substantial confusion and lack of conformity in its application. One court might hold for the plaintiff whose child ran into the street when the parent's attention momentary shifted from the child; or for the defendant, where the parent knew the child liked to run into the street, thinking it was a game.

Two situations allow the uniform application of the doctrine of last clear chance:

- When the plaintiff is helpless; or
- When the plaintiff is inattentive of the peril.

Courts appreciate the nuanced difference between a plaintiff's inattentiveness and a plaintiff's helplessness (see Case in Point 5-6).

CASE IN POINT 5-6

Penn Harris Madison School Corporation v. Howard
861 N.E.2d 1190 (Ind. 2007)

Two decades ago, the Legislature abolished the harsh doctrine of "contributory negligence" by which a man or a woman, injured through the fault of another, was denied any recovery if he or she was even slightly at fault. However, the defense of contributory negligence remains available to government entities like public schools. This case requires our focus on this relatively dormant concept.

Background

David Howard attended Penn High School in the Penn Harris Madison School Corporation ("PHM"). Throughout high school, Howard helped his friend, Jon West, produce theatrical plays and build sets for those plays. West was a music teacher in a PHM elementary school.

During his senior year, Howard, age 17, helped West produce "Peter Pan" at the elementary school. Howard, who had experience rock climbing and rappelling, devised and constructed a pulley mechanism designed to allow the Peter Pan character to "fly" above the audience. Howard made the apparatus from a climbing harness, spring-hinged metal rings (carabiners), fabric webbing, a pulley, and a cable hung from the rafters. Howard himself tested the apparatus several times.

On the night of dress rehearsal, where a number of people were present, Howard climbed a ladder that West was holding and connected himself to the webbing through a loop on the back of the harness. Howard jumped from the ladder. The apparatus failed and Howard fell to the gym floor, suffering serious injuries to his face, spleen, hands, and wrists.

Howard's mother, individually and as his next friend, sued PHM, alleging its negligence caused Howard's injuries.
[...]

Discussion

Prior to 1985, Indiana common law recognized a defense of "contributory negligence" that barred recovery on a plaintiff's negligence claim if the plaintiff was even slightly at fault. In that year, the harsh rule of contributory negligence was substantially revised when a "modified form of comparative fault" took effect. (citation omitted) [footnote omitted.] Although the Legislature dictated that fault could be apportioned between the plaintiff and defendant in many situations, a plaintiff was still barred from recovery if the plaintiff's own fault was greater than fifty percent. (citation omitted). And the Legislature also specified that the provisions of the new comparative fault statute would not apply to governmental entities. (citation omitted) This exemption for governmental entities from comparative fault means that the common law contributory negligence principles apply when a governmental entity is the defendant in negligence litigation. (citation omitted) [footnote omitted]

In this case, the defendant PHM—a public school corporation and, therefore, a governmental entity—asserted the defense of contributory negligence: that it had no liability to Howard because he was at least slightly at fault for the injuries he suffered. As noted above, the jury found in Howard's favor and against the defendant school corporation.

There are three issues in this appeal—two raised by PHM, which is the appellant, and one by the plaintiffs, who are the appellees. First, PHM argues that the trial court's instruction to the jury on the standard of care to which it should hold Howard was too lenient. Second, PHM argues that the trial court should not have allowed the jury to impose liability on it under another common law tort rule, the doctrine of "last clear chance." Third, the plaintiffs argue that the trial court should have instructed the jury that the defense of contributory negligence was not available to PHM in these circumstances because of the special obligation of care that schools have for their pupils. We do not reach the plaintiffs' argument because we affirm the judgment of the trial court.

I

At the plaintiffs' request, the trial court instructed the jury that in deciding whether Howard was guilty of contributory negligence, it must determine whether he had exercised the "reasonable care [that] a person of like age, intelligence, and experience would ordinarily exercise under like or similar circumstances." (citation omitted) The Court of Appeals held that the trial court had committed reversible error in giving the instruction.

The Court of Appeals properly determined that the instruction given by the trial court was not a correct statement of Indiana law. Children over the age of 14, absent special circumstances, are chargeable with exercising the standard of care of an adult. [...]

The plaintiffs make no mention of any of these cases, either in their brief to the Court of Appeals or in their briefs to this Court. They contend instead that the instruction given by the trial court reflects the majority rule in other states and that Indiana's approach is "an obvious hypocrisy," because children over the age of 14 are not treated as adults in certain other areas of Indiana law. (citation omitted) These are respectable arguments but, particularly in the absence of any attempt to distinguish controlling precedent and its policy underpinnings, they are unavailing.

[W]e [have] addressed the standard of care for individuals with mental disabilities. A number of the policy reasons supporting the reasonable person standard adopted in that context also support holding individuals over the age of 14, absent special circumstances, to the standard of care of an adult. First, it provides an incentive to those responsible for children and interested in their estates to prevent harm and restrain those who are potentially dangerous. Second, it avoids the administrative problems involved in courts and juries attempting to identify and assess what a "reasonable person of like age, intelligence, and experience under the circumstances" would do. And third, it imposes on individuals over 14 years of age the cost of the damage they cause if they engage in dangerous activities. (citation omitted).

At bottom, the standard of care we impose on individuals over the age of 14 is a neutral principle of law, operating irrespective of whether the child is plaintiff (as here), defendant (e.g., a 14-year-old or 16-year-old driver), or even a non-party. Howard would be held to this standard of care whether he was plaintiff or defendant—and whether the case was being tried under comparative fault or contributory negligence. We believe that it is the harshness of the rule of contributory negligence, not this neutral standard of care, that imposes the greatest hardship on Howard in this case.

Howard was 17 years old at the time he was injured. As such, the law charged him with exercising the standard of care of an adult, not that of "a person of like age." [footnote omitted] It was error for the trial court to give the jury an incorrect instruction on the law. [...]

The offending instruction asked the jury to determine whether Howard exercised the "reasonable care [that] a person of like age, intelligence, and experience would ordinarily exercise under like or similar circumstances." (citation omitted) Throughout this case, PHM's argument has been that Howard was "an exceptional young man," Appellant's Br. at 35, indeed, that he had been "described by virtually ever[y] witness as being intelligent, mature, and responsible," (citation omitted) Given the way "virtually every witness" and PHM itself characterized Howard, we believe that the jury would have considered the reasonable care that a person of like age, intelligence, and experience—a person who was "an exceptional young man, intelligent, mature, and responsible"—would ordinarily exercise under "like or similar circumstances" to be that of an adult. As this is the standard that the law imposes, we find the error in giving the instruction here to have been harmless.

II

At the plaintiffs' request, the trial court instructed the jury that it could find in favor of Howard, notwithstanding contributory negligence on his part, if the plaintiffs established entitlement to recovery under the "last clear chance" doctrine. [...] The doctrine of last clear chance, as a general proposition, provides that the contributory negligence of a plaintiff does not prevent recovery by that plaintiff for the negligence and injuries caused by the defendant if the defendant by exercising reasonable care might have avoided injuring the plaintiff. In the heyday of contributory negligence, litigation over the applicability of last clear chance was frequent and intense. [footnote omitted] But in the world of comparative fault, where the relative fault of plaintiff and defendant are assessed, the last clear chance doctrine, once the subject of intense debate as to its contours, has been much less at issue during the past two decades.

The Court of Appeals faithfully applied the last clear chance doctrine in this case. It properly noted that Howard had the burden of proving, among other elements, that the defendant "had the last opportunity through the exercise of reasonable care to avoid the injury." (citation omitted). It quoted controlling authority that "the defendant ... must have the last clear chance to avoid the injury to the plaintiff." (citation omitted) And it also quoted one of its own cases for the proposition that no jury instruction on last clear chance should be given if "the undisputed evidence shows that the opportunity of the plaintiff to avoid the injury was as late or later than that of the defendant." (citation omitted).

We think it highly likely that had the Legislature not adopted comparative fault and the contributory negligence regime continued apace, this Court would have adopted the formulation of the last clear chance doctrine embodied in §§479 and 480 of the Restatement of the Law (Second) Torts and hold them to be the law of Indiana today. But the Restatement does not alter the requirement that the defendant have the time to avert the harm to the plaintiff. [...]

We agree with the Court of Appeals that there was no evidence that PHM had the last opportunity to "avert" or prevent Howard's fall. (citation omitted)

[...]

The jury was instructed on the law of last clear chance, including that "[a] plaintiff may recover under the last clear chance doctrine if a plaintiff proves, by a preponderance of the evidence, …[that] the defendant had physical control over the instrumentality and had the last opportunity through the exercise of reasonable care to avoid the injury." (citation omitted). But there simply is no evidence in the record that PHM had either physical control over the pulley mechanism or the last opportunity to avert or prevent the injuries Howard suffered. [I]n the absence of any such evidence, we do not think the jury could have found that the doctrine of last clear chance applied. We find no prejudice to PHM from the instruction.

Conclusion

We affirm the judgment of the trial court.

The court noted that the last clear chance doctrine would allow a plaintiff to recover even if there had been contributory negligence. Also, the contributory negligence defense remained applicable in suits against schools. The school, here, did not have a last clear chance to avert the injury. But the plaintiff was allowed to recover because the issue of "last clear chance" did not affect the trial court's determination that the school was liable.

Plaintiff Helpless

The rule of law for a plaintiff in helpless peril is that, if the defendant had a reasonable opportunity to avoid the injury, the plaintiff's contributory negligence will not bar a recovery for damages. The doctrine requires that the defendant discovered the peril, had an opportunity to avoid the injury, then failed to exercise reasonable care to avoid harm to the plaintiff (see box below).

LAST CLEAR CHANCE: HELPLESS PLAINTIFF

A plaintiff who has negligently subjected himself to a risk of harm from the defendant's subsequent negligence may recover for harm caused thereby if, immediately preceding the harm,

a. the plaintiff is unable to avoid it by the exercise of reasonable vigilance and care, and
b. the defendant is negligent in failing to utilize with reasonable care and competence his then existing opportunity to avoid the harm, when he
   i. knows of the plaintiff's situation and realizes or has reason to realize the peril involved in it or
   ii. would discover the situation and thus have reason to realize the peril, if he were to exercise the vigilance which it is then his duty to the plaintiff to exercise.

Restatement (Second) of Torts §479 (1965)

The driver of a car may not be liable in negligence where a pedestrian abruptly darts in front of the car and is hit but will be liable if the driver has enough time to react to the pedestrian's abrupt turn but does nothing.

Plaintiff Inattentive

Another body of case law concerns the plaintiff's failure to notice the peril of his or her surroundings. When the defendant encounters an inattentive plaintiff and has an opportunity to avoid an injury, the plaintiff's own contributory negligence will not bar a recovery. In such a situation, the defendant is said to have had the last clear chance to avoid the injury. The situation is similar to that of the helpless plaintiff (see box below).

LAST CLEAR CHANCE: INATTENTIVE PLAINTIFF

A plaintiff who, by the exercise of reasonable vigilance, could discover the danger created by the defendant's negligence in time to avoid the harm to him, can recover if, but only if, the defendant

a. knows of the plaintiff's situation, and
b. realizes or has reason to realize that the plaintiff is inattentive and therefore unlikely to discover his peril in time to avoid the harm, and
c. thereafter is negligent in failing to utilize with reasonable care and competence his then existing opportunity to avoid harm.

Restatement (Second) of Torts §480

The circumstances must be such that the defendant *saw* the plaintiff and *knew* that the plaintiff was inattentive. If he or she did not possess such knowledge, there can be no presumption of any last clear chance to avoid the injury. For example, the driver of a car who sees a pedestrian reading a newspaper while crossing the street can use the last clear chance doctrine so long as there is an opportunity to avoid hitting the pedestrian. No recovery would be available to the plaintiff under such circumstances.

■ COMPARATIVE NEGLIGENCE

Many states' dissatisfaction with contributory negligence, as noted above, led them to replace this defense by statutorily providing for the apportionment of damages between the parties. Comparative negligence shifts the focus of the trier of fact from liability to the division of damages between those at fault. A plaintiff who contributed to the negligence would get a recovery, offset by the degree of plaintiff's contribution to the accident. Under contributory negligence, plaintiff would get no recovery even if plaintiff only contributed by one percent.

Nature of Comparative Negligence

Many states have replaced the contributory negligence defense with comparative negligence statutes that require an apportionment of damages whereby both the plaintiff and the defendant share some measure of fault.

A comparative negligence defense requires the following elements (see Table 5-1):

1. actionable negligence by the defendant causing harm or injury to the plaintiff;
2. a negligent act by the plaintiff that contributed to his or her injury;
3. a measurement of the percentage of the relative contribution of the negligence of both plaintiff and defendant; and
4. an award of damages to the plaintiff reduced by the percentage of his or her own negligence.

Table 5-1 Elements Needed to Establish Comparative Negligence
Defendant's negligence
Plaintiff's negligence
Degree that each is responsible for negligence that caused injuries
Damages award to plaintiff, reduced by degree of responsibility for the accident

Under comparative negligence statutes, the plaintiff's recovery is not absolutely barred by his or her own negligence. Instead, the trier of fact measures the negligence of the plaintiff and reduces the amount of any damages to be awarded by the percentage that his or her negligence contributed to the total injury.

Assume, for example, that Parker negligently left his automobile partially blocking a lane of traffic on the street in front of his house. Further assume that Tishawn, driving his car over the speed limit, noticed Parker's automobile but was unable to stop before hitting its rear bumper. Parker sues Tishawn for $20,000 in damages to his automobile. The trier of fact made a finding that Parker was 25 percent negligent and Tishawn was 75 percent negligent. A system of pure comparative negligence would reduce the award to Parker by the amount of his negligence, 25 percent ($5,000), and award the remainder to him. Therefore, under a system of pure comparative negligence, Parker would recover $15,000.

Table 5-2 Accident Involving Teshawn and Parker; Damages Assessed at $20,000	
Tishawn 75% liable	$15,000.00
Parker 25% liable	$ 5,000.00
Total	$20,000.00

Comparative negligence statutes did not appear until early in the twentieth century. By the early 1990s, most jurisdictions in the United States had adopted some form of a comparative negligence system.

Systems of Comparative Negligence

Comparative negligence systems vary among states, and paralegal students should consult local statutes to determine the exact nature of the statutory system. There are three principal types of comparative negligence systems (see Table 5-3):

- Pure comparative negligence—A plaintiff's negligence does not serve to bar a claim, but does reduce damages in proportion to fault; this system forms the basis of the American Law Institute's proposed the law Uniform Comparative Fault Act. The plaintiff can recover for injuries caused by defendant's negligence, offset by the plaintiff's contribution to causing the accident; under contributory negligence, even contributing only one percent to causing the accident would have completely barred the plaintiff from recovery.

- Modified comparative negligence—Sometimes called the *50 percent system;* a plaintiff's contributory fault does not bar recovery under this system so long as it remains below a specified level of contribution, usually 50 percent. If the plaintiff had contributed more than 51 percent to causing the injury, the plaintiff will receive no award in damages.
- Slight-gross system—A plaintiff's contributory negligence does not bar his or her claim as long as his or her negligence is slight and the negligence of the defendant is gross. If the plaintiff contributed even one percent to causing the injury, the plaintiff could recover damages; however, if the plaintiff contributed 40 percent, the plaintiff might not receive an award for damages.

| Table 5-3 Comparison of Types of Comparative Negligence Systems ||
Negligence System	**Damages Awarded**
Pure comparative negligence	Award to the plaintiff offset to the degree that the plaintiff's own negligence caused the injury
Modified comparative negligence	The plaintiff can recover so long as the plaintiff's own negligence does not exceed 49%. If it does, then the plaintiff gets nothing. Otherwise, damages award offset to the degree that the plaintiff's own negligence caused the injury.
Slight-gross system	The plaintiff can recover so long as the plaintiff's own negligence does not exceed perhaps 10% (this may vary and/or may not be a fixed percentage). If it does, the plaintiff gets nothing. Otherwise, damages award offset to the degree that the plaintiff's own negligence caused the injury.

The modified comparative negligence system is the most common. Each system offers an opportunity for the trier of fact to apportion fault, although limiting the scope of apportionment in all but pure comparative negligence.

Joint Tortfeasors

When a negligence action involves more than one defendant-tortfeasor, most jurisdictions enacting a system of comparative negligence have maintained the common law rule of joint and several liability (see Chapter 4). Under that rule, the plaintiff is entitled to recover whatever judgment may be awarded from any defendant found to be liable. Some states have established this by statute (see Case in Point 5-7).

 # CASE IN POINT 5-7

Williams v. White Mountain Construction Company, Inc. v. Permanent Builders, Inc.

749 P.2d 423 (Colo. 1988)

Defendants, third-party plaintiffs-appellants White Mountain Construction Co. and Lloyd Rogers (collectively White Mountain), appeal directly from the Pitkin County District Court order granting summary judgment in favor of Permanent Builders, Inc. (Permanent Builders). [footnote omitted] We affirm.

I.

In the fall of 1981, Permanent Builders subcontracted with White Mountain to dig a trench and install water pipes on Aspen Mountain. White Mountain dug the trench according to the express instructions of Frank Wright, a construction superintendent for Permanent Builders. When advised by White Mountain of the potential hazards of digging the trench in accordance with his instructions, Frank Wright said, "Don't worry about it—we will take care of it if anything happens." On October 7, 1981, Zeke Williams, an employee of Permanent Builders, was seriously injured when the trench collapsed. After the accident, White Mountain again contacted Frank Wright, who made reassurances that Permanent Builders would take care of any problems concerning Williams.

Williams received workmen's compensation benefits which precluded a tort action against Permanent Builders. [footnote omitted] He also filed suit in Pitkin County District Court against White Mountain, alleging that his injuries were caused by White Mountain's negligence.

White Mountain then filed a third-party complaint against Permanent Builders. It claimed that an oral contract of indemnity arose by virtue of Frank Wright's statements. Alternatively, White Mountain claimed that it was entitled to contribution from Permanent Builders. Permanent Builders filed a motion for summary judgment and entered into a stipulation of facts with White Mountain for that purpose. [footnote omitted]

Based on these stipulated facts, the trial court found that no contract of indemnity was created and that, as a matter of law, White Mountain's claim of contribution was barred by [...] the Colorado Workmen's Compensation Act (the Compensation Act). Williams later recovered a jury verdict of $574,586.

White Mountain contends here that (1) the trial court erred in refusing to find that an oral contract of indemnity was created; (2) the Compensation Act does not prohibit White Mountain from claiming contribution from Permanent Builders under the Uniform Contribution Among Tortfeasors Act (the Contribution Act), (citation omitted) [...].

II.

White Mountain first contends that Frank Wright's statement before the accident, "Don't worry about it—we will take care of it if anything happens," when understood in context, together with his reassurance after the accident that Permanent Builders would take care of any problems, was sufficient to create an oral contract indemnifying White Mountain from its own negligence. We do not agree.

Like other contracts, indemnity contracts can arise orally. (citation omitted). The word "indemnity" is not required, (citation omitted) and its presence does not guarantee that an indemnity contract was created. (citation omitted). While such contracts are generally construed to effectuate rather than defeat the parties' intentions, (citation omitted), indemnity contracts holding indemnitees harmless for their own negligent acts must contain clear and unequivocal language to that effect. (citation omitted). Ambiguities will be resolved against the party seeking indemnity. (citation omitted)

[...]

[T]he stipulated facts establish that Frank Wright's statement was ambiguous. The statement arose while he and a White Mountain employee were discussing the hazards of digging the trench in the manner proposed by Frank Wright. Such a discussion might prompt a subcontractor to be concerned not only with the possibility of tort liability as a result of following an unorthodox excavation procedure but also with vicarious liability, [...] and the concomitant responsibility under the Compensation Act to make workmen's compensation payments as an employer. While it is perhaps more plausible that "it" in the statement "Don't worry about *it*—we'll take care of *it* if anything happens" refers to the first possible concern, it is also plausible that "it" refers to the second set of concerns, or to some other concern known only to the parties. We are mindful that it is inappropriate to construe statements so narrowly as to deprive them of any meaning, yet the burden of indemnity is so onerous that we hesitate to impose it unless the language used clearly requires such a result. For the same reasons, the reassurance given by Frank Wright after the injury fails to buttress White Mountain's argument. Resolving these ambiguities against a finding of indemnity, we conclude that the district court correctly found that no express contract of indemnity arose between White Mountain and Permanent Builders. [footnote omitted] [...]

White Mountain advances three arguments supporting its claim that the district court erred in failing to recognize a right to contribution from Permanent Builders for its proportionate liability in the injury to Williams. It maintains first that the primary purpose of the Compensation Act would not be defeated by a judicial interpretation permitting third parties to recover contribution from a negligent employer. White Mountain further claims that such a decision would avoid the unjust result of requiring one tortfeasor to shoulder disproportionate liability because of the fortuity that the other tortfeasor is statutorily immune. White Mountain finally argues that third parties received no benefit under the Compensation Act and should therefore not be burdened by it. Permanent Builders argues that the Contribution Act cannot apply to negligent employers because the exclusive remedy provision of the Compensation Act prohibits employers from being tortiously liable for injuries to their employees. We are persuaded that the rule that best incorporates the design of the legislature and fairness to the parties is one denying all claims of contribution from employers who comply with the Compensation Act.

A.

Whether a third-party tortfeasor sued by an injured employee can recover contribution from a negligent employer who has complied with state workmen's compensation procedures has aptly been called perhaps the most evenly balanced controversy in all of compensation law. [...]

It is undoubtedly true that the legislature has altered traditional theories of loss allocation in tort with the passage of the Uniform Contribution Among Tortfeasors Act, (citation omitted) and with the introduction of a comparative negligence scheme into Colorado law. (citation omitted). The ability of a jury to apportion fault on a percentage basis among plaintiffs and joint tortfeasors alike is now accepted. We also recognize that among joint tortfeasors there is a right of contribution, again according to the relative degree of fault of each. (citation omitted)

The statutory scheme in Colorado closely resembles those in other states. [T]he exclusive remedy provision of Colorado's Compensation Act, provides:

[...]

[E]nacted in 1977, permits one tortfeasor to recover contribution "where two or more persons become jointly or severally liable in tort for the same injury to person or property." (citation omitted) The problem is that a plain reading of the two statutes together does not reveal whether the legislature intended the subsequently adopted Contribution Act to abrogate the exclusive remedy provision of the Compensation Act, thereby permitting third-party claims of contribution from negligent employers. In states with statutory schemes similar to that of Colorado, the majority rule is to prohibit such claims. [footnote omitted] This rule fulfills the twin public policy goals of speedy, predictable determination of job-related injuries and a reluctance to create a judicial remedy that invades the province of the legislature.

B.

The Compensation Act, when read together with the Contribution Act, does not make it clear that the statutory immunity that employers enjoy under the Compensation Act extends to claims for contribution as a result of injury to employees. In the face of statutory silence, questions of interpretation are governed by legislative intent. (citation omitted).

The interpretation urged by White Mountain would frustrate some of the policy concerns that underlie the Compensation Act. It is true that the primary purpose of the Compensation Act is to compensate workers for job-related injuries (citation omitted), and that permitting contribution would not necessarily impede that goal. Yet other concerns are implicated. Questions of employee negligence or employer care are rendered legally irrelevant by the Compensation Act. (citation omitted). Speedy resolution of job-related claims is another purpose. (citation omitted). The Compensation Act is meant to be the exclusive measure of employer liability. (citation omitted) Finally, the Compensation Act is to be liberally construed so as to accomplish these purposes. (citation omitted).

If we were to permit White Mountain to bring a third-party claim for contribution, then Permanent Builders would be forced to litigate the issues of employee negligence or its own due care. This would reinsert issues which the legislature removed when it enacted the Compensation Act, and undermine the express policy of exclusivity upon which so much of the Compensation Act is based. The legislature was presumably aware of the exclusive remedy provision of the Compensation Act when it adopted the Contribution Act. (citation omitted). Therefore, because the Contribution Act demonstrates no intent to abrogate or even alter the allocation of risk assigned to employers in the Compensation Act, we conclude that the Compensation Act remains the exclusive forum for deciding employer liability for job-related injuries.

White Mountain urges us to recognize that prohibiting contribution claims would cause tortfeasors to shoulder a disproportionate share of liability. In light of the recent abolition of joint and several liability, we cannot agree. [...]

Tortfeasors sued by injured employees are now able to present evidence of employer liability at trial so as to reduce whatever damages may be assessed against them to a level proportionate to their liability. The problem of one tortfeasor bearing disproportionate liability has now been eliminated without requiring contribution from negligent employers.

[...] We conclude that the district court was correct in denying White Mountain's claim of contribution. [...] Accordingly, we affirm.

Here, the court determined that assurances made at a work site did not create a basis for indemnification. In this case, White Mountain's seeking to recoup the cost of an award in damages from Permanent Builder. While the claims made at the site seemed to imply contribution to any damages award against the defendant, the court construed the language to apply only to the specific situation on the site and not more broadly to constitute an offer of indemnification if there was an accident.

Once the trier of fact has measured the liabilities of the plaintiff and the defendants, the issue of contribution between the joint tortfeasors arises. Some states allow the apportioning of the damages equally among the defendants according to what is called the **equality rule.** Under this rule, if a partnership is found liable in damages for causing the plaintiff's injuries, each partner will pay an equal portion of the damages.

Other states have adopted a system of apportionment of damages between defendants based upon their respective fault. This system is called **comparative contribution,** and involves an assessment by the trier of fact of the degree of fault of each defendant. Once the defendants' comparative share of fault has been measured, damages are awarded accordingly. If a partnership is found liable in damages for causing a plaintiff's injuries, the partner who was 70 percent responsible for causing the injury will have to pay 70 percent of the damages award assessed against the partnership.

Table 5-4 Equality Rule versus Comparative Contribution, Involving Three Partners	
Equality rule	Partners each responsible for 33 1/3%
Comparative contribution	One partner may be liable for 70% of damages while the other two are liable for 15% each

State laws differ greatly regarding joint and several liability as well as on the issues of contribution and indemnification. To properly apply these principles, paralegal students should consult the law in their state.

■ ASSUMPTION OF RISK

Another major defense to a claim of negligence is the doctrine of **assumption of risk.** Assumption of risk provides a defense to a claim of negligence in cases where the plaintiff knowingly exposes himself or herself to danger and assumes responsibility for any harm. It is based on the premise that an individual is responsible for the consequences of choice, such as when a plaintiff engages in rock-climbing, sky-diving, or bungee-cord jumping.

It finds its rationale in the Latin phrase *violenti non fit injuria*, which means "that to which a person assents is not deemed an injury at law." The doctrine of assumption of risk became established as a legal principle in the late nineteenth century. This defense is an absolute bar to an action for damages similar to the defense of contributory negligence. It requires two basic elements:

- Voluntary assumption of a known risk by the plaintiff; and
- Full knowledge of the danger inherent in the risk.

The presence of these elements relieves the defendant from an obligation to the plaintiff which he or she might otherwise have borne.

Different from Contributory Negligence

Assumption of risk differs slightly from the defense of contributory negligence. It involves knowingly accepting a danger and the voluntarily assenting to exposure. Contributory negligence, on the other hand, involves a departure from the standard of care of an ordinary reasonable person (see Table 5-5).

Table 5-5 Comparison of Assumption of Risk versus Contributory Negligence, Skydiving	
Assumption of risk	Contributory negligence
Decides to go skydiving	Fails to check that parachute is properly packed

If a plaintiff has chosen to engage in skydiving, he or she would be assuming the risk. If the plaintiff had not checked that the parachute was properly packed and sustained injuries upon impact, that would be contributory negligence.

The two defenses may exist in the same case, or they may be available independently of each other. Consider the case of the student teacher injured while participating in a donkey baseball game (see Case in Point 5-8).

CASE IN POINT 5-8

Arbegast v. Board of Education of South New Berlin Central School

65 N.Y.2d 161 (1985)

Plaintiff, a student teacher at the South New Berlin Central School, was injured during a donkey basketball game when the donkey she was riding put its head down and she fell off. The game, sponsored as a fund raising event for the senior class, was staged under contract by the defendant Buckeye Donkey Ball Company, which provided the donkeys, helmets for each of the players, and an employee who transported and handled the animals, gave instructions to the participants, and acted as referee of the games, in return for which the company received a percentage of the receipts. Two games were played; the first pitted the faculty team against the fire department team and was won by the faculty team; the faculty team then opposed the senior class team in the second game. Plaintiff participated in the first game without mishap, but had a different, larger donkey for the second game than she had had for the first. She spent a good deal of the game walking the donkey around but, at the urging of another faculty member, mounted. Soon thereafter she was thrown over the donkey's head when it put its head down as it stopped, with resultant permanent injury to her left arm....

A

Until the enactment in 1975 [New York State law] of CPLR article 14-A, it was, except in an action for wrongful death, a substantive part of the plaintiff's right to recover in a negligence action that plaintiff prove himself or herself free from negligence contributing in the slightest degree to the occurrence.... The theory was that plaintiff's negligence was an intervening cause, which broke the causal connection between the defendant's negligent act and plaintiff's injury....

B

It is against this background that CPLR article 14-A was enacted in 1975, providing that as to all causes of action accruing on or after September 1, 1975, "the culpable conduct attributable to the claimant or to the decedent, including contributory negligence or assumption of risk, shall not bar recovery, but the amount of damages otherwise recoverable shall be diminished in the proportion which the culpable conduct attributable to the claimant or decedent bears to the culpable conduct which caused the damages," and "shall be an affirmative defense to be pleaded and proved by the party asserting the defense."...

Because the Legislature contemplated that article 14-A would "apply to cases where the conduct of one or more of the parties will be found not negligent" and "in which the plaintiff's negligences may be the only negligence," but also that defendant's culpable conduct would include "conduct giving rise to liability upon a theory of strict liability," it is clear that both the basis of liability asserted against the present defendant and the plaintiff's acts may constitute "culpable conduct" within the meaning of the statute.

Thus, what the statute requires comparison of is not negligence but conduct which, for whatever reason, the law deems blameworthy, in order to fix the relationship of each party's conduct to the injury sustained and the damages to be paid by the one and received by the other as recompense for that injury. Comparative causation is, therefore, the more accurate description of the process, ... as is evident both from the wording of CPLR 1411 ("shall be diminished in the proportion which the culpable conduct attributable to the claimant or decedent bears to the culpable conduct which caused the damages" [emphasis supplied]) and from the section of the Judicial Conference Report entitled "Causal Culpability": "Only culpable conduct which was a substantial factor in causing the harm for which recovery is sought is to be considered in determining the amount by which damages are to be diminished. For example, if P accepts a ride in an automobile driven by A, with knowledge that A is intoxicated, and P is injured when B negligently drives his vehicle into the rear of A's vehicle which is properly stopped for a red traffic signal, in P's action against B, there will be no diminution of damages. While P may have engaged in culpable conduct in accepting a ride with A, that conduct was not a substantial factor in causing the damage suffered by P." As that example makes clear, for the statute to operate, plaintiff's conduct must be a cause in fact of his or her injury. When it is, the statute "requires that the culpable conduct attributable to the decedent or claimant be compared with the total culpable conduct which caused the damages."

Neither article 14-A nor its legislative history defines "assumption of risk." The common law distinguished between express and implied assumption of risk. Express assumption, which was held to preclude any recovery, resulted from agreement in advance that defendant need not use reasonable care for the benefit of plaintiff and would not be liable for the consequence of conduct that would otherwise be negligent.... Implied assumption was founded not on express contract, but on plaintiff's voluntarily encountering the risk of harm from defendant's conduct with full understanding of the possible harm to himself or herself....

Here there is evidence from which the jury could have concluded that plaintiff had knowledge of the risk and by participating in the games voluntarily assumed it, and no question that plaintiff's conduct in mounting the donkey from which she was thrown was a cause in fact of her injuries. She would, therefore, have been entitled to a comparative causation charge on implied assumption of the risk had she not conceded that she was told before the games began that "participants are at their own risk." In light of that concession, however, the Trial Judge should have directed a verdict for defendant.

In this case, the court agreed that the plaintiff could not recover because she assumed the risk that, in riding the donkey, she might fall. The plaintiff had ridden a smaller donkey at least once before, so she understood the risk of injury that could arise in this situation.

The defense of assumption of risk applies under two basic circumstances. Those situations are when the plaintiff:

- Expressly consented to the risk (paying to go bungee-cord jumping); or
- Impliedly consented to the risk (when bungee-cord jumping without first reading the defendant's pamphlet on the risks involved in bungee-cord jumping or without first signing a release).

Both situations involve conduct by the plaintiff that may be considered to be reasonable and nonnegligent, and thus do not give rise to a defense of contributory negligence.

Express Consent

The clearest application of the defense of assumption of risk occurs when the plaintiff expressly agrees not to hold the defendant liable for any injury. The courts do not find any violation of public policy in allowing an individual to look out for his or her own welfare before entering into a contract. Limitations on the defense apply in cases where there is an obvious disadvantage in bargaining power between the parties. For instance, an employer may not require employees to enter into a contract limiting the employer's exposure to liability for a job-related injury.

For the assumption of risk defense to apply, two basic express consent elements are required. It is essential that:

- The assent to the risk be freely given; and
- The assent be for the particular risk that led to the injury.

Professor Dobbs offers the contemporary perspective:

A Contemporary Perspective

However formulated, the essential idea was that the plaintiff assumed the risk whenever she expressly agreed to do so by contract or otherwise, and also when she impliedly did so by contract or otherwise, and also when she impliedly did so by words or conduct. Courts bean to think that conduct implied consent whenever the plaintiff had specific knowledge of the risk posed by the defendant's negligence, appreciated its nature, and proceeded voluntarily to encounter it nonetheless. The Restatement and more modern theory added that the risk was assumed only if the plaintiff's conduct in encountering the risk manifested the plaintiff's willingness to accept responsibility for the risk.

Dobbs, *The Law of Torts* §211 (2000)

Express consent (express assumed risk). The plaintiff may expressly assume a risk by accepting the defendant's disclaimer of responsibility or by giving a release or other exculpatory agreement in advance of injury, unless, on the facts, some policy is opposed to such a consensual arrangement. The plaintiff can expressly assume the risk either orally or in writing. If the effect of the agreement is clear and untainted by deceptive behavior or the like [footnote omitted], an express assumed risk ordinarily will relieve the defendant of the duty that otherwise existed. [footnote omitted] Alternatively, it will establish a standard of care that shows he has breached no duty.

Dobbs, *The Law of Torts* §213 (2000)

The principle from contract law of strict construction—where language in an agreement is taken literally from what is said—would apply on the issue of the plaintiff's having provided express consent to assume the risk. So, if the company that flies the airplanes for skydivers requires all passengers to sign a waiver releasing the company from "any and all liability," the court will bar any claim by a passenger who is injured because a parachute didn't open.

The plaintiff in the *Meier* case consented to ride a mechanical bull installed as an amusement ride. The New York state legislature had limited the application of express consent, further restricting the ability of a defendant to avoid responsibility (see Case in Point 5-9).

CASE IN POINT 5-9

Meier v. Ma-Do Bars, Inc.

106 A. D. 2d 143 (N. Y. App. Div. 3d Dep't 1985)

This is an action for serious personal injuries sustained by plaintiff while attempting to ride a "mechanical bull" owned and operated by defendant Clean Snow Corporation. There appears to be no significant issue on this appeal as to the respective liabilities and duties of defendants Paul Solodar and Clean Snow Corporation. It is presumed that Paul Solodar was the owner and in complete control of Clean Snow Corporation. Because their interests are identical insofar as the issue on this appeal is concerned, we shall refer to both defendants collectively as "Solodar."

Solodar obtained permission from defendant Ma-Do Bars, Inc. to install and operate a mechanical amusement device in Hunter Village Inn, a tavern owned by Ma-Do Bars, Inc. The device simulated the spinning and bucking of actual bulls as they perform when ridden in rodeos. The participants attempted to ride the device in the same manner as animals are ridden. It must be assumed that when the device was ridden by patrons of the bar, a rodeo atmosphere was created in which satisfaction was derived from being able to stay on the bull for the predetermined period of time. That it was anticipated that some riders would be unable to stay on the bull was indicated by the fact that air mattresses were spread on the floor surrounding the device.

After observing the mechanical bull being ridden by other patrons, plaintiff talked to the operator and was informed that he could ride the bull upon payment of a $2 fee and execution of a "Liability, Release, Indemnification and Authorization" agreement. He complied with both conditions. He mounted the device and was thrown from it under circumstances not material to the issue before us now.

After commencement of this action and the completion of certain discovery procedures, Solodar moved for summary judgment contending that the agreement was a complete bar to plaintiff's recovery of damages. Special Term granted the motion and plaintiff now appeals. For the purposes of this appeal, we assume that the agreement, if valid and enforceable, was completely exculpatory of any liability on the part of Solodar.

The main thrust of plaintiff's argument is that the exculpatory agreement must be deemed to be void as against public policy and wholly unenforceable because of section 5-326 of the General Obligations Law, which provides:

Every covenant, agreement or understanding in or in connection with, or collateral to, any contract, membership application, ticket of admission or similar writing, entered into between the owner or operator of any pool, gymnasium, place of amusement or recreation, or similar establishment and the user of such facilities, pursuant to which such owner or operator receives a fee or other compensation for the use of such facilities, which exempts the said owner or operator from liability for damages caused by or resulting from the negligence of the owner, operator or person in charge of such establishment, or their agents, servants or employees, shall be deemed to be void as against public policy and wholly unenforceable.

This appears to be a case of first impression involving circumstances such as these. The Legislature's intent in enacting such a statute is the determinative factor in deciding the limits of its application.... It is for the courts to definitively resolve the legal question of the applicability of a statutory enactment to a particular situation....

In our view, the instant case is a classic example of those situations which the Legislature had in mind when it extended the declaration of public policy in the General Obligations Law to apply to places of amusement and similar establishments. The mechanical bull was an amusement device for which plaintiff paid a fee to use and enjoy. That a potential danger existed is exemplified by the owner and operator's requirement that an exculpatory agreement be signed by a user. Defendant created a place of amusement or recreation by the installation of the device.... We conclude from the facts before us that section 5-326 of the General Obligations Law is controlling and that the agreement is null and void.

Professor Dobbs captures the fundamental issue for of this approach:

LIMITING INSTANCES WHERE ASSUMPTION OF RISK CANNOT BE USED

To avoid the harsh applications of assumed risk, courts developed some constraining orders. One of them was that the plaintiff's confrontation of the risk had to be voluntary, which was to say that the plaintiff had to have a reasonable alternative course of action.

Dobbs, *The Law of Torts* §214 (2000)

Implied Consent

In most cases involving the assumption of risk defense, there is no express consent. The consent is usually implied from the plaintiff's conduct. The plaintiff accepts potential consequences by engaging in conduct that entails risk, and proceeds even though injury may result. Unless the defendant tied a bungee cord to the plaintiff then shoved the plaintiff forward, the plaintiff understood that bungee-cord jumping involved an elastic cord and jumping, and a risk of injury.

The defense arises in cases when the defendant offers an activity to the plaintiff without any obligation to accept the offer. The activity carries certain unavoidable danger. The plaintiff, aware of the risks, agrees to participate in the activity, considering the risk worthwhile. For example, assume that Rappel owns an indoor rock-climbing training facility open to the public. Tanesha attempts to scale the wall one afternoon, and is struck and injured by a rock dislodged by another patron. In Tanesha's lawsuit for damages, Rappel would have the defense of an implied assumption of the risk even though there was no express contract between the two parties.

Courts continue to wrestle with the differences between implied and express consent (Case in Point 5-10).

 # CASE IN POINT 5-10

Jagger v. Mohawk Mountain Ski Area, Inc.
269 Conn. 672 (2004)

This case, which comes to this court upon our acceptance of two certified questions [footnote omitted] [...] asks us to consider whether, as a matter of Connecticut law, a skier may bring an action in negligence against a ski area operator and its employee arising out of a collision between the skier and the employee. More specifically, the certified questions require us to decide whether: (1) a skier, pursuant to General Statutes §29-212, [footnote omitted] has assumed the risk, as a hazard inherent in the sport of skiing, of a collision with a ski area employee, acting in the course of his employment with the ski area operator, thereby foreclosing a subsequent action for negligence against the operator and the employee; and (2) our decision in *Jaworski* v. *Kiernan* (citation omitted), in which we concluded that coparticipants in team athletic contests involving contact as a part of the sport owe one another a duty to refrain from reckless or intentional conduct, should extend to the sport of skiing. We conclude that: (1) §29-212 does not bar an action brought by a skier against a ski area operator alleging negligence by an employee of the operator; and (2) the doctrine articulated in *Jaworski* does not extend to the sport of skiing. Accordingly, under the circumstances of the present case, we answer both of the certified questions in the negative.

The following facts and procedural history [...] guide our disposition of the certified questions. During the afternoon of December 4, 1999, the plaintiff, Mary Ann Jagger, a resident of the state of New York, was skiing an intermediate level trail on Mohawk Mountain, located in Cornwall, Connecticut. On that same afternoon, the defendant, Mohawk Mountain Ski Area, Inc. (Mohawk), a Connecticut corporation that operates Mohawk Mountain, was conducting a preseason ski clinic for its ski instructors, one of whom was the defendant James Courtot, a resident of the state of Connecticut. [footnote omitted] As the two skiers negotiated the slopes, the plaintiff and Courtot collided, allegedly as a result of Courtot's failure to exercise reasonable care.

Subsequently, the plaintiff brought this federal diversity action sounding in negligence against the defendants. [footnote omitted] The defendants thereafter moved to dismiss the complaint, claiming that the plaintiff's cause of action is: (1) barred by §29-212, which provides that skiers "assume the risk of and legal responsibility for [injuries] ... arising out of the hazards inherent in the sport of skiing ... [including] collisions with any other person by any skier while skiing," and (2) legally insufficient under our doctrine for coparticipant liability in team contact sports as articulated in *Jaworski v. Kiernan*, (citation omitted). The District Court reserved judgment on the defendants' motion and thereafter certified the questions of law to this court.

I

ASSUMPTION OF RISK

The question as to whether a skier has assumed the risk of a collision with another skier while skiing presents an issue of first impression for this court. In support of her position that a skier may bring such a negligence action, the plaintiff claims that: (1) the negligent operation of a ski area [...] is not limited to the various duties of a ski area operator as enumerated in General Statutes §29-211 [footnote omitted] but rather includes any and all services offered by the ski area operator in the course of its business, including ski instruction and preseason ski clinics, and, accordingly, the operator may be liable in negligence for unreasonable conduct arising from those services; (2) the plain language and legislative history of §29-212 demonstrate that, although skiers may not recover from a ski area operator for injuries arising out of inherent hazards of the sport, skiers do not assume the risk of injuries associated with the negligent operation of the ski area; and (3) other jurisdictions with ski liability statutory schemes similar to that of Connecticut properly have drawn a distinction between collisions not caused in some manner by a ski area operator or its employees, for which an operator is not liable, and collisions somehow caused by the negligence of a operator or its employees, for which an operator may be liable.

In response, the defendants claim that: (1) the statutory exception in §29-212, which provides that a skier assumes the risk of inherent hazards unless the injury was a result of the operator's negligence, is not implicated by the activities associated with ski instruction because ski instruction does not fall within the meaning of "operation of the ski area"; (2) the plain language of §29-212 indicates that collisions with another skier are an inherent risk of the sport assumed by the skier and, therefore, the defendants are statutorily immune from liability as they owed the plaintiff no duty of care; (3) the legislative history surrounding this statutory scheme evinces a legislative intent to place the risk of all injuries arising from the inherent hazards of skiing, including collisions with other skiers, upon the individuals choosing to participate in the sport, while confining the potential liability of a ski area operator to the negligent performance of the various duties enumerated in §29-211, and those functions of a similar nature; and (4) the defendants' position regarding the proper allocation of skiing risk enjoys persuasive support in several decisions of Connecticut trial courts, as well as from the courts of various other jurisdictions. We agree with the plaintiff [...] skier does not assume the risk of a collision with another skier when such collision is caused by the negligence of a ski area operator, its agents or employees. Accordingly, we answer the first certified question in the negative.

We precede our analysis by setting forth the method by which we interpret statutes. "The process of statutory interpretation involves a reasoned search for the intention of the legislature.... In other words, we seek to determine, in a reasoned manner, the meaning of the statutory language as applied to the facts of [the] case, including the question of whether the language actually does apply. In seeking to determine that meaning, we look to the words of the statute itself, to the legislative history and circumstances surrounding its enactment, to the legislative policy it was designed to implement, and to its relationship to existing legislation and common law principles governing the same general subject matter." (citation omitted).

Both parties claim that the statute in question is plain and unambiguous. [...] Thus, a threshold determination must be made as to the meaning of the statutory language at issue. (citation omitted). Because we determine that the language of the statute is not clear and unambiguous, we are not restricted to the text of the statute.

[...]

Whether a Skier Assumes the Risk of a Collision with a Ski Instructor

Having concluded that a preseason clinic for instructors constitutes an activity associated with the operation of a ski area, we turn to the interpretation of §29-212 in order to determine whether a skier, by participating in the sport of skiing, has assumed the risk of collision with a ski instructor. After a thorough review, we conclude that the most reasonable interpretation of §29-212 is that a skier has not assumed the risk of injury associated with the sport of skiing when such risk negligently has been created by a ski area operator or when, in the exercise of due care, the operator could have taken steps to minimize such a risk and unreasonably failed to do so.

[...]

We recognize preliminarily the statutory progression of §29-212. Section 29-212 first indicates that a skier assumes the risk of injury arising out of the hazards inherent in the sport. Subsequently, however, §29-212 provides that those risks are not assumed when "the injury was proximately caused by the negligent operation of the ski area by the ski area operator, his agents or employees." On its face, therefore, the statute invokes the doctrine of assumption of risk for the inherent hazards associated with skiing, placing the burden of such hazards upon voluntary participants in the sport, yet creates an exception for injuries arising out of the negligent operation of the ski area by the operator. [footnote omitted]

Traditionally, the doctrine of assumption of risk provided a defendant with a complete defense to a claim of negligence that centered upon the conduct of the plaintiff; namely, that it was the plaintiff's assumption of a certain risk that subsequently caused an injury. A review of the application of this doctrine [footnote omitted] indicates that the assumption of risk variants fall generally within two separate categories: (1) a negligence defense that the plaintiff's conduct operated so as to relieve the defendant of a duty of care with regard to the plaintiff; [footnote omitted] and (2) a negligence defense that, while conceding that the defendant owed the plaintiff a duty of care and breached that duty, precludes recovery by the plaintiff because the plaintiff was aware of the defendant's negligence and the risk thereby created, but nevertheless chose to confront such risk. [footnote omitted]

[...]

Notwithstanding this analytical morass, closer analysis of the statute reveals that §29-212 provides that a skier assumes the risk of those hazards over which an operator has no control or over which an operator cannot reasonably act so as to ameliorate the potentiality of harm—for such hazards a skier has assumed the risk in the primary sense and an operator has no duty to protect skiers with regard to such hazards. [...] Over those risks which an operator has control, or over which an operator can act reasonably so as to minimize the existence or level of risk, however, an operator owes skiers a duty of care and breach of that duty subjects the operator to liability in negligence under our settled principles of comparative negligence.

[...]

As a result of this standard of care, the doctrine of assumption of risk was infused judicially in order to shield ski area operators from liability arising from the innate danger of the sport.

The plain language of §29-212 itself buttresses this interpretation. [footnote omitted] Section 29-212 provides, as a nonexhaustive enumeration, six examples of risks "inherent in the sport of skiing...." [...] The common thread throughout these examples is that they are either a risk over which an operator has no realistic control—for instance, terrain variations not caused by the operator; General Statutes §29-212 (1); or risks over which the operator has done all that is reasonably required to do to protect skiers—for instance, the conspicuous marking of lift towers to afford notice to skiers of their presence. General Statutes §29-212 (3). [footnote omitted]

[...]

Thus, for inherent hazards, ski area operators owe skiers no duty of care and skiers assume the risk of those hazards in the primary sense. For those hazards which are not an innate part of the sport of skiing, or over which an operator can act reasonably to eliminate or minimize the potential for harm, operators owe skiers a duty of reasonable care. [footnote omitted]

On the basis of this analysis, we conclude that the negligence of an employee or agent of a ski area operator is not an inherent hazard of the sport of skiing. [footnote omitted]

Accordingly, the plaintiff's claim against Mohawk is not statutorily barred by §29-212, and the plaintiff may maintain an action in negligence against Mohawk in accordance with our well settled principles of comparative negligence. [footnote omitted]

II

WHETHER THE STANDARD OF CARE IMPLICATED BY THE SPORT OF SKIING PRECLUDES NEGLIGENCE LIABILITY FOR COPARTICIPANTS

[...]

Applying these same factors to the sport of skiing, we are not persuaded that the duty of care owed to fellow skiers should preclude liability for negligent behavior. As a threshold matter, we recognize [...] that the specific harm alleged by the plaintiff was foreseeable and could have been anticipated as a likely result of the defendants' conduct. Although having passed the initial determination of foreseeability [...] we conclude that the appropriate level of care demanded of coparticipants in the sport of skiing is that of reasonableness.

[...] [W]e recognize that skiing is a dangerous sport and that many injuries sustained during participation in the sport are caused by collisions with other skiers. [footnote omitted] While collisions with other skiers are fairly common, frequency of occurrence is not the ultimate touchstone in evaluating the expectations of participants in the sport. Rather, we perceive the expectations of skiers to be that fellow participants in the sport will conduct themselves in a manner befitting the dangerous potentialities attendant with the sport. Thus, skiers will expect that other skiers will follow the rules and generally accepted practices of the sport of skiing. Indeed, our statutory scheme regarding ski liability confirms that skiers should possess such expectations as they take part in the sport. See General Statutes §29-214 (detailing special defenses for ski area operator based upon failure of skier to engage in appropriate behavior while skiing). [footnote omitted] Although §29-214 deals with special defenses available to a ski area operator in an action brought by a skier, its pronouncements regarding appropriate and reasonable behavior while engaging in the sport are relevant to our inquiry with regard to the expectations of skiers. The normal expectations of skiers will be that fellow skiers will ski in a reasonable and appropriate manner.

Skiing also differs vastly in terms of the expectations of its participants from the more traditional contact sports of soccer, football, basketball and hockey. If skiers act in accordance with the rules and general practices of the sport, at reasonable speeds, and with a proper lookout for others on the slopes, the vast majority of contact between participants will be eliminated. The same may not be said of soccer, football, basketball and hockey; in those activities contact is an inherent part of the game that cannot be eliminated totally.

[...] [W]e conclude that the balancing of the public policy of the encouragement of vigorous participation in the sport of skiing and the protection of the safety of its participants weighs in favor of a negligence standard. We believe that requiring skiers to participate in the reasonable manner prescribed by the rules of the sport actually will promote participation in the sport of skiing. Should the threshold for liability be placed at a level that only reckless or intentional misconduct can serve as grounds for liability, many of the potential harms caused by coparticipants in the sport will go unremedied and, therefore, dissuade potential participants from taking part in the sport. Additionally, a standard of reasonableness also operates to protect the safety of participants in the sport of skiing.

[...]

Both certified questions are answered: No.

No cost shall be taxed in this court to either party.

While collisions could happen at ski resorts, they were not necessarily expected to happen. So, when the plaintiff had a collision at a ski resort, the fact that collisions could happen did not amount to an implied consent not to sue the resort. Collisions are not inevitable when skiing; collisions are not considered part of the sport. The ski resort contended everyone would know that collisions were possible and so would have waived their right to sue a ski resort if there was a collision. The court rejected that logic because it would have effectively made ski resorts immune from almost all lawsuits in negligence.

Knowledge of Risk

Professor Keeton stresses that knowledge of the risk is the watchword for assumption of risk for a plaintiff to provide effective consent:

KNOWLEDGE OF RISK

"Knowledge of the risk is the watchword of assumption of risk." Under ordinary circumstances the plaintiff will not be taken to assume any risk of either activities or conditions of which he has no knowledge. Moreover, he must not only know of the facts which create the danger, but he must comprehend and appreciate the nature of the danger he confronts.

W. Page Keeton et al., *Prosser & Keeton on the Law of Torts* §68 at 487 (5th ed. 1984)

The purely subjective standard to be applied is based on the particular plaintiff and his or her ability to understand the danger. If the plaintiff cannot comprehend the danger, the defense is not available to the defendant.

Consider the following case of a health club patron overcome by fumes (see Case in Point 5-11).

CASE IN POINT 5-11

Larsen v. Vic Tanny International
130 Ill. App. 3d 574 (1984)

Defendant Vic Tanny International, a corporation, appeals the denial of its motion for summary judgment against plaintiff Gregory N. Larsen. The issue upon which defendant's motion hinges is the validity of an exculpatory clause in a contract between plaintiff and defendant. [...]

Plaintiff, a member of defendant's organization, alleged that he was injured while utilizing defendant's health club facilities. Plaintiff's complaint stated that plaintiff sustained serious internal injuries as a result of inhaling gaseous vapors.... Plaintiff's membership contract contained the following provisions:

"By the use of the facilities of Seller and/or by the attendance at any of the gymnasiums owned by Seller, the Member expressly agrees that Seller shall not be liable for any damages arising from personal injury sustained by the Member or his guest in, on or about the premises of the said gymnasiums or as a result of their using the facilities and the equipment therein...."

The courts of Illinois have long held that, under appropriate circumstances, a person may by contract avoid liability for his or her negligence.... In the absence of fraud or willful and wanton negligence, exculpatory contracts will be enforced unless "(1) it would be against the settled public policy of the State to do so, or (2) there is something in the social relationship of the parties militating against upholding the agreement."

The obvious rationale behind this rule is that a plaintiff who expressly consents to relieve a defendant of an obligation of conduct toward the plaintiff assumes the risk of injury as a result of the defendant's failure.... The doctrine of assumption of risk presupposes, however, that the danger which causes the injury is such that it ordinarily accompanies the activities of the plaintiff, and that the plaintiff knows or should know both the danger and the possibility of injury prior to its occurrence.... The standard to be applied is a subjective one geared to a particular plaintiff and her situation, and the determination ordinarily will be made by a jury....

Foreseeability of a specific danger is thus an important element of the risk which a party assumes, and, for this reason, serves to define the scope of an exculpatory clause. This is but another way of stating that, although the type of negligent acts from which a person expressly agrees to excuse another need not be foreseen with absolute clarity, such acts cannot lie beyond the reasonable contemplation of the parties [...] No agreement to assume unknown risks shall be inferred.

Plaintiff in the instant action claims injury resulting from defendant's act of mixing chemical compounds in a manner which produced an explosion of harmful vapors. The question upon which the enforceability of the exculpatory clause hinges is whether defendant's conduct and the risk of injury inherent in this conduct was of a type intended by the parties to fall within the scope of exculpation....

A plaintiff's decision to assume the risk of injury resulting from a defendant's conduct attains efficacy only in a context in which the plaintiff may foresee the range of possible dangers to which he subjects himself, thus enabling the plaintiff to minimize the risk by altering his conduct in order to employ a proportionately higher degree of caution. A plaintiff agreeing to assume a risk of injury in partial exchange for the right to use gymnasium facilities could reasonably contemplate the possibility of injury resulting from slippery surfaces in or around a swimming pool...or a steam room...and could, upon reflection, exercise increased care while utilizing these facilities. The assertion that such a plaintiff would necessarily contemplate the danger of combustible cleaning compounds being mixed in such a manner as to injure the plaintiff's respiratory system, and that the plaintiff could accordingly exercise a more rigid standard of caution either by avoiding certain areas of the gymnasium or by altering his breathing habits while present in those areas is untenable according to the standards of common experience.

[...]

The order of the circuit court denying defendant's motion for summary judgment is affirmed.

While the plaintiff had signed a waiver of liability to join the health club, the waiver encompassed only injuries likely to happen at a health club. The waiver did not apply when there was an accidental gas leak that injured the plaintiff.

Contrasted with Comparative Negligence

Other than in cases of express consent, the defense has been criticized by some as being of little value. Opponents of assumption of risk argue that it is in the public interest to apportion fault—to use a system of comparative negligence—rather than preclude recovery in situations involving an implied voluntary assumption of a known risk like when a fan gets hit by a foul ball during a baseball game. In fact, the comparative negligence statutes of some states have specifically abolished assumption of risk as a defense:

COMPARATIVE NEGLIGENCE STATUTE: NEW YORK

§1411 Damages recoverable when contributory negligence or assumption of risk is established

In an action to recover damages for personal injury, injury to property, or wrongful death, the culpable conduct attributable to the claimant or to the decedent, including contributory negligence or assumption of risk, shall not bar recovery, but the amount of damages otherwise recoverable shall be diminished in the proportion which the culpable conduct attributable to the claimant or decedent bears to the culpable conduct which caused the damages.

New York Civil Practice Law and Rules, Article 14-A

Some courts will still consider allowing for the use of the assumption of the risk doctrine but, mindful that its application serves as a complete bar to recovery, take great care in determining when it would be appropriate to apply such a doctrine (see Case in Point 5-12).

CASE IN POINT 5-12

Hildreth v. Rogers

2006 Ohio 5151 (Ohio Ct. App., Hardin County Oct. 2, 2006)

[…]

In November of 2004, Hildreth initiated a personal injury action against Rogers for injuries he sustained after either falling from or being thrown from the trunk of Rogers' moving vehicle, of which she was driving, in November of 2003. Rogers responded that Hildreth assumed the risk and/or was negligent, and thus any recovery was either completely barred or should be reduced.

In November of 2005, both parties were deposed about the incident. It is undisputed that they were in a relationship and living together when the incident occurred; that their relationship was tumultuous, with arguments sometimes escalating to verbal and physical abuse by both parties; that during the early morning of November 2, 2003, the couple got into an altercation after Hildreth arrived home from a party; that both were yelling and calling each other names; that Hildreth pushed some clay jars off of a bookshelf; that Hildreth slapped Rogers across the face; that Rogers stated that she wanted to leave; that Rogers proceeded outside to her vehicle, a Honda Civic DX with a standard transmission and a spoiler on the back; and, that Hildreth followed her outside and jumped onto the back of the vehicle before Rogers started it.

However, at this point the parties' recollections of events diverged. On cross-examination during her deposition, Rogers testified that upon leaving she did not take any personal belongings with her, other than her purse, because she was too scared of Hildreth's behavior. She stated that Hildreth had told her that one of his friends had given him drugs at the party and that she believed he was either intoxicated or under the influence of something due to his behavior.

Rogers continued that she ran to her vehicle, got inside, and locked it; that, while she attempted to extract her keys from her purse, Hildreth followed her outside, pounded on the driver's side window, and then jumped onto the back of her vehicle; and that she did not pay attention to whether Hildreth said anything to her because she was too scared and thought he might "bust the window out of [her] car and pull [her] out." (Rogers Depo. p. 58).

Rogers also testified that, upon starting her vehicle, she backed out of the driveway and started down the road, keeping the vehicle in first gear and traveling between five to ten miles per hour. She stated that she approached a stop sign at State Route 68 and came to a complete stop before turning right.

Rogers admitted that she was aware that Hildreth was on the back of her vehicle the entire time she was driving, and that he could have gotten hurt if he fell. She also testified that she intended to stop and let Hildreth off the car after crossing a set of railroad tracks on State Route 68, but that he "fell off, or jumped off, or passed out or something" immediately after crossing the tracks. (Rogers Depo. p. 35). She also noted that she did not witness him go off the back of the vehicle.

On recross-examination, Rogers testified that she was not in a hurry because, although she was terrified, * * * "I also have someone on my vehicle and I'm not going to drive like an idiot." (Rogers Depo. p. 65).

Conversely, on cross-examination Hildreth stated that he attended a cookout the evening before the incident, where he consumed two or three beers and a shot of tequila. He testified that, following the cookout, he attended another party, but did not consume any alcohol or drugs. However, Hildreth's rehabilitation therapist recorded on December 2, 2003, that Hildreth "report[ed] that he was drinking alcohol heavily the night of his accident. He chased his girlfriend while she was driving, grabbed on to the back of her car, [and] was eventually thrown from the car to the ground." (Defense Ex. A). Hildreth testified that he did not recall making that statement. Moreover, Hildreth stated that the therapist incorrectly wrote that he ran after the vehicle because he was already sitting on it when Rogers started it.

Hildreth further testified that when Rogers went outside to her vehicle, he followed her, apologized, and asked her to stay. When she proceeded to get into her vehicle, he banged one time on the back window behind the driver's side window. Hildreth continued that he then "jumped on the back of the car. I told her that we needed to talk this out, she didn't need to leave. I told her I was sorry." (Hildreth Depo. p. 50). He also testified that he jumped on the vehicle to prevent Rogers from leaving because he did not believe that she would move it.

Hildreth continued that, once he jumped onto the vehicle, it was a matter of seconds before Rogers started and moved the car. He stated that he did not attempt to get off the vehicle at that time because "it was moving and she put it into gear as soon as she got in." (Hildreth Depo. p. 60). He said that he knew that not attempting to jump off was dangerous at that time, but that he did not have a chance to do so. He later stated that he did not think about the risk of falling off at the time.

Hildreth also testified that Rogers traveled at a speed of fifteen miles per hour after backing out of the driveway, and that he secured himself by holding onto the vehicle's rear spoiler. Hildreth further stated that when Rogers approached the stop sign at State Route 68, he could not jump off the vehicle because she came to a rolling stop rather than a complete stop, and that she was traveling at five to ten miles per hour when she came to the stop sign and turned right. He also stated that after crossing the railroad tracks on State Route 68, he did not fall off of the vehicle, but could only remember that he was hitting on her window, telling her to stop, telling her to slow down, and telling her to pull over, because he wanted off.

On redirect examination, Hildreth clarified that the vehicle's engine was off when he got on the back of the vehicle; that he was on the vehicle for two or three minutes before Rogers started it; and, that once the vehicle was started he could not have gotten off safely because it never stopped and because Rogers was "driving pretty erratic." (Hildreth Depo. p. 95).

On recross-examination, Hildreth admitted that he could not see the speedometer, did not know the distance from the house to the stop sign, did not look at his watch while he was on the vehicle, and that nothing physically prevented him from jumping off of the vehicle. However, Hildreth also testified that when Rogers shifted from reverse to first gear, the movement was too fast for him to jump off, and that if "there was a half of second (sic) when I could have jumped I would have, but I could not jump off." (Hildreth Depo. p. 98).

In February of 2006, Rogers moved for summary judgment, alleging that Hildreth was barred from any recovery because he primarily assumed the risk of injury by climbing onto the trunk of her vehicle. Hildreth replied that, at most, the secondary assumption of the risk doctrine applied, instead of the primary assumption of the risk doctrine, thereby precluding summary judgment.

In March of 2006, the trial court granted Rogers' motion for summary judgment. [...]

It is from this judgment that Hildreth appeals, presenting the following assignment of error for our review.

Assignment of Error

THE TRIAL COURT ERRED IN GRANTING APPELLEE'S MOTION FOR SUMMARY JUDGMENT BASED ON THE DOCTRINE OF PRIMARY ASSUMPTION OF THE RISK.

[...] Hildreth contends that Rogers owed him a duty to refrain from operating her vehicle until she could do so with reasonable safety, and that she breached this duty. Additionally, Hildreth argues that, because he got on a stationary, unstarted vehicle under the belief that Rogers would not move it, he did not primarily assume the risk of injury. We agree.

[...]

Three types of assumption of the risk defenses exist: (1) express or contractual assumption of the risk, (2) primary or "no duty" assumption of the risk, and (3) secondary or implied assumption of the risk (citation omitted). Only primary and secondary assumption of the risk are relevant here.

[...]

Primary assumption of the risk is "a defense of extraordinary strength." (citation omitted) The Ohio Supreme Court noted that a primary assumption of risk defense is different from a typical affirmative defense in a negligence case: "Because a successful primary assumption of risk defense means that the duty element of negligence is not established as a matter of law, the defense prevents the plaintiff from even making a *prima facie* case." (citation omitted). The Court went on to state that because primary assumption of risk negates the duty element of a negligence claim, whether a plaintiff primarily assumed the risk is a question of law to be decided by the court, not a question of fact for the jury (citation omitted).

The Court also emphasized that, given the "great impact a ruling in favor of a defendant on primary assumption of risk grounds carries, a trial court must proceed with caution when contemplating whether primary assumption of risk completely bars a plaintiff's recovery." (citation omitted) The Court further elaborated:

(sic) only those risks directly associated with the activity in question are within the scope of primary assumption of risk, so that no jury question would arise when an injury resulting from such a direct risk is at issue, meaning that no duty was owed by the defendant to protect the plaintiff from that specific risk. In many situations, * * * there will be attendant circumstances that raise questions of fact whether an injured party assumed the risk in a particular situation. In that case, the doctrine of implied assumption of risk, not primary assumption of risk, would be applicable.

(citation omitted) Primary assumption of risk applies when the activity "involves such obvious and unavoidable risks that no duty of care attaches."

[...]

Hildreth testified that he did not get on Rogers' vehicle with the expectation that she would move it, but to keep her from starting and moving the vehicle. Even if, as the trial court noted, Hildreth's belief that Rogers would not leave was mistaken, a genuine issue of material fact still exists as to whether or not Hildreth voluntarily assumed the risk of riding on the vehicle so as to relieve Rogers of any duty she owed him. [...]

Likewise, viewing the evidence in a light most favorable to Hildreth, we cannot say that he voluntarily encountered any risk by jumping on the trunk of Rogers' stationary vehicle if it was in fact not moving. Furthermore, R.C. 4511.38, which mandates that "No person shall start a vehicle, * * * which is stopped, standing, or parked until such movement can be made with reasonable safety," establishes that Rogers owed a duty to Hildreth. Given Hildreth's testimony that he apologized and asked Rogers to stay and work things out, and Rogers' conflicting testimony that she could not hear him and was afraid, whether she breached that duty is a material question of fact precluding summary judgment.

Additionally, the trial court found that Hildreth had several opportunities to safely remove himself from Rogers' vehicle, but chose not to do so. However, a review of the evidence again reveals conflicting testimony. Rogers stated that she steadily drove between five and ten miles per hour, while Hildreth stated that she drove at least fifteen miles per hour and drove erratically. Rogers testified that she stopped after she backed out of the driveway before shifting into first, and that she made a complete stop at the stop sign at the State Route 68 intersection. Hildreth testified that Rogers shifted gears and revved the engine too quickly for him to jump off, that she did not make a complete stop at the stop sign, and that she never slowed enough for him to safely jump off.

Based on the conflicting evidence, we find that genuine issues of material fact exist regarding whether Hildreth assumed the risk and whether Rogers breached a duty, thereby precluding the trial court's application of the doctrine of primary assumption of risk.

Accordingly, Hildreth's assignment of error is sustained.

[...]

In this case, while the plaintiff did hang onto the defendant's car, that action may not have constituted an assumption of the risk of being injured when thrown from the car because the defendant sped away.

Some courts have merged the assumption of risk into contributory negligence, then essentially settled on comparative negligence. Comparative negligence means the recovery is proportional to the actions of the defendant and the plaintiff.

Paralegal students should carefully review individual state statutes to discover the treatment of assumption of risk and comparative negligence. If the statutes are silent, students must review the state's case law.

KEY TERMS

assumption of risk 176	contributory negligence 156
bar to action 156	equality rule 175
comparative contribution 175	last clear chance 165

SUMMARY

The law continues to follow the time-honored principle that a defendant whose conduct would otherwise be negligent toward another may not be liable to the plaintiff for the harm caused by the consent or fault of that plaintiff. The plaintiff's contributory negligence absolutely bars an action for negligence in those jurisdictions that adhere to that principle. The comparative negligence of the plaintiff diminishes his or her recovery in the many jurisdictions that have enacted a comparative negligence law. The defense to an action in negligence of assumption of risk may also negate a plaintiff's claim for recovery if plaintiff appreciated the dangers associated with a particular type of activity. Jurisdictions can take widely varying views on each of these approaches or defenses, so paralegals need to engage in legal research to find out the views of that paralegal's home state. The defenses to negligence actions will continue to receive attention as the various state legislatures further define the issue of preserving the public welfare.

CONCEPT REVIEW QUESTIONS

1. Define *contributory negligence*.
2. Describe the effect of a defense of contributory negligence on a plaintiff's claim.
3. In what way is contributory negligence not really negligence at all?
4. Discuss the doctrine of avoidable consequences.
5. How would a lack of knowledge of a peril on the part of the plaintiff affect a contributory negligence defense?
6. Explain why the last clear chance doctrine has been called the discovered peril doctrine.
7. Define *comparative negligence*.
8. List the elements of a comparative negligence defense.
9. What are the circumstances under which the doctrine of assumption of risk applies?
10. What are the elements of a defense of assumption of risk?

CRITICAL THINKING APPLICATIONS

1. A jockey was thrown from a thoroughbred horse while in a race and hit the inner racetrack rail. Upon impact, the rail splintered and punctured the jockey's lung. The jockey sues the racetrack owners for negligence in maintaining the guard rail. The owners claim that the jockey assumed the risk by participating in a dangerous activity. Assuming that all facts are true, will the owners defeat the lawsuit on a motion for summary judgment on the grounds that the jockey assumed the risk? Why or why not?
2. At a garden party, the host's father said that he had made a cannon to launch fireworks. The child of the host and a few friends followed the host's father into the garage to see the cannon. A friend goes next door and comes back with explosive black powder. The child and the friend pour black powder in the cannon. The child fires the cannon, which explodes. The friend, standing 40 feet away, is injured. The friend's parents sue. The child's parents allege assumption of the risk. Who will win at trial? Why?
3. Jack is a farmer. His friend Clay volunteered to help Jack harvest his crops. Clay grew up on a farm and has used harvesting equipment before. During the harvest, Clay drove a tractor that had an attachment, powered by the tractor, that pulls cornstalks out of the ground. While clearing the field, the machine would occasionally clog. Clay would stop the tractor, go to the machine and, with the tractor still engaged, pull out the stalk or stalks that clogged it. One time Clay did this, the machine pulled him in and seriously injured his arm and leg. The manufacturer's instructions stated that if the machine couldn't be unclogged by pulling the stalk out, the machine would have to be turned off to clear the clog. Clay's friend sued the manufacturer, who filed a motion for summary judgment on the grounds that Clay had assumed the risk when operating the machine contrary to what the instructions had stated. How will the court decide on this motion? Why?
4. One summer afternoon, a plaintiff-motorist pulled off a country road to stop at a farmer's market. Buying some of the freshly picked produce, the plaintiff-driver prepared to get back on the road. When the motorist of vehicle #2 braked

to let the plaintiff back on the road, vehicle #3 rear-ended vehicle #2, which then hit the plaintiff's car. The incident led to a chain-reaction accident, with the driver of vehicle #5 striking vehicle #4, which hits vehicle #3. How should the court determine who is liable for damages to the plaintiff's car, since it seems that the plaintiff played no role in bringing about the collisions and none of the drivers seems to have intended to cause any of the collisions?

5. A homeowner, preparing to change the muffler on the family car, backs the car into the family garage. The homeowner uses a hydraulic powered jack to raise the back of the car, then places jacks on either side; these jacks were of the same height and remained at a fixed height. Crawling under the car, the homeowner disconnected the muffler. That's when he discovered that the tailpipe was too close to the back of his garage to be removed. Rather than move the car forward to make room to remove the tailpipe, the homeowner devised an alternate plan. He applied the emergency jack (intended for changing tires) and slid it next to a stationary jack. By raising the car higher on one side so that it no longer rested on one of the stationary jacks, the homeowner hoped to be able to wiggle the tailpipe out in the extra space he had created. However, wiggling the tailpipe didn't get it loose: instead, it caused the car to slide off the emergency jack. When the car fell, the stationary jack punctured its gas tank, releasing the ten or so gallons of gasoline in the tank. The fumes overcame the homeowner, who lost consciousness for perhaps a half-hour. The homeowner awakened and eventually slipped out from underneath the car. Using the telephone in the garage, he called his neighbor for help before passing out again. The neighbor came over just as the homeowner regained consciousness. The homeowner instructed his neighbor to open the garage door with the electronic opener. Half way up, the gas fumes ignited and caused an explosion. Both men suffered serious burns; the neighbor had third-degree burns on his feet and legs and had to undergo several skin-graft surgeries. His wounds healed months later. At the time of the trial, the neighbor was still taking prescription medications to offset the effects of panic attacks. The homeowner denies liability, claiming that by opening the garage door using the electric door opener, any damages potentially due to the neighbor for the injuries he sustained must be offset by the degree to which the neighbor's opening of the door caused the explosion. How likely is it that the neighbor will be liable in damages to the degree that the neighbor might have helped to bring about homeowner's injuries? Why or why not?

6. In an automobile accident, the passenger in the front seat sustains injuries. She was not wearing a seat belt and the car did not have airbags. If the driver is found negligent at trial, should the passenger's damages be offset by the degree to which the failure to wear a seat belt brought about her injuries? If the injuries could have been completely eliminated by her wearing a seat belt, should the driver be at all liable for damages? Would the situation change if you learned the car could be retrofitted with air bags for less than $500, that the driver knew this, and had chosen not to install this safety equipment?

7. Five years after building a new house, the homeowner discovered that the building encroached on a neighbor's property by a few feet. This error arose due to a mistake made when surveying the boundaries of the property. When the owner sued the surveyor and won, the surveyor sought coverage for damages awarded at trial from an insurance company that had provided malpractice insurance coverage to the surveyor. The insurance company said that the damages awarded to the owner had to be offset by the degree to which the owner failed

to negotiate a settlement that would have been cheaper than to have had the entire matter be resolved by a lawsuit. Would a court grant a request to offset the damages award in proportion to the degree that the owner had failed to negotiate a settlement? Why or why not?

8. An alcoholic is arrested after causing a public disturbance in front of a relative's house. The relative, who had called the police, informed the officers that the alcoholic was very sick, would experience delirium tremens, and needed hospitalization. The alcoholic was brought to the local jail and charged with disorderly conduct. The alcoholic pleaded not guilty and could not make bail. By that point, the relative had gone to the jail to tell the officers in charge that the alcoholic needed medical treatment due to withdrawal and would experience delirium tremens. However, the relative failed to get the alcoholic transferred to a local hospital. That night, the alcoholic jumped off the top bunk bed in the cell where the officers had put the alcoholic for the evening. The alcoholic suffered a broken neck. In a civil suit for negligence, the alcoholic alleges that the officers had been told about the alcoholic's medical condition but had ignored the warning about the delirium tremens. This takes place in a state that is among the few to recognize contributory negligence as an absolute defense to liability. Would this be the right kind of situation for a court to decide to overturn the legal concept of contributory negligence as an absolute bar for the alcoholic's recovery, since the alcoholic was at least to some small degree responsible for producing the fracture? Why or why not?

SKILL-BUILDING APPLICATION

Dr. Hiram Rocker, a psychiatrist, had diarrhea and occasional cramping in the abdomen. When he suddenly experienced great pain, he went to an internist, Dr. Daniel Cutter. After examining Rocker, Dr. Cutter ordered that Rocker ingest a laxative and have an enema. Enemas are never prescribed if there is a risk that the patient has a perforated colon. Rocker went home and did as Dr. Cutter instructed, only to have nausea, chills, and intense abdominal pain. Physicians at the emergency room concluded that Rocker had appendicitis and scheduled surgery two days later. During surgery, the physicians discovered that Rocker actually suffered from diverticulitis and had a perforated colon, so they performed a temporary colostomy. Dr. Rocker had a difficult recovery because of an allergic reaction to medications prescribed to reduce the risk of infection. He needed additional hospitalizations. Rocker brought suit against Cutter, on grounds that included medical malpractice.

The parties disagree about (1) what medical history Rocker reported, (2) when the colon perforation occurred, (3) whether it was caused by Rocker's disease or Dr. Cutter's treatment, (4) why Dr. Cutter did not come to the emergency room, and (5) whether Rocker's progress would have been different had Dr. Cutter chosen a different course of treatment. Dr. Cutter argues that there was contributory negligence, that Rocker neglected to report where his abdominal pain began.

The evidence shows that particular diseases are associated with pain in particular places in the abdomen—gallbladder disease in the right upper quadrant, appendicitis in the right lower quadrant, and diverticulitis in the left lower quadrant. While conceding a patient with diverticulitis should not be treated with enemas, Dr. Cutter says he did not suspect diverticulitis, as it is normally associated with fever, constipation, and pain in the left lower quadrant, while Rocker reported no fever, diarrhea, and pain throughout his abdomen.

A court would conclude that a patient cannot, of course, be negligent because his symptoms fail to fit the usual pattern. Rocker has insisted he told Dr. Cutter his pain started in the left lower quadrant. The latter flatly denies it and claimed, at trial, that Rocker made this point for the first time at trial. In none of the histories taken by medical personnel during his treatment did Rocker ever report that his pain began in the left lower quadrant.

Analyze the facts of this case to determine the applicability of the following defenses:

- Contributory negligence,
- Last clear chance, and
- Assumption of risk.

Private property was the original source of
freedom. It still is its main bulwark.

—Walter Lippman (1889–1974)

CHAPTER 6

Premises Liability

Historically, landholders have enjoyed the protection of their individual interests under the law but also have a responsibility to others on real property. This chapter views the landholder as a potential defendant whose liability depends upon the *use* of the land and the *relationship* between that use and the plaintiff. Historically, the degree of tort liability has varied depending on the injured party's particular purpose and whether he or she had been invited to enter the property. Tort law did not impose the same duty on a landholder toward a trespasser as toward an invited guest or to a lessor as to a vendor, although a uniform approach has developed during modern times.

CHAPTER TOPICS

1. Concepts in Property Law
2. Actions in Tort
3. The Nature of the Duty Owed
4. Scope of Duty, Defined by Common Law
5. Lessor and Lessee
6. Vendor and Vendee

OBJECTIVES

After completing this chapter, you will be able to:

1. Discuss the role of natural conditions in the duty of landholders.
2. Describe the duties of a landholder to all persons entering the property.
3. Examine the liability of a landholder toward trespassers.
4. Understand the concept of licensee in relation to liability to persons entering property.
5. Analyze the liability of a landholder toward an invitee.
6. Examine the liability of landlord and tenant toward persons entering the property.
7. Understand the liability of landholders as sellers of real estate.

■ CONCEPTS IN PROPERTY LAW

Land is known as real property or real estate; personal property is everything else. **Premises** refers to real property, which includes all attached buildings, grounds, facilities, structures, all other things attached to the land, and anything growing from it.

If someone owns a piece of land, with rights to use the property superior to everyone else's in the world, the law considers that person to be the owner. The law regards a possessor of land as someone who has the right to use the land, without lawful interference by anyone save the owner. Under the law, an owner or possessor would be called a **landholder.**

■ ACTIONS IN TORT

If someone interferes with the use and enjoyment of property, the landholder can sue that person for the tort of trespass; look to Chapter 7, where intentional torts are discussed, for more on that course of action.

If a landholder interferes with a neighbor's or the public's use and enjoyment of its real property, the landholder may face suit for nuisance. Chapter 11, on nuisance, considers that tort action in greater detail.

When a landholder engages in an inherently dangerous activity on the property—such as creating a reservoir that breaks and floods adjacent properties—the neighbors would likely have an action in strict liability. Chapter 12 discusses the tort of strict liability in greater detail.

Premises liability is the liability that may arise for a landholder regarding the use of real property. Most actions involving premises liability arise out of negligence, where a landholder has breached a reasonable duty of care that led to the injury of another.

A premises liability claim will most often be an action in negligence. As with any action in negligence, a landholder has a duty to conduct himself or herself as a reasonable person so as to avoid injury for another. This is a duty to act with reasonable care.

■ THE NATURE OF THE DUTY OWED

Having a superior right to use their real property, landholders likely have the best understanding of the property's condition because, as they exercise that right, most likely they would discover any dangers existing on the property. While landholders have the right to the "use and enjoyment" of the property, they also must exercise reasonable care and take into account the interests of other individuals potentially affected by that use.

For example, suppose Cronin has hastily erected a large flagpole in front of his home to hoist the colors in observance of a national holiday. But let's assume Cronin didn't secure the pole sufficiently to support the weight of a heavy, 10- by 20-foot flag. The first time that Cronin raises the flag, the entire pole falls onto a neighbor's property, crushing the neighbor's chinchilla. Cronin's failure to exercise reasonable care when using his property caused harm to another. Cronin will likely be found liable and have to pay damages.

Exception Regarding Natural Conditions

Natural conditions refers to the state of land unaltered by human act. This includes the natural occurrence of trees and vegetation of any kind, along with rock and mineral formations.

Generally speaking, a landholder faces liability for injuries that occur on the landholder's property regardless of whether the landholder's knows of the existence of a dangerous condition. During colonial times, however, when America was agrarian and undeveloped, requiring a landholder to inspect his property and make it safe would have created a significant burden. Thus, an exception arose regarding the general duty of a landholder concerning purely natural conditions on the land (see box below).

NATURAL CONDITIONS

1. Except as stated in Subsection (2), neither a possessor of land, nor a vendor, lessor, or other transferor, is liable for physical harm caused to others outside of the land by a natural condition of the land.
2. A possessor of land in an urban area is subject to liability to persons using a public highway for physical harm resulting from his failure to exercise reasonable care to prevent an unreasonable risk of harm arising from the condition of trees on the land near the highway.

Restatement (Second) of Torts, §329 (1965)

This exception may not apply, even where natural conditions play a significant role in determining a landholder's liability, if other circumstances also exist and contribute to the creation of liability (see Case in Point 6-1).

CASE IN POINT 6-1

Parrott v. United States of America

181 F. Supp. 425 (S.D. Cal. 1960)

This action to recover damages under the Tort Claims Act [footnote omitted] produced evidence of near-gross negligence on the part of Government personnel. Unless the application of some special defensive rule arises to defeat recovery, the plaintiffs should prevail. It is urged by the Government that two such rules completely negative the plaintiffs' case. The first of these is that "*** (A) vendor of land is not subject to liability for bodily harm caused to his vendee or others while upon the land after the vendee has taken possession by any dangerous condition, whether natural or artificial, which existed at the time that the vendee took possession.'' [footnote omitted] [...]

The evidence has established that during World War II the United States Army, as a lessee, occupied certain land in Riverside County, using it as a small arms practice range. The property was released to its private owners in 1947 and the Government has been out of possession since that time. The accident occurred February 12, 1957. Neither the owner nor his successors have been sued. Except during its use by the military, the larger part of the leasehold, consisting of an unfenced peneplain, [footnote omitted] has been used principally for potato farming. [...] Rising rather abruptly from the peneplain is a hill-like formation—largely a residue of boulders from which much of the soil has been eroded by rains. [footnote omitted] This part of the terrain itself is somewhat unusual and apt to invite entry by a young boy.

The only practical purpose for the hill which has been suggested by the evidence is the military one to which it was at one time put by the Government. The almost plain-like land which surrounds it is, however, splendidly adapted to raising field crops, and the area abounds with potato fields, one of which extends to the very base of the monadnock. Most of the fields in the area, including the one formerly a Government leasehold, are unfenced. [footnote omitted] During the Army's use of the land, military personnel were trained upon it in the use of rifle grenades by actually firing them at targets within the area. The only evidence that the property was cleared of unexploded grenades before being returned to civilian occupancy is a certificate [footnote omitted] to the effect that the area has been de-dudded. Ten years elapsed without untoward results following the time when the Government's military personnel made what the court now finds was an exceedingly negligent and cursory search of the portion of the land here involved prior to issuing their certificate. [...] The actual search probably was only conducted on the peneplain. The court's finding of an exceedingly negligent search relates to that made upon the monadnock.

[...]

On the afternoon of February 12, 1957, the three minor plaintiffs [...] had a free afternoon in one of the most fruitful Indian relic areas of California. The property in question is in Riverside County where two years previously an official study [footnote omitted] disclosed that there were still many Indians and eleven active Indian reservations. Of the counties of California, only neighboring San Diego had more Indian reservations at that time. [...] A primitive area like the monadnock in the potato field was a likely place to find such things as arrowheads. What they found, however, was a small rifle grenade not far up the incline and rather conspicuously at rest between rocks. [...] The boys took the grenade home, and, after some futile attempts to take it apart, plaintiff Alvy Parrott threw it upon the pavement. It immediately exploded, inflicting various injuries, all serious, upon the three boys. Plaintiffs base their case upon the assertion that Army personnel failed to properly police or de-dud the firing range prior to its return to civilian use. The court finds that this is true. "The risk incident to dealing with *** explosive *** matters *** requires a great deal of care to be exercised. In other words, the standard of care required of the reasonable person when dealing with such dangerous articles is so great that a slight deviation therefrom will constitute negligence. "[footnote omitted] The same afternoon that the boys were injured, Air Force personnel came a distance of some miles to the area in which the boys found that grenade, and the same day located at least three more which had every appearance of containing a similar explosive. An exhibit in the case [footnote omitted] is a picture of the finder holding five grenades which were found during that afternoon. [...]

[...]

The rationale of non-liability has generally been applied to cases in which there was either a defect in the realty or in some fixture on the premises—conditions for which the owner of the property is responsible. [...]

In the case here decided there was nothing wrong with the land or with any fixtures thereon. Highly dangerous small chattels were negligently left upon the land [...]

Plaintiffs were either trespassers or licensees. They had no express permission to enter the land. Generally, the possessor of land [footnote omitted] owes no duty of affirmative care to a trespasser, and need only abstain from wilfully or wantonly injuring him. [footnote omitted] However, as previously noted, the particular area was one well known as a repository of Indian relics. It had, in addition, a certain attraction to youngsters because of the normal residue of junk which is to be found on an abandoned military range. It was rural, unfenced, and of easy access.

[...]

The duty of care in this case had its origin when what had been a restricted military target range was being readied for return to the unregimented community.

[...]

Many of the cast are, and purport to be, Indians. Any user of explosives contained as in a small grenade and disseminated over land, as would be the custom in a training range, must be guilty of a lack of care in returning such a range to the open countryside in an area where search for Indian relics is frequent, widespread, and inferentially invited. [...]

Plaintiff Alvy Parrott sustained six fractures, numerous lacerations and shock. Pieces of metal still remain in him. He will have some permanent limitation of motion in his right wrist and ankles. Neurological injuries, permanent in nature, will cause him some pain and disqualify him from many types of work. The Court assesses his damages at $ 30,000.

Plaintiff Walter Dwight Anthony suffered multiple punctuate wounds with nerve injuries some of which leave permanent numbness in his left hand. His body still contains shrapnel. His damages are fixed at $ 7,500.

Plaintiff Carlos Pat Anthony suffered injuries comparable in severity to those of his brother. He still has metal in his body, weakness in his left knee, and continued ringing in his ears. His damages are fixed at $ 7,500.

Plaintiff Joe Parrott, the father of Alvy Parrott, and plaintiff Jimmie Faye Anthony, the father of the Anthony boys, claim damages in the amount of medical expenses which they have incurred. Damages in the amount of $ 1,302.50 are allowed Joe Parrott. Damages in the amount of $ 409.50 are allowed Jimmie Faye Anthony.

Even though natural conditions played a role in the decision of the boys to explore the land, it was the negligence of United States in cleaning up the property that was the cause for liability.

Exception Limited in Urban Settings

The exception of a duty of care regarding natural conditions is limited in urban settings. For example, consider a tree with dead limbs. In a rural area, a landholder is under no obligation to remove the dangerous tree limbs as that would require close monitoring of the conditions of the trees. In an urban location, however, a landholder doesn't face an onerous burden in making sure that natural conditions, like fallen branches, do not lead to injury.

The court in *McGarr* specifically used the issue of dead limbs to consider why the exception regarding natural conditions should not apply in an urban setting (see Case in Point 6-2).

 # CASE IN POINT 6-2

McGarr v. United States
736 F.2d 912 (3d Cir. Pa. 1984)

McGarr alleges that his son, Edward Christopher McGarr, was seriously injured when on April 3, 1982, McGarr's automobile went out of control on County Line Road and struck a tree. The road is owned by the Commonwealth of Pennsylvania, but traverses the Valley Forge National Historical Park, which is owned by the United States.

[...]

The dangers of a flooded or washed out or muddy road and bridge are evident and certainly foreseeable where proper runoff and drainage are not secured....McGarr also made clear to the court [...] that discovery may yet reveal the existence of an artificial condition such as grading, drainage course or shoring excavation so as to cause the muddy, slippery and dangerous conditions Plaintiff encountered while crossing County Line Road Bridge....

[...][W]e must therefore consider whether under Pennsylvania law McGarr could recover against an owner of land abutting a highway for the maintenance on the land of an artificial or natural condition causing an unreasonable risk to travelers on the highway....

[...]

The trend in the law is in the direction of imposing a duty of reasonable care upon the possessor of land with regard to natural conditions of land. [...]. Also evident is the lack of congruence between the old common law rule of nonliability and the relevant factors which should determine whether a duty exists. All this leads to but one conclusion. The distinction between artificial and natural conditions should be rejected. "A [person's] life or limb [or property] does not become less worthy of protection by the law nor a loss less worthy of compensation under the law" because that person has been injured by a natural, as opposed to an artificial condition.

It seems evident, therefore, that if McGarr proves either an artificial or a natural condition on land owned by the United States which caused the allegedly dangerous condition he encountered on County Line Road, he may be able to recover from the United States as a landowner.

Thus, for most urban settings, the landholder must exercise reasonable care in the inspection and maintenance of property and may not invoke the defense of natural conditions.

■ SCOPE OF DUTY, DEFINED BY COMMON LAW

The common law has held a landholder to a duty of care to a person on a landholder's property depended on the status of that person in the eyes of the law. The issue of 'status' had to do with the circumstances that had allowed entry to the plaintiff. So, a landholder had a reduced duty to someone illegally on the property—a trespasser—than to a guest who would be there lawfully (and might be considered an invitee). As the status of the person entering the land "improves" from trespasser to invitee, he or she enjoys greater protection from a landholder's negligence.

Yet these designations seemed arbitrary, in part, because it was difficult to see how a landholder could anticipate who would come on the property to know what standard of care had to be followed. The courts and legal scholars have criticized this arbitrary categorization (see box below).

ENTRY UPON LAND

Those who enter upon land are divided unto three fixed categories: trespassers, licensees, and invitees, and there are subdivided duties as to each. They make out, as a general pattern, a rough sliding scale, by which, as the legal status of the visitor improves, the possessor of the land owes him more of an obligation of protection. This system has long made many legal writers, and some of the

PREMISES LIABILITY **203**

courts, quite unhappy because of its arbitrary and sometimes unreasonable character; and there has been some recent movement toward abolishing the distinctions, at least between invitees and licensees. But the traditional entrant classification scheme is well entrenched in the great majority of jurisdictions, and so the categories must be carefully considered one by one.

W. Page Keeton et al., *Prosser & Keeton on the Law of Torts*, §58 at 393 (5th ed. 1984)

Reprinted with permission from Thomson West. All rights reserved.

Table 6-1 lists the different categories of persons and the corresponding duty of care.

Table 6-1 Status, Definition, and Duty Owed by Landholder to a Person on the Premises

Status	Definition	Duty Owed
Trespasser	One who enters upon the land of another without permission or privilege	None
Licensee	One who is granted access to the land	Reasonable care so long as the landholder was aware of the licensee's presence on the property
Invitee	Members of the public on public land, or business visitors	Reasonable care

Trespassers

A **trespasser** is a person who has entered another's land without permission or privilege to be there. To such intruders, the landholder faces no liability for an injury the trespasser suffers from being on the land. Thus, the general rule is that a landholder has no duty to keep that property safe for trespassers:

LIABILITY TO TRESPASSERS

[A] possessor of land is not liable to trespassers for physical harm caused by his failure to exercise reasonable care

a. to put the land in a condition reasonably safe for their reception, or
b. to carry on his activities so as not to endanger them.

Restatement (Second) of Torts, §333 (1965)

Copyright by The American Law Institute. Reproduced with permission. All rights reserved.

The general rule is intended to apply to trespassing adults. The justification for this form of limited immunity is that a landholder should not be expected to anticipate trespassers, and therefore should not be held accountable for their safety on his land.

Exceptions

The general rule has many exceptions that vary from state to state, and paralegal students should consult local statutes and case law on such questions.

Frequent Trespassers

Most jurisdictions hold a landholder to a higher degree of reasonable care when:

- There is frequent trespass and
- The landholder engages in certain activities.

The *Restatement (Second) of Torts* characterizes some people as constant trespassers (see box below).

CONSTANT TRESPASSERS

A possessor of land who knows, or from facts within his knowledge should know, that trespassers constantly intrude upon a limited area thereof, is subject to liability for bodily harm there caused to them by his failure to carry on an activity involving a risk of death or serious bodily harm with reasonable care for their safety.

Restatement (Second) of Torts, §334 (1965)

For example, imagine that factory workers have to cross railroad tracks to get from the parking lot to the factory. The law expects the railroad to be aware of the situation and to exercise reasonable care towards the workers.

Trespassers Discovered by the Landholder

Another exception applies when a landholder discovers a trespasser on the property. Once a trespasser is found, the landholder has a duty to exercise reasonable care to provide for the trespasser's safety.

Whether the landholder knows the specific identity of the trespasser does not matter. If a landholder finds physical evidence of trespass—such as footprints—on the property but does not know specifically who left the footprints, the landholder owes a duty of reasonable care. That means a landholder must refrain from willful or wanton conduct designed to injure trespassers whose presence (though not their identity) is known. The landholder must refrain from intentionally injuring trespassers upon discovery of their presence.

Children: Exception to Rule of Nonliability for the Landholder

Even the common-law rules regarding a landholder's duty to trespassers had an exception regarding age. As you will read in Chapter 7's discussion of intentional torts, the common law has always recognized the need to change expectations depending on a person's age. The younger a person, the less likely the possibility that he or she is capable of forming the intent needed to hold her or him liable. Support for this view has come from the field of developmental psychology, which has shown that a child's developing brain has not yet made the kinds of physical connections that would allow him or her to appreciate the consequences of an action.

Because of their inherent lack of maturity and judgment, children are excepted from the general nonliability rule for trespassers. In the landmark case of *Sioux City & Pacific Railroad Co. v. Stout*, 84 U.S. 657 (1873), a child trespassing on railroad property and injured while playing on a railroad turntable obtained recovery.

Attractive Nuisance

This and other cases led to the development of the doctrine of **attractive nuisance.** (This might involve a public nuisance as well.) Not only would a landholder face liability for injuries to a child who has trespassed on the land, the creation of an artificial condition—an attractive nuisance—would increase the likelihood that the landholder is held liable, since children might be drawn to trespass on the property to investigate further (see box below).

TRESPASSING CHILDREN

A possessor of land is subject to liability for physical harm to children trespassing thereon caused by an artificial condition upon the land if

a. the place where the condition exists is one upon which the possessor knows or has reason to know that children are likely to trespass, and

b. the condition is one of which the possessor knows or has reason to know and which he realizes or should realize will involve an unreasonable risk of death or serious bodily harm to such children, and

c. the children because of their youth do not discover the condition or realize the risk involved in intermeddling with it or in coming within the area made dangerous by it, and

d. the utility to the possessor of maintaining the condition and the burden of eliminating the danger are slight as compared with the risk to children involved, and

e. the possessor fails to exercise reasonable care to eliminate the danger or otherwise to protect the children.

Restatement (Second) of Torts, §339 (1965)

For example, assume that the Dagle family had just recently installed an in-ground swimming pool in their backyard. The little Dagles had friends over to use the pool but only under the supervision of an adult. The Dagles did not erect a fence around the pool. Further, assume that the Dagle children's friend and frequent guest, nine-year-old Butch, decided to go swimming after the Dagles had gone in for the evening. In the dark, Butch tripped over the diving board, falling in and hitting his head against the side of the pool. The Dagles may be held responsible for the injury to Butch because they failed to exercise reasonable care in erecting a fence around the pool.

The fact that an attractive nuisance exists does not automatically make a landholder liable for injuries suffered by a child if it's clear the child understood that trespass meant an increased risk of injury, as shown in the following case (see Case in Point 6-3).

 # CASE IN POINT 6-3

Barnhizer v. Paradise Valley Unified School District

123 Ariz. 253 (1979)

This is a wrongful death action brought by William D. and Georgia B. Barnhizer to recover damages for the death of their son, Steven A. Barnhizer....

The facts of this case are not in dispute. On the evening of May 2, 1975, Steven Barnhizer, then thirteen years old, and two companions went to the Desert Shadows School in Scottsdale where a school sponsored dance was in progress. After telling a teacher chaperone that they were not going to the dance, they were told to leave the area. They left, but later returned to the school from a different direction. Steven suggested to his companions that they climb to the roof of the school building. One of his companions, John Hert, then 15 years old, expressed opposition because he had seen other boys being told by teachers and janitors not to climb onto the roof. However, Steven's suggestion prevailed. Steven fell from the roof, incurring injuries which resulted in his death....

Ordinarily, the duty of a landowner to a trespasser is not to willfully or wantonly injure him [...] Where children are concerned, an exception to this rule has developed, commonly known as the doctrine of attractive nuisance.

[...]

The *Restatement of Torts (Second)* [...] Section 339 [...] provides:

A possessor of land is subject to liability for physical harm to children trespassing thereon caused by an artificial condition upon the land if (c) the children because of their youth do not discover the condition or realize the risk involved in intermeddling with it or in coming within the area made dangerous by it. (citation omitted.)

[...]

We are persuaded [...] that, as a matter of law, plaintiffs failed to meet the condition set forth in part (c) of § 339 of the Restatement, supra, a condition which must exist before a duty arose to protect the decedent against his own folly. Steven was just eight weeks short of his fourteenth birthday and was of the age and intelligence to appreciate the clear danger of falling. The doctrine of attractive nuisance did not, therefore, have application.

Appellants argue that even assuming that Steven was trespassing at the time of his death and that he recognized the danger of falling, because the School District knew that school children could climb to the roof, it had a duty to eliminate or reduce the risk. The problem with this argument is that Steven on this occasion was not an invited school child but a trespasser for whom the School District had no duty except not to willfully or wantonly injure him. The possessor of property is not under a duty to prevent every possibility of harm.

The appellate court did not accept the argument that the roof constituted an attractive nuisance. If it had, the defendant would have owed the plaintiff a duty of reasonable care. But the appellate court ruled that since the plaintiff was too old for the attractive nuisance doctrine to apply here, the defendant owed the trespassing plaintiff no duty of care.

The case law of individual states varies regarding the limitations on the doctrine and should be thoroughly examined if this becomes an issue of law.

Licensees

A **licensee** is anyone who has consent, or license, to enter land. Here, "consent" refers a landholder's willingness to have the licensee on the property. Table 6-2 lists examples of licensees.

Table 6-2 Examples of Licensees by Category

Who	What kind of licensee
Neighbor recovering a baseball hit over the fence by accident	Persons entering the property solely for their own interest
Aunts, uncles, cousins, grandparents	Persons considered family members, but not paying guests or servants
Friends of children over to participate in a birthday party	Persons to whom the use of the premises is a personal favor; not to be confused with invitees simply because they are invited on the premises

The courts often examine custom and usage in an area to determine the existence of a relationship with the landholder. Any visitor who fits one of the categories will be considered a licensee. For example, assume that Detlef was soliciting political campaign contributions door-to-door. As he entered the Thomas family property, he tripped over a skateboard left on the front walk by one of the Thomas children and suffered serious injury. Detlef would fit the first category of a person entering the property and the Thomases would then be held liable (Detlef is a licensee because the Thomas family did not have a 'No solicitors' sign on the property.).

Duty

The general rule of a landholder's liability toward a licensee is similar to that of the responsibility toward trespassers, as Professor Dobbs notes:

> ## DUTY IMPOSED ON THE LANDOWNER WITH NOTICE OF THE LICENSEE'S PRESENCE.
>
> As with trespassers, a duty of reasonable care is imposed once the landowner actually knows or has notice of the licensee's presence and knows or has notice of the danger the licensee is about to encounter.
>
> Dobbs, *The Law of Torts* §233 (2000)

The landholder escapes liability for licensees to the same degree of escaping liability for trespassers because the duty of care owed is minimal.

In the following case, a worker was injured while working on a client's property. The decision in the case hinged upon whether this employee-visitor was a licensee or an invitee: that definition would affect the duty the landholder owed the plaintiff (see Case in Point 6-4).[The *Hundt* case appeared in the previous chapter, but on a different issue.]

 # CASE IN POINT 6-4

Hundt v. LaCrosse Grain Co., Inc.
425 N.E.2d 687 (Ind. Ct.App.1981)

This appeal is from a negligence action brought by [...] Everett Hundt against the LaCrosse Grain Co., Inc. [...] following a fall by Hundt down a flight of stairs on property owned by LaCrosse. Hundt had been employed by LaCrosse for a number of years through an oral agreement to exterminate pests from various buildings located near the company's grain elevator in LaCrosse, Indiana. [...]

When the two arrived, they first went into a small building where the company had an office (and where the misadventure later occurred) and made their presence known to the company's manager, Jim Anderson. They entered the office through the front door, as they always had done in the past. After a few minutes, the Hundts left the building and proceeded to the storage shed located about 180 yards to the rear of the office. [...][I]t was the first time the Hundts had done bird exterminating work on the premises, although the elder Hundt had visited the LaCrosse buildings approximately once a month since 1955 for the purpose of exterminating various other pests. Hundt stated the LaCrosse facility was one of 127 grain elevators (along with various restaurants, farms, stores, and taverns) where he regularly did exterminating.

The particular work they were doing that day required the use of highly toxic chemicals, and after one and one-half to two hours of working with the substance, when the job was complete, Hundt and his son returned to the office building to wash up. This time, however, they entered through the back door of the office building, which was the closest door to the shed where they had been working. Hundt's fall occurred in the building housing the company's office. In this regard, he stated he opened the back door of the building, walked forward a few feet, and then mistakenly opened the door to the basement instead of the washroom door, and his momentum from these actions caused him to fall down the basement stairs. Significantly [...] the basement door opened inward, there was no landing inside the door, and there was no handrail [...] alongside the stairs[...]

One who enters at the owner's express or implied invitation to transact business of mutual benefit to both is an invitee to whom the landowner owes a duty of reasonable care to protect against dangers, while one who enters for his own convenience, curiosity, or entertainment is a licensee by permission, or a mere licensee, who (with certain exceptions) must take the premises as he finds them [...]

LaCrosse contends Hundt was a licensee as a matter of law to whom no duty was breached because, on cross-examination, he acknowledged no one had forced or induced him to open the basement door and that "(t)he washing up would only help me." Even assuming this were the only evidence in the case, we do not believe Hundt must be viewed as a licensee as a matter of law [...].

Moreover [...] Hundt's activity in looking for a place to wash his hands may legally be viewed as a necessary part of the job he was doing for LaCrosse. In this regard, Hundt's son stated the chemicals they were using were "very toxic" and "we had that chemical on us," and thus it was necessary to wash it off "because the chemical burns and if you get enough on you it would permeate your skin and could make you very deathly ill or could kill you." Similarly, Hundt himself testified "(t)here is no way you can keep from getting it (the chemical) on you" despite protective gloves and face shields, and that washing up "is just taken for granted" as "part of the job" and that "(m)y convenience has nothing to do with it." Under these facts, the jury was not required to conclude that Hundt was a mere licensee when he fell.

[...] [T]he decision of the trial court is reversed, and a new trial ordered on the issue of damages only.

Making a further distinction, the *Armstrong* decision states that a licensee relationship is formed when one who is an invitee exceeds the bounds of that relationship. There, the plaintiff had been injured outside of a nightclub that had closed for the evening. At that point, the relationship between the parties has changed, and the resulting duty of care has also changed (see Case in Point 6-5).

CASE IN POINT 6-5

Armstrong v. Sundance Entertainment, Inc.

179 Ga. App. 635 (1986)

Appellant brought suit against appellee to recover damages for injuries suffered when appellant was shot outside appellee's nightclub. Asserting that there are genuine issues of material fact, appellant brings this appeal from the grant of summary judgment to appellee. We affirm.

[...]Under OCGA § 51-3-2, the owner or proprietor of the premises is liable only for wilful or wanton injury to a licensee, whereas under OCGA § 51-3-1 the landowner or occupier owes an invitee the duty to exercise ordinary care in keeping the premises safe....

To determine whether a person is an invitee or a mere licensee, the nature of his relation or contact with the owner or occupier of the premises must be determined. The test is whether the injured person at the time of the injury had present business relations with the owner of the premises which would render his presence of mutual aid to both, or whether his presence on the premises was for his own convenience. [...]

If an invitee does not go beyond that part of the premises to which, as it reasonably appears to him the invitation extends, he does not become a licensee. If, however, he does go beyond that part to which he is invited, he becomes a mere licensee. [...]

It is apparent to us [...] that the requirement that an invitee not go beyond the limits of his invitation extends to the temporal dimension as well as the spatial: one who uses the premises of a merchant at a time beyond that to which an implied invitation extends is a mere licensee. [...]

The uncontradicted evidence in the record shows that appellee's business had closed for the night prior to the occurrence of appellant's injury. [...][T]he nightclub had closed its doors for the night before appellant was accosted and shot. [...][A]ppellant had departed the club and had sat for some time in his car before the events which led to his injury.

Under those circumstances, we find that there are no questions of fact regarding appellant's status at the time of his injury: he was a licensee.

Invitees

The term **invitee** generally refers to visitors for the economic benefit of the landholder or for both parties. Visitors may be considered invitees if:

- they enter by the express or implied invitation of the landholder, who has received an implicit assurance that the landholder has exercised reasonable care to maintain the property,
- the entry is concerned with the nature of the landholder's business, or
- there is a mutual benefit for both the visitor and the landholder.

Table 6-3 lists categories and examples of invitees.

Table 6-3 Types of Invitees	
Category	**Example**
They enter by the expressed or implied invitation of the landholder, receiving implicit assurance that the landholder has exercised reasonable care to maintain the property.	Postal carriers, community property inspectors
	(continued)

Category	Example
Table 6-3 continued	
The entry is concerned with the nature of the landholder's business.	Customers
There is a mutual benefit for both the visitor and the landholder.	Electricians, plumbers, roofers, carpenters

Invitation

An element essential to invitee status is the expressed or implied invitation to enter the premises. An **invitation** is conduct on the part of the landholder that justifies the visitor's belief that his or her entry is sought. The invitation includes the entrance to the premises, the exit, and all parts of the premises that the visitor may be expected to visit. A visitor may be considered an invitee when using restrooms but may lose that status by sneaking into a storeroom or locked closet.

Standard of Care

A landholder has to exercise reasonable care to achieve safety and protection for an invitee. The landholder is not obligated to protect an invitee against his or her own negligence, but is under an obligation not to act negligently toward the invitee and to warn the invitee of any known dangers. The *Restatement* adopts this approach, and is supported by the case law of most jurisdictions, absent statutory modification:

STANDARD OF CARE OWED TO INVITEES

A possessor of land is subject to liability for physical harm caused to his invitees by a condition on the land if, but only if, he

a. knows or by the exercise of reasonable care would discover the condition, and should realize that it involves an unreasonable risk of harm to such invitees, and
b. should expect that they will not discover or realize the danger, or will fail to protect themselves against it, and
c. fails to exercise reasonable care to protect them against the danger.

Restatement (Second) of Torts, §343 (1965)

For example, assume that Brisket Bus Lines regularly discharges its passengers at a designated gate on its premises, allowing passengers to enter the terminal. To enter the terminal, passengers must alight from the bus, traverse three feet of roadway, and step onto a curb. Assume that recent weather conditions had buckled the curb and roadway, leaving a hazardous path to the terminal. Brisket would be liable to any passenger who sustained an injury because of the unsafe entrance to its terminal.

Invitees and Visitors

The distinction between an invitee and a visitor may be so slight that it can cause confusion, although the distinction apparently has some significance (see box on next page).

> ## INVITEE
>
> 1. An invitee is either a public invitee or a business visitor.
> 2. A public invitee is a person who is invited to enter or remain on land as a member of the public for a purpose for which the land is held open to the public.
> 3. A business visitor is a person who is invited to enter or remain on land for a purpose directly or indirectly connected with business dealings with the possessor of the land.
>
> *Restatement (Second) of Torts, §332 (1965)*

Public Invitees

Public invitees are individuals who are lawfully allowed to enter the property to conduct business unrelated to a landholder's business. Examples include meter readers, postal workers, fire inspectors, and garbage collectors. Since they're not on the premises as clients or customers, they are not truly invitees in the strictest sense of the word, but they're not trespassers, either, because they have a lawful purpose to be on the property. Most jurisdictions have held that the landholder has a duty of reasonable care to make the premises safe for public invitees. Some courts have ruled that because public invitees do engage in conduct that affect the conduct of a landholder's business (even if only incidentally), the landholder owes a duty of reasonable care.

Business Visitors

Business visitors are persons invited onto the premises for the purpose of conducting business. The landholder owes business visitors a duty of reasonable care. They have entered the premises for the purpose for which it is open to the public. Examples of business visitors include shoppers, restaurant patrons, theatergoers, and office patrons.

The duty to business visitors extends to protect them from the landholder's employees as well as from other invitees. If a landholder's drunk employee gets into a fight with a customer, the landholder would be liable for damages to the customer. If a drunk customer struck another customer, the landholder would be liable for damages to the customer who was hit.

Social Guests Are Not Invitees

Social guests are licensees and are not considered invitees, even though they have been invited onto the premises. In the following case, the injured party was a child invited over for a birthday party (see Case in Point 6-6). As in this case, some states have statutorily limited liability of a landholder for public invitees who use the property for recreational purposes.

 # CASE IN POINT 6-6

Estate of Gordon-Couture v. Brown

152 N.H. 265 (2005)

This case arises out of the accidental drowning of two-year-old Jaycob Gordon-Couture while attending a birthday party at property owned by the defendants, George and Silvia Brown. [...]

[...] On August 17, 2002, the defendants' daughter held a birthday party for her son at the defendants' property on Half Moon Pond in Kingston. Elizabeth McNeil attended the party and brought her boyfriend's son, Jaycob, with her. McNeil and Jaycob spent some time playing in the water and then returned to the beach. At some point after returning to the beach, McNeil realized that Jaycob was missing. After a search of the area, Jaycob's body was found in the pond. Later, at the hospital, he was pronounced dead due to drowning.

The plaintiff brought suit alleging that the defendants negligently failed "to keep the beach and dock area safe for their guests including providing the proper supervision or, alternatively, placing appropriate limitations upon the use of the beach and dock area." The trial court granted the defendants' motion for summary judgment, ruling that the defendants were not liable under the recreational use statutes, RSA 212:34 and RSA 508:14, I. This appeal followed.

[...]

On appeal, the plaintiff argues that the trial court erred in ruling that the defendants are immune from suit under two recreational use statutes, RSA 212:34 and RSA 508:14, I. Specifically, the plaintiff argues that the recreational use statutes do not apply to private land used for private activities. Rather, the plaintiff argues that the statutes only apply to private land that is open to the general public. We agree.

[...]

Both RSA 212:34 and RSA 508:14 were adopted at a time when many States were enacting recreational use statutes, *i.e.*, statutes that limit the liability of landowners who make their land available for recreational use. [...] The primary impetus behind this trend was "the need for additional recreational areas to serve the general public." (citation omitted).

[...]The recreational use statutes [...] limited the liability of private landowners who make their land available for public recreational uses "on the theory that it is not reasonable to expect such owners to undergo the risks of liability for injury to persons and property attendant upon the use of their land by strangers from whom the accommodating owner receives no compensation or other favor in return." (citation omitted).

[...]

RSA 508:14, I, provides in pertinent part:

An owner, occupant, or lessee of land, including the state or any political subdivision, who without charge permits *any person* to use land for recreational purposes or as a spectator of recreational activity, shall not be liable for personal injury or property damage in the absence of intentionally caused injury or damage.

(Emphasis added.)

The defendants argue that the phrase, "any person," evidences a legislative intent "to broadly immunize landowners in this state" from liability for negligent acts. The plaintiff argues that to construe RSA 508:14, I,as the defendants suggest would be in derogation of the common law. As set forth above, statutes in derogation of the common law are to be interpreted strictly.

[...] [T]o hold otherwise "would immunize even homeowners from the negligence claims of social guests invited for recreational purposes." [...]

RSA 508:14, I, does not clearly eliminate all common law duties of landowners toward all entrants on land. If the legislature wishes to accomplish such a result, it must do so clearly and explicitly. (citation omitted) Therefore, our strict interpretation of RSA 508:14, I, is consistent with our holdings that we will not interpret a statute to abrogate the common law unless the statute clearly expresses that intent. (citation omitted)

[...]

Thus, for RSA 508:14, I, to grant immunity, private landowners must permit members of the general public to use their land for recreational purposes. Here, the defendants' land was not opened to the general public but rather was used for a private birthday party. Accordingly, the trial court erred [...]

We next turn to RSA 212:34 [...]

The defendants argue that under RSA 212:34, the legislature intended "to broadly immunize landowners in this state" from liability for negligent acts. The plaintiff argues that to construe the statute as the defendants suggest would be in derogation of the common law. We look to the language of the statute to determine whether it clearly abrogates all landowners' common law duties owed to all entrants on land for recreational purposes. (citation omitted). We further note that we do not construe statutes in isolation; instead, we attempt to do so in harmony with the overall statutory scheme. (citation omitted). When interpreting two statutes that deal with a similar subject matter, we construe them so that they do not contradict each other, and so that they will lead to reasonable results and effectuate the legislative purpose of the statutes. (citation omitted)

Both RSA 212:34 and RSA 508:14, I, limit the liability of landowners toward entrants on land in circumstances that involve recreational activities. Because RSA 212:34 deals with a similar subject matter as RSA 508:14, I, the statutes should be construed so that they do not contradict each other. (citation omitted) Therefore, RSA 212:34 likewise should be construed to grant immunity only to landowners who open their land to the general public.

[...]

Moreover, RSA 212:34 does not clearly eliminate all common law duties of landowners toward all entrants on land. If the legislature wishes to accomplish such a result, it must do so clearly and explicitly. [...]Thus, for RSA 212:34 to grant immunity, private landowners must permit members of the general public to use their land for one of the listed recreational purposes.

[...]

Here, the defendants did not make their land available to the public. Rather, McNeil and Jaycob were allowed to use their land and swimming area for a private birthday party. Accordingly, the trial court erred [...]

Finally, [...] statutes in derogation of the common law should be narrowly construed. (citation omitted). Because the legislature did not clearly abrogate the common law duties of landowners toward all entrants on land, we narrowly construe RSA 212:34 and RSA 508:14, I, as providing immunity only to landowners who open their land to the general public. [...]

Here, the defendants' land was used for a private birthday party, which was not open to the general public. Therefore, RSA 212:34 and RSA 508:14, I, do not apply.

Reversed and remanded.

The court, here, declined to interpret a statute that limited liability where the landholder opened the premises to the general public, since inviting a child over for a birthday was not the same as making the premises open to the public.

Fireman's Rule

Unlike public invitees, most jurisdictions regard firefighters and police officers as being mere licensees. They are not invitees because these people enter the premises under authority of law. The landholder has the same obligation toward such individuals as toward any licensee: not to intentionally, willfully, or wantonly cause harm or injury. Courts have questioned the wisdom of continuing to apply this rule, such as in the case that follows (see Case in Point 6-7).

CASE IN POINT 6-7

Knoetig v. Hernandez Realty Co., Inc.

255 N.J. Super. 34 (App. Div. 1992)

[...]

Plaintiff is a firefighter employed by the town of Guttenberg. Shortly after midnight on January 31, 1987, and while he was on duty, he received a so-called still alarm indicating a problem that was neither a fire nor a gas leak. He was able to ascertain that the problem was a water leak in a small industrial complex which was causing water to spill out into the public right-of-way where it was starting to freeze. The premises were owned by defendant Anncarl Realty, which had recently purchased them from defendant Lutz Superdyne with the intention of tearing down the old factory structures and building condominiums. Lutz, however, continued to occupy a portion of the premises as a month-to-month tenant while it was making its plans to relocate.

When plaintiff arrived at the scene, he found three Guttenberg police officers waiting for him who told him that they had found the source of the leak within one of the buildings. [...][T]here was an alleyway between two buildings, access to which was barred by a padlocked gate. Since the alley provided the most direct route to the source of the leak, it was plaintiff's plan to cut the padlock, enter the alley, and force an entrance into the building by way of a door leading into the alley. The police officers asked him not to do so since they had already communicated with a representative of the occupant, who was on his way with keys. [...]

In any event, when the agent arrived, it appeared that he had no key to the locked gate. He urged plaintiff not to cut the padlock and told him that they could obtain access by a door some 75 feet down the block, traverse the interior of that building, and then reach the source of the leak. Plaintiff agreed, and started to follow the agent down the street. Before they reached the door, both plaintiff and the agent slipped and fell on accumulated ice and snow on the sidewalk, whose presence, it is conceded, was attributable to the elements and had nothing to do with the water leak. Indeed, the town had issued a summons to defendant Esposito some ten days before this event charging him with violation of the municipal snow removal ordinance.

After having fallen, plaintiff was able to pick himself up, continued to follow the agent, who had also picked himself up, and finally reached the source of the leak, a broken water sprinkler pipe. He turned off the water at the main valve, and the emergency was thus dealt with. The deposition of Lutz' president indicates that sprinkler pipes had broken before, but in the past the repairs, including any required emergency attentions, were performed either by a plumber or a water sprinkler service company. Apparently, the fire department was asked to respond to this break because neither the police nor the agent was able to reach a plumber at that hour of the night.

Plaintiff, claiming to have suffered back and shoulder injuries as a result of the fall, brought this action against defendants. The gravamen of the action is their alleged negligent maintenance of the public sidewalk abutting the commercial premises within their ownership or control. [...]

We are first satisfied that the fireman's rule [...] would not have barred this action. As we have indicated, the original formulation of the rule only barred recovery by a firefighter or police officer whose injury was caused by an act of negligence related to the cause of the emergency requiring his presence at the premises in the first instance. [...] Since the accumulation of ice and snow on the sidewalk in this case was completely unrelated to the water leak which created the emergency to which plaintiff was responding when he fell and was injured, there was no nexus between the negligence causing the emergency and the negligence causing the injury. [...]

We accept this "safe premises" rationale, as indeed we are obliged to. We are convinced, however, that it has no relevance to an area open to the public, and more particularly, to a public right-of-way, including a public sidewalk.

We think the distinction between private premises and public areas is not only obvious but also pertinent to the matter at hand. The class of persons entering upon private premises is limited, and the duty owed to those persons is ordinarily dependent on their individual status, whether licensee, social invitee or business invitee. The class of potential users of areas open to the public is virtually infinite, and each member of the class has the same expectation of reasonable safety. The duty owed to the members of the class should also be the same for each. Thus, for example, an owner of commercial property has, in this jurisdiction, the duty of maintaining the public sidewalk abutting the premises in a reasonably safe condition, and will consequently be liable to a pedestrian who is injured as a result of the failure to do so. [...]. Hence, in this case, any pedestrian, other than a police officer or firefighter, who would have sustained injury as a result of a fall occasioned by defendants' failure to clear the accumulation of ice and snow from the sidewalk, would undeniably have had a good cause of action against them. Even the agent with whom this plaintiff was walking and who also fell on the same icy sidewalk would have had a good cause of action against whomever, as between the owner and the tenant, was not his employer.

We cannot reconcile with any of the articulated bases supporting the fireman's rule [...] including the analysis by *Rosa*, the carving out of this limited class of firefighters and police officers from the general public and withholding from them alone a cause of action which every other pedestrian is entitled to prosecute. This is particularly so when the use then being made of the public sidewalk is no different from that of any other pedestrian and where the negligent maintenance of the sidewalk is entirely separate from the negligent act bringing the firefighter to the scene of the emergency. [...]

We are, moreover, satisfied that the distinction we make here is entirely consonant with the weight of academic and judicial authority addressing the fireman's rule. Indeed, the *Restatement* position is based on just that distinction.

[...]

Where premises are held open for the use of the public, and a fireman or policeman enters upon a part of the premises which is so held open, and at a time when it is open, he may reasonably assume that reasonable care has been used to prepare the land for the reception of the public, and to make it safe for them. [...]

We make this final observation. In adopting the fireman's rule (citation omitted) addressing the traditional status analysis, concluded that the status of a firefighter responding to an emergency is *sui generis*, not strictly that of either a licensee or an invitee. (citation omitted). Consequently, the fireman's rule was not stated in terms of the disparate duty of a landowner owed to licensees and invitees, but rather in terms of the immunity of the landowner from liability for ordinary negligence. [...]

We reach this conclusion because, ordinarily, the duty of a landowner does not encompass the obligation to make the premises reasonably safe for the use of a licensee. [...] Thus, whether liability is formulated in terms of duty to a licensee or duty to a *sui generis* police officer or firefighter, the result is the same.

[...][W]hen a police officer or firefighter sustains an injury on a negligently maintained public sidewalk which he is using in the same manner as any other member of the public at large, we are able to perceive no justification in public policy, logic or legal doctrine for depriving him of the same legitimate expectations and the same reasonable remedies as are accorded to every other member of the public. Such a deprivation would promote none of the public policy concerns underlying the fireman's rule, would serve no jurisprudential imperative and would produce an arbitrarily unfair result.

[...]The summary judgment appealed from is reversed and we remand for further proceedings.

Courts in other jurisdictions will likely also see that these "first responders" should be accorded a lesser duty of care than others in the community might be.

Elimination of Traditional Distinctions under Common Law

Several court rulings have eliminated the distinctions of the duty owed a visitor to premises on the basis of the status of that individual—trespasser, licensee, or invitee. These courts concluded that such arbitrary classifications created too many problems when generating consistent rules on what kind of duty of care to provide. The courts now require landholders to exercise a duty of reasonable care to all persons entering the premises.

For example, when a child injured herself on a neighbor's property, a court concluded that denying recovery to the child because she was a trespasser made sense in the nineteenth century, but not any longer (see Case in Point 6-8).

 # CASE IN POINT 6-8

Ouellette v. Blanchard

116 N.H. 552 (1976)

These are actions to recover for personal injuries to the minor plaintiff, Jaye Ouellette, and consequential damages to her father, Robert Ouellette, in a burning accident on property of the defendant. The plaintiffs allege that on July 23, 1973, the defendant, with a permit, was burning rubbish in an unsupervised fire on his premises. The plaintiff Jaye Ouellette, then ten years of age, went onto the property with other children and with them threw sand on the fire. Jaye stepped on some hot coals and fell forward on her hands burning both her feet and hands.

[...]

Whatever the social and policy considerations that led to the judicial creation of the invitee, licensee and trespasser immunities they no longer retain their viability under modern conditions and it is fitting and proper that they be laid to judicial rest. "The abiding respect of this court for precedent and stability in the law is balanced by an appreciation of the need for responsible growth and change in rules that have failed to keep pace with modern developments in social and juridical thought." (citation omitted). We can no longer justify adherence to a system "which is at the same time complex, confusing, inequitable, and, paradoxically, nonuniform." (citation omitted).

Accordingly, we hold that henceforth in New Hampshire owners and occupiers of land shall be governed by the test of reasonable care under all the circumstances in the maintenance and operation of their property. The character of and circumstances surrounding the intrusion will be relevant and important in determining the standard of care applicable to the landowner. When the intrusion is not foreseeable or is against the will of the landowner many intruders will be denied recovery as a matter of law. In other words, a landowner cannot be expected to maintain his premises in a safe condition for a wandering tramp or a person who enters against the known wishes of the landowner. Essentially the traditional tort test of foreseeability determines the liability or nonliability of the landowner in these cases. "If the defendant could not reasonably foresee any injury as the result of his act, or if his conduct was reasonable in the light of what he could anticipate, there is no negligence, and no liability." (citation omitted)

[...]

In the present case, the jury may properly consider the activity being carried on by the defendant and the foreseeability of children intruding and being injured in determining whether the defendant acted as a reasonably prudent person in the operation of his property. In our opinion, this provides the triers of fact with a simpler and more exact guideline than to require them to first label the status of the plaintiff and then apply the various standards applicable to the found status.

Defendant's exception overruled; remanded.

Because of how society had changed, the court realized that a mechanical application of the arbitrary classifications would have left a child without a recovery. Paralegal students should consult local state statutory and case law treatment of the issue to determine whether the traditional paradigm has begun to change.

Elimination of Traditional Distinctions by Statute

Courts may not solely revise or eliminate the traditional distinctions. Elimination of these distinctions, by statute, means that the standard reflects what the citizenry, through their elected representatives, feels best reflects a consensus about the kind and level of duty imposed.

In the following case, the State of California had imposed the duty as a matter of law by enactment of a statute. The court does not accept that the imposition of such a duty might prove to be financially burdensome; it notes merely that this is a statutorily imposed duty (see Case in Point 6-9).

 # CASE IN POINT 6-9

Jackson v. Ryder Truck Rental, Inc.
16 Cal. App. 4th 1830 (3d Dist. 1993)

Plaintiffs Frances Marie Jackson, individually and as special administrator, etc., et al., appeal from a summary judgment in favor of defendant Ryder Truck Rental, Inc. (Ryder) in plaintiffs' lawsuit for wrongful death. We shall reverse the summary judgment.

[...]

The decedent, Loren Jackson, was an employee of S. B. Thomas Company (Thomas). On August 26, 1985, he was working as a relief driver servicing Thomas customers in Sacramento. Ryder had exclusive responsibility under contract with Thomas for inspection, preventive maintenance, service, and repair of Thomas vehicles in Sacramento. The Thomas employee who normally drove the truck used by the decedent had experienced many problems with the truck's electrical system and had reported those problems to Ryder, but electrical failures had persisted up to the date of the accident.

In the early morning hours of August 26, 1985, when it was still dark, the decedent pulled off eastbound Highway 50 onto the shoulder. After he got out of the truck, while standing on the shoulder about four feet south of the fog line, he was struck and seriously injured by a car driven by Valerie Ferra. Both decedent and Ferra were found unconscious when rescuers arrived at the accident scene. The California Highway Patrol officer who inspected the truck at the scene found its electrical system was completely inoperable.

The investigating officer found no evidence that Ferra had braked or attempted to take evasive action before the accident, indicating that she may have fallen asleep at the wheel. The officer opined that Ferra was speeding at the time of the accident.

The decedent died several months after the accident. Ferra survived, but suffered a complete memory loss as to the accident.

The history of repairs on the truck indicated the battery had been replaced five times in two years, during which time the vehicle had been driven only 30,000 miles. Plaintiffs' expert testified in deposition the vehicle was "eating batteries." The expert stated, "It appears to me that there was a longstanding electrical problem in this van which had not been adequately addressed. It seems like they were repairing or replacing parts, but not really fixing the problem, whatever it was."

[...]

Ryder asserts that imposing a duty or finding proximate cause on these facts would cause future harm because it would encourage people to drive aberrantly and injure others if they knew they could spread their liability for such conduct. We cannot agree. Imposing a duty of due care to protect a foreseeable plaintiff against a foreseeable risk does not encourage negligence in third parties, and if negligent third parties are able to "spread" liability to others who have properly incurred it by failing to exercise due care, those others are encouraged to perform their duties with greater care in the future and to insure themselves against the consequences of any future negligence—a result in keeping with the policy of preventing future harm.

[...]

To find that Ryder had a duty to exercise due care to maintain the trucks entrusted to it for that purpose under contract would impose no financial burden that Ryder did not voluntarily assume by seeking out the maintenance contract.

[...] [T]he "burden" of which Ryder complains is inherent in its chosen function as a company in the truck maintenance business. We will not presume on the strength of a speculative assertion in Ryder's appellate brief that Ryder cannot carry out this function with due care unless it raises its rates prohibitively.

[...]

As the preceding discussion illustrates, the trial court erroneously granted Ryder's summary judgment motion. [...] The judgment is reversed. [...]

■ LESSOR AND LESSEE

In a traditional lease situation, the **lessor** (a landholder) owns or manages the property and is also known as the landlord. The **lessee** is the tenant, who gains a possessory interest in the property. According to the common law, once the lessee occupies the premises, the lessor no longer has responsibility for the property.

For example, assume that Baldwin leased an apartment to Tingle. Baldwin told Tingle to be careful on the front staircase because the top step was loose. The first time Tingle climbed the stairs, Tingle fell on the loose step and was injured. Without an agreement to repair the step and assuming the stairs were not under Baldwin's care, Baldwin's disclosure of the defect would give rise to the general rule, eliminating any liability on his part.

Yet the lessor may be in the best position to know about the condition of the premises and the lessor derives income from the property. Often, someone who rents property won't have many resources, so if someone on the premises—a trespasser, licensee, or invitee—is injured because of the condition of the property, that person will have no real chance at a recovery (see box below).

> ### LESSOR/LESSEE
>
> Modern ideas of social policy have given rise to a number of exceptions to these general rules of nonliability of the lessor, which to a large extent swallow up the general no-duty rule. There is increasing recognition of the fact that the tenant who leases defective premises is likely to be impecunious and unable to make the necessary repairs, and that sometimes the financial burden is best placed upon the landlord, who receives a benefit from the transaction in the form of rent.
>
> W. Page Keeton et al., *Prosser & Keeton on the Law of Torts,* §63 at 435 (5th ed. 1984)

Table 6-4 provides some exceptions that arose to mitigate the harsh consequences of this common-law rule.

Table 6-4 Exceptions Mitigating the Common Law Rule Regarding Lessor Responsibility

Situation	Lessor has
Concealed dangerous conditions	Obligation to disclose
Conditions dangerous to third persons	Ongoing liability
Premises leased for public benefit	A duty to exercise reasonable care
Common areas under the lessor's control	A duty to exercise reasonable care
The lessor had agreed to make repairs	Responsibility to make repairs within a reasonable time

The old common-law rule worked a hardship upon its victims, and the lessor or landholder cannot always expect to escape liability. Consider the following case, in which the landlord was aware that a tenant owned a vicious dog but did nothing to protect others from its attacks (see Case in Point 6-10).

CASE IN POINT 6-10

Strunk v. Zoltanski

479 N.Y.S.2d 175 (1984)

A landlord who, with knowledge that a prospective tenant has a vicious dog which will be kept on the premises, nonetheless leases the premises to such tenant without taking reasonable measures, by pertinent provisions in the lease or otherwise, to protect persons who might be on the premises from being attacked by the dog may be held liable to a person who while thereafter on the premises is bitten by the dog.

Plaintiff here seeks to recover damages from the landlord for injuries suffered when he was bitten by a dog owned by the tenant.[...]

It appears [...] that, about five years prior to plaintiff's being bitten, Sophie Zoltanski inherited from her sister a six-acre parcel of land on which two residences were located. She did not live in either house but rented both. [...] Carl Kenyon, operator of a gas station, was occupying one of the two houses in April, 1979; [...] on one occasion during that month Mrs. Zoltanski was on the premises later leased to Kenyon where the German Shepherd dog which subsequently bit plaintiff was tied in her full view; that at the time the dog was "barking very loudly, jumping up and down, growling and acting ferocious." [...]

On May 8, 1979 plaintiff, then a boy of 14, encountered Kenyon at his gas station and the latter asked him if he wanted the dog. Plaintiff replied that he would have to check with his mother. His mother wanted to see the dog and went with plaintiff to the Kenyon premises. She waited at the residence next door while plaintiff went to get the dog. The boy walked toward the dog to untie it, and it was then that the dog jumped up and bit him on the mouth and later on his arm as he sought to defend himself.

The general rule is that, in conventional settings in which premises are rented by a tenant who acquires exclusive possession and control, the landlord is not liable for attacks by animals kept by the tenant on those premises where the landlord had no knowledge of the animal or its dangerous proclivities at the time of the initial letting of the premises....The aspect peculiar to the present case is the circumstance that here the jury might find [...] that at the time she leased the premises to Carl Kenyon, Mrs. Zoltanski knew that her prospective tenant had a 'vicious' German Shepherd dog which he intended to keep on the leased premises. Notwithstanding this prior knowledge, at a time when she had complete control of the premises she leased them to the tenant, permitted him to keep the dog on the premises, and [...] took no measures by pertinent provisions in the lease or otherwise to protect third persons who might be on the premises from being attacked by the dog.

[...]

The present is a situation in which the landlord, by leasing the premises to the owner of the dog, could be found affirmatively to have created the very risk which was reasonably foreseeable and which operated to injure plaintiff.

[...]

[B]ut landlords as others must exercise reasonable care not to expose third persons to an unreasonable risk of harm. [...]

Considerations of public policy, the appropriate frame of reference for determination of tort liability in situations newly confronted by the courts, require that a landlord who, prior to leasing the premises, has knowledge that the tenant may be expected to carry on activities on the premises in such a manner as unreasonably to expose third persons to risk of physical injury has a duty to take such precautions as lie within the control of the landlord reasonably to protect such third persons from the injuries to be foreseen if such precautions are taken. In the present case, no evidence was tendered [...] that this landlord, aware of the danger of the situation, took any steps to protect this plaintiff [...]

We recognize that in today's world there may be tenants whose interest in keeping a watch or guard dog for protection of person or property, in consequence of the character of the neighborhood in which the leased premises are located or by virtue of the peculiar circumstances of the individual tenant, is legitimate and not necessarily to be discouraged. Nevertheless, the tenant who harbors the dog and derives protective benefit from its presence on the premises will be held strictly liable to third persons for injuries inflicted by the dog [...] In such situations, however, it would defeat what may properly be accepted as a socially useful purpose, namely, provision of housing for persons who may legitimately keep watch or guard dogs, to announce a rule of law which would have the practical effect of discouraging all landlords (who themselves derive no benefit, or at most only an incidental benefit, from the dog's presence) from ever leasing to any tenant who seeks to keep such a dog. The proper accommodation of these interests calls for the imposition on the landlord of a duty, at the inception of the lease when it is known that the tenant will keep a watch or guard dog, to take reasonable precautions for the protection of third persons, by provisions in the lease with respect to confinement or control of the dog or otherwise.

[...]

We do not intend to imply that there must be a finding that this landlord is liable for the injuries suffered by this plaintiff; we do no more than conclude that there are factual questions which foreclose dismissal [...].

The landlord should have realized that the presence of a tenant's vicious dog would likely lead to someone getting injured; the landlord had a duty to reduce that likelihood.

Many states have enacted statutory provisions regarding a lessor's liability toward lessees that have changed the common-law rule. Paralegal students should consult local statutes and case law to resolve questions about the landlord's responsibility.

■ VENDOR AND VENDEE

As a general rule, the **vendor**—that is, the seller—of real property transfers all responsibility for the property to the **vendee,** or purchaser. The vendee had the duty, then, to take care when purchasing real property because of the common law doctrine of *caveat emptor* which, translated, means "Let the buyer beware." This doctrine presumed that everyone is capable of thoroughly inspecting the premises, and a vendee who fails to do so cannot claim ignorance as a defense. Thus, the doctrine of *caveat emptor* meant that the vendor of real property was not liable to the vendee for any condition of the land existing at the time of the sale.

Viewing the doctrine from a modern perspective suggests that *caveat emptor* likely produced harsh and sometimes unfair consequences. For example, a vendor would be likely to know that his property routinely flooded during the rainy season but a vendee might not even think to ask about flooding. However, the vendor would be in a clear position to know this and to advise the vendee about seasonal flooding. Some jurisdictions have limited or eliminated the application of *caveat emptor* and now require sellers to inform prospective buyers of defects or property conditions.

In the alternative, *caveat emptor* has been tempered under contract law. When transferring the property, the vendor grants an implied warranty of habitability to the vendee, a promise that the premises are fit for the vendee's intended use. Failure to disclose conditions that impair habitability, such as seasonal flooding, would mean that the vendee has a cause of action for breach of contract.

The *Restatement* places responsibility on the vendor for notice regarding defects, whether natural or artificial. Yet, the vendee has to have had no reason to know of the defect (hidden) and the vendor has to have failed to disclose the condition (see box on next page).

VENDOR'S LIABILITY

1. A vendor of land who conceals or fails to disclose to his vendee any condition, whether natural or artificial, which involves unreasonable risk to persons on the land, is subject to liability to the vendee and others upon the land with the consent of the vendee or his subvendee for physical harm caused by the condition after the vendee has taken possession, if
   a. the vendee does not know or have reason to know of the condition or the risk involved, and
   b. the vendor knows or has reason to know of the condition, and realizes or should realize the risk involved, and has reason to believe that the vendee will not discover the condition or realize the risk.
2. If the vendor actively conceals the condition, the liability stated in Subsection (1) continues until the vendee discovers it and has reasonable opportunity to take effective precautions against it. Otherwise the liability continues only until the vendee has had reasonable opportunity to discover the condition and to take such precautions.

Restatement (Second) of Torts, §353 (1965)

In the following case, a court examined whether vendors remained liable years after the sale of the property, for a condition they created on the property that subsequent vendees knew of (see Case in Point 6-11).

CASE IN POINT 6-11

Preston v. Goldman

42 Cal.3d 108 (1986)

Should former owners, allegedly negligent in constructing an improvement on their property, be subject to liability for injuries sustained on that property long after they have relinquished all ownership and control? [...]

Defendants Jon and Marion Kubichan bought the subject property in 1968. Around January 1972 [...] they designed and built a pond with a fountain in their backyard for a total cost of approximately $130. The pond was built by excavating the ground to a disputed depth and putting a wall approximately 12 inches above ground around the pond.

In October 1973, Alan Goldman bought the property from the Kubichans. Goldman made no alterations to the pond and maintained water in it. In November 1974, Goldman entered into a lease–option to buy agreement with the Reids who took possession. The Reids, who had two small children, put a new brick facing around the pool's exterior, bricked the patio surrounding it, replaced the flagstone coping with brick, and put a layer of brick around the top of the pool walls. The Reids had emptied the pond and were aware of its depth and configurations.

On May 7, 1976, plaintiff Clinton Preston and his siblings were brought to the property by their parents, Cynthia and Stephen Preston, to visit their aunt and uncle, the Reids. Plaintiff was then 22 months of age. The Prestons had been at the house before and were aware of the pond. At some point Mr. Reid and Mr. Preston went out to the garage, accompanied by the children. The men later returned to the house without them. After some time, the parents looked for the children and found Clinton immersed in the pond. As a result of the accident, plaintiff suffered severe permanent brain damage and quadriplegia....

[...]

After consideration of the relevant variables [...] we have concluded that we should not depart from the existing rules restricting liability of predecessor landowners. [...] The injury here was in a strict sense foreseeable, but at the time the Kubichans built the pool for their own use the prospect that a future landowner who would allow children on the premises would not take appropriate precautions was a tenuous proposition. Unquestionably, plaintiff suffered injury. The closeness of the defendant's conduct and plaintiff's injuries, is, as mentioned in regard to foreseeability, not very great. The Kubichans had no control over the backyard or access to it at the time the injury occurred; nor could they affect the degree of supervision exercised over persons on the premises. They played no direct role in the circumstances of this particular accident, nor would they have been able at the time to take additional precautions to prevent its occurrence. [...] Arguably, however, the greater "blame" should be placed on those in present control of the circumstances who have the power to make changes, take needed precautions, and control the entry of persons on the land.

[...]

The court ruled that liability for the seller's creation of a condition should not exist forever, particularly where subsequent purchasers knew of the condition.

KEY TERMS

Attractive nuisance   205

Business visitors   211

Caveat emptor   221

Invitation   210

Invitee   209

Landholder   198

Lessee   218

Lessor   218

Licensee   206

Natural condition   199

Premises   198

Premises liability   198

Public invitees   211

Social guests   211

Trespasser   203

Vendee   221

Vendor   221

SUMMARY

Questions of liability for injuries on the premises have traditionally been resolved by determining the relationship between the landholder and the person who suffered the injury. Trespassers received little or no protection under the tort law unless the owner was guilty of willful or wanton disregard for the safety of others. Licensees received protection only from a willful disregard for their safety. Invitees received the greatest protection under the tort law since the landholder owed them a duty of reasonable care. The modern trend has been to hold all occupiers of land to the same standard—a duty of reasonable care—for all on the property. State statutes and court decisions have done much to erode the traditional common-law principles. A duty of care may also arise regarding lessors and lessees, and vendors and vendees. Local law must be consulted carefully.

CONCEPT REVIEW QUESTIONS

1. Define premises liability.
2. State the general duty of a possessor of land.
3. Describe the factors used to determine the existence of reasonable care.
4. What is the general rule of liability of a landholder for natural conditions on the land?
5. State the traditional rule of liability a landholder owes to a trespasser.
6. What is a landholder's traditional liability toward licensees?
7. Define the duty of a possessor of land owed to an invitee.
8. What is the fireman's rule?
9. Discuss the general liability a lessor owes to a lessee.
10. What duty does a vendor owe to a vendee of real property?

CRITICAL THINKING APPLICATIONS

1. A parent and child enter a department store on a rainy day. After walking around for twenty minutes, they leave, having purchased nothing. On the way out, the child slips and falls on water tracked into the stores by other rain-soaked patrons. Is the child a licensee or an invitee? In either case, what would be the store's duty of care owed to the child? What would be the contemporary standard?
2. A business operates as a "club" to which those who pay a membership fee can buy items in bulk at reduced rates. The business runs an advertisement to bring in new customers. The ad includes a coupon that can be used for one day. Walker arrives at the store and, after pulling a grocery cart from the line of carts at the entrance, trips on a carpet runner put there by the management. Walker sues. What is the standard of care owed to Walker? Assume that the contemporary standard does not apply. Will Walker succeed? Why or why not?
3. RC stops by the local music store and to RC's chagrin, nature abruptly calls and RC immediately needs a restroom. The only one in the store is for the use of employees and is located in the "employees only" area. Because the staff knows RC, they permit RC to use the facility. RC slips and falls in the "employees only" area. The local music store files for summary judgment on the grounds that as a matter of law and assuming all of what RC says is true, it still won't be found liable. If you're the law clerk to the case's judge and need to draft a response for the judge to this motion for summary judgment, what would you recommend the judge must do? Why?
4. It has snowed hard in the community of Plainfield, and large piles of snow have collected on the streets. Those in charge of municipal services hire heavy equipment to scoop up excess snow and dump it on the athletic field of a middle school. The middle school shares a building with the community's municipal offices and an elementary school. The Saturday after municipal employees have successfully plowed the snow and dumped it onto the athletic field, neighborhood kids start sledding down the newly created snow "mountain." One child slides down the hill but hits a fence pole and is injured. The parents sue the community for damages. If the community files a motion to dismiss, why will that motion be turned down, given the specific facts of this case?

5. The lights at both entrances to a small rental property have burned out, and Daylight Savings Time has ended, so the clocks have just "fallen back," and it has gotten dark an hour sooner. The lights have been inoperative for two weeks. A lessee who occupies one of the three residential units in the rental property comes in after work and is assaulted by a person or persons. Besides having money taken, the lessee is injured and suffered two broken ribs during the robbery. The lessee plans to sue the lessor for the pain and suffering of the assault as well as for the cost of the funds taken, on the grounds that the lessor has breached a duty of care and that such breach proximately caused the lessee's injuries. What is the standard of care that the lessor owes to the lessee? Was it breached in this instance? Why or why not?

6. A real estate agent prepares a property to be shown one Sunday afternoon as an "open house." The owners have left and won't be back until late in the afternoon. A prospective buyer stops to visit. As that potential buyer walks through the front door, he trips on a child's toy and is injured. Are the homeowners liable? If so, what was the duty of care owed? Is the real estate agent liable? If so, what was the duty of care owed? Predict the likelihood of success of a lawsuit brought against both and explain your prediction.

7. For some students, college life isn't all about studying. A senior climbs a street light on campus and starts to unscrew the light bulb. There's an arc of electricity and the senior falls to the ground, suffering injuries from the electrical shock and from hitting the ground. Who should be sued? If there is more than one party, what was the standard of care that each party owed to the senior? Was that duty breached? Why or why not?

8. At a community playground, kids play a game of touch football. Going after a long throw, a child leaps to catch the ball, only to come down on the adjoining property of a lumberyard. The child lands on a pile of scrap wood and is injured from the impact and from having a piece of wood pierce his leg. Who should be sued? If more than one party is involved, what was the standard of care that each party owed to the child? Was that duty breached? Why or why not?

SKILL-BUILDING APPLICATION

Jane's parents got work at Nix-Asbestos, an asbestos removal firm. The company made her parents wear protective clothing at every job site. For their first year at Nix-Asbestos, her parents helped remove asbestos insulation at an old private school that was being converted into high-priced condominiums. Jane helped her parents around the house, including doing the clothes washing, but she never visited her parents while they worked at removing the asbestos from the school. Within a few months after her parents completed that job, Jane contracted mesothelioma, a form of lung cancer that arises primarily from exposure to asbestos. Her parents brought suit against the owners of the old private school, on a theory of premises liability.

What do the parents need to show to establish the liability of the owners of the old private school? What arguments will the owners of the old private school raise against the suit? How will the court likely rule on such requests? Why would the court rule as it would on those arguments?

Slander, Whose sting is sharper than the
sword's.

—William Shakespeare,
The Winter's Tale

Intentional Torts

Tort law is divided into three classes of liability: negligence, intentional torts, and strict liability. For actions in negligence and for intentional tort, one distinction involves the defendant's state of the mind. As defined in Chapter 3, negligence is based upon a breach of a standard of reasonable care and does not require that the defendant intended the consequences of his or her actions. Intentional torts like assault, false imprisonment, or defamation require an intentional state of mind on the part of the actor to cause a harmful result from his or her actions. The defendant's state of mind provides the basis for the classification, and this chapter considers the nature and elements of those intentional actions that the law deems tortious conduct.

CHAPTER TOPICS

1. Intentional Torts
2. Intent
3. Damages for, Harm to Persons
4. Right to Privacy
5. Defamation
6. Misuse of Legal Procedure
7. Damages for, Harm to Property

OBJECTIVES

After completing this chapter, you will be able to:

1. Distinguish between negligence and intentional torts.
2. Discuss the legal effect of intent.
3. Describe the intentional torts that involve an injury or harm to persons.
4. Illustrate each of the intentional torts.
5. Summarize the intentional torts involving an injury to property.

◼ INTENTIONAL TORTS

Intentional tort, in most jurisdictions, consists of the following items:

- a state of mind (intent) to bring about harm to another;
- action based on that desire to cause harm; and
- damages sustained by a victim, who will be the plaintiff in this civil cause of action.

Intentional torts start with a defendant's desire to cause harm. Then, the defendant has to act. The court in the following case looks at the modern understanding of the meaning of "intent" and "act" in a lawsuit about injuries that arose at a workplace (see Case in Point 7-1).

CASE IN POINT 7-1

Bazley v. Tortorich

397 So. 2d 475 (La. 1981)

[...]

Plaintiff, Sidney Bazley, a Jefferson Parish garbage worker filed suit against an unidentified co-employee truck driver, the co-employee's insurer, Sardo Tortorich and Tortorich's insurer as result of work-related injuries Bazley received when he was struck by Tortorich's car [...]

We are called upon to decide [...] whether La.R.S. 23:1032, as amended, prevents an injured employee from seeking recovery in tort for a work-related injury negligently caused by his co-employee [...]

Although the theorists have not always agreed, the words "act" and "intent" now have generally accepted meanings in the fields of tort and criminal law. The word act is used to denote an external manifestation of the actor's will which produces consequences. There cannot be an act subjecting a person to civil or criminal liability without volition. Therefore, a contraction of a person's muscles which is purely a reaction to some outside force, such as a knee jerk or the blinking of the eyelids in defense against an approaching missile, or the convulsive movements of an epileptic, are not acts of that person. (citations omitted). The meaning of "intent" is that the person who acts either (1) consciously desires the physical result of his act, whatever the likelihood of that result happening from his conduct; or (2) knows that that result is substantially certain to follow from his conduct, whatever his desire may be as to that result. Thus, intent has reference to the consequences of an act rather than to the act itself. (citations omitted).

Our criminal and civil codes manifest legislative acceptance of these received meanings of "act" and "intent." As the criminal code articles and reporters' comments make clear, "act" refers to an external manifestation of will which must be voluntary, and "intent" is present when the offender either desires the consequences of his act or when he knew that the consequences were reasonably certain to result from his act. (citations omitted). Although the civil code does not contain definitions of the terms, the word "act" is used many times and must be read in light of the code's underlying civilian concepts. [...] Thus, we see again a basic distinction between intentional and unintentional acts and use of intent in reference to the consequences of the act, rather than the act itself.

Our jurisprudence likewise reflects approval of the general notions of act and intent. This Court [...] approvingly recited the following: "It seems clear that, in the absence of language expressing a contrary meaning, an 'act' involves an exercise of the will. It signifies something done voluntarily." (citation omitted). Only where the actor entertained a desire to bring about the consequences that followed or where the actor believed that the result was substantially certain to follow has an act been characterized as intentional. (citations omitted).

[Since, the plaintiff claimed that the injuries arose due to the defendant's negligence—which would be addressed under the state's worker's compensation law—the plaintiff can only seek relief under that law. The plaintiff needed to claim that defendant acted intentionally to be able to bring a cause of action outside of the scope of the state's worker's compensation law. The plaintiff's claim was dismissed.]

As with an action in negligence, society might excuse conduct that would otherwise create liability for defendant. Chapter 10 and Chapter 11 examine defenses to a cause of action in intentional tort.

Types of Intentional Torts

Intentional torts involve physical harm to another or harm to another's property. Below are some common-law intentional torts or categories of torts involving harm to another:

- assault
- battery
- false imprisonment (also known as false arrest)
- infliction of emotional distress
- invasion of privacy
- defamation
- misuse of the legal process

Following are some common-law intentional torts involving harm to another's property:

- trespass to land
- trespass to chattels (personal property)
- conversion

Chapter 8 focuses on intentional torts related to the operation of a business.

Civil Cause of Action and Criminal Cause of Action

As previously noted, conduct that gives rise to a civil action in tort may also serve as the basis for criminal proceedings. For example, consider the defendant at the bar who hit another patron with a beer mug: this defendant will likely also face charges for the crimes of assault and battery. These legal actions differ from civil actions as to

- who will initiate the suit (in the United States of America, only the government can prosecute),
- the amount of proof (beyond a reasonable doubt is greater than preponderance of the evidence), and
- the nature of the penalty (only a criminal proceeding can result in a sentence of imprisonment, for example).

Difference between Intentional Torts and Actions in Negligence

All intentional torts require that a defendant deliberates before taking action. Negligence turns on a breach of a duty of care. So with negligence, a defendant may not have intended to breach the duty of care. Instead, the defendant has failed to uphold that duty. Negligence focuses on the conduct and not the defendant's state of mind regarding the conduct. Here's how the *Restatement (Second) of Torts* explains the difference:

DIFFERENCE BETWEEN AN ACTION IN NEGLIGENCE OR FOR INTENTIONAL TORT.

The definition of negligence [...] includes only such conduct as creates liability for the reason that it involves a risk and not a certainty of invading the interest of another. It therefore excludes conduct which creates liability because of the actor's intention to invade a legally protected interest of the person injured or of a third person [...].

Restatement (Second) of Torts §282, comment d (1965)

■ INTENT

Intent is the desire to produce a particular result. It comes from the Latin word *intendere*, which means "to form a plan or purpose." Intent requires a degree of deliberation, even if it involves only a moment to think. Intent focuses on the state of mind of a person to cause harm to another or another's property.

Consequences

The *Restatement (Second) of Torts* defines intent as a desire to cause certain consequences (see box below).

INTENT

The word "intent" is used throughout the Restatement of this Subject to denote that the actor desires to cause consequences of his act, or that he believes that the consequences are substantially certain to result from it.

Restatement (Second) of Torts, §8A (1965)

The *Restatement* emphasizes the awareness of a person of the consequences of doing a forbidden act. Engaging in that forbidden action will produce damages. Intent looks to the defendant's appreciation of the consequences for engaging in the forbidden activity.

The Significance of Intent

Many torts have arisen out of the common law. Also, legislatures may create new actions in tort through the enactment of statutes. But courts still may recognize that new torts have developed as society changes. Still, courts that create new torts use the general rationale described in the *Restatement (Second) of Torts* (see box below).

> ## RESTATEMENT (SECOND) OF TORTS § 870 LIABILITY FOR INTENDED CONSEQUENCES—GENERAL PRINCIPLE
>
> One who intentionally causes injury to another is subject to liability to the other for that injury, if his conduct is generally culpable and not justifiable under the circumstances. This liability may be imposed although the actor's conduct does not come within a traditional category of tort liability.
>
> *Restatement (Second) of Torts §870 (1965)*

As an example, consider this action for assault and battery. At a tavern, a defendant stands up and swings a full beer mug at a fellow patron. The patron sees the beer mug coming but cannot avoid the mug, which shatters on the patron's face. In the suit, the patron will need to show that the defendant deliberately sought to put the patron in fear of immediate injury (the tort of assault) and that the defendant struck the patron with the beer mug (the tort of battery).

Intent and Damages

Finally, that action has to result in the plaintiff's suffering an injury. That means that the defendant becomes liable in damages for the harm deliberately caused to the plaintiff. The plaintiff may suffer physical harm or harm to property (which can include harm, such damage to reputation or financial losses). Damages can also arise from the psychological harm that a plaintiff experiences, due to depression, anxiety, embarrassment, humiliation, or even the aggravation of a pre-existing condition. In rare instances, a legislature may have empowered the court to assess punitive damages, as much to discourage a defendant from engaging in the proscribed conduct again as to send a message to others like the defendant.

■ DAMAGES FOR, HARM TO PERSONS

English common law forms the basis for many American laws. Under English common law, most torts took the form of a trespass, since trespass involved an infringement of a plaintiff's rights. Torts of trespass consisted of trespass against the person and against property. Actions for trespass against the individual would then differentiate between a direct injury and an indirect injury.

While American common law has its roots in English law, American jurisdictions tend to differentiate intentional torts according to the type of injury. Intentional torts against the person may regard harm to a person as more grave, since American society has increasingly expressed a concern about infringement of personal safety over infringement of rights in property.

Assault

Under the common law, **assault** involves creating apprehension of harmful contact in the plaintiff. No actual physical contact has to occur. The tort of assault involves a psychological injury; when awarding damages, a court will look at the emotional response of the plaintiff instead of trying to identify any physical injury (see box on next page).

> ## ASSAULT
>
> 1. An actor is subject to liability to another for assault if
>
>   a. he acts intending to cause a harmful or offensive contact with the person of the other or a third person, or an imminent apprehension of such a contact, and
>   b. the other is thereby put in such imminent apprehension.
>
> 2. An action which is not done with the intention stated in Subsection (1, a) does not make the actor liable to the other for an apprehension caused thereby although the act involves an unreasonable risk of causing it and, therefore, would be negligent or reckless if the risk threatened bodily harm.
>
> *Restatement (Second) of Torts §21 (1965)*

To win, the plaintiff would need to prove the following elements by a preponderance of the evidence:

- intent to cause apprehension of physical harm
- an act creating such apprehension
- that harm is imminent
- that results in harm to the plaintiff

Basis for Apprehension

The defendant's act must create in plaintiff an apprehension of physical harm. The fear generated must be reasonable and immediate. The plaintiff has to be aware of the threat: for example, if a gun were pointed at the plaintiff, he or she would have to see the gun. A gun pointed at the plaintiff's back often would not constitute an assault, while one pointed at the plaintiff's face would be. A delay between the act and the plaintiff's reaction would weaken the plaintiff's claim of apprehension of immediate injury.

Words Alone

Most jurisdictions accept the proposition that words alone don't constitute assault. Yet words, taken within a particular context, may be sufficient where the threatened harm is imminent.

For example, if a drunken 300-pound patron tells the 100-pound bartender, "I'm going to rip your arm off and beat you over your head until you're dead," any action by the patron to carry out that threat would constitute assault.

In that example, the bartender may have difficulty assessing the threat. The patron may have made such threats before but never followed through. Or the patron could be so obviously drunk that little likelihood exists of the patron's ability to follow through with the threat. Alas, working as a bartender can involve some grave occupational hazards.

Magnitude of the Threat

The threat's severity, if the defendant acts on the threat, may matter if the court has found the defendant liable. For example, a threat to kill the plaintiff rather than punch the plaintiff in the arm, might warrant a higher award in damages.

Assault as a Crime

As with other intentional torts, the defendant could be liable for damages and could face legal penalties for a crime. But the crime of assault and the tort of assault may differ in subtle ways, as Professor Dobbs notes:

DIFFERENCES BETWEEN CRIME AND TORT OF ASSAULT

Assault may be a crime as well as a tort, but criminal law definitions of assault sometimes emphasize the intent to injure and the risk of escalating violence rather than the victim's apprehension of a battery, (footnote omitted) so criminal assault cases are not necessarily sound authority in the tort setting. For example, under some criminal statutes, the defendant may be criminally responsible for an attempt to batter the victim (footnote omitted). The logic of this kind of provision is that the victim's awareness or lack of awareness is unimportant, since one may attempt to commit a battery the victim does not see or anticipate, as where the victim is hit from behind. Tort law, on the other hand, emphasizes and demands the plaintiffs awareness of the threat.

Dobbs *The Law of Torts* §35 (2000)

Jurisdictions often treat the crime of assault in different ways. If the threat is of serious bodily injury or death and the defendant acts to make good on that threat, some jurisdictions might call it the more serious crime of felonious assault or aggravated assault. For example, use of a weapon like a gun would more easily lend itself to the greater charge. If the threat is that severe, the penalty could be more severe than for a misdemeanor assault, reflecting a societal policy that harsher penalties should work to deter defendants from committing serious crimes.

Battery

Battery involves intentionally making physical contact with another person without that individual's consent. To win, the plaintiff would need to prove the following elements by a preponderance of the evidence:

- intent to cause physical harm
- contact
- done without permission
- resulting in harm to the plaintiff

Touching

Battery focuses on intentionally denying a plaintiff freedom from contact. Contact goes beyond just touching a plaintiff. It includes contact with the plaintiff's clothing, since holding onto a person's clothing could be a way of limiting the plaintiff's freedom from contact just as much as grabbing onto the plaintiff's arm. In the following case, the plaintiff alleged that the defendant grabbed a dinner plate out of the plaintiff's hand; the court had little difficulty ruling that this was battery (see Case in Point 7-2).

CASE IN POINT 7-2

Fisher v. Carrousel Motor Hotel, Inc.

11 Tex.Sup.J. 143 (Tex. 1967)

This is a suit for [...] damages growing out of an alleged assault and battery. The plaintiff Fisher was a mathematician with [...] NASA [...]. The defendants were the Carrousel Motor Hotel, Inc. [...], the Brass Ring Club [...], and Robert W. Flynn, who as an employee of the Carrousel was the manager of the Brass Ring Club. [...] The questions before this Court are whether there was evidence that an actionable battery was committed [...] The plaintiff Fisher had been invited [...] to a one day's meeting regarding telemetry equipment at the Carrousel. The invitation included a luncheon. [...] After the morning session, the group of 25 or 30 guests adjourned to the Brass Ring Club for lunch. The luncheon was buffet style, and Fisher stood in line with others [...] As Fisher was about to be served, he was approached by Flynn, who snatched the plate from Fisher's hand and shouted that he, a Negro, could not be served in the club. Fisher testified that he was not actually touched, and did not testify that he suffered fear or apprehension of physical injury; but he did testify that he was highly embarrassed and hurt by Flynn's conduct in the presence of his associates.

The jury found that Flynn "forceably dispossessed plaintiff of his dinner plate" and "shouted in a loud and offensive manner" that Fisher could not be served there, thus subjecting Fisher to humiliation and indignity. [...] The jury also found that Flynn acted maliciously and awarded Fisher $400 actual damages for his humiliation and indignity [...]

The Court of Civil Appeals held that there was no assault because there was no physical contact and no evidence of fear or apprehension of physical contact. However, it has long been settled that there can be a battery without an assault, and that actual physical contact is not necessary to constitute a battery, so long as there is contact with clothing or an object closely identified with the body. [...]

[U]nder the facts of this case, we have no difficulty in holding that the intentional grabbing of plaintiff's plate constituted a battery. The intentional snatching of an object from one's hand is as clearly an offensive invasion of his person as would be an actual contact with the body. [...]

We hold, therefore, that the forceful dispossession of plaintiff Fisher's plate in an offensive manner was sufficient to constitute a battery, and the trial court erred in granting judgment notwithstanding the verdict on the issue of actual damages.

[...]

The judgments of the courts below are reversed, and judgment is here rendered for the plaintiff [...]

Intent, Not Negligence or Recklessness

Proof of negligence won't be enough to establish liability for an intentional tort. Nor is recklessness sufficient—this is sometimes called *gross negligence*—where a great risk exists of substantial bodily injury or death exists (see box on next page).

> ## RECKLESSNESS NOT ENOUGH TO CONSTITUTE BATTERY
> The act must cause, and must be intended to cause, an unpermitted contact. Mere negligence, or even recklessness, which creates only a risk that the contact will result, may afford a distinct cause of action in itself, but under modern usage of the term it is not enough for battery.
>
> W. Page Keeton et al., *Prosser & Keeton on the Law of Torts*, §9 at 41 (5th ed. 1984)

Consent

Consent, or giving permission, to the touching can work as a complete defense to the tort of battery. Courts limit the use of this defense to only those circumstances that the plaintiff had in mind when granting the consent. For example, while team sports will often involve contact, the players consent to that contact. Yet no sport would regard contact that involves breaking a limb as what a plaintiff intended when granting consent. Or, people traveling on a subway consent to contact if the train is full, but that consent does not mean that a passenger may grope another passenger.

Battery and Assault

A defendant faces liability in tort for battery even when the plaintiff has no idea that the contact will occur imminently. That means making contact when the plaintiff's attention is focused elsewhere will still constitute battery. For the tort of assault, the plaintiff has to know of the imminent harm so that some jurisdictions will find that the defendant's contact to the plaintiff's back amounts only to battery.

Other jurisdictions could find that assault occurred in that fraction of a second when the plaintiff realizes that the contact has suddenly occurred. For example, if a thief runs up behind the plaintiff and grabs a bag the plaintiff was carrying, some jurisdictions would say that a battery occurred the moment the thief grabbed the bag. This interpretation of contact, for purposes of a claim in tort for battery, avoids rewarding the clever thief who might have argued that the contact was so brief that it didn't rise to the level of being a tort action in battery.

For example, back at the tavern, if a drunk defendant swings a full beer mug at another patron and misses, the defendant could face liability in tort for assault. If the drunken defendant hits the other patron, assault and battery has happened. But in some jurisdictions, if the drunken defendant has struck the other patron in the back, so that the other person had no idea what was coming, some jurisdictions might assess liability only for the tort of battery.

False Imprisonment

Liability for **false imprisonment** arises when a defendant has intentionally restrained a plaintiff's freedom of movement, without his consent or legal authority.

To win at suit, the plaintiff would need to prove the following elements by a preponderance of the evidence:

- intent to restrain plaintiff
- done without lawful authority
- resulting in harm to the plaintiff

Restraint includes confinement in any place, such as a room or a vehicle. For example, the plaintiff could sue for false imprisonment if kept in the fenced grounds of a defendant's property

Describing an approach common to many jurisdictions, the *Restatement (Second) of Torts* also adds the requirement that the restraint cause harm or damage (see box below).

FALSE IMPRISONMENT

1. An actor is subject to liability to another for false imprisonment if
   a. he acts intending to confine the other or a third person within boundaries fixed by the actor, and
   b. his act directly or indirectly results in such a confinement of the other, and
   c. the other is conscious of the confinement or is harmed by it.

2. An act which is not done with the intention stated in Subsection (1, a) does not make the actor liable to the other for a merely transitory or otherwise harmless confinement, although the act involves an unreasonable risk of imposing it and therefore would be negligent or reckless if the risk threatened bodily harm.

Restatement (Second) of Torts, §35 (1965)

The *Restatement* requires that the restraint causes a plaintiff harm. That could as easily include psychological harm as it could mean physical harm.

Degree of Restraint

Here, restraint means that no reasonable means of escape exists. The *Restatement* defines confinement as restraint absent a reasonable means of escape (see box below).

CONFINEMENT

1. To make the actor liable for false imprisonment, the other's confinement within the boundaries fixed by the actor must be complete.
2. The confinement is complete although there is a reasonable means of escape, unless the other knows of it.
3. The actor does not become liable for false imprisonment by intentionally preventing another from going in a particular direction in which he has a right or privilege to go.

Restatement (Second) of Torts §36 (1965)

The plaintiff will not have to face undue or unusual risk to escape before being able to make a valid claim for false imprisonment, but the plaintiff must pursue every reasonable option, even if the plaintiff would prefer not to. For example, a plaintiff trapped in a cellar may need to crawl under a porch to escape, but the fact that the plaintiff might get dirty does not change the fact that the plaintiff could escape.

Restraint could arise when a plaintiff must choose between leaving valuable materials behind or staying, as happened in the following case (see Case in Point 7-3).

CASE IN POINT 7-3

Burrow v. K-Mart Corporation

166 Ga. App. 284 (1983)

Store customer brought action for […] false imprisonment against store […]. The Superior Court […] entered judgment for customer on false imprisonment claim […] [The] store appealed from trial court's denial of a new trial on the verdict and judgment for damages for false imprisonment. […]

In an action to recover damages for false imprisonment, the only essential elements of the action are the detention, and the unlawfulness of the detention.[…]The cases have emphasized two points: "Any restraint, however slight upon another's liberty to come and go as he pleases, constitutes an arrest. There is an illegal arrest and false imprisonment of another where he is detained for any length of time against his will."

"The restraint constituting a false imprisonment may arise out of words, acts, gestures or the like, which induce a reasonable apprehension that force will be used if plaintiff does not submit; and it is sufficient if they operate upon the will of the person threatened, and result in a reasonable fear of personal difficulty or personal injuries…." Prosser explains that "imprisonment" was originally intended to have meant stone walls and iron bars, but under modern tort law an individual may be imprisoned "when his movements are restrained in the open street, or in a traveling automobile…or is compelled to go along with the defendant." (citation omitted) […]

Although the Georgia cases have not addressed the problem where one is detained by the act of another exercising dominion over one's personal possessions, other jurisdictions have confronted such issue. As Prosser points out: "A substantial number of cases in recent years have found false imprisonment where the plaintiff surrendered his freedom of motion because of force directed against his valuable property." (citation omitted)

The common thread […] is that where one is deprived of one's property he (or she) need not supinely surrender such possession but is in fact entitled (if not compelled) to remain until repossession is effectuated. Of course, one might always abandon such property but the need to protect one's own property acts as a coercive force in restraining one from leaving. The exercise of dominion over the property serves also to exercise dominion over the person owning such property. We think the rationale of these cases comports with the fundamental purpose and concept of Georgia law which finds false imprisonment in acts which operate upon the will of the person threatened and may result in a reasonable fear of personal difficulty. […] Here, according to the plaintiff's testimony she was told the boxes had to be searched and they were "snatched" from her hands. Furthermore, at the conclusion of the search the plaintiff was told "she could go" by the store employee. Is this not evidence from which the jury as trier of fact might ascertain that the plaintiff, as a result of the actions and language used by the defendant's employee ("I got to search your boxes") and the act of seizing her property, was intimidated into remaining a captive of the store until she was released? The plaintiff did not actually have the choice of leaving since to do so would abandon her property […] Surely the store employee recognized that plaintiff would not leave without the boxes containing valuable merchandise and it may be inferred that the employee intended to restrain and control both the property and the person of the plaintiff until the search was completed. This is further evidenced by the concluding statement addressed to the plaintiff that she "could go" indicating that the plaintiff was now released from custody. […]

Thus, the trial judge did not err in refusing to grant the defendant a new trial as to the false imprisonment […]

Plaintiff's Perception of Restraint

Restraint depends upon a plaintiff's reasonable perceptions; thus, it doesn't require that he or she is actually restrained. For example, a cause of action in false imprisonment exists if a plaintiff reasonably believes that the door to a cell is locked, regardless of whether it actually is locked.

Some jurisdictions would not find sufficient restraint if the plaintiff faces merely the threat of restraint; yet, a threat of violence may prove sufficient. For example, a defendant may tell a plaintiff of the defendant's plan to restrain the plaintiff, but that threat will not be enough to win at trial. If the threat mentioned that restraint would occur as a result of violence, the plaintiff has a greater chance in tort for false imprisonment. If the plaintiff regarded the threat as credible, it does not matter whether the defendant carries out the threat. In the following case, the plaintiff had voluntarily accepted commitment to a psychiatric hospital but found that gaining release against the wishes of a psychiatrist would not happen (see Case in Point 7-4).

CASE IN POINT 7-4

Marcus v. Liebman

59 Ill. App. 3d 337 (1st Dist. 1978)

This is an action for false imprisonment by a patient against a psychiatrist. [...] On appeal the plaintiff contends that the trial court incorrectly entered a [...] verdict for the defendant [...]. We reverse and remand.

Plaintiff testified that in July of 1970 she was having difficulty sleeping, was "completely overwrought" and at the recommendation of her psychologist, Dr. Bass, decided to enter a hospital for several days of rest. On July 20, 1970, plaintiff voluntarily admitted herself as a patient at Lutheran General Hospital where she was placed in the psychiatric wing and introduced to the defendant psychiatrist, Dr. Liebman, for the first time. Plaintiff testified that during one of her first sessions with the defendant she began throwing things at him because she did not want him as her doctor; that she was then placed in restraints after which she began screaming and singing in order to annoy people; and that after a drug was administered to calm her down, she was removed from the restraints.

Plaintiff went on to testify that during her fourth day in the hospital she informed Dr. Liebman that she wanted to sign a release paper which made mandatory her release within five days of signing the form. Dr. Liebman gave her the form and she signed it. Several days later, the defendant told her to rescind her request for release. He instructed her to "sign this piece of paper or you will be committed to Elgin State Hospital." Plaintiff testified that although she told the defendant she wanted to be released and that he had no right to force her to sign that piece of paper, she was frightened and, believing the defendant could actually have sent her to Elgin State Hospital, signed the paper thus rescinding her prior request to be released. Plaintiff admitted that while a patient at Lutheran General Hospital she took trips outside the hospital to see movies and to bowl. She also stated that she was eventually released from the hospital on August 19, 1970. [...] Dr. Liebman denied threatening the plaintiff or telling her he would have her placed in Elgin State Hospital. Dr. Liebman testified that he did tell the plaintiff that if she persisted in her request to leave, a court order could be sought to keep her in the hospital. Dr. Liebman denied telling the plaintiff he would or could seek such an order.

[...]

False imprisonment consists of an unlawful restraint of individual personal liberty or freedom of locomotion against a person's will. (citations omitted) This unlawful restraint may be effected by words alone, by acts alone, or both. (citation omitted) Actual force is unnecessary to an action in false imprisonment. (citation omitted) However, the submission must be to a threatened and reasonably apprehended force. (citation omitted) The defendant contends that the trial court correctly granted his motion for a [...] verdict because plaintiff's apprehension of force or coercion was not reasonable. Defendant cites plaintiff's testimony that she knew she could be released from the hospital within five days and her statement "you have no right to do that" was made in response to Dr. Liebman's alleged threat to have her committed to Elgin State Hospital. Defendant concludes that even at the moment of the alleged threat plaintiff knew she could leave. We disagree and believe that based upon the record before us the question of whether plaintiff's apprehension of force or coercion was reasonable is a question of fact for the jury. On both direct examination and cross-examination, plaintiff testified that she believed Dr. Liebman could have her committed to Elgin State Hospital if she did not sign the piece of paper rescinding her request to leave. Considering plaintiff's mental condition and the fact that she was behind locked doors in a hospital, the jury could find her belief reasonable. It is true that the plaintiff, since she voluntarily admitted herself, knew that she would be released in five days after so requesting. However, plaintiff signed a piece of paper rescinding that request to leave. Plaintiff never testified that she knew she could leave within five days even though she rescinded her request to leave. In fact, her testimony is to the contrary. We do not say as a matter of law plaintiff's belief was reasonable, but we do believe that this was a question of fact for the jury and afforded no basis for the trial court's entering a directed verdict in defendant's favor. Defendant also cites the fact that plaintiff received telephone calls, had visitors, and even made trips outside the hospital during her last weeks there in support of the contention that plaintiff's actions were not the result of a reasonably apprehended threat. While the above facts may be relevant to a determination of whether plaintiff's apprehension was reasonable, they are not sufficient [...] and are better left to the jury to consider in light of the other evidence.

[...]

The instant threat is unlike one to prosecute in the future, one to cause a person to fear a loss of his job in the future, or apply force appreciably later than the time at which one attempts to escape confinement. The instant threat to have plaintiff committed to Elgin State Hospital was a present threat. The defendant could have initiated commitment procedures immediately. The fact that these procedures could not have been concluded immediately does not change the threat to one in the future. At the time the alleged threat was made plaintiff was already confined. It was certainly reasonable for the plaintiff to believe that before her release commitment procedures could have been concluded.

[...]

Order reversed; cause remanded.

Legal Authority to Confine as a Defense

In many jurisdictions, legal authority may exist to confine a plaintiff, such as when a law enforcement officer has arrested him or her. Some jurisdictions grant businesses the privilege of holding alleged thieves until law enforcement arises—a practice known as the *shopkeeper's privilege*.

Holding a suspected thief, however, brings questions about the accuracy of the merchant's belief that the person was in fact a thief and how long is a reasonable period to hold someone until law enforcement arrives. In the *Gortarez* case, the court described in greater detail the kind of analysis that a business had to engage in to justify an exercise of the shopkeeper's privilege as a defense to a claim in tort for false imprisonment (see Case in Point 7-5).

CASE IN POINT 7-5

Gortarez v. Smitty's Super Valu, Inc.

Supreme Court of Arizona 140 Ariz. 97 (1984)

[…] Plaintiffs brought suit against defendants for […] false imprisonment […] after Gortarez and his cousin, Albert Hernandez, were detained in the parking lot of Smitty's.

[…]

Ernest Gortarez, age 16, and his cousin, Albert Hernandez, age 18, went to Smitty's store on January 2, 1979, around 8:00 p.m. They visited the automotive department, where Hernandez selected a power booster which cost $22.00. While Hernandez was paying for the power booster, Gortarez picked up a 59-cent vaporizer used to freshen the air in cars. Gortarez asked if he could pay for it in the front of the store when he finished shopping. The clerk said yes, but decided that the request was suspicious and had a "hunch" that Gortarez would try to leave the store without paying for the item.

The two cousins wandered through the store, looking at other merchandise, and finally left the store through an unattended check-out aisle. The clerk, Robert Sjulestad, had followed the two through the store, in aisles parallel to where the young men were walking, so that there were occasions when he could not observe Gortarez below shoulder level. Since Sjulestad did not see them dispose of or pay for the vaporizer, he concluded that Gortarez or Hernandez took the item without paying for it.

Sjulestad then told the assistant manager and the security guard, Daniel Gibson, that "[t]hose two guys just ripped us off." According to Gibson's testimony, Sjulestad explained that "they had picked up a vaporizer and asked to pay for it in the front, and then didn't pay for it, as I watched them walk through, and they obviously did not pay for anything at that time."

Gibson and Scott Miller, the assistant manager, along with two other store employees, then ran out of the store to catch the two young men as they were about to get inside their car in the parking lot. Miller went to the passenger side to intercept Gortarez, while Gibson went for Hernandez, who was about to open the car door on the driver's side. Gibson said that he identified himself "as an officer" by showing his badge as he ran up to Hernandez. (Gibson was an off-duty police officer working as a security guard for Smitty's.) (footnote omitted) Gibson told Hernandez: "I believe you have something you did not pay for." He then seized Hernandez, put his arms on the car and began searching him. Hernandez offered no resistance even though Gibson did not ask for the vaporizer, nor say what he was looking for. In cross-examination, Gibson admitted that Hernandez did nothing to resist him, and, as Gibson searched him, Hernandez kept repeating that he did not have anything that he had not paid for.

Meanwhile, on the other side of the car, flanked by Miller, Gortarez saw Gibson grab Hernandez, push him up against the car, and search him. Gortarez was outraged at this behavior and used strong language to protest the detention and the search—yelling at Gibson to leave his cousin alone. According to Gortarez, he thought the men were looking for the vaporizer because he heard Gibson tell the others to watch out for the bottle, and to look under the car for the bottle. Gortarez testified that he told the men that Hernandez did not have the vaporizer—it was in the store. No one had stopped to check at the counter through which the two exited, where the vaporizer was eventually found in one of the catch-all baskets at the unattended check-out stand. Seeing Gibson "rousting" Hernandez, Gortarez came to the defense of his cousin, (footnote omitted) ran around the front of the car and pushed Gibson away. Gibson then grabbed Gortarez and put a choke hold around Gortarez' neck until he stopped struggling. Both Hernandez and Gortarez testified that the first time that Gibson identified himself to them was after he had restrained Gortarez in a choke hold. There was testimony that Gortarez was held in the choke hold for a period of time even after Gortarez had advised the store employees that he had left the vaporizer in the store. When a carry-out boy told the store employees that he had found the vaporizer in a basket at the check-out stand, the two cousins were released.

Gortarez later required medical treatment for injuries suffered from the choke hold. Plaintiffs sued Smitty's and Gibson for [...] false imprisonment [...] At the close of all the evidence, the court directed a verdict for the defendants on the false imprisonment [...] count. [...]

FALSE IMPRISONMENT [...]

Arizona has codified the common law. So far as relevant here, the statute provides that a private person may make an arrest for a misdemeanor when the person to be arrested has committed a misdemeanor amounting to a breach of the peace in the presence of the person making the arrest. (citation omitted) Thus, at common law and by statute, the privilege to arrest for misdemeanors without a warrant is limited to those misdemeanors which constitute a breach of the peace. (footnote omitted) In the case of misdemeanors such as shoplifting, there is no breach of the peace, and no common law privilege to arrest. Therefore any common law privilege would exist only for recapture of chattel. There is a limited privilege for an owner whose property has been wrongfully taken, while in fresh pursuit, to use reasonable force to recapture a chattel. (citation omitted) An important caveat to this privilege is that the actor must be correct as to the facts which he believes grant him the privilege, and faces liability for damages resulting from any mistake, however reasonable. (citation omitted) The force privilege must be reasonable under the circumstances, and not calculated to inflict serious bodily harm. Ordinarily, the use of any force at all will not be justified until there has been a demand made for the return of the property. (citation omitted)

Thus, privileges for misdemeanor arrest traditionally available at common law recognize no privilege to arrest for ordinary "shoplifting."

[...]

There have been a number of decisions which permit a business person for reasonable cause, to detain a customer for investigation. (citation omitted.) This privilege, however, is narrow; it is confined to what is reasonably necessary for its limited purpose, of enabling the defendant to do what is possible on the spot to discover the facts. There will be liability if the detention is for a length of time beyond that which is reasonably necessary for such a short investigation, or if the plaintiff is assaulted, insulted or bullied, or public accusation is made against him, or the privilege is exercised in an unreasonable manner....

[...] Arizona has adopted the shopkeeper's privilege by statute, which provides in pertinent part:

C. A merchant, or his agent or employee, *with reasonable cause, may detain* on the premises *in a reasonable manner and for a reasonable time* any person suspected of shoplifting...*for questioning or summoning a law enforcement officer.*

D. Reasonable cause is a defense to a civil or criminal action against a peace officer, merchant or an agent or employee of such merchant for false arrest, false or unlawful imprisonment or wrongful detention.

(citation omitted) (emphasis supplied).

The trial court was evidently of the view that by the terms of subsection D, reasonable cause, alone, was a defense. We disagree; we believe that the statutory shopkeeper's privilege [...] involves all of the elements noted in subsection C. Subsections C and D [...] must be read together. Applying subsection (D) by recognizing the privilege defense upon a showing of "reasonable cause" without the limitations contained in subsection (C), would render the latter meaningless. Where the language of the statute is susceptible of several interpretations, the court will adopt one which is reasonable and avoids contradictions or absurdities. [...]

To invoke the privilege, therefore, "reasonable cause" is only the threshold requirement. Once reasonable cause is established, there are two further questions regarding the application of the privilege. We must ask whether the purpose of the shopkeeper's action was proper (*i.e.*, detention for questioning or summoning a law enforcement officer). (footnote omitted) The last question is whether the detention was carried out in a reasonable manner and for a reasonable length of time. If the answer to any of the three questions is negative, then the privilege granted by statute is inapplicable and the actions of the shopkeeper are taken at his peril. If the shopkeeper is mistaken and the common law recapture privilege is therefore also inapplicable, the seizure is tortious.

[…]

In the case at bench, the facts supporting reasonable cause are as follows: the clerk saw Gortarez with the item when he asked if he could pay for it at the front. The clerk followed the two young men through the store, and did not see them either deposit the item or pay for it as they left. Although the question of reasonable cause in the instant case may have been close (footnote omitted) we defer to the trial court's better opportunity to see and judge the credibility of witnesses and uphold it on the specific finding that conflicting inferences could not be drawn from the facts and that reasonable cause existed as a matter of law.

Purpose of the Detention

The statute provides this privilege for the express and limited purpose of detention for investigation by questioning or summoning a law enforcement officer. A finding of detention for the proper purpose could not have been made as a matter of law on the state of the evidence before the trial judge, since there was no evidence of either questioning or summoning of officers. At best, […] it is possible that the intent of the employee was to question or call officers.

Reasonableness of the Detention

Assuming there was reasonable cause for the detention, and that the detention was for a proper purpose, the privilege still may not attach if the merchant does not detain in a reasonable manner and for a reasonable time. […]

Reasonable force may be used to detain the person; but […] the use of force intended or likely to cause serious bodily harm is never privileged for the sole purpose of detention to investigate, and it becomes privileged only where the resistance of the other makes it necessary for the actor to use such force in self-defense. In the ordinary case, the use of any force at all will not be privileged until the other has been requested to remain; and it is only where there is not time for such a request, or it would obviously be futile, that force is justified.

[…]

Under the restrictions given above, there was a question whether the use of force in the search of Hernandez, and, more importantly, in the restraint of Gortarez, was reasonable. There was no request that the two young men remain. No inquiry was made with regard to whether Hernandez had the vaporizer. Gibson testified that Hernandez gave no indication of resistance and made no attempt to escape. The possible theft of a 59 cent item hardly warrants apprehension that the two were armed or dangerous. There was, arguably, time to make a request to remain before Gibson seized Hernandez and began searching him. (footnote omitted) Also, there is no indication that such a request would *obviously* have been futile. The evidence adduced probably would have supported a finding that the manner of detention was unreasonable as a matter of law. […] We hold that the court erred in its findings with respect to both the purpose and manner of detention. This requires reversal and retrial. At the new trial evidence on the three issues should be measured against the principles set forth in this opinion.

[…]

The appeals court reversed the initial verdict for the defendant and ordered a new trial on the reasonableness of the use (or threat of use) of force to support the defendant's claiming of the shopkeeper's privilege, although there seems little reason to doubt how the trial court will rule.

Consent as a Defense

That false imprisonment relies on detention implies that the plaintiffs had not consented to the confinement. As the following case shows, it doesn't matter how the detention occurred if it turns out that plaintiffs had no opportunity to consent to the detention (Case in Point 7-6).

 ## CASE IN POINT 7-6

Scofield v. Critical Air Medicine, Inc.
45 Cal. App. 4th 990 (Cal. App. 2d Dist. 1996)

Defendants and appellants, Critical Air Medicine, Inc., Executive Air Services, Inc., Harry A. Metz, and Kenneth Malcomson (collectively Critical Air), appeal the judgment entered following a jury verdict in favor of plaintiffs and respondents Erin Scofield (Erin) and Laura Scofield (Laura) [...] The jury awarded Erin and Laura $60,000 each in damages for their claims of false imprisonment. (footnote omitted)

[....]

On December 29, 1990, Nancy Scofield, the mother of Erin, Laura, and David, was killed in a truck accident in Baja California, Mexico. Thirteen-year-old David was seriously injured, and eleven-year-old Erin and eight-year-old Laura suffered minor injuries. [...] Jackie and William Dalton [...] drove the children to the nearest medical facility in Guerrero Negro, Mexico. Robert Scofield (Scofield), Nancy's husband and the father of the children, was contacted in the Los Angeles area.

Scofield telephoned the Daltons at the clinic in Guerrero Negro, and was informed his son had suffered a head injury and was in a coma. Scofield then called several air transport services. Each of the air charter companies informed Scofield the Guerrero Negro airstrip had no lights and it would be impossible to fly the children out until the next morning. Believing his son might not live through the night, Scofield contacted the American Consulate and spoke with Kathleen List (List).

List contacted Cindy Clemment (Clemment) at the Bi-National Health Committee. Clemment called Hartsen's Ambulance Service. When Clemment was informed Guerrero Negro was approximately 600 miles south of San Diego, she determined an air transport would be necessary. Clemment told the representative of Hartsen's, who suggested Critical Air could make the transport, she " '[was] going to take care of it,' " and " 'if she need[ed] further assistance, [she would] call [Hartsen's] back.' "

The Bi-National Health Committee utilized the services of several air transport companies, including Schaeffer's, Air Evac and Critical Air. The usual practice was to rotate the companies as services were needed. Since Air Evac was next on the list, Clemment called that company. Clemment then telephoned Scofield and informed him that at 8:15 that evening, an "Air Evac 421 flight team" would be ready to depart from Montgomery Field in San Diego to retrieve his children. Clemment instructed him to be in San Diego at 1 o'clock the next morning when the children were scheduled to arrive.

As soon as she had finished making the arrangements, Clemment received a call from a Critical Air employee, Carlos Ayala. When Clemment told Ayala she already had arranged for Air Evac to transport the children, Ayala stated, " 'Don't bother, we're going to go pick them up. We already have the information.' " Clemment informed Ayala she was " 'taking care of [the situation].' " Clemment then contacted a Red Cross worker named Francisco Amador in Guerrero Negro. She told Amador "the [Scofield] children were not to be discharged to anybody other than this specific [Air Evac] crew."

Air Evac pilot, Richard Jones, got a crew ready to fly to Guerrero Negro. Jones obtained a United States customs number, and was informed Critical Air was also planning a flight to Guerrero Negro. Jones telephoned the Air Evac flight coordinator for clarification. The flight coordinator told Jones to continue with his flight plan and at approximately 8 p.m. on December 29, 1990, Jones and his crew left Montgomery Field, flying toward Tijuana, Mexico. Immediately after the Air Evac plane completed its take-off, Critical Air's plane took off from a different runway at Montgomery Field.

The Critical Air pilot, Stuart Bachman, knew an Air Evac plane was also flying to Guerrero Negro. As the two planes approached the Tijuana airport, Bachman maneuvered his plane in front of and below Air Evac's plane, forcing the Air Evac plane to turn to avoid a collision. As a result, the Critical Air plane landed first, proceeded through customs, and left ahead of the Air Evac plane.

Critical Air's plane, which bore no distinctive markings or logo, arrived in Guerrero Negro about 20 minutes before the Air Evac flight. Bachman did not tell anyone on the ground the plane was from Critical Air, not Air Evac. The Daltons watched as the Critical Air crew, whose clothing had no distinctive markings, quickly loaded the three Scofield children onto the plane. Before the Air Evac plane landed in Guerrero Negro, Bachman had taken off.

Scofield had spoken with Erin on the telephone and told her he was sending a plane to take her, Laura and David back to the United States. Had anyone told Erin the plane was not the one her father had sent for her, she would not have boarded.

Clemment met Scofield in San Diego. Clemment told him although she had dispatched the Air Evac plane to retrieve his children, Critical Air had interfered and also had sent a plane to Mexico. Clemment informed Scofield she was not sure which service would transport the children, and at which airstrip they would be landing. Scofield was extremely upset; he had authorized Air Evac to transport his children, not Critical Air.

At approximately 1 a.m., Critical Air's plane landed at Montgomery Field. The children were taken off the plane, loaded into an ambulance and taken to Sharp Hospital. David was later transferred to Children's Hospital. (footnote omitted)

[...]

The president of Critical Air, Harry Metz (Metz), first learned of the Scofields' accident in Mexico when a Hartsen's Ambulance Service employee telephoned a Critical Air employee. When Metz contacted the United States Consulate about the situation, he was informed arrangements to transport the children already had been made. Metz indicated later he was led to believe he could continue to pursue the matter. (footnote omitted)

Although Metz understood Air Evac was sending a plane to Mexico, he made arrangements for the Critical Air plane to fly to Guerrero Negro, and eventually spoke with a Dr. Rodriguez at the clinic there. Metz admitted Critical Air never obtained permission from Scofield or his representative to transport the three children. Metz, however, believed Dr. Rodriguez had authorized Critical Air to fly the children from Guerrero Negro to San Diego.

[...]

Here, the evidence established the girls' consent to their confinement on the aircraft was procured through a misrepresentation by Critical Air as to its authority. The confinement therefore was nonconsensual. (citation omitted) Because "the tort consists of the ' "nonconsensual, intentional confinement of a person, without lawful privilege, for an appreciable length of time," ' " (citation omitted), the jury properly found Critical Air's conduct amounted to a false imprisonment.

[...]

The judgment is affirmed. The Scofields to recover costs on appeal.

Because Critical Air misrepresented its authority, any grant of consent because of that misrepresentation was not valid.

As jurisdictions may construe the concept differently, a paralegal should review case law and statutes to determine the rule of law in a particular jurisdiction.

Emotional Distress (Intentional Infliction)

The **intentional infliction of emotional distress** means the defendant has deliberately sought to cause psychological harm to the plaintiff by engaging in outrageous conduct. For example, if the defendant, the dorm roommate of the plaintiff, said the plaintiff had a mole that looked cancerous, repeated this observation over months, and showed the plaintiff photos of how skin cancer progressed, the plaintiff has a claim for intentional infliction of emotional defense, regardless of the nature of the mole.

To win, the plaintiff would need to prove the following elements by a preponderance of the evidence:

■ intent to cause emotional distress
■ action, outrageous in nature
■ resulting in emotional distress (psychological harm)

Harm

As with the tort of assault, intentional infliction of emotional distress involves psychological, not physical, harm. The harm can take the form of horror as well as of embarrassment, anxiety as well as humiliation. For example, a plaintiff may receive damages for having heard that his or her child had been hit by a school bus, even if the plaintiff learns a few hours later that this did not happen.

Different from Assault

Intentional infliction of emotional distress differs from assault because it deals with a broader range of psychological harm. Assault focuses on apprehension of imminent physical harm while intentional infliction of emotional distress could deal with a great range of psychological harm. For example, if during an interview an interviewer copies the interviewee-plaintiff's lisp, the plaintiff might have a good claim for intentional infliction of emotional distress (see box below).

THE NATURE OF HARM WITH EMOTIONAL DISTRESS, ACCORDING TO PROFESSOR DOBBS.

Although stand-alone emotional harm is real and an important concern, and many cases leave us in no doubt about the reality of the distress, emotional harm does have some special characteristics that call for a degree of caution.

First, emotional harm, as distinct from the financial costs of treatment, cannot ordinarily be represented in dollar awards. [...]

Second, we may be confident that distress is real but quite uncertain how deep-seated it is and what to expect of the plaintiff herself by way of mitigation. [...]

Third, we cannot at this juncture be confident about whether awards for distress accomplish compensation. [...]

Finally, in some situations (but not all) courts do not see any reasonable limit on the number of emotional harm claims that can be brought as the result of a single tort. [...]

continued

> [...] a large number of people might suffer some degree of distress as a result of a single tort. A negligent or intentional killing or beating might shock millions who watch it on television or read about it.
>
> Dobbs *The Law of Torts* §302 (2000)

Going beyond "Trivial" Annoyances

Recovery for the intentional infliction of mental distress has gained acceptance only in the past few decades. The reticence of courts to recognize such a cause of action arose out of concern that trivial or minor annoyances would serve as a valid basis for recovery. Thus, courts usually will not find a defendant liable for a trivial annoyance. For example, while driving, a defendant might express displeasure at a plaintiff's driving style with a gesture intended to offend. Yet courts would find that recipient of such a gesture merely to be a function of driving in America and would see no basis for an award of damages.

Distress Regarding Another Person

The *Restatement (Second) of Torts* also notes that liability may arise when the outrageous conduct was directed at an individual other than the one distressed. If a defendant tells a grandparent that the plaintiff's child has suffered an injury due to a school bus traffic accident, even if the account is false, the defendant could face liability (see box below).

CONDUCT DIRECTED AT THIRD PERSON

Where such conduct is directed at a third person, the actor is subject to liability if he intentionally or recklessly causes severe emotional distress

a. to a member of such person's immediate family who is present at the time, whether or not such distress results in bodily harm, or
b. to any other person who is present at the time, if such distress results in bodily harm.

Restatement (Second) of Torts, §46 (1965)

If the defendant acted so as to suggest that physical harm would come to the plaintiff's child and the plaintiff sees the menacing, the plaintiff has a claim for intentional infliction of emotional distress.

Emotional Distress (Negligent Infliction)

Some jurisdictions have gone so far as to recognize a cause of action for **negligent infliction of emotional distress.** That means the defendant breached a duty of care owed to the plaintiff, which caused psychological harm to the plaintiff. The following elements are needed to make a claim for negligent infliction of emotional distress:

- The defendant owed the plaintiff a duty of care
- The defendant breached that duty
- The breach of duty caused emotional distress (psychological harm)

If during a magic show, the magician-defendant gets a volunteer from the audience to participant in a magic trick and then carelessly performs the act so as to give the volunteer-plaintiff reason to think that the magician will saw off the volunteer's limb, that will be negligent infliction of emotional distress. It is not assault, nor intentional infliction of emotional distress, because the magician had a duty of care to perform the trick so as not to alarm the plaintiff.

Nature of Harm

Many jurisdictions often limit the cause of action for negligent infliction of emotional distress only to those instances where there is a threat of physical harm. But in *Dillon v. Legg* 68 Cal.2d 728(1968), a California court ruled that there was harm when the plaintiff saw a relative killed when hit by the defendant's car. In this instance, the plaintiff suffered tremendous psychological pain but no physical injury.

Outrageous Conduct

No set definition exists for what constitutes outrageous conduct that amounts to breach of a duty of care because that seems to depend heavily upon the specific facts. The plaintiff in the following case had little difficulty in establishing the outrageousness of the defendant's conduct, since the defendant was a surgeon who was to repair damage in the plaintiff's eye but performed surgery on the wrong eye (see Case in Point 7-7).

 # CASE IN POINT 7-7

Triano v. Fitzpatrick
2000 Conn. Super. 508 (Conn. Super. Ct. Feb. 17, 2000)

[...]

Beginning in May of 1997, the plaintiff consulted with Fitzpatrick, an eye specialist, for vision problems. [...] By August 1997, the plaintiff had lost most of the vision in his left eye and relied exclusively on his right eye. At Fitzpatrick's office on August 19, 1997, Fitzpatrick examined the plaintiff, treated the plaintiff's right eye with a laser and advised the plaintiff that it was necessary for the plaintiff to have an operation performed immediately on his left eye. The plaintiff agreed to the operation and Fitzpatrick prescribed medications for the plaintiff to place in his left eye prior to surgery. Fitzpatrick scheduled the surgery for the following day, August 20, 1997, at the hospital.

The plaintiff arrived at the hospital the next day where he signed the hospital's informed consent form authorizing Fitzpatrick to perform an operation only on his left eye (footnote omitted). While the plaintiff was under anaesthesia, Fitzpatrick operated upon the plaintiff's right eye. After the operation, the plaintiff was discharged with a bandage over his only sighted eye, his right eye. On the following day, August 21, 1997, the plaintiff returned to Fitzpatrick's office for a post-operative follow-up visit, where it was determined that the plaintiff's right eye no longer had any vision. As a result of this conduct on the part of the defendants, the plaintiff is totally and unexpectedly blind.

The first five counts of the plaintiff's revised complaint are directed towards Fitzpatrick. The [...] third count sounds in negligent infliction of emotional distress.
[...]

Reading the plaintiff's complaint in the light most favorable to the plaintiff, the court finds that the conduct the plaintiff alleges fits within the parameters of extreme and outrageous conduct from which emotional distress would likely result. The plaintiff alleges that Fitzpatrick, who had been treating both of the plaintiff's eyes for four months prior to surgery, who knew that his patient only had vision in his right eye and had consented only to the operation for the left eye, knowingly operated on the sighted right eye, rendering it sightless and causing the plaintiff severe emotional distress.

[...]

In sum, Fitzpatrick's motion to strike the plaintiff's complaint in its entirety is denied [...]

Given the loss of sight in this case, courts clearly need to witness truly unusual conduct to satisfy the "outrageous conduct" of the tort.

Paralegal students should check a jurisdiction's laws to determine what those courts have determined as sufficient defendant's actions constituting outrageous conduct for negligent infliction of emotional distress (see box below).

OUTRAGEOUS CONDUCT

So far as it is possible to generalize from the cases, the rule which seems to have emerged is that there is liability for conduct exceeding all bounds usually tolerated by decent society, of a nature which is especially calculated to cause, and does cause, mental distress of a very serious kind. The requirements of the rule are rigorous, and difficult to satisfy.

W. Page Keeton et al., *Prosser and Keeton on the Law of Torts* §12 at 60-61 (5th ed. 1984)

■ RIGHT OF PRIVACY

The tort of **invasion of the right of privacy** recognizes that individuals may wish to keep confidential those things to which the public should not freely have access.

To win a claim for the invasion of the right of privacy, a plaintiff would need to prove the following elements by a preponderance of the evidence:

- intent to commit an action
- action that amounts to an interference with the right to privacy
- harm arising out of that invasion

Origin

The origin of the tort for invasion of a right to privacy arose because of a prescient 1890 *Harvard Law Review* article by Samuel D. Warren and Louis D. Brandeis, titled "The Right of Privacy." Recognizing that an increasingly industrialized society would mean an increasingly intrusive society, the authors saw the need for individuals to have protection from the inquiries of others. With the current ubiquity of popular entertainment media, the need for individuals to escape the unblinking gaze of the public seems even more necessary.

Types of Intrusion

Although not actually a right—rights arise only out of the U.S. Constitution or state constitutions—this tort sweeps broadly to include four types of intrusion, as noted in the *Restatement (Second) of Torts* (see box on next page).

> ## RIGHT OF PRIVACY
>
> 1. One who invades the right of privacy of another is subject to liability for the resulting harm to the interests of the other.
> 2. The right of privacy is invaded by
>   a. unreasonable intrusion upon the seclusion of another…or
>   b. appropriation of the other's name or likeness…or
>   c. unreasonable publicity given to the other's private life…or
>   d. publicity that unreasonably places the other in a false light before the public.
>
> *Restatement (Second) of Torts, §652A (1965)*

Consider, then, the four distinct actions in tort for invasion of privacy.

For Appropriation

The **invasion of privacy for appropriation** involves using the plaintiff's name or likeness, without permission, to gain economic advantage. For decades, having the smiling image of a celebrity on a box of wheat cereal has made a fortune for the cereal manufacturer, so the manufacturer, at least, believes this picture has economic value. If the manufacturer uses the picture to increase sales, it must pay for the privilege of using it.

This cause of action goes just the endorsement of a product. It also could involve a separate action in tort for copyright infringement, where a defendant has taken the plaintiff's picture or likeness from some sort of display or presentation and used it to generate income.

For Unreasonable Intrusion

The **invasion of privacy for unreasonable intrusion** involves the invasion of solitude and seclusion. For this type of tort, the plaintiff must show that the defendant invaded the solitude and seclusion the plaintiff had enjoyed. In a modern society overwhelmed by the entertainment media's insatiable need for "news," freedom from such scrutiny most closely corresponds to what people mean when they think about the tort of invasion of privacy.

Some might argue the cliché, "There's no such thing as bad publicity." Those whose celebrity enables them to earn a living may be said to have little to complain of if, for example, pictures of their private honeymoon at a remote location show up in the supermarket tabloids or TV programs.

Defendant's Public Disclosure of Private Facts

This type of invasion of privacy deals with the deliberate, unpermitted, and offensive release of private information for which no legitimate public interest exists. A cause of action for **public disclosure of private facts** seems more likely when the plaintiff is a private, not public, figure. Most people prefer that the details of their life remain private. For example, most people prefer to keep their medical records confidential. Yet for someone who relies on publicity to make money, the disclosure of this person's criminal record, for example, would seem almost inevitable. By seeking the public's attention, a public figure provides others with the incentive to dig up embarrassing information.

For Holding a Plaintiff in a False Light in the Public Eye

Another type of invasion of privacy is **holding a plaintiff in a false light in the public eye.** In this action, the defendant has made material misrepresentations to the public about the plaintiff. For example, a caption accompanying a movie star's photo might wrongly say that the star had just walked away from a drunk driving accident, when in fact he or she was going in for surgery to straighten a childhood injury, a broken nose.

In the following case, the court notes that the publication of a photo in a newspaper the day after an accident was not an invasion of privacy. Rather, the invasion occurs when the photo is published years later and implies that the plaintiff brought about the injuries depicted in the photo (see Case in Point 7-8).

 # CASE IN POINT 7-8

Leverton v. Curtis Pub. Co.

192 F.2d 974 (3d Cir. Pa. 1951)

This case involves the extend (sic) of the right of privacy. [...]

The plaintiff in 1947, when she was a child of ten, was involved in a street accident in the city of Birmingham, Alabama. A motor car nearly ran over her. A newspaper photographer who happened to be on the spot took a photograph of the child being lifted to her feet by a woman bystander. The picture was dramatic and its effect was heightened by the fact that it was an action picture, not one posed for the camera.

The photograph appeared in a Birmingham newspaper the day following. Twenty months later it was used by the Curtis Publishing Company as an illustration for an article on traffic accidents, with emphasis on pedestrian carelessness, under the title, 'They Ask To Be Killed' by David G. Wittels. The print was purchased by Curtis from a supplier of illustration material. Plaintiff claims that the publication of her picture this long after the accident in which she was involved, was a violation of her right of privacy.

[...]

It is agreed on all sides that the original publication of the picture of this traffic accident was not actionable. If it invaded the right of the plaintiff to stay out of public attention, it was a privileged invasion, her interest in being left alone being overbalanced by the general public interest in being kept informed. As we see the questions in this case, they are two. (1) Is the privilege involved in the original publication lost by the lapse of time between the date of the original publication immediately following the accident and the reappearance of the plaintiff's picture in the Saturday Evening Post twenty months later? (2) The second question is whether, if the privilege has not been lost by lapse of time, it is lost by the using of the plaintiff's picture, not in connection with a news story, but as an illustration heading an article on pedestrian traffic accidents?

[...]

It could be easily agreed that the plaintiff in this case, because she was once involved in an automobile accident does not continue throughout her life to have her goings and comings made the subject of newspaper stories. That, however, is a long way from saying that the occasion of her once becoming a subject of public interest cannot be brought again to public attention later on. Suppose the same newspaper which printed the plaintiff's photograph the day after her accident printed a resume sometime later of traffic accidents and supplied pictures dealing with them, including this one, which photographers on its staff had compiled. We cannot think that their publication under those circumstances would subject the publisher to liability.

[...]

We conclude that the immunity from liability for the original publication was not lost through lapse of time when the same picture was again published.

Now to the second point. The first publication of the plaintiff's photograph was purely news. The second publication was a sort of a dramatic setting for the discussion of a traffic problem by Mr. Wittels. Does that much of a change in the purpose of the publication lose the privilege?

Something was made at the argument of the point that the use of the photograph by Curtis was 'commercial'. Of course it was. So was the original publication in the Birmingham newspaper. People who run newspapers and magazines as commercial enterprises, run them to make profit if they can. What adds to reader interest adds to circulation and that adds to profit. [...] [W]e think this particular publication was an actionable invasion of plaintiff's right of privacy. Granted that she was 'newsworthy' with regard to that particular accident for an indefinite time afterward. This use of her picture had nothing at all to do with her accident. It related to the general subject of traffic accidents and pedestrian carelessness. Yet the facts, so far as we know them in this case, show that the little girl, herself, was at the time of her accident not careless and the motorist was. The picture is used in connection with several headings tending to say that this plaintiff narrowly escaped death because she was careless of her own safety. [...] But we are not talking now about liability for defamation. We are talking about the privilege to invade her interest in being left alone.

The heading of the article was called 'They Ask To Be Killed'. Underneath the picture of the little girl was the heading 'Safety education in schools has reduced child accidents measurably, but unpredictable darting through traffic still takes a sobering toll.' In a box beside the title appears the following: 'Do you invite massacre by your own carelessness? Here's how thousands have committed suicide by scorning laws that were passed to keep them alive.' The sum total of all this is that this particular plaintiff, the legitimate subject for publicity for one particular accident, now becomes a pictorial, frightful example of pedestrian carelessness. This, we think, exceeds the bounds of privilege.

[...]

The judgment of the District Court will be affirmed.

Since the defendant publisher stated that the accident and injury depicted in the picture was the plaintiff's fault, when it was clearly not, and the court easily found for the plaintiff on a claim of false light invasion of privacy.

Different than Defamation.   While this cause of action overlaps to some extent with the tort of defamation, it differs in that it focuses on a statement that proved "highly offensive to a reasonable person." For example, for some, saying that the plaintiff practiced one type of religion instead of the actual faith that the plaintiff subscribes to might prove sufficient to prevail at trial in tort for invasion of privacy, specifically in an action for holding the plaintiff in a false light in the public eye.

Professor Dobbs describes the distinction:

THE DISTINCTION BETWEEN A TORT ACTION FOR FALSE LIGHT INVASION OF PRIVACY VERSUS DEFAMATION

The tort theoretically goes beyond defamation because the objectionable false light is not necessarily a defamatory one, only false and offensive. For example, a false light claim was established when a newspaper feature article made false statements about the plaintiffs (sic) poverty and her stoic attitude following the death of her husband in a disaster. Likewise, a false light claim was made out when a television program, by splicing shots, falsely depicted the plaintiff as a hunter who shot wild geese on the ground rather than in flight. Possibly, but not certainly, these are cases in which defamation could not be established.

Dobbs *The Law of Torts* §428, (2000)

The First Amendment and Freedom of Speech

The ability to bring a successful suit can prove quite difficult because of the afore-mentioned right of freedom of speech contained in the First Amendment to the U.S. Constitution. That right protects such a range of speech under the belief that the free flow of information benefits a democratic society. Only when a defendant knowingly distributes information maliciously, with the knowledge of its falsity, will a plaintiff stand a decent chance at winning in court.

■ DEFAMATION

The tort of **defamation** involves the disclosure of information with the intent to cause harm to the plaintiff. The damage arises from the way the information changes the public's perception of the plaintiff (for example, the public's perception of the plaintiff's reputation). Defamation can take the form of a written statement **(libel)** or an oral one **(slander).**

How Libel and Slander Differ

The *Restatement (Second) of Torts* makes clear the distinction between slander and libel (see box below).

LIBEL AND SLANDER DISTINGUISHED

1. Libel consists of the publication of defamatory matter by written or printed words, by its embodiment in physical form or by any other form of communication that has the potentially harmful qualities characteristic of written or printed words.
2. Slander consists of the publication of defamatory matter by spoken words, transitory gestures or by any form of communication other than those stated in Subsection (1).
3. The area of dissemination, the deliberate and premeditated character of its publication and the persistence of the defamation are factors to be considered in determining whether a publication is a libel rather than a slander.

Restatement (Second) of Torts, §568 (1965)

Libel involves communications that can be seen or touched while slander involves communications that are heard. This distinction can break down, for example, when someone reads a defamatory statement aloud. Regardless of the oral form of publication, the plaintiff still would file a claim for libel because the defamatory statement exists in permanent form: writing.

Elements Needed for a Defamation Claim

To win a defamation claim, a plaintiff would need to prove the following elements by a preponderance of the evidence:

- publication
- of information about the plaintiff
- with the intent to damage the plaintiff's reputation or good standing in the community and that
- the plaintiff experiences harm as a result of the publication of that information

Nature of a Defamatory Statement

A **defamatory statement** involves information whose release damages the plaintiff's reputation in the eyes of the community. The formulation offered in *the Restatement (Second) of Torts* covers a very broad range of statements that could prove defamatory (see box below).

DEFAMATION

To create liability for defamation there must be:

a. a false and defamatory statement concerning another;
b. an unprivileged publication to a third party;
c. fault amounting at least to negligence on the part of the publisher; and
d. either actionability of the statement irrespective of special harm or the existence of special harm caused by the publication.

Restatement (Second) of Torts, §558 (1965)

The information in a defamatory statement may damage a plaintiff's financial or social standing. The impact of defamation could include, for example, the plaintiff's being ostracized or being unable to find employment opportunities.

In the following case, the court makes clear a distinction between a defamatory statement and disclosures—no matter how embarrassing—made during a legal proceeding (see Case in Point 7-9).

 # CASE IN POINT 7-9

Carniol v. Carniol

288 A.D.2d 421 (N.Y. App. Div. 2d Dep't 2001)

[...]

The parties to this appeal have been involved in protracted and acrimonious divorce proceedings (citation ommitted). In the course thereof, the defendant made certain allegations, inter alia, in her statement of net worth and during her deposition, about the plaintiff's "income, assets and net worth," which he considered to be "false, prejudicial, scandalous and defamatory." As a result, the plaintiff commenced the instant action seeking damages for defamation and for prima facie tort. The complaint sought damages of $83,449, which was the identical amount set forth in a Qualified Domestic Relations Order the defendant had obtained in the divorce action. The gist of the instant action was that the defendant made misrepresentations to the matrimonial court to obtain greater support than she was genuinely entitled to receive. [...]

We now reverse.

[...]

Assuming that the defendant's statements were otherwise actionable, they all were pertinent to the parties' divorce litigation and thus were absolutely privileged (citation ommitted). As a matter of public policy, they may not serve as the basis for the imposition of liability in a defamation action (citation ommitted).

While the plaintiff might not like the defendant's statement about the plaintiff's finances, it did not rise to the level of a defamatory statement. Even if they had, the statements were made in the context of a legal proceeding. And because a legal proceeding is intended to bring together all information needed to resolve a legal issue, the statements made there generally do not form the basis of an action in tort.

Publication

While an injurious statement may cause emotional harm to the one at whom it was directed, if it is not communicated to a third person it is not a defamatory statement. A critical element in the tort is **publication**—what the law refers to as the communication of a defamatory statement to a third person. The plaintiff's emotional upset alone will not support a claim in tort for defamation; publication of the information to others has to have occurred. As the following case shows, publication need not be limited to the print or electronic media. Here, a jewelry business sent a postcard to a customer, which reasonably would have led the customer's wife to conclude that he was engaging in conduct that challenged the integrity of their marriage (see Case in Point 7-10).

 ## CASE IN POINT 7-10

Freeman v. Busch Jewelry Co., Inc.,
98 F. Supp. 963 (D. Ga. 1951)

In this action plaintiff seeks to recover $25,000 damages for wounded feelings and marital difficulties growing out of this transaction. It appears without dispute that the plaintiff, a young married man of LaGrange, Georgia, and his wife purchased from defendant company a radio for the sum of $19.95, on which payments of $ 1.25 per week were made for many weeks, there remaining on September 16, 1948, a small balance of $ 4.20.

Plaintiff at the time of the purchase was living at 912 Todd Street and working at Almond's Service Station, and continued to work and reside at the same places on September 15, 1948. On that date there came to plaintiff's residence through the mail, a postal card from defendant company bearing the following writing: 'Dear Milford, I'll be in LaGrange next week. Call me at 9693. Love, Mary.' Defendant was then at work. On returning home for lunch his wife showed him the post card. He attempted to explain to her that he did not understand its contents, that he knew no girl by the name of Mary and that he had had no affair with any person. After lunch he went to defendant company and caused its agent to phone his wife and make an explanation which, at that time, she apparently accepted. Upon further reflection, however, the wife, who was then in a delicate condition, worried considerably over the matter and later in the evening packed up her personal belongings, and, taking their child with her, went to live with her mother. Some two weeks later plaintiff was able to induce his wife to return home, she being then sick and apparently in need of help.

Prior to the receipt of this postal card this young couple were living happily together, with no other than the usual trivial domestic disagreements. After this time, however, things began to change. The wife could not free her mind from the thought that plaintiff might have been unfaithful to her and she did not trust him as before. When he would come home, after being out, she would ask him questions, and he, being irritated at her distrust, would decline to answer. His drinking, before this time only moderate, tended to increase as sometimes happens under the same or similar circumstances. He even struck his wife on one occasion. There have been other separations. It so happened that prior to the receipt of this postal card, plaintiff had been pursuing studies in Atlanta under the G.I. Bill of Rights, and, on two week-ends, instead of returning to his home, he remained in Atlanta, explaining to the satisfaction of his wife that he was busy studying.

There is no evidence that his stay in Atlanta over the week-end was anything but innocent. However, coupled with the other circumstances, it caused his wife to worry, and to distrust the husband. It does not appear that even to this time the confidence of his wife which plaintiff formerly enjoyed has been restored.

Plaintiff's wife [...] trusted her husband prior to September 16th, and since that time on some occasions thought that she continued to trust him, and on other occasions, including the time of the trial, stated very frankly she just doesn't know what to think.

From the evidence in the case it is clear to the court that the receipt of this postal card was definitely the beginning of plaintiff's marital difficulties, that it caused plaintiff's wife for the first time to distrust him, and to leave him, that her distrust of plaintiff was the source of great annoyance and disappointment to plaintiff, and that subsequently thereto plaintiff has been more addicted to drink, according to his wife's own testimony, than previously.

While the parties have resumed their marital relationship and their cohabitation along with their two small children, it seems clear that the status of mutual respect and affection existing prior to September 16th does not now exist, though it is possible that the husband's exoneration by the judgment in this case might assist in its restoration in the future; at least the Court hopes so. Defendant was guilty at least of a great degree of negligence in sending to this husband at his home an open postal card which on its face would convey to his wife no other impression than that the husband had a clandestine relationship with some person named Mary. The reactions of plaintiff's wife were to be reasonably anticipated. [...]

The plaintiff undoubtedly had the right as alleged in his petition 'the legal right to personal security in his home, including the right of enjoyment of life, and the enjoyment of the happiness of home and the love and confidence of his wife.' The defendant injured plaintiff in the enjoyment of the above right by representing to plaintiff's wife in effect, that plaintiff was unfaithful to her. Defendant should have reasonably anticipated that the open postal card would fall into the hands of plaintiff's wife, would be read by her and would cause such a reaction as it actually did cause in this case. [...]

From the above it follows that judgment should be rendered in favor of plaintiff in the sum of $5,000.

This case shows that, if someone learns of a defamatory statement, even through a communication as seemingly insignificant as a postcard, publication has occurred.

Libel

Libel is a written defamatory statement communicated to a third person. The writing can take any form, from a postcard to a newspaper article. The writing can be any type of communication that has been preserved, so an electronic broadcast of any sort usually qualifies as a writing. As the following case illustrates, changes in technology may mean that the means of communicating the libelous statement have changed, yet a statement still may be libelous (see Case in Point 7-11).

CASE IN POINT 7-11

Doe v. Cahill

884 A.2d 451 (Del. 2005)

The defendant-appellant, John Doe No.1, anonymously posted allegedly defamatory statements about the plaintiff-appellee, Cahill, on an internet blog. Cahill brought a defamation action. [...] On November 2, 2004, the plaintiffs below, Patrick and Julia Cahill, both residents of Smyrna, Delaware, filed suit against four John Doe defendants asserting defamation and invasion of privacy claims. [...] Using the alias "Proud Citizen," Doe posted two statements on an internet website sponsored by the Delaware State News called the "Smyrna/Clayton Issues Blog" (footnote omitted) concerning Cahill's performance as a City Councilman of Smyrna. The "Guidelines" at the top of the blog stated "this is your hometown forum for opinions about public issues." The first of Doe's statements, posted on September 18, 2004, said:

If only Councilman Cahill was able to display the same leadership skills, energy and enthusiasm toward the revitalization and growth of the fine town of Smyrna as Mayor Schaeffer has demonstrated! While Mayor Schaeffer has made great strides toward improving the livelihood of Smyrna's citizens, Cahill has devoted all of his energy to being a divisive impediment to any kind of cooperative movement. *Anyone who has spent any amount of time with Cahill would be keenly aware of such character flaws, not to mention an obvious mental deterioration.* Cahill is a prime example of failed leadership—his eventual ousting is exactly what Smyrna needs in order to move forward and establish a community that is able to thrive on its own economic stability and common pride in its town. (footnote omitted)

The next day, Doe posted another statement:

Gahill [sic] *is as paranoid* as everyone in the town thinks he is. The mayor needs support from his citizens and protections from unfounded attacks.... (footnote omitted)

These were the only two internet postings attributed to Doe or mentioned in the Cahills' complaint.

[...]

The internet is a unique democratizing medium unlike anything that has come before. The advent of the internet dramatically changed the nature of public discourse by allowing more and diverse people to engage in public debate. Unlike thirty years ago, when "many citizens [were] barred from meaningful participation in public discourse by financial or status inequalities and a relatively small number of powerful speakers [could] dominate the marketplace of ideas"(footnote omitted) the internet now allows anyone with a phone line to "become a town crier with a voice that resonates farther than it could from any soapbox." (footnote omitted) Through the internet, speakers can bypass mainstream media to speak directly to "an audience larger and more diverse than any the Framers could have imagined." (footnote omitted) Moreover, speakers on internet chat rooms and blogs can speak directly to other people with similar interests. [...]

Internet speech is often anonymous. "Many participants in cyberspace discussions employ pseudonymous identities, and, even when a speaker chooses to reveal her real name, she may still be anonymous for all practical purposes." (footnote omitted) For better or worse, then, "the audience must evaluate [a] speaker's ideas based on her words alone." (footnote omitted) This unique feature of [the internet] promises to make public debate in cyberspace less hierarchical and discriminatory" than in the real world because it disguises status indicators such as race, class, and age. (footnote omitted) It is clear that speech over the internet is entitled to First Amendment protection. (footnote omitted).

This protection extends to anonymous internet speech. (footnote omitted) Anonymous internet speech in blogs or chat rooms in some instances can become the modern equivalent of political pamphleteering. As the United States Supreme Court recently noted, "anonymous pamphleteering is not a pernicious, fraudulent practice, but an honorable tradition of advocacy and dissent." (footnote omitted) The United States Supreme Court continued, "the right to remain anonymous may be abused when it shields fraudulent conduct. But political speech by its nature will sometimes have unpalatable consequences, and, in general, our society accords greater weight to the value of free speech than to the dangers of its misuse."

It also is clear that the First Amendment does not protect defamatory speech. [...] Certain classes of speech, including defamatory and libelous speech, are entitled to no Constitutional protection. [...] Accordingly, we must adopt a standard that appropriately balances one person's right to speak anonymously against another person's right to protect his reputation.

[...]

Under Delaware law, a public figure defamation plaintiff in a libel case must plead and ultimately prove that: 1) the defendant made a defamatory statement; 2) concerning the plaintiff; 3) the statement was published; and 4) a third party would understand the character of the communication as defamatory. (footnote omitted) In addition, the public figure defamation plaintiff must plead and prove that 5) the statement is false (footnote omitted) and 6) that the defendant made the statement with actual malice. (footnote omitted) Finally, "proof of damages proximately caused by a publication deemed libelous need not be shown in order for a defamed plaintiff to recover nominal or compensatory damages." (footnote omitted)

[...]

We agree that the context in which the statements were made is probative [...] Given the context, no reasonable person could have interpreted these statements as being anything other than opinion. The guidelines at the top of the blog specifically state that the forum is dedicated to *opinions* about issues in Smyrna. If more evidence of that were needed, another contribution to the blog responded to Doe's second posting as follows: "Proud Citizen, you asked for support, I don't think you are going to get it here. Just by reading both sides, your tone and choice of words is [that of] a type of person that couldn't convince me. You sound like the person with all the anger and hate…"

At least one reader of the blog quickly reached the conclusion that Doe's comments were no more than unfounded and unconvincing opinion. Given the context of the statement and the normally (and inherently) unreliable nature of assertions posted in chat rooms and on blogs, this is the only supportable conclusion. Read in the context of an internet blog, these statements did not imply any assertions of underlying objective facts. Accordingly, we hold that as a matter of law a reasonable person would not interpret Doe's statements as stating facts about Cahill. The statements are, therefore, incapable of a defamatory meaning. [...] Doe's statements simply are not sufficient to give rise to a *prima facie* case for defamation liability.[78]

FOOTNOTES

[78] We do not hold as a matter of law that statements made on a blog or in a chat room can never be defamatory. We hold only that in order to recover, a plaintiff having a defamation claim based on a statement made in an internet chat room or on a blog must prove that a statement is factually based and thus capable of a defamatory meaning. (citation omitted) ("[A] statement of opinion would be actionable if it implies the allegation of undisclosed defamatory facts as the basis for the opinion.")

The court did not dwell on the location of the allegedly defamatory statements but instead looked to see whether such statements fairly could be statements of opinion. It concluded that they were and so, dismissed the plaintiff's claim.

Public or Private Figures?

Standards for proving defamation will vary depending upon the plaintiff's status. A public figure has been brought to the public's attention, while a private figure generally does not merit such attention. Given the protection for freedom of speech in the First Amendment to the U.S. Constitution, public figures should then expect to be the target of more harmful statements. For a public figure to make a successful claim of defamation, the plaintiff will need to show that the defendant knew the statement was false and published it or acted with such recklessness as to its truth, a level of intent known as *actual malice* (see *New York Times v. Sullivan*, 376 U.S. 254 (1964)). Thus, for example, a magazine cartoon suggesting a well-known minister's first sexual encounter was with his mother would not be actionable, where the cartoonist used the word "parody" repeatedly, to serve as a border to the cartoon, clearly indicating that the statement was not true [see *Hustler Magazine, Inc. v. Falwell*, 485 U.S. 46 (1988)].

For a private figure, however, the plaintiff need only prove the falsity of the statement and that the defendant intended to print it, regardless of the motive.

Damages

A court will award damages according to the degree to which a plaintiff's reputation has been damaged due to the release of the defamatory statements.

Unlike libel, where the defamatory statement appears in writing, a statement made orally is ephemeral and would be limited as to the population that heard it. To garner damages for slander, a plaintiff has to show actual damages.

In showing actual damages in a slander claim, however, four exceptions exist in the common law and are classified in Table 7-1 as **slander** *per se.* All focus on a measure of impropriety, a value not held as dearly by contemporary society as in historical times.

Table 7-1 Slander *per se* Exceptions	
• Crime—implies the corruption of plaintiff's soul. • Loathsome disease—implies improper sexual relations.	• Chastity—also implies improper sexual relations. • Business or profession—implies improper activities in the course of operating a business.

Defenses

Truth as a Defense

The tort of defamation focuses on the impact that a statement has on a plaintiff's reputation. So the common law made truth to be an absolute defense, since the statement would give a full accounting of plaintiff's reputation.

Complications arise, however, when the defendant's statements are substantially true. If a reasonable person would decide that the statement, on the whole, was indeed defamatory, the truth will operate as a defense. For example, if the defendant calls the plaintiff "a no-good, lying cheat" and can provide evidence of the plaintiff's lying or cheating, the truth will be a valid defense, even if the defendant could not show that plaintiff was also "no good."

Paralegals should take care with the use of truth as a defense, taking note of what the legislature and the courts in their specific jurisdiction say about how much truth a statement must contain for use as a defense.

Privilege as a Defense

Because some statements can serve as the basis for heated debate about great public issues, a privilege exists that completely bars liability for statements made during such a debate. Given venues where such debate can arise, the privilege applies to members of Congress, legislators, and judges and attorneys in a courtroom, so long as the statements were made in Congress or in the courtroom only (see, for example, *The Restatement (Second) of Torts*, §590A Witnesses in Legislative Proceedings). The law of privilege as a defense is considered in greater detail in Chapter 11.

■ MISUSE OF LEGAL PROCEDURE

The intentional use of legal process or procedure to harm another forms a class of torts known as the misuse of legal procedure. That class includes three actions in tort:

- Malicious prosecution involves the use of the criminal process to harm another person;
- Wrongful civil proceedings provides a remedy for malicious civil claims; and
- Abuse of process involves the use of the civil process beyond its intended purpose.

All three actions share an interest in freedom being free from unjustifiable litigation.

Malicious Prosecution

Malicious prosecution involves charging a plaintiff with a crime where no valid basis exists to prosecute. To win, the plaintiff would need to prove, by a preponderance of the evidence, the following elements:

- malicious filing of a criminal charge against the plaintiff;
- done without a valid basis in law (no "probable cause" to arrest or to prosecute); and
- resulting in harm to the plaintiff (such as inconvenience)
- ending of the proceedings in favor of the plaintiff (i.e., charges dropped; plaintiff found "not guilty").

The Role of Law Enforcement Officials

This suit typically will involve direct action by a law enforcement officer. The following case demonstrates, however, that a defendant need not be part of the law-enforcement community to institute baseless criminal proceedings against a plaintiff. Anyone could ask for a prosecution for which no valid legal basis existed. This case involves the forcible eviction of a plaintiff because he did not look as though he should have been where he was (see Case in Point 7-12).

CASE IN POINT 7-12

Griswold v. Hollywood Turf Club

106 Cal. App. 2d 578 (1951)

Plaintiff was forcibly evicted from the race course of Hollywood Turf Club, arrested, charged with breach of the peace, tried and acquitted. He sued the turf club and certain others for malicious prosecution, false imprisonment, and assault and battery. [...] On a summer afternoon in 1947 he was admitted to the track as a paying customer. He entered the exclusive clubhouse premises with friends who, he testified, had bought a clubhouse ticket for him. He did his betting unmolested until shortly after the seventh race. He had not dressed up for the occasion; he had on the clothes of a workingman and his appearance excited the suspicion of a member of the track's Security Police [...]. This guard asked him to show a clubhouse ticket stub which he did not have. (These are usually thrown away by persons entering the clubhouse gate.) Plaintiff endeavored to persuade the guard that he had entered on a ticket, but did not succeed. The guard grabbed him and attempted to forcibly eject him from the clubhouse premises. They went through the gate and a scuffle occurred, either after plaintiff had reentered or was attempting to reenter the clubhouse premises. [...] Other guards came, held him, tripped him to the ground, tore his clothes, broke his glasses, handcuffed him and placed him under arrest. [...] He was taken to a police substation on the turf club premises, later to the Inglewood police station, released on bail, charged with breach of the peace, tried and acquitted.

The alleged offense for which plaintiff was placed under arrest consisted of fighting and offering to fight, and using bad language. The private officers involved testified that while plaintiff was being handcuffed he said: "You bastards are all alike," and used other expressions of a similar nature, which might be expected of an uninhibited and articulate citizen under the circumstances. As plaintiff was taken to the police substation, curious bystanders followed. Two strange women appeared in an outer room of the station, and other persons, including women, sensing excitement, were peeking through the station door to see and hear what went on. It was claimed that plaintiff, at the station, offered to whip any of the officers if the handcuffs were removed, and used language similar to that previously mentioned, which presumably shocked the sensibilities of the curious onlookers. [...]

Plaintiff sued the turf club, defendants Long, an Inglewood police officer, [and] Jones, a Hawthorne police officer (who was on vacation and working for the turf club) [...] One form of verdict furnished the jury was in favor of plaintiff on the malicious prosecution charge [...] Each of the forms contained the following: "(Draw a line through the name of any defendant not to be included in this verdict.)" [...] The verdict for malicious prosecution was against the turf club and Long for $ 1,995 damages [...] The court refused to accept the verdicts [...]

The court granted the motion of the turf club and Long for a new trial, specifying insufficiency of the evidence [...] Plaintiff appeals from the judgment, and from all orders made, whether appealable or nonappealable.

[...] A [...] sufficient reason is that the evidence would have justified a verdict for these defendants on the malicious prosecution count. [...]

The [...] order granting a new trial as to Hollywood Turf Club and Long is affirmed [...]

The court agreed with the trial court that insufficient evidence supported a claim for malicious prosecution as, nominally, it seems the plaintiff acted in a way to justify at least some of the charges he faced, regardless of his being acquitted on all of them.

Damages

The harm to a plaintiff can include loss of freedom, since the plaintiff may not have the option to be released before trial by posting bail. Also, a plaintiff may develop a reputation based on this prosecution, regardless of when the false charges are dropped.

A plaintiff can receive an award in damages by providing evidence of actual harm. That could include damage to reputation, loss of employment, and legal expenses.

Initiating Wrongful Civil Proceedings

The tort of **wrongful civil proceedings** mirrors the tort of malicious prosecution in all but one way. It involves the initiation of legal action, such as filing a civil suit or initiating a baseless appeal, which would not succeed because it lacked sufficient supporting evidence. To win, the plaintiff would need to prove, by a preponderance of the evidence, the following elements:

- filing a civil suit
- done without sufficient legal basis
- resulting in harm to the plaintiff (such as costs) and
- resolution of the civil suit in favor of the plaintiff

By initiating a baseless civil suit, the defendant usually seeks to coerce a plaintiff into a course of action. In criminal law, such an action would constitute extortion, a crime.

In the following case, an insurance company that provided a workers' compensation policy wanted to avoid paying the plaintiff. The plaintiff was an employee injured while working for the business that had purchased the workers' compensation insurance policy. While an agreement for payments had been reached, the insurance company, the business, and counsel for the business filed legal actions to delay payment of the benefit, effectively denying the coverage the employee was entitled to under the policy. Repeatedly, the state's highest court and other judicial personnel rejected the unnecessary litigation by the defendants that led to the delay of payment even though the defendants continued to undertake other legal actions to prevent payment to the plaintiff (see Case in Point 7-13).

CASE IN POINT 7-13

McGee v. Feege, Hayes & Feege, P.C.
517 Pa. 247 (1987)

The principal issues raised in this appeal are: (1) whether a seizure or deprivation of property is an essential element of the tort of abuse of process, and (2) if a seizure or deprivation of property is necessary, are the facts in this case sufficient to establish such a seizure or deprivation of the property of the appellant, Mary Jane McGee.

The genesis of this action was the protracted and bitterly fought workmen's compensation case appellant, Mary Jane McGee, successfully prosecuted against her employer L.F. Grammes & Sons, Inc. On August 28, 1968 the appellant sustained a work related injury to her right thumb while she was working as a welder in the employ of L.F. Grammes & Sons, Inc. Shortly after she suffered the injury, appellant and her employer entered into an agreement for compensation at the rate of $60.00 per week. The compensation agreed to was payable for an indefinite period commencing September 4, 1968.

In July of 1970, appellant's employer filed a petition for termination of the Compensation Agreement on the grounds that appellant had recovered and was able to return to work as of November 26, 1968. We [...] held that based upon the record, the employer had failed to satisfy its burden of proof in that the evidence did not show either that appellant's disability had ceased or that her continued disability was the result of an independent action. (citation omitted) We reversed the order of the Commonwealth Court that affirmed the order of suspension and remanded the case to the Board. Upon remand, the Board, on July 13, 1978, set aside the suspension order of the referee and ordered that compensation be re-instated at the rate of $85.51 a week. [...].

Despite the finality of the Board's order for payment of compensation at $85.51 a week, the appellant's employer [...] participated in the initiation and pursuit of a series of frivolous and meritless legal maneuvers designed to delay and frustrate payment to the appellant. Those maneuvers included, inter alia, filing of the following: a Petition for Rehearing; a Petition to Amend Termination Petition; an Amended Petition for Review; Petitions for Stay; Petitions for Supersedeas; Petitions to Open and Strike Judgment; a Motion for a Hearing (footnote omitted), and an Answer and New Matter in response to appellant's Petition to Enforce Judgment.

On March 23, 1979, after considering the appellant's petition to enforce judgment and the answer and new matter filed thereto, this Court entered an order as follows:

We now grant the petition to enforce judgment and direct that the July 13, 1978 Order of the Workman's Compensation Board be complied with forthwith. All other proceedings conflicting with this order are hereby dismissed.

In spite of this Court's Order of March 23, 1979 as quoted above, the employer continued to resist payment of the compensation due appellant. The employer [...] filed in this Court an Application for Reargument and a Motion for a Stay of Proceedings. In addition, Motions to Reconsider the Dismissal of the Petitions to Open and/or Strike Judgment were filed [...] On April 20, 1979 we entered a Per Curiam Order denying the Application for Reargument and Motion for a Stay.

Nonetheless, the employer [...] persisted in refusing payment to appellant and filed yet another petition in this Court. This time it was a Petition for Clarification of our Order of April 20, 1979. In the meantime, appeal proceedings from the denial of one of the various motions, that had been brought to the Commonwealth Court by the appellees, were still pending. In May of 1979, the Commonwealth Court issued a briefing schedule, set an argument date and indicated that the parties were expected to comply notwithstanding the previous recent orders of this Court. The appellant responded by filing in this Court a petition for a Writ of Prohibition and an Application for a Stay.

Both the appellees' petition for Clarification and the appellant's Petition for a Writ of Prohibition came before us for disposition. In a Per Curiam Order of July 6, 1979, the appellant's Petition for Prohibition was granted and appellee's Petition for Clarification was denied.[5]

On October 18, 1979, the appellant commenced an action [...] against the appellees alleging abuse of process. Basically, in her complaint, the appellant charges that the appellees conspired and agreed to pursue a series of successive dilatory legal maneuvers for the sole purpose of avoiding payment to her as ordered by the Board and mandated by this Court. Appellant alleges that all of the legal proceedings initiated and maintained by the employer after March 23, 1978 were commenced pursuant to the alleged conspiracy to deny payment to the appellant. [...] The trial court refused appellant's motion and granted appellees' motion, entering summary judgment in favor of the appellees.

When the legal process is perverted and directed toward a victim for a purpose other than that for which the process was designed, a cause of action for abuse of process exists [...] We will not countenance the use of the legal process as a tactical weapon to coerce a desired result that is not the legitimate object of the process [...]

The Order of the Superior Court is reversed and this case is remanded to the Court of Common Pleas [...] for proceedings consistent with this opinion (footnote omitted).

FOOTNOTES

[5] In disposing of these petitions we said:

On March 23, 1978, this Court filed an opinion in which we reversed a Commonwealth Court order affirming the Workmen's Compensation Board's (Board) decision which would have sustained a referee's suspension of a compensation agreement between McGee and her employer, L.F. Grammes & Sons, Inc. (Grammes). (citation omitted). Grammes had initially petitioned on July 1, 1970 to terminate the agreement alleging that the disability had ended on November 26, 1968. We held that the record did not support an order terminating the agreement and remanded the cause to the Board to reinstate the agreement and to compute the payment and interest due McGee for the period during the litigation when no compensation was being paid. Pursuant to our mandate, the Board entered an order on July 13, 1978 vacating the prior suspension order and directed that compensation be continued pursuant to the compensation agreement.

While this should have terminated the matter, Grammes, and now the intervening insurer, have deliberately protracted this litigation in an attempt to avoid payment to McGee in accordance with our mandate. [n1] The dilatory tactic that has been employed in this lawsuit to avoid a legitimate obligation has already forced this Court to issue a supplemental order on March 23, 1979 directing that the Board's July 13, 1978 order "be complied with forthwith", and "[a]ll other proceedings conflicting with this order are herewith dismissed." Therefter (sic), Grammes filed an Application for Re-Argument and Motion for Stay which was denied by this Court on April 20, 1979. In view of the three definitive expressions of the position of this Court, a Petition for Clarification at this time is impertinent and frivolous and is dismissed out of hand. [n2]

[n1] This record presents a despicable example of a blatant misuse of the legal process to avoid payment of a legal obligation. On July 12, 1978, Grammes requested the Board for a re-hearing, alleging inter alia that "in view of the fact that the Referee, the Board and the Commonwealth Court and one of the Justices of the Supreme Court held that the Defendant had met its burden of proving it was entitled to a termination" the Board had the right to relitigate an issue *finally decided* by this Court. When the Board properly rejected the request as being "tantamount to a negation of the most recent holding of the Supreme Court", Grammes compounded the situation by appealing this frivolous claim to the Commonwealth Court. Concurrently, Grammes filed a new petition for termination with a Referee again alleging that the disability terminated as of November 26, 1968.

[n2] The question raised in the petition for clarification relates to the appropriate weekly rate at which McGee was entitled to compensation. The July 13, 1978 order set the weekly rate at $85.51 although the original compensation agreement had established the rate at $ 60.00 per week. We note that neither Grammes or the intervening insurer has appealed from the Board's July 13, 1978 order [...] The first complaint relating to the weekly rate of compensation as established by the order of July 13, 1978 was raised in a Petition for Rehearing which was filed with the Board on October 26, 1978 long after the thirty day period for appeal of the July 13, 1978 order had expired. Thus any objection to the weekly compensation order as established by the July 13, order was waived. We also note that the question as to the rate of weekly compensation set forth in the July 13, 1978 order was not raised in the answer to the Petition to Enforce Judgment entered on the July 13, 1978 order but was first set forth in the Application for Re-Argument after our grant of the Petition to Enforce Judgment.

The court found that the protracted litigation regarding the plaintiff's worker's compensation claim amounted to a flagrant abuse of process.

Anti-SLAPP Suits

Some jurisdictions have found it necessary to go beyond this tort by enacting legislation that prohibits the filing of a suit with the goal of limiting public participation. Strategic Litigation Against Public Participation (SLAPP) often involves a powerful party's filing a law suit to intimidate people from engaging in some kind of public discourse. Statutes designed to prevent efforts to stifle public debate were enacted as *anti-SLAPP laws*.

For example, if a business wanted to operate a waste-to-energy power facility and saw that local opposition had formed to challenge the operation of the business, the business might sue the leaders of the local opposition for defamation. The defamation suit will prove groundless, but meanwhile, the leaders of local opposition would still need to prepare a defense against such a claim. An anti-SLAPP law establishes that there is no merit to the claim of defamation, then requires the plaintiff-business to pay the defendants' legal costs and, perhaps, even damages.

In the following case, a citizen wrote letters for publication about a politician's actions in a public works project in a local newspaper, only to learn that the politician had filed suit in defamation. The citizen, believing that the defamation suit was baseless, used the anti-SLAPP law (see Case in Point 7-14).

CASE IN POINT 7-14

Alves v. Hometown Newspapers, Inc.
857 A.2d 743 (R.I. 2004)

Are litigants in Rhode Island SLAPP-happy? This is the second case in as many months that calls upon us to determine whether summary judgment was granted properly in favor of the defendants when the defendants asserted an affirmative defense under General Laws 1956, chapter 33 of title 9, the Limits on Strategic Litigation Against Public Participation Act (the anti-SLAPP statute). The plaintiff, Stephen Alves (Alves or plaintiff), appeals from a Superior Court grant of summary judgment in favor of the defendant, Alan G. Palazzo (Palazzo or defendant), on his anti-SLAPP defense, including an award of attorneys' fees and costs.

This case came before the Supreme Court for oral argument pursuant to an order directing the parties to show cause why the issues raised in this appeal should not summarily be decided. [...] [W]e are of the opinion that cause has not been shown, and we summarily affirm the judgment entered in the Superior Court.

Facts and Procedural History

The facts are largely undisputed. At the time this action was filed, Alves represented the 19th Senatorial District in the Rhode Island General Assembly, and he also served on the Town of West Warwick's school building committee (building committee). Palazzo is a resident of West Warwick. The complaint in this case arose out of remarks made at public meetings and a series of letters to the editor published by Hometown Newspapers, Inc., d/b/a The Kent County Daily Times (Daily Times), and penned by [...] Alan G. Palazzo [...] (footnote omitted) concerning the West Warwick Town Council's (town council) and School Committee's (school committee) handling of a proposed school building project (the project). [...]

Alves filed a nine-count complaint, five counts of which were directed at acts that defendant conducted. Count 1 alleged that Palazzo libeled plaintiff in a "Letter to the Editor" of the Daily Times on October 1, 2001. Count 3 alleged that Palazzo again libeled plaintiff in a "Letter to the Editor" of the Daily Times on October 9, 2001. Count 5 alleged that Palazzo slandered plaintiff at a school committee meeting on September 26, 2001. Count 6 alleged that Palazzo maliciously placed plaintiff in a false light before the public by preparing the letter of October 1, 2001. Count 8 repeated a false-light allegation for the letter of October 9, 2001. [...]

Palazzo filed a motion to dismiss the complaint [...] and seeking an order for costs and attorneys' fees [...]. [...] Palazzo argued that plaintiff's complaint constituted a "SLAPP suit," seeking to punish Palazzo for writing letters to the editor discussing public matters and criticizing plaintiff. Palazzo maintained that his letters merely were commentary "that is typical of opinions regarding public events that aired in any public forum such as a town council meeting or a newspaper." [...]

Alves argued that Palazzo [...was] adequately apprised of the charges [...] Alves further asserted that Palazzo's activities were not protected under the anti-SLAPP statute because it was not enacted "to cloak false accusations of criminal activity in legislatively-created immunity." [...] Palazzo's letters were a self-styled "series of informational updates relative to our Town Council and SBC's ['school building committee] handling of the 'Natick' School project."(footnote omitted) Palazzo's letter of October 1, 2001, was a strongly worded warning to West Warwick taxpayers to look disfavorably on the potential increased cost of the project from $ 10.5 million to $ 12 million. Palazzo printed questions he put to the town council and excerpted some of the answers. The questions covered topics such as the council's plans in case developing the site went over budget and whether the taxpayers would be responsible for additional money if the project site had to be moved. In the letter, Palazzo also questioned the wisdom of spending $ 1.5 million for a school site. In the context of urging the taxpayers to become concerned about this issue, he wrote, "it is your hard earned tax dollars that are being spent in this manner. Yes, we need a new school but perhaps you might ask Mr. Rousselle, Sen. Alves, Ms. DiMasi et al., why the fiasco?" With respect to this letter, plaintiff based his amended complaint on the following statements:

"I've also heard from a member of the Council that Sen. Alves seems to be exerting a lot of pressure to keep this project moving along.

"* * *

"I challenge anyone involved with this project today, especially Mr. Rousselle, Sen. Alves and Ms. DiMasi to deny the facts as I have presented them."

Palazzo's letter of October 9, 2001, to the editor continued to criticize the cost of the project. He took issue with a proposed new site for the school and questioned whether the town "really looked into the site from a Geo-technical perspective." Palazzo alleged that the town was paying $425,000 more for a construction manager than was originally noted at a school committee meeting in November 2000. He also said that additional costs would be associated with using Eric Ahlborg as the construction manager on the project. He further noted that the council president, Mr. Rouselle, was the guest of honor at a recent fundraiser that Alves hosted. With respect to the letter of October 9, 2001, (footnote omitted) plaintiff based his amended complaint on the following statements:

"At several SBC and Town Council Meetings, I've noticed what I'd call a 'close' relationship between Sen. Alves and Mr. Eric Ahlborg. If you have attended some of these same meetings, you may have also taken note of this. Has anyone on our Council also taken note and asked some hard questions? Given the progress of this project to date and the possible additional costs to the taxpayers, isn't it prudent to at least ask?

"Think about it—could it be possible that the taxpayers of this town are being used to bankroll and advance the personal and financial agendas of a 'chosen few'?

"I challenge anyone involved with this project to date, especially Mr. Rouselle, Sen. Alves and Ms. DiMasi, to deny the facts as I have presented them."

In both his original and amended complaints, Alves alleged that Palazzo slandered him on or about September 26, 2001, "while speaking at the Town of West Warwick School Building Committee Meeting." Alves did not specify the particular slanderous statements in either complaint, but instead incorporated the newspaper statements included in the previous counts by reference. In response, Palazzo denied that he spoke at the meeting on September 26, 2001, and submitted minutes from that meeting to support that. Alves did not directly hear Palazzo say anything defamatory at that meeting, but submitted an affidavit from DiMasi. She averred that after the committee meeting, she heard Palazzo say that Alves had "rigged" the bids on the project. However, Palazzo attested that DiMasi could not have heard him say anything after the meeting because he left the meeting just when it ended because of family obligations.

[...] [T]he hearing justice filed a decision granting Palazzo's motion [...] She ruled in her decision that the anti-SLAPP statute barred plaintiff's claims [...] she wrote, "With respect to A. Palazzo's letters to the editor of the Daily Times, it is clear that the activity was of a type envisioned by the Legislature in enacting [***] § 9-33-1 et seq." She observed that it was Alves's burden to prove that both of Palazzo's letters were objectively and subjectively baseless. In applying the anti-SLAPP statute, she found as follows:

"Although Plaintiff bases his action on a few statements lifted from the letters, the Court must consider the publications in their entirety to determine whether they rise to the level of sham. In his letters, A. Palazzo addressed a matter that was under review and consideration by a local governmental body. The statements addressed an issue of public concern in his community. He sent the letters to the editor of a local newspaper. A. Palazzo expressed concern over the potential increased cost of the Natick school project. His statements concerning Plaintiff related to his position as a School Building Committee member and his alleged role with respect to the project."

The motion justice reasoned that because Palazzo's statements related to an issue of public concern and were not objectively baseless, they were entitled to conditional immunity under the statute.

The motion justice also awarded Palazzo costs and reasonable attorneys' fees and ordered counsel to file affidavits specifying the costs and legal fees that they incurred by working on Palazzo's case. [...]

Discussion

On appeal, Alves asserts that the hearing justice erred in finding that Palazzo's letters of October 1, 2001, and October 9, 2001, were protected by the anti-SLAPP statute. Specifically, Alves asserts that the two letters, when read together, constitute defamation because Palazzo "did not outline any factual basis for his conclusions that Alves either bankrolled and advanced the personal and financial agendas of a chosen few or had a close relationship with the project manager." [...]

[...]

The Anti-SLAPP Defense

The anti-SLAPP statute was enacted to prevent vexatious lawsuits against citizens who exercise their First Amendment rights of free speech and legitimate petitioning by granting those activities conditional immunity from punitive civil claims. (citation omitted) The anti-SLAPP statute (citation omitted) contains an explicit findings section that elucidates this purpose:

Findings.

The legislature finds and declares that full participation by persons and organizations and robust discussion of issues of public concern before the legislative, judicial, and administrative bodies and in other public fora are essential to the democratic process, that there has been a disturbing increase in lawsuits brought primarily to chill the valid exercise of the constitutional rights of freedom of speech and petition for the redress of grievances; that such litigation is disfavored and should be resolved quickly with minimum cost to citizens who have participated in matters of public concern."

The next section of the statute, (citation omitted), explains that the grant of conditional immunity will bar any civil claim, counterclaim, or cross-claim directed at the protected activities unless the petition or speech constitutes a sham:

Conditional Immunity.

(a) A party's exercise of his or her right of petition or of free speech under the United States or Rhode Island constitutions in connection with a matter of public concern shall be conditionally immune from civil claims, counterclaims, or cross-claims. Such immunity will apply as a bar to any civil claim, counterclaim, or cross-claim directed at petition or free speech as defined in subsection (e) of this section, except if the petition or free speech constitutes a sham. The petition or free speech constitutes a sham only if it is not genuinely aimed at procuring favorable government action, result, or outcome, regardless of ultimate motive or purpose."

When an exercise of free speech or right of petition in connection with a matter of public concern is implicated, a plaintiff must prove that such conduct is a sham to defeat an anti-SLAPP defense. [...]

"The petition or free speech will be deemed to constitute a sham * * * only if it is both:

1. Objectively baseless in the sense that no reasonable person exercising the right of speech or petition could realistically expect success in procuring the government action, result, or outcome, and
2. Subjectively baseless in the sense that it is actually an attempt to use the governmental process itself for its own direct effects. Use of outcome or result of the governmental process shall not constitute use of the governmental process itself for its own direct effects."

[...]

"As used in this section, 'a party's exercise of its right of petition or of free speech' shall mean any written or oral statement made before or submitted to a legislative, executive, or judicial body, or any other governmental proceeding; any written or oral statement made in connection with an issue under consideration or review by a legislative, executive, or judicial body, or any other governmental proceeding; or any written or oral statement made in connection with an issue of public concern." (citation omitted)

The motion justice produced an extensive written analysis of Alves's complaint for libel [...] as [they] pertained to Palazzo's affirmative defense under the anti-SLAPP statute. She found that "with respect to A. Palazzo's letters to the editor of the Daily Times, it is clear that the activity was of a type envisioned by the Legislature in enacting [the anti-SLAPP statute]." [...] S[he noted that "speaking to a newspaper reporter is a frequently used method for members of the general public to communicate concerns to governmental authorities who are considering or reviewing a matter of public concern." [...]

We previously have upheld the constitutionality of the anti-SLAPP statute. (citation omitted) Moreover, we have held that making public complaints to newspapers on matters of public concern is protected activity within the meaning of the anti-SLAPP statute. (citation omitted)

[...]

The motion justice based her ruling on plaintiff's failure to satisfy the first part of the test to prove that Palazzo had engaged in sham petitioning. She explained her decision as follows:

"In his letters, A. Palazzo addressed a matter that was under review and consideration by a local governmental body. The statements addressed an issue of public concern in his community. He sent letters to the editor of a local newspaper. A. Palazzo expressed concern over the potential increased cost of the Natick school project. His statements concerning Plaintiff related to his position as a School Building Committee member and his alleged role with respect to the project. The Plaintiff has failed to demonstrate that the letters were objectively baseless in the sense that no reasonable person making those statements could have realistically expected success in procuring the government action, result or outcome."

Having found that Palazzo's statements in the letters to the editor were not objectively baseless, the motion justice did not address the subjective part of the test, and granted summary judgment [...] [for] libel [...].

{...}[W]e conclude that the hearing justice did not err and that summary judgment in favor of Palazzo was appropriate.

Alves contends that Palazzo's two letters, when read together, constitute actionable defamation. Specifically, he contends that Palazzo's statement, "I've noticed what I'd call a 'close' relationship between Sen. Alves and Mr. Eric Ahlborg," insinuates that the close relationship is the reason why Ahlborg's company was awarded the contract to build the Natick School. There is no doubt that one may infer an allegation of *quid pro quo* between Alves and Ahlborg based on that comment. However, considering this comment in the larger context of the letter, it is clear that Palazzo made it for the larger purpose of calling the taxpayers' attention to the costs of the building project. Other inflammatory comments in the letter reveal this overall purpose. For instance, further in that same letter, Palazzo says "Mr. Rousselle and Sen. Alves believe that you really don't care how your money is spent." These comments clearly constitute a general, albeit hyperbolic, appeal to the affected taxpayers to examine the expense of the project.

Furthermore, the statement serves as a challenge to the members of the school committee to examine and justify the expenditures the project entailed, especially with regard to potentially changing sites for the school. In the same letter, Palazzo issued the following challenge:

"I challenge anyone involved with this project to date, especially Mr. Rousselle, Sen. Alves and Ms. DiMasi, to deny the facts as I have presented them. Hopefully, you have noticed that they have not responded to the specific issues I have raised.

"Why not? Because all the information relative to this Council, the SBC and the warnings about the school site, are a matter of public record."

All of the characterizations that Palazzo drew in the letter of October 9, 2001, were based on known or disclosed facts, and are clearly his interpretation of such facts. Saying that two people involved in a public project appear to have a "close" relationship only hints that there is an improper relationship; it does not elucidate the nature of the relationship.

Palazzo invited everyone who was present at the school committee meetings to observe what he had observed and inquire whether there was something improper going on between Alves and Mr. Ahlborg. Palazzo drew his opinion from their appearances at public meetings. Anyone present at those meetings could have drawn the same or a different conclusion about their relationship. Furthermore, Palazzo enclosed his description of what he called a "close" relationship between

Alves and Ahlborg in quotes, signaling that he was merely characterizing their relationship and not stating it as fact. Palazzo's opinion was just that—an opinion, and it does not rise to the level necessary to constitute actionable defamation. (citation omitted)

[...]

Alves also alleges that Palazzo's suggestion that "the taxpayers of this town are being used to bankroll and advance the personal and financial agendas of a 'chosen few'" supports his libel claim because it suggests that Alves rigged the bidding for the school project. The allegation falls apart when the above quote is read in context. The offending remark was introduced by the following opinion:

"What I cannot support nor condone is what appears to be the Council's intention to go ahead with the current plan based upon phone calls and pressure exerted by political allies to the detriment of all other West Warwick taxpayers. Think about it—could it be possible that the taxpayers of this town are being used to bankroll * * *."

Examining the greater context of Palazzo's statement reveals that his *suggestion* that the taxpayers are being used to bankroll personal and financial agendas was leveled at the town council, and not at Alves. By implication, Alves may be a beneficiary of this cabal, one of the "chosen few," but the charge is clearly leveled against the town council. Moreover, all of Palazzo's cautionary language of "what appears to be the Council's intention * * *" and "could it be possible that the taxpayers * * *" makes clear that these are impressions of events concerning the funding of the project, as *he* saw them. They are his mere opinions, and not the stuff of which defamation and false light are made.

We also conclude that plaintiff's allegations based on Palazzo's statement that Alves was "exerting a lot of pressure to keep this project moving along * * *," must fail because the statement was mere hyperbole. Public officials are accused of and, often, do exert pressure to keep projects that they support "moving along." Such action would be commendable if the project is in the public interest. With respect to this particular project, Palazzo obviously believed it to be contrary to the public interest. The statement, however, is hardly defamatory.

[...]

Once the motion justice determined that the statements were protected, Alves's defamation claim could not proceed.

[...]

We do not intend any of the foregoing analysis to dismiss defamation and false-light claims out of hand when a defendant claims conditional immunity under the anti-SLAPP statute. We merely wish to highlight the deliberately high hurdle that a public official must clear to proceed under these common-law claims when citizens criticize public officials on issues of public concern.

[...]

For the foregoing reasons, we affirm the Superior Court judgment and remand the record in this case thereto.

The appeals court found that all of the plaintiff's statements were made as part of a larger public discourse and enjoyed conditional immunity from liability. Therefore, any claim for defamation could not possibly result in verdict for the plaintiff, so the defendant properly used the Anti-SLAPP statute to defeat the defamation claim. Further, the defendant was entitled to recover the legal costs incurred to rebut the meritless defamation claim.

Engaging in Abuse of Process

The tort of **abuse of process** is the use of any facet of the litigation process for an improper end, something beyond the stated goal. The civil proceedings will be properly filed, but the defendant's motives for filing suit do not focus primarily on seeking relief for a wrong.

To win, a plaintiff would need to prove the following elements by a preponderance of the evidence:

- filing of a civil suit
- goal other than to gain recovery of damages at law
- harm to plaintiff

In Case in Point 7-15, the court recognized that abuse of process has occurred and notes how it differs from malicious prosecution.

CASE IN POINT 7-15

T.B. Proprietary Corp. v. Sposato Builders, Inc.
1996 U.S. Dist. 17335 (E.D. Pa. 1996)

In 1994, a developer of expensive houses contended another developer's less expensive houses were too much like its own. A bench trial [...] ended in favor of the defendants, Sposato Builders and Heyser Estates ("Sposato"). A year later, a jury decided in favor of Sposato on its counterclaim against T.B. Proprietary ("TB") and third-party claim against its corporate parent, Toll Brothers ("Toll"), for abuse of process [...]

[...]

In 1994, Toll transferred its copyrights in the architectural plans and brochures for two houses, the "Philmont" and the "Cornell," to its wholly-owned subsidiary, TB. TB filed suit against Sposato for violations of the Copyright Act and the Lanham Act. It alleged the "Drexel," built by Sposato, was substantially the same as the Cornell and its construction proved copyright infringement, either by copying the Cornell architectural plans or the brochure. TB also claimed that the Brunos, a couple who had previously contracted with Toll to build a Philmont house but were excused from compliance, used the Philmont brochure and other materials to have the Sposatos build them a similar but less expensive house. (footnote omitted)

[...]

The counterclaim against TB and third-party claim against Toll for common law abuse of process were severed from plaintiff's intellectual property claims. (footnote omitted)

[...]

At the abuse of process trial, there was evidence that TB and Toll sought more than protection of their copyrights in the underlying litigation. In-house counsel for TB and Toll admitted that having Sposato "agree to stop making the Drexel house" was a purpose of the litigation. (citation omitted) However, in July, 1994, four months before the complaint was filed, TB's law firm, Panitch, Schwarze, Jacobs and Nadel (hereafter "Panitch"), informed TB in writing the architectural plans for the Philmont and Cornell were copyrighted, but the houses constructed from those plans were not, so that building the Drexel might not be illegal. (citation omitted) Panitch attorney James Meyer testified, "We started out with a rather modest objective of trying to protect the copyright...in the architectural plans and brochures and it turned out that this case had gotten completely out of hand and I frankly didn't know why." (citation omitted)

Vincent Sposato (footnote omitted) testified that Meyer told him at his deposition, "Toll Brothers, how big they were and…that it would be possible that we could put ourselves out of business by spending the money to litigate this…case." (citation omitted) After the deposition, the Sposato attorney received a letter from Panitch stating the case could be settled if Sposato paid a license fee of $ 90,000 and redesigned the facades of the Drexel and the Bruno house. (citation omitted) Vincent Sposato testified that such measures would put Sposato out of business. The Panitch letter also listed damages TB would seek at trial, if Sposato did not agree to settle. Included in that list were lost profits and reconstruction of existing Sposato houses. The letter also suggested that current owners of Sposato houses might be added as defendants in the copyright infringement action. Vincent Sposato testified that such action would "basically give us a bad name in the business" and "wouldn't really allow us to…build homes anymore." (citation omitted)

A jury found TB and Toll liable for abuse of process and awarded Sposato $148,003.34 in compensatory damages […]

B. Abuse of Process

Sposato's abuse of process claim is that TB and Toll used the Copyright and Lanham Act litigation to force Sposato to stop building similar, less expensive, houses in a development geographically close to one of Toll's developments. […] [A]buse of process is "the improper use of process after it has been issued, that is, a perversion of [the process]…where the party employs it for some unlawful object, not the purpose for which it is intended by the law to effect…" (citation omitted)

In the original 1838 English abuse of process case […] the defendants used a debt to force plaintiff to surrender his ship so that he could not sail and make enough money to repay the debt. Forcing plaintiff to surrender the ship was "effecting an object not within the scope of the process…" (citation omitted) […]

The elements of abuse of process are "(1) an 'abuse' or 'perversion' of process already initiated (2) with some unlawful or ulterior purpose, and (3) harm to the plaintiff as a result." (citation omitted) Sposato presented sufficient evidence of each element to support the verdict.

There was evidence of abuse of the underlying lawsuit. Vincent Sposato and Richard Sposato, Jr. testified that they were told at their depositions they risked losing their business if they didn't agree to TB's terms. The threats at the depositions were followed by a letter regarding the terms of settlement: pay a $ 90,000 license fee and redesign the Drexel and Bruno house. The Sposato brothers testified they would go out of business if they settled on those terms; TB claimed it would ask the court to order Sposato to reconstruct already-built houses and pay lost profits if they refused those settlement terms. The settlement letter could be construed as a threat. TB and Toll claimed at trial they were only protecting their copyrights in the plans and brochures, but their failure to submit certified copies of the copyright registration during a week-long bench trial suggested they had always intended to withdraw at the last minute their unjustified claim that Sposato had infringed the plans. The jury was entitled to find TB and Toll's threats and litigious behavior proof of "abuse" or "perversion" of civil litigation.

There was evidence TB and Toll had an unlawful or ulterior goal not only in initiating but pursuing the litigation. Toll's in-house counsel admitted that a purpose of the litigation was to stop Sposato from building the Drexel; the Sposato development was geographically close to a Toll development, although it was not as expensive or attractive. Former Toll customers, Mr. and Mrs. Bruno, had decided to have a house similar to the Philmont built for less money. The Bruno house built by Sposato was not of the same quality as the Philmont they originally contracted for Toll to build.

It was reasonable for the jury to have concluded that TB and Toll, by making threats and forcing Sposato to incur sizeable legal defense fees, was trying to eliminate or hamper a competitor undercutting them in price.

TB and Toll argue that TB was only protecting its monopoly in the underlying copyrights, a legitimate goal of the litigation (citation omitted), but TB and Toll's conduct did not reflect the low probability of success. The Drexel was far from identical to the Cornell. [...]

Even if Richard Sposato, Sr., had copied the floor plans of the Cornell in building the Drexel, TB and Toll would not have accomplished the results they threatened to achieve at trial. Reconstruction of existing structures has not been a remedy in copyright infringement cases involving house plans. Even where the architectural plans were copied and used to build an infringing house, injunctive relief has been limited to impounding the infringing plans, preventing construction of new houses, and awarding lost profits, not reconstruction of the existing house. (citation omitted). In its settlement letter to Sposato, TB sought both a license fee and redesign of the Drexel and Bruno house, but the substantial amount of the license fee ($ 90,000) would ordinarily suggest the licensee would get the right to use the design in the future, instead of having to redesign.

[...]

Sposato presented sufficient evidence that TB and Toll abused or perverted the underlying litigation to obtain a result not countenanced under copyright law. There was sufficient evidence for a jury reasonably to find liability for abuse of civil process.

C. Malicious Use of Process

TB and Toll argue that Sposato confused the tort of abuse of process with that of malicious use of civil process, which "has to do with the wrongful initiation of such process, while abuse of civil process is concerned with a perversion of a process after it is issued." (citation omitted). TB and Toll claim that Sposato's confusion prejudiced the jury.

The torts are not mutually exclusive. (citation omitted) Sposato met its burden of proving the elements of an abuse of process claim. The court was not confused about the distinction between abuse of process and malicious use of process and confined the evidence to that relevant to the former. The court instructed the jury specifically not to regard the defendants' motive in initiating the copyright infringement action except as it related to the purpose for which the action was continued. Sposato might have believed that TB and Toll had an improper reason for bringing the underlying lawsuit, and may have also elicited evidence supporting that belief, but the evidence was presented as it related to the improper conduct of the litigation. The court is not persuaded the jury was confused.

[...]

TB and Toll argue that any abuse of process was the result of unauthorized actions of the Panitch attorneys. There was substantial evidence TB and Toll authorized those actions, and no evidence of repudiation; to the contrary, in-house counsel was present to observe the offensive conduct at the Sposato depositions, voiced no objection, and made no effort to stop it. Without repudiation, TB and Toll ratified the actions of the Panitch lawyers. (citation omitted)

TB and Toll can hardly characterize themselves as unsophisticated clients blindly following counsel's advice. Robert Toll, Toll's chief executive officer, is a lawyer, and two lawyers of Toll's in-house legal department admitted their involvement in the litigation. The jury reasonably concluded that the strategy and tactics employed in the copyright infringement litigation were TB and Toll's responsibility.

> [...]
>   The evidence of TB and Toll's abusive conduct during the copyright litigation was sufficient for the jury to find them liable and to award punitive damages. The verdict was not against the weight of the evidence. The law governing the common law abuse of process was presented to the jury correctly. [...] TB and Toll have failed to show any reason why the jury's verdict on liability or award of punitive damages should be set aside. Accordingly, TB and Toll's motion for judgment as a matter of law or, in the alternative, for a new trial is denied.

While some courts use the *terms abuse of process* and *malicious prosecution* interchangeably, the court took pains to distinguish them here. Paralegals should review the usage in their jurisdiction.

■ DAMAGES FOR, HARM TO PROPERTY

For centuries, the law has granted owners of real property (land) and personal property (everything else) exclusive use and possession of their property. Not only does the law protect the owner's right to own, but also to control the property as he or she sees fit. Torts that interfere with the control of property include trespass to land (real estate) and trespass to chattels (interference with the control of personal property).

Trespass to Land

A defendant's intentional entry onto another's real property without consent could result in a suit for the tort of **trespass to land.** The violation focuses on an interference with the owner's right to control the property, so the owner does not have to show actual damages to support a valid claim. For example, a trespass could include crossing the plaintiff's land as a short-cut.

To win a claim for civil trespass in most jurisdictions, a plaintiff would need to prove, by a preponderance of the evidence, the following elements:

- intent to enter onto real property of another
- entry onto real property of another
- interference with the exclusive control of that land
- without the consent of the party who has the interest in the land

Entry

Going across a plaintiff's land, without consent, interferes with the plaintiff's exclusive right of control of the property. Examples of entry include the defendant entering the property, causing a third party to enter it, or entering it through some tangible thing, such as throwing a baseball onto the plaintiff's property.

Since the entry must involve some tangible contact, having noise or light enter the plaintiff's property will not support a cause of action in trespass to land. It may well turn out, however, that the plaintiff has a cause of action in private nuisance for the invasion of the music and the light. For a discussion of nuisance, see Chapter 9.

Intent

Liability exists upon proof that the defendant intended to invade the plaintiff's property. If the trespass occurs by accident, the plaintiff may have instead a cause of action in nuisance.

Some jurisdictions might accept the notion of negligent trespass, but that may mean only that the conduct is characterized as negligent; the tort will still focus on the interference of the use of the land, which is an action in trespass. The court makes this point in Case in Point 7-16, when the plaintiff sought recovery for a fire that spread onto the plaintiff's property.

CASE IN POINT 7-16

Martin v. Union Pacific Railroad Company
256 Ore. 563 (1970)

This is an action to recover damages for property damage caused by a fire which originated on or near a railroad right of way and spread onto plaintiffs' land. [...]

Plaintiffs' complaint alleges that the defendants negligently caused the fire to occur and negligently permitted it to escape and spread onto plaintiffs' range land. [...]

A trespass arises when there is an intrusion upon the land of another which invades the possessor's interest in the exclusive possession of his land. The intrusion may be caused by either intentional, negligent, reckless or ultrahazardous conduct.[3] Whether the invasion of the plaintiff's interest is direct or indirect is immaterial in determining whether the invasion is trespassory. (footnote omitted.)

The spread of the fire from defendants' land onto plaintiffs' land was an intrusion of a character sufficient to constitute a trespass. [...] A fire, although once regarded as a "tenuous material substance, and anciently classified with air, earth and water as one of the four elements" (Webster's Dictionary) is now deemed only a process—the process of combustion capable of operating to cause harm to a person's interest in the exclusive possession of land [...].

We hold that the invasion in the present case resulting from defendants' negligent conduct constituted a trespass. [...]

FOOTNOTES

[3](citation omitted) In Furrer v. Talent Irrigation Dist., 90 Or Adv Sh 399, 466 P2d 605 (1970), we explained that negligence and trespass are not comparable concepts: "The briefs treat negligence as if it were a coordinate with trespass and nuisance. As explained in the Restatement of Torts, Introduction to Chapter 40 at 221 (1939), negligence describes the defendant's conduct whereas trespass and nuisance describe the invasion of plaintiff's interest in land. Thus either a trespass or nuisance may arise out of intentional, negligent, reckless, or ultrahazardous conduct." (citation omitted.)

Possession

An occupier of the land will have a basis for and action in trespass. An owner, at law, has absolute control over the property until the owner transfers that property permanently.

Lease as a Means of Transferring Possession. An owner may transfer possession of the land temporarily, however, by entering into a contract to lease the property. That transfer would mean transferring the right to sue for interference with possession. So a tenant, who now has a right of possession would be the sole party to sue if a trespass occurred. But if the tenant stays on the property beyond the period of the lease, the owner may bring an action for trespass against the tenant.

Scope and Vertical Possession. The possessor's interest in the control of land goes to the sky and to the earth's core. But to accommodate modern society, many jurisdictions have enacted legislation that limits the interest in the sky to the degree that it would not otherwise adversely affect air travel or impede the running of power and telecommunication lines. The possessor's rights to the control of anything under the soil recognizes that the possessor has mineral rights to the property. Courts and legislatures in jurisdictions with great mineral resources have developed a sophisticated and complicated perspective regarding mineral rights, so paralegals in those jurisdictions would need to study this law thoroughly to gain an understanding of how subservice trespass could occur.

Damages

The act of invasion, alone, proves sufficient to award damages only when the invasion interfered with the plaintiff's control of the property. An invasion need not cause any actual harm to the property, only interference with its control. The invasion alone is sufficient to maintain an action. This technical trespass may entitle the plaintiff only to nominal damages instead of compensatory or punitive damages, but it still provides sufficient grounds for action.

For example, going to the wrong house to deliver a package constitutes trespass but filing suit because of attempting to make a delivery seems too trivial to justify the time and expense involved for a suit that likely would generate only nominal damages.

Case in Point 7-17 shows that a court will assign slight damages when there has been a clear but slight interference.

 # CASE IN POINT 7-17

McKean v. Alliance Land Company
200 Cal. 396 (1927)

Plaintiffs own the northern one-half of lot 9, Alice Park Property, Oakland, California. Defendants own lot 10, adjoining. Plaintiffs claim the common boundary between said lots is located 1182.84 feet from the point of intersection of Twelfth and Harrison Streets; defendants contend it is located 1182 feet from the same point, and relying upon this contention caused to be erected upon their property a brick and tile garage building, which building upon completion, according to the testimony of their own witness Mr. Prather, encroached beyond the boundary claimed by them a distance of from one-half to five-eighths of an inch.

Plaintiffs sued to enjoin defendants from depriving them of their property, being the said 84/100 of a foot, [...] for damages in amount of $ 5,000.

[...] [A]n experienced surveyor gave testimony in support of plaintiffs' contention. Plaintiffs also introduced certain old city ordinances in an effort to prove that subsequent to the filing for record of the map of Alice Park there had been a change made of about one foot in the monument line of Twelfth Street and certain old maps purporting to show a variation of one foot in the location of Twelfth Street. None of these exhibits show a difference of .84 of a foot and at most they appear to be but proof of inaccuracy in the surveys.

On the other hand [...] an experienced surveyor, gave testimony fully supporting defendants' claim, and they further introduced evidence showing that every conveyance of lot 9 and lot 10 from 1868 to date of the trial gave the distance from Twelfth Street, or Fourteenth Street, in accordance with the filed map distance and as found by the court. Mr. Prather stated he had first surveyed the tract in question six years prior to the commencement of this action; that at the request of defendants he surveyed lot 10 in December, 1921, and again went over the survey after construction of the garage; that as his initial point he took the northerly line of Twelfth Street, as fixed by the city monuments, at its intersection with the easterly line of Harrison Street; that he found the distance along Harrison Street from said point to the point of intersection with the southerly line of lot 10 to be 1182 feet. This distance is corroborated by the map of Alice Park and is .84 of a foot less than the distance testified to by Mr. Boardman. It is conceded that Mr. Prather's survey is right, and Mr. Boardman's wrong, if the northerly line of Twelfth Street is located now where it was in 1868. In other words, it is a disputed question of fact as to whether the monument line of Twelfth Street was changed subsequent to 1868. [...] From the record it appears that no convincing proof of such change was given.

The trial court found that the boundary line was, as claimed by defendants, 1182 feet from the above-described point of intersection, and found further that defendants' building encroached from one-half to five-eighths of an inch on plaintiffs' lot, by reason of which encroachment plaintiffs had been damaged in the sum of $10, and no more, and gave judgment accordingly.

[...]

Here the correct boundary line is established protecting the rights of appellants. The court further specifically found that "a judgment for said sum of $10 is an adequate remedy for said damage and will afford said plaintiffs, and each of them, full, complete, and adequate relief." There was no direct evidence that the encroachment of from one-half to five-eighths of an inch caused any actual damage to plaintiffs, and to our mind the award of the trial court is both wise and just.

Judgment affirmed.

Given the minor degree of interference, the court found that damages adequately compensated the plaintiff for the loss.

Defenses

Consent.   Since the tort of trespass to land involves physically interfering with plaintiff's use and enjoyment of the land, consent to enter the property will serve as a complete defense. Courts may differ as to the scope of consent, whether consent can be withdrawn, and whether consent was provided at all.

Mistake.   If a defendant makes a mistake as to the location of a boundary and crosses onto the plaintiff's property in a good-faith belief that no trespass occurred, the court will not excuse the defendant's liability. However, it might award only nominal damages.

Toxic Torts

A byproduct of an industrial society is toxic waste. Toxic waste can contaminate water, earth and air. Our country continues to manage the proper disposal of these wastes through the use of a number of laws, such as the federal "Superfund" law: CERCLA, the Comprehensive Environmental Response, Compensation, and Liability Act of 1980 (42 U.S.C. 9601 et seq.).

The invasion of toxic compounds onto a plaintiff's property can give rise to an action in trespass of land. Additional theories for establishing liability include actions for negligence and nuisance. These causes of action, however, exist under state law, so paralegals should research local law to determine what options exist for filing suit in tort for a recovery.

Many cases turn on evidence of trespass in the following case, where a business regularly released airborne pollutants (see Case in Point 7-18).

CASE IN POINT 7-18

Bradley v. American Smelting and Refining Company
104 Wn.2d 677 (1985)

[...]

Plaintiffs, landowners on Vashon Island, had sued for damages in trespass and nuisance from the deposit on their property of microscopic, airborne particles of heavy metals which came from the American Smelting and Refining Company (ASARCO) copper smelter at Rushton, Washington....

The parties have stipulated to the facts as follows: Plaintiffs Michael O. Bradley and Marie A. Bradley, husband and wife, are owners and occupiers of real property [...]. The Bradleys purchased their property in 1978. Defendant ASARCO, a New Jersey corporation doing business in Washington, operates a primary copper smelter on real property it owns [...]

On October 3, 1983, plaintiffs brought this action against defendant alleging a cause of action for intentional trespass and for nuisance. Plaintiffs' property is located some 4 miles north of defendant's smelter. Defendant's primary copper smelter [...] has operated in its present location since 1890. It has operated as a copper smelter since 1902, and in 1905 it was purchased and operated by a corporate entity which is now ASARCO. As a part of the industrial process of smelting copper [...] various gases such as sulfur dioxide and particulate matter, including arsenic, cadmium and other metals, are emitted. Particulate matter is composed of distinct particles of matter other than water, which cannot be detected by the human senses....

As a part of defendant's smelting process, the Tacoma smelter emits into the atmosphere gases and particulate matter. For the purposes of resolving the certified questions, the parties stipulate that some particulate emissions of both cadmium and arsenic [...] have been and are continuing to be deposited on plaintiffs' land....

Does an intentional deposit of microscopic particulates, undetectable by the human senses, upon a person's property give rise to a cause of action for trespassory invasion of the person's right to exclusive possession of property as well as a claim of nuisance?

The courts have been groping for a reconciliation of the doctrines of trespass and nuisance over a long period of time and, to a great extent, have concluded that little of substance remains to any distinction between the two when air pollution is involved [...]

The basic distinction is that trespass can be defined as any intentional invasion of the plaintiff's interest in the exclusive possession of property, whereas a nuisance requires a substantial and unreasonable interference with his use and enjoyment of it. That is to say, in trespass cases defendant's conduct typically results in an encroachment by "something" upon plaintiff's exclusive rights of possession.

[...]

Both of these concepts are nonsensical barriers, although the courts are slow to admit it. The requirement that the invasion be "direct" is a holdover from the forms of action, and is repudiated by contemporary science of causation. Atmospheric or hydrologic systems assure that pollutants deposited in one place will end up somewhere else, with no less assurance of causation than the blaster who watches the debris rise from his property and settle on his neighbor's land. Trespassory consequences today may be no less "direct" even if the mechanism of delivery is viewed as more complex....

The view recognizing a trespassory invasion where there is no "thing" which can be seen with the naked eye undoubtedly runs counter to the definition of trespass expressed in some quarters. (citation omitted). It is quite possible that in an earlier day when science had not yet peered into the molecular and atomic world of small particles, the courts could not fit an invasion through unseen physical instrumentalities into the requirement that a trespass can result only from a direct invasion. But in this atomic age even the uneducated know the great and awful force contained in the atom and what it can do to a man's property if it is released. [...] If these observations on science in relation to the law of trespass should appear theoretical and unreal in the abstract, they become very practical and real to the possessor of land when the unseen force cracks the foundation of his house. The force is just as real if it is chemical in nature and must be awakened by the intervention of another agency before it does harm....

The measure of damages for a permanent trespass, like a nuisance, is depreciation of market value. [...]

We hold that the defendant's conduct in causing chemical substances to be deposited upon the plaintiffs' land fulfilled all of the requirements under the law of trespass. [...] We hold that theories of trespass and nuisance are not inconsistent, that the theories may apply concurrently, and that the injured party may proceed under both theories when the elements of both actions are present.

Later legal action, however, determined that the presence of the particulate matter, alone, was not sufficient to support a claim for trespass or nuisance. Others downwind of the plant described in this case sued and one class of claims resulted in a settlement.

Trespass to Chattels

Any intentional interference with another's personal property is considered a **trespass to chattels.** Another term for personal property is a **chattel.** As mentioned earlier in this chapter, real property is land; personal property is everything else.

To win a claim for trespass to chattels, plaintiff would need to prove the following elements by a preponderance of the evidence:

- intent to interfere with the exclusive possession of personal property of another
- interference
- damages to the chattel caused by that interference

The tort action involves an intentional interference with a right to possess the property. The plaintiff must have had a legal right of possession that was intentionally interfered with by the defendant. The defendant must intend to deprive the plaintiff of the control of the personal property. Recovery is limited to the loss of the plaintiff's not being able to control the chattel.

This cause of action goes back centuries, to common law. Courts, however, continue to examine this cause of action as a modern society brings potentially new types of chattel into existence, as the following case illustrates (see Case in Point 7-19).

 ## CASE IN POINT 7-19

Intel Corporation v. Hamidi
30 Cal. 4th 1342 (2003)

Intel Corporation (Intel) maintains an electronic mail system, connected to the Internet, through which messages between employees and those outside the company can be sent and received, and permits its employees to make reasonable nonbusiness use of this system. On six occasions over almost two years, Kourosh Kenneth Hamidi, a former Intel employee, sent e-mails criticizing Intel's employment practices to numerous current employees on Intel's electronic mail system. Hamidi breached no computer security barriers in order to communicate with Intel employees. He offered to, and did, remove from his mailing list any recipient who so wished. Hamidi's communications to individual Intel employees caused neither physical damage nor functional disruption to the company's computers, nor did they at any time deprive Intel of the use of its computers. The contents of the messages, however, caused discussion among employees and managers.

On these facts, Intel brought suit, claiming that by communicating with its employees over the company's e-mail system Hamidi committed the tort of trespass to chattels. [...]

After reviewing the decisions analyzing unauthorized electronic contact with computer systems as potential trespasses to chattels, we conclude that under California law the tort does not encompass, and should not be extended to encompass, an electronic communication that neither damages the recipient computer system nor impairs its functioning. Such an electronic communication does not constitute an actionable trespass to personal property, i.e., the computer system, because it does not interfere with the possessor's use or possession of, or any other legally protected interest in, the personal property itself. (citation omitted) The consequential economic damage Intel claims to have suffered, i.e., loss of productivity caused by employees reading and reacting to Hamidi's messages and company efforts to block the messages, is not an injury to the company's interest in its computers–which worked as intended and were unharmed by the communications–any more than the personal distress caused by reading an unpleasant letter would be an injury to the recipient's mailbox, or the loss of privacy caused by an intrusive telephone call would be an injury to the recipient's telephone equipment.

[...]

Hamidi, a former Intel engineer, together with others, formed an organization named Former and Current Employees of Intel (FACE-Intel) to disseminate information and views critical of Intel's employment and personnel policies and practices. FACE-Intel maintained a Web site (which identified Hamidi as

Webmaster and as the organization's spokesperson) containing such material. In addition, over a 21-month period Hamidi, on behalf of FACE-Intel, sent six mass e-mails to employee addresses on Intel's electronic mail system. The messages criticized Intel's employment practices, warned employees of the dangers those practices posed to their careers, suggested employees consider moving to other companies, solicited employees' participation in FACE-Intel, and urged employees to inform themselves further by visiting FACE-Intel's Web site. The messages stated that recipients could, by notifying the sender of their wishes, be removed from FACE-Intel's mailing list; Hamidi did not subsequently send messages to anyone who requested removal.

Each message was sent to thousands of addresses (as many as 35,000 according to FACE-Intel's Web site), though some messages were blocked by Intel before reaching employees. Intel's attempt to block internal transmission of the messages succeeded only in part; Hamidi later admitted he evaded blocking efforts by using different sending computers. When Intel, in March 1998, demanded in writing that Hamidi and FACE-Intel stop sending e-mails to Intel's computer system, Hamidi asserted the organization had a right to communicate with willing Intel employees; he sent a new mass mailing in September 1998.

The [...] record contains no evidence Hamidi breached Intel's computer security in order to obtain the recipient addresses for his messages [...] Hamidi stated he created the recipient address list using an Intel directory on a floppy disk anonymously sent to him. Nor is there any evidence that the receipt or internal distribution of Hamidi's electronic messages damaged Intel's computer system or slowed or impaired its functioning. Intel did present uncontradicted evidence, however, that many employee recipients asked a company official to stop the messages and that staff time was consumed in attempts to block further messages from FACE-Intel. According to the FACE-Intel Web site, moreover, the messages had prompted discussions between "[e]xcited and nervous managers" and the company's human resources department.

Intel sued Hamidi and FACE-Intel, pleading [...] [an]action for trespass to chattels [...] seeking both actual damages and an injunction against further e-mail messages. [...] The trial court entered default against FACE-Intel upon that organization's failure to answer. The court then granted Intel's motion for summary judgment, permanently enjoining Hamidi, FACE-Intel, and their agents "from sending unsolicited e-mail to addresses on Intel's computer systems." Hamidi appealed; FACE-Intel did not (footnote omitted).

[...]

[T]he tort of trespass to chattels allows recovery for interferences with possession of personal property "not sufficiently important to be classed as conversion, and so to compel the defendant to pay the full value of the thing with which he has interfered." (citation omitted)

In modern American law generally, "[t]respass remains as an occasional remedy for minor interferences, *resulting in some damage*, but not sufficiently serious or sufficiently important to amount to the greater tort" of conversion. (citation omitted)

[...]

The dispositive issue in this case, therefore, is whether the undisputed facts demonstrate Hamidi's actions caused or threatened to cause damage to Intel's computer system, or injury to its rights in that personal property, such as to entitle Intel to judgment as a matter of law. To review, the undisputed evidence revealed no actual or threatened damage to Intel's computer hardware or software and no interference with its ordinary and intended operation. Intel was not dispossessed of its computers, nor did Hamidi's messages prevent Intel from using its computers for any measurable length of time. Intel presented no evidence its system was slowed or otherwise impaired by the burden of delivering Hamidi's electronic messages. Nor was there any evidence transmission of the messages imposed any marginal cost on the operation of Intel's computers. In sum, no evidence suggested that in sending messages through Intel's Internet connections and internal computer system Hamidi used the system in any manner in which it was not intended to function or impaired the system in any way. Nor does the evidence show the request of any employee to be removed from FACE-Intel's mailing list was not honored. The evidence did show, however, that some employees who found the messages unwelcome asked management to stop them and that Intel technical staff spent time and effort attempting to block the messages. A statement on the FACE-Intel Web site, moreover, could be taken as an admission that the messages had caused "[e]xcited and nervous managers" to discuss the matter with Intel's human resources department.

Relying on a line of decisions, most from federal district courts, applying the tort of trespass to chattels to various types of unwanted electronic contact between computers, Intel contends that, while its computers were not damaged by receiving Hamidi's messages, its interest in the "physical condition, quality or value" (citation omitted) of the computers was harmed. We disagree. The cited line of decisions does not persuade us that the mere sending of electronic communications that assertedly cause injury only because of their contents constitutes an actionable trespass to a computer system through which the messages are transmitted. Rather, the decisions finding electronic contact to be a trespass to computer systems have generally involved some actual or threatened interference with the computers' functioning.

[...]

Intel connected its e-mail system to the Internet and permitted its employees to make use of this connection both for business and, to a reasonable extent, for their own purposes. In doing so, the company necessarily contemplated the employees' receipt of unsolicited as well as solicited communications from other companies and individuals. That some communications would, because of their contents, be unwelcome to Intel management was virtually inevitable. Hamidi did nothing but use the e-mail system for its intended purpose—to communicate with employees. The system worked as designed, delivering the messages without any physical or functional harm or disruption. These occasional transmissions cannot reasonably be viewed as impairing the quality or value of Intel's computer system. We conclude, therefore, that Intel has not presented undisputed facts demonstrating an injury to its personal property, or to its legal interest in that property, that support, under California tort law, an action for trespass to chattels.

[...]

Since the e-mail did not interfere with the use or enjoyment of the computer system, no trespass occurred.

Conversion

The tort of **conversion** involves taking possession of personal property so that an owner may not use it. As a crime, this kind of taking would be known as theft.

To win a claim for conversion, a plaintiff would need to prove the following elements by a preponderance of the evidence:

- intent to interfere with the exclusive control of personal property of another
- interference so as to put the personal property in the defendant's exclusive control
- damages caused by the interference with exclusive control

The *Restatement (Second) of Torts* expands on the scope of the common law tort by also taking into account a defense to tort liability in conversion (see box below).

CONVERSION

1. Conversion is an intentional exercise of dominion or control over a chattel which so seriously interferes with the right of another to control it that the actor may justly be required to pay the other the full value of the chattel.
2. In determining the seriousness of the interference and the justice of requiring the actor to pay the full value, the following factors are important:
   a. the extent and duration of the actor's exercise of dominion or control;
   b. the actor's intent to assert a right in fact inconsistent with the other's right of control;
   c. the actor's good faith;
   d. the extent and duration of the resulting interference with the other's right of control;
   e. the harm done to the chattel;
   f. the inconvenience and expense caused to the other.

Restatement (Second) of Torts, §222A (1965)

This definition hints at the ways a defendant can act so as to convert the plaintiff's personal property.

Examples of Conversion

The tort of conversion makes it impossible for the owner or lawful possessor of an item to regain its possession and, so, the ability to use it. Examples of actions that can underlie the basis for liability in tort liability appear in Table 7-2.

Table 7-2 Examples of Actions Giving Rise to Tort of Conversion (Where Defendant Operates a Dry Cleaning Business)

• Destroying (incinerates plaintiff's garment)	• Refusing to turn it over to the owner (if a dry cleaner refuses to return a garment to the owner who has paid for the cleaning)
• Severely damaging the personal property (when ironing the garment, leaves a large, prominent scorch mark)	• Disposing of the personal property (defendant dry cleaner throws out plaintiff's garment)
• Making material alterations to the personal property (Taking plaintiff's long-sleeved shirt and making it into a short-sleeved shirt	• Receiving the personal property (defendant takes plaintiff's property knowing that owner did not authorize such a transfer)
• Misdelivering the personal property (if dry cleaner gives owner's garment to another customer)	• Going beyond the scope of authority to use (using plaintiff's dress suit to interview for a job in a new industry)

Conversion Is Different from Trespass to Chattels

While no universal standard exists for knowing when an action goes from trespass to chattels to conversion, a court would look to the extent of the interference with the owner's or possessor's control and the duration of such interference. The greater the interference in degree or time, the greater the likelihood that the plaintiff will have a valid claim for conversion. For example, at a party, if the defendant takes the plaintiff's coat by accident, discovers the mistake shortly thereafter, and then returns it, that might give rise to an action for trespass to chattels (although a suit based on such conduct would provide the plaintiff with nominal damages, at best). At that same party, if the defendant took the plaintiff's coat, knowing that it was not the defendant's to take, this would give rise to an action for conversion (see Case in Point 7-20).

 ## CASE IN POINT 7-20

Roberson v. Kunzli, Gott, LLC
2006 Conn. Super. 377(Conn. Super. Ct. Feb. 9, 2006)

On June 2, 2005, the plaintiffs, Dale C. Roberson and Cynthia B. Roberson filed a four-count complaint against the defendants, Werner O. Kunzli, Gott, LLC (Gott), The Hideout Trust Association, Inc. (Hideout), and Donald R. Bunce alleging [...] trespass (count two); conversion (count three) [...]. Pending before the court is the defendants' motion to strike all [...] counts of the complaint on the grounds that they each fail to state a claim upon which relief may be granted.

The complaint alleges the following facts. Between January and April 2000, the plaintiffs negotiated the purchase of a 3.93-acre parcel of land from Gott, which was adjacent to the plaintiffs' residence. [...]

Gott conveyed the property to the plaintiffs on April 11, 2000. On December 15, 2000, Gott conveyed its easements to Hideout. On May 13, 2003, pursuant to the direction of the other defendants, Bunce and his employees entered the plaintiffs' parcel and cut down fifty-six trees and other vegetation.

[...]

Count Two: Trespass

[...] The defendants argue that the plaintiffs do not have an exclusive possessory interest in the property and therefore, cannot state a claim for trespass because the defendants retained the right to enter upon the parcel and were merely exercising this right. The plaintiffs counter that the defendants went beyond the scope of the easement and committed a trespass when Bunce entered the plaintiffs' property and cut down fifty-six trees and other vegetation.

[...]

Although the defendants argue that the plaintiffs do not have an exclusive possessory interest in the property and thus, defendant Bunce's entry [...] cannot constitute a trespass, the Supreme Court [...] has stated that possession does not have to be exclusive. Actual possession of real estate is always sufficient to sustain an action of trespass to real property against an individual who does not have a superior right.

[...]

In the present case, the plaintiffs allege that they hold title [aside: title refers to ownership of property] to the property in question [...]; the defendant, Bunce, entered the plaintiffs' property under the direction of the other defendants and clear cut and removed fifty-six trees and other vegetation belonging to the plaintiffs [...]; "The defendants knew, or should have known, that they were trespassing" on the plaintiffs' property [...]; and, the defendants' actions caused a direct injury to the plaintiffs including making "the property more susceptible to erosion…a visual nuisance…and…[destroying] the habitat for wildlife that were on the plaintiffs' property" [...]. Because the plaintiffs have sufficiently stated a cause of action for trespass, the defendants' motion to strike count two is denied.

Count Three: Conversion

The defendants move to strike count three on the grounds that: (1) the defendants maintained the right [...] to remove trees and vegetation from the plaintiffs' property to create and/or maintain their view and to landscape the property and therefore, cannot be held liable for conversion, and; (2) severing plants and trees from the land cannot be considered conversion because the plants growing on the plaintiffs' land are considered real property, not personal property. [...] [T]he defendants argue that conversion does not apply to the removal of trees.

[...] Trees and other vegetation, when attached to the land, are considered real property. Once the trees and vegetation have been removed from the land, they become personal property; thus, conversion applies. (citation omitted)

In Count Three, the plaintiffs alleged that they owned the fifty-six trees and other vegetation that the defendants clear cut [...]; they were deprived of this property when it was cut down [...]; the defendants were not authorized to remove the trees and vegetation from the plaintiffs' property [...]; and, they were harmed in that the trees and vegetation had significant monetary value of which they were deprived by the defendants [...]. Based on the foregoing allegations, the plaintiffs have sufficiently stated a cause of action for common-law conversion. Therefore, the motion to strike count three is denied.

[...]

For all the foregoing reasons, the defendants' motion to strike counts two and three is denied [...]

Once the court clarified how a grant of access to property—an *easement*—did not include the right to remove trees and vegetation, the court concluded that the plaintiffs had stated valid causes of action for trespass to land and for conversion.

Since the differences between conversion and trespass to chattels can depend upon the extent and duration of the interference, standards regarding the degree of interference resulting in a particular tort may differ by state. Paralegals should examine the law within specific jurisdictions before characterizing a plaintiff's cause of action as one or the other.

KEY TERMS

Abuse of process   270

Assault   231

Battery   233

Chattel   278

Consent   235

Conversion   281

SUMMARY

Intentional torts emphasize the defendant's state of mind when committing the tortious conduct. When a defendant sets out deliberately to cause harm to a plaintiff, liability will arise. The plaintiff may experience physical harm, psychological harm, harm to the plaintiff's property, or to the plaintiff's reputation. Intentional torts differ from an action in negligence, where an intentional tort requires a deliberate action or omission and negligence involves a breach of duty, regardless what the defendant thought when breaching the duty owed to the plaintiff.

CONCEPT REVIEW QUESTIONS

1. Discuss the role of intent in an intentional tort.
2. Describe the difference between an assault and a battery.
3. What is the extent of confinement required for liability for false imprisonment?
4. What is the state of mind of the plaintiff necessary to sustain a finding of intentional infliction of emotional distress?
5. List the four tort actions based upon the right of privacy.
6. Describe the interest that is to be protected by the torts of defamation.
7. What is the key element in all defamation?
8. List the elements necessary to maintain an action for trespass to land in most jurisdictions.
9. Discuss the distinction between a trespass to a chattel and the tort of conversion.

CRITICAL THINKING APPLICATIONS

1. It's the height of another Presidential campaign season. One private organization decides to attack the candidate of a major political party. Instead of showing the candidate's face, the organization uses on its Web site an image of an old doll, common a century earlier, which is a racial stereotype. What

cause(s) of action may the candidate file against this organization? What are the candidate's chances for success at trial? Why?

2. A defendant operates a home-based business, buying and reselling small consumer goods via the Internet. That means that package delivery trucks come at least three and sometimes up to seven times a day during the business week. Sometimes the delivery trucks pull into the driveway of the plaintiff, a next-door neighbor, since the defendant has no driveway for the trucks to park and turn around. Of the torts discussed in this chapter, which cause(s) of action in tort(s) could the plaintiff use as the grounds to file suit against defendant? Why? What are the plaintiff's chances of prevailing on any of them at trial? Why?

3. A plaintiff is jammed in a crowded subway car, by an entrance. The train stops at a platform, but no one gets out. The defendant tries to push into the crowded car, against the plaintiff. Assume that the plaintiff sues the defendant for battery. How will a judge rule if the defendant files a motion to dismiss? Why?

4. A debt collection agency tells a plaintiff that unless she pays an outstanding debt, the debt collection agency will file suit. The plaintiff does not pay. The debt collection sues the plaintiff. Does the plaintiff have a cause of action for abuse of process? Why or why not?

5. After the hometown team wins a game, ending a long string of losses, one fan in the stands holds up a sign, "Finally, we've won!" A photographer for a major hometown daily newspaper takes a picture of this fan and the sign. The photo runs on the front page of the next day's edition of the newspaper. The fan sues the newspaper for invasion of privacy. What type of invasion of privacy should the fan allege in the complaint? Counsel for the newspaper moves for summary judgment. Will the court grant the newspaper's request? Why or why not?

6. A defendant finds a puppy at a playground; the dog is of an unusual and rare breed. The next day, "lost" signs go up on telephone poles for the dog. Would the owner have a cause of action for one of the torts mentioned in this chapter? If so, what would the likelihood be that the owner would prevail at a trial regarding that tort?

7. Kids cut through the property of people who live adjacent to a school. Could those people sue the kids (actually, the parents of the kids)? Under what tort? What's the likelihood of success for the people who bring suit?

8. A plaintiff is riding in the subway. As the subway approaches a station, the car abruptly stops and the electricity goes out. The plaintiff and the other passengers have to sit in the hot, dark subway car for 45 minutes before the electricity suddenly comes back on, the train pulls into the station, and all passengers can get out. The subway system offers not a word of explanation for the delay. Does the plaintiff have a cause of action against the subway system for false imprisonment? Why or why not?

SKILL-BUILDING APPLICATION

Dido and Aeneas have decided to end their marriage, although one was more interested in the divorce than the other. In fact, Aeneas decided to monitor all phone calls to the family home, where Dido still resided, with the hope of getting information that could be used in the divorce. When Dido was at work, Aeneas entered the house, using the spare house key that was always kept under a rock by the door, and went in to program the phones to allow for the monitoring. While inside, Dido's Chihuahua, Dr. Woo, started barking at Aeneas. Aeneas, who had never liked the dog, takes it, kills it, and leaves with its carcass, disposing of it without leaving any trace of having killed the pet in the house. Given the torts mentioned in this chapter, identify all potential causes of action that Dido may have, under tort law, against Aeneas.

"It is always right to detect a fraud, and to perceive a folly; but it is very often wrong to expose either. A man of business should always have his eyes open, but must often seem to have them shut."

—*Philip Stanhope (1694–1773)*

Misrepresentation, Interference with Economic Relations, and Other Business–Related Torts

Commerce underlies the existence of a capitalist society. Business activities can generate the kind of income that leads to the creation of stable communities, which in turn become the bedrock of a functioning society.

The torts described in this chapter recognize that economic losses from tortious conduct can undermine the viability of a business. Torts like intentional misrepresentation (fraud) undermine the creation of dependable business relationships; reasonable reliance on misstatements can lead a business to engage in activity that can challenge the viability of a business. Under the concept of interference with economic relations, the law recognizes that finding and retaining new business can draw so heavily upon a firm's resources that without having recourse to an action to tort law, more businesses could fail. Business activities play such a significant role in a society's functioning that even the bad faith of parties to a contract can lead to the destabilization of business relations that exist under contract law.

CHAPTER TOPICS

1. Misrepresentation
2. Interference with Economic Relations
3. Wrongful Discharge
4. Bad Faith Breach of Contract

OBJECTIVES

After completing this chapter, you will be able to:

1. Better appreciate the differences between intentional torts and torts of negligence.
2. Recognize the value of the "good name" of a business to its ongoing operation.
3. See how business opportunities can be curtailed.
4. Understand the significance of representation and misrepresentation on the operation of a business.
5. Comprehend that even parties to a valid contract can engage in tortious conduct.
6. Learn the elements, and consequences, of wrongful discharge of an employee.

■ MISREPRESENTATION

Misrepresentation focuses on those torts that caused a plaintiff to act based on incorrect information.

The defendant may have known or doubted the accuracy of a statement but made it anyway: that action constitutes fraud. The critical element is a measure of deliberateness in producing an effect, a level of intent often called *scienter*.

Another type of misrepresentation involves failure of a duty to determine the accuracy of information: it is known as negligent misrepresentation.

Fraud

Fraud (sometimes called *deceit, fraudulent misrepresentation,* or *intentional misrepresentation*) involves an action that misleads the plaintiff and causes economic loss. For example, if the defendant tells the plaintiff an $10,000 investment will double to $20,000 in a month but there is no sign of the defendant at the end of the month, the plaintiff has a claim for the tort of fraud. In order to win a claim of fraud, plaintiffs need to show proof by a preponderance of the evidence on each of the following elements (see box below).

ELEMENTS NEEDED TO MAKE A CLAIM OF FRAUD

1. an intentional misrepresentation
2. of fact or opinion (as distinct from a promise)
3. that is material and
4. intended to induce and
5. does induce reasonable reliance by the plaintiff
6. proximately causing pecuniary harm to the plaintiff.

Dobbs The Law of Torts §470 (2000)

For example, suppose a defendant dining in a restaurant intentionally and falsely claimed to have found broken glass in his food. The restaurant owner saw bits of glass and the defendant's bloodied mouth—both of which arose because of the defendant's actions—and paid the defendant to avoid a lawsuit. Because the defendant has deliberately misrepresented the cause of the injury, the defendant could be found liable for the tort of fraud.

Consider the following case that describes fraud in the sale of land. While the plaintiffs could have found out about a restriction on the use of the land, the defendant had led them to believe no restriction existed, so that the plaintiffs had no reason to investigate further (see Case in Point 8-1).

CASE IN POINT 8-1

Letellier v. Small

400 A.2d 371 (Me. 1979)

[...]
In October 1976 the Letelliers purchased from Small a parcel of undeveloped land known as "lot 8" located in Biddeford. In 1974 Small had sought approval of the lot along with others as a subdivision from the Biddeford Planning Commission. After

receiving the results of a soil analysis test, the Biddeford Planning Commission imposed two restrictions on lot 8; namely, that the lot had to be serviced by the municipal water system and that no subsurface sewage disposal system would be permitted. The commission entered these restrictions upon a subdivision plan which included lot 8, and Small's attorney filed that plan with the Registry of Deeds in York County.

It is uncontroverted that the Letelliers did not know of the restriction prohibiting use of a subsurface sewage system on lot 8 until after the purchase. [...]

As to the first factual issue, plaintiffs established that defendant at times had in his possession the soil report and a copy of the subdivision plan including the restrictions. Small denies having obtained knowledge of the restrictions prior to the sale of the land, either through his attorney or from his own examination of the subdivision plan or the soil report.

As to the second factual issue, plaintiffs testified that (a) they asked Small whether the lot passed the soil test and defendant replied, "Yes, it has"; (b) defendant offered to show plaintiffs a copy of the soil analysis, but later said that he was unable to find the report; and (c) defendant showed plaintiffs a copy of the subdivision plan that did not include the restrictions. Small admitted that he could not find the soil report and that he showed plaintiffs a copy of the subdivision plan that did not contain the restrictions. However, defendant testified that he also showed plaintiffs a copy of the subdivision plan that did include the restrictions and that in answering plaintiffs' question regarding the soil report, he had replied, "I must have done something right. I can sell a piece of land." While admitting this response was ambiguous, defendant argues that plaintiffs could not have justifiably relied upon it.

Upon learning of the proscription against a subsurface sewage system, plaintiffs abandoned their plans to build a house on lot 8 and brought the instant suit seeking damages for fraud and deceit. Defendant now appeals from the jury's verdict in favor of the plaintiffs.

[...]

[A] defendant is liable for fraud or deceit if he (1) makes a false representation (2) of a material fact (3) with knowledge of its falsity or in reckless disregard of whether it is true or false (4) for the purpose of inducing another to act or to refrain from acting in reliance upon it, and (5) the plaintiff justifiably relies upon the representation as true and acts upon it to his damage. A plaintiff may justifiably rely on the fraudulent misrepresentation of a defendant, whether made intentionally or recklessly, without investigating the truth or falsity of the representation. Reliance is unjustified only if the plaintiff knows the representation is false or its falsity is obvious to him.

It remains only to apply this analysis to the case before us. [...] [I]n order to recover for deceit, the Letelliers had to establish they could not have discovered the falsity of Small's representation regarding the soil report through the exercise of reasonable care. Consequently, in rendering a verdict in favor of the Letelliers, the jury found they had met a standard of diligence that we here conclude the law does not require of plaintiffs in deceit actions. Nevertheless, defendant argues that plaintiffs' reliance on his representation regarding the soil report was not justifiable since plaintiffs failed to (1) check a copy of the subdivision plan in the Registry of Deeds which contained the restriction on a subsurface sewage system, (2) conduct an independent investigation to determine the results of the soil test once defendant aroused plaintiffs' suspicions by failing to produce the report as promised, and (3) learn of the restrictions through the attorney hired to conduct the title search by the credit institution financing the Letelliers' purchase.

We reject defendant's contentions. None of these alleged oversights by the Letelliers establish the actual knowledge of falsity, or the obvious falsity, necessary to render their reliance unjustifiable. Nor is there any doubt of the sufficiency of the evidence to support the jury's finding that the Letelliers met the stringent due diligence requirement [...]. Although the deed passing title to lot 8 referred to the subdivision plan recorded in the Registry of Deeds, which contained the restrictions, plaintiffs' failure to consult the recorded plan is understandable in light of the fact that defendant showed plaintiffs a copy of the subdivision plan—one that did not contain the restrictions. Similarly, while Small's failure to produce the soil report as promised might have aroused suspicions, Small himself dampened any suspicions by showing plaintiffs the subdivision plan and by answering that the lot had passed the soil test. [...] In short, the record contains ample evidence to support the jury's verdict that the Letelliers were justified in relying on Small's misrepresentation.

[...]Judgment affirmed.

The plaintiffs reasonably relied on the defendant's statement about the use of the land, and the defendant's statement gave them no reason to investigate whether restrictions noted elsewhere would have applied.

The Crime of Fraud

There is also a criminal version of the tort of fraud. Prosecuted by the government, it requires that the plaintiff provide enough evidence to establish the defendant's guilt beyond a reasonable doubt. It carries the possibility of imprisonment. Thus, a plaintiff can sue a defendant for the tort of fraud in the hope of getting damages; in addition, the defendant can face prosecution for the crime of fraud, which could lead to imprisonment.

Consumer Protection Laws

Some states have expressly responded to consumer fraud by the enactment of **consumer protection laws.**

For example, a law—sometimes called a *lemon law*—might outline specific steps that an automobile buyer can take to get the seller to restore the automobile to the condition that the buyer reasonably expected it to be in when the buyer purchased it.

Another consumer protection law might allow any purchaser to state in a letter what was wrong with the item or service purchased; if the seller doesn't respond within 30 days, the purchaser then can file suit and could receive compensatory and punitive damages. While these laws create protections for the purchase of many goods and services, they also provide a means for the seller to "make it up" to the purchaser's satisfaction without resorting to the courts. In that way, buyers and sellers could reach a more satisfactory result. The Massachusetts Consumer Protection Law below is an example (see box below).

MASSACHUSETTS CONSUMER PROTECTION LAW, CH. 93A.

Section 9. (1) Any person, other than a person entitled to bring action under section eleven of this chapter, who has been injured by another person's use or employment of any method, [...] as the court deems to be necessary and proper. [...]

(3) At least thirty days prior to the filing of any such action, a written demand for relief, identifying the claimant and reasonably describing the unfair or deceptive act or practice relied upon and the injury suffered, shall be mailed or delivered to any prospective respondent. Any person receiving such a demand for relief who, within thirty days of the mailing or delivery of the demand for relief, makes a written tender of settlement which is rejected by the claimant may [...] limit any recovery to the relief tendered if the court finds that

the relief tendered was reasonable in relation to the injury actually suffered by the petitioner. In all other cases, if the court finds for the petitioner, recovery shall be in the amount of actual damages or twenty-five dollars, whichever is greater; or up to three but not less than two times such amount if the court finds that the use or employment of the act or practice was a willful or knowing violation of said section two or that the refusal to grant relief upon demand was made in bad faith. [...]

(6) Any person entitled to bring an action under this section shall not be required to initiate, pursue or exhaust any remedy established by any regulation, administrative procedure, local, state or federal law or statute or the common law in order to bring an action under this section [...]

(8) [...] [R]ecovering or failing to recover an award of damages or other relief in any administrative or judicial proceeding, except proceedings authorized by this section, by any person entitled to bring an action under this section, shall not constitute a bar to, or limitation upon relief authorized by this section.

Damages

When trying to determine the amount in damages a plaintiff should get from the defendant, the courts will look to a number of factors. For example, the *Restatement (Second) of Torts* provides a list of factors that a court might consider when calculating the appropriate amount of damages arising from fraud (see box below).

MEASURE OF DAMAGES FOR FRAUDULENT MISREPRESENTATION

1. The recipient of a fraudulent misrepresentation is entitled to recover as damages in an action of deceit against the maker the pecuniary loss to him of which the misrepresentation is a legal cause, including
   a. the difference between the value of what he has received in the transaction and its purchase price or other value given for it; and
   b. pecuniary loss suffered otherwise as a consequence of the recipient's reliance upon the misrepresentation.
2. The recipient of a fraudulent misrepresentation in a business transaction is also entitled to recover additional damages sufficient to give him the benefit of his contract with the maker, if these damages are proved with reasonable certainty.

Restatement (Second) of Torts §549 (1965)

Negligent Misrepresentation

Negligent misrepresentation involves a defendant's breach of duty in providing the plaintiff with accurate information, where that breach of duty resulted in misleading the plaintiff and cause economic harm.

For example, assume the defendant says an oil well will be a "gusher" once the final drilling is done. However, the defendant has not checked with a geologist to determine whether a large pool of oil lies at the bottom of the well. The plaintiff buys an interest in this new well, and it turns out there was only a small amount of oil. The defendant has engaged in negligent misrepresentation. To win a claim in negligent representation, the plaintiff would need to prove the following elements by a preponderance of the evidence:

- a false representation
- made by the defendant who had a duty to make a correct statement
- that causes the plaintiff reasonably to rely on it
- where there is a breach of that duty
- resulting in damages to the plaintiff

Negligent Misrepresentation Is Different from Fraud

The difference between this tort and fraud is that in fraud, the defendant deliberately set out to deceive the plaintiff. With negligent misrepresentation, the defendant breached a duty to provide accurate information to a plaintiff.

Advice Provided to Others

The defendant's liability to the plaintiff may arise when the defendant has negligently failed to provide proper information (see box below).

INFORMATION NEGLIGENTLY SUPPLIED FOR THE GUIDANCE OF OTHERS

1. One who, in the course of his business, profession or employment, or in any other transaction in which he has a pecuniary interest, supplies false information for the guidance of others in their business transactions, is subject to liability for pecuniary loss caused to them by their justifiable reliance upon the information, if he fails to exercise reasonable care or competence in obtaining or communicating the information.
2. Except as stated in Subsection (3), the liability stated in Subsection (1) is limited to loss suffered
   a. by the person or one of a limited group of persons for whose benefit and guidance he intends to supply the information or knows that the recipient intends to supply it; and
   b. through reliance upon it in a transaction that he intends the information to influence or knows that the recipient so intends or in a substantially similar transaction.
3. The liability of one who is under a public duty to give the information extends to loss suffered by any of the class of persons for whose benefit the duty is created, in any of the transactions in which it is intended to protect them.

Restatement (Second) of Torts §552 (1965)

For example, assume that a soft-drink provider sweetened its product with a low-calorie compound that, in very rare instances, would trigger an allergic reaction in those who suffer from a particular ailment, and did not disclose that fact on their beverage label. If the company intended not to disclose the existence of this compound, that is fraud. If due to mechanical failure this information was not printed on the beverage container, the provider has negligently misrepresented the safety of the soft drink.

Fiduciary Relationship and Negligent Misrepresentation

Often, when someone solicits advice from a person engaged in a profession, that person will have a superior understanding about the topic that the person seeks advice about (which is why that person sought advice from the 'professional'). Since that professional has superior information, a risk exists that the professional could mislead the person and that the person who had caught the advice might never have known of this. Therefore, that professional has a **fiduciary duty,** a duty that requires exercising great care in offering advice, since the person seeking the advice likely would not detect any inaccuracy. A breach of this duty might give rise to an action for negligent misrepresentation.

In the following case, an auditing firm argued that it had no duty to a lender to provide an auditing report commissioned by a third party, so that there was no negligent misrepresentation. So, if the auditing firm did not have an obligation to turn over the report, there could be no breach of duty. Thus, in Case in Point 8-2, the question is: did a duty exist?

CASE IN POINT 8-2

Abrams Centre National Bank v. Farmer, Fuqua & Huff, P.C.
225 S.W.3d 171 (Tex. App. El Paso 2005)

ESS College of Business, Inc. was a for-profit business college located in Dallas, Texas and directed by Jan V. Friedheim. The College trained students to work as secretaries, paralegals, and administrative assistants. Most of the students received financial aid through federal programs which were administered by the Department of Education (DOE). In fiscal years 1999 and 2000, the DOE imposed the Ninety Percent Rule, which prohibited the College from deriving more than 90 percent of its revenue from federal funding.

Although the College received federal funding for its programs, it also borrowed money from various lenders in 1998, 1999, and 2000. On November 5, 1998, it incurred the maximum credit line of $950,000 from Chase Bank of Texas [...]. In March 1999, Abrams Centre National Bank, (Abrams) replaced Chase as the lender for the 1998 debt. The $950,000 debt was rolled into a new seven-year term loan of $1,000,000 which was guaranteed by the Small Business Administration. Abrams also provided the College with a $300,000 credit line on April 22, 1999. The $300,000 credit line was renewed on April 22, 2000 and again on September 29, 2000. At that point, the credit line was increased by $200,000. On January 22, 2001, Abrams loaned an additional $250,000. All of the promissory notes were guaranteed by Jan V. Friedheim and her husband and secured by liens on personal property which primarily consisted of the College's accounts receivable for funds due under federal educational programs for student loans.

The College hired Farmer, Fuqua & Huff, P.C. as an independent auditor. Farmer audited the College at fiscal year end in 1998, 1999, and 2000. [...] The College informed Farmer that copies of the audit would be sent to Chase as required by their line of credit.

Following an open audit by the DOE in July 2000 indicating a high default rate on Perkins loans, the College was placed on provisional certification. When a school is placed on provisional certification, the DOE can take action without allowing for due process. The College never notified Abrams that it had been placed on provisional certification. The DOE placed the school on "reimbursement status" in December 2000 for failure to comply with the Ninety Percent Rule. While on reimbursement status, the College could only obtain Title IV reimbursement by submitting complex documentation every thirty days showing what funds had been earned during the prior period. As a consequence, the school suffered an adverse affect on its cash flow. ESS sought additional funds from Abrams and it agreed to the two-month short term loan of $250,000 in January 2001.

On March 27, 2001, the DOE revoked the school's provisional certification to participate in Title IV programs. ESS ceased operations, defaulted on all three loans to Abrams, and filed for bankruptcy. Because all of the loans were guaranteed by the Friedheims, Abrams filed suit against both of them. Abrams obtained a judgment for $1,600,000. This judgment remains unsatisfied.

Abrams then filed suit against the accounting firm for negligent misrepresentation, claiming Abrams had relied on the financial status of the school as reflected in the audits when it loaned money to ESS.

[...]

Abrams [...] argues Farmer knew the audit was being formulated for the general purpose of obtaining a bank loan. It fell within the class of lenders Farmer knew the College intended to supply with the audits. Farmer also knew that ESS had to provide its audited information to Chase Bank as a requirement of the credit line and that once ESS changed lenders, the new lender would be receiving and relying upon the audited reports.

On the other hand, [...] Farmer was hired by ESS to provide audits for the Department of Education. The purpose of the audits was explicitly stated in each of the compliance letters: "This report is intended for the information of management and the U.S. Department of Education. However, this report is a matter of public record and its distribution is not limited." This caveat is not surprising. The purpose of providing compliance letters to the DOE was to establish that no more than 90 percent of the College's funding came from federal programs. The remaining 10 percent had to come from another source. Indeed, the funds came from a credit line. The 1998 audit was provided for a specific party—Chase Bank—in order to comply with the credit line terms. [...] William Huff was in charge of the 1999 and 2000 audits and had knowledge of the 1998 audit. In his affidavit, he maintained that Farmer knew ESS had a revolving credit line with Chase Bank but the firm did not know that ESS intended to give a copy of its reports to Abrams in order to secure replacement or extensions of existing loans. Huff also stated that had the firm known Abrams would be relying on the reports, Farmer would have charged more to compensate for the additional risk of liability. Audits conducted for purposes of governmental agencies involve less risk. If problems arise, there generally are no repercussions since the risk is shifted to the client. Munselle, Huff, and Friedheim all insisted that ESS never informed Farmer of its intent to give the audits to Abrams or to any bank other than Chase.

While Farmer undoubtedly owed a duty to Chase, it owed no duty to Abrams.

[...]

■ INTERFERENCE WITH ECONOMIC RELATIONS

Interference with economic relations encompasses a number of torts most commonly associated with the operation of a business. They include creating falsehoods about such facets of a business such as ownership or quality of a firm's property. Interference with economic relations can also involve acts that interfere with or impair the operation of a business.

Disparagement of Title

Disparagement of title involves making injurious falsehoods about the ownership of land. An ownership interest in real property (real estate or land) is referred to as *title*, a document that officially and publicly establishes ownership. Disparagement of title (also known as *slander of title*) involves making false statements regarding a firm's ownership interest (that is, its title) in a piece of real property.

For example, assume that a plaintiff is trying to sell a piece of land. Another person who intentionally and falsely claims to be the owner of the plaintiff's property could sabotage the plaintiff's efforts. This person could be found liable for the tort of disparagement of title.

To win a claim in disparagement of title, the plaintiff must prove the following elements by a preponderance of the evidence:

- the making of a false statement about the plaintiff's title to property
- communication of that false statement to another
- with the intent to do so that the plaintiff may lose out on business opportunities (such as the sale of the real estate)
- which result in damages

In the initial complaint, the plaintiff must demonstrate that the impairment of the value of the property was significant, material, and sufficient. If some question exists whether a seller of land has an unfettered and unencumbered title to the property, the property is said to have a "cloud on the title." Case in Point 8-3 focuses on the blocking of a potential sale due to the existence of such a 'cloud'.

CASE IN POINT 8-3

Davis v. Wood

61 Cal. App. 2d 788 (1943)

Appellant commenced an action against respondents for slander of title to real property. [...]

"That on or about the 29th day of May, 1935, plaintiff herein and one J. Henry Wood, made and executed a certain agreement in writing by the terms and provisions of which the said J. Henry Wood leased and let unto plaintiff herein and plaintiff hired and took possession from said J. Henry Wood, all that certain real estate with the equipment thereon situate in Siskiyou County, State of California, which property is mining property and known as the Portuguese Mine" [...]

III

"That during the months of January and February, 1941, all [...] defendants unjustly, maliciously and unlawfully conspired together to obtain plaintiff's real property [...] the said defendants falsely represented and pretended that they had some valid claim upon the land [...] and thereupon said defendants prepared or caused to be prepared what purported to be notices of Location of Mining Claims covering and describing the same real property [...] and on or about the 19th day of February, 1941, said defendants maliciously caused [...] mining claims to be recorded in the office of the County Recorder of Siskiyou County, State of California, and the same have ever since remained of record in said county and apparently in full force and effect and a cloud upon plaintiff's title".

IV

"That the pretense of said defendants in making said purported notices of location of mining claims [...] was to create a cloud upon and claim against the property [...] when in truth and in fact said defendants and each of them well knew and had notice that said land was leased to said plaintiff and well knew and had notice that plaintiff was in actual possession of said land [...] and was actually and honestly working said mining ground in compliance with the terms of said lease and the defendants well knew and had notice that the annual work was done [...]; that defendants [...] had no interest in the lands [...] and the statements [...] were wholly false and known to be so by [...] defendants [...] that by reason of said conspiracy, representations, pretenses and false claims [...] the plaintiff has been greatly embarrassed in the free enjoyment, use and disposition of his aforesaid property and the interest of the plaintiff has been [...] greatly depreciated and plaintiff greatly damaged by reason of the said pretended claims of said defendants" [...]

V

"That the defendants never had and have not now any interest, right, title or claim directly or indirectly to said land [...] and that these defendants in recording said instruments acted maliciously and in order to vex and harass plaintiff herein."

VI

"That said defendants, in recording said instruments, cast a cloud upon and a slander upon plaintiff's title to the lands [...]; that the recording of said notices of locations of mining claims by defendants decreased the value of said leasehold interests and rendered it unmarketable, all to the damage of said real estate and to plaintiff in the sum of Ten Thousand dollars".

VII

"That the acts of said defendants [...] have been actuated by malice, and that said defendants [...] have been guilty of oppression and malice in their actions, as aforesaid; that this is a proper case for punitive damages and this plaintiff has sustained exemplary or punitive damages in the sum of Five Thousand dollars."

[...]

The trial court stated:

[...]

"In the instant case no pleading of malice or of facts indicating actual or implied malice exists, and above all, no pleading of proper damages is made. There is absolutely no showing [...] that any deal of plaintiff was interfered with nor any other matter than would justify damages in a slander of title action.

[...]

The most usual manner in which a third person's reliance upon disparaging matter causes pecuniary loss is by preventing a sale to a particular purchaser. The disparaging matter may prevent a sale by causing a purchaser to break an agreement already entered into for the purchase of the thing."

[...] "The disparaging matter may, if widely disseminated, cause pecuniary loss by depriving its possessor of a market in which, but for the disparagement, his land or other thing might with reasonable certainty have found a purchaser. In such case the impossibility or the great difficulty of showing [...] the particular person or persons who were dissuaded from purchasing the thing by the publication of the disparaging matter makes evidence of the owner's inability to avail himself of a ready market for the thing in question sufficient proof of the loss and often of its extent; indeed, this inability to dispose of readily marketable things is also sufficient evidence that the defamatory matter has come to the knowledge of unknown possible purchasers and has led them to refrain from buying."

[...]

From the foregoing statements of the law relating to damages for slander of title, or, to state it more accurately, for wrongful disparagement of title, it is apparent that the elements of damages are the loss caused by the impairment of vendibility and the cost of clearing the title. (citation omitted)

Therefore, in our opinion, a complaint which alleges that by reason of the recording of a notice of location by respondents the leasehold interest of appellant was greatly depreciated in value and was rendered unmarketable, to appellant's damage in the sum of $10,000, states the ultimate fact of damages and is sufficient [...]

In view of the foregoing we conclude that the trial court abused its discretion in sustaining respondents' demurrer [...]

The judgment is reversed.

By filing a false "loss of mining" claim, the defendants hoped to impair the transfer of title of the plaintiff's interest in the land. At trial, the court dismissed the plaintiff's case on the grounds that it wasn't clear as to the damages suffered. The appeals court disagreed with the trial court, saying the plaintiff sufficiently alleged an amount in damages and returned the case to the trial court so that a trial could be held.

Disparagement of Title Is Different from Defamation

Disparagement of title differs from the tort of defamation in one significant way: defamation is a false statement *about a person* and disparagement of title is a false statement made *about property*. Disparagement of title could result in denying the seller his right to sell his land free and clear of impediments. Defamation, on the other hand, could involve a statement about the seller being a liar and a cheat—a statement about the seller, not the property.

Type of Evidence Needed to Win a Suit for Disparagement of Title

As with defamation, the freedom of speech protections in the First Amendment to the U.S. Constitution apply to disparagement of title. The principles set forth in the U.S. Supreme Court's ruling in *New York Times v. Sullivan* applies to disparagement of title. To establish liability, the plaintiff must show that the defendant acted with "actual malice" when disparaging the title of the plaintiff's real estate. The "actual malice" standard means that the defendant knew (or should have known) that the information was false, yet went ahead and released the information.

Commercial Disparagement

Commercial disparagement involves making injurious falsehoods about other aspects of a business. For example, a defendant places an advertisement in a newspaper claiming that the plaintiff made inferior goods.

Types of Disparagments

Such falsehoods could focus on any of three aspects of a business:

- Disparagement of goods, regarding a firm's property other than real estate;
- Disparagement of services, regarding the services a business provides; and
- Disparagement of business, about the nature of the plaintiff's business.

Some jurisdictions refer to this tort as *trade libel*; both torts refer to falsehoods about a business.

An example of disparagement of services in Case in Point 8-4 looks to the impact statements about the skills and competencies of a physician have upon his business prospects.

CASE IN POINT 8-4

Patel v. Soriano and Irvington General Hospital
369 N.J. Super. 192 (App.Div. 2004)

Plaintiff Kumar A. Patel, M.D., a board certified surgeon with a subspecialty in vascular surgery, sought vascular surgical privileges at defendant Irvington General Hospital (IGH). According to plaintiff, defendant Jaime R. Soriano, M.D., the chief of vascular surgery at IGH, sabotaged plaintiff's application and communicated false statements about plaintiff to other members of IGH's medical staff—all to continue his own monopolistic control over IGH's vascular surgery department. As a result, plaintiff filed an action [...] seeking [...] damages for both Soriano's and IGH's misconduct.

[...] [T]he trial judge found in favor of plaintiff and concluded that both IGH and Soriano had defamed plaintiff and had tortiously interfered with plaintiff's reasonable expectation of economic advantage. [...]

Trade libel identifies the tort addressing aspersions cast upon one's business operation. [...] It is similar to the tort of intentional interference with one's economic relations, rather than a branch of the general harm to reputation involved in libel and slander. [...]

A plaintiff alleging trade libel must prove publication of a matter derogatory to the plaintiff's property or business, of a kind designed to prevent others from dealing with him or otherwise to interfere with plaintiff's relations with others. (citation omitted) The communication must be made to a third person and must play a material part in inducing others not to deal with plaintiff. [...]

Distinguishing between personal defamation of a plaintiff and disparagement of plaintiff's property may be difficult. (citation omitted) Generally, the latter tort has been applied to statements that are injurious to plaintiff's business, but cast no reflection on either plaintiff's person or property. (citation omitted) For example, if the statement charges plaintiff with personal misconduct, or imputes to plaintiff reprehensible personal characteristics, it is regarded as libel or slander. (citation omitted) If, however, the aspersion reflects only on the quality of plaintiff's product, or on the character of plaintiff's business as such, it is disparagement. [...]

The elements of a disparagement action include proof of publication of material derogatory to the quality of a plaintiff's business, or to his business in general, of a kind calculated to prevent others from dealing with him, or otherwise to interfere adversely with his relations with others (citation omitted). To establish loss of trade or other dealings, plaintiff must show the falsehood was communicated to a third person and played a material and substantial part in leading others not to deal with plaintiff. *Ibid.* Plaintiff must also prove that the statement is false, and that defendant made the statement knowingly or recklessly (citation omitted). Finally, plaintiff must prove special damages, such as the loss of a present or prospective advantage, in the form of pecuniary loss. (citation omitted) .

[...] The necessary showing is specific: plaintiff must establish pecuniary loss that has been realized or liquidated, such as lost sales, or the loss of prospective contracts with customers. (citation omitted) Traditionally, plaintiff was required to identify particular business interests who have refrained from dealing with him, or explain the impossibility of doing so (citation omitted). However, where requiring such identification is unreasonable, proof of lost profits resulting from breach of contract may suffice, especially where the loss is shown with reasonable certainty and where the possibility that other factors caused the loss is satisfactorily excluded. (citation omitted)

[...]

Applying these principles here, we conclude that plaintiff established a cause of action for trade libel, in that he established that false statements made knowingly or recklessly about him by defendant caused him to lose referrals at IGH. The statements pertained solely to the character of the medical services provided by plaintiff and essentially charged plaintiff with negligence. Since the statements did not imply that plaintiff was personally dishonest, reprehensible, or lacking in integrity, they fall under the tort of trade libel, as opposed to personal defamation (citation omitted). [...]

The statements regarding such matters as mortality and morbidity, aneurysm-related deaths, and even plaintiff's relationship with others on staff all were focused on his performance as a surgeon as opposed to personal defamation. We hold that plaintiff proved a trade libel cause of action.

[...] Affirmed in part; reversed in part and remanded for consideration of damages consistent with this opinion. [...]

The defendant's statements about the plaintiff's competencies led to the loss of business for the plaintiff.

Type of Evidence Needed to Win a Suit for Commercial Disparagement

As with disparagement of title, to establish liability for commercial disparagement, the plaintiff must show that the defendant acted with "actual malice" when disparaging some aspect of the plaintiff's business.

Interference with a Contractual Relationship

When a business has entered into a contract and a defendant acts to interfere with the completion of that contract, the defendant has committed the tort of **interference with a contractual relationship.** For example, the defendant commits the tort when he or she induces an employee to break an employment contract.

To win a claim of interference with a contractual relationship, a plaintiff must prove, by a preponderance of the evidence, these elements:

- A valid contract exists
- An intent to interfere with the completion of that contract
- Interference
- Which results in damages.

In another form of interference with a contractual relationship, the plaintiff is hindered from completing a contract to sell property (see box below).

THE DEGREE OF DEFENDANT'S INTERFERENCE WITH THE PERFORMANCE OF A CONTRACT

The defendant makes the plaintiff's performance impossible or more burdensome. For example, the defendant intentionally and without justification interferes with his tenant's right to assign the lease, making it impossible for the tenant to sell his business to a buyer.

Dobbs, *The Law of Torts* §446 (2000)

In Case in Point 8-5, the issue involves whether the plaintiff had been offered an opportunity, as per a partnership agreement, to purchase a greater interest in the partnership.

 # CASE IN POINT 8-5

Cacciola v. Nellhaus

49 Mass. App. Ct. 746 (2000)

The plaintiff is the widow of Salvatore J. Cacciola, one of four brothers who were partners in a real estate investment business. She is also the executrix of her late husband's estate. The defendant is the lawyer who represented the partnership. The plaintiff filed suit against the defendant after learning that he had also represented one of the other brothers, Edward, in Edward's purchase of the partnership share of another brother, Anthony, who had died. The complaint was in [...] interference with contractual relationship [...]

During his lifetime, Antonio Cacciola acquired considerable residential and commercial real estate. On January 1, 1985, as part of his estate plan, he set up a partnership called Cacciola Associates (partnership). As established, the partnership, to which he conveyed his real estate interests, had five partners: Antonio and his four sons, Edward, David, Anthony, and Salvatore. Two years later, the father died. His four sons assumed responsibility for the partnership. Each then held a twenty-five per cent interest. Anthony died in January, 1988, eight months after his father.

The partnership agreement provided that if a partner died, the surviving partners could continue the partnership. The agreement also set out the procedure for the partnership to purchase the partnership share of a deceased partner. Each partner had equal authority in the management of the partnership, and all decisions affecting the conduct of partnership affairs were to be made by majority vote. Edward and Anthony were in charge of the daily management of the partnership, for which they each received compensation of two and one-half per cent of the gross income of the partnership. They did not have authority over matters requiring the agreement of the partners.

Howard Nellhaus, the defendant, served as legal counsel to the partnership from 1985 until at least 1995. Following Anthony's death, the defendant advised the three remaining partners to execute a document entitled "Exercise of Option to Continue Partnership." The document provided that Anthony's estate would become successor-in-interest to Anthony's partnership interest. The surviving partners discussed having Anthony's son, Anthony Jr., succeed his father as a full partner if that were feasible or arranging for the partnership to purchase Anthony's share from his heirs. No action was taken on either of these alternatives.

In March of 1992, Edward, Salvatore, and Salvatore's son and daughter met at the partnership office. Edward reported that Anthony's heirs appeared ready to sell their share of the partnership. He said the partnership "might be able to 'pick up' those interests for an amount as low as $250,000, which...Edward...thought would be a very favorable figure." Salvatore responded that the partnership should acquire Anthony's share, but emphasized that the partnership should pay a fair and equitable price to Anthony's heirs. Edward said nothing further to Salvatore on this subject.

In August, 1993, Salvatore received a financial statement from the partnership's accountant showing Edward with a fifty per cent interest in the partnership. It was then Salvatore learned that two months before, Edward had purchased Anthony's share from Anthony's heirs. The purchase price was $300,000, which was substantially less than the fair-market value of Anthony's share of the partnership and its assets. Edward had falsely represented to Anthony's heirs that Salvatore was not interested in buying Anthony's share, and secretly had purchased Anthony's share of the partnership for his own personal benefit. Anthony's heirs testified [...]

Several months after learning of Edward's purchase, Salvatore discovered that the defendant had served as Edward's lawyer in the transaction. The defendant had advised Edward that Edward had the "right and authority" under the partnership agreement to purchase Anthony's share without notice to Salvatore. When Salvatore sought information about the transaction, the defendant refused to provide any details, claiming the information was confidential and that as an attorney he could not disclose it.

[...] Salvatore filed an action against Edward in January, 1994. In July, 1995, Salvatore died. In June, 1996, Salvatore's wife, Erasmia (plaintiff), filed this action in her role as executrix claiming that the defendant "in representing and protecting the interests of Edward and withholding key information from Salvatore, while purportedly acting as counsel for the partnership, violated the obligations he had as counsel to Salvatore, a partner in the partnership." The complaint [...] alleged [...] interference with a valuable opportunity of the partnership [...].

The judge dismissed the interference count on the ground that the claim of damage belonged to the partnership and that therefore Salvatore (sic) lacked standing to bring that action as an individual. The judge also concluded that the defendant did not know of Salvatore's interest in buying Anthony's share of the partnership, and therefore could not have intentionally interfered with Salvatore's contractual opportunity.

[...]

As to Salvatore's claim as an individual, the judge ruled that the plaintiff's complaint did not allege facts necessary to prove a claim of intentional interference with contractual relations. The elements of such a claim are: "(1) a business relationship or contemplated contract of economic benefit; (2) the defendant's knowledge of such relationship"; (3) the defendant's intentional interference through improper motive or means; and "(4) the plaintiff's loss of advantage directly resulting from the defendant's conduct." [...] "A 'probable future business relationship from which there is a reasonable expectancy of financial benefit is enough.' " (citation omitted) In dismissing the plaintiff's individual claim, the judge found that "since plaintiff admits that Salvatore never had conversations with Nellhaus regarding the disposal of Anthony's shares, it is clear that Nellhaus did not know of Salvatore's possible willingness to acquire those shares for himself."
[...]

The allegations of the complaint make clear that Edward knew of Salvatore's probable interest in Anthony's share. The partners had discussed the possibility of the partnership buying the share. Edward not only kept secret his own intentions, but also misinformed Anthony's heirs about Salvatore's interest. It is a fair inference that Salvatore's interest was the occasion for the defendant's advice to Edward that he was not legally bound to consult with Salvatore about the sale and for his later secretiveness when Salvatore sought information about the transaction. As counsel to the partnership, the defendant was familiar with the provisions of the partnership agreement, which gave the partnership the first option to buy Anthony's share and required a vote of the partners owning at least fifty-one per cent of the shares for "all determinations affecting the conduct of the affairs of the partnership." The defendant's advice to Edward, which violated the terms of the partnership agreement as well as Edward's fiduciary duty to his partners, led directly to Salvatore's loss of opportunity to buy Anthony's share of the partnership if the partnership did not exercise its right to do so.

[...]

Accordingly, the judgment [...] is reversed, and the plaintiff is to have thirty days [...] for leave to file an amended complaint on behalf of the partnership.

[...]

Since the defendant's control of information impaired the plaintiff's ability to buy out a partner's interest in a partnership, the court concluded that the defendant had interfered with a contractual relationship.

Interference with Prospective Economic Advantage

The tort of **interference with prospective economic advantage** involves sabotaging another's efforts to acquire new business. Some refer to this as the tort of *unfair competition*.

An example of this tort occurs when a plaintiff car salesman, on the verge of his customer signing a contract to buy a car, is undercut by a competing dealer who offers the customer the same kind of car at a lower price. The plaintiff car salesman could sue to recover at least the lost profit expected from the sale.

To win a claim for interference with prospective economic advantage, the plaintiff must prove, by a preponderance of the evidence, these elements:

- Expecting reasonably to secure an economic advantage
- An intent to interfere with taking that advantage
- Interference
- Which result in damages (but may be limited only to loss of economic benefits)

Part of the difficulty in establishing liability for this tort involves the plaintiff's ability to provide sufficient evidence that the contractual relationship came close enough into being that the defendant's interactions substantially contributed to the loss of that potential contractual relationship.

Case in Point 8-6 shows just how difficult it can be to set forth a valid claim based on this tort. The plaintiff alleges that a nonprofit testing organization interfered with the plaintiff's effort to get customers to purchase its preparation materials for taking the nonprofit organization's tests.

 # CASE IN POINT 8-6

United Educational Distributors, LLC v. Educational Testing Service

350 S.C. 7 (Ct. App. 2002)

Educational Testing Service ("ETS"), a nonprofit corporation [...] administers, scores, and prepares testing materials for, among others, the College-Level Examination Program ("CLEP"). UED sells study aids for the CLEP test, which it markets primarily to military personnel.

On October 9, 1998, UED filed its original complaint [...] alleging ETS wrongfully interfered with UED's present and future sales contracts of its study materials. Essentially, UED alleged [...] intentional interference with prospective economic advantage.

[...]

UED named several people from ETS specifically and alleged they participated in ETS's "concerted effort to prevent [UED] from obtaining new business." However, UED failed to allege that ETS interfered with any specific contracts it had received or was certain to enter into. Rather, UED alleged that it "would have continued to receive responses from at least 10% of the lead cards [it] mailed."

[...]

Businesses selling products on military bases are prohibited from selling door to door. Instead, with addresses only obtained from the military through the

Freedom of Information Act (no names or telephone numbers are provided), [UED] sends out lead cards (in the Beaufort area, normally 4 mailings a year, 1500 cards mailed at a time) to all the addresses inviting calls if the recipients have an interest in the product being sold ([UED] does not have a store front, it is a direct sales company whose business is completely dependent on generating new customers through these lead cards). As a result of [ETS's] interference, [UED] has seen the average expected response (per past history) to its lead cards in the Beaufort area drop from 10% in 1996 and 1997 to virtually none in 1998 (when the interference began) and none in 1999.

[…] [UED], not having names or phone numbers, couldn't do follow-up to see why they have not been receiving the normal percentage of lead card responses, as they had in the past (i.e. [UED] has no way of knowing who didn't respond and why, they only know they don't receive responses anymore). Meanwhile, the only change in circumstances from 1996 to present, and therefore the only possible cause for this quantifiable, precipitous drop in responses/business (to nothing), is [ETS's] interference.

[…]

South Carolina only recently recognized the tort of intentional interference with prospective contractual relations […] The elements of the cause of action are (1) the intentional interference with the plaintiff's potential contractual relations, (2) for an improper purpose or by improper methods, and (3) causing injury to the plaintiff. (citation omitted) "As an alternative to establishing an improper purpose, the plaintiff may prove the defendant's method of interference was improper under the circumstances." (citation omitted) Generally, there can be no finding of intentional interference with prospective contractual relations if there is no evidence to suggest any purpose or motive by the defendant other than the proper pursuit of its own contractual rights with a third party. (citation omitted).

Upon a review of our limited South Carolina precedent, a cause of action for intentional interference with prospective contractual relations generally stands following the loss of an identifiable contract or expectation. […]

The plaintiff must actually demonstrate, at the outset, that he had a truly prospective (or potential) contract with a third party. This does not require plaintiff to prove the tort in his initial pleadings; rather, the allegations must present facts that give rise to some reasonable expectation of benefits from the alleged lost contracts.

[…]

The agreement must be a close certainty; thus, a mere offer to sell, for example, does not, by itself, give rise to sufficient legal rights to support a claim of intentional interference with a business relationship (citation omitted). Likewise, the mere hope of a contract is insufficient. […]

These contracts cannot be speculative. […]

[…]

Here, UED has redrafted its complaint twice and still has not alleged that it had a reasonable probability of entering into a specific contract but for the interference of ETS. Rather, UED merely asserts, based on past experience, it would have received a response from approximately 10% of its mailings. Further, UED asserts that *everyone* on the military bases it tried to serve constitutes a potential customer and, therefore, prospective contracts. Even with these alleged potential customers, however, UED acknowledges it "has no way of knowing who didn't respond and why." Moreover, UED does not allege that any of its past customers provided repeat business. Therefore, UED has failed to plead any potential contract was thwarted by any alleged tortious conduct on the part of ETS.

For the foregoing reasons, the decision of the circuit court dismissing UED's action for intentional interference with prospective contractual relations pursuant to Rule 12(b)(6) is

AFFIRMED

Since the only evidence the plaintiff had of alleged interference was that they were not getting the same level of response to their mailings as before, the court upheld the dismissal of the claim because it was not clear the drop in responses was due to action by the nonprofit testing organization.

Different from Interference with a Business Relationship

With the tort of interference with a contractual relationship, a contract already exists. With the tort of interference with prospective economic advantage, however, no valid contract yet exists. Not surprisingly, finding evidence to prove this claim can prove more difficult than finding evidence when there is a contract.

The Difficulty in Establishing Damages

If the plaintiff can show there was interference in a potential business opportunity, the plaintiff now has the difficult task of showing damages from being unable to take advantage of the opportunity. The plaintiff also must explain just how much value was lost due to the interference.

Negligent Interference with Prospective Economic Advantage

A growing trend recognizes that a defendant has breached a duty of care, negligently causing interference with the plaintiff's economic advantage. If the defendant neglected to determine that the plaintiff was in the process of entering into a contract and the defendant's interference prevented the finalizing of that contract, the plaintiff may have a claim for negligent interference with prospective economic advantage. A critical element, however, involves whether the defendant owed the plaintiff a duty of care

To make a claim for negligent interference with prospective business economic advantage, the plaintiff must prove, by a preponderance of the evidence, these elements:

- A reasonable expectation of securing an economic advantage
- Duty of care owed by the defendant
- Breach that creates an interference
- That results in damages (but may be limited only to loss of economic benefits).

In Case in Point 8-7, the court takes care to explain how a breach of contract can give rise to an action in tort for negligent interference with prospective economic advantage. When a shipping company negligently failed to properly pack the plaintiff's goods for shipping to a customer, the customer sustained damages and suffered losses, which in turn disrupted the plaintiff's business arrangement with the customer.

 CASE IN POINT 8-7

North American Chemical Company v. The Superior Court of Los Angeles County

59 Cal. App. 4th 764 (2d Dist. 1997)

[...]

In its complaint, North American sought recovery of sums it paid as damages in settlement of a customer's claim that arose from a contaminated North American product packaged and shipped for North American by Harbor Pac. Harbor Pac contends that North American can state no claim for negligence, but only one for a breach of contract. North American responds that it is entitled to pursue both remedies until such time as an election may be required by law. The issue is important as it impacts both the applicable statute of limitations and the proper measure of damages. Harbor Pac also raises the objection that North American is claiming only an economic loss and such damages are not recoverable in the absence of physical injury to person or property.

We hold that North American's packaging and shipping contract with Harbor Pac imposed a duty on Harbor Pac which required it to reasonably and carefully perform its contractual obligations; it is this duty North American has alleged was breached. In addition, because this case arises from a contract for the performance of services rather than the sale of goods, and the negligent performance of that contract allegedly resulted in a *foreseeable* economic loss to North American, the so-called "economic loss rule" does not bar recovery even though (1) the only damages that North American seeks are based solely on economic loss and (2) contractual privity is present. As a result, we conclude that North American has stated a viable cause of action for negligence. We therefore will grant the requested writ.

[...]

On or about February 1, 1993, North American, a manufacturer of a large variety of chemicals, including boric acid, entered into an oral agreement with Harbor Pac in which Harbor Pac agreed to bag, containerize and transport chemicals to North American's customers at a fixed price per short ton. This agreement was confirmed in writing by Harbor Pac in a letter dated February 5, 1993. By its terms, the agreement was effective through December 31, 1993.

On or about May 20, 1993, North American shipped approximately 46 metric tons of bulk boric acid to Harbor Pac from its facility in Trona, California. The shipment was accompanied by bills of lading which provided that Harbor Pac was to package and seal the boric acid into one-ton Flecon bags. The packaged boric acid, as reflected in the bills of lading, was destined for ultimate delivery to North American's customer, N. H. Techno Co., Ltd. (NHT), in Nagoya, Japan. In accordance with the terms of its contract with North American, Harbor Pac received the bulk boric acid on May 21, 1993, and packaged and sealed it. Unfortunately, Harbor Pac utilized the same silo that had previously been used to package a product known as "V-bor," and North American's boric acid became contaminated. Harbor Pac shipped the sealed one-ton bags to Japan on May 23 and May 30, 1993. The last part of that shipment arrived in Japan on June 11, 1993.

NHT produces specialty glass for thin filter resistors, a key component of liquid crystal displays. It began using North American's boric acid in its manufacturing process on or about October 12, 1993. Within two weeks, it discovered that the boric acid was contaminated with V-bor and it was forced to stop production for approximately twelve days. A provisional claim for damages in the sum of $254,600 was submitted by NHT to North American on or about October 25, 1993. A formal demand by NHT for payment of this sum was made two weeks later on November 8. After some investigation by North American and negotiation with NHT, it was agreed on December 27, 1993, that North American would pay $203,550 [...] to compensate NHT for the damages and loss caused by the contaminated boric acid. [...]

On January 28, 1994, North American provided documentation supporting the damages claimed by NHT to Harbor Pac together with a demand for payment of that claim. North American asserted that it was Harbor Pac, not North American, which had caused the boric acid to become contaminated with V-bor and this was the direct and legal cause of NHT's loss. Harbor Pac (and its insurer) ignored North American's claim and demand for payment. As a result, North American filed this action on June 9, 1995. [...] North American alleged that Harbor Pac had held itself out as qualified to properly bag, containerize and transport bulk chemical products and that its failure to do so, i.e., to carry out its contract with North

American in a reasonable and professional manner, constituted negligence for which Harbor Pac was liable.

Harbor Pac [...] argued to the trial court that North American was attempting to convert what was at most a contract breach into a tort and this was not legally permissible. In addition, Harbor Pac argued that it could not be held liable for a claimed loss by North American which consisted solely of economic damages. The trial court agreed [...]

There are essentially two issues presented by North American's petition: (1) Can the negligent performance of a contractual obligation give rise to an action in tort? (2) Is North American entitled to recover under a negligence theory for injury solely to its economic interests without any need to allege or prove injury to person or property? We answer both of these questions in the affirmative.

[...]

A Contractual Obligation May Create a Legal Duty the Breach of Which Will Support an Action in Tort

Harbor Pac's principal argument is that whatever its contractual liability to North American may be, it cannot be held liable in tort for negligence. It is certainly true that contract and tort are different branches of the law. Contract law exists to enforce the intentions of the parties to an agreement while tort law is designed to vindicate social policy. (citation omitted) However, the same wrongful act may constitute both a breach of contract and an invasion of an interest protected by the law of torts. (citation omitted)

This court recently endorsed the general rule that where the "negligent" performance of a contract amounts to nothing more than a *failure* to perform the express terms of the contract, the claim is one for contract breach, not negligence. (citation omitted) However, for over 50 years California has also recognized the fundamental principle that " '[a]ccompanying every contract is a common-law duty to perform with care, skill, reasonable expedience, and faithfulness the thing agreed to be done, and a negligent failure to observe any of these conditions is a tort, as well as a breach of the contract.' The rule which imposes this duty is of universal application as to all persons who by contract undertake professional or other business engagements requiring the exercise of care, skill and knowledge; the obligation is implied by law and need not be stated in the agreement [citation]." [...] A contract to perform services gives rise to a duty of care which requires that such services be performed in a competent and reasonable manner. A negligent failure to do so may be both a breach of contract and a tort. (citation omitted) In such a hybrid circumstance, the plaintiff is entitled to pursue both legal theories until an occasion for an election of remedies arises. (citation omitted)

[...]

In a case that is factually very close to the one before us, the court applied these principles and found the tort remedy available. In *Allred v. Bekins Wide World Van Services* (citation omitted), plaintiff had been employed on a West Pakistan construction project. Upon its completion, his employer entered into a contract with the defendant Bekins to transport plaintiff's personal belongings back to the United States. Bekins negligently packed plaintiff's property in rancid and contaminated straw which subsequently resulted in damage to plaintiff's property and personal injury to plaintiff and members of his family. While plaintiff did not contract directly with Bekins, he acquired enforceable contractual rights by virtue of his obvious status as an intended third party beneficiary of his employer's contract with Bekins. [...] The *Allred* court had no trouble concluding that plaintiff's complaint, alleging the facts summarized above, pleaded the negligent violation of a contractually created legal duty owed by Bekins to plaintiff which proximately resulted in property damages and bodily injuries to plaintiff and his family. The court stated, "The purpose of Bekins' contract with the employer [...] was the delivery of the Allred family's goods to their home in the United States. In this undertaking Bekins was bound, as a matter of law, to use at least reasonable care and skill. [Citations.] And: '"[N]egligent failure to observe [such] conditions is a tort, as well as a breach of the contract." The rule which imposes this duty is of universal application as to all persons who by contract undertake professional or other business engagements requiring the exercise of care, skill and knowledge; the obligation is implied by law and need not be stated in the agreement....' [Citation.]" (citation omitted)

Harbor Pac asserts that the decision in *Allred* is inapplicable to the facts of this case. It argues that *Allred* involved personal injuries and property damage and not the purely economic loss claimed here; and it was NHT which suffered property damage in this case, not North American. However, that argument really goes to the damage issue which we discuss below. *Allred* is important here because it provides a closely analogous application of the general rule which we apply that a tort remedy may arise from the negligent performance of a contractual commitment.

In essence, Bekins contracted to pack and ship goods. It performed that contract in a negligent manner and caused damage to one of the parties entitled to enforce the contract. It is of no significance that the plaintiff in *Allred* was a third party beneficiary. That status simply gave him a right to claim the benefit of Bekins's contractual promise which, as we have shown, necessarily included the legally imposed duty to perform with due care. Bekins's failure to do so gave rise to a cause of action for negligence in favor of one of the "contracting" parties.

In accordance with these well-established principles, we conclude that North American's contract with Harbor Pac imposed upon the latter a duty of reasonable care in carrying out and performing that contract.

[...]

[T]he critical issue to be determined before allowing recovery of an economic loss is the foreseeability of the risk of that loss flowing from a defendant's negligent conduct. In cases involving the negligent performance of services, it would seem to matter little whether that foreseeability is established, at least in part, by a contractual relationship. It is the foreseeability of the economic loss resulting from the defendant's conduct, not the plaintiff's inability to contractually anticipate and provide for such loss, which serves as the foundation for imposition of liability. Moreover, the emphasis placed on the ability of contracting parties to allocate the risk of economic loss in the context of the sale or distribution of goods has no logical application here. No party contracting for the services of another need negotiate with the other regarding the latter's burden to perform the contract reasonably and competently. Absent an express contractual provision to the contrary, such burden is already imposed by law upon the performing party and, as we have shown, enforced in tort with a more expansive measure of damages. Thus, a plaintiff has no reason to bargain for a standard of performance already imposed by law and, absent very unusual circumstances, is not likely to agree to accept the risk of a defendant's negligent performance when the defendant's reasonable and competent performance is the whole purpose of the contract and is a necessarily implied covenant therein. Obviously, in a contract for the performance of services, any reallocation of economic losses away from the negligently performing defendant would, in all but the most unusual case, defeat the contract's purpose.

[...]

The tort of negligent interference with prospective economic advantage is established where a plaintiff demonstrates that (1) an economic relationship existed between the plaintiff and a third party which contained a reasonably probable future economic benefit or advantage to plaintiff; (2) the defendant knew of the existence of the relationship and was aware or should have been aware that if it did not act with due care its actions would interfere with this relationship and cause plaintiff to lose in whole or in part the probable future economic benefit or advantage of the relationship; (3) the defendant was negligent; and (4) such negligence caused damage to plaintiff in that the relationship was actually interfered with or disrupted and plaintiff lost in whole or in part the economic benefits or advantage reasonably expected from the relationship. [...]

North American has alleged facts (or claims it can do so) which plainly show that (1) Harbor Pac's performance of its packaging and shipping contract was expressly intended to affect North American—the purpose of such performance was to facilitate a sale of North American's product to its Japanese customer; (2) if Harbor Pac did not perform that contract properly there was a reasonably foreseeable harm to North American's economic interests—indeed, the delivery of contaminated boric acid to Japan would have an immediate and predictable negative impact on North American's relationship with its Japanese customer; (3) North American clearly suffered injury here as it was allegedly required to make good on the damage done to its customer's business and economic interests by reason of Harbor Pac's negligent conduct; (4) the injury resulted directly from Harbor Pac's negligent acts; (5) whether or not moral blame could be placed on Harbor Pac, its wrongful conduct was plainly responsible for the loss suffered by North American; and finally, (6) future harm to others can clearly be avoided by enforcement of a rule that imposes a burden of due care on all persons in the performance of their contractual undertakings. [...]

The satisfaction of these factors is sufficient to demonstrate a "special relationship" between North American and Harbor Pac thereby creating a basis for liability even in the absence of other injury or contractual privity. [...]

North American has alleged sufficient facts to demonstrate that Harbor Pac had a legal duty to perform its contract in a reasonable and competent manner and that it negligently failed to do so. In addition, it has also alleged [...] facts demonstrating the existence of the special relationship [...] so as to justify the recovery of the economic losses which it claims legally resulted from Harbor Pac's negligent acts. [...] All we decide is that North American is entitled to pursue its claims of negligence and/or negligent interference with prospective economic advantage and the trial court's order [...] was error.

[...]

Given the possibility that the plaintiff had incurred damages arising from the loss of a prospective business opportunity because of a failure to fulfill the terms of a contract an existing relationship had been disrupted, the appellate court returned the case to the trial court to resolve this question of fact.

Not Universally Recognized as a Tort

The tort of **negligent interference with prospective economic advantage** has been recognized relatively recently. For that reason, a difference of opinion still exists as to how widely it has been accepted by the courts (see boxes below).

NEGLIGENT INTERFERENCE WITH A PROSPECTIVE ECONOMIC ADVANTAGE

The defendant does not intentionally interfere but does so negligently. For example, the defendant negligently spills a dangerous chemical, requiring the neighborhood to be evacuated with resulting loss of business to the plaintiff. A few courts have recognized such claims, but negligently caused economic harm is generally not actionable.

Dobbs, *The Law of Torts* §446 (2000)

> **NEGLIGENT INTERFERENCE WITH CONTRACT OR PROSPECTIVE CONTRACTUAL RELATION**
>
> One is not liable to another for pecuniary harm not deriving from physical harm to the other, if that harm results from the actor's negligently
>
> a. causing a third person not to perform a contract with the other, or
> b. interfering with the other's performance of his contract or making the performance more expensive or burdensome, or
> c. interfering with the other's acquiring a contractual relation with a third person.
>
> *Restatement (Second) of Torts, §766C*

■ WRONGFUL DISCHARGE

The employment relationship between employer and employee is generally "at will"—that is, both the employer and employee can end the relationship at any time. However, state and federal laws have limited the exercise of this option, as a matter of social policy such as ending an employment relationship because of a worker's religious beliefs.

To make a claim for **wrongful discharge,** a plaintiff must prove, by a preponderance of the evidence, these elements:

- an employment relationship
- termination by the employer
- in violation of certain laws designed to advance a social policy
- that results in damages.

For example, the plaintiff would have a claim for wrongful discharge if the termination of employment:

- meant violating law against discrimination
- interfered with an employee's fulfillment of a civil obligation, such as jury duty
- came in retaliation for filing a worker's compensation claim
- was the result of filing a lawsuit.

Different from Wrongful Interference with a Contractual Relationship

The tort of wrongful discharge is not the same as interference with a contractual relationship, because that tort involves a third party. Wrongful discharge, on the other hand, involves only an employer and employee.

Whistleblowers

Whistleblower laws encourage workers to come forward and disclose violations of the law or business policy without having to fear losing a job in retaliation for having "blown the whistle" on their employer. Some states and the federal government have enacted such laws (for example, 31 U.S.C. § 3729 (1982), The False Claims Act).

Case in Point 8-8 involves a university professor who sought the audit of an account at his school. The professor alleged that calling for the audit may have led to his termination. In talking about the tort of wrongful discharge, the trial court notes that Ohio had created its own "whistleblower" law.

CASE IN POINT 8-8

Marcuso v. University of Cincinnati

150 Ohio App. 3d 69 (Franklin County 2002)

On October 29, 1999, appellant, Dr. Marc Marcuso, filed a complaint in the Ohio Court of Claims against appellee, the University of Cincinnati ("University"), alleging that he had been wrongfully terminated in violation of Ohio public policy. [...]

Appellant received his Ph.D. in physics from the University in 1979 and became employed in its physics department in 1984. In April 1985, appellant donated $400 to the University and deposited it into a restricted gift fund called the Physics Educational Laboratory Fund. When appellant set up the fund, he specified that the general purpose of the fund and restriction on the use of the fund were as follows: "Shall be used solely to meet hardware expenses involved in the development of new physics-related experiments for undergraduate students." [...]

In 1990, appellant also donated $150 to the fund [...] Beginning in 1986, a third contribution to the fund came from an agreement [...] by which ten percent of the royalties from the sales of a lab manual were deposited into the fund. [...]

In July 1997, appellant wanted to purchase some overhead projector systems for use in classrooms [...] and contacted the University of Cincinnati Foundation to determine how much money remained in the fund. He was told the fund was depleted. Appellant began to investigate how the money had been spent and contacted the internal audit services department to request a transaction history of the fund. The money had been spent in February 1992, on new carpet for the laboratory in which appellant worked.

As a result of appellant's request, the audit department sent an inquiry and the transaction history to the Dean of the College of Arts and Sciences. The Dean contacted the head of the physics department, who consulted with the physics department business manager and determined that the expenditure of funds was legitimate.

Appellant testified that he became aware of a rumor that he was trying to get the head of the physics department, Dr. Peter Suranyi, in trouble by instituting the audit. He attempted to discuss his concerns with Dr. Suranyi, regarding the use of the fund and his belief that the fund was misused. Appellant believed that a conflict of interest existed between his supervisors, Dr. Richard G. Gass and Dr. Richard Newrock, and himself since he believed that Dr. Gass attempted to take credit for his idea regarding image capture experiments using video. His relationship with his other supervisor, Dr. Newrock, deteriorated because appellant believed that Dr. Newrock broke promises to develop a budget for appellant's lab. Appellant argued as well that Dr. Newrock objected to the passage of rights from the University to appellant to a data acquisition instrument that appellant designed. The two had a disagreement in 1991 over appellant's job duties and Dr. Newrock had threatened to fire appellant. Appellant believed that one or both of his supervisors wanted him fired as retaliation for his initiating the audit.

In appellant's review dated June 1998, Dr. Gass listed one of the problems appellant was having was working with other members of the department, and an example given was that he filed a complaint with the University alleging misuse of funds without bringing the problem to the attention of the department head first. Dr. Gass wanted to meet with appellant to discuss his yearly evaluation, but appellant refused to meet in Dr. Gass' office because they had met in appellant's office in the past and appellant feared a confrontational meeting.

Dr. Gass delivered a letter to appellant on June 15, 1998, rescheduling the evaluation meeting for Tuesday, June 16, 1998, in Dr. Gass' office but appellant again failed to appear. In July 1998, appellant received another letter [...] which outlined the need for his cooperation in the renovation of the physics department building and stated his new responsibilities, including supervising a new staff member. Appellant was expected to sign the letter as an acknowledgement of his agreement by July 9, 1998; however, appellant refused to sign the letter and, in a letter dated July 28, 1998, appellant's services were terminated with six-months notice.

[...]

Appellant contends that [...] public policy is jeopardized if an employer can ignore a statute and then fire an employee for complaining about it, as in this case where appellant contends that his employment was terminated because he complained about how the money in the physics fund was spent. [...]

In this case, the trial court found that appellant may have been attempting to assert a claim under R.C. 4113.52, Ohio's Whistleblower Protection Act, and he did not comply with that statute and, therefore, the claim lacked merit; however, the trial court also analyzed appellant's claim, pursuant to R.C. 3345.16, which appellant argues is the only public policy that his claim is based upon. The trial court found that, assuming appellant had met the first two elements of the tort, the clarity element and the jeopardy element, he failed to prove by a preponderance of the evidence that the termination of his employment was motivated by his conduct in instituting the internal audit and, thus, he failed to prove the fourth element, the overriding justification element, of his tort claim.

[...]

In his 1996 performance evaluation, before his audit request, Dr. Gass advised appellant of the need to have better communication with the other members of the department. In his 1997 performance evaluation, Dr. Gass noted that appellant behaved unprofessionally during the preparation of the department's Ohio Board of Regents' request by repeatedly ignoring requests for information that would have strengthened the request. Dr. Gass also noted that appellant needed to improve cooperation and communication with other members of the department. In his 1998 performance evaluation, there were several instances listed of appellant's refusal to cooperate with other members of the department. For example, Dr. Gass listed that appellant had filed a complaint with the University alleging misuse of department funds before approaching the department head, he refused to attend a meeting until instructed to do so by the department head, he failed to respond to his supervisor's and the facility committee chairman's requests for a list of goals for 1999, he failed to respond to a request for input on the renovation of Braunstein Hall in which he worked, he failed to respond to two requests to attend a meeting to discuss his evaluation, and was generally insubordinate to everyone except the department head. Dr. Gass also noted that cooperation and collaboration with other department members has been a continuing problem and had not improved, even though it had been mentioned in his last two evaluations. His numerical rating on his performance evaluation decreased in each of these years.

Both Dr. Gass and the department head at that time, Dr. Suranyi, testified that appellant's employment was terminated because he was insubordinate and refused to sign the letter which outlined his new duties. [...] Dr. Gass testified that mentioning the incident in appellant's performance evaluation was a form of discipline. Dr. Suranyi testified that, at the conclusion of the investigation into the use of the fund, it was determined that there was no impropriety.

> [...]
>   The trial court concluded, and we agree, that [...] appellant did not prove that his dismissal was motivated by his action in instituting the internal audit. Appellee had a legitimate overriding business justification for its decision to terminate appellant's employment. Appellant's lack of cooperation for several years and his refusal to accept his new duties constituted a legitimate overriding business justification for its decision to terminate appellant's employment. Thus, appellant failed to present evidence on all of the elements of the tort for wrongful discharge in violation of public policy [...].
>   For the foregoing reasons, appellant's assignment of error is overruled, and the judgment of the Ohio Court of Claims is affirmed.

Since there was a valid, independent business reason to end the professor's employment, the appellate court upheld the determination that no wrongful discharge had occurred.

■ BAD FAITH BREACH OF CONTRACT

A contract is a legally enforceable agreement (see box below).

DEFINITION OF CONTRACT

A contract is a promise or a set of promises for the breach of which the law gives a remedy, or the performance of which the law in some way recognizes as a duty.

Restatement (Second) of Contracts §1 (1965)

When a breach of contract has occurred, the usual remedy involves giving the non-breaching party what was promised under the contract as a form of damages.

For the plaintiff to make a claim of bad faith breach of contract, the plaintiff must prove, by a preponderance of the evidence, the following elements:

- a valid contract exists
- the defendant's intentional failure to honor the terms of the contract
- the failure causes harm to plaintiff
- where no good faith defense exists for such a failure

The tort of **bad faith breach of contract** goes beyond a mere breach of the legal agreement. Here, "bad faith breach" suggests that the breaching party may have even entered into an agreement only to cheat the non-breaching party.

This tort often arises when a claim is filed under an insurance policy (although it is not limited to this). For example, a plaintiff files a claim according to the terms of the policy and the defendant refuses to honor the terms of the contract and pay the claim. The plaintiff files suit for this tort, contending that the insurance company either never intended to honor the policy or acted in so derelict a manner that even if the company paid out under the policy, the difficulty in obtaining payment effectively neutralized the terms of the policy.

More Than Just a Claim for Breach of Contract

The tort of bad faith breach of contract recognizes that the breaching party has acted in a fashion so extremely wrong that the remedy needs to be greater than that for a simple breach of contract. This arises, in part, out of an implicit promise that the parties have acted in good faith. The tort of bad faith breach of contract recognizes that the defendant has gone beyond a breach of a contractual obligation to act in good faith. The existence of this tort gives the plaintiff a remedy in addition to an equally valid claim for breach of contract (see box below).

WHEN BAD FAITH BREACH OF CONTRACT IS ACTIONABLE UNDER TORT LAW INSTEAD OF CONTRACT LAW

Courts generally recognize that contracting parties are under a duty to act in good faith so as not to deprive the other party of the benefits expressly implicitly allocated to him by the contract and contemplated by the parties. This is usually called an implied covenant of good faith and fair dealing.

Under the traditional rule, the defendant who breaches the implied covenant of good faith is liable in contract, not in tort and the remedies are circumscribed accordingly.

The insurer would…be required to honor its contractual obligation to defend the insured as well as to pay judgment against him up to the policy limits. If the insurer breaches these obligations, so that the insured is subject to liability beyond the policy limits, the insurer is liable in tort, not merely in contract.

Dobbs, *The Law of Torts* §453 (2000)

Courts have tended to recognize the need to apply this tort outside of an insurer's bad faith in honoring an insurance policy.

Case in Point 8-9 illustrates how an insurance company in bad faith might avoid honoring the terms of a policy for injuries that would arise out of an automobile accident.

 # CASE IN POINT 8-9

Goodson v. American Standard Insurance Company of Wisconsin

89 P.3d 409 (Colo. 2004)

I.

In May, 1995, Dawn Goodson and her two minor children were involved in an automobile accident. They were stopped at a red light when a vehicle struck them from behind. Chet Weber owned the vehicle that Goodson was driving at the time of the accident. Weber gave Goodson authorization to drive his vehicle. Weber was a named insured of American Standard Insurance Company of Wisconsin ("American Standard"). Goodson timely notified American Standard of the collision.

Goodson delayed seeking medical treatment for herself and her children for over a year because she was concerned about the cost of medical bills and was unaware of the personal injury protection ("PIP") benefits available under Weber's policy. In July, 1996, Goodson and her children began receiving chiropractic treatment for their injuries. Around that time, Goodson learned of the possibility of receiving PIP benefits and submitted to American Standard an application for PIP benefits. Around October, 1996, Goodson submitted her outstanding chiropractic bills to American Standard for payment. American Standard disputed Goodson's claim from the outset. First, American Standard took the position that the PIP benefits under Weber's policy were subject to reduction because Goodson and her children received treatment from a provider that was not a member of American Standard's preferred provider organization ("PPO"). [...] Third, in December, 1997, American Standard agreed that the policy was effective at the time of the collision, but asked Goodson and her children to undergo an independent medical evaluation ("IME") to determine whether their injuries were related to the accident and whether their medical treatment was reasonable and necessary. In April 1998, American Standard finally paid the full amount of the outstanding medical bills, which totaled slightly over $8,000.

In July, 1998, Goodson filed suit against American Standard, alleging the following claims: breach of contract; bad faith breach of insurance contract; outrageous conduct; and willful and wanton breach of insurance contract [...] The case was submitted to the jury solely on the tort claim of bad faith breach of insurance contract. [...]

The jury returned a general verdict against American Standard, awarding Goodson and her children $75,000 in actual damages. Moreover, the jury found beyond a reasonable doubt that American Standard's breach was willful and wanton, and awarded $75,000 in punitive damages.

[...]

Here, American Standard delayed the payment due under the policy for a year and a half after Goodson submitted her outstanding bills for payment. Goodson proved to the jury that she suffered emotional distress as a result of this delay. The anxiety, fear, stress, and uncertainty she experienced occurred as a result of her worry about whether she would be financially responsible for her medical bills, which American Standard refused to pay.

An insured purchases insurance in the first place so as not to suffer such anxiety, fear, stress, and uncertainty. The fact that an insurer finally pays in full does not erase the distress caused by the bad faith conduct. Damages for emotional distress the insured proves are therefore available in actions for bad faith breach of insurance contract upon the showing of the insurer's liability [...].

Insureds such as Goodson should be able to proceed to the jury on all damages that flow from a breach of the duty of good faith and fair dealing. [...]

Accordingly, we [...] remand the case to that court with instructions to reinstate the trial court's judgment entered on the jury verdict [...].

The court found the defendant's resistance and delaying on the payment of the claim was so extreme as to go beyond a mere claim of breach of contract, and agreed that the plaintiff should receive additional damages just for extreme conduct.

KEY TERMS

SUMMARY

Our capitalist society recognizes the difficulty a business operator faces just to stay in operation. It has provided relief from certain types of business-related torts. For example, deception can raise costs to the point of bankrupting a business. Disparagement of a business's reputation or product can increase the cost of competition. Society also knows that an imbalance of power can develop in an employment relationship and guards against practices that violate social policies for equality. Even where parties to a contract engage in egregiously inappropriate conduct, society has provided options to stem the damages that can arise out of the tortious bad faith conduct of a party.

CONCEPT REVIEW QUESTIONS

1. What must a plaintiff allege to win at trial an action for fraud?
2. Explain the differences between intentional and negligent misrepresentation.
3. Contrast disparagement of title with commercial disparagement; what unique aspects of a business do they focus on?
4. What are the ways that a defendant can interfere with a plaintiff's contractual relations?
5. Explain the differences between intentional and negligent interference with prospective economic advantage.
6. In an action for intentional or negligent interference with prospective economic advantage, why does a plaintiff have a significant problem in establishing damages?
7. Identify at least three reasons why, as a matter of public policy, an employer may not terminate an "at-will" employment.
8. What level of conduct must a defendant reach to go beyond a breach of contract to the level of a bad faith breach of conduct?

CRITICAL THINKING APPLICATIONS

1. A manufacturer claims as a business expense payments made to a parts supplier. The manufacturer claims to have paid the supplier an extra $10,000 beyond what it paid. The supplier does not know this, and when it files its federal tax return, the IRS assesses a penalty against the supplier for failing to note

the additional $10,000. Will the manufacturer be liable to the supplier? Under what theory of tort law? Why?

2. A radio station lures a popular programmer from a competitor while the programmer was still under contract with the competitor. Assume that the competitor files suit and the radio station files for a motion to dismiss. What is the tort theory that the competitor alleges against the radio station? Will the court grant the radio station's motion? Why or why not?

3. A business operator buys a list of potential sales contacts. An employee of the business operator copies the list and sells it to the business operator's competitor. Will the business operator be able to bring suit using any of the tort theories of recovery mentioned in this chapter? Which, if any? Why or why not? Whom should the operator sue?

4. Using the scenario in Problem 3: The business operator has been on the lookout for potential investors. After the employee copied the list of sales contacts, the employee e-mailed it to a prospective investor. Also, the employee unintentionally e-mailed the list to all prospective investors, even those that the business operator had rejected. Have any of the theories of tort here occurred? If so, which one? Why?

5. A business offers its employees a pension but makes it available only if the employee has been with the business for five years. An employee is terminated after four years and eleven months, on the grounds that the employee has been coming to work drunk. This is not true. If the employee sues the employer, what would the theory of recovery be? If the employer files for a summary judgment against the employee, what ruling will the court likely grant? Why?

6. A driver gets into an automobile accident and files a claim for recovery under the insurance company the driver purchased from an insurance company. Over the years, the insurance policy has found that it can deny claims and that sometimes people do not object to the denial of coverage. It institutes a policy to deny coverage against all claims related to automobile accidents. The driver wants to sue the insurance company. Among the theories mentioned in this chapter, which would be the best one to use? Why?

7. Because the child of a barbershop owner has chosen to date a business owner's child, the business owner has arranged to open a barbershop next door. The business owner does not expect to make money by operating this new barbershop. Will the barbershop owner have a theory in tort, among those mentioned in this chapter, for a suit against the business owner? Why or why not? What would be the most likely theory of tort recovery, from the torts mentioned in this chapter?

8. A contractor has entered into a legally binding agreement with a community to repair a stretch of the community's main road. The contractor begins to repair the road. One of the contractor's competitors, who had also bid on the project but was not hired, visits the work site during early-morning hours and wrecks the contractor's work from the day before. Among the theories of tort mentioned in the chapter, what would be the most likely one for the contractor to bring against the competitor whose bid had been rejected? Why?

SKILL-BUILDING APPLICATION

TEF Company, an insurance brokerage company, provides its corporate clients an array of services, including but not limited to risk management. TEF agrees to purchase the Davis Risk Management (DRM) Company. As part of the deal, DRM's CEO Jason Davis was given a personal services contract for five years to work for

TEF. Two years after the completion of the purchase, TEF's CEO announced her retirement. In the running as her replacement was TEF's Chief Operating Officer Jocelyne Bonin and Davis. The TEF board of directors select Bonin. Davis does not like this decision, and through a series of e-mails, contacted Russell and Curtis Durrenberger, two high-level management employees who had come from DRM. The e-mails focus on starting a new risk management company made up of all former DRM employees as well as selected members of TEF's management team. Davis and the Durrenbergers resigned from TEF to start up DDD Risk Management Services. The new business immediately solicits business from New England Breeze, LLC, New England's premier alternative-energy business and TEF's very first customer.

TEF sues DDD. What cause or causes of action can TEF file against DDD from those torts mentioned in this chapter? Indicate what evidence, from the facts provided, would support each element of the tort or torts that TEF can bring against DDD. Predict an outcome at trial for TEF, and explain why a court likely will rule as it does on the cause or causes of action filed by TEF.

It is from the level of calamities, not that
of every day life, that we learn impressive
and useful lessons.

—William Makepeace Thackeray
(1811–1863)

Doctrine of Nuisance | CHAPTER 9

The doctrine of nuisance occupies a unique place in the law of torts. Virtually *any* interference with an individual's interests has been termed a nuisance by the courts at one time or another. Such generalization and lack of clear definition has resulted in a tangled web of fact and principle that makes the doctrine of nuisance difficult to grasp. Technically, the doctrine of nuisance does not offer a specific cause of action but rather refers to the harm caused by the use of one's property that interferes with the interests of another. This chapter deals with the origins and fundamental principles of the nuisance doctrine, the distinction between a private and a public nuisance, and the interests to be protected.

CHAPTER TOPICS

1. Doctrine of Nuisance
2. Private Nuisance
3. Public Nuisance
4. Remedies

OBJECTIVES

After completing this chapter, you will be able to:

1. Discuss the nature and history of the concept of nuisance.
2. Analyze the interests and requirements of a private nuisance.
3. Define the invasion of rights involved in a nuisance.
4. Discuss how a nuisance interferes with the use and enjoyment of land.
5. Identify the nature of a public nuisance.
6. Discuss the remedies available for a nuisance.

■ DOCTRINE OF NUISANCE

A substantial or unreasonable interference with another's property interests may constitute a **nuisance.** A nuisance might involve any activity that causes annoyance or inconvenience or endangers life or health, but not necessarily or automatically any of those activities (see box below).

NUISANCE AS DESCRIBED IN THE RESTATEMENT (SECOND), COMMENT TO § 821A.

The term frequently is used in several different senses. In popular speech it often has a very loose connotation of anything harmful, annoying, offensive or inconvenient, as when it is said that a man makes a nuisance of himself by bothering others. Occasionally this careless usage has crept into a court opinion. If the term is to have any definite legal significance, these cases must be completely disregarded.

In its legal significance, "nuisance" has been employed in three different senses:

1. It is often used to denote human activity or a physical condition that is harmful or annoying to others. Thus it is often said that indecent conduct or a rubbish heap or the smoking chimney of a factory is a nuisance.
2. It is often used to denote the harm caused by the human conduct or physical condition described in the first meaning. Thus it may be said that the annoyance caused by loud noises or by objectionable odors is a nuisance to the person affected by them.

    When the word is used in either of these two senses it does not necessarily connote tort liability. The courts that use the word in either sense will often proceed to discuss whether the particular "nuisance" is actionable and may conclude that it is not.
3. Often, however, the term has been used to denote both the conduct or condition and the resulting harm with the addition of the legal liability that arises from the combination of the two.

    Thus the courts may say that a person is maintaining a nuisance, meaning that he is engaged in an activity or is creating a condition that is harmful or annoying to others and for which he is legally liable [...]

Restatement Second of Torts, §821A

According to this definition a wide range of conduct can constitute a nuisance. That makes sense in light of the nature of the tort, since the type of interference can change according to the time, place, and individuals affected.

Private or Public

Interference can affect an individual (private nuisance) or a community (public nuisance). It can apply to so many situations that courts have used the term to describe the impact of the harm rather than label any one activity a nuisance. The courts have also found it easier to fashion a remedy by focusing on the harm caused, since the character of the interference may change. For example, a barking watchdog might be welcomed by neighbors who want safety but regarded as a nuisance if they want to sleep with the windows open. Thus, some nights, the dog may need to be kept inside.

Elements for Recovery

To win in court on a claim of nuisance, the plaintiff will have to show, by a pre-ponderance of the evidence, the following elements:

- an intentional act
- that causes substantial and unreasonable interference with the **use and enjoyment** of real or personal property
- that causes substantial harm

A nuisance focuses less on a defendant's conduct and more on the degree to which a plaintiffs interest in property is impaired.

In the *Padilla* case, the New Mexico appeals court looked at the impact of the defendant's conduct on the plaintiffs, who owned property adjacent to that of the defendant, where the defendant operated a business that generated noise and noxious fumes(see Case in Point 9-1).

 # CASE IN POINT 9-1

Padilla v. Lawrence

101 N.M. 556 (Ct. App. 1984)

Atanacio Padilla, Juanita Padilla, and their son, Johnny E. Padilla ("plaintiffs"), long-term residents of Bernalillo, New Mexico, filed a class action complaint against defendant Amy Lawrence and defendant Sun Country Garden Products, a corporation ("the plant"). Lawrence is the owner of the plant, also located in Bernalillo, which processes bark and manure for the purpose of packaging soil conditioner for sale. Plaintiffs requested an injunction against the plant and sought money damages based upon theories of trespass, public nuisance, private nuisance, negligence, and personal injury....

Plaintiffs Atanacio and Juanita Padilla own real property on which their residence is located, which is approximately 600 feet from the nearest boundary of the plant. They have resided in the house for over twenty-five years. The plant has been in operation for approximately five years. It is located in the industrial park of Bernalillo and covers over nine acres. Plaintiffs' house is among several residences near the plant. The record indicates that these residences are outside the industrial park.

[...]

The witnesses testified that the plant's operation has resulted in plaintiffs' exposure to odors, dust, noise, and flies, which were not in evidence prior to construction and operation. The witnesses testified that an odor, variously described as that of a dead animal, of a pig pen, and of rotten fish, permeated the air, and that dust, noise, and flies were also a problem. The odor prohibited cooking in the summer, prevented use of evaporative cooling, and generally interfered with normal residential activities. Plaintiff Atanacio Padilla testified that the odor and dust caused him to have nosebleeds and fits of choking.

Mr. Padilla also testified that he and his wife finally moved from the residence in 1982 because of the problems associated with the plant's operation and that the nosebleeds and choking have stopped. Plaintiff Johnny E. Padilla testified that he began renting the residence at that time and that the problems continue. The realtor testified that the plant's operation caused problems that affected the property's value as a residence [....]

A private nuisance has been defined as a non-trespassory invasion of another's interest in the private use and enjoyment of land [....] It is a civil wrong based on a disturbance of rights in land [....] The elements of proof depend on whether the conduct is intentional or unintentional. Liability for intentional conduct requires that the conduct be unreasonable.[...]

[...]

[T]he evidence would support a finding that the invasion was intentional because defendants knew or should have known that their conduct in operating the plant interfered with plaintiffs' use and enjoyment of their land. (citation omitted) Evidence also supports the finding that the operation of the plant was unreasonable.

[...]

The trial court found that the operation of the plant deprived plaintiffs from enjoying the use of their property and caused plaintiffs Atanacio and Juanita Padilla to move away from their residence of twenty-five years. Further, there was evidence that the property would be difficult to sell for residential purposes and the court found that the value of the residence has been diminished. Plaintiffs Atanacio and Juanita Padilla established their home long before defendants began operating the plant, and priority of occupation is a circumstance of considerable weight in determining unreasonableness....There was substantial evidence to support the trial court's finding of unreasonableness. The finding of a private nuisance is affirmed. Given the noise and smells that would accompany the combination of bark mulch and manure into a type of conditioner for soil, the court had no difficulty finding that defendant's conduct substantially impaired plaintiffs' use and enjoyment of plaintiffs' adjacent residential property.

The court ruled that the plaintiffs really could not enjoy their property with the business operating next door. Perhaps more importantly, they had lived there before the business began, so in legal parlance it could be said that "the nuisance came to them." Conversely, property owners who move in next door to a business might expect to experience some impairment of the ability to enjoy and use that property.

Nature of Interference

The doctrine of nuisance provides a remedy only if an interference is substantial and unreasonable.

Substantial

For interference to be **substantial,** the plaintiff must suffer more than a trivial injury. No set definition for "trivial" exists, but some courts have construed the term in light of the appropriateness of using the courts to issue a remedy; no judge would want to delay a criminal trial, for example, because of a plaintiff's suit about a defendant's trivial nuisance. As a famous legal scholar has noted, "The law does not concern itself with trifles." For example, setting off fireworks may be a trivial nuisance if your neighbors do it only on the Fourth of July, but it might be substantial if they do it every night (and, of course, this assumes that setting off fireworks is legal).

Unreasonable

A court might find that an **unreasonable** interference goes beyond what many people would consider appropriate for the use of property (see box below).

Courts could consider several factors in trying to determine whether an interference is unreasonable:

- Whether the plaintiff has suffered substantial harm
- The defendant's ability to bear the loss (for example, being able to pass the cost on to customers or to carrying insurance against such a loss)
- How the defendant used his or her property
- Whether the defendant's conduct suited that locale
- Which interest arose first?

The courts have not settled on a single definition of what constitutes unreasonable, in part because the facts used to determine unreasonableness can vary widely. For this reason, the courts examine the larger context in which the interference has occurred. In the *Rodrigue* case, the Louisiana Supreme Court determined the unreasonable interference of a large Christmas display in a noncommercial neighborhood (see Case in Point 9-2).

CASE IN POINT 9-2

Rodrigue v. Copeland

475 So.2d 1071 (La. 1985)

Plaintiffs, three residents of the Pontchartrain Shores Subdivision in Jefferson Parish, instituted this action to enjoin defendant, Alvin C. Copeland, from erecting and operating his annual Christmas display. The plaintiffs sought injunctive relief...due to problems associated with an enormous influx of visitors to their limited access, residential neighborhood [....]

Since 1977 defendant has annually maintained a Christmas display on his premises at 5001 Folse Drive. The display has grown in size and popularity since the year of its inception. The display consists of an extravagant array of lights and lighted figures accompanied by traditional Christmas music. The neighborhood is a limited access area which is zoned solely for single-family residences [....]

Since 1982 defendant's exhibition has drawn numerous spectators to the neighborhood during the hours while the display is in operation. The spectators view the display either from their automobiles or on foot after parking their vehicles in the surrounding neighborhood. The increased congestion in the neighborhood has created numerous problems for some of the defendant's neighbors such as restricted access to their homes, noise, public urination, property damage and a lack of on-street parking [....]

As a general rule, the landowner is free to exercise his rights of ownership in any manner he sees fit. He may even use his property in ways which "...occasion some inconvenience to his neighbor." However, his extensive rights do not allow him to do "real damage" to his neighbor [....]

At issue in this case is whether Copeland's light and sound display has caused a mere inconvenience or real damage to his neighbors and their right to enjoy their own premises.

In determining whether an activity or work occasions real damage or mere inconvenience, a court is required to determine the reasonableness of the conduct in light of the circumstances. This analysis requires consideration of factors such as the character of the neighborhood, the degree of the intrusion and the effect of the activity on the health and safety of the neighbors.

[...] [W]e conclude that defendant's display has occasioned real damage, not mere inconvenience, upon plaintiffs. Likewise, we conclude that plaintiffs will be irreparably harmed unless injunctive relief is granted.

Defendant's exhibition constitutes an unreasonable intrusion into the lives of his neighbors when considered in light of the character of the neighborhood, the degree of the intrusion and its effect on the use and enjoyment of their properties by his neighbors.

[...]

The damage suffered by plaintiffs during the operation of defendant's display is extensive, both in terms of its duration and its size. Defendant's display becomes operative in early December and remains in operation until January 5. During this period, plaintiffs are forced to contend with a flow of bumper to bumper traffic through their limited access neighborhood. In addition, they must endure the noise and property abuse associated with the crowd of visitors who congregate near the display.

The display begins operation at dusk each evening and continues until 11:00 p.m. on weekdays and 12:00 midnight on weekends. The display is occasionally operational beyond midnight. While in operation, it features an extravagant display of lights which are located across the front of defendant's residence, on the roof and in the enclosed yard to the west of the residence. Some of the lights comprising the display are shaped into figures such as a star, a reindeer, a snowman, three angels and a depiction of Santa and his reindeer. Lights are also located in the trees and shrubs. In addition to the lights, the display features a tapestry proclaiming "Glory to God in the Highest" and a creche.

Noise emanates from the display and from the visitors. The display is accompanied by traditional Christmas music which is amplified through loudspeakers located on the second floor of defendant's residence. The music is audible inside the home of Mary Borrell. The plaintiffs also complain of noise emanating from car engines, car horns, the slamming of car doors and police whistles.

The record clearly indicates that traffic in the neighborhood is congested due to the slow progress of vehicles carrying spectators by the display. The traffic has seriously impaired the ability of plaintiffs to gain access to and from their premises. Furthermore, on-street parking for plaintiffs or their guests becomes virtually nonexistent. As a result of the traffic congestion and lack of parking, plaintiffs and children of defendant's neighbors cannot have their own Christmas celebrations and gatherings....

Plaintiffs' injury stems from the nature and size of the display which render it incompatible with a restricted access, residential neighborhood. Defendant is enjoined from erecting and operating a Christmas exhibition which is calculated to and does attract an unusually large number of visitors to the neighborhood.

The court concluded that while some might celebrate a holiday with displays of light and music, such displays go beyond a reasonable use of the property when the display attracts viewers and runs late into the night for six weeks.

Significant Harm and the "Normal Person" Standard

Taking a different perspective, the courts may consider what a normal person would think amounts to significant harm.

The *Restatement (Second) of Torts* takes the position that liability for nuisance exists only if a "normal" person in a community would feel the intrusion produced significant harm (see box below).

SIGNIFICANT HARM

There is liability for a nuisance only to those to whom it causes significant harm, of a kind that would be suffered by a normal person in the community or by property in normal condition and used for a normal purpose.

Restatement (Second) of Torts, §821F

The harm must be of some importance and involve more than slight annoyance. If the harm involves some detrimental change to the land itself, there can be little doubt that a cause of action in nuisance exists. When the invasion involves only personal discomfort, it becomes more difficult to determine whether an action for nuisance can be maintained. The standard to be applied is that of how a normal person is affected by the invasion and is similar to the reasonable person standard applied in negligence cases.

As an example, assume that Alphonse celebrated Independence Day with a fireworks display for his family and friends. The fireworks display lasted two hours and produced brilliant colors and loud noise that could be seen and heard by his neighbor, Semple. In fact, Semple was deprived of sleep while the display lasted. While Semple may have been annoyed, absent an ordinance that deals with creating such displays in a community, Semple would not likely prevail in an action for nuisance. Had Alphonse repeated the display for the next four days, well beyond the holiday period, Semple may have reasonable grounds for an action for nuisance.

States vary on whether to use the normalcy test. Most do, but paralegals should research a jurisdiction's laws to see whether that test applies.

Legality of Actions

That a defendant has engaged in a legal activity does not necessarily prevent a plaintiff from winning an action in nuisance (see box below).

DEFENDANT'S CONDUCT NEED NOT NECESSARILY BE ILLEGAL TO CREATE LIABILITY.

The question is not whether the activity itself is an improper, unsuitable or illegal thing to do in the place where it is being carried on, but whether the actor is carrying it on in a careful manner or at a proper time.

Restatement (Second) of Torts, §830 comment c.

Conduct of Others

If multiple persons or businesses severely and unreasonably interfer with a plaintiff's use and enjoyment of property, the plaintiff may face a difficult task in having to choose whom to sue. In addition, a court might find it difficult to conclude that the particular defendant's interference, individually, was substantial enough to merit recovery.

Worse, the fact that two or more parties engage in the interference can complicate the issue about the unreasonableness of the interference. For example, a plaintiff living next door to an industrial park will have less of a chance at recovery than if he lived in a residential area where one business had already operated. In Case in Point 9-3, the plaintiffs sued the defendants whose street parking, while legal, made it difficult for the plaintiffs to get out of their driveway.

CASE IN POINT 9-3

Cunningham v. Quintanilla

2004 Tex. App. 1077 (Tex. App. Tyler Feb. 4, 2004)

This case had its genesis in a dispute over the parking on Windomere Avenue in the Winnetka Heights Addition of Dallas, Texas.

Appellees Leonore Quintanilla ("Quintanilla") and Christine Escobedo ("Escobedo") brought suit against Gary Penn, D.D.S. ("Penn"), his employee Sarah Cunningham ("Cunningham"), and Appellees' next door neighbor, Johnny Wayne Howard ("Howard"), asserting causes of action for private nuisance [...] We affirm the judgment of private nuisance [...]

In November 1994, Appellee Escobedo bought the house located at 205 South Windomere Avenue in the Winnetka Heights subdivision in Oak Cliff near its intersection with West Jefferson Boulevard. On the other side of Windomere, Appellant Penn had practiced dentistry since 1981, although the address of his clinic is 1418 West Jefferson Boulevard. There is no off-street parking for Penn's clinic, and Penn, his employees, and patients parked on Windomere immediately behind the clinic. At that time, parking was allowed on both sides of Windomere.

When she moved in, Escobedo noticed that it was difficult to get in and out of her narrow driveway in her Toyota Camry if cars were parked on both sides of the street. The roadway had a high crown which frequently caused the bottom of her car to scrape the street surface when she tried to enter or leave her driveway. The high curbs and narrow driveways further aggravated the situation.

When Escobedo bought the house, Penn and his office manager frequently parked in front of her house on her side of the street. Escobedo approached Penn about the problem, and he initially seemed sympathetic, but did nothing to alleviate the problem and continued to park in front of her house. Escobedo turned to the City of Dallas Department of Transportation in an effort to obtain a no-parking zone on both sides of the street in front of her house. The Department of Transportation told her, however, that Penn's signature on the petition would be necessary if parking was to be restricted on his side of the street. She did not or could not obtain Penn's signature on the petition, but, in June of 1996, she did succeed in having the area adjacent to her driveway on her side of the street designated as a no-parking zone. The curb on the clinic side of the street remained a legal parking zone. Although this improved access somewhat, according to Escobedo, Penn, his staff, and patients frequently parked in the no-parking area. There matters stood without incident for two-and-a-half years because Escobedo's time was devoted to caring for two sick parents in addition to her work.

Appellee Quintanilla moved in with Escobedo as a tenant in January of 1999. She drove a Nissan 300 ZX, and it was especially difficult for her to enter or leave her driveway without the car's undercarriage scraping the street or driveway. Early during the summer of 1999, Quintanilla began leaving notes on cars parked legally across the street from her driveway demanding that they not park there.

[...]

Escobedo and Quintanilla [...] procured several surveillance cameras [...] in January of 2000 to watch the street and the dental clinic. During the next year, Escobedo had six flat tires all caused by screws or nails. The Escobedo-Quintanilla videos showed one instance of Cunningham "shooting the bird" at Escobedo and Quintanilla as they videotaped her leaving work at the clinic. It also recorded Cunningham kicking something off the street in the direction of Escobedo's car which was parked on the street. That same day, Escobedo had a flat. Although not captured on video, Quintanilla testified that on one occasion, Cunningham called her a "bitch."

[...]

The trial court found for Escobedo and Quintanilla [...] granting judgment as follows:

1. That the Defendants' actions in parking in a legal parking zone located across the street from the Plaintiffs' driveway constituted a substantial interference with the Plaintiffs' use of their property located at 205 South Windomere and thereby constituted a private nuisance;
2. That the Defendants [...] be permanently enjoined from parking directly across from the driveway of the residence of the Plaintiffs located at 205 South Windomere [...];
3. That the Defendants are to take necessary precautions to prevent others that are visiting or working with them from parking directly across from the driveway located at 205 South Windomere [...]
7. That the Plaintiff Quintanilla recover from the Defendants Cunningham and Penn, jointly and severally, the sum of $ 11,265.35;
8. That the Plaintiff Escobedo recover from the Defendants Cunningham and Penn, jointly and severally, the sum of $ 753.42;

[...]

Appellant Cunningham [...] contends that the evidence does not support Appellees' recovery on the theory of private nuisance. In his first issue, Appellant Penn also contends that the evidence does not support the trial court's finding of private nuisance.

[...]

But in order to constitute a private nuisance, the condition or acts of the defendant must interfere substantially with the use and enjoyment of the plaintiff's land by causing unreasonable discomfort or annoyance to persons of ordinary sensibilities attempting to use it. (citation omitted)

There is a great deal of evidence that it is difficult to get in and out of Escobedo's drive when cars are parked on the street opposite her residence. There is some evidence that because of the Winnetka Heights Historical Area restriction, Escobedo cannot widen her drive, that Quintanilla was once late to an examination because she could not get out of her driveway, and also evidence that Appellees' cars as well as Appellant Cunningham's vehicle have suffered some damage as a result of the parking problem on the street in front of Escobedo's house. The record also supports the underlying findings that Cunningham continued to park across from Appellees' driveway and has also encouraged vendors and patients of the clinic to do so.

Appellants point out that several factors other than cars legally parked across the street make entry into the Escobedo driveway more difficult. Because of the high crown on the roadway, a car will scrape the street surface or "bottom out" whether there are cars across the street or not. Appellants' driveway is very narrow and the curbs are high. [...] Exit and entry in Quintanilla's Nissan 300 ZX sports car presents a special challenge. Appellants complain that there is no evidence establishing how much narrower, if any, the street in question is than other Dallas residential streets. They argue that a finding that parking in a legal parking zone across the street from the Escobedo driveway constituted a substantial "interference" with Appellees' use of the property would serve as a precedent to preclude on-the-street parking generally.

There is evidence that others have complained to Penn about the parking on Winnetka, but apparently no one had petitioned the city to change the on-street parking situation for at least thirty years. Although one cannot ordinarily acquire a prescriptive right to maintain a nuisance (citation omitted), the fact that on the street parking has been permitted for at least twenty-five years without incident is evidence supporting a conclusion that the condition is not seriously offensive, or intolerable to a person of ordinary sensibilities. Moreover, entry into and exit from the Escobedo driveway became easier after the establishment of a no-parking zone in front of the Escobedo house on her side of the street.

There is, however, more than a scintilla of evidence supporting the trial court's finding of nuisance. Considering all the evidence, we also conclude that the finding is not so against the great weight and preponderance of the evidence as to be manifestly wrong and unjust.

Cunningham's issues one and two and Penn's issue one are overruled.

[...]

IT IS THEREFORE ORDERED ADJUDGED AND DECREED that Defendants Cunningham, Penn, Allen, Maldonado, Howard [...] are permanently enjoined from parking directly across from the driveway for the residence at 205 S. Windomere, Dallas, Texas.

IT IS FURTHER ORDERED ADJUDGED AND DECREED that for so long as Defendants Cunningham, Penn, Allen, and Maldonado, own or work at the Dental Clinic, and so long as Defendant Howard lives next door to 205 S. Windomere, such Defendants shall take necessary precautions to prevent others visiting or working with them, from parking directly across from the residence driveway.

[...]

The trial court's finding of private nuisance is affirmed. The portion of the trial court's judgment ordered in abatement of the nuisance and permanently enjoining Appellants and others from parking directly across from Appellees' residence is affirmed. [...]

By issuing an injunction applicable to all defendants, the court made sure that the nuisance ended and that plaintiffs could exit the driveway.

A court may apportion liability among defendants for a nuisance, so long as it can clearly identify each defendant's degree of responsibility for the nuisance. However, the courts will apportion liability among multiple defendants so long as the contribution of each is definable. Further, joint and several liability—which could mean holding a defendant for all the damages or for that part caused by the specific defendant—may exist even when a court cannot apportion the liability according to the responsibility of each defendant (see box below).

> ## CONDUCT OF OTHERS
>
> A dozen nuisances do not each obtain immunity because they all interfere with the plaintiff's use of his land. Where the damage done is incapable of any practical division, as where a river polluted with oil burns a barn, or poisons cattle, each will be liable for the entire loss.
>
> W. Page Keeton et al., *Prosser & Keeton on the Law of Torts,* §88B at 634 (5th ed. 1984)

As in the case of a negligence action, the actions of plaintiff that aggravate the situation may prevent any recovery in a cause of action for nuisance.

Basis for Recovery

The types of losses occurring in a nuisance action will vary greatly depending upon the nature of the invasion and the extent of the interference with the property's use and enjoyment, and may take any of the following forms:

- harm to real property
- physical injury
- psychological disturbance
- economic loss

Courts could provide recovery for any single type of loss or in combination with other types of losses.

Actions in Nuisance Are Different from Actions in Trespass

Actions in trespass differ from actions in nuisance. One difference focuses on the nature of the interest involved. For example, a defendant who physically enters another person's land without permission involves trespass. The entry violates the plaintiff's interest in exclusive possession of the land. On the other hand, interfering with the use and enjoyment of another person's land is a nuisance. The interference impairs the plaintiff's interest in using and enjoying the land and need not involve physically entering the land.

A nuisance requires significant harm to the plaintiff, while trespass does not. A defendant may cross a plaintiff's property without permission so that there is liability for trespass (although likely little basis for recovery, because little damage would likely occur if the trespass happened only once). With a nuisance, the interference has to go so far beyond something slight or fleeting for plaintiff to win in nuisance. For example, to constitute a nuisance, a neighbor's loud music must go on for days, not just minutes.

■ PRIVATE NUISANCE

A **private nuisance** is an interference with an individual's interest in the use and enjoyment of land. That individual's interest would include ownership. It could be for possession as well, so that a tenant could have a basis for an action in private nuisance (see box on next page).

> ### PRIVATE NUISANCE
> A private nuisance today is a condition or activity that interferes with the possessor's use and enjoyment of her land by incorporeal or non-trespassory invasions to such an extent that the landowner cannot reasonably be expected to bear without compensation.
>
> Dobbs, *The Law of Torts* §463 (2000)

Interest Protected

The interest protected by this action in tort emphasized the individual's using the property comfortably and conveniently. Convenience could include using the interest in the land in various ways. Besides living on the land, the individual could engage in agricultural or commercial uses. Or the interference might include a loss of value due to the defendant's carelessness leading to a contamination of ground water, as Case in Point 9-4 points out.

 # CASE IN POINT 9-4

Adkins v. Thomas Solvent Company
440 Mich. 293 (1992)

The question before us is whether a claim for relief may be maintained by plaintiffs who claim the right to damages in nuisance for property depreciation caused by environmental contamination of ground water despite testimony by both plaintiffs' and defendants' experts that their properties were not and would never be subject to ground water contamination emanating from the defendants' property.

[...]

We are persuaded that the boundaries of a traditional nuisance claim should not be relaxed to permit recovery on these facts. Compensation for a decline in property value caused by unfounded perception of underground contamination is inextricably entwined with complex policy questions regarding environmental protection that are more suitably resolved through the legislative process.

[...]

In 1984, the plaintiffs sued the Thomas Solvent Company in the Calhoun Circuit Court for damages and injunctive relief from injuries allegedly resulting from the improper handling of chemicals and industrial waste. Claiming that the Thomas Solvent Company's and other defendants' improper handling and storage of toxic chemicals and industrial waste had contaminated the ground water, the plaintiffs brought claims sounding in negligence, continuing nuisance, continuing trespass, strict liability, and ultrahazardous activities.

Originally, approximately fifty plaintiffs brought suit against the Thomas Solvent defendants, [footnote omitted] the Grand Trunk Railroad defendants, [footnote omitted] Wesley E. Carter, a private individual doing business as Raymond Road Landfill and O.K. Wrecking Company, and Hannah's Cement Products, Inc., the lessor of the land used as Raymond Road Landfill. The plaintiffs claimed that toxic chemicals and industrial wastes were released accidentally or intentionally at sites owned by the defendants. The plaintiffs complained of contaminants emanating from two sites owned or operated by the Thomas Solvent defendants. The plaintiffs alleged that contamination issued from a facility on Raymond Road which included an office building, a warehouse, a dock for storing drums, and twenty-one underground bulk storage tanks. In addition, the plaintiffs complained that contamination stemmed from a facility on Emmett Street, which the Thomas Solvent defendants allegedly leased from Grand Trunk Western Railroad. The Emmett Street facility included two underground bulk storage tanks, one aboveground tank, and a loading dock adjacent to a railroad spur. The plaintiffs also complained that contamination originated at the Raymond Road Landfill.

[...]

As discovery continued, it became clear that contaminants allegedly discharged into the ground water by the defendants never reached these plaintiffs' property. The plaintiffs' expert [...] concluded that a ground water divide separated the flow of ground water in the area, with water on the north side of the divide flowing generally north or northwesterly and the water on the south side of the divide flowing in a westerly direction. He testified that no contaminants from the Thomas Solvent facilities had any effect on the properties of these plaintiffs, which were located south of the divide.

This appeal involves the claims of twenty-two plaintiffs who live over 2000 feet south and east from the Thomas Solvent facilities [...] The plaintiffs argued that a tortious event and a range of damages occurred when toxic substances left the defendants' property. They conceded that no contaminants ever reached these twenty-two plaintiffs' property, but urged the court to impose liability on the defendants for any loss in property values due to public concern about the contaminants in the general area. Concluding that any damages that these plaintiffs suffered resulted from unfounded public perception that their ground water was contaminated, the trial court dismissed their claims. [...]

[...]

Historically, Michigan has recognized two distinct versions of nuisance, public nuisance and private nuisance. (citation omitted) A private nuisance is a nontrespassory invasion of another's interest in the private use and enjoyment of land. (citation omitted) [...] [T]he gist of a private nuisance action is an interference with the occupation or use of land or an interference with servitudes relating to land. [footnote omitted] There are countless ways to interfere with the use and enjoyment of land including interference with the physical condition of the land itself, disturbance in the comfort or conveniences of the occupant including his peace of mind, and threat of future injury that is a present menace and interference with enjoyment. The essence of private nuisance is the protection of a property owner's or occupier's reasonable comfort in occupation of the land in question. (citation omitted) [...]

The plaintiffs alleged that the defendants' improper handling and storage of toxic chemicals and hazardous waste contaminated underground water in the area, thus supporting their recovery of money damages for nuisance. [...]

The crux of the plaintiffs' complaint is that publicity concerning the contamination of ground water in the area (although concededly not their ground water) caused diminution in the value of the plaintiffs' property. This theory cannot form the basis for recovery because negative publicity resulting in unfounded fear about dangers in the vicinity of the property does not constitute a significant interference with the use and enjoyment of land. [footnote omitted]

[...]

Just as the development of nuisance on the case responded to the limitations of trespass by recognizing a cause of action when there was damage, but not injury amounting to use, the modern formulation of nuisance in fact, acknowledges changing conditions by declining to recognize a cause of action where damage and injury are both predicated on unfounded fear of third parties that depreciates property values. The rationale may be expressed by observing that reasonable minds cannot differ that diminished property value based on unfounded fear is not a substantial interference in and of itself. [...]

This response also corresponds with the historical premise underlying tort liability for nuisance in fact, i.e., that when some significant interference with the use and enjoyment of land causes the property value loss, courts of law accommodate conflicting interests by recognizing claims designed to shift the loss. [footnote omitted] However, on the present state of the record, plaintiffs do not contend that the condition created by the defendant causes them fear or anxiety. Thus, not only have these plaintiffs not alleged significant interference with their use and enjoyment of property, they do not here posit any interference at all.

Plaintiffs correctly observe that property depreciation is a traditional element of damages in a nuisance action. (citation omitted) We are not persuaded, however[...] that an allegation of property depreciation alone sets forth a cognizable claim in private nuisance of significant interference with the use and enjoyment of a person's property. Diminution in property values caused by negative publicity is [...]—a loss without an injury in the legal sense.

[...]

We agree that different considerations apply to the remedies appropriate, and that injunctive relief is sometimes available when a tort is merely threatened or denied on the basis that damage is the more appropriate relief. In both law and equity, however, there must be a cognizable claim of a substantive interest invaded or threatened. [...] Our point is that unfounded fears cannot constitute an allegation of a nuisance in fact with regard to these plaintiffs. [footnote omitted]

[...]

[W]e would think it not only "odd" (citation omitted) but anachronistic that a claim of nuisance in fact could be based on unfounded fears regarding persons with AIDS moving into a neighborhood, the establishment of otherwise lawful group homes for the disabled, or unrelated persons living together, [footnote omitted] merely because the fears experienced by third parties would cause a decline in property values. [footnote omitted]

[...]

If any property owner in the vicinity of the numerous hazardous waste sites that have been identified [footnote omitted] can advance a claim seeking damages when unfounded public fears of exposure cause property depreciation, the ultimate effect might be a reordering of a polluter's resources for the benefit of persons who have suffered no cognizable harm at the expense of those claimants who have been subjected to a substantial and unreasonable interference in the use and enjoyment of property. [footnote omitted] Thus, while we acknowledge that the line drawn today is not necessarily dictated by the spectral permutations of nuisance jurisprudence, if the line is to be drawn elsewhere, the significant interests involved appear to be within the realm of those more appropriate for resolution by the Legislature. [footnote omitted] (citation omitted)

[...]

We reverse [...] and remand to the trial court for a continuation of proceedings with regard to the remaining plaintiffs.

With no evidence of actual contamination, the court found that a potential loss of value due to the possibility of groundwater contamination did not rise to the legal definition of a private nuisance. By implication, the court would have more likely found an action in nuisance if there had been contamination. The court felt it was not in a position to create a cause of action due to the perception that a nuisance existed.

Freedom from interference and annoyance in the use and enjoyment of an individual's property could extend to the ability to receive electronic transmissions, as seen in the following case. (see Case in Point 9-5).

CASE IN POINT 9-5

Page County Appliance Center, Inc. v. Honeywell, Inc.
347 N.W.2d 171 (Iowa 1984)

Plaintiff Page County Appliance Center, Inc. (Appliance Center), sued Honeywell, Inc. (Honeywell), and ITT Electronic Travel Services, Inc. (ITT), for nuisance [...]. Appliance Center has owned and operated an appliance store in Shenandoah, Iowa, since 1953.

In 1975 the store was acquired from his father by John Pearson, who sold televisions, stereos, and a variety of appliances. Before 1980 Pearson had no reception trouble with his display televisions. In early January 1980, however, ITT placed one of its computers with Central Travel Service in Shenandoah as part of a nationwide plan to lease computers to retail travel agents. Central Travel was separated by only one other business from the Appliance Center. This ITT computer was manufactured, installed, and maintained by Honeywell.

Thereafter many of Pearson's customers told him his display television pictures were bad; on two of the three channels available in Shenandoah he had a difficult time "getting a picture that was fit to watch." After unsuccessfully attempting several remedial measures, in late January 1980, he finally traced the interference to the operations of Central Travel's computer. Both defendants concede Pearson's problems were caused by radiation leaking from the Honeywell computer.

Pearson discussed the problem with Kay Crowell, owner of Central Travel. She placed a call to ITT's president in New York. Although he was unavailable, ITT personnel apparently notified Honeywell. ITT's only contact with Pearson was through a telephone call some ten months later. At that time Pearson told ITT's sales representative that Honeywell was working on the problem; he made no effort to follow up on ITT's interest in the problem.

Honeywell indeed was working to correct the situation, and had been since February 1980. Honeywell technicians made repeated trips to make various unsuccessful adjustments to the computer. They found the computer was operating properly; the interference-causing radiation was a design and not a service problem. Pearson then telephoned Armando Benitez, the technicians' supervisor. Pearson testified Benitez told him Honeywell was "way over budget" on the Central Travel computer and that "if you don't like it, you can move." Nonetheless, in early fall of 1980 Honeywell sent out Phil Brzozoski, one of its engineers from Boston. According to Pearson, when he asked Brzozoski why it had taken him so long to come, the latter replied he would not have been there at all had Pearson not instituted suit; that was the way big business worked. Kay Crowell, admittedly Pearson's friend, testified Brzozoski told her the delay was "good business." Pearson in fact did not bring suit until December 22, 1980, although his counsel sent demand letters to Honeywell and ITT in October 1980. At trial a top Honeywell employee testified it was not company policy to await lawsuits before taking remedial action.

The Honeywell engineers effected a 70 percent improvement in the television reception by certain modifications of the computer in the fall of 1980. Pearson, still dissatisfied, started this action in December. While the suit was pending, Honeywell further modified the computer, finally alleviating Pearson's problems in May 1982.

At trial a Honeywell senior staff engineer admitted the technology to manufacture a non-radiation-emitting computer was available long before it developed this computer, but opined it would have been neither cost nor consumer effective to utilize that technology. He testified Honeywell believed it had corrected Pearson's problems in the fall of 1980.

The Appliance Center's case against Honeywell and ITT finally was submitted to the jury on the theor[y] of nuisance [...] The jury found for the Appliance Center against the remaining defendants on both theories, and further found the Appliance Center should recover $71,000 in compensatory damages [...]

Narrowing our focus, we note the Appliance Center is alleging a "private nuisance," that is, an actionable interference with a person's interest in the private use and enjoyment of his or her property [....] It also is apparent that if Central Travel's computer emissions constitute a nuisance it is a "nuisance per accidens, or in fact"—a lawful activity conducted in such a manner as to be a nuisance [....]

Principles governing our consideration of nuisance claims are well established. One's use of property should not unreasonably interfere with or disturb a neighbor's comfortable and reasonable use and enjoyment of his or her estate. A fair test of whether the operation of a lawful trade or industry constitutes a nuisance is the reasonableness of conducting it in the manner, at the place, and under the circumstances shown by the evidence. Each case turns on its own facts and ordinarily the ultimate issue is one of fact, not law.

The existence of a nuisance is not affected by the intention of its creator not to injure anyone. Priority of occupation and location—"who was there first"—is a circumstance of considerable weight [....]

When the alleged nuisance is claimed to be offensive to the person, courts apply the standard of "normal persons in a particular locality" to measure the existence of a nuisance [....] This normalcy standard also is applied where the use of property is claimed to be affected. "The plaintiff cannot, by devoting his own land to an unusually sensitive use [...] make a nuisance out of conduct of the adjoining defendant which would otherwise be harmless." (citation omitted) [...]

In the case before us, ITT asserts the Appliance Center's display televisions constituted a hypersensitive use of its premises as a matter of law, and equates this situation to cases involving light thrown on outdoor theater screens in which light-throwing defendants have carried the day....

We cannot equate the rare outdoor theater screen with the ubiquitous television that exists, in various numbers, in almost every home. Clearly, the presence of televisions on any premises is not such an abnormal condition that we can say, as a matter of law, that the owner has engaged in a peculiarly sensitive use of the property. This consideration, as well as related considerations of unreasonableness, gravity of harm, utility of conduct, and priority of occupation, are factual determinations that should have been submitted to the jury in this case. We find no trial court error in refusing to direct a verdict on this ground [....]

The court had no difficulty finding that the computer gave off interference sufficient to impair the appliance store's ability to "use and enjoy" its property, that is, to be able to have working television sets on display.

Another approach would not limit the use to only certain activities but would look toward how the individual feels about using the interest in land. The following are examples of what "use and enjoyment" involves, as the creation or existence of:

- a physical condition
- convenience or comfort
- peace of mind
- freedom from the possibility of future harm

■ PUBLIC NUISANCE

A **public nuisance** can harm the entire public. This involves an interference with the rights and interests of all. Under the common law, a public nuisance would have an effect upon the public's comfort and convenience (see box on next page):

PUBLIC NUISANCE

1. A public nuisance is an unreasonable interference with a right common to the general public.
2. Circumstances that may sustain a holding that an interference with a public right is unreasonable include the following:
   a. Whether the conduct involves a significant interference with the public health, the public safety, the public peace, the public comfort, or the public convenience, or
   b. whether the conduct is proscribed by a statute, ordinance or administrative regulation, or
   c. whether the conduct is of a continuing nature or has produced a permanent or long-lasting effect, and, as the actor knows or has reason to know, has a significant effect upon the public right.

Restatement (Second) of Torts §821B

For example, blocking the entrance to a state park would be a public nuisance.

In the following case, the plaintiff claimed the adjacent parking lot constituted a public nuisance (see Case in Point 9-6).

CASE IN POINT 9-6

B & W Management, Inc. v. Tasea Investment Co.
451 A.2d 879 (D.C. 1982)

B & W Management, Inc. (B & W) and Tasea Investment Company (Tasea) own property in the same "CR" zone in Northwest Washington, D.C. B & W operates a two-story parking garage in the CR zone. [footnote omitted] B & W appeals from the trial court's order dismissing its amended complaint, which sought [...] to recover compensatory [...] damages on a common law nuisance theory. [footnote omitted]

[...]

"A public nuisance is an unreasonable interference with a right common to the general public." (citation omitted). [footnote omitted] At common law, the term "public nuisance" covered a variety of minor criminal offenses that interfered, for example, with the public health, safety, morals, peace, or convenience. (citation omitted) As applied to land use, therefore, public nuisance theory provides the common law underpinning (subject to statutory modification) for injunctive and damage actions based on zoning violations. (citation omitted)

In contrast, a "private nuisance" is a substantial and unreasonable interference with private use and enjoyment of one's land, (citation omitted)—for example, by interfering with the physical condition of the land, disturbing the comfort of its occupants, or threatening future injury or disturbance. (citation omitted) [footnote omitted]. [...]

While a private nuisance claim is thus inherently a private right of action, as a general proposition only governmental authorities or other representatives of the general public have standing to attack a public nuisance in court (absent statutory authorization). (citation omitted)

[...]

The question here thus becomes: has appellant stated a claim for private nuisance or—its equivalent in this context—a claim for special damage from a public nuisance? [footnote omitted]

> In its amended complaint, B & W alleged the following damages attributable to Tasea's unlawful parking lot: [...] damage to "the aesthetics of the area surrounding [B & W's] property" from "increase[d] air pollution, motor vehicle traffic, urban blight, and visual unsightliness of surface parking lots."
>
> [...]
>
> B & W's claim for damage to "the aesthetics of the area" based on neighborhood "blight" does not amount to an assertion of the substantial interference with B & W's use and enjoyment of its land required to sustain a private nuisance action. (citation omitted) Nor is this an allegation of [...] damage attributable to a public nuisance. As the trial court stated, "there is nothing alleged which suggests that [B & W's] claimed interest in such aesthetics is in any way different from that of other persons who own or occupy real property in that section of the city generally." [...]
>
> B & W accordingly has failed to state a claim on which relief could be granted, and the trial court properly dismissed the amended complaint. [footnote omitted]
>
> Affirmed.

Since the plaintiff could not show that the defendant's parking lot constituted an interference with everyone's use and enjoyment of the area, the plaintiff had no valid claim based on public nuisance.

■ IDENTIFYING THE TYPE OF NUISANCE

Courts have struggled to establish a precise dividing line between a private and public nuisance. Often, it depends on who is affected. That difference could affect the remedy the court could provide.

For example, a property owner who lived adjacent to a cement-mixing plant could sue for private nuisance because fumes from the plant killed that person's garden; the court could order the plant's owners to pay the property owner for the loss of the ability ever to grow a garden. But those same noxious fumes could prevent people from using a public pond so that the remedy could involve damages for the loss of the use and enjoyment of that public pond.

The issue before the court in Case in Point 9-7 involved a road on private property. Had the property owner's occasional, permitted use turned this road into a public road, so that putting up an obstacle on it created a public nuisance? Or did the fact that the property owner occasionally granted access on the roadway mean the public had no interest and so, no valid basis, for suing if the property owner erected an obstacle on the roadway?

 # CASE IN POINT 9-7

Roberie v. VonBokern

2006 Ky. 186 (Ky. Aug. 24, 2006)

This case concerns a dispute over access to an unimproved dirt road in Owen County, Kentucky. Appellants, Steve Roberie and Joyce Roberie, husband and wife, appeal a judgment of the Owen Circuit Court, which determined that the road is a public road and awarded punitive damages of $5,000.00 to the primary Appellees, their neighbors Robert VonBokern and Victoria VonBokern. The Roberies make two arguments in this appeal: (1) that the VonBokerns' cause of action was improper in that it amounted to an action to quiet title in a third party, and (2) that there was no legal or factual basis for the trial court's award of punitive damages. [...] We granted the Roberies' motion for discretionary review and now hold that this was a proper cause of action, though for a different reason than was given by the Court of Appeals, and that the punitive damages award to the VonBokerns was appropriate given the circumstances.

II. Background

In May 1996, the Roberies purchased an approximately 35-acre tract from the Goderwis family, which had subdivided a single piece of property into three smaller tracts. The Roberie property contained a home and was situated between the two remaining Goderwis tracts—one lying to the east, and the other lying to the northwest and not relevant to this dispute. All three properties are bordered on the northeast by Fairview Road, which is open to the public. The unimproved dirt road, which is the subject of this dispute, runs from Fairview Road in a roughly southerly direction and forms the boundary between the Roberies' property to the west and the Goderwises' property to the east. The disputed road continues to the south, forming the eastern border of a farm owned by the VonBokerns. Although the VonBokerns' property is not landlocked, the disputed road provides the best access to the northern section of the farm.

[...]

By all accounts, the parties seem to have coexisted peaceably for some months after the Roberies purchased the property. During this time, the VonBokerns occasionally used the road, though they did so, at least initially, with the permission of the Roberies. Later the VonBokerns began to use the road without permission. Eventually, the two families became embroiled in a dispute over access to the road.

Sometime in 1998, Mr. VonBokern told the Roberies that he believed the unimproved dirt road was actually a county road. The conflict escalated after Mr. Roberie observed Mr. VonBokern taking measurements of the road, presumably to make improvements to it. Mr. Roberie ordered Mr. VonBokern to leave his property and used threatening language, prompting Mr. VonBokern to call the state police. Next, Mr. VonBokern graded a portion of the road with his bulldozer. Mr. Roberie again objected and questioned county officials as to whether the county had any claim to the road, but they were unable to give him any information on its status. The Roberies erected fenceposts along their side of the road to prevent Mr. VonBokern from widening the road, but this did not prevent Mr. VonBokern from spreading a load of gravel on the road. Additional incidents occurred between the families, including exchanges of harsh language and at least one incident of allegedly harassing behavior by the Mr. Roberie—Mrs. VonBokern testified that on one occasion Mr. Roberie had frightened her deliberately by driving closely behind her on a winding road. Finally, the Roberies erected fenceposts at the entrance of the road completely blocking access.

In September 1999, the VonBokerns filed suit against the Roberies and Goderwises in Owen Circuit Court contending that the road mentioned in the deeds to their property was a turnpike road that was owned by the county and was, therefore, open to public use. The VonBokerns demanded a declaration of rights, injunctive relief, and compensatory damages. [...]

The Roberies filed their answer to the complaint, counterclaiming against the VonBokerns for trespass and demanding injunctive relief, compensatory damages, and punitive damages. [...]

The VonBokerns [...] amended their complaint in January 2001, demanding punitive damages from the Roberies for a course of conduct that was "designed and calculated to intimidate" them from using the disputed road. [...]

The case came to trial in July 2002. Although the VonBokerns argued that several legal theories supported their claim for access to the road, testimony from the parties and their expert witnesses focused primarily on whether the disputed road was, in fact, the Pleasant Home and Clay Lick Turnpike as the VonBokerns had alleged. Ultimately, the jury found that the disputed road was the same road which had been acquired by the county pursuant to the 1897 deed. In addition, the jury awarded $5,000 in punitive damages to the VonBokerns, presumably for the Roberies' intimidating, abusive behavior and for blocking access to the road. Despite the award of punitive damages, the jury did not award compensatory damages to the VonBokerns.

[...]

[W]e affirm the decision of the Court of Appeals insofar as it concluded that the VonBokerns stated a valid cause of action. However, we believe that the claim is more appropriately categorized as a public nuisance action.

[...]

The fundamental issue in this case is whether the VonBokerns stated a valid cause of action against the Roberies. [...] [W]e believe the VonBokerns' claim is valid and amounts to a private action for public nuisance.

[...]

It must be noted, however, that the class of individuals that is eligible to maintain a private action for public nuisance is limited.

1. In order to recover damages in an individual action for a public nuisance, one must have suffered harm of a kind different from that suffered by other members of the public exercising the right common to the general public that was the subject of interference.
2. In order to maintain a proceeding to enjoin to abate a public nuisance, one must
   a. have the right to recover damages[...] or
   b. have authority as a public official or public agency to represent the state or a political subdivision in the matter, or
   c. have standing to sue as a representative of the general public, as a citizen in a citizen's action or as a member of a class in a class action. (citation omitted)

[...]

In this case, the VonBokerns alleged that the disputed dirt road was actually a public turnpike that was owned by the county and that the Roberies' efforts to prevent their access to the road amounted to an "interference with a public right." The VonBokerns also alleged that the Roberies' act of blocking the road interfered with the use and enjoyment of their property in that it prevented one means of access to their farm. This is precisely the sort of special harm envisioned by the drafters of the Restatement who note the following [...]:

The right of access to land, that is, the right of reasonable and convenient ingress and egress, is itself a property right in the land. If the public nuisance interferes with immediate ingress and egress to the plaintiff's land, the nuisance is a private as well as a public one and the harm suffered by the plaintiff is particular harm differing in kind from that suffered by the general public, so that the plaintiff can recover for the public nuisance. Complete deprivation of access, so that the land of the plaintiff is completely cut off is obviously sufficient particular damage. But the deprivation need not be complete and it is enough that the ingress or egress is made unreasonably burdensome or inconvenient or unsafe. Access by a particular entry is still a valuable property right even though there may be another entry left open; and the fact that there is access from the north left open does not prevent the recovery when the plaintiff is deprived of access from the south. (citation omitted)

[...]

In light of the foregoing, we hold that the VonBokerns' claim was a valid private action for public nuisance. [...]

The court found that since there was a public road involved, the VonBokerns' inability to use it to get to their property constituted a public nuisance, brought individually only on their behalf.

■ REMEDIES

After determining that liability exists, a court has a number of potential remedies available for use:

- Damages: available in an amount equal to the decrease in the market value of the property due to the nuisance and/or the costs of repairs and/or damages arising out of personal harm
- Injunction: court order limiting the defendant's future conduct, usually to stop engaging in tortious conduct, which can be combined with other remedies
- Abatement: permission for the plaintiff to enter the defendant's land and use of reasonable force, in a reasonable manner, so as to end the nuisance although most jurisdictions require the plaintiff to provide notice before entering the defendant's property.

Yet a defendant may be willing to pay damages in an action for private nuisance but continue to interfere with the plaintiff's use and enjoyment in the plaintiff's property. The court in the *Baldwin* case, where the plaintiff was a neighbor to a pig farm, suggested a method for determining damages where the nuisance continued (see Case in Point 9-8).

 CASE IN POINT 9-8

Baldwin v. McClendon

292 Ala. 43 (1974)

The respondents, Robert Baldwin and W. J. Bottcher, appeal [...] The appellees, James E. McClendon and Ethel McClendon, are husband and wife. Their home, for some fifteen years, has been a forty-seven acre farm, located in a rural agricultural area of Blount County, about seven miles southeast of Oneonta on the road to Springville. In early 1970, the appellants commenced hog production on a large commercial scale on the appellant Baldwin's property which adjoins the appellees. In their business, the appellants operate two hog parlors each with a separate connecting lagoon. One hog parlor will house something over a thousand hogs and a second smaller one will accommodate approximately four hundred. There is also a third servicing lagoon. The hog parlor is a covered shelter with a concrete floor, laid on a plane, slightly declining toward the adjoining lagoon. The hogs are fed and watered in the parlors, and there they live, sleep and grow to a desired weight, when they are topped out. The lagoons which adjoin the hog parlors are related facilities, designed for the purpose of retaining the disposing of the waste material excreted by the hogs on the floor in their parlors. These lagoons are entrenched bodies of water into which the hog waste is flushed down with water in cleaning the parlor floors. In the lagoons, the waste material, commingling with the water, creates a chemical reaction resulting in a disintegration of the waste. This causes the emission of offensive odors. During the trial, the extent and intensity of the odor was the subject of much conflicting testimony. The appellees and witnesses offered by them, in general, said that the odor was so bad that they had to keep the doors and windows in the house closed, that it sickened them at the stomach, caused loss of appetite and practically ruined all outdoor recreation about the home-place. The appellees' residence was said to be at distances varying from two hundred to a thousand feet from the nearest hog parlor and adjoining lagoon. Witnesses testified that these facilities adjoined the appellees' land near the division line between the parties.

[...]

After stating that he visited the appellees' premises and inspected the stream in their pasture, the rock formation from which part of it flowed, the hog parlors and lagoons operated by the appellants, and the poultry houses and hog pasture of an adjacent neighbor, the trial judge found 'with no doubt about it' that the appellants' operations emitted foul odors which had a detrimental effect on the appellees' enjoyment of their home and the value of their property [....]

The court further found that the operation of the hog parlors and lagoons was an obnoxious nuisance subject to abatement [...] and that the appellees suffered damages from the nuisance because of its proximity to their home, one of the lagoons being about as close to the appellees' property line as it could be built. The court also observed that the appellants had spent some $31,300 in creating the hog parlors and lagoons, and that an injunction would bring a severe blow to them. The court concluded that the appellees were entitled to have the nuisance abated, or else, be compensated in damages, if the nuisance is allowed to continue.

Accordingly, the court ordered and decreed that the appellants be enjoined, prohibited and restrained from operating the hog parlors and lagoons, provided that, if the appellants paid into the court the sum of $3,000 as damages for the use of the appellees, the injunction would not go into effect, and the appellees' only relief would be compensation for damages, but, if not paid within thirty days, the injunction would go into full force and effect without further orders of the court.

The appellants argue that their operation is carried on in a rural community given over almost entirely to agricultural pursuits, such as the growing of farm produce, the raising of turkeys and chickens, the dairy business, and hog and cattle production, and that it follows that fowl and animal odors will permeate the area to some degree. They assert that the appellees should endure some unpleasantness and not be permitted to enjoin a lawful business, the facilities for which were constructed according to approved plans and specifications, and the operation of which is conducted in a reasonable manner.

While these contentions must be considered in deciding the case, we think the decision also hinges on other factors, such as the location and proximity of the operation to the appellees' home, the intensity and volume of the odors, their interference, if any, with the appellees' own well-being and the enjoyment of their home, and any consequential depreciation in value of their home. It appears that the trial judge considered these matters [...]

On several occasions, we have defined a private nuisance as "any establishment, erected on the premises of one, though for the purposes of trade or business, lawful in itself, which, from the situation, the inherent qualities of the business, or the manner in which it is conducted, directly causes substantial injury to the property of another, or produces material annoyance and inconvenience to the occupants of adjacent dwellings, rendering them physically uncomfortable, is a nuisance. In applying this principle, it has been repeatedly held that smoke, offensive odors, noise, or vibrations, when of such degree or extent as to materially interfere with the ordinary comfort of human existence, will constitute a nuisance...."

We have read the evidence in the record, as well as the condensed recital of the testimony in the appellants' brief. We allude to this only to say that ample legal evidence appears to support the trial judge's finding and conclusion that a private nuisance did in fact exist [...].

Affirmed.

In this case, the court saw that issuing an order forbidding the continued operation of the hog farm would damage a profit-making business. Instead of shutting the farm down, the court ordered the defendants to pay plaintiffs for the permanent loss in value of their property because of the hog-farming operations. That court order—an injunction—would prohibit the defendant from engaging in the interference. If a court enjoined a defendant from continuing to create a nuisance and that defendant persisted, the defendant could then face criminal charges for disobeying a court order.

The problem facing the court in the following case, however, involved determining against whom the order should be issued, where the parties used their land lawfully but in incompatible ways (see Case in Point 9-9).

CASE IN POINT 9-9

Silva v. Melville

12 Mass. L. Rep. 611 (Super. Ct. 2001)

[...]
How should the law resolve the conflict that arises when adjoining landowners pursue incompatible uses of their own property?

Background

The defendant, Donald Melville ("Melville"), is a cranberry farmer who owns roughly thirty acres of land in Carver, on which he operates a number of cranberry bogs. The plaintiff, Cornelia Silva Romboli ("Silva"), owns roughly four acres of land, which she uses solely as her residence, that partially abuts Melville's land. In 1992, after buying a new parcel of land that abutted the rear portion of Silva's property, Melville built a cranberry bog on what he believed to be his own property. In fact, the bog extended onto roughly 1/10th of an acre of Silva's property, on the portion of her property furthest from her house. From 1992 until at least 1997, when Silva first notified Melville that he was encroaching on her property, Melville farmed this cranberry bog, including the 1/10 acre belonging to Silva. After he learned of the encroachment, Melville retreated onto his own property and built a dirt dike road separating Silva's land from his own. However, Melville continues to farm the part of the cranberry bog that rests on his own property, which means that, twice each year, in the fall and again in the winter, he floods the bog with water. [footnote omitted] As a result of this flooding, water seeps below the ground on Melville's property and percolates onto the rear of Silva's adjoining property, raising the water level.

[...]
The jury [...] found that water from Melville's property had entered onto Silva's property after March 11, 1995, but that this entry of water did not result from the unreasonable use of Melville's land. The jury was told that an unlawful

trespass by water existed only if the entry of water from Melville's land onto Silva's land was caused by an unreasonable use of Melville's land or, phrased differently, that Melville's negligent use of his land caused the flow of water onto Silva's land. Therefore, in view of the jury's finding on this issue, the jury found no negligent trespass of water.

As a result of the jury's findings as to liability, the jury was permitted to award damages only for Melville's continuing physical trespass onto Silva's property that occurred after March 11, 1995. Pragmatically, this meant that the jury needed to evaluate the damages caused to Silva as a result of Melville's continued farming of her 1/10 of an acre of cranberry bog after March 11, 1995 until he built the dirt dike road on that bog separating his property from hers.

[...]

The jury found that the entry of water onto Silva's property did not result from the unreasonable use of Melville's land. In making this finding, the jury recognized that Melville could farm his cranberry bog successfully only if he flooded it twice each year, that his flooding of his property would inevitably raise the water level on her adjoining 1/10th of an acre, and that there was nothing that Melville reasonably could do to stop this from happening except to stop farming his bog. The jury concluded that it was more reasonable for Melville to continue to farm his bog and for Silva to put up with the increased water level, than for Melville to abandon his bog so that Silva's adjoining 1/10th of an acre would have a lower water level. This Court concurs with that finding. In view of this factual finding, it would not be equitable to order Melville to cease and desist from allowing water to percolate from his land onto Silva's, because to do so would require Melville to stop flooding his adjoining cranberry bog, which effectively would require Melville to stop farming that bog.

[...]

The court's ruling in this case might not please the owner whose property flooded periodically.

An alternative remedy, in the form of a *compensated injunction*, might be a better solution (see box below).

REMEDIES; "COMPENSATED INJUNCTION"

The remedies potentially available for a private nuisance (or a public nuisance with special harm to the private plaintiff) are (1) compensatory damages, (2) punitive damages in egregious case, (3) injunctions abating or modifying the nuisance, and (rarely) (4) a "compensated injunction" that abates the nuisance but requires the plaintiff to pay the costs of the abatement.

Dobbs, *The Law of Torts* §468 (2000)

However, a court will issue an injunction only where a remedy in damages would fail to provide adequate relief. Paralegals should review their jurisdiction's laws regarding damages, injunctions, and abatement.

KEY TERMS

Nuisance   322

Private nuisance   331

Public nuisance   336

Substantial   324

Unreasonable   324

Use and enjoyment   323

SUMMARY

The law of nuisance is based on two separate forms of tort liability: private nuisance and public nuisance. Both involve conduct invading another's use and enjoyment of property.

Public nuisances affect the public's interest in the use and enjoyment of property, often property commonly used by all. Private nuisances affect an individual's interest in the use or enjoyment of property. If the court finds the existence of a nuisance, it may issue an injunction (a court order) compelling the termination of the interference. Alternatively, the court may assess damages in the amount of the defendant's loss of enjoyment and use of the property. Courts sometimes face the thorny issue of shutting down a business where it creates a nuisance and so, might favor a damages award, recognizing the loss in value of the plaintiffs' property but also serving a community interest by allowing a business to continue to operate.

CONCEPT REVIEW QUESTIONS

1. Describe the concept of nuisance.
2. What is the purpose behind the doctrine of nuisance?
3. Describe the nature of the harm that is the subject of an action for nuisance.
4. What are the two principal types of nuisance?
5. Define a private nuisance.
6. Discuss the nature of the use and enjoyment of property.
7. What are the four requirements for a recovery for a private nuisance?
8. Define a public nuisance.
9. What are the three remedies available for a nuisance?

CRITICAL THINKING APPLICATIONS

1. A plaintiff drives to work along a toll road; using public roads would add an hour, in each direction, to her commute. The defendant's employee is driving a tanker truck filled with solvents. The truck tips over, blocking the toll road for the entire day. The plaintiff learns of the accident before getting on the toll road and takes public roads. If the plaintiff filed suit for a private nuisance against the tanker's owner, will that defendant's motion to dismiss be granted? Why or why not?

2. Five days a week from 9 a.m. to 5 p.m., a defendant walks up and down the sidewalks of a particular neighborhood carrying a loud radio blasting at maximum volume. The defendant has been doing this for the last six months. If a homeowner sues defendant for creating a public nuisance, would the homeowner win if the matter went to trial? Why or why not?

3. A new restaurant is opening up on the ground floor of a city block. That means around 6 a.m. every day, a produce truck stops to deliver what the restaurant would need for that day's business. Next door is a condo complex. One of the condo owners wants to sue the restaurant for creating a private nuisance. If the restaurant files a motion for summary judgment, what is the court's likely ruling?

4. The defendant, a condo owner, has started a new business providing services via the Internet. The defendant has hired two employees who put in regular working hours but occasionally come and go late. The condo association rules prohibit owners from operating a home business where people are employed. The neighbor adjacent to the defendant's unit wants to file suit to stop the operation of this business. Would the neighbor do better in court by filing a claim based in a private nuisance or a public nuisance? Why that particular type of lawsuit in nuisance?

5. A gang operates in a neighborhood. Local law enforcement has not succeeded in prosecuting any gang member. Would the presence of this gang in the neighborhood constitute a public nuisance? Why or why not?

6. In a neighborhood of row houses, the owner of one house has let his building fall into disrepair. From the street, it's obvious that the building is filled with old newspapers. If a neighbor wanted to sue on the grounds that the building is a nuisance, would the neighbor characterize this situation as one involving a private nuisance or a public nuisance? Why?

7. A plaintiff owns thousands of acres of forested lands that are regularly logged. The defendant operates a laboratory in the back of a van, making illegal drugs. The manufacturing process creates toxic waste, which the defendant dumps out of the back of the van and drives away. Law enforcement succeeds in catching the defendant manufacturing the illegal drugs and charges the defendant for having committed crimes related to the manufacture of the illegal drugs. Could the plaintiff-landowner sue the defendant for private nuisance because of the toxic waste dumped on the property? Why? Would the situation change materially if the defendant dumped the toxic waste elsewhere but used the private logging roads to manufacture the illegal drugs? Why?

8. After meeting all the requirements at law, a defendant opens a child care service. Twice a day, parents come by for their children, blocking traffic occasionally for up to a half-hour at a time. Should a neighbor file an action in private or public nuisance? Why? Why might it make sense to sue the defendant for creating a private nuisance and a public nuisance?

SKILL-BUILDING APPLICATION

Chris and Mark Johnson purchased their first home, on Harrison Avenue in Presidential Heights. On the other side of the Heights, four miles away, Michael's Hog Farms continued its century-long tradition of family farming. The

Johnsons discover that during the summer months whenever the temperature rises above 90 degrees, the aroma of the Michael's Hog Farm would reach their house about one out of three days. Describe the elements of each action in nuisance that the Johnsons could bring against Michael's Hog Farms. Then offer a prediction about the Johnsons' chances for success for each action in nuisance, taking note specifically of any defenses available to Michael's Hog Farm.

We judge ourselves by what we feel capable
of doing, while others judge us by what we have
already done.

—*Henry Wadsworth Longfellow*
(1807-1882)

Defenses to Intentional Torts

A plaintiff must establish, by a preponderance of the evidence, a *prima facie* case of liability against a defendant to receive an award of damages. If the plaintiff satisfies this requirement, the defendant may then offer up a legally valid explanation—a defense—to excuse liability. Defenses vary according to the tort. They may also vary in their degree of impact, so that some may only mitigate damages while others completely excuse the defendant's actions. This chapter reviews some defenses to intentional torts; additional defenses appear in other chapters. Defenses to actions in negligence have been addressed in Chapter 5.

CHAPTER TOPICS

1. Defenses
2. Necessity
3. Consent
4. Mistake
5. Statute of Limitations

OBJECTIVES

After completing this chapter, you will be able to:

1. Demonstrate the concept of defense to intentional tort.

2. Classify the traditional defenses available in an action for intentional tort.

3. Summarize the elements of each defense to an intentional tort.

4. Illustrate the defenses that are applicable to each of the intentional torts.

■ DEFENSES

Defenses as a Way of Advancing a Social Policy

Society has determined that once a plaintiff has proven that the defendant caused a tort, the defendant may not face liability under certain circumstances. Society's allowing for defenses recognizes the risk that a mechanistic application of liability under tort law can unfairly penalize a defendant and, thus, not serve a societal goal. For example, if a plaintiff has consented to a defendant's conduct, why should the plaintiff then complain of an injury? If the plaintiff has had the opportunity to file suit but waited for years before doing so, thereby putting the defendant at a disadvantage to find evidence for a defense, should society allow the plaintiff to create such an advantage?

Pleadings

Defenses are part of the pleadings of a case, and many are affirmative defenses. In an affirmative defense, the defendant admits to engaging in the tortious conduct but also claims the existence of a defense that would excuse any liability. Affirmative defenses must be raised in the answer filed in response to the complaint. If this claim of defense is not raised in the answer to the complaint, a court may consider it to be waived.

■ NECESSITY

When a defendant uses the defense of **necessity,** he or she acknowledges causing harm. Yet the defendant claims that causing the injury avoided an immediate threat that would have resulted in greater injury (see box below).

> ### NECESSITY AS A DEFENSE
> In a limited group of situations, partial or complete privileges protect defendants whose acts in emergencies would otherwise count as trespass to land or chattels or as conversion. The emergency and privilege it generates are both called 'necessity.' The privilege can be invoked only to avert a public disaster or serious imminent harm to the defendant or to others.
>
> Dobbs, *The Law of Torts* §107 (2000)

Reprinted with permission from Thomson West. All rights reserved.

For example, if a defendant needed to enter into an unoccupied home to avoid extremely harsh weather, the defendant might escape liability where the alternative, exposure to the severe weather, could have led to death. Severe environmental conditions may regularly compel a defendant to have to choose "the lesser of two evils."

To successfully use necessity as a defense, a defendant must show the following elements at trial:

- an imminent threat exists
- the threat may involve serious bodily harm or injury
- steps can be taken to avoid or minimize the harm from the threat
- those steps involve committing an intentional tort against the plaintiff's person or property
- the defendant commits this intentional tort only so as to avoid the threat of greater harm

Imminent Threat

For a court to allow a defendant to claim necessity as a defense, the threat of harm must be so imminent that no reasonable alternative course of action exists. For example, if the defendant could have saved a pedestrian from an oncoming car by simply yelling at the pedestrian to jump out of the way, the defendant will not escape liability for assault and battery by instead choosing to shove the plaintiff out of the car's path.

The Necessity of Using Force

The use of force to protect property, oneself, or another is sometimes regarded as a privilege. The use of force in such instances will be addressed in Chapter 11.

Private Necessity

Private necessity, as a defense, involves violating tort law to avoid greater harm to a specific individual or property. For example, a defendant could jettison cargo from a ship if doing so would prevent the ship from capsizing during a storm and save the passengers. Because the defendant acted to avoid greater harm to the passengers, the defendant will prove successful in claiming the defense of private necessity when the cargo's owners sue for damages. Case in Point 10-1 provides a variation on that example: the claim of private necessity involved containing a fire on a ship that might have spread and ignited a grain silo.

 # CASE IN POINT 10-1

Protectus Alpha Navigation Co. v. North Pacific Grain Growers, Inc.
585 F. Supp. 1062 (D. Or. 1984)

Protectus Alpha Navigation Co. (Protectus) is the owner of the M/V PROTECTOR ALPHA, a diesel-driven bulk grain carrier of Cypriot registry. The ship came up the Columbia River on February 13, 1982 to load wheat at a grain facility owned by North Pacific Grain Growers, Inc. (North Pacific). The ship docked shortly before midnight, and about twenty hours later a fire broke out. Protectus asserts that as a result of the negligence of North Pacific, the ship became a total loss.

Protectus filed an action against North Pacific for: (1) compensation for the loss of the ship; (2) expenses incurred in firefighting and salvage and pollution control; and (3) indemnity for third-party claims arising from the death and injuries to the Coast Guardsmen and the loss of the ship's cargo. [...] A court trial was held, limited primarily to the issue of liability.

Facts

On February 14, 1982 at about 7:00 p.m., an oil barge operated by Don Stein began to pump diesel fuel into the PROTECTOR ALPHA. About thirty minutes later, Jose Travenia, an oiler for the ship, went into the engine room where he saw flames nine to ten feet high in the generator flat. The fire apparently started when diesel fuel spilled from an overflowing tank and ignited on the hot exhaust manifold of the generator. Travenia tried to put out the fire with a portable fire extinguisher. He became lost in heavy black smoke.

Shore personnel telephoned the fire department. Richard Merz, a volunteer fireman with the Kalama Fire Department, was the first firefighter to arrive at the dock. Assisted by crew member Arturo Miralles, Merz located and rescued Travenia, the lost oiler. Meanwhile, firefighters and firefighting equipment from Cowlitz County, Kalama, and Longview arrived at the dock. After Travenia was rescued, the firefighters attempted to seal off and discharge CO_2 into the engine room. There was testimony that if the firefighters had been able to release CO_2 when the fire was discovered, the fire would have been extinguished, but they could not do it while Travenia was trapped in the area for fear of killing him.

At about 8:30 p.m., and after the CO_2 had been applied, Chief Dan Baxter and Assistant Chief Donald McWain of Cowlitz County Fire District entered the generator flat. The generator flat is an area approximately $20' \times 20'$ open on one end. They observed from the crosswalk that the CO_2 had reduced the fire from flames to an orange glow.

When Captain Greiner of the Coast Guard arrived at 9:15 p.m., Chief Baxter explained his plan to shoot Aqueous Film Forming Foam (AFFF) onto the fire from the crosswalk. 75 gallons of 3% AFFF and 130 gallons of 6% AFFF were on the dock. Another 200 gallons were on the way from Vancouver, Washington. Three fire engines and other equipment necessary to pump the foam were on the dock. The hoses, connectors, and attachments were in place and foam was about to be introduced into the line.

Shortly before 9:30 p.m., North Pacific's dock foreman, Harry "Swede" Anderson, arrived at the dock. Within five minutes, Anderson, without consulting any of the firefighters, ordered the ship cast off from the dock. He gave the order in spite of the fact that Curtis LaRoy, a substitute foreman who had been at the dock for an hour, had urged Anderson to consult with the firefighters before he released the ship.

Chief Baxter and Assistant Chief Robert Mesneak of the Longview Fire Department shouted to Anderson and urged him not to cast off the ship. Anderson shouted an obscenity and released the last line that held the ship at the dock.

When fireman Merz saw that the fire hoses attached to the ship had become taut as the ship was moving away from the dock, he ordered the lines released.

Smoke had choked the ship's engines so that she was without power. A tugboat steered the ship to the edge of the channel but could not hold her there. The ship's anchor was dropped to keep her from drifting in the river. The ship was then about 1,000 yards downstream from the dock. The firefighters' substitute plan to fight the fire was unsuccessful. They had intended to shoot high expansion foam into the engine room, but equipment from the dock had to be ferried out to the ship and raised on ropes to the deck. By the time the necessary equipment reached the ship, the engine room was too hot to enter. It was decided to pump the foam through a hole into the engine room.

At 5:12 a.m., when Coast Guard workers were cutting a hole into the bulkhead in the engine room, a crankcase in the engine room exploded. One Coast Guardsman was killed and another was seriously injured. The explosion broke open the sealed engine room, and fed by oxygen, the fire spread rapidly to the ship's superstructure. At 5:55 a.m., Captain Greiner abandoned firefighting efforts, and the burning ship was beached downstream. The fire burned for three more days.

Claims

Protectus argues that North Pacific's employees were guilty of negligence as a matter of law when, in violation of Washington statutes which prohibit interference with public officials in the performance of their duties, they released the PROTECTOR ALPHA from the dock.

North Pacific contends that the loss of the PROTECTOR ALPHA and her cargo was caused by plaintiff's own negligence. The defendant also asserts that it was reasonable and prudent for its employees to cast off the ship, and that their conduct was justified by necessity.

[...]

The Necessity Defense

North Pacific contends that Anderson's decision to release the mooring lines and cast off the ship was a prudent response to the emergency created by the fire. North Pacific asserts that its conduct was justified by necessity because Anderson and Van Skike had reason to fear that the fire would trigger an explosion in the grain storage facility.

The defense of public necessity excuses a defendant from liability when, in an attempt to avert a public danger, he destroys the property of another. The defense applies only when the emergency justifies the action and when the defendant acts reasonably under the circumstances.

The doctrine of private necessity allows a defendant to interfere with another's property to protect himself, his property, or some other person. But the private necessity defense also requires that the defendant's conduct be reasonable. Private necessity does not excuse the infliction of harm on another's property. (citation omitted)

Here, the danger of explosion was not sufficiently imminent to justify Anderson's conduct, and his conduct was not reasonable under the circumstances. It is true that if North Pacific's grain elevator had exploded, it would have had a devastating effect on life and property in the area. Therefore, if there had been some likelihood that a spark from the fire would cause an explosion in the grain elevator, Anderson would have been justified in taking extreme action to prevent such a contingency. But an explosion at the time Anderson acted was extremely unlikely. It is highly improbable that a spark could have been carried from the ship to the grain gallery since a steady drizzle was falling and the wind was blowing away from the dock. The fire was small and confined to the engine room.

Nor is it likely that the vapors necessary for a combustion explosion were present. The grain had been loaded seventeen hours before the fire; the combustible grain dust had had time to settle. The substances which fed the ship's fire were diesel, lubricating oil, and bunker fuel, all of which are heavy and slow to vaporize. North Pacific's own expert, Roger Strehlow, testified that he had never heard of an explosion from these substances. There were no acetylene tanks in the engine room. The presence of smoke and CO_2 in the engine room would have eliminated most of the oxygen so that it would not be available to mix with vapors to form an explosive mixture. Vernon Clancey, another expert witness for North Pacific, acknowledged that he knew of no occasion in which a shipboard fire triggered a grain elevator explosion.

There was no reasonable basis, even with the information available to him, for Anderson to believe that an explosion was likely. But even if there had been, his decision to cast off the ship was not reasonable. The grain facility could have been protected by much less drastic methods. The inside of the grain elevator could have been hosed down with water. North Pacific's employees did this routinely before welding to prevent sparks from igniting the grain dust.

As a second alternative, Anderson could have followed LaRoy's suggestion, approved by the firefighters, that the ship be pivoted on its stern line so that the stack would be moved farther away from the grain gallery. Firemen and ship crewmen had loosened the lines with this objective.

Anderson's conduct was not justified by necessity.

[...]

Since other measures existed to address the possibility of a threat that had never occurred before, the court did not accept that private necessity applied.

Public Necessity

The defense of **public necessity** involves protecting a broader, public, interest. For example, a fire department may destroy a home if doing so would stop a forest fire from engulfing a neighborhood. Yet the government has to show that evidence existed to support such action, something lacking in the following case (see Case in Point 10-2).

CASE IN POINT 10-2

Barton-Barnes Inc. v. State of New York
180 A.D.2d 4 (3d Dep't 1992)

In 1980, Wesley Pawlowski leased a car from Kresge Leasing Corporation. During the early morning hours of February 5, 1981, when the car was parked in the basement of a State office building in the City of Binghamton, Broome County, a fire erupted in a transformer which contained the chemical pyranel. The heat generated by the fire converted the pyranel into polychlorinated biphenyls (PCBs), dibenzofurans (furans) and dibenzodioxins (dioxins) which spread throughout the building. All of these chemicals are considered toxic at low levels. Initial testing performed on the car on February 18, 1981 by State officials uncovered the presence of PCB contamination [footnote omitted] in the front seat and on the hood and the State notified Pawlowski that it was being held for decontamination. While it was believed that several attempts were made at decontamination, the record is unclear as to the dates such cleaning occurred, who attempted it and, with the exception of one attempt at decontamination with the cleaner Lestoil, what materials or methods were used. Retests of the car conducted in March and April 1981 showed decreased levels of PCBs but that some contamination remained. Apparently no further action was taken until October 1, 1981 when Pawlowski received a letter from the State Office of General Services advising that "State personnel charged with disposition in this matter" had determined not to return the vehicle. Ultimately, the vehicle was destroyed by or at the direction of State officials. It was unclear who made the determination to destroy the vehicle or the rationale for it.

Thereafter, Kresge transferred title to the car to claimant, its insurer, for fair market value. Claimant, in turn, commenced this action seeking damages for conversion. In its answer, the State asserted, *inter alia*, that its actions were privileged under the common-law doctrine of public necessity because the car contained toxic contaminants. The Court of Claims concluded after trial that the State bore the burden of proving that reasonable procedures were used to clean the car and that the ultimate decision to terminate decontamination attempts and dispose of the vehicle was reasonable in order for its acts to fall within the ambit of the privilege. Finding that the evidence submitted failed to satisfy either of these showings, the court granted judgment for claimant. The State appeals.

The doctrine of public necessity operates to avoid liability for what would otherwise constitute an actionable conversion "if the act is or is reasonably believed to be necessary for the purpose of avoiding a public disaster" (citation omitted). Ordinarily, invocation of the doctrine requires only a showing that the chattel itself has become dangerous and that intervention is necessary (citation omitted); there is no preliminary requirement that attempts be made to eradicate the condition giving rise to the threatened public peril prior to effecting the actual conversion (citation omitted). However, in situations such as the one herein where, following an initial admittedly privileged confiscation, the converter reasonably believes that an alternative less extreme than actual destruction of the chattel may suffice to eliminate the public threat and undertakes such measures to rid it of the pestilence with the view toward ultimately restoring it to its rightful owner, before the converter can rely upon the public necessity doctrine to justify ultimate destruction of the chattel it must demonstrate that reasonable efforts, albeit unsuccessful, were made at eradication, thus rendering destruction reasonably necessary (citation omitted).

> We agree with the Court of Claims that the evidence presented falls woefully short of establishing that reasonable efforts were made to eradicate the toxic contamination of this car. The State was able to provide no details of the cleaning methods used other than the fact that on one occasion a common household cleaner was used. Moreover, because at least some cleaning was attempted and it had the effect of reducing the degree of contamination, the testimony of the State's expert that *no* amount of cleaning or scrubbing could render the vehicle safe because of the many intricate surfaces on the car, standing alone, is in our view insufficient to satisfy its burden of proof of the doctrine's applicability.

The State of New York needed to show that its efforts at decontamination so substantially failed that the only recourse was to take the vehicle out of public necessity.

■ CONSENT

Consent involves a plaintiff agreeing to accept the consequences of a defendant's otherwise tortious conduct. To raise this defense of consent to liability, the defendant has to show the following elements:

- sanctioning of an invasion of an interest
- based upon a full understanding of the consequences

By agreeing, the plaintiff effectively waives any right to recovery from the defendant. Consent negates the wrongfulness of the act so that no tort actually occurs. For example, if professional athletes could bring suit for battery arising out of the playing of a game, most professional sports could not happen because the participants could not come into physical contact with one another.

When Consent Is Not Available

A plaintiff may not grant consent to an injury of his or her interests under any of the following conditions:

- The plaintiff lacked the capacity to consent—that is, the ability to form the intent necessary to hold the defendant liable for committing the tort. For example, a child cannot consent to engage in sports where contact might arise
- The plaintiff lacked complete knowledge of relevant facts when granting the consent. A person planning to play touch football won't be prepared to engage in the full-contact version of the sport.
- The plaintiff's agreement came as a result of the defendant's threat to injure or from mistake—for example, when a kid turns over his lunch money to the school bully to avoid getting beaten up.

Consent to Crime

Society precludes a plaintiff from granting consent to injury arising out of criminal behavior. Otherwise, people might consent to injury for a price, something that our society would clearly wish to avoid, as noted in the *Restatement (Second) of Torts* (see box below).

> ## CONSENT TO CRIME
>
> 1. Except as stated in Subsection (2), consent is effective to bar recovery in a tort action although the conduct consented to is a crime.
> 2. If conduct is made criminal in order to protect a certain class of persons irrespective of their consent, the consent of members of that class to the conduct is not effective to bar a tort action.
>
> *Restatement (Second) of Torts* §892C

Consider the plight of the acting students whose consent arose out of trust that the defendant, an acting coach of great repute, misused when he compelled the students to engage in sexual activity (see Case in Point 10-3).

CASE IN POINT 10-3

Micari v. Mann

481 26 Misc. 2d 422 (Sup. Ct. 1984)

Plaintiffs, students in defendant's acting school, instituted this action to recover damages based on allegations of sexual abuse and harassment. At trial the moving plaintiffs (all of whom were in their early twenties at the time of the incidents complained of) testified that defendant (who was then in his mid sixties) caused them to perform at school various sexual acts with him or in his presence, including fellatio upon him and masturbating and engaging in lesbian acts in his presence. Plaintiffs acknowledged that no physical force was employed or threatened by defendant to cause them to perform these acts. They asserted, however, that defendant individually told them that this sexual activity was intended to release their inhibitions and thus improve their acting skills. They indicated that, in light of defendant's outstanding reputation as an acting teacher who had taught many famous members of the profession, they trusted him, although they each professed doing so with a certain amount of trepidation.

Defendant denied that any of the alleged sexual activity occurred except for one instance of fellatio which he stated was initiated by one of the plaintiffs. [...]

[...]

Here the wrongs which the jury found defendant to have committed are most reprehensible. The jury [...] determined that defendant misrepresented the reason he requested the performance of the sexual acts about which the plaintiffs testified. Thus, defendant, a person with a distinguished reputation as an acting teacher, abused the relationship which he, as a teacher with overpowering influence over his students, possessed. [...]

Here the testimony indicated that defendant, playing upon the emotional needs of his insecure students, actively sought to be ensconced as their trusted father figure—indeed, one of the plaintiffs described defendant's behavior after a sexual experience as "fatherly." It is this studied effort at domination under the guise of acting *in loco parentis,* coupled with both his actual and apparent ability to affect plaintiffs' dearest aspirations, that renders defendant's actions so heinous. This gross violation was not merely of their bodies but of their trust as well, an invasion so reprehensible as to cry out for the imposition of a sanction expressing the moral outrage of society. [...]

By exploiting a position of authority that arose out of reputation and age, the defendant coerced the plaintiffs to grant consent. The defendant's exploitation of that position meant that the plaintiffs did not in fact have the opportunity to grant meaningful, valid consent to receive tortious injury. This kind of abuse of a position of trust, involving sexual activity, justifiably led to prosecution.

■ MISTAKE

The mistake defense deals with action based on incorrect information or an erroneous belief about facts. That an individual made a mistake does not automatically excuse the person from liability; he or she must have genuinely believed the inaccurate information was valid. If the defendant chose a course of action based on a mistake of fact, the defendant lacked the intent necessary for establishing liability.

For example, suppose a partygoer defendant mistakenly takes another person's coat home, having confused it with the defendant's own coat. The defendant would not face liability for conversion since the defendant did not intend to take the plaintiff's coat, only the defendant's own.

To establish the defense of mistake of fact, the defendant will have to show the following elements:

- inaccurate information that the defendant genuinely believes is accurate
- intent to act based upon that information
- intentionally engaging in tortious conduct

Reasonable Person Making Such a Mistake

Mistake may provide a defense in cases involving intentional torts. When a defendant raises this as a defense at trial, the critical issue for the judge or jury is whether a reasonable person, under the specific circumstances, would likely have made such a mistake. A jury can draw on the experience of the jurors to determine whether the defendant acted like a "reasonable person" (see box below).

> ### MISTAKE
> The law is, then, that if the defendant entertained the intent necessary for the particular tort, such as trespass to land, battery, or false imprisonment, it will be no excuse, ordinarily, that he was mistaken as to something justifying his conduct. But this generality does not apply when the defendant is regarded as having a justifiable reason for the exercise of a privilege. If, in other words, the defendant's motive or purpose is that of self-defense, or defense of another, then even though he may be acting under an erroneous belief as to the necessity for the exercise of this defense, he may be justified.
>
> W. Page Keeton et al., *Prosser & Keeton on the Law of Torts* §17 at 111 (5th ed. 1984)

In Case in Point 10-4, a mistake of fact could negate liability for the tort conversion. The issue that the trial court faced, however, had to do with the reasonableness of the defendant's belief that he had authority to act as he did.

CASE IN POINT 10-4

Walker v. Brown

501 So. 2d 358 (Miss. 1987)

Ralph Walker individually and Ralph Walker, Inc. appeal from a jury verdict holding them jointly liable [...] for the conversion of a refrigerated trailer. The adverse judgment in the Circuit Court of Rankin County held the[m...] liable for $5,000 actual damages [...]

On September 2, 1981, Raymond Brown, Jr. began hauling a perishable load of lettuce and celery from Salinas, California to destinations in Harrisburg, Pennsylvania and Bedford, Ohio. He only made it as far as Mississippi where his trailer containing the perishable load was taken. The trailer was returned after four to five days, but its detention formed the basis for this suit in conversion.

Raymond Brown, Jr., a Virginia resident, and his father, Raymond Brown, Sr., operated more or less as trucking partners. Brown, Sr. rented a refrigerator trailer under a lease/purchase agreement and had given the trailer to his son to make a living.

On September 2, 1981, the younger Brown was traveling with his wife and son when he learned through Valentine Truck Brokers, Inc., a shipping broker that drew commissions for bringing shippers, receivers and carriers together, that a load needed shipment east. The younger Brown contracted with Valentine to haul the load. Though no delivery date was discussed, Brown was aware that the highly perishable load of lettuce should reach Pennsylvania and Ohio before September 9, 1981.

Not having permits to drive a more northern route, Brown intended to drive a southern route which would take him through Arkansas, Tennessee or Mississippi. Brown realized at the time the trailer was loaded that it would be too heavy to meet the more restrictive weight limits in those states. He decided to drive through Mississippi and avoid the multiplied risk.

Brown encountered several problems along the way.

[...]

It was September 9 when Brown pulled into Vicksburg, Mississippi. He knew he was late, but when he called to inform Valentine of his plan to circumvent the scales, he said he was told to just get going. Brown did, but he got caught by tax commission enforcement officers. He followed them to a weigh station, where it was determined that the rig was overweight. Brown learned that the fine would be $126.00 and he would need an additional $300.00 advance to pay this fine, and to hire someone to haul the overweight part of the load to the state line and reload it onto his trailer.

He disconnected the trailer and drove his cab to a nearby truck stop on U.S. Highway 49 to call Valentine Truck Brokers to ask for money. He spoke with dispatcher Robert Knipe. There was a dispute as to whether Knipe stated the money would be or might be wired but Knipe told Brown to go to the S.O.S. Truck Stop in Clinton, Mississippi, where Valentine did business. Brown proceeded to the truck stop and waited for approximately four hours, but no money arrived. Brown then returned to the scales to check on the load and discovered that the trailer had been moved.

Knipe testified that after receiving Brown's call, he telephoned the buyers in Pennsylvania and Ohio who cancelled the orders because they were late. Knipe then found a dealer for the perishable produce on a consignment basis in Atlanta. To get the load sold, attempting to minimize their joint loss, Knipe called Ralph Walker's trucking business, located on U. S. Highway 49 South, because Walker had helped Valentine pick up troubled loads on several previous occasions. He did not tell Walker who owned the trailer, but he told him that there was a overloaded trailer with perishable lettuce which needed to be taken to Atlanta for salvage immediately. Walker would be reimbursed for paying the fine and services.

Walker testified that he sent one tractor trailer and another cab to handle the job. The excess load was placed on the tractor trailer and the cab towed Brown's trailer. Once past the scales, Walker's men reloaded Brown's trailer and drove it on to Atlanta.

Walker testified that he knew the trailer wasn't Knipe's, but he thought it belonged to somebody "that was affiliated with Mr. Robert (Knipe)," so it would be alright. Walker said he did not ask permission to take the trailer because he didn't know the owner and he doubted that the owner knew him.

Knipe testified that on September 9 he spoke with Brown, Sr., who gave him permission to take the trailer. However, he wasn't sure whether that conversation preceded or followed his call to Walker. Raymond Brown, Sr. testified and denied he ever gave Knipe permission, and stated that, in any event, he did not speak with Knipe until September 12 because he was out of town.

After dropping the produce in Atlanta, Walker had Brown's trailer returned to Mississippi but taken to Houston, Mississippi and left at a plant where Walker did a lot of business. Walker thought he would leave Brown's trailer there because he often ran loads from Houston to Jackson, so it could easily be returned. He thought this would allow Brown and Valentine Truck Brokers to conclude their business as to who owed whom with regard to the lateness of the load of perishable lettuce resulting in the cancellation by the recipients.

Workers at the scales told Brown who took his trailer. On the same day it was taken, Brown went to Walker's office. Brown testified that he told Walker that his trailer was stolen and he wanted it back. Walker testified that he explained to Brown that the load of perishable produce was being salvaged in Atlanta, and Brown seemed satisfied with this. Walker told him to call Valentine Truck Brokers and speak with Knipe because it was Brown and Knipe's deal and not his.

Walker heard nothing more from Brown until September 12, when a Mississippi Highway Patrol Investigator and a Richland police officer questioned Walker about the trailer. Brown had reported it stolen, but Walker agreed to have it back within eight hours. The trailer was returned to the truck stop on U. S. Highway 49 near the weigh station about 2:00 a.m. on September 13. The trailer was undamaged. Walker was never charged.

The younger Brown spent $420.00 on food and hotel bills while in Jackson, and resorted to asking trucker friends to buy meals for his family when he ran out of money. Brown even accepted the Highway Patrol Investigator's offer to buy his son a meal.

[…]

Walker and Ralph Walker, Inc. argue here that they cannot be liable for conversion because Ralph Walker, at worst, acted on the mistaken belief that Robert Knipe had authority to order the trailer moved and the produce salvaged. We are told that Walker reasonably believed Knipe had this authority.

Conversion requires an intent to exercise dominion or control over goods which is inconsistent with the true owner's right. (citation omitted) Walker's good faith reliance does not absolve him from liability as to actual damages […]

Walker can take no solace in a claim that he was the innocent agent or servant of Valentine Truck Brokers. Though an agent or servant who innocently receives or transports goods on behalf of his principal may be insulated (citation omitted), that protection is not afforded the agent who negotiates the transaction. We hold there was sufficient evidence that Walker, in a legal sense, negotiated the transaction through which he wrongfully gained possession of Brown's trailer. The jury was justified in finding that this was done with the intent to exercise dominion and control over the trailer, which was in fact inconsistent with Brown's rights. We affirm the $5,000.00 judgment holding Walker liable for the actual damages for conversion […]

We cannot say the jury verdict in this case is such that it must be set aside. The jury was instructed that it could award actual […] damages. The jury could have considered the amount of money lost on the shipment not being delivered, the

Browns' expenses in staying in Mississippi for nearly five days and the consequential harm resulting from the trailer's detention. The Browns expended $420.00 on food and hotel bills and Brown had to sell his four-month old CB radio at a loss to obtain cash. The jury also could have considered lost business because of the extended stay in Jackson. Raymond Brown, Jr. testified that he intended to deliver the produce and then contract to carry another load, but could not because the trailer was gone. Brown testified that he could have delivered the produce by September 10, giving him two to three days during which he could have obtained and possibly delivered another load. We find no error in the jury award.

[...]

We hereby affirm the jury's verdict of liability for actual damages in the amount of $5,000.00

[...]

Walker had received orders from Knipe to take a trailer. Knipe never mentioned who owned the trailer and Walker never asked. Although the risk of uncertainty as to ownership was small, Walker—who owns a trucking company and may well have heard of trailers getting hijacked—could have easily asked Knipe about this.

Mistake may depend greatly upon the specific circumstances and fact of the tort. A paralegal should review state law to determine when the defense of mistake might apply.

■ STATUTE OF LIMITATIONS

A **statute of limitations** is a law that specifies the maximum length of time a plaintiff has in which to file a suit. By creating such laws, states recognize that with time, evidence becomes more difficult to uncover and memories can fade. If a defendant is sued two years after the tort supposedly happened, he or she operates at a distinct disadvantage when trying to find information that could free him or her from liability. The following box lists reasons for imposing statutes of limitations:

REASONS FOR IMPOSING A STATUTE OF LIMITATION

1. Evidence will deteriorate as memories fade or even become distorted in ways that cannot be convincingly tested, so "stale claims" should be barred.
2. Renewal of an ancient grievance in court may initiate more conflicts than it resolves; and in any event society should not use its judicial resources to reignite a conflict that had been quieted by time.
3. The defendant, who may not in fact have been a wrongdoer, is entitled at some point in time to peace of mind that comes from knowing the potential conflict has burned out.
4. The defendant's ability to manage business or personal affairs is clouded by a potential law suit; for instance, he may be unable to borrow money or make business commitments until claims are resolved; if he does not in fact know of the potential claims, he may make financial commitments that prove disastrous in the light of a late-asserted claim.

5. For similar reasons, insurers find it costly to insure against a defendant's liability for an indefinite time into the future; these costs represent real costs to society (in the form of increased premiums for insurance or increased costs of goods); if these costs can reasonably be avoided by requiring prompt suit, society in general is better off.

6. In some cases, stability of transactions or relationships has other important social values; a consent to adoption of a child should not be subject to revocation or attack long after the child has established a relationship with adoptive parents, for example. In greater or lesser degree the same stability or security interests affect other potential litigations as well.

7. Over time, society's expectations and standards change, sometimes in ways that society itself does not perceive immediately; without a limitation, judges or juries might unjustly impose today's standards on events that took place twenty, thirty or fifty years ago [...]

Dobbs, *The Law of Torts* §216 (2000)

Regardless of the merits of a plaintiff's claim, the defendant's use of the lapse of a statute of limitations can work as a complete defense to tort liability. For example, suppose a plaintiff is injured in an automobile accident in a state with a three-year statute of limitations. If the plaintiff does not file within three years of the accident, the defendant may raise the defense of statute of limitations and bar any recovery, no matter whether the defendant actually caused the accident.

Time

The starting point for a claim of a statute of limitation from liability is the moment that the tort occurs. The courts often use the metaphor of a clock that starts to run at the moment the injury occurs. From that moment on, a plaintiff has only a certain amount of time to file suit, and that amount may vary by the kind of cause of action. Failing that, the plaintiff's claim is barred once time has elapsed. Paralegals should check for the appropriate statute of limitation with any tort.

Case in Point 10-5, about a claim of ownership to the rights of a famous song, focuses on the risks of letting too much time pass before filing suit.

 # CASE IN POINT 10-5

Newsome v. Brown

2005 U.S. Dist. 4088 (S.D.N.Y. 2005)

Plaintiff Betty Newsome brings this copyright action alleging claims about her song entitled "It's a Man's World," which challenge defendants' rights in two other songs, as will be described. The defendants are James Brown (the world-renowned singer and performer), Bert Jones, Dynatone Publishing Company, Leonard S. Mietus Management Co., Clamike Music, Inc., and Warner/Chappell Music, Inc.

[...]

The complaint contains four counts. Count I alleges that defendants have infringed Newsome's copyright in "It's a Man's World." However, Count I does not describe what the infringement consisted of. Count II is about the song "It's a Man's Man's Man's World." It essentially alleges that certain of the defendants made improper copyright registrations to the latter song, at first indicating that defendant Brown was the sole composer and later stating that both defendant Brown and Newsome jointly composed this song. Count II essentially challenges any claim of right to this song on the part of any of the defendants. Count III deals with a song entitled "It's a Man's Man's Man's World (But It Wouldn't Be Nothing Without a Woman or a Girl)." Count IV seeks an accounting.

Although the notice of motion states that summary judgment is sought as to all claims against the moving defendants, the arguments presented by these defendants do not deal at all with Count III. Thus, the court must construe the motion as addressed only to Counts I, II and IV. [...] The Court grants the motion as to Count II and that count is dismissed. As to Counts I and IV, the court dismisses these counts to the extent that they relate to Count II [...]

Facts

The facts set forth herein are derived from the complaint, declarations and depositions, and documents.

Creation and Registration of "It's a Man's World" and "It's a Man's Man's Man's World"

As the complaint states, Newsome wrote the words and music to the song "It's a Man's World," [...]

Newsome hummed the melody of "It's a Man's World" to defendant Brown while in a limousine leaving New York City. On that occasion Newsome and Brown made some efforts to come up with a new song, and ultimately Brown developed "It's a Man's Man's Man's World." Brown performed and recorded the song in 1966, which became an international hit.

Brown assigned his rights in "It's a Man's Man's Man's World" to defendant Dynatone on April 14, 1966 for the initial copyright term of 28 years and the renewal term of 28 years. Dynatone registered the song for copyright on the same day, crediting Brown as the sole author.

The 1966 Action and 1967 Settlement

After discovering that Brown had recorded and released the song "It's a Man's Man's Man's World," Newsome inquired of Clamike why she was not given credit on the recording. Clamike then commenced an action in this court in June 1966 against Brown, Dynatone, and King Records, Inc. alleging that "It's a Man's Man's Man's World" was an infringement of "It's a Man's World." (citation omitted.) The only defendant to appear in that action was Brown, who denied all allegations and interposed a counterclaim alleging that Clamike was infringing the copyright to "It's a Man's Man's Man's World."

A settlement agreement was reached in 1967. The agreement credited Newsome and Brown as co-authors of "It's a Man's Man's Man's World" and provided that Clamike and Dynatone were co-owners of the copyright. Dynatone had a 2/3 interest, and Clamike had a 1/3 interest. They were to receive royalties from the song in these proportions, and disburse them to Brown and Newsome respectively. In the settlement agreement there were signature lines for Clamike, Dynatone, and Brown, and also for the attorney for the plaintiff and the attorney for the defendants. The agreement was signed on behalf of Clamike by Clarence Jackson, but there was no signature on behalf of Dynatone. Brown signed. An attorney for the plaintiff signed. No attorney for the defendants signed.

Despite the lack of complete signatures, it appears that the terms of the settlement agreement were carried out. Dynatone collected the royalties from performances of "It's a Man's Man's Man's World." Dynatone retained a 2/3 share, which was disbursed to Brown, and paid a 1/3 share to Clamike, which was disbursed to Newsome.

[...]

The Renewal of Copyrights

At some point Warner/Chappell succeeded to the duties of Dynatone in collecting royalties and dispersing them as Dynatone had done.

Defendant Mietus was connected with Clamike beginning in June of 1968. From 1968 to December 31, 1992, on behalf of Clamike, Mietus collected the royalty share from Dynatone, and later Warner/Chappell, and paid the royalties to Newsome.

The copyright for "It's a Man's World" was renewed as of January 8, 2001. Although the renewal application referred to Clamike as the original copyright claimant, Newsome is referred to as the renewal claimant. Based on the copyright laws enacted in 1976, the initial term of the copyright expires after 28 years, and then can be renewed. *See* 17 U.S.C. § 304(a)(2)(B)(ii). The renewal rights belong to the proprietor or the author as of the time of expiration of the original copyright. The copyright for "It's a Man's World" expired January 1, 1993. As the registered author of the words of the song "It's a Man's World," Newsome claims that she became the owner of the renewal rights of the copyright on this day, rather than on the renewal registration date of January 8, 2001.

Warner/Chappell renewed the copyright for "It's a Man's Man's Man's World" on January 24, 1994, continuing to credit Brown as the lone author.

[...]

On December 1, 1994, Janet Raines, an employee of Warner/Chappell, wrote to Bob Crews, of the renewal section of the Copyright Office. The letter noted that the original registration of "It's a Man's Man's Man's World" was solely in the name of Brown. The letter stated that this needed to be corrected, because in fact Newsome had a 1/3 interest in the song, as a result of the settlement of litigation. The letter enclosed a Supplementary Registration form in accordance with the letter, and this registration became effective December 13, 1994.

Mietus also took steps in December 1994 to have Newsome included as author of "It's a Man's Man's Man's World" in the copyright registration. He wrote the Copyright Office on December 6, 1994, sending a renewal registration form for that song, which listed both Brown and Newsome as authors. [...] The Copyright Office accepted this registration and it became effective on the same date as the Raines registration—December 13, 1994. The evidence before the court provides no explanation as to why, in December 1994, Raines and Mietus took steps to have Newsome included in the copyright registration of "It's a Man's Man's Man's World." Newsome claims that she gave no authority to either Raines or Mietus to take the steps which they took.

[...]

Civil actions under the Copyright Act of 1976 are subject to a three-year statute of limitations as provided by *17 U.S.C. § 507(b)*, which states that "no civil action shall be maintained under the provisions of this title unless it is commenced within three years after the claim accrued." A copyright claim accrues when the plaintiff "knows or has reason to know of the injury upon which the claim is premised." (citation omitted). This three-year statute of limitations generally applies to claims of copyright infringement on a "rolling" basis, since "each act of infringement is a distinct harm giving rise to an independent claim for relief." (citation omitted). In other words, if a series of infringing acts constitutes a "continuing wrong," there can be liability for the acts which occur within the three-year statutory period. (citation omitted).

Count II of the complaint asserts that the lyrics and music to "It's a Man's Man's Man's World" "were created by Plaintiff" but copyrighted by defendant Dynatone, listing defendant Brown as author.

[...]

Newsome's ownership claim accrued when she knew or had reason to know of the injury upon which the claim was premised. (citation omitted).

It is conclusively established that this occurred nearly 40 years ago. Brown recorded "It's a Man's Man's Man's World" in 1966, and it became an international hit. At Newsome's instance (sic), Clamike commenced a lawsuit in June 1966 against Brown and others. In the 1967 agreement settling that action, both Newsome and Brown were formally credited as being co-authors of the song. Although Newsome now attacks that agreement as not binding on her, she sure knew of the agreement at the time, and has admitted receiving $250,000 in royalties pursuant to the agreement and has admitted receiving accounting statements accompanying those royalties. She has specifically admitted that, sometime within three years of the date of the agreement, she was aware that she and Brown were credited in the agreement as co-authors of the song in question.

It is also relevant to note the January 9, 1996 agreement entered into between Clamike and Newsome. Newsome signed this agreement. It expressly recognizes Newsome and Brown as co-authors of "It's a Man's Man's Man's World." It purported to revise upward the royalties to be received by Newsome, as described earlier in this opinion.

Since this action was commenced April 3, 2001, any copyright claim which accrued prior to April 3, 1998 is barred. The ownership claim Newsome is asserting regarding "It's a Man's Man's Man's World" accrued in 1966 or within a very few years thereafter. Newsome not only knew that Brown was asserting a claim of ownership or co-ownership, but indeed she acquiesced in this. But, for statute of limitations purposes, the crucial fact is her knowledge. At the very latest, Newsome's claim accrued in 1996. At this time she again agreed to Brown's claim of co-ownership. But again for statute of limitations purposes is Newsome's knowledge. Although the 1996 events occurred almost 30 years after the transactions of 1966 and 1967, 1996 is still more than three years before the time Newsome commenced her lawsuit.

For these reasons, the court holds that defendants are entitled to summary judgment dismissing Count II as barred by the statute of limitations.

The court concluded that the plaintiff and Brown had resolved the issue of authorship in the 1960s. Since the plaintiff received payments for some years, she had had plenty of time to keep track of when the copyright needed to be renewed, but filed suit too many years after the time for renewal and to object to Brown's claim that he was the sole author of the song.

The Discovery Rule

Public policy recognizes, however, that the passage of time may put a plaintiff at a disadvantage. While it may be obvious that the "clock" starts to run from the moment of injury, sometimes the exact moment of injury is not immediately clear. Then, the issue becomes, at what point in time did the plaintiff become aware of the injury? Some jurisdictions apply a **discovery rule,** which says the "clock" starts to run once the plaintiff reasonably becomes aware of the injury and "discovers" the need to file suit.

The Discovery Rule and Claims of Sexual Abuse

How should the courts apply the discovery rule when the alleged victim is a minor? Consider a child who was sexually abused. The experience may have so traumatized the individual that it becomes clear only years after the abuse occurred. Yet, several years later, the alleged abuser will not have a timely chance to find timely and valid evidence.

Courts have had difficulty balancing the interests of the plaintiff in gaining recovery with a defendant's ability to investigate the facts to provide a defense. Some courts, recognizing that the statute of limitations was the result of legislative action, suggest that the legislature address the problem. So some legislatures have enacted laws that extend the length of the statute of limitations. Other states' legislatures "start the clock" to run—usually for three years, a common span for many other torts—once the plaintiff has reached the age of majority.

Case in Point 10-6 involved allegations of child abuse: assault, battery, and intentional infliction of emotional distress, among others. Finding no statute indicating any decision by that state's legislature to handle this kind of situation, the court determined that the traditional measurement of time in which to file a tort suit applied.

 CASE IN POINT 10-6

Doe v. Maskell

342 Md. 684 (1996)

In this case we are asked to decide whether the "discovery rule" applicable to the time-bar of the statute of limitations on civil actions at law found in Maryland Code (citation omitted) applies to cases of allegedly "repressed" and "recovered" memories. We hold that repression of memories is an insufficient trigger to compel the application of our discovery rule, and we shall affirm the summary judgment entered in favor of the defendants.

I

Reviewing the record in a light most favorable to the plaintiffs, the facts of the case are as follows: Jane Doe, from 1967 to 1971, and Jane Roe, from 1968 to 1972, were students at Seton Keough High School [hereinafter "Keough"], a parochial school in Baltimore City. During their tenure at Keough, both girls, individually were referred for counseling to the school chaplain, Father A. Joseph Maskell. According to the complaints filed in the cases, Maskell subjected the girls to repeated sexual, physical, and psychological abuse [...]

Both girls were allegedly threatened with extreme punishments if they informed anyone of the abuse, which continued until the girls graduated and left Keough in 1971 and 1972 respectively. At some point [footnote omitted], both plaintiffs claim that they ceased to recall the abuse suffered at the hands of Father Maskell, due to a process they term "repression." (footnote omitted). Both plaintiffs began to "recover" memories of this abuse in 1992.

Plaintiffs filed suit [...] on August 24, 1994 allege battery, negligent supervision, negligent misrepresentation, intentional infliction of emotional distress, fraud, and loss of consortium. (footnote omitted) [...]. Prior to trial, the trial judge conducted a hearing to consider defendants' motions for summary judgment based on the time-bar of the statute of limitations.

At the hearing, both plaintiffs testified, as did expert witnesses offered by both plaintiffs and the defendants. [...] At the conclusion of the hearing, Judge Caplan entered summary judgment for the defendants. [...] The defendants agreed that the petition should be granted, and we issued our writ of certiorari to consider the important issues raised by this case.

II

The general Maryland statute of limitations and the one applicable in this case is Md. Code [...] § 5-101 [...]. That section provides:

"A civil action at law shall be filed within three years from the date it accrues unless another provision of the Code provides a different period of time within which an action shall be commenced."

Statutes of limitations [...] are intended simultaneously to "provide adequate time for diligent plaintiffs to file suit," (citation omitted) to "grant repose to defendants when plaintiffs have tarried for an unreasonable period of time," (citation omitted) and to "serve societal purposes," (citation omitted) including judicial economy. There is no magic to a three-year limit. It simply represents the legislature's judgment about the reasonable time needed to institute suit. We have also observed that:

"Statutes of limitation find their justification in necessity and convenience rather than in logic. They represent expedients rather than principles." (citation omitted) Historically, our cases have held that a cause of action "accrued" on the date of the wrong. (citation omitted) Under this "date of wrong" rule, claims that were not discovered until after the limitations period had expired were automatically barred. This traditional rule did not distinguish between a "blamelessly ignorant" plaintiff and one who had acted negligently and "slumbered on his rights." (citation omitted).

To ameliorate this harsh result, this Court (footnote omitted) developed the "discovery rule," which holds that a cause of action "accrues" when plaintiff knew or should have known that actionable harm has been done to him. [...] We held that in order to "activate the running of limitations [it must be proven that the plaintiff had] actual knowledge—that is express cognition, or awareness implied from 'knowledge of circumstances which ought to have put a person of ordinary prudence on inquiry [thus, charging the individual] with notice of all facts which such an investigation would in all probability have disclosed if it had been properly pursued.'"(citation omitted).

But the discovery rule, by necessity, must operate differently in different contexts. To retain the requisite flexibility to apply the rule to different situations, this Court has always retained to itself the power to shape the contours of the discovery rule. [...] It is, therefore, for the trial court initially, and ultimately for this Court, to determine how the discovery rule will be applied to cases involving repressed memories. In so doing, we are mindful that "in determining the application of the statute [of limitations] to particular actions, we do so with awareness of the policy considerations unique to each situation." (citation omitted) Therefore, the determination of the applicability of the discovery rule in a memory loss or repression case is a legal determination for this Court to make. (footnote omitted)

III

We find that the critical question to the determination of the applicability of the discovery rule to lost memory cases is whether there is a difference between forgetting and repression. It is crystal clear that in a suit in which a plaintiff "forgot" and later "remembered" the existence of a cause of action beyond the 3-year limitations period, that suit would be time-barred. Dismissal of such a case reflects our judgment that the potential plaintiff had "slumbered on his rights," should have known of his cause of action, and was blameworthy. To permit a forgetful plaintiff to maintain an action would vitiate the statute of limitations and deny repose for all defendants.

Plaintiffs in this case, however, claim that in order to avoid the pain associated with recalling the abuse they suffered, their memories were "repressed," not merely "forgotten," and later "recovered," rather than "remembered." They argue that this difference renders them "blamelessly ignorant" and excuses their failure to file suit in a timely manner. To aid in an understanding of plaintiffs' argument, we have extracted two implicit assumptions:

1. That there is a qualitative and quantitative difference between "repression" and mere "forgetting"; and
2. that this difference is of a sufficient quality to compel us to find that plaintiff is excused by operation of the discovery rule and had no reason to have known about the existence of her cause of action.

We have reviewed the expert testimony provided at the summary judgment hearing, and reviewed numerous scientific journals submitted by the parties. [...] The plaintiffs have provided us with several studies purporting to validate the diagnosis of repression. [...] The Defendants have also offered significant scientific information tending to discredit the concept of repression and its application in this setting. These arguments against repression take several forms.

First, the adversaries of repression stress that there is no empirical, scientific evidence to support the claims that repression exists. The studies purporting to validate repression theory are justly criticized as unscientific, unrepresentative, and biased. (citation omitted) The reason for the failure of repression enthusiasts to obtain empirical evidence may be the nature of the process itself. [...]

Just because there is so far no empirical validation for the theory of repression is not alone sufficient reason to discount the concept, yet it does cast some doubt.

Second, critics of repression theory point out that the scientific, and specifically, the psychological community has not embraced repression theory, and that, in fact, serious disagreement exists. While the existence of consensus (or lack thereof) in the scientific community is a more familiar inquiry within the context of determining the admissibility of scientific evidence [...], it is also a useful measure for this Court to evaluate the acceptance, and acceptability of a scientific theory. [footnote omitted.]

[...]

After reviewing the arguments on both sides of the issue, we are unconvinced that repression exists as a phenomenon separate and apart from the normal process of forgetting. Because we find these two processes to be indistinguishable scientifically, it follows that they should be treated the same legally. Therefore we hold that the mental process of repression of memories of past sexual abuse does not activate the discovery rule. The plaintiffs' suits are thus barred by the statute of limitations. If the General Assembly should wish to rewrite the law, that is its prerogative and responsibility. [footnote omitted.]

[...]

[W]e shall affirm the summary judgment in favor of the defendants on the ground that plaintiffs' claims were barred by the statute of limitations three years after they reached their eighteenth birthdays, for Doe after August 11, 1974 and for Roe, after April 29, 1975.

Although the court noted that some legislative action had taken place regarding adjusting the statute of limitations for a tort claim of child abuse, it noted that the legislature had enacted no new law dealing with this issue. Therefore, the claims of the plaintiffs were barred under the statute of limitations. Note that this case took place in 1975 and the law in many states has changed because of a growing body of evidence indicating that the trauma of such violence can cause the victim to repress memories of the experience. The following example of the law in West

Virginia, represents how a legislature could strike a balance in protecting the rights of all parties involved (see box below).

STATUTE OF LIMITATIONS FOR TORTS AGAINST A CHILD IN WEST VIRGINIA

§ 55-2-15. General saving as to persons under disability.

If any person to whom the right accrues to bring any such personal action, suit or scire facias, or any such bill to repeal a grant, shall be, at the time the same accrues, an infant or insane, the same may be brought within the like number of years after his becoming of full age or sane that is allowed to a person having no such impediment to bring the same after the right accrues, or after such acknowledgment as is mentioned in section eight [§ 55-2-8] of this article, except that it shall in no case be brought after twenty years from the time when the right accrues.

W. Va. Code §55-2-15 (2007)

Tolling

Using the metaphor of a running clock to measure the statute of limitations, **tolling** refers to "stopping the clock" to suspend the elapsing of time on a statute of limitations. The clock might stop, for example, if the court lacks jurisdiction over the defendant or if the plaintiff suffered some incompetence, such as being a minor or insane.

Suppose a defendant injured a plaintiff, then fled overseas, returning only after the statute of limitations had passed. When the plaintiff files suit, the defendant claims the statute of limitations has run out. Because the defendant was overseas and outside the court's ability to compel defendant to respond to allegations of abuse, the "clock" stopped while the defendant was overseas. As a matter of policy, society does not want to reward defendants who flee from a jurisdiction simply to have "the clock run out."

Some states may not have statutes of limitations for certain types of legal actions. This will not necessarily expand the defendant's tort liability; the plaintiff will still need to meet the burden of proof, by a preponderance of the evidence, on all elements of the tort.

Table 10-1 Available Defenses

Tort	Available Defenses
Assault	Consent, Defense of Self, Immunity, Mistake, Necessity, Privilege, Statute of Limitations
Battery	Consent, Defense of Self, Immunity, Mistake, Necessity, Privilege, Recapture of Chattel, Statute of Limitations
Conversion	Consent, Defense of Property, Immunity, Mistake, Recapture of Chattel, Statute of Limitations
Deceit	Consent, Immunity, Mistake, Statute of Limitations

(continued)

Defamation	Consent, Immunity, Mistake, Privilege, Statute of Limitations, Truth
Emotional Distress	Consent, Immunity, Mistake, Privilege, Reasonable Discipline, Recapture of Chattel, Rightful Possession, Statute of Limitations
False Imprisonment	Consent, Defense of Self, Immunity, Privilege, Reasonable Discipline, Statute of Limitations
Injurious Falsehood	Consent, Defense of Self, Immunity, Privilege, Reasonable Discipline, Statute of Limitations
Misuse of Legal Procedure	Consent, Immunity, Mistake, Privilege, Statute of Limitations
Privacy	Consent, Immunity, Mistake, Necessity, Privilege, Reasonable Discipline, Recapture of Chattel, Rightful Possession, Statute of Limitations

See Chapter 7 and 8 for more about the torts listed here. See Chapter 11 for defenses involving immunity and privilege (including the privilege to use force, and to use force to discipline).

KEY TERMS

Consent   355

Discovery rule   364

Necessity   350

Private necessity   351

Public necessity   353

Statute of limitations   360

Tolling   368

SUMMARY

It is the plaintiff's obligation to make a *prima facie* case of liability for an intentional tort. Once that obligation has been met, the burden of proof shifts to the defendant to establish a legal excuse or privilege for his or her conduct as a defense to the tort action. The traditional common-law defenses to intentional torts involve a legal excuse, or justification, for the defendant's acts that caused injury to the plaintiff. This reflects the recognition, as a matter of social policy, that granting the means for a defendant to escape liability is, in some instances, more important than the individual interests of an injured plaintiff. Social policy also mandates that a defendant be excused from liability when the plaintiff has consented to the risk of injury. It may excuse liability where necessity dictates that committing a tort may mean avoiding a greater injury. Sometimes, a defendant's mistake of fact keeps the defendant from forming the intent needed to establish liability against the defendant. Any liability for an intentional tort may be avoided by statutory time limits on filing an action. This chapter lists the defenses available for certain intentional torts; some of these defenses are discussed in other chapters.

CONCEPT REVIEW QUESTIONS

1. Describe the doctrine of informed choice.
2. List the circumstances under which consent is ineffective.
3. List the elements of the defense of mistake.
4. Distinguish between public necessity and private necessity.

CRITICAL THINKING APPLICATIONS

1. During a hockey game, the defendant slashes at the plaintiff with a hockey stick. When the plaintiff later sues the defendant for battery, the defendant claims that the plaintiff consented to playing hockey and the defendant files a motion to dismiss. Will a court grant this motion? Why or why not?
2. The plaintiff rents a locker at a local storage business. A few months later, the plaintiff fails to pay rent on the locker for two months. Per the terms of the rental contract, the storage business cleaned out the locker. After waiting 30 days, also according to the rental contract, the storage business auctioned off the contents to pay the rent owed. The plaintiff, who had been in a very serious automobile accident and incapacitated for four months, returns to the storage business to discovery that the contents of the locker have been auctioned off. The plaintiff sues for the recovery of the items or damages. The storage business claims that the plaintiff should have responded to the letters sent about non-payment of rent and the auctioning of the contents. Because the plaintiff did not respond, the defendant claims the statute of limitations defeats any claim the plaintiff had. Do you agree or disagree? Why?
3. Behind the plaintiff's house, a commuter train collides with an empty freight car. People from the community repeatedly cross through the plaintiff's property to give medical aid to the train's passengers. These repeated crossings have damaged the plaintiff's land so that it needs landscaping. If the plaintiff sues the townsfolk who came to the aid of the passengers, what will be the outcome at trial? Why?
4. The plaintiff is walking in a public park and sees two people trying to subdue a third person. The plaintiff jumps into the fray, pushing against the attackers. One falls to the ground and suffers a nasty gash to the forehead. The other attacker then announces that they are law-enforcement officers who had been trying to arrest the third person. The injured officer files suit against the plaintiff for battery. The plaintiff files a motion for summary judgment, claiming it was a mistake and the plaintiff genuinely believed the person being arrested needed help. Will the court grant the plaintiff's motion? Why or why not?
5. During a bar fight, the plaintiff strikes the defendant. The plaintiff wants to sue the defendant but discovers that the defendant has left on a military tour of duty. By the time the defendant returns and can be served process, the statute of limitations has passed. In the defendant's answer to the complaint, the defendant says because the statute of limitations has passed, he cannot be held liable. Then, he files a motion for summary judgment. Will the court grant the motion? Why or why not?
6. During a pick-up game of basketball, the plaintiff leaps upward to sink a jump shot. Swatting at the ball, the defendant knocks the plaintiff down. The plaintiff suffers injuries and sues the defendant for damages. Will a court find the defendant liable for damages? Why or why not?

7. A wildfire has started to burn a house at the edge of a neighborhood. Firefighters stop spraying down that house and douse the adjacent house with water, to prevent the fire from spreading into the neighborhood. They succeed. The owner of the burnt-out home sues for damages because the fire department deliberately refused to put out the fire consuming his house. How likely is it that the owner will recover damages because of the firefighter's actions?

8. The plaintiff, a law-enforcement officer, comes upon two people fighting and arrests one of them. After a few hours of investigating, the officer discovers this person was trying to defend himself against the other's attack. The person wrongfully arrested sues for false imprisonment. Will the officer, and the community that employs this officer, be found liable? Why or why not?

SKILL-BUILDING APPLICATION

Ganymede owned the building that shared an alleyway with Total Grocer. Recent modifications to Total Grocer now made it possible for Total Grocer to take in supplies from the alleyway. Ganymede lived in the ground floor unit of the building and complained to Total Grocer about the delivery of meat to Total Grocer, saying that occasional drippings from the meat gave the alleyway an unpleasant odor. No shipment of any other supplies to Total Grocer, via the alleyway, constituted a reason for Ganymede to complain to Total Grocer.

Over a weekend, Ganymede had installed chain-link fencing at either end of the alleyway. On one end was a closed gate. When the delivery from the wholesale supplier of meat came and the driver couldn't get into the alley, the driver went into Total Grocer to complain. The store manager on duty at that time, Hsin, went out to the alleyway and pushed the gate open. The driver then started down the alley, carrying a crate of frozen chicken breasts, only to find that Ganymede did put out a kitchen chair and was sitting in it. The driver went by the seated Ganymede, and may have brushed Ganymede's arm. The driver returned to the truck, accompanied by Hsin. Getting more supplies from the truck, the driver went down the alleyway. Hsin was standing next to Ganymede, who was still seated. The driver walked by without touching Ganymede, dropped the supplies off, then headed back to the truck. Hsin went into Total Grocer by the alleyway door.

Considering the defenses mentioned in this chapter, what chance does the driver have of escaping liability by using any of them? Define the defense and explain why it could help the driver to avoid liability.

Any law that takes hold of a man's daily life
cannot prevail in a community, unless the vast
majority of the community are actively in favor
of it. The laws that are the most operative are
the laws which protect life.

—Henry Ward Beecher (1813—1887)

Privilege and Immunity from Tort Liability | CHAPTER 11

Government bodies, public officers, or family members may enjoy immunity from liability. Immunity frees a defendant from having to justify or excuse one's behavior. The granting of immunity reflects a social policy, of the need to protect individuals or governments, while properly fulfilling an obligation or responsibility.

Privilege exists to excuse liability. Under certain circumstances, a defendant may escape liability for otherwise tortious conduct also as a matter of public policy.

CHAPTER TOPICS

1. Immunity and Privilege
2. Immunity and Public Policy
3. Sovereign Immunity
4. Sovereign Immunity under Federal Law
5. Sovereign Immunity for Other Government Entities
6. Privilege and Public Policy
7. Privilege and the Rules of Evidence

OBJECTIVES

After completing this chapter, you will be able to:

1. Define the doctrine of immunity from tort liability.

2. Examine the rationale behind the concept of immunity from tort liability.

3. Understand the nature of immunity within a family structure.

4. Analyze the doctrine of governmental immunity.

5. Understand the concept of immunity for public officers.

6. When an adult is *in loco parentis* to a child, what privilege may exist regarding the use of force towards a child?

7. Discuss the concept of privilege.

8. What is meant by privilege, within the context of the rules of evidence?

■ IMMUNITY AND PRIVILEGE

If a court finds a defendant liable in tort, the defendant must compensate the plaintiff for the loss through the payment of damages. Sometimes, however, society sees a greater benefit in not compensating the plaintiff, for example, when the defendant committed the tort while fulfilling certain responsibilities.

The Difference between Immunity and Privilege

Immunity protects individuals or governments from liability when they are engaged in fulfilling official obligations. **Privilege** arises, on a case-by-case basis, where finding a defendant liable would work contrary to social policy.

Often, immunity as a defense means freedom from liability for someone serving in an official, governmental capacity. For example, a court will not allow a suit where evidence shows that an official acted to fulfill the duties of the office. The threat of liability might otherwise discourage people from working in government.

A defense of privilege excuses the defendant's liability when society's interest in helping the injured party would be otherwise frustrated. The application of privilege depends very much on the circumstances involved. For example, imagine when a thief sues a victim for assault and battery because the victim fought back and injured the thief. Society might want to grant a privilege for the use of reasonable force in self-defense, so that the victim of an assault can legally fight back against his attacker.

Here's how Professor Dobbs contrasts the two:

THE DIFFERENCES BETWEEN IMMUNITY AND PRIVILEGE

Immunities tend to shield defendants because of their legal status, while privileges tend to shield defendants because their actions were justified in the particular case. Privileges raise fault issues and go to the merits of the case, while immunities may be accorded even to wrongdoers.

[...]

Courts sometimes emphasize the bright-line quality of immunity by saying that an immunity is an immunity from suit, not merely an immunity from liability. The point of that saying is to assert that the value of the immunity is to save the defendant from the costs and uncertainties of a grail and hence to claim that courts can rightly avoid considering the merits of the case.

Dobbs, *The Law of Torts* §225 (2000)

■ IMMUNITY

Traditional Basis for Policy

Immunity as a defense means absolute freedom from liability otherwise created by an intentional tort. The absolute excusing of liability arose out of the historical need for the proper wielding of power for the greater good. A king, for example, could not face suit for his actions since it was presumed the king would always have the country's best interests in mind when engaging in an action. In a more contemporary situation, a father might need to use force to protect his family. Today, society accords far less deference to leaders and their actions. Although immunity still exists, it is provided only in certain limited situations, as defined by statute. It exists chiefly to allow public officials to fulfill their obligations without constant concern regarding the risk of facing personal liability for performing the duties of an office.

Sovereign (Governmental) Immunity

The doctrine of **sovereign immunity,** or governmental immunity, exempts from liability any government entity and those who work for it or act on its behalf. The concept's continued existence relies, in part, on the principle of separation of powers. Freeing the government from such suits spares it from the risk of excessive judicial scrutiny. Another rationale claims this immunity protects governments from damage awards that could overwhelm their budget.

Yet, most jurisdictions recognize that because government employees can cause tortious injury—for example, getting into an accident while driving a government vehicle—a grant of immunity simply because the driver is a government employee, working at the moment of injury, seemed arbitrary. Those jurisdictions have modified the absolute protection of sovereign immunity by statute. In that way, an injured plaintiff may have an opportunity to recover for some types of torts. Note that states may vary widely on the degree of limitation of the absolute protection of sovereign immunity (see box below).

ABROGATION OF SOVEREIGN IMMUNITY

Almost all states have now enacted tort claims statutes waiving the blanket common law immunity of the state and its agencies. Besides these general statutes, other statutes may affect immunities in particular cases, and of course both kinds of statutes must be consulted for details. As a matter of structure, about thirty states abolish the tort immunity generally, but retain it in specified circumstances. [footnote omitted] A second group works in reverse, retaining the immunity generally, but abolishing it for a list of cases in which liability is permitted. In several states, a tort claim against the state must be presented to an administrative body instead of to a court. [footnote omitted] Some states set up a separate court of claims for hearing tort claims against the state [footnote omitted]. About three states appear to retain a very broad sovereign immunity. [footnote omitted]

Dobbs, *The Law of Torts* §268 (2000)

National Government

In 1946, Congress ended the federal government's absolute protection from suit because of sovereign immunity when it enacted the **Federal Tort Claims Act (FTCA).** This law allowed injured parties to sue the federal government as if it were a private individual (see box on next page).

> ## FEDERAL TORTS CLAIM ACT
>
> a. The district courts shall have original jurisdiction, concurrent with the United States Claims Court [United States Court of Federal Claims], of:
>   1. Any civil action against the United States for the recovery of any internal-revenue tax alleged to have been erroneously or illegally assessed or collected, or any penalty claimed to have been collected without authority or any sum alleged to have been excessive or in any manner wrongfully collected under the internal-revenue laws;
>   2. Any other civil action or claim against the United States, not exceeding $10,000 in amount [...] upon any express or implied contract with the United States, or for liquidated or unliquidated damages in cases not sounding in tort [...]
> b. (1) [...] the district courts [...] shall have exclusive jurisdiction of civil actions on claims against the United States, for money damages [...] for injury or loss of property, or personal injury or death caused by the negligent or wrongful act or omission of any employee of the Government while acting within the scope of his office or employment, under circumstances where the United States, if a private person, would be liable to the claimant in accordance with the law of the place where the act or omission occurred.
>
> 28 U.S.C.S. §1346

This statute broadly addresses the instances where sovereign immunity might apply. The list below illustrates a sense of the breadth and range of this law (see box below).

> ## HEADINGS FOR INTERPRETIVE NOTES AND DECISIONS INVOLVING THE FEDERAL TORT CLAIMS ACT
>
> 1. IN GENERAL
> 2. TAX REFUND CLAIMS (28 USCS § 1346(a)(1))
> 3. CLAIMS FOUNDED ON FEDERAL LAW; CONTRACT CLAIMS; CLAIMS NOT SOUNDING IN TORT (28 USCS § 1346(a)(2))
> 4. TORT CLAIMS (28 USCS § 1346(b))
> 5. SETOFFS, COUNTERCLAIMS AND OTHER CLAIMS (28 USCS § 1346(c))
> 6. MISCELLANEOUS CLAIMS (28 USCS § 1346(d), (e), (f))

As in those states that modified sovereign immunity, Congress required certain conditions to exist before allowing suits against the federal government. These important requirements are listed below:

- Plaintiffs had a two-year statute of limitations from the time of injury filing successfully a claim against the Federal government.
- The government rejected the claim.
- Such a claim must be filed in a Federal court of claims or any federal district court.

Immunity and the Military

The federal government has not consented to having U.S. military personnel face liability in tort while in the service. For one thing, the risk of lawsuit might impair the ability of these people to follow orders. For another, since the nature of the military involves national defense, society considers national defense to be a more pressing concern than to allow for individuals to gain compensation due to injury by service personnel.

In Case in Point 11-1, the U.S. Supreme Court acknowledged the importance of military commanders having the ability to manage service personnel.

CASE IN POINT 11-1

United States v. Shearer

473 U.S. 52 (1985)

[...]

Respondent is the mother and administratrix of Army Private Vernon Shearer. While Private Shearer was off duty at Fort Bliss and away from the base, he was kidnaped and murdered by another serviceman, Private Andrew Heard. A New Mexico court convicted Private Heard of Shearer's murder and sentenced him to a term of 15 to 55 years' imprisonment.

Respondent brought this action under the Federal Tort Claims Act [...] claiming that the Army's negligence caused Private Shearer's death. Respondent alleged that Private Heard, while assigned to an Army base in Germany in 1977, was convicted by a German court of manslaughter and sentenced to a 4-year prison term. Upon his discharge from that confinement in Germany, the Army transferred Private Heard to Fort Bliss. Respondent alleged that, although the Army knew that Private Heard was dangerous, it "negligently and carelessly failed to exert a reasonably sufficient control over" him and "failed to warn other persons that he was at large."

[...] The Federal Tort Claims Act's waiver of sovereign immunity does not apply to "[a]ny claim arising out of assault [or] battery," (citation omitted) and it is clear that respondent's claim arises out of the battery committed by Private Heard. No semantical recasting of events can alter the fact that the battery was the immediate cause of Private Shearer's death and, consequently, the basis of respondent's claim.

[...]

It is clear that Congress passed the Tort Claims Act on the straightforward assurance that the United States would not be financially responsible for the assaults and batteries of its employees....

To permit this type of suit would mean that commanding officers would have to stand prepared to convince a civilian court of the wisdom of a wide range of military and disciplinary decisions; for example, whether to overlook a particular incident or episode, whether to discharge a serviceman, and whether and how to place restraints on a soldier's off-base conduct.

We hold that Congress has not undertaken to allow a serviceman or his representative to recover from the Government for negligently failing to prevent another serviceman's assault and battery.

While the Court's ruling left the mother of the victim unable to recover damages, the Court affirmed the principle that the military needs a measure of freedom from the civil law to accomplish its primary mission.

Activities Involved in Running a Government

The U.S. Supreme Court in *Dalehite v. United States*, 346 U.S. 15 (1953), addressed the issue of whether the Federal Tort Claims Act (FTCA) lifts sovereign immunity when the federal government engages in the exercise of discretion. It focused specifically on the regulation of the use of fertilizer. More broadly, the Court focused on why the government and its employees should enjoy immunity for the tort of negligence, when engaging in a discretionary function (see Case in Point 11-2).

CASE IN POINT 11-2

Dalehite v. United States

346 U.S. 15 (1953)

Petitioners seek damages from the United States for the death of Henry G. Dalehite in explosions of fertilizer with an ammonium nitrate base, at Texas City, Texas, on April 16 and 17, 1947. [...]

The suits were filed under the Federal Tort Claims Act (citation omitted). That Act waived sovereign immunity from suit for certain specified torts of federal employees. It did not assure injured persons damages for all injuries caused by such employees[....]

Suing under this grant of jurisdiction, the plaintiffs claimed negligence, substantially on the part of the entire body of federal officials and employees involved in a program of production of the material—Fertilizer Grade Ammonium Nitrate (FGAN hereafter)—in which the original fire occurred and which exploded. [...]

Since no individual acts of negligence could be shown, the suits for damages that resulted necessarily predicated government liability on the participation of the United States in the manufacture and the transportation of FGAN. Following the disaster of course, no one could fail to be impressed with the blunt fact that FGAN would explode. In sum petitioners charged that the Federal Government had brought liability on itself for the catastrophe by using a material in fertilizer which had been used as an ingredient of explosives for so long that industry knowledge gave notice that other combinations of ammonium nitrate with other material might explode. The negligence charged was that the United States, without definitive investigation of FGAN properties, shipped or permitted shipment to a congested area without warning of the possibility of explosion under certain conditions. The District Court accepted this theory. His judgment was based on a series of findings of causal negligence which, for our purposes, can be roughly divided into three kinds—those which held that the Government had been careless in drafting and adopting the fertilizer export plan as a whole, those which found specific negligence in various phases of the manufacturing process and those which emphasized official dereliction of duty in failing to police the shipboard loading. [...] Even assuming their correctness arguendo, though, it is our judgment that they do not establish a case within the Act. This is for the reason that as a matter of law the facts found cannot give the District Court jurisdiction of the cause under the Tort Claims Act[....]

The Federal Tort Claims Act was [...] the offspring of a feeling that the Government should assume the obligation to pay damages for the misfeasance of employees in carrying out its work. [...] Some simplified recovery procedure for the mass of claims was imperative. This Act was Congress' solution, affording instead easy and simple access to the federal courts for torts within its scope[....]

One only need read § 2680 in its entirety to conclude that Congress exercised care to protect the Government from claims, however negligently caused, that affected the governmental functions. [...] An analysis of § 2680(a), the exception with which we are concerned, emphasizes the congressional purpose to except the acts here charged as negligence from the authorization to sue. It will be noted from the form of the section [...] that there are two phrases describing the excepted acts of government employees. [...] The second is applicable in this case. It excepts acts of discretion in the performance of governmental functions or duty whether or not the discretion involved be abused. "Not only agencies of government are covered but all employees exercising discretion." It is clear that the just-quoted clause as to abuse connotes both negligence and wrongful acts in the exercise of the discretion because the Act itself covers only "negligent or wrongful act or omission of any employee, within the scope of his office where the United States, if a private person, would be liable...."

[...]

Affirmed.

The Court upheld judgment for the federal government because the FTCA exempted the negligent exercise of discretion, and where this activity involved such an exercise of discretion.

Often the issue involves a government agency's need to formulate and apply a policy. For example, a federal agency might be charged with improving the security of U.S. passports. The agency adopts a faulty security standard that renders passports less secure. If this failure slows down the ability of U.S. citizens to travel, none of those disgruntled citizens will have a claim in negligence against the federal agency.

If those disgruntled travelers claimed a violation of their civil rights, however, they could bring suit under **42 USC §1983,** which limits governmental immunity for officials who have violated civil rights while performing their official duties.

State Government

State governments also could exercise sovereign immunity. Just as the federal government has curtailed its sovereign immunity, states have expressly lifted immunity in some instances. Of course, governments retain the immunity unless otherwise they've expressly waived it (see box below).

STATE GOVERNMENTAL IMMUNITY

1. A State and its governmental agencies are not subject to suit without the consent of the State.
2. Except to the extent that a State declines to give consent to tort liability, it and its governmental agencies are subject to the liability.
3. Even when a State is subject to tort liability, it and its governmental agencies are immune to the liability for acts and omissions constituting
   a. the exercise of a judicial or legislative function, or
   b. the exercise of an administrative function involving the determination of fundamental governmental policy
4. Consent to suit and repudiation of general tort immunity do not establish liability for an act or omission that is otherwise privileged or is not tortuous.

Restatement (Second) of Torts §895B (1965)

Table 11-1 describes some instances where states will limit their immunity.

Table 11-1 How States Might Address the Issue of Immunity from Suit	
Immunity	**No Immunity**
• For typical governmental activities, like collecting taxes • Exercise of discretionary functions	• Abuse of exercise of discretionary functions (But the state then provides an alternative means to get a remedy, through the creation of state agencies to review and decide such claims; and so long as the plaintiff has complied with procedural requirements, such as complying with a statute of limitation.)

Exercise of discretionary authority often occurs when the executive branch of government attempts to do its job. The executive branch of government often fulfills its legal obligations through its agencies. If an agency had to defend a suit for the exercise of all discretionary actions it undertook, then the government could not function. Allowing for suit would put the courts in the awkward position of having to second-guess decisions of the executive branch of government. That would violate the doctrine of the separation of powers, wherein each branch of our government is sufficiently free of interference from other branches so that it can fulfill its legal obligations. (For more on this topic, see 'Ministerial or Proprietary Function,' below.)

Eminent Domain

Governments may confiscate real or personal property if doing so would advance a public good. However, it must pay the owner for the loss of property. The threat of arbitrary government confiscation of property seemed obvious to our nation's founders. The Fifth Amendment to the U.S. Constitution provides for **eminent domain**—that is, the notion that when the government takes property for the public good, it must compensate the owner.

The act of taking property may provide instances where officials have to exercise discretion, such as deciding whether a taking should occur, what should be taken, and the amount of compensation appropriate for such a taking. To allow government to engage in such necessary takings of property, states and the federal government have retained immunity from suit for the exercise of discretion in taking property under eminent domain. A government employee, then, should not expect to face liability in such a situation, as noted in Case in Point 11-3, where the city manager initiated an action in eminent domain.

 # CASE IN POINT 11-3

Weast v. Budd

186 Kan. 249 (1960)

This was an action to recover damages from the city of Parsons, Kansas, and Bernard T. Budd, the city manager, alleged to have been sustained by the plaintiff as a result of the city's commencement and abandonment of an eminent domain proceeding to take his entire farm for water works improvement. The defendants filed a motion to strike certain allegations of the plaintiff's second amended petition, which was sustained in part, and the plaintiff has appealed. The allegations of the second amended petition are briefly summarized: On September 18, 1957, pursuant to proper resolution and ordinance and applicable statutes of the state of Kansas, the defendant city commenced an eminent domain proceeding in the district court of Neosho County, to condemn the plaintiff's 100-acre farm, together with other lands, for a water reservoir. [...]

On November 19, 1957 [...] the city [...] abandoned the eminent domain proceeding to all of the plaintiff's farm except a two-acre strip of land.

Between the time of the commencement of the eminent domain proceeding and its abandonment, the plaintiff was told, informed, instructed and directed by Budd that the city was taking and would take his entire farm. The plaintiff relied upon Budd's representations and instructions that he not cut his sorgo crop, which he was then prepared to do, since its value would be included in the commissioners' award; that he immediately remove himself, his family, and his 77 head of cattle from his farm and do no further work on a gas well then being drilled on the farm, all of which resulted in the loss of his sorgo crop destroyed by frost on or about October 20, 1957; loss from the forced sale of his 77 head of cattle because he had no feed for them; loss from being unable to use his growing rye, wheat and barley crops as pasture; loss of the gas well by reason of its caving in because plaintiff's lessee did no further work on it, and expenses incurred in trying to find a place to move. Plaintiff prayed for damages against both defendants in the amount of $3,000 for loss of the sorgo crop, $2,400 for loss of rye, wheat and barley pasture, $8,700 for loss from the sale of his cattle, $10,000 for loss of the gas well, and $500 for expenses incurred in trying to find a place to move.

[...]

Since the second amended petition alleged the city commenced a proceeding in eminent domain to acquire land for water works improvement, and inasmuch as it was further alleged the proceeding was abandoned by the city by proper resolution within ten days after the commissioners filed their appraisement in the district court of Neosho County, and, assuming, *arguendo*, that the plaintiff sustained the damages alleged, the question arises, is the city liable?

The answer to the question is conditioned upon the answer to the further query: In what capacity was the city acting? If it acted as an agent of the sovereign upon a subject of general public concern, dissociated from any private, proprietary right, it shares the sovereign's immunity from suit (citation omitted).

It is unnecessary to write a treatise on the law of eminent domain. Suffice it to say eminent domain is the right to take private property for public use without the owner's consent upon payment of just compensation.

[...]

Since the power of eminent domain is an inherent power and springs from the necessity of government, it is exercised by a municipal corporation only as a governmental power or function irrespective of the purpose for which the property acquired for public use is to be put [...]

Assuming, without deciding, that the statements, representations and instructions of Budd were tortious, it has been consistently held by this court that a city is not liable for negligent acts or misconduct of its officers or employees when acting in the performance of its governmental function absent a statute expressly imposing liability. The rule is based upon the doctrine that the state is not liable except as made so by statute, and that municipalities, as an agent of the sovereign, when acting in a governmental capacity, are arms of the state and likewise not liable.

[...]

As has been determined, the city was acting in a governmental capacity when it commenced and abandoned the eminent domain proceeding. As city manager, Budd was responsible to see that the ordinances of the city were enforced and carried out (citation omitted), and in conferring with the court's commissioners and the plaintiff at the farm on October 16, 1957, he was carrying out those duties. Budd was a city officer acting for the city. Consequently, in seeing to it that the ordinances of the city were carried out he was performing an executive or administrative function and, in the absence of a statute imposing liability, any injuries the plaintiff may have sustained as a result of the city's or Budd's actions were *damnum absque injuria,* and the trial court did not err in sustaining the motion to strike the items of damages heretofore enumerated.

The judgment is affirmed.

The court noted that immunity applied to the city manager since he was fulfilling a legal obligation as a government employee.

Suit in Federal Court against States for Abuse of Discretion

The **Eleventh Amendment to the United States Constitution** limits instances where suit may be brought against a state. It prohibits citizens from using the federal trial courts to sue a state (see box below).

ELEVENTH AMENDMENT

The Judicial power of the United States shall not be construed to extend to any suit in law or equity, commenced or prosecuted against one of the United States by Citizens of another State, or by Citizens or Subjects of any Foreign State.

U.S. Const. amend XI

States may, but are not required to, consent to make themselves subject to the authority of the federal trial courts. Individuals who sue states likely will find that the state has limited its traditional sovereign immunity to allow for suit.

States may sue one another in the federal system. Those suits often have to do with defining boundaries or the sharing of common resources. The trial for such a suit is done before the U.S. Supreme Court. Rather than hold the trial, the Court usually appoints someone to examine the issues and make a recommendation to the Court about how to rule.

Local Government

State law may require communities to provide certain services but then gives the community discretion in fulfilling those mandates. The required activities may be common and expected of any community, such as providing law enforcement or emergency services. For those kinds of activities, states often extend immunity to the community as it works to fulfill such mandates (see box below).

MUNICIPAL GOVERNMENT

1. Except as stated in Subsection (2), a local government entity is not immune from tort liability.
2. A local government entity is immune from tort liability for acts and omissions constituting
   a. the exercise of a legislative or judicial function, and
   b. the exercise of an administrative function involving the determination of fundamental governmental policy.

> 3. Repudiation of general tort immunity does not establish liability for an act or omission that is otherwise privileged or is not tortious.
>
> *Restatement (Second) of Torts* §895C (1965)

In Case in Point 11-4, the plaintiff lived adjacent to a school and when it rained, the rain run-off from the schoolyard poured onto the plaintiff's property. The plaintiff contended that sovereign immunity did not exempt the school board from having to compensate him for damage caused by the run-off.

 # CASE IN POINT 11-4

Vento v. Strongsville Board of Education
2007 Ohio App. 3785 (Ohio Ct. App., Cuyahoga County 2007)

Plaintiff-appellant Charles Vento appeals from a common pleas court order dismissing his complaint against defendant-appellee Strongsville Board of Education for failure to state a claim. [...] He also contends that in maintaining its property, the appellee was engaged in a proprietary function, so his claim was one for which the city could be liable under the exception to sovereign immunity [...] The complaint in this case was filed March 30, 2006. It alleged that the defendant school board owned Muraski Elementary School and the real property located at 20270 Royalton Road in Strongsville, Ohio. The complaint alleges that, "since at least April of 2002 and continually through the present," the school board "negligently, recklessly and carelessly maintained its real property***, causing excessive water and drainage to flow upon the real property owned by [plaintiff-appellant]." [...] Plaintiff-appellant asserted that this conduct caused him to suffer damage to his property and to incur expenses to correct the damage. He further claimed that the school board's actions deprived him of the use of his property and diminished its value.

[...] [T]he school board argued [...] that its maintenance of school grounds was a governmental function as to which it was immune, and [...] that appellant's complaint alleged an intentional tort, which was not a claim excepted from sovereign immunity. The court granted this motion without opinion, so we address all of these contentions.

[...]

The only school board action which the plaintiff challenges here is the maintenance of the real property on which Muraski Elementary School is located. Therefore, it is important to discern, first, whether the maintenance of real property upon which an elementary school is located constitutes a governmental function or a proprietary one.

[...] "[G]overnmental functions" encompass the maintenance of school grounds, regardless of how the grounds themselves are used. By contrast, "proprietary functions" are defined, in part, as functions not included in the statute's list of governmental functions. (citation omitted). (footnote omitted) Because the maintenance of school grounds is a governmental function it is, by definition, not a proprietary function.

[...]

There is also an exception to sovereign immunity for negligent performance of governmental functions, but that exception applies only to "injury, death, or loss to person or property that is caused by the negligence of [a political subdivision's] employees *and that occurs within or on the grounds of,* and is due to physical defects within or on the grounds of, buildings that are used in connection with the

> performance of a governmental function * * *." (citation omitted)(emphasis added). The injury to plaintiff-appellant's property did not occur "within or on the grounds of" school property, but on adjacent property. Therefore, this exception does not apply to allow appellant to pursue his claim. (citation omitted)
>
> [...]
>
> Plaintiff-appellant could prove no set of facts pursuant to his complaint which would have entitled him to relief. Therefore, the court correctly granted the school board's motion to dismiss for failure to state a claim.
>
> Affirmed.
>
> [...]

Since the schoolyard was used for a government function—education—the fact that incidental rainwater flooded the plaintiff's property was not enough to lift sovereign immunity in that case.

Ministerial or Proprietary Function

When the U.S. government, as an organization, fulfills obligations uniquely reserved to it, the government is exercising a **ministerial function.** Often, immunity applies in the performance of a ministerial duty. Making decisions on how best to fulfill the agency's ministerial duties involves the reasonable exercise of discretion.

Contrast that with when a jurisdiction engages in a proprietary activity. At the state level, a state may grant communities the option of providing additional services. These proprietary functions include waste management, water, power/energy, or other services that a nongovernment entity could provide. When providing such services, and using discretion to fulfill such duties, communities usually do not enjoy sovereign immunity.

Table 11-2 offers examples of government functions for which communities likely enjoy sovereign immunity, and proprietary functions where sovereign immunity likely does not apply.

Table 11-2 Examples of Ministerial Functions (Immunity) and Proprietary Functions (No Immunity)

Ministerial Functions (Immunity)	Proprietary Functions (No Immunity)
• Municipal courts • Town management • Law enforcement • Emergency services	• Power/energy generation • Cable • Water/sewerage • Trash collection • Medical services/clinics • Natural resources (lakes, beaches, etc.) • Housing

What constitutes a proprietary or ministerial function will vary by state. Some states may even say that these functions can substantially, even completely, overlap. When that happens, courts may well have to determine the predominant characteristic of the activity to determine whether the community enjoys sovereign immunity from suit. As the question of sovereign immunity can involve the common law, statutes, or both, paralegals should thoroughly research how a state regards sovereign immunity.

Immunity for Law Enforcement Officers

Those acting on behalf of a government agency have historically enjoyed immunity from suits for negligence while acting in their official capacity (see box below).

Without such immunity, who would want to work in law enforcement, since every contact with the public could result in an action in tort?

Immunity for acts of negligence by such personnel arises also due to the exercise of discretion, since law enforcement officers need to use discretion when working to fulfill their obligations. To help them, officers receive training and gain experience so that the exercise of discretion builds off the special understanding they have developed for the job.

The concept seems clear, yet determining when a law enforcement officer has discretion and properly exercises discretion could prove more difficult. When engaging in this analysis, such as in Case in Point 11-5, the court clarified who would enjoy immunity and under what circumstances.

 # CASE IN POINT 11-5

Ross v. Consumers Power Company
420 Mich. 567 (1985)

These nine cases require us to reexamine the extent of immunity from tort liability which the governmental tort liability act [...] and the common law provide to the state and its agencies, non-sovereign governmental agencies, and the officers, agents and employees of these state and local governmental agencies. We hold:

1. All governmental agencies (state and local) are statutorily liable for injuries arising out of the failure to keep highways in reasonable repair [...] negligent operation of a government-owned motor vehicle by an officer, agent, or employee [...] and dangerous or defective conditions in public buildings under the agency's control [....]
2. All governmental agencies (state and local) have tort liability for injuries arising out of the performance of a proprietary function. "Proprietary function" is defined as any activity conducted primarily for pecuniary profit, excluding activities normally supported by taxes or fees.

3. All governmental agencies (state and local) are immune from tort liability for injuries arising out of the exercise or discharge of a non-proprietary, governmental function. "Governmental function" is defined as any activity which is expressly or impliedly mandated or authorized by constitution, statute, or other law. An agency's *ultra vires* activities are therefore not entitled to immunity.

4. All governmental agencies (state and local) are vicariously liable for the negligent operation of government-owned motor vehicles by their officers, employees, and agents.... Vicarious liability for all other torts may be imposed on a governmental agency only when its officer, employee or agent, acting during the course of his employment and within the scope of his authority, commits a tort while engaged in an activity which is non-governmental or proprietary, or which falls within a statutory exception.

5. Judges, legislators, and the highest executive officials of all levels of government are absolutely immune from all tort liability whenever they are acting within their respective judicial, legislative, and executive authority. Lower level officers, employees, and agents are immune from tort liability only when they are

    a. acting during the course of their employment and are acting, or reasonably believe they are acting, within the scope of their authority;

    b. acting in good faith; and

    c. performing discretionary-decisional, as opposed to ministerial-operational, acts.

"Discretionary-decisional" acts are those which involve significant decision making that entails personal deliberation, decision and judgment.

"Ministerial-operational" acts involve the execution or implementation of a decision and entail only minor decision making.

[...]

The court's analysis acknowledged that the immunity applied with the exercise of discretion, by all government officials. The state legislature disagreed with the court's analysis. It enacted legislation that allowed for a broader application of absolute immunity for governmental officials, according to the court in *Nalepa v. Plymouth-Canton Community. Sch. Dist.*, 207 Mich. App. 580 (1994).

A paralegal must review a state's law specifically on this issue when determining whether liability under tort exists over the actions of a government employee.

Warrantless Arrests

Should law enforcement officials making a **warrantless arrest**—that is, an arrest without first obtaining a warrant—be immune from a suit for liability in tort?

According to the Fourth Amendment to the U.S. Constitution, law enforcers must obtain a warrant to arrest a person. Law enforcers would secure a warrant from a judicial official after showing that probable cause exists to make an arrest. Probable cause is a measure of evidence, much lower than what would be needed to convict a person. Still, it requires some facts to support arresting someone and charging that person with the commission of a crime.

Quite often, law enforcers may not have time to secure a warrant. Given the training they receive, and their experience, law enforcers may make an arrest without a warrant if the officer believes that probable cause exists. If the officer is wrong, however, and the person arrested sues for the tort of false imprisonment, would immunity apply for the officer so as to escape liability?

Violation of Federal Civil Rights under 42 U.S.C. §1983 and the Issue of Immunity

The immunity of a law enforcer—or any government official—may be overruled by federal law. Specifically, under 42 U.S.C. §1983, any government official may not successfully raise immunity as a defense against an allegation that the official acted so as to deprive the civil rights of a plaintiff. This means that if any government official acts to violate the rights of another, such as the right to be free from unreasonable arrest, that official might not escape personal liability on a theory of sovereign immunity.

In Case in Point 11-7, the court had to determine whether law enforcement officers who made a warrantless arrest would enjoy immunity from a claim of violation of rights under 42 U.S.C. §1983.

CASE IN POINT 11-7

Goines v. James

189 W. Va. 634 (1993)

This case is before the Court upon the appeal of Sarah Goines and Curtis Goines from an April 16, 1992, order of the Circuit Court of Wood County denying the Appellants' motion to set aside a jury verdict and grant a new trial. The Appellants filed suit on June 13, 1988, pursuant to 42 U.S.C. A. § 1983 (West 1981) based upon alleged violations of their Fourth Amendment rights. (footnote omitted) [...] The Appellants' primary contention turns upon the single issue of whether a police officer's conduct in following a misdemeanant in hot pursuit into the residence of a third party, (footnote omitted) with neither a search warrant authorizing such entrance nor with permission of the owner, in order to effect the arrest of the misdemeanant constitutes a civil cause of action for which damages may be recovered. (footnote omitted) The Appellants argue that this warrantless search to effect a misdemeanor arrest was unconstitutional. The Appellees maintain that the police officers had the right to enter the Appellants' premises to effect the arrest. Moreover, the Appellees argue that regardless of what this Court decides on this underlying issue, the officers are entitled, as a matter of law, to the defense of qualified immunity in the civil action for damages because their conduct did not violate clearly established constitutional law. [...] [W]e hold that the officers involved were entitled to qualified immunity (footnote omitted) for their actions since the law concerning this constitutional issue was not clearly established. Accordingly, we affirm the decision of the circuit court.

[...]

On June 14, 1986, Officer Jeffrey James of the Parkersburg City Police Department was dispatched to respond to a complaint of disorderly conduct. Upon his arrival at the scene, Officer James observed a subject, later identified as Gary Shaffer, standing in front of the Appellants' home holding an open beer bottle. The officer testified that he observed Mr. Shaffer consume the contents of a beer bottle he had in his hand, while Mr. Shaffer stood in the street. Mr. Shaffer then broke the bottle by throwing it onto the street. Officer James exited his vehicle, approached Mr. Shaffer, and requested his identification. Mr. Shaffer refused to show the officer the requested identification and walked away from the officer into the Appellants' backyard.

Officer James followed Mr. Shaffer, but encountered the Appellant, Sarah Goines, before reaching him. The officer asked Ms. Goines if he could question Mr. Shaffer. When Ms. Goines responded that he could, the officer proceeded to enter the Appellants' backyard where Mr. Shaffer was standing in the middle of an ongoing party. When Officer James reached Mr. Shaffer in the backyard, he again asked Mr. Shaffer for identification. Mr. Shaffer again refused and walked away. At Appellant Sarah Goines' direction, Mr. Shaffer entered the Appellants' home through the back door.

Officer James followed Mr. Shaffer and when he reached him, the officer grabbed Mr. Shaffer in the doorway to the porch of the Appellants' home, but Mr. Shaffer pulled away, retreating into the house. Officer James proceeded into the home. At trial, the officer testified that he was arresting Mr. Shaffer for public intoxication. The officer also testified that he had no warrant for Mr. Shaffer's arrest, no search warrant to enter the premises, and no resident of the home had consented to or invited the officer to enter the premises.

Mrs. Goines alleges that the officer made an unprovoked assault upon her during his entry of the home, which caused serious bodily injury. Further, while Officer James was attempting to arrest Mr. Shaffer, the officer was confronted by Steven Goines, Appellant Sarah Goines' son. Steven Goines demanded that the officer produce a warrant and that the officer leave the premises. When the officer tried to explain that he had a right to be in the home to arrest Mr. Shaffer, a fight between the two ensued. Steven Goines was then arrested.

[...] [I]t is sufficient in this case to conclude that even if such an arrest was unconstitutional, the law thereon was not clearly established at the time of the officer's conduct, and consequently, the officer is entitled to qualified immunity from civil liability.

Consequently, we hold that under the doctrine of qualified immunity, a police officer is absolved from civil liability for following a misdemeanant in hot pursuit into the residence of a third party, with neither a warrant nor the permission of the third party, in order to effect a warrantless arrest of the misdemeanant, so long as such entry violates no clearly established statutory or constitutional rights.

For the foregoing reasons, the judgment of the Circuit Court of Wood County is affirmed.

Having found that the officers had a valid basis for making a warrantless arrest and that the law was not clear on this point, the court found that the officers enjoyed immunity and would not be liable on a claim of violation of civil rights.

Citizen's Arrest

As seen previously, in certain instances government employees in the course of fulfilling their duties enjoy immunity from a law suit. Jurisdictions often recognize that nongovernmental employees may make an arrest, often referred to as a **citizen's arrest.** When making a citizen's arrest without an arrest warrant, should that private citizen enjoy immunity from suit? The *Restatement (Second) of Torts* describes procedures that jurisdictions may adopt concerning valid circumstances under which a citizen may make a warrantless arrest (see box below).

WARRANTLESS ARREST

[...] a private person is privileged to arrest another without a warrant for a criminal offense

 a. if the other has committed the felony for which he is arrested, or
 b. if an act or omission constituting a felony has been committed and the actor reasonably suspects that the other has committed such act or omission, or

c. if the other, in the presence of the actor, is committing a breach of the peace or, having so committed a breach of the peace, he is reasonably believed by the actor to be about to renew it, or

d. if the other has attempted to commit a felony in the actor's presence and the arrest is made at once or upon fresh pursuit, or

e. if the other knowingly causes the actor to believe that facts exist which would create in him a privilege to arrest under the statement in Clauses (a) to (d).

Restatement (Second) of Torts §119 (1965)

If a private citizen faces suit in tort for having made a warrantless citizen's arrest, the question of immunity depends upon the citizen's having actual authority for the arrest. The private citizen will lose the immunity if, in fact, no probable cause existed. This mistake of fact will mean that the citizen has no authority to arrest and, without that authority, cannot raise immunity as a defense.

In Case in Point 11-8, the court looked first to see whether probable cause existed to make an arrest under applicable state law. Finding that, it then looked to see whether immunity should apply during a citizen's arrest.

CASE IN POINT 11-8

Fraser v. County of Maui

855 F. Supp. 1167 (D. Haw. 1994)

On September 30, 1992, Plaintiff Loretta Fraser ("Plaintiff") filed a complaint against Defendants Wendell Loo ("Loo"), County of Maui ("County"), David Firestine ("Firestine"), and Napili Ridge Association of Apartment Owners ("Napili Ridge"), asserting federal causes of action under 42 U.S.C. §1983 [...] and state causes of action under false imprisonment, malicious prosecution, and intentional and negligent infliction of emotional distress. Against Napili Ridge, Plaintiff also asserts state negligent employment and supervision claims.

[...]

Facts

This action arises out of the citizen's arrest of Plaintiff by Firestine on January 23, 1992. Firestine arrested Plaintiff for harassing him. At the time of the arrest, Firestine was the Resident Manager of the condominium complex in which Plaintiff lived. Unhappy with his work, Plaintiff began conducting an informal surveillance of Firestine's job performance. Plaintiff then complained about his performance to the complex's board, of which Plaintiff was a member, and asked that Firestine be fired. The other board members disagreed with Plaintiff's assessment of Firestine's performance and refused to fire him. As a result, Plaintiff began an intensive surveillance of Firestine's activities. For a 3 1/2-day period, she followed Firestine around during his job and took notes of his activities. Frustrated, Firestine called the Maui Police Department after the first day of Plaintiff's surveillance and complained to the police about her behavior. Loo was the officer responding to Firestine's complaint.

Loo's affidavit testimony reveals the following about the events leading to Plaintiff's arrest:

Firestine called the Maui Police Department on January 20, 1992 to complain about Plaintiff's conduct. Firestine complained that Plaintiff was following him, sometimes as close as 10 feet behind him, and that she was writing down everything he did. Furthermore, when Firestine entered his apartment, Plaintiff waited outside watching what he was doing inside. Loo arrived at the scene to investigate the complaint. He spoke with both Plaintiff and Firestine. Plaintiff told Loo that she had a right to follow Firestine because she was a member of the condominium complex's board and it was her job to make sure Firestine was doing his job as Resident Manager. Loo told Plaintiff she could not follow Firestine if it was interfering with his work and annoying him, because the situation could escalate to a confrontation. Plaintiff then told Loo she would follow Firestine at a distance so as not to bother him or interfere with his work. Loo spoke with Firestine to be sure Firestine was satisfied with this resolution. Firestine stated he did not want to pursue the matter further. He did, however, tell Loo that Plaintiff was no longer a member of the board.

Early in the morning of January 23, 1992, Firestine again called the Maui Police Department to again complain about Plaintiff's surveillance. Loo went to the complex and saw Plaintiff standing at the bottom of the stairs leading to Firestine's apartment. Firestine was in his apartment. Loo spoke with Firestine, who told him that Plaintiff continued to follow him and that he was getting angry and was liable to hit Plaintiff if she did not stop. Loo talked to Plaintiff and told her he believed she was harassing Firestine and that she could be arrested. Plaintiff stated that she did not believe she was doing anything wrong, but that she would leave the area. Firestine then told Loo that, as long as Plaintiff left him alone, he did not wish to pursue prosecution.

Loo returned to the police station and discussed the situation with his supervisor. They decided that Plaintiff's conduct came within Haw. Rev. Stat. § 711-1106, dealing with the criminal offense of harassment. Later in the morning of January 23, 1992, Loo was again dispatched to the complex to investigate another complaint from Firestine. Upon arriving, Loo saw Plaintiff sitting on the lawn outside Firestine's office. She was surrounded by several tenants, who were telling her to leave Firestine alone. Firestine told Loo that, after Loo left, Plaintiff came back and told Firestine she was going to continue her surveillance. Loo approached Plaintiff, gave her a copy of § 711-1106, and told her she was violating this code section. Firestine then arrested Plaintiff.

[…]

§ 1983 Claim

In her complaint, Plaintiff asserts that both Firestine and Loo unlawfully arrested her. She claims the arrest was made without probable cause. An arrest without probable cause violates the Fourth Amendment and gives rise to a cause of action for damages under 42 U.S.C. § 1983. (footnote omitted) (citation omitted).

The Court now separately examines whether Plaintiff has met her summary judgment burden with regard to the § 1983 claims against each of the defendants.

[…]

Plaintiff argues that both Firestine and Loo unlawfully arrested her. Defendants Loo and County maintain that Firestine, not Loo, arrested Plaintiff. Nevertheless, they maintain that, assuming arguendo that Loo did arrest Plaintiff, Loo is protected by qualified immunity from liability for the alleged unlawful arrest because he had a reasonable belief that probable cause existed to arrest Plaintiff. He therefore seeks summary judgment on Plaintiff's § 1983 claim against him.

[…]

When a police officer asserts qualified immunity from liability under § 1983 for an unlawful arrest, "the district court must determine whether, in light of clearly established principles governing the conduct in question, the officer objectively could have believed that his conduct was lawful." (citation omitted) To resolve this issue, the district court must decide (1) whether the law governing the official's conduct was clearly established, and (2) whether, under the law, a reasonable officer could have believed the conduct was lawful. Id.

Neither party disputes that at the time Loo arrested Plaintiff clearly established constitutional law specified that, absent probable cause, Loo could not make a warrantless arrest of Plaintiff. (citation omitted) The dispute here focuses on the second part of the qualified immunity inquiry: Whether, under the law, a reasonable officer could have believed that Loo had probable cause to arrest Plaintiff.

[...]

"The test for probable cause is whether 'facts and circumstances within the officer's knowledge...are sufficient to warrant a prudent person, or one of reasonable caution, [to believe]...that the suspect has committed, is committing or is about to commit an offense.'" (citation omitted).

Plaintiff was arrested for allegedly committing the act of harassment under Haw. Rev. Stat. § 711–1106. At the time of Plaintiff's arrest, § 711–1106 provided in pertinent part that:

1. A person commits the offense of harassment if, with intent to harass, annoy, or alarm another person, that person:

...

    (b) Insults, taunts, or challenges another person in a manner likely to provoke an immediate violent response...;
        Haw. Rev. Stat. § 711-1106 (1985). (footnote omitted)

If Loo had probable cause, or a reasonable belief that probable cause existed, to arrest Plaintiff under § 711-1106, then he is shielded from liability. As discussed in detail below, this Court finds that probable cause did exist and that a reasonable police officer would have believed that probable caused existed. This Court therefore GRANTS summary judgment on Plaintiff's § 1983 claim against Loo.

[...]

The undisputed facts in this case show that probable cause existed to arrest Plaintiff for harassment under § 711-1106(1)(b) in that a person of reasonable caution would have believed Plaintiff challenged Firestine in a manner likely to provoke a violent response in Firestine. Plaintiff's continual surveillance of Firestine for 3 1/2 days before her arrest was done for the expressed purpose of finding ways in which Firestine's job performance was lacking. In essence, Plaintiff was challenging Firestine's ability to perform his job. (footnote omitted.) The manner in which Plaintiff expressed her challenge was likely to provoke a violent response from Firestine. Plaintiff followed Firestine for 3 1/2 consecutive days, watched his job performance and other activities, and took notes. Plaintiff presents no evidence that Firestine had received notification from his employers that his job performance would be under surveillance by Plaintiff. In fact, Plaintiff's own deposition testimony indicates that Firestine's employers did not sanction Plaintiff's surveillance in that Firestine's supervisor, the assistant manager at Napili Ridge, called Plaintiff's husband and told him that Plaintiff could not continue her surveillance. Furthermore, Firestine was aware of Plaintiff's surveillance and found it so intrusive that he contacted the police on three separate occasions in an effort to get Plaintiff to stop. Firestine told Loo that he was becoming so annoyed that he might hit Plaintiff if she did not stop. (footnote omitted)

[...]

[T]his Court finds that Loo had probable cause to arrest Plaintiff for harassment under § 711-1106, and therefore did not unlawfully arrest Plaintiff. Furthermore, the Court also specifically finds that, from the evidence detailed above, a reasonable police officer would have believed that probable cause existed, and therefore Loo is protected from liability under the doctrine of qualified immunity. Consequently, the Court GRANTS summary judgment as to Plaintiff's § 1983 claim against Loo.

[...]

b. Defendant County

Because this Court has found that Loo did not unlawfully arrest Plaintiff, the County cannot be liable to Plaintiff. [...]

[...] [T]his Court finds the undisputed facts discussed in connection with the issue of whether Loo had probable cause to arrest Plaintiff show that Firestine also had probable cause to arrest her. Plaintiff challenged Firestine's ability to perform his job when she conducted a surveillance of his activities for 3 1/2 consecutive days. Her surveillance was likely to provoke a violent response in Firestine, as shown by the facts that Firestine called the police to get Plaintiff to stop her surveillance, he threw away her furniture to retaliate against her, and he told Loo he thought he might hit her if she did not stop. Given these undisputed facts, a person of reasonable caution would have believed Plaintiff challenged Firestine in a manner likely to provoke a violent response in Firestine.

Moreover, Firestine's evidence indicates that Loo advised him that he could make a citizen's arrest of Plaintiff [...]. Plaintiff does not controvert this evidence. Because Plaintiff has presented no evidence showing that Firestine had some reason to doubt Loo's advice, (footnote omitted) this Court finds that, under the facts and circumstances known to Firestine, in particular, Loo's advice, a person of reasonable caution would believe Plaintiff was committing an offense. Plaintiff cannot sustain a false imprisonment claim against Firestine.

[...]

This Court has found that Firestine had probable cause to arrest Plaintiff for harassment, and therefore Plaintiff cannot sustain a malicious prosecution claim against Firestine. Even if the Court had not specifically found that probable cause existed, it would find that Plaintiff could not sustain a malicious prosecution claim.

Plaintiff cannot sustain either a false imprisonment or malicious prosecution action against Firestine. Consequently, the Court GRANTS summary judgment on Plaintiff's § 1983 claim against Firestine.

[...]

Once the court found the existence of probable cause for an arrest under Hawaii law, it had no difficulty determining that immunity applied, regardless of who made the arrest.

Once again, states may vary regarding when lifting of sovereign immunity may occur. Paralegals need to check their jurisdiction's law to establish those situations where a jurisdiction has consented to the removal of sovereign immunity.

■ PRIVILEGE

If a defendant raises the defense of privilege, he or she has caused some measure of harm to the plaintiff. But the harm caused by the defendant is small compared to the harm that otherwise might have befallen the plaintiff so that the defendant is not liable in tort.

As a Matter of Public Policy

Society recognizes the defense of privilege when excusing a defendant's liability would serve a societal purpose (see box on next page).

> ## PRIVILEGE
> [Privilege] is applied to any circumstance justifying or excusing a *prima facie* tort, such as a battery, assault, or trespass; it signifies that the defendant has acted to further an interest of such social importance that it is entitled to protection, even at the expense of damage to the plaintiff. The defendant is allowed freedom of action because his own interests, or those of the public, require it, and because social policy will best be served in permitting it. The privilege is bounded by current ideas of what will most effectively promote the general welfare.
>
> W. Page Keeton et al., *Prosser & Keeton on the Law of Torts* §16 at 109 (5th ed. 1984)

With privilege, society has determined that the defendant's actions could result in less of a loss to the party who could have instead suffered a greater loss. For example, when using force in self-defense, society has decided that having the victim act so as to reduce the magnitude of injury makes more sense than for the victim to suffer injury and then go to court to recover in damages.

Motive

One way to see if a privilege applies is to examine the defendant's motive. A defendant has to want to avoid a greater harm, regardless of whether he or she accomplishes that goal. For example, suppose a defendant sees that a speeding car is about to hit an unsuspecting pedestrian. By shoving the pedestrian aside, the defendant has committed at least a battery. Yet the defendant will not face any liability for that tort; shoving the pedestrian out of the way meant saving the pedestrian from potentially greater damages. And if the defendant shoves the potential victim out of the way of the path of the oncoming car but the victim then hits a lamppost and breaks a wrist, the defendant will not face liability. In that instance, even though the defendant injured the plaintiff, the harm undoubtedly would have been greater had the potential victim been hit by the car.

Applicability

A court will not automatically recognize a defendant's claim of privilege. In its analysis, it could look at the following factors to decide whether the defendant had a privilege against liability:

- Was defendant's motive to avoid a greater harm?
- Did the defendant engage in conduct that would reduce the risk of greater harm?
- If the defendant was mistaken in committing a tort to avoid a greater harm, would a societal purpose be served if such a mistaken motivation and action were excused?

That could include the use of force in self-defense, as noted above.

The court, then, faces a balance of interests. That involves weighing the harm caused by the defendant against the societal benefit gained by the defendant's actions.

Paralegals should take care to research case law on privilege in their states. The scope and application of privilege may vary widely by jurisdiction.

Use of Force

In Defense of Self, Persons, and Property

Society has recognized that an individual should have the right to use force in self-defense in response to a threat. The force used must be proportional to the force arising from a threat. **Use of force** depends upon a reasonable belief that the threat exists. The law allows for the use of force for self-defense, in defense of another, and for possession of personal property (also known as *chattels*). The defendant has the burden of showing that circumstances justified the use of force.

As the following list shows, the use of force in defense may apply for a cause of action with certain torts (see box below).

TORTS WHERE THE USE OF FORCE IN SELF DEFENSE TYPICALLY APPLIES:

- assault
- battery
- conversion
- false imprisonment
- infliction of emotional distress
- toxic torts
- trespass to land and chattels

Proportionality of Force Used in Defense

The law requires **proportionality of force** in stopping an assailant. That is, the force used against an alleged assailant must not exceed the force applied against the defendant. For example, to stop an assailant in a bar fight, the defendant may only hit the assailant hard enough to end the attack. The defendant may not use force to kill the assailant if doing so went beyond what the defendant needed to do to stop the assailant (see box below).

FORCE NOT THREATENING DEATH OR BODILY HARM

1. An actor is privileged to use reasonable force, not intended or likely to cause death or serious bodily harm, to defend himself against unprivileged harmful or offensive contact or other bodily harm which he reasonably believes that another is about to inflict intentionally upon him.
2. Self-defense is privileged under the conditions stated in Subsection (1), although the actor correctly or reasonably believes that he can avoid the necessity of so defending himself,
   a. by retreating or otherwise giving up a right or privilege, or
   b. by complying with a command with which the actor is under no duty to comply or which the other is not privileged to enforce by the means threatened.

Restatement (Second) of Torts §63 (1965)

No question exists, however, about the privilege to use deadly force. The defendant may use it in self-defense or in defense of another person so long as the threatened force would likely cause death or bodily harm. Most jurisdictions use the formulation described below.

> ## FORCE THREATENING DEATH OR BODILY HARM
>
> 1. Subject to the statement in Subsection (3), an actor is privileged to defend himself against another by force intended or likely to cause death or serious bodily harm, when he reasonably believes that
>   a. the other is about to inflict upon him an intentional contact or other bodily harm, and that
>   b. he is thereby put in peril of death or serious bodily harm or ravishment, which can safely be prevented only by the immediate use of such force.
>
> *Restatement (Second) of Torts* §65 (1965)

In most states, the law recognizes this approach of matching the allowable force to the degree needed to end the interference.

Retreat

Because society wishes to avoid the use of force whenever possible, a defendant may not use force in self-defense if he or she had the opportunity to retreat safely from the threat. The retreat, however, should not expose the defendant to an unreasonable risk of injury.

This rule applies even when the defendant faces a threat of injury at home. The defendant is required to leave the house if it would be reasonable to do so. In some jurisdictions, however, the (historical) rule of law is "A man's home is his castle," and is specifically called the **castle doctrine.** According to the castle doctrine, a defendant does not have to retreat from his or her own home when confronted with a threat that could be avoided by retreating safely (see box below).

> ## FORCE THREATENING DEATH OR BODILY HARM
>
> (2) The privilege stated in Subsection (1) exists although the actor correctly or reasonably believes that he can safely avoid the necessity of so defending himself by
>   a. retreating if he is attacked within his dwelling place, which is not also the dwelling place of the other, or
>   b. permitting the other to intrude upon or dispossess him of his dwelling place, or
>   c. abandoning an attempt to effect a lawful arrest.
>
> (3) The privilege stated in Section (1) does not exist if the actor correctly or reasonably believes that he can with complete safety avoid the necessity of so defending himself by
>   a. retreating if attacked in any place other than his dwelling place, or in a place which is also the dwelling of the other, or
>   b. relinquishing the exercise of any right or privilege other than his privilege to prevent intrusion upon or dispossession of his dwelling place or to effect a lawful arrest.
>
> *Restatement (Second) of Torts* §65 (1965)

In Case in Point 11-9, a court found that the use of force made sense where it seemed as if the defendant lived on the premises. (Note: Given the age of this case, the law may have changed as times have changed).

CASE IN POINT 11-9

Scheuerman v. Scharfenberg

163 Ala. 337 (1909)

This appeal presents but one question, which is as novel as it is difficult. The question is this: Is the owner of a storehouse, in which goods and other valuables are kept by him for sale and deposit liable in trespass to a would-be burglar of such store, who is shot by means of a spring gun [Author's note: A spring gun is merely a regular gun which has been rigged up so that if a door or window is opened the gun automatically fires in the direction of the opening door or window.] placed in the store by the owner for the purpose of shooting persons who might attempt to burglarize it—the gun being discharged by the would-be burglar while in the attempt to enter, but after the breaking is completed?

[...]

A man's place of business (such as the defendant's store in this case) is pro hac vice his dwelling, and he has the same right to defend it against intrusions, such as burglary, as he has to protect his dwelling. (citation omitted) Burglary of a store house, such as the one attempted to be burglarized in this case, or in which goods, etc., are kept for sale or in deposit, is by statute made a felony punishable as if it were of a dwelling. (citation omitted) Applying these principles of law, we hold that the owner of such a store is not liable in trespass to a would-be burglar thereof, who is shot by means of a spring gun by such owner placed in the store for the purpose of shooting persons who might attempt to burglarize it; the gun being discharged by the would-be burglar in attempting to enter.

Affirmed.

The court's ruling in favor of the shopkeeper did not depend upon the way that force was used to repel the invader. Instead, the court regarded the place of business as the equivalent of a home. So, the castle doctrine obviated the need for the shopkeeper to retreat before using force in defense of his place of business.

Reasonable to Use Force

A defendant's privilege of self-defense requires that the force used be only as much as needed to end the threat and where no other reasonable alternative exits. No privilege applies with the excessive use of force. The court in the 1864 case of *Morris v. Platt* emphasized the need for the defendant to show that the use of force was reasonable in that particular situation (see Case in Point 11-10).

CASE IN POINT 11-10

Morris v. Platt

32 Conn. 75 (1864)

[...]

It appears from the evidence offered on the trial that the defendant wounded the plaintiff in two places by two shots fired from a pistol; and from the nature of the weapon, and the other conceded circumstances, the jury were authorized to find, and doubtless did find, that the wounds were inflicted with a design to take the life of the plaintiff. It was incumbent on the defendant to justify or excuse their infliction. He in the first place attempted to justify them, and the obvious attempt to take life which aggravated them, by offering evidence to prove that he was assailed by the plaintiff and others in a manner which indicated a design to take his life, and "that he was in great bodily peril and in danger of losing his life by means of the attack," and that he fired the pistol "to protect his life and his body from extreme bodily injury." If these facts were proved and found true, they fully justified the attempt of the defendant to take the life of the plaintiff as matter of law, and entitled the defendant to a verdict in his favor. And so the court were bound to tell the jury, if properly requested to do so by the defendant.

The motion further shows that the defendant did in substance request the court to charge, that if they found the fact proved as claimed, he would be justified in self-defense in using the pistol as he did—that the rule of law is "that a man may lawfully take the life of another who is unlawfully assailing him, if in imminent peril of losing his life or suffering extreme bodily harm, & c." What a man may lawfully do he may lawfully attempt to do, and that request embodied in substance, and with sufficient distinctness, a well-settled specific rule of law, applicable alike in criminal prosecutions and civil suits and to the facts of the case as claimed.

[...]

A man who is assailed, and under such circumstances as to authorize a reasonable belief that the assault is with design to take his life, or do him extreme bodily injury which may result in death, will be justified in the eye of the criminal law if he kill his assailant [...] for the killing would have been lawful and of course the attempt lawful; and no man is liable in a civil suit or criminal prosecution for an injury lawfully committed in self-defense upon an actual assailant. Doubtless the question whether the belief was reasonable or not, must, in either proceeding, be ultimately passed upon by a jury; and the assailed judges at the time, upon the force of the circumstances, when he forms and acts upon his belief, at the peril that a jury may think otherwise and hold him guilty.

[...]

We advise that a new trial be granted. [...]

In this historic case, the court recognized the long tradition of allowing for the use of deadly force, so long that the defendant had a reasonable belief that the use of such force was necessary.

In Defense of Another

Courts have long recognized that a defendant may have the privilege to use force to defend another so long as the facts support using force. In Case in Point 11-11, a wife feared for the life of her husband and acted to defend against the threat.

CASE IN POINT 11-11

Farmers and Mechanics Mutual Insurance Company of West Virginia v. Cook

210 W. Va. 394 (2001)

In this case from the Circuit Court of Hardy County, we address a situation where a wife, in the defense of her husband, shot and killed a third-party aggressor. The wife has been acquitted of any criminal responsibility, but the alleged aggressor's widow has sued the couple for wrongful death.

The couple gave notice of the lawsuit to their homeowners' insurance company. The homeowners' insurance company has refused to provide liability coverage or a legal defense to the homeowners, citing to an "intentional acts" exclusion in the policy. The insurance company does not contest that the homeowners acted together in self-defense, but does, nevertheless, contend that the shooting of the third party was intentional, and as such it could be expected that there would be bodily injury.

[...]

We conclude that when an individual acts in self defense or in defense of another, an insurance company may not rely upon an intentional acts exclusion to deny coverage or a legal defense.

[...]

The instant case is [...] filed by an insurance company, appellee Farmers and Mechanics Mutual Insurance Company of West Virginia ("Farmers and Mechanics"), against the purchasers of a homeowners' liability insurance policy, appellants Gerald and Brenda Cook, and against appellant Leah Buckler, an individual who has sued the Cooks for the wrongful death of her husband, Homer Buckler.

[...]

Mr. and Mrs. Cook owned a home and a tract of land in Moorefield, West Virginia. The Cooks were repeatedly harassed and threatened by neighbors due, in part, to the Cooks' placement of a fence and rocks along the edge of their property bordering Hickory Ridge Road. At various times, the fence was torn down, roofing nails were placed in the Cooks' driveway, and piles of rocks and dirt dumped on their property.

One of the individuals who harassed and threatened the Cooks was Homer Buckler. Mr. Buckler was a huge man, standing 6 feet, 4 inches and weighing in excess of 300 pounds. The Cooks repeatedly sought the help of law enforcement authorities to stop the intimidation by Mr. Buckler, to no avail. For example, after the Cooks' fence was torn down, the sheriff investigated and spoke with Mr. Buckler, and as a result, Mr. Buckler agreed to apologize to the Cooks. However, instead of apologizing, Mr. Buckler visited the Cooks and threatened to kill them if they ever called the authorities again regarding his conduct.

On May 7, 1997, Mrs. Cook spoke with a state trooper by telephone about an investigation into the vandalism of the Cooks' nearby cabin. The trooper indicated he was going to come out to the area and speak to Mr. Buckler about the matter. Shortly after the conversation ended, Mrs. Cook heard a truck outside her house, and looking outside saw Mr. Buckler throwing rocks onto her property in the direction of Mr. Cook.

Mr. Cook—who was 5 feet, 6 inches tall and weighed 140 pounds—approached Mr. Buckler and asked that he not throw rocks on his property. At the same time, Mrs. Cook loaded a shotgun and walked outside, fired a warning shot in the air, and then hurried to her husband's side. Mrs. Cook contends she asked Mr. Buckler to leave, and told him she had already called the police. Mr. Buckler immediately looked at Mr. Cook and said, "You're a G-- d----- dead man. I warned you, I told you never to call them."

Witnesses indicate that Mr. Cook began to walk away, but that Mr. Buckler pursued and attacked him. Mr. Cook responded by swinging his fist at Mr. Buckler; Mr. Buckler threw Mr. Cook to the ground and began beating him.

As Mr. Buckler beat Mr. Cook, Mrs. Cook held the shotgun in one hand and tried to pull Mr. Buckler off her husband. Mr. Buckler paused long enough to strike Mrs. Cook and rip her shirt open. Mrs. Cook again plead with Mr. Buckler to stop, but she was ignored.

Mrs. Cook claimed she was afraid her husband would be killed, so she pointed the shotgun at Mr. Buckler's right arm. [...] As Mrs. Cook fired, Mr. Buckler raised up and raised his right arm, causing the shot to land under his right armpit. Mr. Buckler later died of his injuries, and Mrs. Cook was charged with and convicted of second-degree murder.

In *State v. Cook*, supra, Mrs. Cook appealed her conviction to this Court. After carefully examining the record, we concluded that Mrs. Cook had established that she acted in defense of her husband Gerald in shooting Mr. Buckler, and that the State had failed to rebut this defense beyond a reasonable doubt. We reversed Mrs. Cook's conviction and remanded the case for the entry of a judgment of acquittal.

Subsequent to this Court's opinion, Mrs. Buckler filed a wrongful death action against the Cooks for the death of her husband. The Cooks sought liability insurance coverage and defense counsel for the wrongful death action from their homeowner's insurance carrier, appellee Farmers and Mechanics.

[...]

In West Virginia, we have plainly recognized that individuals are permitted to use a reasonable degree of force to defend themselves or others. (citation omitted) While the individual may be acting "intentionally," lashing out against an attacker, the individual is not invading the interests of the attacker in a way that the law forbids. To the contrary, the public policy of this State favors the right of individuals to act in defense of themselves and others. [...]

Mrs. Cook contends she did not intend to shoot and kill Mr. Buckler, but instead acted in defense of her husband. The record does not conclusively establish that Mr. or Mrs. Cook acted with wrongful intent toward Mr. Buckler, but instead can be read to show they acted purely in self-defense. [...]

The record in the instant action is otherwise sparse, but suggests that issues remain for a factfinder to resolve regarding whether, in the context of a wrongful death action, the Cooks acted within their legal rights. The Cooks have sufficiently alleged that Mrs. Cook was acting in defense of her husband, so as to trigger the insurance company's duty to provide a defense. But whether the insurance company will be required to indemnify the Cooks for any liability they may have to Mrs. Buckler is a factual issue that must await resolution in the underlying wrongful death action.

[...]

After careful examination of the record, we find that genuine issues of fact remain regarding whether, in the context of the wrongful death action, the Cooks acted in self-defense, and thereby, whether they are entitled to liability insurance coverage. We therefore conclude that the circuit court erred in granting summary judgment to Farmers and Mechanics, and the judgment must be reversed.

While the court had to determine whether liability coverage applied for the homeowners, it made clear that, if sufficient facts existed, the wife's use of deadly force to end a perceived deadly threat against the husband, the insurance company would need to cover any award of damages, since the wife's use of force was lawful in this instance.

When using force in defense of another, a defendant must have a reasonable belief that the potential victim also had a valid basis to use force in defense. For example, if the defendant sees two men attacking a third, the defendant may use force to defend the third man. If it turns out, however, that the two attackers were undercover officers trying to arrest the third man, the defendant acted on an incorrect belief and can face liability for assaulting the officers.

In Defense of Property

A defendant may use force in defense of property, so long as he or she has a reasonable belief about the need to use such force. As with the use of force in defense of one's self or others, a defendant may use only so much force as is necessary to end the threat directed towards the property. Finally, a defendant may use such force if he or she has no reasonable opportunity to go to court to end the threat (see box below).

DEFENSE OF PROPERTY

The interest in peaceful possession and enjoyment justifies protection by self-help, in situations where there is usually no time to resort to the law. The limitations upon the privilege are much the same as in the case of self-defense: the force must be, or reasonably appear to be, necessary, and not excessive in view of the interest involved.

W. Page Keeton et al., *Prosser & Keeton on the Law of Torts* §21 at 131 (5th ed. 1984)

Repossession of Property

One instance where a defendant may not use force in self-defense involves repossession. For example, suppose the defendant has borrowed money to purchase a car. As a condition for getting the loan, the defendant may have to provide the lender with the option to retake the car if the defendant fails to make a loan payment. That option might be referred to as a *chattel mortgage* on the car, which is similar to a home mortgage except it applies only to cars. (A car is personal property; only land is known as real property.) Since the defendant has authorized the lender's act of repossessing, the defendant then cannot legally use force to prevent the repossession (see Case in Point 11-12).

 ## CASE IN POINT 11-12

Westerman v. Oregon Automobile Credit Corporation
168 Ore. 216 (1942)

This is an action, as asserted by the plaintiff, "for trespass to a motor vehicle and its contents." [...] The complaint alleges in substance that on the 13th day of January, 1940, the plaintiff, being the owner of a Ford car, borrowed money from the defendant, Oregon Automobile Credit Corporation (hereafter called the company), and to secure the loan executed a chattel mortgage upon the car. [...]

[...] [T]the plaintiff makes [...] allegations and charges that the defendant on the 17th day of April, 1940, took possession of the same automobile, maliciously and without plaintiff's consent, "and while so doing trespassed on said property, all to plaintiff's damage in the sum of $100." [...]

The mortgage provides that in the event of default the note shall become immediately due and payable, and the mortgagee is authorized to foreclose, at its option, by taking immediate possession of the car wherever the same shall be found without prior notice or demand for performance, said notice being waived, and to sell the same at private sale. While the plaintiff was in default, defendant company, by its agent, the defendant Hoffmiller, went to the plaintiff's home to get the payment or get the car. Defendant Hoffmiller advised the plaintiff that he was going to take the car, whereupon the plaintiff said, "You can't take the car without law." Defendant Hoffmiller then left plaintiff's home [...]

The foregoing is a fair summary of the testimony favorable to the plaintiff.

[...] We will consider first the alleged trespass of March 9th. The condition of the mortgage having been broken, defendant was entitled to foreclose in the manner provided by that instrument. (citation omitted) By the terms of the mortgage, as well as by statute, the defendant company then had a qualified ownership of the chattel, together with a right to immediate possession thereof. (citation omitted)

[...]

The plaintiff contends that the right of a mortgagee upon condition broken to repossess a chattel without the aid of legal process can be exercised only if the plaintiff consents and that if possession is taken in defiance of plaintiff's objection, the taker becomes a trespasser. On the contrary, we hold that, where there is no invasion of plaintiff's rights relative to real property and no force is involved against the person, one having an immediate contractual right to the possession of the chattel may take the same notwithstanding the absence of consent or the verbal refusal to consent by the mortgagor. In doing so, he commits no trespass.

[...]

We shall next consider the manner in which one having the immediate right to possession may take it. In general terms it may be said that he must not commit a breach of the peace in the process of taking. [...]

Again, where the taking is on the land of the mortgagor, the law wisely imposes restrictions which do not apply when the taking is in a public place. A chattel mortgagee entitled to immediate possession and having the contractual right to take the chattel "wherever it may be found" has a right to enter the land of the mortgagor for the purpose of taking possession and removing the chattel, but he is privileged to do so only at reasonable times and in a reasonable manner. [...]

The mere use of force upon the chattel as in the lifting or removing thereof or in the entry of a car is not tortious when committed by a mortgagee having immediate right of possession. His duty in this respect is merely to deal with the chattel in such manner as not to damage it, thereby lessening its value as security. These principles will, we think, harmonize the authorities which at first appear to be in hopeless confusion. [...]

To permit one who agreed, for a valuable consideration, that in the event of default the mortgagee may take possession wherever the chattel may be found, to revoke that consent by mere words would be permitting him to destroy the contract by his own wrong. The rule which prohibits the mortgagee to use force was not adopted for the purpose of protecting the mortgagor in the wrongful withholding of a chattel; it was adopted to prevent a breach of the peace by the mortgagee.

[...] In this case, although there was refusal to consent, there was no physical obstruction. No violence would have occurred if plaintiff had not interfered after defendants had taken possession. The taking of possession was in fact consummated by defendants without assault, battery or intimidation and during the absence of the plaintiff.

[...] The judgment of the circuit court is affirmed.

As this case notes, the act of repossession cannot involve the use of force to regain the chattel. Rather, repossession will occur as a result of court action.

Deadly Force Used in Defense of Property

A defendant may not use deadly force in defense of property unless the property plays a vital and critical role in the defendant's life. There, society balances the life of the assailant with the ability to replace chattel. In the following case, the homeowner wanted to end a series of burglaries that happened at his vacation property, by using a spring gun (see Case in Point 11-13).

CASE IN POINT 11-13

Katko v. Briney

183 N.W.2d 657 Iowa (1971)

The primary issue presented here is whether an owner may protect personal property in an unoccupied boarded-up farm house against trespassers and thieves by a spring gun capable of inflicting death or serious injury.

We are not here concerned with a man's right to protect his home and members of his family. Defendants' home was several miles from the scene of the incident to which we refer infra.

Plaintiff's action is for damages resulting from serious injury caused by a shot from a 20-gauge spring shotgun set by defendants in a bedroom of an old farm house which had been uninhabited for several years. Plaintiff [...] had broken and entered the house to find and steal old bottles and dated fruit jars which they considered antiques.

At defendants' request plaintiff's action was tried to a jury consisting of residents of the community where defendants' property was located. The jury returned a verdict for plaintiff and against defendants for $20,000 actual and $10,000 punitive damages.

[...]

Thus we have this appeal by defendants.

[...]

Most of the facts are not disputed. In 1957 defendant Bertha L. Briney inherited her parents' farm [...] [,] an 80-acre tract [...] where her grandparents and parents had lived. No one occupied the house thereafter. Her husband, Edward, attempted to care for the land. He kept no farm machinery thereon. The outbuildings became dilapidated.

For about 10 years, 1957 to 1967, there occurred a series of trespassing and housebreaking events with loss of some household items, the breaking of windows and "messing up of the property in general". The latest occurred June 8, 1967, prior to the event on July 16, 1967 herein involved.

Defendants through the years boarded up the windows and doors in an attempt to stop the intrusions. They had posted "no trespass" signs on the land several years before 1967. The nearest one was 35 feet from the house. On June 11, 1967 defendants set "a shotgun trap" in the north bedroom. After Mr. Briney cleaned and oiled his 20-gauge shotgun, the power of which he was well aware, defendants took it to the old house where they secured it to an iron bed with the barrel pointed at the bedroom door. It was rigged with wire from the doorknob to the gun's trigger so it would fire when the door was opened. Briney first pointed the gun so an intruder would be hit in the stomach but at Mrs. Briney's suggestion it was lowered to hit the legs. He admitted he did so "because I was mad and tired of being tormented" but "he did not intend to injure anyone". He gave no explanation of why he used a loaded shell and set it to hit a person already in the house. Tin was nailed over the bedroom window. The spring gun could not be seen from the outside. No warning of its presence was posted.

Plaintiff lived [...] seven miles from the old house. He had observed it for several years while hunting in the area and considered it as being abandoned. He knew it had long been uninhabited. In 1967 the area around the house was covered with high weeds. Prior to July 16, 1967 plaintiff [...] had been to the premises and found several old bottles and fruit jars which they took and added to their collection of antiques. On the latter date about 9:30 p.m. [plaintiff] made a second trip to the Briney property. [Plaintiff] entered the old house by removing a board from a porch window which was without glass. [...] As he started to open the north bedroom door the shotgun went off striking him in the right leg above the ankle bone. Much of his leg, including part of the tibia, was blown away. [...] He remained in the hospital 40 days.

Plaintiff's doctor testified he seriously considered amputation but eventually the healing process was successful. Some weeks after his release from the hospital plaintiff returned to work on crutches. He was required to keep the injured leg in a cast for approximately a year and wear a special brace for another year. He continued to suffer pain during this period.

[...]

The record discloses plaintiff to trial time had incurred $710 medical expense, $2056.85 for hospital service, $61.80 for orthopedic service and $750 as loss of earnings. In addition thereto the trial court submitted to the jury the question of damages for pain and suffering and for future disability.

[...]

Plaintiff testified he knew he had no right to break and enter the house with intent to steal bottles and fruit jars therefrom. He further testified he had entered a plea of guilty to larceny in the nighttime of property of less than $20 value from a private building. He stated he had been fined $50 and costs and paroled during good behavior from a 60-day jail sentence. Other than minor traffic charges this was plaintiff's first brush with the law.

[...]

The main thrust of defendants' defense in the trial court and on this appeal is that "the law permits use of a spring gun in a dwelling or warehouse for the purpose of preventing the unlawful entry of a burglar or thief" [...]

The fact that the trespasser may be acting in violation of the law does not change the rule. The only time when such conduct of setting a 'spring gun' or a like dangerous device is justified would be when the trespasser was committing a felony of violence or a felony punishable by death, or where the trespasser was endangering human life by his act." (citation omitted)

[An] instruction [to the jury] stated: "To entitle the plaintiff to recover for compensatory damages, the burden of proof is upon him to establish by a preponderance of the evidence each and all of the following propositions:

1. "That defendants erected a shotgun trap in a vacant house on land owned by defendant, Bertha L. Briney, on or about June 11, 1967, which fact was known only by them, to protect household goods from trespassers and thieves.
2. "That the force used by defendants was in excess of that force reasonably necessary and which persons are entitled to use in the protection of their property.
3. "That plaintiff was injured and damaged and the amount thereof.
4. "That plaintiff's injuries and damages resulted directly from the discharge of the shotgun trap which was set and used by defendants."

The overwhelming weight of authority, both textbook and case law, supports the trial court's statement of the applicable principles of law.

[...]

In Wisconsin, Oregon and England the use of spring guns and similar devices is specifically made unlawful by statute.

[...]

Study and careful consideration of defendants' contentions on appeal reveal no reversible error.

Affirmed.

[...]

While the court acknowledged the property owner's frustrations, it noted that deadly force could not be used to protect the farmhouse as long as it was unoccupied at the time of a break-in.

A common situation that may arise, however, if a burglar breaks into a house to steal property and the defendant occupies the property at that time. Courts may accept the use of deadly force in defense of self but not if used solely in defense of property.

Common law has recognized that a possessor of personal property may use force in the **recapture of chattels.** The force used must not exceed the amount needed only to recapture the chattels (see box below).

THE AMOUNT OF FORCE PERMITTED TO RECAPTURE CHATTELS

The use of force against another for the purpose of recaption is not privileged unless the means employed are

a. not in excess of those which the actor correctly or reasonably believes to be necessary to effect the recaption, and
b. not intended or likely to cause death or serious bodily harm.

Restatement (Second) of Torts, §106 (1965)

The lawful possessor of personal property may have the authority to use force to recapture the personal property, but only in certain situations:

- Wrongdoer has taken the chattels from the possessor by force or fraud.
- Possessor may lawfully recapture chattels immediately.
- Possessor has requested the return of the chattel.
- Possessor has recaptured the chattel from the wrongdoer.

By specifying when the use of force may be used to recapture personal property, states hope that this kind of "self-help" can occur quickly and without injury.

Many kinds of takings by a wrongdoer justify the use of force to recapture the chattel. The possessor may use a reasonable amount of force against a thief. In some jurisdictions, if the wrongdoer used fraud, the lawful possessor can use force to recapture personal property.

But the lawful possessor may not use force in any other way to repossess the chattels. So, the lawful possessor may not use force against another where that battery was unnecessary to recapture the chattels.

The possessor may not use force that could result in death or serious bodily injury.

The Tort of Trespass

A lawful owner may trespass onto a wrongdoer's property to regain his or her possession. This act is known as **trespass to regain chattels.** If the lawful possessor could go onto a wrongdoer's land to recapture the chattel, does that mean that the lawful possessor can trespass on to the land of an innocent third party to catch a fleeing thief? In some states, the courts might find that acceptable as long as the trespass was brief and the use of force appropriate to recapture the personal property.

In Case in Point 11-14, the chattel is only a document, but the trespass committed to recapture the chattel involved delicate circumstances.

 # CASE IN POINT 11-14

McLean v. Colf

179 Cal. 237 (1918)

Action to recover damages for personal injuries resulting from an alleged assault and battery by the defendants upon the plaintiff. [...]

It appears that the defendant Guy V. Colf, as contractor, had undertaken to construct a dwelling-house for the plaintiff. A dispute arose concerning the completion of the contract, and the owner agreed with the contractor that if the latter would do certain specified work, Mrs. McLean would consider the contract as completed. This understanding was embodied in a letter signed by Mrs. McLean and her husband, and addressed to Colf. On the following day Colf, with his codefendants, came to the house to do the work agreed upon. Mrs. McLean met them, and requested certain other changes in place of those specified in her letter. To this the contractor assented. He proceeded to write a new agreement embodying the new terms. He laid the letter of the preceding day on a table, and was proceeding to write the new agreement when the plaintiff took the letter and placed it inside her bodice, stating that she would keep it. Colf demanded its return, which was refused, and he thereupon attempted to take it from her by force. The plaintiff resisted, and Colf called his codefendants to his aid. The three men continued their efforts to take the paper from the plaintiff, she meanwhile resisting and screaming, until a neighbor appeared on the scene, whereupon the defendants desisted. According to the plaintiff's testimony, which was in some degree corroborated, the defendants treated her with considerable roughness, not to say brutality, inflicting bruises and swellings upon her person, and causing her pain from which she suffered for two weeks or more.

The claim of the appellants that the paper was the property of the appellant Guy V. Colf [...] and that said Colf had the right to use force to protect his possession, or to regain his momentarily interrupted possession, may be conceded. But the right to use force, particularly as against the person of another, is always limited by the condition that the force must be no more than is reasonably adequate and necessary to the occasion. (citation omitted) In this case the court made a finding "that the amount of force and violence used by the defendants in committing the assault and battery upon the plaintiff was unreasonable and excessive and unduly violent." [...]

> Although Colf may have had a technical right to the paper, its ownership and possession were of little or no substantial value. The claim of the appellants that their failure to regain the paper conclusively establishes that they did not use more than the "necessary" force is without merit. Their want of success may have been due to a variety of causes other than their own moderation. The question whether excessive force has been used is peculiarly one of fact for the trial court or the jury, and, under the circumstances here shown, we cannot interfere with the conclusion reached.
>
> The judgment is affirmed.

While the contractor had a valid legal interest in the contract, the appeals court agreed that he used too much force to excuse liability for assault and battery arising out of an attempt to regain possession of the letter.

States vary as to what procedures should apply for recapture, so paralegals must examine state law to determine those procedures available for the peaceful recapture of chattel.

Reasonable Discipline

Maintaining Family Order

Under common law, the head of the family could use reasonable force to achieve reasonable discipline over all family members. States no longer allow such force to be used against a spouse or other adult to create order and discipline, as this would be considered domestic violence and would involve criminal charges arising from such a use.

Disciplining of a Child

Society has recognized the need for the use of reasonable force to maintain order and discipline over children. Any use of force, however, must fit the circumstances. Only those charged with the care and custody of children may use force. As society has developed a better understanding about the problem of domestic violence, states may impose very precise and strict limits on the appropriateness of the use of force to discipline children.

To successfully raise the defense of use of force for reasonable discipline, a defendant will need to show the following elements:

- The force is necessary
- The force is reasonable to maintain discipline
- The force is not going to put the child at substantial risk of death or extreme physical injury, pain, or mental distress

Anyone formally granted legal authority to care for the child may use force in this way.

In Loco Parentis

Adults who have temporary care and custody over a child may use force to discipline a child, if allowed by statute. This temporary grant of authority, *in loco parentis,* is Latin and means literally "in place of a parent." Possessors of such a grant of authority would include a teacher or another person charged with educating and taking care of the child. Temporary custody is not the same as full custody, which only a court could grant.

Any person with temporarily custody possess authority to use force to discipline, subject to the same rules that apply when a parent would use force to discipline a child. State law may presume, then, that adults using such force have the best interests of the child in mind (see box below).

THE USE OF FORCE AGAINST A CHILD FOR REASONABLE DISCIPLINE

1. A parent is privileged to apply such reasonable force or to impose such reasonable confinement upon his child as he reasonably believes to be necessary for its proper control, training, or education.
2. One other than a parent who has been given by law or has voluntarily assumed in whole or in part the function of controlling, training, or educating a child, is privileged to apply such reasonable force or to impose such reasonable confinement as he reasonably believes to be necessary for its proper control, training, or education, except in so far as the parent has restricted the privilege of one to whom he has entrusted the child.

Restatement (Second) of Torts §147 (1965)

A special instance where *in loco parentis* applies arises in the classroom. Teachers may use *corporal punishment*, that is, force, to discipline a child. Because the use of force may occur frequently, clear limits may exist for the application of corporal punishment. So, some states might have adopted the principles similar to those described in the *Restatement (Second) of Torts* sets forth (see box below).

FACTORS A TEACHER MAY NEED TO CONSIDER BEFORE ADMINISTERING CORPORAL PUNISHMENT

In determining whether force or confinement is reasonable for the control, training, or education of a child, the following factors are to be considered:

a. whether the actor is a parent;
b. the age, sex, and physical and mental condition of the child;
c. the nature of his offense and his apparent motive;
d. the influence of his example upon other children of the same family or group;
e. whether the force or confinement is reasonably necessary and appropriate to compel obedience to a proper command;
f. whether it is disproportionate to the offense, unnecessarily degrading, or likely to cause serious or permanent harm.

Restatement Second of Torts, §150 (1965)

In Case in Point 11-14, where a physical education teacher used force to discipline a student, the trial court looked at these specific criteria to conclude that the teacher properly and legally used corporal punishment.

CASE IN POINT 11-15

LaFrentz v. Gallagher

105 Ariz. 255 (1969)

Joseph LaFrentz [...] sued Frank Gallagher [...] for assault and battery alleged to have been committed by defendant Gallagher on February 25, 1964. [...]

The case was tried by the court with a jury [...], resulting in a verdict in favor of defendant. Plaintiff at the time of the trial was twelve years old and in the seventh grade in the Desert View School [...] Plaintiff was about five feet tall, and weighed approximately eighty pounds. He was attending a physical-education class at the time of the incident. Frank Gallagher, a teacher in the school, was coach in charge of the class. The students were playing softball, and Gallagher was umpiring the game.

According to the testimony of the plaintiff, he was at bat and had hit a ground ball, and the call at first base was close, but Gallagher called him out. He stated that while he was walking back, "kicking the dust," Gallagher came up to him, grabbed him by the throat and slammed him into the backstop, with the words:

"I don't want any more of your Little League lip, punk!"

This testimony was corroborated at least in part [...]

It is a well-established principle of law in an action against a school teacher for damages for battery that corporal punishment which is reasonable in degree administered by a teacher to a pupil as a disciplinary measure is "privileged," and does not give rise to a cause of action for damages against the teacher. The courts have held that the teacher is in loco parentis, so that the crucial question that arises is the reasonableness of the punishment. (citation omitted) [...] This question of reasonableness was submitted to the jury under proper instruction. The jury accepted Gallagher's version.

[...]

Judgment affirmed.

The trial court agreed that in light of the circumstances, the teacher used reasonably appropriate force to discipline the rude child.

Given the risks that teachers use excessive force or mistakenly discipline the wrong child, states that allow for corporal punishment often create procedures to minimize the risk of such misuse.

Paralegals should examine a state's laws in detail to appreciate that jurisdiction's position on the use of force to discipline a child. A jurisdiction may make it illegal for any teacher to use force to discipline a child.

■ PRIVILEGE AND EVIDENCE

A specialized application of the concept of privilege applies within the context of evidence. Evidence involves any information, accepted at trial, that when used, helps to resolve the issue of law before a court. The application of privilege, on the issue of the admissibility of information evidence, looks to see whether allowing this information into will benefit society overall. So, for example, the attorney-client privilege exempts from evidence any communication between a lawyer and the lawyer's client. In that way, clients may feel that they can speak more frankly, which in turn means that the lawyer will get all possible information so as to fashion the best possible legal strategy on the client's behalf.

In Case in Point 11-16, a mother wished to regain custody of her child. The trial court judge asked that the mother undergo an examination to gain a better understanding of her mental illness. The mother cited the Fifth Amendment to the U.S. Constitution, claiming the privilege to be free from having to make incriminating statements.

CASE IN POINT 11-16

In the matter of Sloan

84 Misc. 2d 306 (1975)

In this proceeding to transfer guardianship and custody of an infant, respondent mother moves to vacate the court's order that she undergo psychiatric examination on the ground of her Fifth Amendment privilege against compulsory self incrimination. (footnote omitted)

The infant herein was born May 11, 1972 and has been in the care of petitioning agency since April 17, 1973. Her father has signed a surrender for her adoption. [...]

The court ordered that respondent submit to a psychiatric examination [...]

The court conceives respondent's objection [...] as a twofold claim of denial of her privilege against self incrimination. On the one hand, she claims the privilege for any statements made to the psychiatrist which might reveal a crime or tend to connect her with a criminal act. More fundamentally, she is asking the court to treat mental illness as equivalent to a crime, since proof of that condition will have grave consequences for her, and to expand the privilege to information given a psychiatrist which might prove mental illness.

[...]

The New York courts have not hesitated to compel psychiatric examinations when relevant to the action. (citation omitted) (footnote omitted) In applying the testimony-conduct distinction, the courts have protected the accused by treating statements made to the psychiatrist as "verbal acts," relevant only to the issue of mental condition, and not as evidence of the truth or falsity of the facts asserted. (citation omitted) Any incriminating statement made by respondent during psychiatric examination would be similarly protected.

In order for the claim of privilege to be honored, the threat posed must be criminal. (citation omitted) (footnote omitted) A finding of mental illness in this proceeding cannot subject respondent to either criminal penalty or loss of freedom. [...] Nor can statements made by respondent to the psychiatrist be evidence against her in a civil commitment proceeding [...]

In all legislation permitting the termination of parental rights, the basic and vexing issue is where to draw the line between the conflicting rights of parent and child. Looked at from the standpoint of the community, the question is how to ensure that children will receive the guidance and affection they need to become responsible and productive members of society without denying the parent due process of law.

The policy of the Legislature is to end foster care and free the child when a parent will never be able to give the child a home. That policy could be frustrated by transplanting a criminal doctrine to this proceeding, which is nonpunitive and in which respondent's rights are safeguarded. The parent's interest in freedom from the intrusion of a psychiatric examination must give way to the interest of the child and society in knowing whether the parent is mentally ill. The court concludes that the privilege against self incrimination cannot be asserted to prevent a psychiatric examination of respondent in this action.

Respondent's motion is denied.

The privilege against self-incrimination, as described in the Fifth Amendment, is unusual because it is a constitutional right and not a protection arising out of common law or from statute. Here, the trial court judge acknowledged the importance of the privilege against self-incrimination, but ruled that since this was a civil case involving a mother's effort to regain custody of her child, she did not risk punishment. Thus, the privilege did not apply.

Listed below are other instances where privilege to exempt certain communications from disclosure in court may apply.

Examples of Other Forms of Privilege and Evidence:
Between: • Attorney and client • Husband and wife • Physician and patient (but only as pertains to receiving medical treatment) • Religious official and member of that official's faith

KEY TERMS

42 USC §1983   379

Castle doctrine   397

Citizen's arrest   390

Eleventh Amendment to the United States
    Constitution   382

Eminent domain   380

Federal Tort Claims Act (FTCA)   375

Immunity   374

In loco parentis   408

Ministerial function   384

Privilege   374

Proportionality of force   396

Recapture of chattels   406

Sovereign immunity   375

Use of force   396

Trespass to regain chattels   407

Warrantless arrest   386

SUMMARY

To advance public policy, the legal system may free from liability parties or organizations that might otherwise be liable under tort law.

Immunity frees the defendant from having to justify or excuse the behavior. It may apply when individuals have possibly incurred liability while fulfilling official duties or obligations. A government may limit its exposure to liability on the grounds that having to face suits could prove to be too expensive so as to affect, materially and adversely, the operation of the government. Immunity often arises out of the status of the defendant, so that a government official may not have to face liability when trying to fulfill the responsibilities of government.

Privilege tends to excuse liability when certain situations arise. A defendant may escape liability for a claim of assault, for example, by saying that defendant used only so much force as was necessary to end an unlawful interference. In that instance, however, the privilege ends when the defendant no longer faces a threat of injury. Privilege may often involve the use of force, so the legal system allows such use of force only in very specific situations and circumstances. One such instance might be with the use of force to discipline a child. Also, the issue of privilege, within the context of the use of information as evidence at trial, is different than the privilege that may apply to negate tort liability.

CONCEPT REVIEW QUESTIONS

1. Define the concept of immunity.
2. Discuss the origins of the doctrine of immunity.
3. What is sovereign immunity?
4. Discuss the primary limitation imposed upon the general tort liability of the United States government under the Federal Tort Claims Act.
5. Explain the public policy behind the concept of privilege.
6. Why may an adult use reasonable force to discipline a child?
7. Within the context of the use of force, what does *in loco parentis* mean?
8. What does privilege mean, within the context of rules of evidence?

CRITICAL THINKING APPLICATIONS

1. During a particularly violent thunderstorm, a lightning strike disabled part of the police department's telephone system, so that "Caller ID" did not work. A 911 operator received a call and took down the information by hand, but got the address wrong. By the time local law enforcement discovered the mistake, the caller had been murdered by a burglar. The victim's family sued the police department because of the operator's negligence in recording the information. The lawyer for the police department files a motion for summary judgment. Is it likely that the judge will grant the motion? Why or why not?
2. At a fair held on the grounds of a federal park, U.S. park rangers arrested Ajax. Since no federal facilities existed in the park, the rangers turned Ajax over to local law enforcement. Overwhelmed with crowd control in the area surrounding the fair, the rangers and chief of local law enforcement decided to release Ajax at the opposite end of town, after issuing him a summons to appear at court. After Ajax is dumped there, he murders a hitchhiker. The hitchhiker's family sues local law enforcement and the federal government for negligence. Local law enforcement settles the suit. The federal government claims that it is immune from suit in this matter. Do you agree or disagree? Why?
3. In a local community, the head of the Department of Public Works has resigned to take a better-paying position. The community immediately advertises for a replacement. Among the department head's duties was checking all vehicle maintenance. A week after the head has quit, a Department of Public Works employee fails to repair the brakes on a village truck. The next day, a

heavy fog settles on the community. An employee takes the vehicle out to a road-repair project and within half a mile, the brakes fail, creating an automobile accident. The driver of the car hit by the Public Works truck sues for damages. The community says that it is immune from suit in this instance. Do you agree or disagree? Why?

4. State police officers attempt to subdue a suspect of an armed robbery. Since the alleged robber has dropped the gun, the officers use their batons to stop the suspect, who has failed to obey repeated calls to halt. A bystander videotapes the entire chase, including when the officers rain dozens of baton blows to end the suspect's resistance. The suspect sues, saying the officers violated the alleged robber's Fourth Amendment right to be free from unreasonable searches and arrests. Why won't immunity protect the officers in this instance?

5. Firefighters respond to a call of a cat stuck in a tree. They forward the call to the animal control officer. An hour later, the fire department gets a second call asking that someone come to rescue the cat. Again, the firefighters forward the call to Animal Control. An hour later, a third call comes. This time, the fire department forwards the call but also sends a ladder out to retrieve the cat. Later, the cat's owner sues the animal control officer for negligent infliction of emotional distress because of the owner's suffering while waiting for someone to arrive. Lawyers for the fire department file for summary judgment, claiming immunity. How do you think the court will rule on this motion? Why?

6. A commuter feels a sudden tugging and realizes someone is trying to pull a briefcase off his shoulder, with his laptop inside. He gives the briefcase a strong jerk, surprising the thief, who loses her balance, falls, and suffers a head injury. The thief files suit against the commuter, alleging battery. Will the commuter be liable in damages for the thief's injuries? Why or why not?

7. A plaintiff agrees to undergo surgery to repair a torn ligament in the plaintiff's leg. During surgery, the physician discovers a new problem and performs surgery to correct that problem as well as to repair the ligament. The repaired ligament heals without a problem. To correct the other problem, the physician had to cut through nerve tissue, which caused permanent injury to plaintiff. The plaintiff sues the surgeon for battery. Will the court rule that the plaintiff should receive compensatory damages? Why or why not?

8. A shoplifter grabs a ham from a display in the delicatessen's window. An employee gives chase and catches the shoplifter, knocking him to the ground and taking the ham back. The shoplifter sues the owner of the delicatessen for injuries he sustained when the deli employee knocked him down. How likely is it that the shoplifter will win? Why?

SKILL-BUILDING APPLICATION

In a dangerous part of town, Kersh approached a parked car, its windows rolled down. Thinking he recognized a prostitute in the front passenger seat, Kersh goes to the driver's side and stabs the driver twice, in the leg and along the face. The driver yells, "Freeze, police!" to Kersh, who is retreating rapidly. The officer pulls out his badge, then says, "Freeze or I'll shoot!" Kersh turns to the officer and says, "Look, you go your way and I go mine," then turns and resumes retreating. The officer calls out, "Freeze and drop your weapon." Kersh ignores the officer, who fires a drawn service weapon twice, hitting Kersh once in the leg.

Kersh files suit against the officer under 42 USC §1983 on the grounds that the officer used excessive force, a violation of Kersh's Fourth Amendment rights. Did the officer have the privilege to use such force? Why or why not? Does the officer enjoy immunity? Why or why not?

Man is never watchful enough against the
dangers that threaten him every hour.
                          —Horace (B.C. 65–8)

Strict Liability

The law of strict liability imposes responsibility for damage to an individual or property *without regard* to a defendant's intent or negligence. This separate body of tort law protects persons and property from harm due to abnormally dangerous things or activities. Defenses like assumption of the risk may be available statutorily.

CHAPTER TOPICS

1. Liability without Fault
2. Animals
3. Abnormally Dangerous Things
4. Scope of Liability
5. Defenses

OBJECTIVES

After completing this chapter, you will be able to:

1. Illustrate the development of the law of liability without fault.
2. Discuss the elements of strict liability.
3. Analyze the doctrine of strict liability as applied to animals.
4. Discuss the nature of abnormally dangerous things.
5. Discuss the scope of strict liability.
6. Consider available defenses.

■ LIABILITY WITHOUT FAULT

A tort action in **strict liability** focuses only on the wrongful act. In contrast, liability for an intentional act reflects the concept in social policy that someone who commits a tort should be responsible for the consequences. Liability for negligence reflects a social policy of liability when there is a breach of duty of care. But liability under the tort theory of strict liability reflects a social policy that certain activities carry such abnormally high risk that merely engaging in them is enough to establish liability.

This may seem harsh, especially where theories of intentional liability or liability due to negligence allow at least for the use of defenses where imposing liability would not advance a societal goal. For example, consider imposing liability in an automobile accident where the driver dodged a pedestrian who was suddenly in the road and scraped an oncoming car. Should the driver's actions to avoid greater harm limit or even negate liability? Yet, society takes a different approach with the theory of strict liability (also known as *absolute liability*).

Underlying this theory is the notion that those who are best able to bear the cost of the consequences should bear those costs if an injury occurs. For example, a business that uses dynamite in its work will face strict liability for any harm arising out of its use. To handle the cost of this liability, the business could purchase an insurance policy—since not all uses of dynamite will necessarily result in injury—and pass along the cost of the insurance premiums to customers, in the form of higher prices. In that way, the party most likely to benefit from the use of the dynamite—the customer—effectively "pays" for any liability that might arise. When a zoo exhibits wild animals for public display, some small portion of its admission price goes toward the insurance premium for the policy that protects the zoo in the event of an injury caused by a wild animal.

The theory of strict liability also arises in product liability suits, a topic best reserved for Chapter 13.

■ SCOPE OF LIABILITY

Whether the doctrine of strict liability applies in a given situation may depend on any one of several relevant factors, as noted below.

Factors to Consider When Determining if Strict Liability Should Apply
• Harm must have been clearly foreseeable.
• Actions by third parties or as a result of the force of nature will relieve the defendant from strict liability.
• The plaintiff's knowing and unreasonable exposure to a risk of harm means that the defendant will not be strictly liable for the injuries.
• When permitted by privilege, such as activity undertaken to advance a public function, the theory of strict liability may not apply.

Because of these factors, the theory of strict liability is not "automatically" applied. Instead, the court can consider these factors and decide whether to impose strict liability—a nuance that works to advance social policy.

Paralegal students should consult a state's law on these questions, since this doctrine usually exists as a matter of statute or from the common law.

■ ANIMALS

Under the common law, owners faced strict liability for any harm caused by their animals. The rationale was that certain types of animals present so obvious a danger that an owner is unconditionally responsible for injuries, no matter what degree of care is practiced.

Most jurisdictions have tempered the severity of this rule. Instead, liability will depend on the type of animal and the risk represented. For example, an owner of a dog known for its aggressiveness should have it tied up, whereas the owner of a breed better known for its docile nature should not.

Depending on whether the animal is a domesticated pet, wild animal, or livestock, the law of a given jurisdiction may vary on the issue of the owner's legal responsibility.

Domestic Animals

Strict liability generally does not apply to **domesticated animals** like dogs or cats. Generally, these animals do relatively minor harm, provide great social benefit, and would impose too heavy a burden upon owners where too small a risk of injury exists.

However, an owner of domesticated animals would face strict liability if the animals have a propensity for causing harm and the owner knows this. That might seem to hold an owner liable under a theory of negligence for injuries caused by a domesticated animal, where the owner knew of this propensity for violence but failed to exercise reasonable care. Strict liability applies because an owner of a domesticated animal with a known propensity for violence is held liable regardless of whether an owner has taken reasonable care to protect the public from the animal. After all, no one has a right to own any kind of pet. Liability might also arise where a jurisdiction has by statute imposed liability for the harm caused by the domesticated animal regardless of its propensity to cause harm but for only certain type of injuries. For example, many jurisdictions have a dog-bite liability statute (see box below).

> ## STRICT LIABILITY FOR INJURIES CAUSED BY A DOMESTICATED ANIMAL
>
> Strict liability is imposed when the keeper of the animal knows or has reason to know that his animal is abnormally dangerous in some way and injury results from that danger.
>
> For example, if a dog owner knows that his dog has an abnormal or vicious propensity to attack and bite, or his horse to kick, he is liable for the dog's biting and the horse's kicking. The owner would be liable for ordinary negligence or an intentional tort, but strict liability based upon the owner's knowledge of a dangerous propensity differs from ordinary negligence. Although the knowledge or scienter requirement necessarily means that harm is foreseeable in light of the animal's known propensity, liability is imposed even if the defendant exercised reasonable care to keep the dog penned and horse stabled.
>
> Dobbs, *The Law of Torts* §343, (2000)

Jurisdictions may vary as to their definition of a domesticated animal; some look at whether these animals have customarily served the interests of humanity. Table 12-1 has examples of how jurisdictions can seem arbitrary in deciding which category an animal falls into.

Table 12-1 Some Domesticated and Wild Animals, According to the Courts	
Domesticated	Bull, cat, stallion, bees, horse, parrot, steer, mule
Wild	Wolf, leopard, coyote, chimpanzee, snakes, deer, zebra, lion, bear

Restatement (Second) Torts §506 (1965), Reporter's Comment

The old saying "A dog is entitled to the first bite" was never the law. If it were, the animal's first victim would be prevented from seeking recovery. If that old saying is at all relevant, it might apply to hold owners liable for injuries caused by domesticated animals with a known propensity to cause harm.

Wild Animals

Most jurisdictions impose strict liability on the owners of wild animals for any harm caused. Regardless of the care they exercise, owners of wild animals expose the community to an unreasonable risk by keeping such animals (see box below).

WILD ANIMALS

1. A possessor of a wild animal is subject to liability to another for harm done by the animal to the other, his person, land or chattels, although the possessor has exercised the utmost care to confine the animal, or otherwise prevent it from doing harm.
2. This liability is limited to harm that results from a dangerous propensity that is characteristic of wild animals of the particular class, or of which the possessor knows or has reason to know.

Restatement (Second) of Torts, §507 (1956)

Strict liability exists for owners of wild animals based on the animals' inherently dangerous nature. If the animal presents some form of abnormal risk to the community where it is kept, the owner exposes others to that risk and must bear the burden for any harm. Keepers of lions, tigers, bears, wolves, elephants, and other wild animals face strict liability. The law in most jurisdictions holds that such animals can never be domesticated, and therefore strict liability is imposed. Professor Dobbs explores this point in detail (see box below).

THE DIFFERENCE BETWEEN DOMESTICATED AND WILD ANIMALS

An animal is instead wild or domesticated according to whether, by local custom, it is devoted to 'the service of mankind' or commonly treated by the community as a tame or domestic animal.

Dobbs, The §343, at page 949

In Case in Point 12-1, the court had to determine whether imported boars were wild animals. If they were, the owner would face strict liability for damages caused by the animals.

CASE IN POINT 12-1

King v. Blue Mountain Forest Association

100 N.H. 212 (1956)

This case poses the problem as to what remedies exist in this state by statute or at common law for damage to property allegedly caused by wild animals. The four counts in each declaration present different grounds of liability but certain historical background is common to all counts.

The defendant corporation was organized in 1891 by Austin Corbin [...] for the purpose of enabling him to conveniently manage the park owned by him, consisting of about 25,000 acres of land, including Croydon and Grantham mountains, all fenced and stocked with wild animals, located in the towns of Newport, Cornish, Croydon, and Grantham, in establishing and maintaining which he expended in the vicinity of $500,000 [....] Included among the animals imported into Corbin park were Prussian wild boar from the Black Forest of Germany [....] Generally the boar could survive the climate of this state only if fed in the winter [....] By special act of the Legislature the defendant was given special game privileges within the park upon the erection of a fence enclosing the entire area. [T]hat statute provided that "all fish, birds, and game of, in, or upon" the park "shall be the property" of the defendant, its successors or assigns. The Blue Mountain Forest Association is the only one to have imported wild boar into the northeastern part of the United States and they are not indigenous to the North American continent [....] Beginning in 1938, and thereafter from time to time, some boar escaped from the park. It is alleged that the escaped boar and their progeny, bred and born during the period of their escape, caused damage to the plaintiffs' lands and crops, which damage was characteristic of wild boar as a class and normally expected of them if at large. It is also alleged that several years prior to the trespasses in September 1954, the boar and their progeny had from time to time passed back and forth from the defendant's park on to land of others, through holes in the fenced enclosure and that the boar habitually returned to defendant's enclosure for the winter or at seasons of food shortage to be fed or cared for by the defendant.

1. The [...] rule of strict liability for animal trespasses to real estate is still in effect in many of the eastern states today and the tendency has been to restore the common law rule, either by statute or by decision. (citation omitted) There has been no legislative attempt to modify this doctrine and it is still the law in this state [....] As already indicated, strict liability for animal trespasses to real estate was firmly established in the jurisprudence of this state prior to the enactment of this statute.

   If a farmer who owns or possesses contented cows is held to strict liability for trespass to real estate it would be a strange doctrine that would not impose at least the same liability upon the owner of battering boar which were imported into the state for the purposes of exclusive and private hunting. [...]

2. The fourth count [...] is predicated on the theory that the possessor of wild animals is held to a standard of strict liability. It is conceded that there is no case in this jurisdiction imposing strict liability for damage to persons or property by escaped wild animals but it is urged that a rule should be adopted in this state [...]

It is true that strict liability for the keeping of dangerous wild animals is supported by a large number of jurisdictions and that the English courts have

> regarded this liability as a mere phase and specific application of the rule in
> *Rylands v. Fletcher*, (1868) LR 3 HL 330....[...] In view of the consistent policy
> evidenced by an unbroken line of decisions in this state which, with the exception
> of cases of cattle trespass to real estate, impose liability at common law for negligence only, we do not now adopt a rule of absolute liability for injuries to persons
> and property caused by wild animals, as a general principle of law. The demurrer
> to the fourth count of the declaration should be sustained.

The court held the owner not liable under a theory of strict liability only because
that policy had not been adopted. Instead, the court ruled that under a common-
law theory of negligence, the property owner would be liable for failing to exercise
reasonable care for such animals.

Livestock

Most jurisdictions hold the owner of **livestock** strictly liable for the damage done by
the animals for any trespass. If the animal is of the type likely to roam and do damage, the keeper of such livestock is strictly liable for the harm caused (see box below).

TRESPASSING LIVESTOCK

1. Except as stated in Subsections (3) and (4) a possessor of livestock
   intruding upon the land of another is subject to liability for the intrusion
   although he has exercised the utmost care to prevent them from intruding.
2. The liability stated in Subsection (1) extends to any harm to the land or to
   its possessor or a member of his household, or their chattels, which might
   reasonably be expected to result from the intrusion of the livestock.
3. A possessor of land who fails to erect and maintain a fence required by the
   applicable common law or by statute to prevent the intrusion of livestock,
   can not recover under the rule stated in Subsection (1).

Restatement (Second) of Torts, §504 (1965)

Thus, an owner of livestock faces strict liability for damages because the owner has
the ability to exercise control over the animals.

Because owners are in the best position to maintain proper enclosures for their
livestock, they bear the burden of protecting the community from their horses,
cattle, pigs, sheep, fowl, and other such animals. Also, as owners typically maintain livestock for some commercial purpose, they would be in the best position to
insure against the risk of loss. The owner can best pass along the cost of insuring
against loss through a slight increase in the selling price of the livestock. Here
again, the ultimate beneficiaries—the customers—effectively pay the insurance
premium to guard against losses caused by the animals.

In the western United States, the rule of strict liability for wandering livestock
has not applied. The courts have allowed ranchers with cattle grazing on the range
a great deal of latitude. With the encroachment of civilization on traditional grazing

land, however, the legislatures of many states have revisited this issue and decided to enact legislation imposing strict liability on livestock owners. The statutes of any such jurisdiction must be reviewed to determine the extent, if any, to which livestock owners may be liable for the harm done by their grazing animals.

Case in Point 12-2 shows how state law has created strict liability on livestock owners. It examines whether assumption of the risk could be a defense to the imposition of strict liability.

CASE IN POINT 12-2

Madrid v. Fifth Judicial District Court

312 Mont. 517 (2002)

These parties were previously before this Court in *Madrid v. Zenchiku Land and Livestock*, (citation omitted). In that case, this Court [...] imposed strict liability on owners of livestock for injuries sustained by persons injured by their trespassing livestock. We therefore reversed and remanded the case to the District Court for a determination of the damages sustained by Madrid when he was injured by Zenchiku's trespassing bull. On remand, Zenchiku sought leave to pursue its previously raised affirmative defense of assumption of the risk, claiming that the viability of that defense was not addressed in our *Madrid* opinion, and that even if the owner of livestock may be held strictly liable for another's injuries, the owner of the livestock may nonetheless seek to mitigate his liability by establishing that the plaintiff assumed the risk of his injuries. The District Court, after considering briefs from both parties, concluded that Zenchiku should be allowed to present affirmative defenses, including assumption of the risk, at trial. Madrid filed this Application.

[...]

We did not address the viability of Zenchiku's assumption of the risk defense in *Madrid* for the simple reason that neither party brought it to our attention.

Zenchiku argues now that this Court has always permitted the defendant to raise the defense of assumption of the risk in strict liability cases. It is true that in strict *products* liability cases, we have approved the defense, because such a defense is expressly authorized by statute. [...]

A different result is compelled here. We have previously held that if a strict liability statute does not expressly provide for the defense at issue, it may not be raised.

[In] *Stroop v. Day* (citation omitted), we were asked to consider whether the defense of contributory negligence could be raised in a case brought under § 27-1-715, MCA, which imposes strict liability on a dog owner if the owner's dog bites, without provocation, anyone in a public place or who is lawfully present on the dog owner's property. The statute contains no "assumption of the risk" or other affirmative defense language similar to that found in § 27-1-719, MCA. We reviewed two lines of cases from other jurisdictions in *Stroop*—one allowing affirmative defenses such as comparative fault to be raised in strict liability dog-bite cases governed by statute, and the other limiting defenses to only those expressly provided in the statute. We were persuaded by the latter line of authority, concluding that the only defenses available to the dog-owner were those *expressly* set forth in the statute—provocation and unlawful presence. We stated: "Ideas of comparative or contributory negligence are inapplicable under such a strict liability scheme." (citation omitted)

> This same analysis applies in the case at bar. [...]
>
> The only defense supplied by the statute arises if the enclosure breached by the animal is not legal. No such defense exists here. Because the statute does not expressly provide for an assumption of the risk defense [...] we conclude that the District Court erred in allowing Zenchiku to interpose the defense of assumption of the risk, and that the District Court therefore has proceeded under a mistake of law.

By statute, the livestock owner was found liable under a claim of strict liability. Since that same statute did not make available the defense of assumption of the risk, the livestock owner could not raise the defense to avoid strict liability.

■ DEFENSES TO CLAIMS BASED ON A THEORY OF STRICT LIABILITY

The social policy behind strict liability holds owners liable when they have control over animals that are too dangerous for society. For that reason, a plaintiff's conduct should not matter; the animal is dangerous no matter what the plaintiff does.

However, that would mean a plaintiff who knowingly and deliberately came into contact with an owner's wild animal and suffered injury would receive damages. So, the owner would be liable for injuries that could be reasonably avoided by the plaintiff's conduct.

Contributory negligence (a concept introduced in Chapter 5) is not available as a defense in strict liability situations involving wild animals unless the plaintiff knowingly and unreasonably subjected himself or herself to an abnormally dangerous animal (see box below).

PLAINTIFF'S CONDUCT

1. Except as stated in Subsection (2), the contributory negligence of the plaintiff is not a defense to the strict liability of the possessor of an animal.
2. The plaintiff's contributory negligence in knowingly and unreasonably subjecting himself to the risk that a wild animal or an abnormally dangerous domestic animal will do harm to his person, land or chattels, is a defense to strict liability.
3. The plaintiff's assumption of the risk of harm from the animal is a defense to the strict liability.

Restatement (Second) of Torts, §515 (1965)

Using defenses in negligence recognizes that a plaintiff has some control over the circumstances. Yet these defenses arose in response to an owner-defendant's breach of a duty of care. Since an owner with a wild animal has absolute liability, application of these defenses relates to the apportionment of damages. In some instances, the plaintiff's actions could act as a complete bar to recovery, as noted below.

◼ ABNORMALLY DANGEROUS THINGS

Origin of the Rule; *Rylands v. Fletcher*

The notion of strict liability for engaging in **abnormally dangerous activity** arises out of the old English case of *Rylands v. Fletcher*, L.R. 3 H.L. 330 (1868). In *Rylands*, the defendants, who owned a mill, created a reservoir on their property to provide a steady flow of water to power the mill. When the reservoir burst, the mill owners faced strict liability for damages because constructing a reservoir was not a natural use of their land.

> ### ABNORMALLY DANGEROUS
>
> In short, what emerges from the English decisions as the "rule" of *Rylands v. Fletcher* is that the defendant will be liable when he damages another by a thing or activity unduly dangerous and inappropriate to the place where it is maintained, in the light of the character of that place and its surroundings.
>
> W. Page Keeton et al., *Prosser & Keeton on the Law of Torts* §78 at 547-8 (5th ed. 1984)

Since the court's decision, the non-natural use of land has been broadened to include things abnormal, requiring some special use that increases the danger to others (see box below).

Application of the Rule

In the United States today, most jurisdictions accept the decision in *Rylands v. Fletcher* as applying the law of strict liability to abnormally dangerous things and activities.

> ### ABNORMALLY DANGEROUS ACTIVITIES
>
> 1. One who carries on an abnormally dangerous activity is subject to liability for harm to the person, land or chattels of another resulting from the activity, although he has exercised the utmost care to prevent the harm.
> 2. This strict liability is limited to the kind of harm, the possibility of which makes the activity abnormally dangerous.
>
> *Restatement (Second) of Torts,* §519 (1965)

The defendant's liability arises from engaging in activities where a risk of serious harm cannot be eliminated even through the practice of utmost care.

Determining whether strict liability applies depends upon the existence of certain factors (see table below).

Determining Strict Liability Due to Abnormally Dangerous Activity: Factors to Consider	
• that a high degree of risk exists of that some harm will occur; • the chance that any harm will be great; • that reasonable care cannot eliminate this risk;	• how uncommon this activity is; • the appropriateness of engaging in this activity in a particular location; and • how much the community will benefit to the community will outweigh the danger.

These factors tend to distinguish strict liability for abnormally dangerous things from pure negligence. If the risk outweighs an activity's social utility, the defendant will face strict liability no matter what degree of due care was practiced.

Blasting

A common example of an abnormally dangerous activity is blasting, usually to clear land or to mine. No amount of reasonable care can eliminate the risk of serious harm.

Other Instances

Other activities can be so great a risk that a theory of strict liability may apply. In Case in Point 12-3, the court considered the question of strict liability as it applies to the spraying of weed killer.

CASE IN POINT 12-3

Young v. Darter

363 P.2d 829 (Okla. 1961)

[...]

In 1957, in order to kill weeds growing therein, defendant caused his pasture lying immediately to the south and west of plaintiff's thirty acre field of cotton to be sprayed with 2-4D poison. Such poison allegedly drifted and spread across such cotton, damaging it.

[...]

Donald Young (defendant's brother) testified that he did the spraying, using a mixture of 2-4D poison and water; that he did not know it would damage cotton or that the spray would drift; that he stopped spraying before he got close to the cotton because he did not know whether it would hurt the cotton or not; that he thought if he sprayed the mixture on the cotton it might kill it; that at the time he did the spraying there was a little breeze out of the south; that there could have been quite a bit out of the southwest.

An inspector in the entomology division of the State Board of Agriculture testified that he had some experience and training with 2-4D; that he was familiar with the reaction of a plant to 2-4D; that the mixture used as a spray would drift and the distance depended upon the wind; that one should know the wind currents when he used it and should not use it when there is any possibility for it to drift and get on any other broad leaf plant; that it has a detrimental effect on cotton; that he examined plaintiff's field of cotton one or two months after the spraying; that, in his opinion, the cotton had been damaged by 2-4D or 2-45T.

[...]

Spraying poison on weeds growing upon one's own land is a lawful operation, and, when done in a manner not hazardous to rights of another, is not a nuisance per se. Under proper conditions, the spraying would cause no invasion of the adjacent lands....

When one in an operation lawful and proper in itself, but cognizant of existing conditions and with knowledge that injury may result to another, does an act with the result flowing therefrom that damage is done to the other as the direct and proximate consequence of the act, the one who does the act and causes the injury should be required to compensate the other for the damage done[....]

[W]e believe [...] that the promiscuous spraying of poisonous substances in a manner calculated to endanger the rights of one's neighbors is an activity not commonly regarded as consonant with the principles of natural and common justice.

[...]

The use, by the defendant, of a poison on his land, which, if it escaped, would cause damage to plaintiff, was done at defendant's peril. He is responsible for its drifting and thereby trespassing on plaintiff's land where it damaged the cotton. Any precautions defendant's agent may have taken to prevent the injuries to plaintiff's cotton, in view of the results, do not serve to extinguish his liability. The question in general is not whether defendant acted with due care and caution, but whether his acts occasioned the damage....

For the reasons that we are holding that the evidence was sufficient to the jury in finding defendant liable [...]

Where no amount of reasonable care could eliminate the risk that spraying the pesticide would damage a neighbor's crops, the court held the defendant strictly liable for the use of the pesticide.

■ DEFENSES TO ACTIONS BASED ON A THEORY OF STRICT LIABILITY

Defenses like assumption of the risk and contributory negligence should not reduce or eliminate the strict liability. A plaintiff who knowingly and unreasonably faces exposure to an abnormally dangerous activity should not recover damages.

But when a court allows a defendant to use these defenses, it is in the context of assessing damages and not whether they would eliminate an action in strict liability.

Assumption of Risk

On occasion, the courts have allowed for the recognition of **assumption of risk.** However, this relates more to the apportionment of damages than to the issue of a defendant being strictly liable. Some suggest that assumption of risk would completely relieve a defendant of liability for damages arising from an abnormally dangerous activity. This would depend, of course, on whether the plaintiff knew or should have known of the risk (see box below).

A DEFENSE TO STRICT LIABILITY: ASSUMPTION OF THE RISK

The plaintiff's assumption of the risk of harm from an abnormally dangerous activity bars his recovery for the harm.

Restatement (Second) Torts, §523 (1965)

Instead of looking to how a defendant can minimize risks associated with activity where there could be recovery under a theory of strict liability, the courts have recognized that a plaintiff can play some role in creating liability. In effect, the recognition that a plaintiff can participate to bring about injuries does nothing to relieve the defendant's responsibilities but does recognize that the defendant should not face liability where some plaintiffs should have known better.

Contributory Negligence

This defense applies for the same reason as with assumption of the risk, that where a plaintiff knowingly engages in an abnormally dangerous activity, the defendant should not become absolutely liable (see box below).

A DEFENSE TO STRICT LIABILITY: CONTRIBUTORY NEGLIGENCE

1. Except as stated in Subsection (2), the contributory negligence of the plaintiff is not a defense to the strict liability of one who carries on an abnormally dangerous activity.
2. The plaintiff's contributory negligence in knowingly and unreasonably subjecting himself to the risk of harm from the activity is a defense to the strict liability.

Restatement (Second) Torts, §524 (1965)

Comparative Fault

Without relieving a defendant of absolute liability, courts have looked to **comparative fault** as a potential defense. Under this defense, a damages award is offset by an amount proportional to the degree to which the plaintiff brought about the injury. While this arrangement might make sense in terms of the imposition of damages, the courts will not permit this apportionment of damages to relieve defendant liability under a cause of action in strict liability.

Applying that defense has led to strong disagreement about the wisdom of permitting the use of comparative negligence as a defense against an action in strict liability. Professor Dobbs captures the sense of allowing the use of a defense that would otherwise fly in the face of holding someone strictly liable for injuries (see box below).

DEFENSES TO STRICT LIABILITY

The difference in the treatment of the plaintiff who confronts known danger lies largely in the question of contract, consent, or apparent consent. In the context of strict liability, the person who foolishly tries to pet the defendant's tiger is assuredly foolish and her recovery should probably be reduced, but she has almost certainly not consented to accept the risk and to relieve the defendant of all responsibility. In contrast, the plaintiff who accepts employment as trainer of the defendant's wild animals apparently consents to the abnormal risks that entails and hence should not recover on a strict liability basis;" certainly this is true if she expressly contracts to assume the risk.

Dobbs, *The Law of Torts* §350 (2000)

KEY TERMS

Abnormally dangerous activity   425

Assumption of risk   427

Comparative fault   428

Domesticated animals   419

Livestock   422

Strict liability   418

SUMMARY

The doctrine of strict liability imposes liability on a defendant who engages in an abnormally dangerous activity or who owns wild animals. Strict liability has no concern for the fault of the defendant. It exists where the risk of harm outweighs the benefit to society. When engaging in an abnormally dangerous activity, liability depends on a consideration of economic reality: if an activity is beneficial but dangerous, a defendant would likely pass along the cost of liability to those who gain the benefit. This liability comes about even though defendant has no intent to cause harm nor has failed to exercise reasonable care.

Defenses to this absolute liability arise when a plaintiff knew of the risk but acted in spite of it. However, the courts permit such defenses only to reduce an award in damages and not to release the defendant from liability in certain situations for which strict liability applies.

CONCEPT REVIEW QUESTIONS

1. Define strict liability.
2. List the main categories of strict liability.
3. Do the principles of strict liability apply to trespassing animals?
4. How do most jurisdictions treat the liability of an owner for damages caused by domestic animals?
5. Discuss the rationale behind imposing strict liability on owners of wild animals.
6. What is the leading case in the law of strict liability for abnormally dangerous things?
7. What is the reasoning behind imposing strict liability for abnormally dangerous things?
8. Discuss the application of the defense of assumption of the risk in determining strict liability for abnormally dangerous things.

CRITICAL THINKING APPLICATIONS

1. At a roadside gas station, the owner has put a tank of rattlesnakes on display. A plaintiff lifts the lid to the tank that holds the snakes and puts his hand in, only to get bitten. The plaintiff sues the gas station owner in strict liability. Will the owner's motion to dismiss be granted? Why or why not?

2. A plaintiff grew up on a cattle ranch. While working one summer as a ranch hand, the plaintiff waded into a shallow river to rescue a newborn calf. As the plaintiff tried to get the calf onto dry land, the calf's mother attacks and injures the plaintiff. The defendant, who owns the ranch and the cattle, moves for summary judgment. Will the trial court grant the motion? Why or why not?

3. Among the animals a circus brings to town is a bear trained to balance on a large ball. While the bear is being guided onto its ball, it takes a swipe at its handler. That causes the handler to turn away from the bear for a second. The bear turns and then takes a swipe at a rider doing tricks on a horse being led around the ring where the bear is. Can the rider, as the plaintiff, successfully sue in strict liability? Will the defendant circus owner succeed in arguing that the rider assumed the risk by working in a circus?

4. A defendant owns and operates a pig farm. The pigs produce a lot of waste, so the defendant stores the waste in big lagoons, where it eventually dries out and can be sold as fuel. When an earthen wall around one of the lagoons fails, untreated pig waste flows into a river, contaminating it. The plaintiff is a city that relies on the river for its drinking water. Will the plaintiff succeed in a suit against the defendant on the grounds of strict liability? Why or why not?

5. A defendant shipping company stores 55-gallon drums of toxic waste in one of its warehouses, before shipping the containers to be destroyed. Kids break into the warehouse over the weekend. One accidentally knocks over a drum and gets a severe burn. Will the child, in a suit filed on his behalf by his parents, win in a suit for damages based on a theory of strict liability? Why or why not? If the drums have on their sides, in prominent letters, 'Toxic Waste,' would your answer change? If so, then why?

6. A motorist loses control of her car and drives into a warehouse filled with toxic waste. Some of the toxic waste splashes onto the driver, who is burned. Can the plaintiff recover under a theory of strict liability? Why or why not?

7. A cow from a defendant farmer's property crosses onto a neighbor's backyard to eat the daisies the plaintiff has planted there. When the plaintiff tries to shoo the cow away, it instead charges her and does as much harm as a cow can do, short of death. Will the defendant be liable under a theory of strict liability? Why or why not?

8. A plaintiff is walking down the street. A defendant motorist is momentarily distracted by a story on his car radio and drives into the plaintiff. Will the plaintiff succeed in seeking damages from the defendant under a theory of strict liability? Why or why not?

SKILL-BUILDING APPLICATION

Jerry Thompson and Dean Jefferies worked for a moving company. Driving a truckload of a client's home furnishings to the client's new home, their truck's engine stalled just as they were crossing railroad tracks. A train owned and operated by

Bristol & Eastern Railway struck the truck, killing Jerry instantly and leaving Dean with severe, life-altering injuries. Jerry's family sues Bristol & Eastern under a theory of strict liability. Based on the material in this chapter, what would be the best argument to be made to make a claim of strict liability? What is the likelihood of Jerry's family prevailing at trial on this theory, and why?

Of all inventions, the alphabet and the printing
press alone excepted, those inventions which
abridge distance have done most for the
civilization of our species.

— *Thomas Babington Macaulay*
(1800–1859)

CHAPTER 13

Product Liability

Product liability deals with injuries that arise from the use or sale of a product. Plaintiffs can recover damages under theories of negligence, breach of warranty, or strict liability, allowing them a variety of theories for recovery, a rarity in the legal field. This chapter examines all of these theories.

CHAPTER TOPICS

1. *Caveat Emptor*
2. Contracts
3. Warranty
4. Negligence
5. Strict Liability
6. Unreasonably Dangerous
7. Defenses
8. Consumer Product Safety

OBJECTIVES

After completing this chapter, you will be able to:

1. Explain the concept of privity of contract.
2. Provide a history of the development of the law of product liability.
3. Analyze the various theories of recovery in product liability actions.
4. Determine the proper parties for a product liability action.
5. Discuss the concept of warranty.
6. Summarize the role of the law of negligence in product liability actions.
7. Discuss the role of the law of strict product liability.
8. Analyze the liability of a manufacturer for inherently dangerous products.
9. Explore the relationship of defenses to an action for product liability.
10. Discuss consumer product safety.

■ HISTORY OF PRODUCT LIABILITY

Product liability focuses on injuries that arise because of a defect in a product. Historically, an injured party had no basis for recovery. As society underwent industrialization, the possibility of recovery became available to a purchaser and, soon, to virtually anyone injured by a product. Today, plaintiffs may recover under such theories as breach of contract, negligence, and under strict liability.

■ *CAVEAT EMPTOR*

The original rule of law about purchasing goods was *caveat emptor*. **Caveat emptor**—which in Latin means "let the buyer beware"—arose during a time when people would go daily to market to purchase produce and goods. The purchaser would learn which vendors consistently sold goods with minimal defects and which were not as scrupulous. More importantly, a purchaser would quickly learn the difference between ripe and rotten produce. It made sense, then, to require a purchaser to inspect the produce before buying or to suffer the consequences of not taking the trouble to learn about the produce. After all, the thinking went, if the plaintiff had an opportunity to examine the object thoroughly and failed to detect a defect, whose fault was that?

Given the advances of industrialization, where specialization of trade and industry likely meant that purchasers could become experts on only a narrow range of topics, *caveat emptor* has given way to a modern view. The merchant—or any seller—who knows or should know more about the product, has an obligation to provide safe goods. That obligation has arisen as a matter of law, and such law provides the basis for learning about theories for recovery based on product liability.

■ CONTRACT

The relationship between buyer and seller involves a **contract,** an exchange of value for value. In early days, parties had a face-to-face relationship, which made the transaction a personal one. Recovery under breach of contract, which focused on the sale of the goods, virtually precluded a recovery under tort law, where a contract could more readily contain a means for assessing damages.

Because only buyer and seller negotiated for the sale of the product, under the common law only the buyer would have a right of recovery; anyone outside the relationship had no valid basis for recovery. The legal concept of **privity of contract** meant that the buyer, and only the buyer, could sue the seller if the product subsequently turned out defective in some way. This view is consistent with *caveat emptor*, where the purchaser was supposed to use personal experience as a guide when conducting the transaction.

However, requiring privity of contract meant that some injured parties would have no valid basis for recovery. For example, if parents buy their child a bicycle helmet that fails to protect the child in an accident, the child would have no legal basis for recovery. Privity of contract meant that only if *the parent* experienced injury—even though this was a child's bicycle helmet—would the parent have a basis for recovery.

■ WARRANTY

For commercial transactions, the courts wanted to avoid the limitations imposed under *caveat emptor* and privity of contract. Staying with such limitations of recovery could mean slowing the pace of commercial transactions, since each buyer would need to make a thorough examination of the goods.

Because commercial transactions involved goods manufactured by mass production and because of the need to generate income quickly from sales, courts found another basis for recovery. Under a **warranty,** the manufacturer and/or the seller makes a promise regarding the quality of some aspect of the product, so that the buyer reasonably can rely on the truthfulness of that statement. While courts found that an implied warranty existed with each commercial transactions, manufacturers and/or sellers also began to make clear promises about the nature and quality of the goods. Such express promises would reassure buyers that if the goods proved to be defective, a ready and obvious remedy existed for a buyer.

The Uniform Commercial Code (U.C.C.)

Merchants lobbied each state to enact a **Uniform Commercial Code (U.C.C.)** that created standard business laws to facilitate making sales through the country. While each state has its own version—there is no federal version—these nearly identical state laws deal with transactions for the sale of goods worth more than $500 between merchants.

The U.C.C. expressly provides for a theory of recovery for breach of warranty. This encompasses promises made explicitly during the sale (under U.C.C. § 2-313). Also, the U.C.C. imposed an implicit **warranty of merchantability** (under U.C.C. § 2-314) that what the manufacturer and/or seller provides is what the purchaser reasonably expects to buy. It also imposed an implicit **warranty of fitness** that the products will work in a specific way and are fit for a particular use (under U.C.C. § 2-315).

For example, an automobile dealership might provide a power train warranty with each vehicle it sells, which explicitly provides for the repair of the car's transmission system. If the dealer sells an automobile, it implicitly warrants that the car being sold is what it is, in terms of not only the features but also in terms of the actual ownership. Finally, when an automobile dealership sells an "all terrain" vehicle, it is making an implicit promise regarding the use of the vehicle under a broad range of conditions.

Limiting a Seller's Liability under a Theory of Warranty

Two provisions in the U.C.C. help sellers mitigate damages involving a transaction for the sale of goods. A customer cannot bring a claim in warranty without having first notified the seller within a reasonable time that the customer knew or should have known, of the defect (see box below).

**BUYER'S OBLIGATIONS UNDER THE U.C.C. TO MAKE OUT
A CLAIM FOR BREACH OF WARRANTY**

1. The buyer must pay at the contract rate for any goods accepted.
2. Acceptance of goods by the buyer precludes rejection of the goods accepted and if made with knowledge of a non-conformity cannot be revoked because of it unless the acceptance was on the reasonable assumption that the non-conformity would be seasonably cured but acceptance does not of itself impair any other remedy provided by this Article for non-conformity.

continued

3. Where a tender has been accepted
   a. the buyer must within a reasonable time after he discovers or should have discovered any breach notify the seller of breach or be barred from any remedy; and
   b. if the claim is one for infringement or the like (subsection (3) of Section 2-312) and the buyer is sued as a result of such a breach he must notify the seller within a reasonable time after he receives notice of the litigation or be barred from any remedy over for liability established by the litigation.
4. The burden is on the buyer to establish any breach with respect to the goods accepted.
5. Where the buyer is sued for breach of a warranty or other obligation for which his seller is answerable over
   a. he may give his seller written notice of the litigation. If the notice states that the seller may come in and defend and that if the seller does not do so he will be bound in any action against him by his buyer by any determination of fact common to the two litigations, then unless the seller after seasonable receipt of the notice does come in and defend he is so bound.
   b. if the claim is one for infringement or the like (subsection (3) of Section 2-312) the original seller may demand in writing that his buyer turn over to him control of the litigation including settlement or else be barred from any remedy over and if he also agrees to bear all expense and to satisfy any adverse judgment, then unless the buyer after seasonable receipt of the demand does turn over control the buyer is so barred.

The Uniform Commercial Code, §2-607, the American Law Institution

Notifying the seller of a defect provides the seller with the opportunity to correct the defect without the plaintiff having to file suit.

Also, the U.C.C. provides sellers the freedom to limit or even to disclaim any warranty. Courts may invalidate such disclaimers or limitations if they were not clearly presented to the plaintiff (see box below).

EXCLUSION OR MODIFICATION OF WARRANTIES

1. Words or conduct relevant to the creation of an express warranty and words or conduct tending to negate or limit warranty shall be construed wherever reasonable as consistent with each other [...]
2. [...] [T]o exclude or modify the implied warranty of merchantability or any part of it the language must mention merchantability and in case of a writing must be conspicuous, and to exclude or modify any implied warranty of fitness the exclusion must be by a writing and conspicuous. Language to exclude all implied warranties of fitness is sufficient if it states, for example, that "There are no warranties which extend beyond the description on the face hereof."
3. Notwithstanding subsection (2)
   a. unless the circumstances indicate otherwise, all implied warranties are excluded by expressions like "as is", "with all faults" or other

continued

> language which in common understanding calls the buyer's attention to the exclusion of warranties and makes plain that there is no implied warranty; and
> b. when the buyer before entering into the contract has examined the goods [...] as fully as he desired or has refused to examine the goods there is no implied warranty with regard to defects which an examination ought in the circumstances to have revealed to him [...]
>
> U.C.C. §2-316 (2004)

So disclaimers may prove a defense in a claim for breach of warranty. Yet, disclaimers might not negate a claim for personal injury under a theory of recovery in strict liability (see box below).

> **THE EFFECT OF DISCLAIMERS OF LIABILITY**
> So far as a personal injury case is considered to be a warranty case under the UCC and not a strict tort claim in disguise, the disclaimer or limitation of the implied warranty might preclude suit.
>
> Dobbs, *The Law of Torts* §371 (2000)

While every state has created statutes that impose the U.C.C. in that jurisdiction, states may adopt a version that doesn't contain the identical provisions in the version used in another state. Therefore, paralegal students should examine the version of the U.C.C. enacted in their state, to ascertain that certain provisions, if they have been adopted, apply for a claim of breach of warranty (see table below).

Warranties under Article 2 of the Uniform Commercial Code	
§2-313	creation of
§2-314	implied warranty of merchantability
§2-315	implied warranty of fitness for a particular purpose

Defenses

Many jurisdictions do not allow a defendant to avoid liability under a breach of warranty claim when the defendant has disclaimed all warranties. Allowing for such a rule would effectively eliminate the entire theory of recovery based on breach of warranty. Some jurisdictions might allow that a disclaimer negates recovery for a purchaser but that such a disclaimer may not apply to all users of the product. Procedural defenses may also exist, such as failure to file within a specific statute of limitation or to comply with a statute that requires a plaintiff to provide a defendant with notice prior to filing suit—which would then give defendant an opportunity to repair the defective item or replace it with a reasonable substitute.

■ NEGLIGENCE

Courts in the nineteenth and twentieth centuries began to recognize that creating exceptions to the limitation of privity of contract failed to address the actual losses incurred by those who were not original parties to the contract. For this reason, the courts began to move away from basing recovery on breach of contract—did the parties understand everything about the product at the time of sale?—to asking whether the product was "imminently dangerous." This meant recovery under tort law, not contract law.

Most notably Justice Cardozo, in *MacPherson v. Buick Motor Co.*, 217 N.Y. 382 (1916), rejected the continued limitation of the requirement of the privity of contract doctrine. *MacPherson* signaled that modern society could not expect every subsequent user or purchaser to have privity with the seller or to keep creating exceptions for people who were injured yet weren't in privity. Instead, the court imposed a duty of care to inspect the goods, upon the party who had the best chance of knowing all about the product: the manufacturer and/or seller. Courts used the theory of negligence to provide recovery when defective products turned out to be unreasonably dangerous (as described in Case in Point 13-1).

CASE IN POINT 13-1

MacPherson v. Buick Motor Company
217 N.Y. 382 (1916)

Cardozo, J.

The defendant is a manufacturer of automobiles. It sold an automobile to a retail dealer. The retail dealer resold to the plaintiff. While the plaintiff was in the car, it suddenly collapsed. He was thrown out and injured. One of the wheels was made of defective wood, and its spokes crumbled into fragments. The wheel was not made by the defendant; it was bought from another manufacturer. There is evidence, however, that its defects could have been discovered by reasonable inspection, and that inspection was omitted. [...] The question to be determined is whether the defendant owed a duty of care and vigilance to any one but the immediate purchaser.

The foundations of this branch of the law, at least in this state, were laid in *Thomas v. Winchester* (6 N.Y. 397). A poison was falsely labeled. The sale was made to a druggist, who in turn sold to a customer. The customer recovered damages from the seller who affixed the label. "The defendant's negligence," it was said, "put human life in imminent danger." A poison falsely labeled is likely to injure any one who gets it. Because the danger is to be foreseen, there is a duty to avoid the injury. [...]

If the nature of a thing is such that it is reasonably certain to place life and limb in peril when negligently made, it is then a thing of danger. Its nature gives warning of the consequences to be expected. If to the element of danger there is added knowledge that the thing will be used by persons other than the purchaser, and used without new tests then, irrespective of contract, the manufacturer of this thing of danger is under a duty to make it carefully. [...] There must be knowledge of a danger, not merely possible, but probable. It is possible to use almost anything in a way that will make it dangerous if defective. That is not enough to charge the manufacturer with a duty independent of his contract. [...] There must also be knowledge that in the usual course of events the danger will be shared by others than the buyer. Such knowledge may often be inferred from the nature of the transaction. But it is possible that even knowledge of the danger and of the use will not always be enough. [...] We are dealing now with the liability of the manufacturer of the finished product, who puts it on the market to be used without inspection by his customers. [...]

Beyond all question, the nature of an automobile gives warning of probable danger if its construction is defective. This automobile was designed to go fifty miles an hour. Unless its wheels were sound and strong, injury was almost certain. [...] The defendant knew the danger. It knew also that the care would be used by persons other than the buyer. This was apparent from its size; there were seats for three persons. It was apparent also from the fact that the buyer was a dealer in cars, who bought to resell. [...]

The manufacturer who sells the automobile to the retail dealer invites the dealer's customers to use it. The invitation is addressed in the one case to determinate persons and in the other to an indeterminate class, but in each case it is equally plain, and in each its consequences must be the same.

If danger was to be expected as reasonably certain, there was a duty of vigilance, and this whether you call the danger inherent or imminent [...]

We think the defendant was not absolved from a duty of inspection because it bought the wheels from a reputable manufacturer. It was not merely a dealer in automobiles. It was a manufacturer of automobiles. It was responsible for the finished product. It was not at liberty to put the finished product on the market without subjecting the component parts to ordinary and simple tests [....] Under the charge of the trial judge nothing more was required of it. The obligation to inspect must vary with the nature of the thing to be inspected. The more probable the danger, the greater the need of caution.

The court escaped the need for privity of contract, or the reliance on convoluted exceptions to a requirement of privity, and allowed for recovery due to negligence. Virtually all other jurisdictions allowed for recovery under a theory of negligence. [Author's Note: A few years later, Judge Cardozo also wrote the majority opinion in the *Palsgraf* case, mentioned in Chapter 3, so his views helped to shape a modern view on tort liability. He subsequently served as a U.S. Supreme Court Justice.]

Who Has a Duty?

In many instances, sellers as well as manufacturers are liable since they have control over the item as it travels through the stream of commerce (see box below).

NEGLIGENCE

So far as liability for negligence is concerned, there is no longer any doubt that it attaches to any seller of a product, including the maker of a component part of the final product, and an assembler of parts supplied by others, or even a mere processor under contract with the maker. It applies to dealers, whether at wholesale or retail, and to a second-hand dealer who reconditions automobiles for sale. It is obvious that less in the way of care may be required of some of these sellers than of others; but if reasonable care has not been exercised, there may be liability.

W. Page Keeton et. al., *Prosser & Keeton on the Law of Torts*, §100 at 704 (5th ed. 1984)

Nature of Duty

The specific duty owed applies to any defect in a problem that reasonably could harm a party. Manufacturers and sellers must exercise the level of care expected of a reasonably prudent person under the same circumstances (see box below).

> ### NEGLIGENT MANUFACTURE
>
> A manufacturer who fails to exercise reasonable care in the manufacture of a chattel which, unless carefully made, he should recognize as involving an unreasonable risk of causing physical harm to those who use it for a purpose for which the manufacturer should expect it to be used and to those whom he should expect to be endangered by its probable use, is subject to liability for physical harm caused to them by its lawful use in a manner and for a purpose for which it is supplied.
>
> *Restatement (Second) of Torts*, §395 (1965)

This approach respects the limits imposed by the court in the *Palsgraf* case in Chapter 3: recovery exists only for a reasonably foreseeable plaintiff. This is not like privity of contract, which involves just buyer and seller. Rather, this approach allows for other foreseeable users of the goods. Whether under a theory of strict liability or negligence, the determination of the proper plaintiff in a product liability action is based on the issue of foreseeability, as shown in Case in Point 13-2.

CASE IN POINT 13-2

Hampshire v. Ford Motor Company

155 Mich. App. 143 (1986)

[...]

On December 17, 1976, plaintiff was driving his 1966 Cadillac on Franklin Avenue in the County of Los Angeles, California. Plaintiff sustained serious injuries when his vehicle was struck head-on by a 1973 Lincoln Continental, manufactured by defendant Ford Motor Company, which had crossed over the center line. [...] [P]laintiff merely alleges that Ford was negligent in the design of the ignition locking system on the 1973 Lincoln such that it failed to operate as an effective anti-theft device which made Ford vehicles more subject to theft than other types of cars. At the time of the accident in this case, the Lincoln was a stolen car. The car had been stolen several hours prior to the accident. [...]

Plaintiff asserted that stolen cars are more likely to be involved in injury-causing collisions with other members of the public. Plaintiff alleged that defects in the ignition locking system encourage car thefts that result in injuries to motorists who are struck by stolen cars. The trial court determined that [...] the defendant did not owe a duty to the plaintiff under the facts of this case as alleged by plaintiff. [...]

In regard to the substantive issue of this appeal, plaintiff argues that the trial court erred in determining that California law did not impose a duty on defendant under the facts of this case. We disagree.

A manufacturer's duty to use reasonable care to design a product such that it is reasonably safe for its intended and foreseeable use does not extend to the protection of the whole world. The scope of the duty often depends primarily on whether the injuries to a particular plaintiff are foreseeable [...]

[T]he trial court relied on California authority which precludes recovery against the owner of a vehicle when he leaves his keys in his car, the car is stolen and an innocent third party is injured when he is involved in an accident with the stolen vehicle....

The trial court reasoned that, since California law did not recognize a duty under those facts, California would not impose a similar duty on an automobile manufacturer. We agree....

[...]

The lower court merely reasoned that, since California did not impose a duty on the owner of a vehicle to prevent theft for the benefit of third parties, it would therefore not impose a similar duty on the automobile manufacturer under similar circumstances. We are persuaded by this reasoning. Defendant owed no duty to plaintiff in this case. [...]

[A]ffirmed.

Breach of Duty

When has a manufacturer and/or seller breached such a duty? Courts have generally settled on three instances where a breach has occurred: 1) where manufacturers or sellers have created or failed to detect a defect, 2) where manufacturers or sellers have a duty to warn of defects, and 3) where manufacturers or sellers have liability even after a warning has been given.

Creating or Failing to Detect a Defect

Courts have imposed liability on a manufacturer and/or seller for breaching a duty of reasonable care in the design and/or inspection of the goods. Since the manufacturer has control over the product's design and manufacturing process, the courts look to see that the manufacturer has followed the safety practices common to the industry and, those duties imposed under the law (see Case in Point 13-3).

CASE IN POINT 13-3

Hohlenkamp v. Rheem Manufacturing Company
134 Ariz. 208 (Ct. App. 1982)

[...] [I]n February 1958, Mr. and Mrs. Hohlenkamp purchased and took up residence in their new home in Tucson. It contained a Rheem gas-fired hot water heater which was located in a 6' X 10' utility-storage room along with a washing machine and a furnace. For the four years prior to the fire which occurred in this case, Mr. Hohlenkamp also kept a gas-powered lawnmower and a can of gasoline in the room.

Adjacent to the utility room, Mr. Hohlenkamp had constructed a screened-in porch area. On May 22, 1962, Steven Hohlenkamp was playing in this screened-in porch area when Mrs. Hohlenkamp heard a "terrible whoosh" and "the whole house shook." She immediately ran to the porch and found her son, Steven, engulfed in flames.

The Tucson Fire Department determined that the cause of the blaze was the ignition of flammable gasoline vapors by the pilot light on the Rheem water heater.

At the time of this investigation the gasoline can which Mr. Hohlenkamp kept in the utility room was found on its side three feet from the water heater. The cap to the gas can was off and the can was charred on the three exposed sides but had neither exploded nor imploded as a result of the fire. There was a conflict in the evidence as to whether the fire was caused by the seepage of gasoline fumes from the lawnmower gas tank or by gasoline spilled from the can.

Appellant presented expert testimony that the water heater was defective in design because it did not have a flame arrestor screen (Davy screen) to prevent flashback explosions and because the water heater did not contain a warning about the dangers of storing flammable substances in or about the area where the water heater was located. Appellant further presented testimony that the general lay public does not know that gasoline fumes are heavier than air and can leak out from gasoline cans and lawnmower tanks, run along the floor for long distances and be sucked into the pilot light and burner area of a hot water heater because of a draft created by the heater's design and operation.

Mr. and Mrs. Hohlenkamp were aware that the hot water heater had a constantly burning pilot light and Mr. Hohlenkamp lit the pilot light himself on at least two occasions when the wind had blown it out. He also knew from his automotive background that gasoline or any flammable liquid should not be stored near an open flame, that gasoline was dangerous when it was in a vaporized form and that gasoline fumes were heavier than air. However, there was also testimony that Mr. Hohlenkamp did not understand that gasoline fumes could be sucked into the pilot light by the draft created in the design and operation of the heater.

Appellant presented evidence that water heater manufacturers had knowledge before the Hohlenkamp accident of the danger presented in residential homes by vapor-like substances coming in contact with the open flame at the bottom of their water heaters. Evidence was also presented that flame arrestor screens had been patented in this country since the beginning of the century and were used widely throughout the petroleum and gasoline industry to prevent flashback explosions.

Rheem put on expert testimony that the Davy screen has never been incorporated into the design of a gas-fired water heater of any make. Several defense experts testified that the use of the screen would significantly increase the risk associated with a hot water heater because the screen would tend to act as a filter and if it became clogged, carbon monoxide poisoning would result. Expert testimony was also presented by Rheem that different types of flammable vapors required different size pores or holes in the Davy screen device in order to prevent fire. Thus, a particularly sized Davy screen would not prevent the ignition of all flammable vapors that could be present in or around a water heater. They also testified that the screen itself, if in contact for a period of time with a flammable vapor, would eventually glow red and become an ignition or detonation force in itself. Rheem also presented testimony that it had no notice of any similar accident involving one of its water heaters igniting a flammable vapor until it received notice of the lawsuit in 1975.

[...]

I. DID APPELLEE PROVE A STRICT LIABILITY CASE FOR A DESIGN DEFECT?

There is strict liability for a design defect if the product is in a defective condition. A defective condition is a condition not contemplated by the ultimate consumer which will be unreasonably dangerous to him. The term "unreasonably dangerous" means "dangerous to an extent beyond that which would be contemplated by the ordinary consumer who purchases it, with the ordinary knowledge common to the community as to its characteristics." (citation omitted)

[...] The design defect which forms the basis of a claim in strict liability views the defect from the viewpoint of the consumer. The design defect upon which a negligence claim can be based views the defect from the standpoint of the manufacturer. [...] [W]hen faced with a design defect, in order to determine whether the claim for relief is based on strict liability or negligence, one must ask whether the product, because of the alleged design defect, is "dangerous to an extent beyond that which would be contemplated by the ordinary consumer who purchases it, with the ordinary knowledge common to the community as to its characteristics." [footnote omitted] (citation omitted). If reasonable minds could differ on the answer to this question, or if the answer is in the affirmative, a claim for relief is based on strict liability. If the answer is in the negative, the defect must be judged upon negligence principles using the standard of a reasonably prudent manufacturer.

We pose the strict liability "test question." Would the ordinary consumer know that the water heater had an open pilot light and appreciate the fact that the light could cause a fire if gasoline fumes came in contact with it? [footnote omitted.]

[...]

We are unable, as a matter of law, to answer the strict liability "test question" in the affirmative or negative because we believe reasonable minds could differ. The issue was, therefore, a strict liability issue, and if the jury believed there was a design defect, but that the defect was not "unreasonably dangerous" [...] then the issue sounded in negligence. The trial court erred in not letting the issue of strict liability for design defect be decided by the jury.

II. EVIDENCE OF INDUSTRY STANDARDS AND STATE OF THE ART IN STRICT LIABILITY CASES

[...] Appellee was allowed to present evidence that it complied with all the standards of the American National Standard Institute. Did the trial court err when it allowed evidence of industry standards and state of the art into evidence? We think not. While state of the art is not, strictly speaking, a defense in strict liability actions, it may be considered in determining whether a product is defective.

[...]

Industry standards have also been found to be admissible in strict liability cases on the ground that these standards often constitute substantive evidence on the strict liability issue of whether a product is in a defective condition, unreasonably dangerous to the user.

[...]

"In our view, these safety standards are relevant, especially in design defect cases. In cases of defects in manufacture, the jury is frequently able to judge the defective item by comparing it to others similarly produced by the manufacturer. However, as the California Supreme Court has noted: '...A design defect, by contrast, cannot be identified simply by comparing the injury-producing product with the manufacturer's plans or with other units of the same product line, since by definition the plans and all such units will reflect the same design.' (citation omitted.). By reason of the nature of the case, the trier of fact is greatly dependent on expert evidence and industry standards in deciding whether a defect is present.

* * *

These codes were formulated by groups of experts in the conveyor designing and manufacturing field, and were approved by many organizations. They are likely to be more probative than a single learned treatise or an expert opinion, as they represent the consensus of an entire industry. There is no motive for the formulators to falsify, and there is no danger that the standards will be subsequently altered or incorrectly remembered by a witness. Finally, since we require that the safety standards be introduced through an expert witness, the average party will have a fair opportunity to cross-examine the experts on any inconsistencies, misrepresentations or other limitations of the standards. Given these guarantees of trustworthiness, we approve the admission of industry safety codes as substantive evidence on the strict liability issue of whether a product is in a 'defective condition unreasonably dangerous.' (citations omitted)".

The evidence of industry standards was introduced here by an expert witness [...] There was no error by the court in admitting evidence of state of the art and industry standards for the limited purpose of showing whether the product was defective and unreasonably dangerous.

[...]

Our conclusion is supported by the close similarity between negligence and strict liability. The elements of both are the same with the exception that in negligence plaintiff must show a breach of a duty of due care by defendant while in strict liability plaintiff must show that the product was unreasonably dangerous. The distinction between the two lessens considerably in failure to warn cases since it is clear that strict liability adds little in warning cases. Under a negligence theory the issue is whether the defendant exercised due care in formulating and updating the warning, while under a strict liability theory the issue is whether the lack of proper warning made the product unreasonably dangerous. Though phrased differently the issue under either theory is essentially the same: was the warning adequate? (citations omitted)"

[...]

The directed verdict on the issue of strict liability for a design defect is vacated and set aside and the case is remanded for a new trial on that issue only. The case is affirmed in all other respects.

Since the plaintiff had made the case that a design defect could exist that resulted in subsequent injury, a jury needed then to assess the evidence and the plaintiff's theory of recovery.

Since a seller has control over the goods, courts have concluded that the seller reasonably should take the time to inspect the goods, consistent with practices in the industry and as imposed by law. Although the case described in Case in Point 13-4 predates revisions to the *Restatement of Torts*, it does capture a court's construction of the issue of whether a duty to inspect exists.

CASE IN POINT 13-4

Bower v. Corbell

408 P.2d 307 (Okla. 1965)

[...]

2. The uncontroverted facts disclose that on December 7, 1959, plaintiff's husband purchased an MBS power saw from defendant. This saw, mounted on bicycle-type wheels, was powered by a 5 3/4 horsepower gasoline engine. Power was transmitted to a 20-inch circular blade attached to a rigid shaft at the front of the machine by means of a belt and pulley. The mechanical design was such the blade could be so positioned as to allow the saw to be operated either horizontally or vertically. The saw was operated from two handle bars at the rear, which formed part of the frame, upon which the controls were mounted. The position of the blade presumably would be maintained by means of setscrews intended to hold the shaft in the desired position. When the setscrews were loosened the shaft would turn, thus permitting the saw blade to change position.

3. The morning following purchase plaintiff's husband, assisted by one Stephens, operated the saw for approximately one hour with the blade in horizontal position, felling trees which varied in diameter from 2-6 inches. The limbs then were trimmed in preparation for the logs, or poles, to be sawed into firewood. After noon they returned to work accompanied by plaintiff and Stephens' wife. Plaintiff's husband was operating the saw with the blade in a vertical position cutting the poles into stove lengths, as Stephens fed the poles into the saw at right angles. This was accomplished by pushing the logs across another log laid upon the ground, which kept the saw above the ground and allowed the sawed lengths to roll away from the saw.

4. Plaintiff and Stephens' wife had been working some distance away piling brush, but plaintiff returned to where the men were working, approaching the saw from the right side. Plaintiff then went a slight distance in front of and to the right of the saw and stopped over to pick up a stick of wood. While in this position, the saw "screamed" and she felt it cut her body. The blade struck plaintiff, cutting her head and back and causing severe and permanent injuries, the nature and extent of which are not involved herein. After the accident the setscrews were found to have vibrated loose, allowing the saw blade to tilt some 5-10 degrees to the right of the vertical position in which it was being operated prior to the accident.

5. [...] The petition alleged negligence on part of the manufacturer in failing to use due care in construction, inspection and testing of the machine. Negligence was charged against defendant in that, having assembled the machine, at the time of sale and delivery the saw was in a defective condition and dangerous both to the operator and persons in the vicinity of the operation, which facts could have been ascertained by proper inspection which defendant had neglected to make. Further, that the saw was defective in that the setscrews, which held the shaft supporting the blade, had no recess in which to fit, making it impossible to tighten the screws sufficiently to prevent the shaft from turning when the saw was in operation. Plaintiff alleged her injuries resulted from her husband's use of the saw, in that when attempting to cut a log the saw, because of defective construction, turned on its side, began vibrating violently and clawed its way over the log and struck plaintiff, causing injury solely by reason of negligent construction and inspection of the power saw.

6. Defendant's answer alleged plaintiff's contributory negligence, concurrent negligence of plaintiff's husband in failing to use ordinary care in use of the equipment, failure to inspect the saw prior to attempting to use same and failure to make certain the saw was safe prior to permitting his wife to work in close proximity. Further, if the saw were defective in any particular, same was a latent defect which defendant could not have discovered by exercise of ordinary care; hazards coincident to use of the saw should have been apparent to person of ordinary intelligence so that plaintiff's conduct amounted to assumption of risk. [...]

7. The evidence, including the factual matters stated above, was not in serious conflict. When the accident occurred the saw "jumped" sideways several feet, struck plaintiff and landed bottom side up. When running, the saw was too powerful to hold, and vibrates so that it shakes the operator. The seller did not advise the purchaser about the setscrews, and that this was the only means of holding the shaft in place, but only advised the saw was ready to go.

8. Some time after the accident Stephens bought the saw from Corbell. When he operated the saw he carried a wrench and tightened the setscrews about every 15 minutes. If this were not done the screws became loose and the blade would turn because the saw vibrates all the time it is in operation. Stephens, who was helping saw wood at the time of the accident did not hear the saw "scream", but did see the saw jump sideways. After buying the

saw he never used it as much as an hour without checking. Sometimes the screws did not need tightening but at other times this would be needed. On one occasion a setscrew was gone. Prior to the accident he did not know that vibration of the saw would shake the setscrews loose and thus allow the blade to turn. He also testified the saw would "buck" when in use and, although it had never gotten away from him, he learned to hold it with a very tight grip.

9. A witness experienced with gasoline-powered machines of this type testified he had examined the saw; the setscrews were intended to keep the shaft locked in position and prevent the blade from turning; if the setscrews became loose the shaft and blade could turn a complete circle; the vibration would cause the setscrews to become loose within 15-30 minutes. The witness stated in his opinion the setscrews were not recessed into the shaft, because he examined the machine before trial and was able to twist the shaft which could not be done if they were recessed.

10. Defendant's evidence concerning the sale coincided with the purchaser's (Corbell) testimony, except for testimony that before sale the machine was started, he was shown the service points and how to operate the machine, and the saw was engaged in demonstration. There also was testimony that a pamphlet and booklet describing servicing of the engine and the manufacturer's warranty probably were tied on the machine. The purchaser's testimony was that the machine neither was demonstrated nor the means of operation shown him at the time of purchase, but that he relied upon what he was told by the seller.

11. Defendant's shop foreman testified he assembled these saws on a commission basis. The engine was bolted to the frame and he installed the belt and blade on the saw, then checked all bolts and the setscrews to see if same were tight. The machine would be started, allowed to run a few minutes, then shut down and checked over again. Following this the foreman affixed a decal to the saw "Sale and Services by Bower Implement Company." The witness had assembled approximately 150 machines over the years and never had known of any difficulty with the setscrews before this instance.

12. Defendant's contentions on appeal are based upon the premise the evidence did not establish failure to recess the setscrews into the shaft would be a defect; that, even assuming the setscrews were not recessed and this was a defect, same would be a defect in design only and would constitute a latent defect for which a retailer could not be liable.
[…]

15. The primary argument […] is that a vendor of a chattel manufactured by a third person, who neither knows nor has reason to know, that it is, or is likely to be, dangerous, is not liable for harm resulting from the dangerous character or condition of the chattel although the seller could have discovered this by inspection or test before the sale. […]

16. This action is founded upon negligence alone, and not upon products liability as commonly understood. […] However, it is observed that the comments in the original statement dealing with Sec. 402, noted that a retailer, in the cursory inspection given to goods which are handled for purposes of sale, may have opportunity to observe indications which as a competent dealer in such goods should cause him to realize that such goods are, or are likely to be, in a dangerous condition for use. Thus it is said that a retailer must utilize both the special opportunity to observe the condition of the goods and the special competence that such a dealer should have to realize the dangerous implications of conditions which, though observable, are not likely to be appreciated by the purchaser.
[…]

19. The cogent answer to the argument premised upon whether inherently or imminently dangerous is found in *MacPherson v. Buick Motor Co.*, (citation omitted) wherein Cardozo, J., said:

"*** Subtle distinctions are drawn by the defendant between things inherently dangerous and things imminently dangerous, but the case does not turn upon these verbal niceties. If danger was to be expected as reasonably certain, there was a duty of vigilance, and this whether you call the danger inherent or imminent. ***"

[…] We are convinced that an instrumentality such as involved herein, which from its very nature and operation makes possible injury or death at any instant to those in the area of use, necessarily must be denominated as inherently dangerous. An automobile is not inherently dangerous within itself. But when serviced and set in motion it becomes a contrivance of an inherently dangerous nature. Where reasonably certain to place life and limb in danger if negligently made or serviced it is a thing of danger. (citation omitted) […]

21. Liability in this case must depend upon whether the retailer owed any duty of care to plaintiff, and if so whether such duty was breached. The evidence relative to handling the saw prior to recommending it to the purchaser as "ready to go" has been mentioned. Admittedly defendant partially assembled the components. Defendant's shop employees were paid for rendering this service. From this it must follow that some duty devolved upon defendant to test and inspect properly before sale. The evidence was that defendant's employee purportedly tested the saw by running the engine and again checking the belts before placing the "sold and serviced" decal thereon. There was no effort to make an actual test of the saw by an effort to use it for the intended purpose. The only evidence of defendant's use or experience with the saw was lack of knowledge of any bad experience with others previously sold. Such evidence neither can be classed as positive proof these saws always were safe for the intended purpose nor proof that even if defective such defect would not have been discovered by exercise of proper care.

22. The real question presented is whether defendant, by simply making the inspection and test noted, fulfilled the duty owed to a prospective purchaser, or whether the accepted rules of care required further inspection and tests of the working parts. The reasonableness of the inspection and tests used must depend upon the circumstances of the particular case. The inherently dangerous character of the machine must be acknowledged. It is further argued that neither defendant nor the employee (foreman) had knowledge, or from known facts should have realized, this saw was dangerous or had latent defects, or that they knew anything more about power saws than the purchaser. However, since the foreman had assembled 150 saws, the jury undoubtedly considered defendant, through this employee, either knew far more about power saws than the purchaser, or that defendant was negligent in placing responsibility in such employee's hands.

[…]

27. Defendant had under its control, for retail sale to the general public, a mechanical device which was dangerous unless properly constructed, completely maintained and carefully operated during use. In these circumstances defendant owed to the purchaser, and others who might reasonably be expected to be within proximity to the machine during use for the purpose for which intended, the duty of using the degree of care to see that it operated safely commensurate with the danger to which such persons would be exposed when the machine was in use. The evidence was such that the jury was required to decide whether the dangerous defect in the machine could, or would, have been discovered upon reasonable observation, inspection or

testing, and thus defendant should have imparted notice to the purchaser of the potential danger to those rightfully using the instrumentality for the purpose intended.

[...]

30. This appeal presents an issue as to which we are required, by exigencies of the present era, to determine and declare a sound and legally defensible rule of conduct applicable in cases of vendors of inherently dangerous items sold to the general public. The reason and need were succinctly stated in *MacPherson*, supra, thus:

"*** Precedents drawn from the days of travel by stagecoach do not fit the conditions of travel today. The principle that the danger must be imminent does not change, but the things subject to the principle do change. They are whatever the needs of life in a developing civilization require them to be."

[...]

32. Evolved from text principles and judicial declaration in modern cases [...] we are of the opinion a rule consonant with reason and justice may be stated: Where a vendor supplies a purchaser with a device or instrumentality, and in exercise of ordinary care knows or should know if same is defective it will be dangerous to all who come in contact therewith during use for the purpose for which intended, the vendor owes a duty to ascertain the condition of the instrumentality by exercising reasonable care to see that it is safe for the use for which intended. A vendor who fails to exercise ordinary care to ascertain the true condition and safety of the instrumentality, and chooses to sell without notice or warning of the dangerous characteristics and dangers inherent in use thereof is liable for injuries proximately caused by use of the instrumentality.

33. The conclusion stated removes need for discussion of defendant's argument relative to liability herein being that of the manufacturer. Neither is it necessary to deal with the error asserted in the giving of an instruction dealing with defendant's duty to inspect the power saw prior to sale. However, having pointed out that inspection and testing do not require a factory-type inspection but rather that which would, or should, make defects which reasonably could be expected to cause injury apparent to a dealer, the claim that to require any inspection or testing would create an unreasonable burden is not persuasive.

[...]

37. Plaintiff's evidence was not required to exclude every conclusion inconsistent with defendant's liability. Where the circumstances disclosed by evidence and legitimate inferences remove the case from the realm of conjecture or speculation and bring it within the sphere of legitimate and rational inferences, a jury verdict based thereon is properly supported by competent evidence. (citation omitted.) [...]

The court upheld the ruling in favor of the plaintiff consistent with the spirit of the *MacPherson* case, supra, that recognized a manufacturer and seller owe certain duties to all purchasers and that, specifically, a seller involved in the assembly of the goods needs to test the goods adequately before sale.

Duty to Warn

Since the manufacturer and/or seller have a duty to inspect goods, they also have the responsibility to warn of such a defect if it is discovered during the inspection (see box on next page).

FAILURE TO WARN

One who supplies directly or through a third person a chattel for another to use is subject to liability to those whom the supplier should expect to use the chattel with the consent of the other or to be endangered by its probable use, for physical harm caused by the use of the chattel in the manner for which and by a person for whose use it is supplied, if the supplier

a. knows or has reason to know that the chattel is or is likely to be dangerous for the use for which it is supplied, and

b. has no reason to believe that those for whose use the chattel is supplied will realize its dangerous condition, and

c. fails to exercise reasonable care to inform them of its dangerous condition or of the facts which make it likely to be dangerous.

Restatement (Second) of Torts, §388 (1965)

A breach can occur when the defendant provides no warning, when the warning provided was inadequate, or where the warning dealt insufficiently with the defect.

The duty to inspect is limited to what the manufacturer and/or seller would reasonably expect the item to be used for. Case in Point 13-5 illustrates just how far-reaching the duty goes.

CASE IN POINT 13-5

Brown v. Glade and Grove Supply, Inc.

647 So. 2d 1033 (Fla. Dist. Ct. App. 4th Dist. 1994)

[...]

On March 27, 1985, plaintiff's decedent, Daniel Brown, Jr., died as a result of injuries sustained when the tractor he was operating for his employer, U.S. Sugar Corporation (U.S. Sugar), rolled over. The tractor, manufactured by MRS had a separate steering system to control the rear wheels. When operating the tractor in the field, this rear steering system was desirable as it would enable the operator to make tighter turns and allow "crabbing," a four-wheel steering technique used in the field. On the road, however, operation of the tractor without a lock-out pin in place to prevent the inadvertent engagement of the rear wheel steering system and to stabilize the rear wheels would render the tractor unreasonably dangerous and prone to roll-over. One of the few undisputed facts in this case is that at the time of this accident a lock-out pin was not in place.

Following the accident, plaintiff filed suit against MRS, Glades Equipment, and Glade and Grove, under strict liability and negligence theories. Plaintiff's theory of defective design is two-pronged. First, plaintiff asserts defects in the design of the rear wheel steering system. Plaintiff's experts [...] specifically criticized the design of the lock-out pins, the overall design of the hydraulic steering system, which could cause rear wheel shifting at normal road speeds, and the placement of the lever for the rear wheel steering, which could cause inadvertent actuation of the rear wheels. Second, plaintiff asserts design defects in the warnings, including the failure to apprise the user of the dangers of driving the vehicle on the road without the proper lock-out of the rear wheel steering system.

[...]

WARNINGS

[...]

Plaintiff's expert testified that failure to place the warnings on the tractor was "contrary to safe custom and practice." The mere existence of warnings in an instruction manual is not dispositive of the adequacy of the warnings for several reasons. A warning may be defective not only by virtue of inadequate wording, but as a result of its location and the manner in which the warning is conveyed. (citation omitted.) For example, even if the language contained in the instruction manual adequately apprised a user of the dangers, a jury could find the warning defective because it was not permanently affixed to the tractor. (citation omitted) (manufacturer owes a duty to the user to warn of its producer's dangerous propensities and, therefore, that an employer or supervisor has been warned is of little import where the employee-user has not received the warning).

Had the instruction manual been kept with the tractor by the employer and thus available to plaintiff's decedent, which it was not, a question of fact still exists as to whether the "warning" language contained in the manual adequately apprises a user of the serious risk of injury or death resulting from nonuse of lock-out pins. The instruction manual provided by MRS gave no warning of the risk of roll-over. It contained, the following language: CAUTION

DO NOT USE THE REAR WHEEL STEERING LEVER AT HIGH SPEEDS. WHEN TRAVELLING, INSTALL THE REAR STEERING LOCKOUT.

Advising a user to operate a tractor with the lock-out pins in place is an instruction, not a warning. A warning should contain some wording directed to the significant dangers arising from failure to use the product in the prescribed manner, such as the risk of serious injury or death. [...]

Further, the danger of roll-over from nonuse of a lock-out pin is not the type of "obvious" danger [...] so as to lead to the conclusion that no warning was required. Rather, a manufacturer and supplier of a product who knows or has reason to know that the product is likely to be dangerous in normal use has a duty to warn those who may not fully appreciate the possibility of such danger.

Causation[...]

Plaintiff's experts testified as to the alleged design defects in the subject tractor, and stated that they believed these defects contributed significantly to cause the tractor roll-over and the death of plantiff's (sic) decedent. Although one of plaintiff's experts conceded that he could not identifiy (sic) a specific defect which could be identified as the singular, legal cause of the accident, as a matter of law, we find the affidavit and deposition testimony of plaintiff's experts sufficient to raise issues of material fact with regard to the defective design of the tractor and the causal connection between the defects in design and warnings and the death of plaintiff's decedent.

Liability of Glades Equipment

In addition to the manufacturer, Glades Equipment, as the seller of the tractor, may be held responsible for the defects under strict liability, as well as for its own negligent failure to inspect the subject tractor. Glades Equipment, and not Glade and Grove, was the seller and distributor of this tractor based on the uncontroverted evidence. [...]

Regarding inspection, if there was a duty to inspect the tractor at the time of delivery, Glades Equipment, not Glade and Grove, is charged with that duty. However, should the facts adduced at trial demonstrate conclusively that the manufacturer shipped the tractor directly to the purchaser with no opprtunity (sic) for inspection by Glades Equipment, we see no basis for imposing an additional duty of inspection on the seller of the product. (citation omitted) Because, at this point, the facts are controverted as to whether the manufacturer expected its distributors to perform a pre-delivery inspection and whether an inspection should have been performed in this case, we decline to affirm summary judgment in favor of Glades Equipment [...]

The court found that the duty existed, for manufacturer and seller alike.

Both the manufacturer and/or seller (who would have had an opportunity to inspect the product before releasing it into the stream of commerce) can be held liable for failing to warn about a product's known defect—when the product is used as intended—or giving an inadequate warning (see table below).

Theories of Recovery in Products Liability Due to Negligence For:
• creating or failing to discover a flaw in the goods,
• failing to adequately warn about a risk or hazard in how goods are designed, or
• sale of defectively designed goods.

Liability Regardless of Any Warning

Under certain circumstances, liability for negligence may arise even when a warning has been given. The case in Case in Point 13-6 recognized that regardless of providing a warning, the manufacturer of the handgun could be liable for injury out of an accidental discharge, since the weapon had a known propensity to fire accidentally.

 # CASE IN POINT 13-6

Johnson v. Colt Industries Operating Corporation
797 F.2d 1530 (10th Cir. Kan.1986)

[...]

In May 1974 appellee purchased a .22 caliber Colt single action revolver from a gun store near his home town of Junction City, Kansas. The gun had been manufactured by appellant in 1969 and sold to the gun store in that year. The gun model was the famous Colt "six-shooter," first produced by appellant in 1873. The gun model has achieved a certain notoriety as a result of its association with the Old West and the United States Army. Appellant has not altered the design of the gun model significantly since its inception. The gun has a revolving cylinder with six chambers that accept six bullets. The gun has an exposed hammer that must be cocked manually before each shot is fired. Appellee, an experienced handler of guns, testified that he purchased the gun for personal protection.

On July 31, 1981 appellee took the gun with him on a fishing trip to a nearby creek. While appellee was seated on a rock in the creek the gun fell from its holster and struck the rock. The impact caused the gun to discharge. The bullet entered appellee's right buttock and lodged in his bladder. Although surgery was successful in removing the bullet, appellee's doctor testified that the bullet had traumatized certain nerves and rendered appellee permanently impotent. [...]

Both parties' expert witnesses testified that exposed hammer single action revolvers expose the user to a hazard known as "drop-fire." Drop-fire occurs when the gun is carried with a bullet in the chamber over which the hammer rests. In this situation, regardless of the cock position of the hammer, a sharp blow to the hammer, such as when the gun is dropped and lands hammer first, will cause the gun to discharge. When appellee's gun discharged, all six chambers were loaded but the hammer was uncocked.

[...]

Appellee alleged that appellant was liable for his injuries because of the defective design of the gun. [...] Appellee's theory of the case was that the gun was unreasonably dangerous when fully loaded because of the drop-fire hazard.

[...]

Appellant claims that it should have been held only to a duty of reasonable care and not to the "highest degree of care." This claim is without merit. [...] [O]ne who engages in dangerous activities is held to a higher standard of care to avoid negligence liability [....] It requires little imagination to include gun manufacturing in this category of dangerous activities. [...] Likewise, in a recent strict products liability case the Kansas Supreme Court stated that "we also think that the duty of the manufacturer must be commensurate with the seriousness of the danger. The greater the danger, the greater the duty."...It is entirely reasonable to believe that the Kansas courts would hold the manufacturers of deadly hand guns to the most exacting duty of care.

We hold that the court properly instructed the jury on appellant's duty of care....

Kansas tort law provides a remedy and a punishment for unreasonably dangerous defectively designed products that injure consumers while in normal use. Since appellee convinced a properly instructed jury of the gun's defective design and appellant's indifference to the known risk of drop-fire, the judgment must stand.

In this case, the handgun manufacturer knew this model could accidentally discharge, to the point that it even had a name for it: "drop-fire." Regardless of informing the plaintiff about this aspect of the handgun, the court saw the risk of injury as so great that no amount of warning could allow the manufacturer to escape liability.

Since this was a well-known design defect, the court said that, effectively, only one question had to be settled at trial: did the defendant manufacture the item? This new theory, which emphasizes a defect that a manufacturer and/or seller knew or have known of, is called *strict liability*. Chapter 12 covers the topic of strict liability.

Defenses

A defendant may raise the traditional defenses available against any action in negligence. The following table talks about only a few of these (see table below).

Defenses to an Action in Negligence, Regarding Use of a Product	
• Contributory negligence—When extreme misuse of a product occurs, beyond what a defendant could have reasonably anticipated. • Comparative negligence—Also, when extreme misuse has occurred.	• Assumption of the risk—When the plaintiff knew of the risk and voluntarily used the product. • Misuse—This is available as a defense only under those circumstances when the misuse was extreme and beyond what should have been contemplated or reasonably anticipated by the defendant.

Of course, procedural defenses like the statute of limitations—arising out of the plaintiff's failure to file within the time allowed under law—apply.

■ STRICT LIABILITY

Also in reaction to the limitations of recovery provided under *caveat emptor* and the principle of privity of contract, courts considered another way to provide recovery for an injured party. Under a theory of strict liability, a plaintiff needed only to show that the defendant was responsible for making the product available. That would mean the manufacturer could be deterred from putting defective products on the market. The manufacturer could be expected to include the cost of insurance premiums for a policy that could be used to pay damages as part of the selling price of the product.

Applicability to a Product Liability Claim

The first use of the principles of strict liability, discussed in detail in Chapter 12, arose under common law. Early applications of the theory involved the sale of food intended for human consumption. Since the harm could be great and, in many instances, could be avoided through the use of proper food preparation processes, courts effectively made producers of food strictly liable for injuries arising out of the use of the food as was intended. For example, in the landmark decision of *Mazetti v. Armour & Co.*, the Supreme Court of Washington departed from the general rule that a supplier of goods was not liable in the absence of negligence (see Case in Point 13-7).

CASE IN POINT 13-7

Mazetti v. Armour & Co.

75 Wash. 622 (1913)

The complaint alleges that the plaintiffs were operating a profitable restaurant in the city of Seattle [...]; that defendant Armour & Co. is engaged in the business of manufacturing and selling to the public generally meats and products to be used as food; that it maintains a place of business in Seattle, Wash., from which it sells and distributes its goods, representing and holding out to the general public that its goods are pure, wholesome, and fit food for human beings; that on June 16, 1912, plaintiffs, in the usual course and conduct of their business, purchased from the Seattle Grocery Company a carton of cooked tongue, prepared and ready to be used for food without further cooking or labor; that such package had been manufactured and prepared by defendant Armour & Co. [...] that in making such purchase plaintiffs relied upon the representations of Armour & Co. that said food was pure and wholesome and fit for food; that Armour & Co. were guilty of negligence in manufacturing and preparing the foods purchased, in that in the center of the carton was a foul, filthy, nauseating, and poisonous substance; that in the due course of trade plaintiffs served to one of their patrons a portion of the tongue; that the patron ate of it; that he then and there became sick and nauseated, and did then and there in the presence of other persons publicly expose and denounce the service to him of such foul and poisonous food; that the incident became known to the public generally; that plaintiffs had no knowledge or means of knowing the character of the food served; that its condition could not be discovered until it was served for use–all to the damage of the plaintiffs, etc., for loss of reputation, business, and lost profits during the life of their lease. [...]

The suit was brought by the retailer against his immediate vendor, so that we still have to meet the question of whether the retailer who has lost his trade can sue over the head of his immediate vendor, or join him with the manufacturer as in this case. In the light of modern conditions we see no reason why he should not. He has been damaged. He and all others who in the course of trade handled the unwholesome goods purchased them relying upon the name and reputation of the manufacturer. The goods were designed for ultimate consumption by an individual patron, and packed to facilitate and make convenient such resales as might be made pending ultimate consumption. Every tradesman, whether wholesaler or retailer, is in a sense a consumer, for he buys to resell. In a way he risks his reputation. He stakes it upon either an express warranty, as printed on the package, or an implied warranty that the goods are wholesome and fit for food. He is injured by the fault or a breach of duty of the manufacturer, for his immediate vendor, like himself, has no way to test every sealed package [....]

To the old rule that a manufacturer is not liable to third persons who have no contractual relations with him for negligence in the manufacture of an article should be added another exception, not one arbitrarily worked by the courts, but arising [...] from the changing conditions of society. [...]

Plaintiffs have been injured. No other person or firm had an opportunity to check the offensive package after it was sealed and sent on its way. Right and reason demand that any party injured should have a right of recovery against the first offender without resorting to that circumlocution of action against intervening agents, which is demanded where the product as well as the market is open, and the rule of caveat emptor should in justice apply.

[...]

The consumer purchases prepared food products to sustain life and health. The retailer purchases the same products, depending upon established brands to sustain his reputation as a dealer in clean and wholesome food. We would be disposed to hold on this question that, where sealed packages are put out, and it is made to appear that the fault, if any, is that of the manufacturer, the product was intended for the use of all those who handle it in trade as well as those who consume it. Our holding is that, in the absence of an express warranty of quality, a manufacturer of food products under modern conditions impliedly warrants his goods when dispensed in original packages, and that such warranty is available to all who may be damaged by reason of their use in the legitimate channels of trade.

We regard this case, in so far as the dealer is permitted to sue the manufacturer, as one of first impression. We think the complaint states a cause of action.

Other courts adopted the rationale of the *Mazetti* court, which eliminated the need for privity of contract between seller and consumer.

Scope of Liability

Recent decisions have extended the principles of strict liability to include the sale of any defective product causing physical harm. Since the court's decision in *Greenman v. Yuba Power Products, Inc.*, nearly all courts have adopted the principles of strict liability in tort for product liability, when an issue arose that had to do with the design of manufacturing equipment used in the home (see Case in Point 13-8).

CASE IN POINT 13-8

Greenman v. Yuba Power Products, Inc.

59 Cal. 2d 57 (1963)

Plaintiff brought this action for damages against the retailer and the manufacturer of a Shopsmith, a combination power tool that could be used as a saw, drill, and wood lathe. He saw a Shopsmith demonstrated by the retailer and studied a brochure prepared by the manufacturer. He decided he wanted a Shopsmith for his home workshop, and his wife bought and gave him one for Christmas in 1955. In 1957 he bought the necessary attachments to use the Shopsmith as a lathe for turning a large piece of wood he wished to make into a chalice. After he had worked on the piece of wood several times without difficulty, it suddenly flew out of the machine and struck him on the forehead inflicting serious injuries.

[...]

Plaintiff introduced substantial evidence that his injuries were caused by defective design and construction of the Shopsmith. His expert witnesses testified that inadequate set screws were used to hold parts of the machine together so that normal vibration caused the tailstock of the lathe to move away from the piece of wood being turned permitting it to fly out of the lathe. They also testified that there were other more positive ways of fastening the parts of the machine together, the use of which would have prevented the accident. The jury could therefore reasonably have concluded that the manufacturer negligently constructed the Shopsmith. The jury could also reasonably have concluded that statements in the manufacturer's brochure were untrue, that they constituted express warranties, and that plaintiff's injuries were caused by their breach [...]

Moreover, to impose strict liability on the manufacturer under the circumstances of this case, it was not necessary for plaintiff to establish an express warranty [....] A manufacturer is strictly liable in tort when an article he places on the market, knowing that it is to be used without inspection for defects, proves to have a defect that causes injury to a human being. [...]

We need not recanvass the reasons for imposing strict liability on the manufacturer [....] The purpose of such liability is to insure that the costs of injuries resulting from defective products are borne by the manufacturers that put such products on the market rather than by the injured persons who are powerless to protect themselves. Sales warranties serve this purpose fitfully at best [...] Implicit in the machine's presence on the market, however, was a representation that it would safely do the jobs for which it was built [...] To establish the manufacturer's liability it was sufficient that plaintiff proved that he was injured while using the Shopsmith in a way it was intended to be used as a result of a defect in design and manufacture of which plaintiff was not aware that made the Shopsmith unsafe for its intended use [....]

The judgment is affirmed.

The court determined that when the seller has marketed a product for use and consumption, he or she has undertaken a special responsibility toward the consumer. Consumers have the right to expect the seller to stand behind the goods, and demands that the cost of any harm be insured by the seller.

Restatement (Second) of Torts §402A

The principle articulated in *Greenman* and other cases led to the widespread acceptance of the application of strict liability for product liability. The **Restatement**

(Second) of Torts §402A—a document that reflects what scholars and others in a field have concluded is the ideal statement of the law on a topic—provides the general rule of liability that is followed in virtually every state today (see box below).

STRICT LIABILITY THEORY APPLYING IN PRODUCT LIABILITY CLAIMS

1. One who sells any product in a defective condition unreasonably dangerous to the user or consumer or to his property is subject to liability for physical harm thereby cause to the ultimate user or consumer, or to his property, if
   a. the seller is engaged in the business of selling such a product, and
   b. it is expected to and does reach the user or consumer without substantial change in the condition in which it is sold.
2. The rule stated in Subsection (1) applies although
   a. the seller has exercised all possible care in the preparation and sale of his product, and
   b. the user or consumer has not bought the product from or entered into any contractual relation with the seller.

Restatement (Second) of Torts, §402A (1965)

Note that the scope of §402A of the *Restatement* applies to unreasonably dangerous products but only up until when these items leave the seller's control. Subsequent modifications that interfere with the safe use of the product may mean the seller no longer faces liability. Yet, the manufacturer and/or seller might face liability where such modifications were reasonably foreseeable, as depicted in Case in Point 13-9.

CASE IN POINT 13-9

Merriweather v. E. W. Bliss Company
636 F.2d 42 (3rd Cir. Pa. 1980)

[...]

On January 14, 1975 the appellant, plaintiff below, was severely injured when the jaws of the 45 ton press he was operating descended, crushing his hands. At the time of the accident the appellant had been attempting manually to remove some fabric from the bottom die of the press. While he was attempting to remove this fabric, the appellant's foot inadvertently came into contact with the electric foot switch which operated the press, causing that press to descend and injure him.

This power press had been manufactured by E. W. Bliss Company some nineteen years earlier. At the time of its manufacture the press had been equipped to operate by means of a mechanical foot treadle. At that time it was also the practice of E. W. Bliss Company to manufacture and deliver these presses without any point of operation guards whatsoever.

After its delivery to the appellant's employer, General Electric Corporation, several modifications were made to this press by General Electric. First, the mechanical foot treadle was removed and the press was equipped with electric operating controls. These controls permitted the press to operate in one or two ways, by either: (1) simultaneously pressing two palm buttons, one by each hand;

or (2) pressing an electric foot switch. In addition General Electric installed hairpin or finger guards around the pinch points of the press. However, these guards could be removed by the operator or adjusted in such a manner as to enable the operator to place his hands under the ram of the press.

[...] Following his injury the appellant brought this action against E. W. Bliss Company in the United States District Court. At trial the appellant proceeded under the theory that Bliss was strictly liable for his injury because Bliss' failure to install adequate point of operation guards rendered the press unsafe for its intended use at the time it left the manufacturer's hands.

In its defense Bliss relied principally upon the doctrine of substantial change, as set forth in §402A(l)(b) of the *Restatement (Second) of Torts*. According to Bliss it could not be held liable for the injuries suffered by Mr. Merriweather because the press in question had been substantially changed by General Electric after it had left Bliss' control.

[...] [T]he trial court, in its charge to the jury, referred extensively to the concept of substantial change. The court refused, however, to charge that reasonably foreseeable changes in a product would not absolve the manufacturer of liability for injuries caused by that product. Instead, over the appellant's objections, the court instructed the jury on substantial change without any reference to reasonable foreseeability. Given these instructions, the jury returned with a verdict for the defendant.

In its motion for new trial the appellant raised the arguments which are made here [...] (2) that, in this case, the question before the jury was one of proximate cause and not of substantial change; and, (3) that, if instructions were given on the question of substantial change, then those instructions must also discuss the foreseeability of such change. Appropriate requests for instructions and objections to the charge were timely made by appellant. The trial court denied this motion and the instant appeal followed.

Because we believe that the appellant is correct on the last of these three contentions we will reverse and remand for a new trial.

[...]

Since the adoption by Pennsylvania's courts of §402A the doctrine of substantial change has been an integral part of that state's law of products liability. (citations omitted) [...] Moreover, we have, [...] concluded that, under Pennsylvania law, the question of substantial change is properly one for the jury's consideration. (citations omitted). In fact, in our review of Pennsylvania law on this issue we have failed to find any appellate decisions [...] which have challenged the propriety of this practice. Accordingly we must conclude, in the absence of any clear precedent to the contrary, that the concept of substantial change remains part of the law of Pennsylvania under §402A.

We also conclude that the trial judge acted correctly in this case in choosing to instruct the jury on the doctrine of substantial change. In its brief the appellant argued that an instruction on substantial change is only appropriate when that change occurs before the product reaches its ultimate user. Therefore, changes in a product occurring after that product reaches its user do not raise questions of substantial change but rather present problems of causation. (citations omitted).

In this case it is clear that the modifications of the power press occurred after it reached General Electric. Therefore, given this fact, the appellant argues that E. W. Bliss is not entitled in this case to an instruction on substantial change.

[...]

[T]he Restatement indicates that the seller of a product will be liable for injuries caused by that product if "it is expected to and does reach the user or consumer without substantial change in the condition in which it is sold" See §402A(l)(b) *Restatement (Second) of Torts*. Therefore, by its very terms, §402A seems to indicate that only unexpected substantial changes will absolve the seller of a product from liability for injuries caused by that product. [...]

Furthermore the notion of reasonable foreseeability has been incorporated into the concept of substantial change by the courts of Pennsylvania. (citations omitted) Moreover, in a leading Pennsylvania appellate decision on this question, (citations omitted), the Superior Court specifically endorsed the use of the phrase "reasonably foreseeable" in jury instructions dealing with substantial change, stating: The test in such a situation is whether the manufacturer could have reasonably expected or foreseen such an alteration; such determination is for the fact-finder unless the inferences are so clear that a court can say as a matter of law that a reasonable manufacturer could not have foreseen the change. [...]

Were we to adopt the approach to the substantial change doctrine accepted by the district court in this case we would significantly undercut this policy. If the manufacturer is to effectively act as the guarantor of his product's safety, then he should be held responsible for all dangers which result from foreseeable modifications of that product. Yet under the view taken by the court below this would not occur. Rather, once the modification of the product was shown to be substantial the manufacturer would be excused from all liability for injuries caused by that product, even if that modification was clearly foreseeable. As a practical matter, therefore, the district court's decision broadens considerably the scope of the substantial change defense. [...] [T]he broadening of this defense is inconsistent with the concept of the manufacturer as the guarantor of his product [...]

Finally we note that, on the record presented in this case, the issue of the foreseeability of the modification of this press was properly a question for the jury's determination. Therefore, we will reverse and remand this case for further proceedings in accordance with this opinion.

The appellate court concluded that to read the "substantial change" rule to negate any liability of manufacturer misread the view of the Pennsylvania courts.

The "Unreasonably Dangerous" Standard

The rule set forth in §402A of the *Restatement*—"in a defective condition **unreasonably dangerous** to the user or consumer"—underlies the specific theory of strict liability for products. That standard shifts the issue of fault away from the parties and on to product alone. So it does not matter whether the defendant is a manufacturer or a seller; rather, did the defendant expose the plaintiff to a defective product that carried an unreasonable risk of harm?

What constitutes a defective product? The *Restatement (Second) of Torts* does not define it simply under §402A or elsewhere, perhaps recognizing that courts will want some flexibility, even though that might mean no clear standard would develop.

Most courts came to define "defective product" in one of three ways (see box below).

UNREASONABLY DANGEROUS

This simply means that the product must be defective in the kind of way that subjects persons or tangible property to an unreasonable risk of harm....A product is defective as marketed in the kind of way that makes it unreasonably dangerous for any of the following reasons: (1) a flaw in the product that was present in the product at the time the defendant sold it; (2) a failure by the producer or assembler of a product adequately to warn of a risk or hazard related to the way the product was designed; or (3) a defective design.

W. Page Keeton et. al., *Prosser & Keeton on the Law of Torts* §99 at 695 (5th ed. 1984)

This three-part formulation looked beyond what a customer might ordinarily expect when using the product. For example, although consuming alcohol may injure one's health, no one expects alcohol to contain some toxic ingredient, like arsenic, that would be itself harm to all drinkers.

Flaw in the Product

A flaw in a product makes the product more dangerous in the course of ordinary use. That flaw might arise during the manufacturing or distribution of the product. It does not matter whether the defendant was negligent in the execution of these activities; instead, did the flaw in the product result in harm to the plaintiff?

The seller may not have been at all negligent in creating a product or failing to discover a flaw in it. Under a theory of negligence, the plaintiff would need to show that the defendant had breached a duty of care regarding the product's safety. But under strict liability, the court will not have to measure the duty that the defendant owed to the plaintiff as it will focus only on a defect that causes harm to the plaintiff. In Case in Point 13-10, the court avoided entirely the issue of whether the defendant owed a duty of care that was breached as to the manufacture of the soda bottle. It looked, simply, at whether a flaw existed that made it unreasonably dangerous.

CASE IN POINT 13-10

Paducah Coca-Cola Bottling Company v. Harris
316 S.W.2d 128 (Ky. 1958)

[...]

Harris purchased a case of mixed soft drinks, including a dozen Coca-Colas, from a country store. He placed the case in the trunk of his automobile and drove to his place of employment. Upon arrival there he opened the trunk and set the case of drinks on the ground. He then went into a nearby shack and brought out a wooden keg, which the workers customarily used as a receptacle for cooling soft drinks. The keg was empty. Harris picked up two Coca-Cola bottles between the fingers of one hand and set them in the keg. He testified that he did not drop or strike the bottles against anything while he was placing them in the keg. As he 'started to raise up,' one of the bottles exploded and particles of glass struck him in the eye. The bottle separated diagonally into two main pieces, one being the top one-third, with the cap still intact, and the other being the bottom two-thirds. The pieces were preserved and were introduced in evidence in the trial.

[...]

It is the contention of the bottling company that the plaintiff failed to prove that the bottle was in a defective condition when it was in the control of the company, or that the bottling operation was negligently conducted [...]

Since the bottle did break [...] without any material external impact at the time, and since [...] a sound bottle could not break from internal pressure even though hot and violently agitated, the conclusion is reasonable that the bottle was defective when it was filled by the appellant bottling company. The question then remains as to whether the bottling company was negligent in not discovering the defect.

The evidence for the bottling company was that its inspection procedures and devices were designed to disclose cracked or chipped bottles, and that a substantial number of such bottles were discovered and rejected each day. The testimony of the plaintiff's expert witness was that a structural flaw in a bottle, such as in his opinion existed in the bottle in question, could have been discovered if the bottles were revolved when passing the inspection point, and particularly if the conveyor belt was operated more slowly. There was no evidence for the company that causing the bottles to revolve or move more slowly on the conveyor belt would be unreasonably burdensome.

[...]

The evidence here would warrant the conclusion that there was a failure of duty on the part of the bottling company, either in the form of an omission of duty by an inspector or in the form of inadequate inspection procedures and devices.

[...]

Since the normal consumer use of a Coca-Cola bottle involves close contact with hands and face, we think it is obvious that the risk of danger of personal injury from explosion of the bottle is extremely high. The manufacturer's duty of care is commensurate with the risk. Accordingly, the manufacturer of Coca-Cola has the duty to exercise the greatest care to guard against defects that might cause explosion [...]

The judgment is affirmed.

The court ruled that the flaw existed in the bottle and made it unreasonably dangerous so that the defendant was strictly liable. The defendant also failed to inspect the bottle for such flaws, and that was a breach of duty of care, so that the plaintiff could have proceeded also on a claim of negligence.

Failure to Warn

A defendant may face strict liability for introducing an unreasonably dangerous product into the stream of commerce by not providing a plaintiff with information about the product's potential for dangerousness. Courts see strict liability for **failure to warn** as not involving just a theory of negligence. If anyone introduces a defective product into a stream of commerce, not providing a warning increases the potential for harm to plaintiff. In Case in Point 13-11, the court considered the risks associated with the manufacture and sale of a mini-trampoline.

 CASE IN POINT 13-11

Richter v. Limax International, Inc.

45 F.3d 1464 (10th Cir. Kan. 1995)

[...]

Richter purchased a mini-trampoline from Limax on February 1, 1989. There were no instructions in or on the box containing the mini-trampoline, although the trampoline did have sticker on it stating: "This product was designed to be used only as an exercise device. It is not designed to be used for acrobatics, trampolining or any springboard type activities." Richter stated she only used the trampoline for jogging. She began by jogging for short periods of time but eventually increased her time up to sixty minutes per day. She used the product until March 10, 1989. [footnote omitted.] The next day she experienced severe pain in her ankles while walking. A doctor diagnosed her as having stress fractures in her ankles. Richter testified the pain forced her to discontinue her work as a sales representative for a furniture manufacturer.

The plaintiff produced expert testimony which established relatively simple tests would have revealed that because the surface of a mini-trampoline depresses furthest in the center and decreasingly towards the edges, as a jogger's feet strike the trampoline's surface and it gives way, the inside of each foot drops further than the outside. This rotation of the foot, which is termed "eversion," occurs to a lesser degree in normal jogging, but rebound jogging markedly accentuates the degree of rotation.

Further testimony established it has long been known that lateral pulling on a bone by ligaments or muscles can cause microscopic fractures. If the bone is not allowed time to heal and the stress on the bone continues, these tiny fractures can coalesce into a stress fracture. The eversion of the feet caused by the mini-trampoline results in certain tissues pulling laterally on particular ankle bones. Richter's expert witnesses testified that longterm use of the trampoline could cause stress fractures in the affected ankle bones.

Limax admitted it conducted no tests relating to the long-term effects of jogging on the mini-trampoline and did not systematically review published studies of mini-trampolines by sports medicine and exercise specialists. The CEO of Limax testified the company had sold approximately two million mini-trampolines world-wide and Richter's complaint about stress fractures was the first Limax had received. Further, although mini-trampolines had been in use since 1975, by the time of Richter's purchase no one had yet suggested their use entailed a risk of stress fractures. No expert testifying at trial could identify any study or article on rebound jogging or mini-trampolines that reported ankle stress fractures or pointed out the risk joggers faced of incurring such an injury.

Richter, however, produced testimony by experts that observations from very simple tests, interpreted in light of well-established knowledge about the structure of the foot and the causes of stress fractures, would have made it apparent that the repetitive use of the mini-trampoline for jogging could cause stress fractures. [...] One Of Richter's experts pointed out that although there were no known reports concerning mini-trampolines as a cause of stress fractures, sport and exercise magazines as well as scientific and medical journals have long published articles establishing that repetitive jogging can cause stress fractures. The testimony verified that such repetitive jogging on a mini-trampoline exaggerates the stresses that result from repetitive jogging on a flat surface. Although the mini-trampoline was found by the jury not to have a defective design, Richter's expert witness testimony established that the marked accentuation of eversion caused by the design of the mini-trampoline could result in her kind of injury developing from her repetitive jogging.

[...]

The rule is that a manufacturer has a duty to make such tests and inspections, during and after the process of manufacture, as should be recognized as being reasonably necessary to secure the production of a safe product; and a manufacturer who negligently fails to use reasonable care in making such tests and inspections, and thereby produces a defective article which causes damage while being put to an ordinary, anticipated use, is liable for such damage. (citation omitted) [...]

Ordinarily, a manufacturer has a duty under Kansas law to warn consumers and users of its products when it knows or has reason to know that its product is or is likely to be dangerous during normal use.

The duty to warn is a continuous one, requiring the manufacturer to keep abreast of the current state of knowledge of its products as acquired through research, adverse reaction reports, scientific literature, and other available methods. A manufacturer's failure to adequately warn of its product's reasonably foreseeable dangers renders that product defective under the doctrine of strict liability. (citation omitted)

[...]

In 1976, Kansas adopted the rule set out in the *Restatement (Second) of Torts* §402A (1965) [...]

Comment h to section 402A states that where a seller "has reason to antici-pate that danger may result from a particular use,...he may be required to give adequate warning of the danger (see Comment 7), and a product sold without such warning is in a defective condition." Kansas courts have relied on both com-ments j and k to section 420A in concretizing the duty to warn announced in com-ment h [footnote omitted].

[...] [A] product may not be defectively designed, but may nonetheless be defective because the manufacturer failed to adequately warn the users of the product of a reasonably foreseeable hazard. [...] Under the strict liability theory, a plaintiff is not required to establish misconduct by the maker or seller but, instead, is required to impugn the product. The plaintiff must show the product is in "a defective condition unreasonably dangerous," which means that it must be defective in a way that subjects persons or tangible property to an unreason-able risk of harm. (citation omitted). A product can be defective in one of the fol-lowing three ways: (1) a flaw is present in the product at the time it is sold; (2) the producer or assembler of the product fails to adequately warn of a risk or haz-ard related to the way the product was designed; or (3) the product, although perfectly manufactured, contains a defect that makes it unsafe. (citation omitted) [footnote omitted]

[...]

The mini-trampoline was specifically intended for exercise, and in particular, for jogging. When used for this purpose, however, the mini-trampoline's design results in the foot turning in a way that places stress on the ankle bones. That the design is not defective, within the state of the known art, does not detract from the manufacturer's duty to warn the consumer of foreseeable dangers that can arise from normal use.

[...]

Richter presented a substantial amount of expert testimony to the effect that visual observation of a person jogging on the mini-trampoline by someone with expertise in biomechanics, would reveal eversion and further that relatively simple tests could measure the degree of eversion. A comparison of that measurement with a measurement of the eversion caused by jogging on a flat surface would have revealed mini-trampolines cause users' feet to evert to a markedly greater degree. [footnote omitted.]

Testimony established that it is well known that such stresses, experienced on a repetitive basis, could cause fractures. We hold the jury could have reasonably found Richter's injury was causally related to repetitive jogging on the mini-trampoline, the use for which Limax's product was intended. The jury could also reasonably have concluded Limax should have warned users of this danger because the danger was eminently knowable given the state of the art and Limax should have known of it.

[...]

Kansas imposes on manufacturers a duty to research and make such tests and inspections as reasonably necessary to make their products safe or to estab-lish a basis for warning consumers of a product's unavoidable dangers.

Under Kansas law, both strict liability and negligence require warnings only for dangers which are reasonably foreseeable in light of the intended use of a product. The jury could reasonably have concluded that a simple consultation with a biomechanics expert would have given Limax sufficient information to arrange for appropriate testing of the mini-trampoline. No expert witness for ei-ther side expressed any doubt that the mini-trampoline accentuates eversion of the ankles or that eversion could cause stress fractures. It is true that no one ap-pears to have considered the problem until Richter's injury occurred, but it is also true that plaintiffs (sic) evidence demonstrated that the danger was patently obvi-ous to any expert who had a reason to look for it. [...] Limax conceded that it did no testing or research to consider foreseeable harm arising out of the uses to which the mini-trampoline would be put.

Manufacturers do not have a duty to test for inconceivable dangers, nor do they have a duty to test for every conceivable danger. They do have a duty to warn of dangers of harmful effects arising from the foreseeable use and misuse of a product that are known or are readily foreseeable in the state of art. [...]

In the present case, plaintiffs (sic) experts testified that the accentuated eversion of the foot caused by prolonged jogging on the mini-trampoline made Richter's injury foreseeable and that the manufacturer should have warned the user of the product of the possible foreseeable harm she encountered. [...] A fair and impartial jury concluded under the evidence that because of the specific design of the mini-trampoline, Richter's harm was foreseeable. We simply conclude there was sufficient evidence to allow the jury to make that finding.

We find that the district court erred in granting a judgment [...] and we therefore hold that the verdict and judgment in favor of the plaintiff should be reinstated.

[...]

Since experts agreed that an intended use of the mini-trampoline could result in injury, the defendant faced liability for not warning that this was an unreasonably dangerous product.

Defective Design

In product liability cases, proving **defective design,** that is, that a product is unreasonably dangerous, involves an interpretation of the meaning of the term *defect* as it applies to design hazards.

Existence.   In order for liability to exist for the manufacture or sale of an unreasonably dangerous product, the plaintiff must prove the existence of a defect (see Case in Point 13-12).

 # CASE IN POINT 13-12

Humphrey v. Diamant Boart
556 F. Supp. 2d 167 (E.D.N.Y. 2008)

Humphrey was employed as a Labor Supervisor by the Village of Garden City, New York. He had worked for the Village of Garden City since 1984 and was originally hired as a laborer. By September 2005, Humphrey had been promoted to Labor Supervisor, which involved the supervision of a crew of one to two co-employees responsible for, among other things, the replacement and repair of street lights in the Village of Garden City.

The saw at issue in this case is a Quickie Super 60 handheld portable saw (hereinafter, "saw," "Quickie saw," or "Quickie Super 60 saw") designed and manufactured by EMAK International ("EMAK"), an Italian corporation. In April 2001, EMAK sold the saw to Diamant Boart, for resale. On September 21, 2001, Diamant Boart sold the saw to Fastenal, which was an independent distributor of professional contractors' construction products. In April 2002, Fastenal sold the saw to the Village of Garden City.

Humphrey began using the Quickie Super 60 saw in 2002 soon after it was purchased by the Village of Garden City. He was the sole user of the saw and stored it on his crew truck. Humphrey was given no formal training as to the operation of the Quickie Super 60 saw or any of the other power equipment he used in his work. Moreover, he was not given any formal instruction with respect to the type of blade he should use with the saw when cutting concrete, asphalt, or wood. Instead, Humphrey learned about the operation of the saw by personal observation of other Village of Garden City employees, starting in 1984 when he was first hired. Humphrey used the Quickie saw to cut wooden poles two or three times per week for approximately three and one-half years prior to his accident without the saw recoiling or malfunctioning during use. According to Humphrey, beginning in 2002 and throughout the three and one-half year period that he used the Quickie saw prior to the accident, he observed that the saw's blade guard would loosen during operation, and Humphrey would stop and re-tighten the guard before continuing its use. Humphrey knew that he needed to re-tighten the blade guard because he could actually see the guard rotate back and expose more of the blade. Humphrey never advised his employer that the blade guard was loosening during operation, nor did he ever request service or maintenance on the blade guard.

At the time of the sale of the saw by defendants, the saw had several on-product warning and instruction labels. Among other warnings, the labels on the blade guard of the saw warned the user as follows:

WARNING

FAILURE TO FOLLOW ALL WARNINGS AND INSTRUCTIONS MAY RESULT IN SERIOUS INJURY OR DEATH

Read entire operator's manual before operating this machine. Understand all warnings, instructions, and contents.

Use only reinforced abrasive or high speed diamond blades having an operating speed above or equal to the maximum spindle speed and specifically designed for use with hand-held, portable, high speed cut off machines.

Do not use damaged or carbide tipped blades.

Machinery hazard—Always keep all guards in place properly adjusted and in good condition. A warning on the top of the saw console repeated the direction to the operator to read the manual before operating the saw. The operator's manual contained two warnings to the operator not to use carbide tipped blades on the saw.

Humphrey observed and was aware of the on-product warnings and instruction labels, but did not read them. Humphrey also was aware that the saw had an operator's instruction manual and that on-product labels instructed him to read the manual, but he did not read it.

According to the former President of Diamant, the Quickie saw (1) is used by, and marketed to, professional contractors, and (2) is intended to be used to cut hard materials, such as steel, concrete, brick, and asphalt, not to cut soft materials, like wood. Moreover, as stated on the label and Operating Instructions, it is intended for use only with diamond and abrasive blades, not carbide tipped blades.

On September 23, 2005 [...] Humphrey and a two-person crew were removing and cutting up a 20-foot wooden light pole from a parking lot [...] in the Village of Garden City. The crew had removed the bolts securing a metal shoe which attached the pole to its concrete base and laid the pole horizontally on the surface of the parking lot to be cut into more manageable pieces. Humphrey was using the saw for approximately 8 minutes prior to the accident, during which time he cut the top T bar on the wooden pole off and had cut two section lengths along the top of the pole. According to Humphrey, as he began a third cut in the top of the pole, the saw "bound up" in the cut for a "second" and kicked back, striking him in the face.

[...]

A. The Design Defect Claim

Strict products liability requires proof that "(1) the product is 'defective' because it is not reasonably safe as marketed; (2) the product was used for a normal purpose; (3) the defect was a substantial factor in causing the plaintiff's injuries; (4) the plaintiff by the exercise of reasonable care would not have both discovered the defect and apprehended its danger; [and] (5) the plaintiff would not have otherwise avoided the injury by the exercise of ordinary care." (citation omitted.)

"[T]o establish a *prima facie* case in strict products liability for design defects, the plaintiff must show that the manufacturer breached its duty to market safe products when it marketed a product designed so that it was not reasonably safe and that the defective design was a substantial factor in causing plaintiff's injury." (citation omitted). In determining whether a design defect existed, an assessment must be made as to "whether it is a product which, if the design defect were known at the time of manufacture, a reasonable person would conclude that the utility of the product did not outweigh the risk inherent in marketing a product designed in that manner." Moreover, the burden is on the plaintiff to present "evidence that the product, as designed, was not reasonably safe because there was a substantial likelihood of harm and it was feasible to design the product in a safer manner." [...]

Plaintiff asserts [...] that the Quickie Super 60 saw was defective in design. Specifically [...] plaintiff identifies [...] the following defects: (1) the blade guard is defective because the locking knob was positioned too close to the arbor shaft, was difficult to tighten, and loosened during operation; and (2) the saw's on-product warning and instruction labels are defective because they did not warn a user, among other things, that the saw could "kickback." [...]

B. The Failure to Warn Claim

Defendants argue that the plaintiff's failure to warn claim cannot survive summary judgment because plaintiff testified at his deposition that (1) he was aware that the blade guard rotated back during use for more than three years prior to the accident, and (2) he did not read the warnings on the saw or the operator's manual. [...] [T]he Court disagrees and finds that there are material issues of disputed fact on this claim that preclude summary judgment.

[U]nder New York law [...] a plaintiff must show the following: (1) the manufacturer had a duty to warn; (2) the manufacturer breached the duty to warn in a manner that rendered the product defective, *i.e.*, reasonably certain to be dangerous; (3) the defect was the proximate cause of the plaintiff's injury; and (4) the plaintiff suffered loss or damage. (citation omitted.)

It is well-settled that a manufacturer has a duty to warn (1) "against latent dangers resulting from foreseeable uses of its product of which it knew or should have known," and (2) "of the danger of unintended uses of a product provided these uses are reasonably foreseeable."

[...]

Moreover [...] the standard for evaluating "failure-to-warn" liability as "intensely fact-specific, including but not limited to such issues as feasibility and difficulty of issuing warnings in the circumstances; obviousness of the risk from actual use of the product; knowledge of the particular product user; and proximate cause." (citation omitted.) Given this fact-intensive inquiry [...] "[t]he adequacy of the instruction or warning is generally a question of fact to be determined at trial and is not ordinarily susceptible to the drastic remedy of summary judgment." (citations omitted.)

[...] [P]laintiff contends [...] that the warnings on the saw guard and in the Operating Instructions did not conspicuously state the hazards associated with the saw, including tooth separation/fracture and kickback, and were misleading with regard to the potential risks associated with the use of the incorrect blade. [...]

First, the warning to be proper, must be conspicuous and state the associated hazard(s). In this case possible hazards are tooth separation/fracture and kickback—neither of which is addressed by the warning on the saw guard, or in the OPERATING INSTRUCTIONS. By contrast, the kickback hazard and it [sic] means of avoidance are described in the Homelite Manual on page 18.

Secondly, the warning on the guard and the associated pictogram, which shows a broken blade, mixes with it the warning about carbide-tipped blades, rather than clearly separating the two. There is ample space on the label [...] to include a separate conspicuous and proper warning against using toothed or car-bide-tipped blades. This is particularly important because similar saws made by other manufacturers allow the use of carbide-tipped blades in certain special cir-cumstances [...] and frequent users of such equipment, such as Public Works Departments, encounter a variety of brands over time, and can be expected to transfer usage experience across brands of substantially similar products.

Based upon this report and the circumstances surrounding the alleged acci-dent and use of the saw, there are issues of fact on this claim that must be decided by a jury.

[...]

In short, these factual issues as they relate to the conspicuousness and sub-stance of the warnings, and whether Humphrey's employer or co-workers would have conveyed to him any additional warnings that plaintiff claims should have been utilized to make the warnings adequate, cannot be decided [...] but rather need to be submitted to a jury.

[...]

Although the court did not rule specifically on whether the warnings were suffi-cient, it did point out that enough questions of fact existed about warnings that a jury needed to sort out the facts and issue a verdict.

Tests Used.   The courts use two specific tests to determine design hazards:

- Consumer expectation test—A product is defectively dangerous if it is dan-gerous beyond what a consumer expected at the time of purchase.
- Risk-utility test—A product is unreasonably dangerous when the magnitude of the dangerousness outweighs the utility of the product.

In Case in Point 13-13, where the plaintiff brought suit under strict liability for a design defect, the court considered both theories.

 # CASE IN POINT 13-13

Halliday v. Sturm, Ruger & Company, Inc.
368 Md. 186 (2002)

This case arises from the tragic death of Jordan Garris. In June, 1999, Jordan shot himself while playing with his father's handgun. Jordan's mother, petitioner here, seeks to hold the manufacturer of the handgun, respondent Sturm, Ruger & Co. (Sturm Ruger), liable for Jordan's death.

[...]

The handgun in question is a Ruger P89 semi-automatic pistol. To fire the gun, one must place a loaded magazine into it, pull the slide at the top of the gun as far to the rear as possible and then release it, ensure that a safety lever is in the "fire" position, and then pull the trigger. Even when loaded, the gun will not fire unless the trigger is pulled with the safety lever in the "fire" position.

Jordan's father, Clifton Garris, purchased the gun in March, 1999, from On Target, Inc., a retail firearms store. With the purchase of the gun came an instruction manual, the offer of a free safety course, which Garris declined, a pamphlet entitled "Youth Handgun Safety Act Notice" published by the Federal Bureau of Alcohol, Tobacco and Firearms, a lock box in which to store the gun and the magazine, and a padlock for the box. There was a dispute as to whether On Target recommended that Garris purchase a separate trigger lock for the gun […]

The instruction manual provided multiple warnings and instructions regarding the storage and use of the gun. On the cover of the manual, and embossed on the barrel of the gun itself, was an admonition to read the manual before using the gun. Among other warnings and instructions in the manual is a highlighted box entitled "WARNING - STORAGE" in which, in red letters, is the statement "Firearms should always be stored securely and unloaded, away from children and careless adults" and the statement, in capital letters, "STORE SECURELY AND UNLOADED." In the part on "THE BASIC RULES OF SAFE FIREARMS HANDLING," which itself is in red capital letters, is a section headed, in red capital letters, "FIREARMS SHOULD BE UNLOADED WHEN NOT IN USE," and in that section is the warning:

"Firearms and ammunition should be securely locked in racks or cabinets when not in use. Ammunition should be safely stored separate from firearms. Store your firearms out of sight of visitors and children. It is the gun owner's responsibility to be certain that children and persons unfamiliar with firearms cannot gain access to firearms, ammunition, or components."

Garris signed an acknowledgment that the On Target salesperson explained the instruction manual, the safety lever, and the action of the gun. The Youth Handgun Safety Act Notice warned Garris, in highlighted letters, that the misuse of handguns was a leading contributor to juvenile violence and fatalities and that "safely storing and securing firearms away from children will help prevent the unlawful possession of handguns by juveniles, stop accidents, and save lives."

Garris disregarded virtually every one of these warnings and opportunities. He did not store either the gun or the magazine in the lock box but rather placed the gun under his mattress and kept the loaded magazine on a bookshelf in the same room, so that it was visible and accessible to Jordan. Jordan found the handgun under his father's mattress. He also found the loaded magazine. From watching television, the child knew how to load the magazine into the gun, and he did so. While playing with the gun, he apparently pulled the slide and thereby placed a bullet into the chamber. Either the safety lever was in the "fire" position already or Jordan moved it there. He then pulled the trigger, shot himself in the head, and died two days later. He was three years old.

[…]

Petitioner alleged that the gun was defective and unreasonably dangerous because its design "failed to incorporate reasonable devices to prevent its use by young children," in particular "one or more of the following: a grip safety, a heavy trigger-pull, a child-resistant manual safety, a built-in lock, a trigger lock, and/or personalized gun technology that would have substantially reduced the likelihood that a child could fire the gun...." Citing data released by the Centers for Disease Control and Prevention to the effect that 1,641 children under ten were accidentally killed by handguns between 1979 and 1996, petitioner averred in her complaint that "it was foreseeable that the gun would be found and handled by a young child, and that it would be fired by a young child, with resulting foreseeable grievous or fatal injury to the child and/or others." Petitioner contended that the handgun industry was aware of the problem of young children finding and injuring themselves with handguns and, in the 1880's, had developed a childproof grip safety, but that Sturm Ruger manufactured the gun without that, or any other, childproof device.

Sturm Ruger responded to the complaint with [...] assertions that (1) as a matter of law, the gun was not in a defective condition or unreasonably dangerous, and (2) it was used in a manner that was contrary to the clearly worded instructions and warnings that accompanied the product when sold, and was therefore *mis*used. [...] Sturm Ruger argued that the gun did not malfunction but rather performed exactly as it was designed to function, and that the accident occurred because of Garris's failure to heed clear warnings.

In response, petitioner argued that it is "inconsistent with the proper function of a gun to design it so that it can be fired by young children." The lack of child-resistant features, she claimed, made the gun foreseeably dangerous to small children, and, "because firing by small children is not one of the proper functions of a gun, a gun fired by a small child has not performed properly." She urged that Garris's failure to heed the warnings and keep the gun securely locked was not a defense to liability because that also was foreseeable. [...]

The essence of petitioner's case was that, when dealing with design defects in a strict liability claim, the court should apply a "risk-utility" analysis in lieu of a "consumer expectation" test and hold that the gun in question failed that preferred test because (1) the risk of excluding child safety features outweighs the utility of that exclusion, and (2) alternative safer designs could have been adopted economically. She argued [...] that "the central thing that Sturm Ruger did wrong in designing this gun...is to sell a gun a three year old could shoot." The court rejected that argument, holding instead that, under Maryland law, the risk-utility test applied only when the product malfunctioned and that the gun in question did not malfunction. Although at times indicating that the warnings given in the instruction manual and Federal notice were not really adequate, the court concluded that Garris clearly knew that the gun was dangerous.

[...]

The principal issue presented here is whether, in examining whether a product in general, or a handgun in particular, is defective for purposes of a strict liability action, this Court should continue to apply the "consumer expectation" test [...] or should adopt instead a version of the "risk-utility" analysis [...]. It would be helpful, therefore, at the outset, to define these two standards.

The consumer expectation test emanates from §402A of the RESTATEMENT (SECOND) OF TORTS which, under certain circumstances, makes the seller of a product that is in a "defective condition unreasonably dangerous" to the consumer liable for the physical harm caused to the consumer by that product. The test defines what is meant by the terms "defective condition" and "unreasonably dangerous." Comment g to §402A defines "defective condition" as a "condition not contemplated by the ultimate consumer, which will be unreasonably dangerous to him." Comment i, in speaking to the term "unreasonably dangerous," states that the article must be dangerous "to an extent beyond that which would be contemplated by the ordinary consumer who purchases it, with the ordinary knowledge common to the community as to its characteristics." Thus [...] under the consumer expectation or contemplation test set forth in §402A, a product is defectively dangerous "if it is dangerous to an extent beyond that which would be contemplated by the ordinary consumer who purchased it with the ordinary knowledge common to the community as to the product's characteristics." (citation omitted)

The "risk-utility" test, which has been applied principally to alleged defects in the *design* of a product, regards a product as defective and unreasonably dangerous, for strict liability purposes, if the danger presented by the product outweighs its utility. Where this test is applied, the issue usually becomes whether a safer alternative design was feasible, for, if so, that would likely alter the balance by reducing the extent of the danger.

[…]

Indeed, § 2 of the RESTATEMENT (THIRD) OF TORTS: PRODUCT LIABILITY, which adopts this test for design defect cases, goes directly to that issue:

"A product…is defective in design when the foreseeable risks of harm posed by the product could have been reduced or avoided by the adoption of a reasonable alternative design by the seller…and the omission of the alternative design renders the product not reasonably safe."

This Court first adopted the concept of strict liability, as articulated in RESTATEMENT (SECOND) OF TORTS §402A, in *Phipps v. General Motors Corp.*, (citation omitted). Paraphrasing the language in that section, we said that, to recover in an action for strict liability,

"it must be established that (1) the product was in a defective condition at the time that it left the possession or control of the seller, (2) that it was unreasonably dangerous to the user or consumer, (3) that the defect was a cause of the injuries, and (4) that the product was expected to and did reach the consumer without substantial change in its condition." (cite omitted)

Expounding upon those conditions and the nature of the action, we added that, for a seller to be liable under §402A, the product must be both in a "defective condition" and "unreasonably dangerous" at the time it was placed on the market and that both of those conditions were "explained in the official comments in terms of consumer expectations." In that regard, we called attention, in particular, to Comments g and i to §402A. (citation omitted).

Phipps involved an alleged design defect in an automobile […] We observed […] that there were certain kinds of conditions that, whether caused by design or manufacture, would never be said to involve a reasonable risk […] Those kinds of conditions, we said, whether resulting from a defect in design or manufacture, were defective and unreasonably dangerous "without the necessity of weighing and balancing the various factors involved." (citation omitted). […] The holdings […] that the risk-utility test does not apply to a design defect unless the product malfunctions in some way and that a handgun does not malfunction when it shoots a bullet into a person in whose direction it is fired, remain the law of Maryland.

Petitioner raises four questions in her brief but really presents five propositions. First, she urges that we […] abandon the consumer expectation test, and adopt the risk-utility test in strict liability actions based on design defects […] Second, she asks either that, in applying that test, we do not require that a product malfunction as a prerequisite or that we regard the use of the gun by a three-year-old as a malfunction. Third, she requests that we not carve out an exception to the risk-utility test for handguns. Fourth, she contends that, because Garris's conduct in leaving the gun and the magazine accessible to Jordan was foreseeable, it did not constitute a misuse of the product, and, finally, she argues that the warnings contained in the instruction manual do not suffice to shield Sturm Ruger from liability.

[…]

The concept of strict liability, especially as formulated in §402A of RESTATEMENT (SECOND), was regarded as an important pro-consumer advance; relieving persons injured by products from the requirement of proving negligence on the part of manufacturers or others in the distribution chain and focusing, instead, on the product itself, made it easier to obtain a recovery for a defectively designed or manufactured product. Substitution of a risk-utility analysis, however, especially as formulated in the RESTATEMENT (THIRD), has attracted considerable criticism and has been viewed by many as a retrogression, as returning to negligence concepts and placing a very difficult burden on plaintiffs. (citations omitted)

[…]

In his comprehensive article, John Vargo, (cite omitted) notes the wide range of tests, and permutations of tests, used by the various States. Vargo concluded that, as of 1996, ten States continued to apply the ordinary consumer expectation test for strict liability design defects, (citation omitted), and that six States applied a modified consumer expectation test, which, according to Vargo, engrafts on the consumer expectation test certain risk-utility balancing factors and substitutes the "reasonable consumer" for the "ordinary consumer." (citation omitted). Nine States, according to Vargo, have adopted a version […] which imputes knowledge of the product's dangerousness to the manufacturer and then balances the product's risks against its utility, the question being whether, with the imputed knowledge of the product's dangers, the manufacturer was negligent in marketing the product (citation omitted).

[…] California adopted the consumer expectation and risk-utility tests as parallel alternatives:

"[A] product may be found defective in design, so as to subject a manufacturer to strict liability for resulting injuries, under either of two alternative tests. First, a product may be found defective in design if the plaintiff establishes that the product failed to perform as safely as an ordinary consumer would expect when used in an intended or reasonably foreseeable manner. Second, a product may alternatively be found defective in design if the plaintiff demonstrates that the product's design proximately caused his injury and the defendant fails to establish, in light of the relevant factors, that, on balance, the benefits of the challenged design outweigh the risk of danger inherent in such design." (citation omitted).

Several States have followed that approach. Others have modified the second part so as not to shift the burden to the defendant. […]

Mr. Vargo observes that only seven States apply a pure risk-utility analysis in design defect cases, (citation omitted), and that four States have adopted strict liability rules that do not fit neatly into any of these various tests. (citation omitted). Thirty-two States, he contends, apply a risk-utility analysis under *any* test for design defects, and he includes Maryland in that category. (citation omitted). In Vargo's view, only three States (Alabama, Maine, and possibly Michigan) require evidence of a reasonable alternative design in all design defect cases. (citation omitted).

[…]

It is clear that, under the consumer expectation test that we applied […], no cause of action had been stated in this case. There was no malfunction of the gun; regrettably, it worked exactly as it was designed and intended to work and as any ordinary consumer would have expected it to work. The gun is a lawful weapon and was lawfully sold. What caused this tragedy was the carelessness of Jordan's father in leaving the weapon and the magazine in places where the child was able to find them, in contravention not only of common sense but of multiple warnings given to him at the time of purchase.

We are asked to […] permit an action to proceed against the manufacturer of the weapon. We are asked to modify the common law to impose liability on gun manufacturers who have failed to incorporate into their products one or another kind of device that would make the weapon childproof, quite apart from the inclusion of other safety devices, clear warnings regarding the storage of the weapon, and the offer of a lock box in which to store it. Although, as we noted, some courts have done that, there is no consensus in that regard. We were asked […] to extend and create new theories of liability, which we declined to do, noting that "we have consistently recognized that common law principles should not be changed contrary to the public policy of the State set forth by the General Assembly of Maryland." (citations omitted).

> That caution is especially appropriate here. Given the controversy that continues to surround the risk–utility standard articulated for design defect cases in §2 of the RESTATEMENT (THIRD), we are reluctant at this point to cast aside our existing jurisprudence in favor of such an approach on any broad, general basis. Nor is there a need to do so in this case, which deals with more specific issues that have been presented on several occasions to the General Assembly and have been considered and debated in that arena. So far, the Legislature has chosen not to place these burdens on gun manufacturers but has attempted to deal with the problem in other ways. We shall respect that policy choice.
> JUDGMENT OF COURT OF SPECIAL APPEALS AFFIRMED, WITH COSTS.

Here, the court saw that where the legislature has not created such a duty, it could not impose one because issues of policy are better addressed by elected officials.

The courts have considered other tests in an attempt to define a defect as it relates to an unreasonably dangerous product. The tests have involved an application of the principles of both negligence theory and strict liability to produce a favorable result for the consumer. Paralegal students must consult individual state laws to ascertain how products are determined to be defective.

Restatement (Third) Torts: Product Liability

Over time, the widespread use of the "unreasonably dangerous" language in the *Restatement (Second) of Torts* §402A generated issues that suggested a need to refine the principles there. In 1998, the American Law Institute, a private, not-for-profit organization responsible for issuing all *Restatements of Law*, released the **Restatement (Third) Torts: Product Liability.**

This new *Restatement* addressed some of the issues raised when courts sought to apply the provisions of the *Restatement (Second) of Torts* §402A. For example, it clarified that the issue of product liability depended upon the fact of a defect and not of the theory of recovery (see box below).

CHANGES IN THE *RESTATEMENT (THIRD) TORTS: PRODUCT LIABILITY*

No manufacturer or distributor is liable for harm caused by a product unless the product is defective. The language of defectiveness encompasses negligence, warranty, and strict tort liability. Although each theory was historically of separate importance, the *Restatement*'s "defect" analysis makes it possible to discuss the rules of liability without necessarily identifying the negligence or warranty basis for them.

Dobbs, *The Law of Torts* §352, (2000)

The *Restatement (Third) Torts* seemed to make radical changes, but in fact merely characterized the way that courts had interpreted §402A (see box on next page).

> ### RESTATEMENT (THIRD) TORTS: PRODUCT LIABILITY AND RECOVERY UNDER A THEORY OF STRICT LIABILITY
>
> The Products Restatement drops all references to strict products liability. Its view is that courts have mostly come to apply negligence standards in determining design and warning defects, even when they maintained the language of strict liability. The effect, although not the language of the Products Restatement is that strict liability is retained when it comes to product flaws, but negligence or something very much like it, is the test of liability when it comes to design and warning defects.
>
> Dobbs, *The Law of Torts* §353 (2000)

Some of the changes are listed here (see table below).

> Some Changes in the *Restatement (Third) Torts: Product Liability* Made from the Principles Found in *Restatement (Second) of Torts* §402A
>
> - Abandonment of the "unreasonably dangerous" standard
> - The possibility of liability even if the product is unavailable
> - Specifically addressed design defect claims of prescription drugs

Following is a summary of the table of contents for the *Restatement (Third) Torts: Product Liability* (see box below).

> ### TABLE OF CONTENTS FOR THE *RESTATEMENT (THIRD) TORTS: PRODUCT LIABILITY*
>
> Chapter 1– Liability of Commercial Product Sellers Based on Product Defects at Time of Sale
>> Topic 1– Liability Rules Applicable to Products Generally
>> [...]
>> Topic 2– Liability Rules Applicable to Special Products or Product Markets
>> [...]
>> Chapter 2– Liability of Commercial Product Sellers Not Based on Product Defects at Time of Sale
>> [...]
>> Chapter 4– Provisions of General Applicability
>> Topic 1– Causation
>> [...]
>> Topic 2– Affirmative Defenses
>> [...]
>> Topic 3– Definitions
>> [...]
>
> American Law Institute (1998)

A paralegal must remember that the *Restatement (Third) Torts: Product Liability*, like the *Restatement (Second) of Torts* §402A, does not have the force of binding law unless a court or legislature adopts its provisions. States will differ as to what provisions of the *Restatement (Third) Torts: Product Liability*, if any, constitute controlling law, just as with the *Restatement (Second) of Torts* §402A. Paralegals therefore must determine through research what theories a particular state has adopted.

Defenses

One defense may arise where the risk was obvious, then the absence of a warning may not automatically confer liability, as Professor Dobbs notes:

> ### DEFENSES: KNOWN OR OBVIOUS RISK
> One reason a warning may not be required is that the risks involved are either generally known or are obvious to a purchaser or user. One function of a warning is to alert the product user to risks. A warning may not be needed if people already know of the risks.
>
> Dobbs, *The Law of Torts* §363 (2000)

A defendant might avoid liability when the plaintiff fails to meet the burden of proof. That is, the plaintiff has an obligation to provide, by a preponderance of the evidence, that strict liability actually arose. Failing that, the defendant will escape liability.

A defendant might have available a statute of limitations, which bars recovery for a fixed period of time after the defect was discovered. Or jurisdictions might impose a statute of respose, which limits liability for a period of years from the date of manufacture.

A plaintiff may have failed to provide the defendant with notice prior to filing suit. Such a statutory requirement reflects the hope by a legislature that a defendant can avoid litigation if given the opportunity to repair or replace the defective item.

■ ALTERNATIVE THEORIES OF RECOVERY

Besides the above-mentioned theories, states may have adopted consumer protection laws that might reasonably include claims under product liability. They may have even enacted statutes that specifically address product liability, thereby creating a new type of cause of action in that jurisdiction. Again, paralegals should research the status of product liability law in their particular state.

Since 1972, the federal government has regulated unsafe products through its Consumer Product Safety Commission. The authority vested in that body includes issuing warnings regarding the safety of products and, in some instances, orders mandating a recall of the dangerous products.

KEY TERMS

Caveat emptor   434

Contract   434

Defective design   463

Failure to warn   460

Privity of contract   434

Restatement (Second) of Torts §402A   457

Restatement (Third) of Torts: Product Liability   471

Uniform Commercial Code (U.C.C.)   435

"Unreasonably dangerous"   458

Warranty   435

Warranty of fitness   435

Warranty of merchantability   435

SUMMARY

An action for product liability arises out of injuries resulting from using a product that has been placed in the stream of commerce. A cause of action may be based on a theory of breach of warranty or on a theory of strict liability in tort. The law of product liability has advanced substantially since the days of *caveat emptor*, and it now offers the consumer a great deal of protection from products that are unsafe or that fail to meet safety standards. The paralegal student will find this to be a challenging and constantly evolving area of the law.

CONCEPT REVIEW QUESTIONS

1. What is the meaning of the phrase *caveat emptor*?
2. Discuss the concept of privity of contract.
3. How are the parties to a product liability action determined?
4. Discuss the concept of warranty.
5. In what way is the concept of negligence reflected in the law of product liability?
6. What is the reasoning behind the application of the theory of strict liability in product liability cases?
7. What is meant by the phrase *unreasonably dangerous*?
8. List the traditional defenses to be considered in a product liability action.
9. What was the purpose of establishing the Consumer Product Safety Commission?

CRITICAL THINKING APPLICATIONS

1. During college, Courtney drinks so much "light" beer that she neglects her studies and flunks out of school. Courtney files suit against the three major U.S. breweries on the grounds of failing to provide adequate notice that drinking light beer could lead to alcoholism. Each brewery files for summary judgment. What is the likely outcome on all three motions?
2. Tristan purchases a number of government-surplus weather balloons, fills them with helium, attaches them to a lawn chair, sits in the chair and, armed with a .22-caliber gun, rises up into the air. When trying to descend, Tristan fires at the balloons but the bullets do not pierce the thick-skinned balloons. Eventually, the helium leaks out and Tristan comes to earth, hard, resulting in a broken arm. Tristan sues the seller of the government-surplus balloons. If this matter were to go to trial, what would the likely outcome be?
3. Carlos signs up for membership at a local health club. After receiving training from the health club staff, Carlos regularly visits the club. One day, Carlos let the weight down too fast on a weight machine. The impact damaged a weight and sent it onto Carlos's foot, breaking a toe. Carlos plans to sue the manufacturer of the equipment. Will the manufacturer be found liable? Why or why not?
4. For Halloween, Rich wants to go as a ghost. Unable to find any white powder to smear on his body and make himself white as a ghost, Rich sprays white paint on himself. The next day, Rich has difficulty getting the paint off and

develops a skin rash. If Rich sues the manufacturer of the white spray paint, will a court find in Rich's favor? Why or why not?

5. The temperature gauge on the dashboard of Li's car indicates that the engine is too hot. Li can see steam coming from under the hood. Pulling over to the side of the road, Li opens the hood and sees tendrils of steam rising from where the cap is joined to the radiator. Using napkins to remove the cap, Li is hit in the face by the cap when Li twists it open. Li sues the cap manufacturer on the grounds that it failed to warn that removing the radiator cap after the car's engine is running could lead to injury from the sudden release of pressure built up in the radiator. Will the manufacturer face liability in damages?

6. On a small tube of lip balm, the manufacturer has placed a warning: Do not eat. Taylor puts the tube down on the kitchen table, and Taylor's baby reaches over, grabs the tube, removes the top, and takes a big bite out of it. After treatment in an emergency room, the baby is fine but Taylor now has to pay for the medical expenses. Taylor sues the manufacturer of the lip balm to recover in damages the cost of those expenses. How likely is it that Taylor will win? Why?

7. Without paying attention, Brandon reaches into a supply cabinet to grab some liquid soap. Finding a bottle that seems like the right one, Brandon sprinkles some on himself only to see that he's grabbed a lye-based cleaner. Brandon suffers from second-degree burns. He sues the manufacturer of the cleaner on the grounds that it failed to configure the bottle so that someone couldn't accidentally get burned by just pouring the cleaner out onto flesh. The manufacturer files a motion to dismiss. Will the trial court grant the request? Why or why not?

8. Jake is driving along an empty interstate highway one night. He decides to see how fast his compact car can go and pushes all the way down on the gas pedal. The car races past 80 mph but suddenly stops with an awful clanging because a piston has shot through the wall of the engine, ruining it. Jake sues on the grounds that the car manufacturer failed to include a warning that operating the vehicle at more than 80 mph could cause the destruction of the engine. Will Jake win at trial? Why or why not?

SKILL-BUILDING APPLICATION

Early in July, workers from the city's Department of Public Works were completing the repaving of a stretch of road. Whinging, who had driven heavy machinery for the DPW for fifteen years, felt the brakes give way on the ten-ton roller he was driving. Yelling to the other DPW employees to get out of the way, that the brakes of the roller no longer worked, Whinging succeeded in steering the vehicle off the road into an empty field, but was crushed to death the first time the roller tumbled as it turned a half-dozen times before stopping. Whinging's family sued, claiming that the roller manufacturer failed to install a roll bar "cage" around the driver's seat, and that this failure was a design defect that had resulted in Whinging's death. What theory of product liability would the family mostly succeed at arguing to win at trial? Define that theory and explain why that theory would be better than all other possible theories of liability for the manufacturing of a ten-ton roller without a "cage" around the driver's seat. Offer a prediction of the family's actually winning at trial using that particular theory.

Men at some time are masters of their fates:
The fault, dear Brutus, is not in our stars, but
in ourselves, that we are underlings.

William Shakespeare (1564–1616)

Vicarious Liability

Vicarious liability imposes liability for the tortious behavior of one person acting on behalf of another. Historically, an employer was liable for the tortious actions of an apprentice, when this employee committed a tort while under the control of the employer. So, an employer could owe a duty of care to the world regarding the actions of an employee when a tort occurred. The critical elements focus on the nature of the relationship and the degree of control exercised of the actions of the other. This chapter acquaints paralegal students with the concept of vicarious liability, examining the extent of one's liability to another for the acts of a person acting on behalf of the original party.

CHAPTER TOPICS

1. Doctrine of Vicarious Liability
2. Principal–Agent Relationship
3. Independent Contractor
4. Joint Enterprise
5. Automobile Ownership
6. Dram Shop Liability

OBJECTIVES

After completing this chapter, you will be able to:

1. Understand the doctrine of vicarious liability.
2. Discuss the principle of *respondeat superior*.
3. Analyze the principal–agent relationship.
4. Distinguish between a frolic and a detour in determining vicarious liability.
5. Comprehend the distinction between an independent contractor and an employer.
6. Summarize the nature of a joint enterprise.
7. Discuss the principles of liability that attend ownership of an automobile.
8. Analyze the concept of dram shop liability in a contemporary commercial setting.

■ DOCTRINE OF VICARIOUS LIABILITY

Vicarious liability simply means holding someone liable for the actions for another. The liability arises out of the relationship between the individuals and authority one party has given to another.

For a court to recognize that there is vicarious liability, the plaintiff will have to show that:

- A relationship exists
- Where one (an agent) is granted authority to act on behalf of another (the principal)
- That the principal had some control over how the agent exercised that grant of authority
- When that agent exercised that grant of authority, a tort happened

For example, a popular sports figure hires an agent to negotiate a contract with a new employer. Time is of the essence because certain financial restrictions require that a contract has to be negotiated within twelve hours. As the sports agent speeds towards a meeting with the new employer, the agent hits a pedestrian. The pedestrian should be able to hold the sports figure liable for any damages caused by the agent's negligence, since at the time of the collision, the agent was acting on behalf of the sports figure.

Yet liability may be difficult to prove if the agent was driving at an unlawful rate of speed. Or if it turns out that the agent stopped at an ATM that was a mile away from the quickest route. The injured pedestrian, in a suit for negligence against the sports figure, would need to show that a relationship exists between the sports figure and the agent. Then, the pedestrian has to show that in the relationship, the sports figure gave the agent authority to negotiate on behalf of the sports figure. Finally, the pedestrian will need to show that the agent was exercising that authority in trying to negotiate the new contract within the specific time frame.

Historically, the courts have recognized the principle of *respondeat superior,* a Latin phrase that means "let the master answer," which looks to an employer, or "master," as legally responsible for the behavior of someone in his or her employ.

Terms

Some jurisdictions refer to the principle of vicarious liability by various terms. As shown in Table 14-1, all of the terms focus on the existence of a relationship and the granting of authority that arose out of the creation of that relationship.

Table 14-1 Other Terms for the Concept of Vicarious Liability

Term	Definition
Imputed negligence	The negligence of one person is imputed (assigned) to another.
Master–servant	The master is responsible for the conduct of his or her servant.
Principal–agent	The principal is responsible for the conduct of his or her agent.
Employer–employee	The employer may be responsible for the conduct of his or her employee.
Respondeat superior	"Let the master answer."

The most common usage is "principal–agent." The term **master–servant** carries a connotation associated with this country's history of slavery, so it has increasingly fallen out of favor.

Why Courts Have Recognized This Doctrine

Perhaps the critical reason, as a matter of policy, to hold the principal liable for the actions of an agent has to do with allocation of responsibility and risk. The relationship exists for the benefit of the principal. Since the agent's actions will benefit the principal, the principal should also be responsible for the actions of the agent. If the principal gets the benefits, the principal should also bear the risk. Further, the principal usually has more resources than the agent and has more control over the nature of the relationship and the control of the granting of authority. So, according to social policy, the person who has the most to gain should also be the person who could better bear the loss.

Principals will have more options on how to manage the risk. If a principal sells goods, then the retailer can charge a few more cents more for the item so as to pay a premium for an insurance policy that would provide funds if there was an accident that arose when the agent sold the goods.

In the *Reed* case, the court found that an occasional employee was not acting within the scope of employment at the time of the plaintiff's injury. With only a nominal link between the defendant and its occasional employee during this specific activity, the business would not reasonably expect to have to secure insurance to cover a situation like the plaintiff's (see Case in Point 14-1).

CASE IN POINT 14-1

Reed v. House of Decor, Inc.
468 So.2d 1159 (La. 1985)

We granted certiorari to determine whether the intermediate court erred in reversing a judgment which held that House of Decor, Inc. was vicariously liable for plaintiff's injuries caused by Chuck Williams, an alleged employee of House of Decor. The critical issue is whether Williams was an employee of the House of Decor in the course and scope of that employment at the time of the accident.

William Cusack and Steven Tomoletz, as individuals, leased certain immovable property in the Vieux Carré section of New Orleans. The lower floor of the main building on the property was used as a gift shop operated by the House of Decor, Inc., a corporation in which Cusack and Tomoletz were the sole shareholders. The two men resided on the upper floor of the main building. The leased property also included slave quarters in the rear. Cusack and Tomoletz sublet the upper apartment in the slave quarters to Williams on a two-year lease for a monthly rental of $125, executing the sublease in their individual capacities and not as officers of the corporation. [...]

The day before the accident, Cusack asked plaintiff, an employee of a hotel across the street from the House of Decor, to help move a refrigerator from Williams' upper apartment to the new residence. The accident occurred on a Sunday, before the hour that the gift shop opened. While Williams and plaintiff were attempting to move the refrigerator down the stairs of the slave quarters to Williams' truck, Williams lost his grip, and the refrigerator fell onto plaintiff's ankle.

Plaintiff filed suit against the House of Decor and Gulf Insurance Company as the corporation's liability carrier, alleging that the House of Decor was vicariously liable for the negligence of its "employee," Chuck Williams. Neither Cusack nor Tomoletz was ever named or served as an individual defendant, nor was any argument made to the jury that they were individually liable. Both sides restricted their opening and closing arguments to the jury (except for the issue of damages) to the issue of the House of Decor's vicarious liability for the negligence of Williams as a corporate employee. After trial on the merits, the jury answered written interrogatories and found that Williams was an employee of House of Decor at the time of the accident and that his negligence caused plaintiff's injuries [....] Judgment was rendered in favor of plaintiff and against the House of Decor and Gulf Insurance. Both sides appealed.

We granted certiorari, being primarily concerned about an employer's liability for the off-duty torts of an employee who was performing (perhaps under subtle economic coercion) tasks at the request of and for the personal benefit of a principal officer and shareholder of a corporate employer [....]

Whether a party is liable for the act of a tortfeasor on the basis that the tortfeasor was the party's employee in the course and scope of employment depends upon the proof and assessment of several factors, including payment of wages by the employer, the employer's power of control, the employee's duty to perform the particular act, the time, place and purpose of the act in relation to service of the employer, the relationship between the employee's act and the employer's business, the benefits received by the employer from the act, the motivation of the employee for performing the act, and the reasonable expectation of the employer that the employee would perform the act [....]

In summary, Williams did not receive any wages from the House of Decor. The corporation had no power of control or power of discharge over his work activities. The act of moving the refrigerator occurred at a time when the business operated by the corporation was closed and at a place away from the corporation's business premises. The moving of the refrigerator from an apartment occupied by Williams to another residence provided no apparent benefit to the corporation and had no relationship with the corporation's business. Indeed, the corporation was just about to close down the business permanently, and it is difficult to perceive any purpose in moving the refrigerator that was in any way related to the corporation [....]

Determination of the course and scope of employment is largely based on policy. The risks which are generated by an employee's activities while serving his employer's interests are properly allocated to the employer as a cost of engaging in the enterprise. However, when the party (the alleged employer) upon whom vicarious liability is sought to be imposed had only a marginal relationship with the act which generated the risk and did not benefit by it, the purpose of the policy falls, and the responsibility for preventing the risk is solely upon the tortfeasor who created the risk while performing the act.

In the present case, the jury found that Williams was an employee of the House of Decor. The evidence arguably supports this limited determination that he was an occasional employee [....] If Williams were a regular employee of the small corporation, perhaps policy would dictate that he should be viewed as being in the course and scope of his employment when performing a task at the request of and for the personal benefit of the holder of 51% of the corporate shares in the two-shareholder corporation. However, there is no compelling policy reason for a similar conclusion in the case of someone who at best was an occasional employee [....]

We therefore conclude that Williams' act of moving the refrigerator, during the performance of which plaintiff was injured, was not performed by an employee of House of Decor in the course and scope of employment.

While the accident occurred, Williams, the occasional employee, might, at best, be indirectly acting on behalf of corporate ownership. The court therefore felt it unfair to allocate the risk of having to cover costs for plaintiff's injury because the defendant really would not have cause to expect to bear this cost for this kind of injury.

■ PRINCIPAL–AGENT RELATIONSHIP

The creation of the **principal–agent relationship** and the doctrine of holding a principal vicariously liable for the actions of the agent has long been recognized (see box below).

---

§ 7.03 PRINCIPAL'S LIABILITY–IN GENERAL

(1) A principal is subject to direct liability to a third party harmed by an agent's conduct when
   (a) as stated in § 7.04, the agent acts with actual authority or the principal ratifies the agent's conduct and
     (i) the agent's conduct is tortious, or
     (ii) the agent's conduct, if that of the principal, would subject the principal to tort liability; or
   (b) as stated in § 7.05, the principal is negligent in selecting, supervising, or otherwise controlling the agent; or
   (c) as stated in § 7.06, the principal delegates performance of a duty to use care to protect other persons or their property to an agent who fails to perform the duty.
(2) A principal is subject to vicarious liability to a third party harmed by an agent's conduct when
   (a) as stated in § 7.07, the agent is an employee who commits a tort while acting within the scope of employment; or
   (b) as stated in § 7.08, the agent commits a tort when acting with apparent authority in dealing with a third party on or purportedly on behalf of the principal.

Restatement (Third) of Agency, §7.03 (2006)

The Relationship: When Does It Arise?

Courts have looked to different factors when determining whether a principal–agent relationship exists to recognize vicarious liability. Those factors can include those listed in Table 14-2.

Table 14-2 Factors a Court Will Consider When Determining Whether Vicarious Liability Exists.

Term	Definition
Control	The principal has some presumed control over the actions of the agent.
Origination	The principal has initiated the process that led to the harm.

(continued)

Table 14-2 *continued*	
Entrustment	The principal has delegated the responsibility for some task to the agent.
Privilege	Responsibility for another person accompanies the privilege of hiring.
"Deep pocket"	Damages are awarded against the party most likely able to bear the loss.

These factors underscore how the principal has vested authority in the agent, so that the principal may benefit by the agent's actions. Issues may exist about the degree of authority that the principal has provided to the agent. Yet that issue presumes the principal has acted so as to empower agent. So, the relationship arises when the principal grants power to the agent to act on behalf of the principal.

Control

Control relates to the ability of the principal to dictate how the agent can serve the principal's interests best when exercising the authority granted from the principal. It is not enough that the principal has empowered the agent to act on behalf of the principal. To hold the principal liable for a tort committed by an agent, the principal had to have some say in how the agent would act. If the principal is telling the agent to act so that the principal's interests are served, the principal becomes liable for the agent's actions. In some states, the greater the degree of control by the principal means the greater the likelihood of responsibility for the consequences of the agent's actions.

State courts have established a set of criteria to determine the nature and extent of control that the principal has in the relationship. No single factor predominates in inferring control; all factors must be assessed to establish the nature and degree of control that a principal exercises in the relationship. A court might look to the following criteria:

Factors a Court Considers When Determining the Extent of Control in a Principal–Agent Relationship
• the extent to which the employer may determine the details of the work • the nature of the occupation • custom of the community • skill required • who supplies the tools or other instrumentalities used in the work • period over which the employment is to last • method of payment

Establishing the degree of control can involve simply looking at a series of instructions. It might be established due to a tradition, such as when a principal was teaching an apprentice a craft, where the apprentice might need to order supplies. It might arise indirectly, where the principal's payment of funds, such as with amount and frequency, can guide the agent's exercise of authority. The paralegal student must consult state statutory and case law to determine the factors stressed in individual states.

Employment

An agency relationship may exist during the course of employment. A manager might tell an employee to purchase supplies. It does not automatically exist. At a grocery store, a cashier would not have any authority to order enough to stock the shelves full of goods. A court, then, will look at the nature of the relationship that has arisen. If a manager hires a cashier to work at the grocery store, the scope of employment is limited to checking out the customer's order (see box below).

---

§7.07 EMPLOYEE ACTING WITHIN SCOPE OF EMPLOYMENT
[...]

2. An employee acts within the scope of employment when performing work assigned by the employer or engaging in a course of conduct subject to the employer's control. An employee's act is not within the scope of employment when it occurs within an independent course of conduct not intended by the employee to serve any purpose of the employer.
3. For purposes of this section,
   a. an employee is an agent whose principal controls or has the right to control the manner and means of the agent's performance of work, and
   b. the fact that work is performed gratuitously does not relieve a principal of liability.

Restatement (Third) of Agency, §7.07 (2006)

Scope of Employment

Vicarious liability applies to those torts committed by the agent. That could include torts occurring within the **scope of employment.** No set definition exists for what constitutes the scope of employment. When trying to determine the scope, a court might consider not only those essential tasks the employee has to complete but may include those acts that would help to accomplish the employer's objectives (see box below).

SCOPE OF EMPLOYMENT

As in the case of the existence of the relation itself, many factors enter into the question: the time, place and purpose of the act, and its similarity to what is authorized; whether it is one commonly done by such servants; the extent of departure from normal methods; the previous relations between the parties; whether the master had reason to expect that such an act would be done....

W. Page Keeton et. al., *Prosser & Keeton on the Law of Torts* §70 at 502 (5th ed. 1984)

Generally, the agent remains within the scope of employment if the act serves the principal's purposes. It is not enough that the agent forbids the agent to commit a certain act or for the agent to "act carefully." If the agent is furthering the interests of the principal, the principal will be held responsible regardless of instructions.

In the *Baird* case, the court is concerned with the control of the surgeon over the acts of his nurse-anesthetist (see Case in Point 14-2).

 # CASE IN POINT 14-2

Baird v. Sickler

69 Ohio St. 2d 652 (1982)

On January 26, 1976, appellee Maxine Baird underwent a laminectomy at Good Samaritan Hospital in the city of Dayton, Ohio. The procedure was performed to alleviate blocked vertebrae in her spine resulting from the Klippel-Feil syndrome. Appellees, Maxine and Richard Baird, employed Donald M. Sickler, M.D., to supervise and conduct the operation. J. A. Nichol, a registered nurse and trained nurse-anesthetist licensed under the laws of the state of Ohio to administer anesthesia [...], assisted Dr. Sickler as the anesthetist during the laminectomy. At the time of the operation, Nichol was an employee of Anesthesia Associates. Dr. Sickler was aware that, because appellee Maxine Baird suffered from spondylosis as well as Klippel-Feil syndrome, her spinal cord might be compromised if the operation were done with appellee in a sitting position. Cognizant of the difficulties of intubating, i.e., inserting an endotracheal tube in the airway, of an individual so afflicted, Dr. Sickler helped position—prepare the head and torso—and otherwise assist in appellee's intubation. Dr. Sickler did not perform the actual insertion of the tube in appellee's trachea; nurse Nichol performed that task. Dr. Sickler was, however, present at all times during the intubation.

As a result of the operation, appellee was rendered permanently a paraplegic from the C-6 level down. Evidence adduced at trial indicated that the paralysis had two possible geneses: (1) the faulty intubation and positioning of appellee or (2) the aggravation, through fallen blood pressure of a sustained duration during the laminectomy itself, of a minor injury initially precipitated by appellee's intubation and positioning.

At the close of appellees' case, the trial court directed a verdict in favor of appellant. On appeal, the Court of Appeals reversed the lower court's decision, holding the directed verdict to be improper on grounds that reasonable minds could find appellant liable under the doctrine of *respondeat superior* and that appellant, by failing properly to direct the nurse-anesthetist, had breached a statutory duty[....]The cause is now before this court pursuant to the allowance of a motion to certify the record.

[...]

This cause presents a novel question in Ohio: is a chief surgeon ever legally accountable for the negligence of an assisting nurse-anesthetist, not directly employed by him? If an operating physician may never be held liable in such a factual context, then the trial court in the instant case acted properly in directing a verdict in favor of the appellant, Dr. Sickler. We find, however, that a chief surgeon's immunity for the negligent acts of an assisting nurse-anesthetist is not a matter of law and, thus, that the trial court erred in directing the verdict [....]

Under the doctrine of *respondeat superior*, the "master" is liable for the negligence of his "servant" when the latter is engaged in performing the work of the former [....] A master—servant relationship is extant only when one party exercises the right of control over the actions of another and those actions are directed toward the attainment of an objective which the former seeks [....] For the relationship to exist, it is unnecessary that such right of control be exercised; it is sufficient that the right merely exists.

All requisite indices of the master–servant diad were present in the relationship between appellant Dr. Sickler and J. A. Nichol, the nurse-anesthetist who assisted him. That appellant exercised and possessed the right to control Nichol's actions is reflected in appellant's own testimony at trial. Dr. Sickler admitted that, before the intubation, he instructed Nichol as to the procedures he wished to follow because of appellee Baird's special condition. He stated that, during the intubation, he watched to ensure that Nichol did not hyperflex or hyperextend appellee's neck and admitted that had he observed any misfeasance in the conduct of the intubation, he would have possessed the right and duty to halt the procedure. Appellant testified that, following the intubation, he held appellee's head as she was turned and placed on the operating table and monitored her positioning to ensure that neither her airway nor eyes were compromised. Appellant clearly not only controlled but also participated in the administering of the anesthetic. Moreover, even if he had failed to exercise control over the intubation, he clearly, as he himself admitted, had the right to control it. Appellant contends that the doctrine of *respondeat superior* is inapplicable to the present case because Nichol, the nurse-anesthetist, was an employee and servant of Anesthesia Associates, not of Dr. Sickler. The loaned servant rule, however, compels us to reject this argument [....]

Appellant finally argues that the Court of Appeals' decision in the instant case resurrects the now abjectly discredited "captain of the ship" doctrine which held a chief surgeon responsible for all that transpires in the operating room. Our ruling, which affirms the appellate court's determination, in no way breathes new life into that now prostrate doctrine. We make no attempt to impose upon an operating physician the duty of overseeing all that occurs in the highly technical milieu in which he works. Instead, we seek only to ensure that where, in the operating room, a surgeon does control or realistically possesses the right to control events and procedures, he does so with a high degree of care [....]

The court found, in this case, that the physician would supervise the actions of the nurse-anesthetist and would have an obligation to assist the nurse if difficulties arose during the surgery. In fact, the physician played a role in the administering of the anesthesia. This court refused to rely on "the captain of a ship" doctrine, which held the captain liable for any misconduct that occurs. Because the physician did have a high degree of control over the actions of the nurse-anesthetist during the administration of the anesthesia, the court ruled that the physician was vicariously liable for the plaintiff's injuries.

Liability When There Is "Frolic and Detour"

When the agent acts outside the boundaries of the grant of authority, the law will not hold the principal responsible. It could be that the agent has chosen to pursue personal interests and not to advance the principal's interests. In the English case of *Joel v. Morrison*, 172 Eng. Rep. 1338 (1834), Baron Parke stated that the master is not liable when the servant is "going on a frolic of his own." So **frolic**—a material deviation from the grant of authority—has since become a part of American jurisprudence.

A frolic will deal with something significant, such as doing work for another principal. It generally would not apply to something trivial, like using a restroom. Yet a frolic can occur even at work, as Professor Dobbs notes:

FROLIC AND DETOUR EVEN IN THE WORKPLACE

Although frolic and detour terminology is often associated with an employee's geographical or temporal deviation from employment, employees may depart from employment without leaving the situs of their work. They may do so by undertaking tasks alien to the work they were employed to do. An employee hired to cut down an elm tree on the employer's property undertakes to cut down an oak on the neighbor's land. That may enhance the employer's view and hence benefit the employer in some sense, but it is outside the employment.

Dobbs, *The Law of Torts* §335 (2000)

An agent might not be on a frolic if having only chosen a roundabout way to complete an assignment. Determining whether a frolic has occurred depends heavily upon the facts of the circumstances.

Contrast a frolic with a detour. A **detour** would involve a short or limited deviation from completing an assignment on behalf of the principal and then a return to that assignment. Determining this, too, depends heavily on the facts and circumstances. Some courts have held principals liable for the actions of an agent on a detour, where a reasonably expected, slight departure from an assignment could have been expected.

For example, suppose that Arliss worked as Theodore's general agent, out of Theodore's office. On the way to a local restaurant to pick up some sandwiches for lunch, Arliss struck Mrs. Mantooth, a pedestrian. The question of fact would revolve around what was customarily expected of agents such as Arliss and whether Theodore permitted the act. A court may hold Arliss to have been on a frolic and not on the principal's business or it may rule that Arliss engaged in an act of personal interest that was reasonably expected to happen. The answer to the question will generally be based on whether the deviation was major or minor. If the departure was minor, then the employer will be held liable as a necessary risk to his or her business.

By way of contrast, consider the New York Supreme Court's decision in the *Cowin* case, where the agent reported for work in an intoxicated condition, and the principal, although aware that the agent's means of transportation was an automobile, sent him home in that condition (see Case in Point 14-3).

 # CASE IN POINT 14-3

Cowin v. Huntington Hospital

130 Misc. 2d 267 (Sup. Ct. 1985)

Upon a motion to dismiss a complaint for failure to state a cause of action, the Court must accept the facts alleged in the complaint as true and determine whether these facts fit within any cognizable legal theory [....]

The complaint in the instant action alleges, in effect, that defendant's employee JAMES THOMAS reported for work in an intoxicated condition, and that defendant, although aware his means of transportation was an automobile, sent THOMAS home in that condition. Shortly afterwards, the automobile driven by THOMAS was the cause of a motor vehicle accident causing personal injury to plaintiff. While the Court agrees with the contentions of both parties that under the facts alleged defendant owed no duty to the public to control THOMAS' actions under General Obligations Law a 11-101, commonly known as the Dram Shop Act, it does not agree with plaintiff that a separate common law duty to protect the general public from the actions complained of exists.

In order to establish tort liability, the plaintiff must demonstrate the existence and breach of a duty owed to him by defendant [....] While, as a general rule a person is under no duty to control the conduct of another, certain relationships, such as that between master and servant, do create such a duty. This duty, however, is a narrow one and under the doctrine of respondeat superior, an employer will be liable for the negligence of an employee only while the employee is acting within the scope of his employment [....] An employee acts within the scope of his employment when he is doing something in furtherance of the duties he owes to his employer and where the employer is, or could be, exercising some control, directly or indirectly, over the employee's activities[....]Driving to and from work is not considered to be acting within the scope of one's employment except in those instances where such travel has been found to be within the scope of the employee's duties [....] In the instant case, defendant was not, as a matter of law, acting within the scope of his employment since his actions in becoming intoxicated prior to reporting for work can in no way be viewed as having been performed in furtherance of the employer's requirements and the employer did not participate in creating his condition. Nor can this Court find a duty on the part of the defendant, premised independently of an employment relationship, which would require it to take reasonable measures to protect the public at large from the off-duty torts of its employee. Plaintiff cites *Restatement (Second) of Torts* § 319 as a basis for imposing such a duty. That section provides:

"One who takes charge of a third person whom he knows or should know to be likely to cause bodily harm to others if not controlled is under a duty to exercise reasonable care to control the third person from doing such harm."

This section requires more than mere knowledge of a person's dangerous propensities. "Taking charge" within the meaning of Section 319 requires a custodial relationship, one in which the person charged with controlling the conduct of another voluntarily assumes responsibility for that person. This the defendant specifically and unequivocally declined to do. In the absence of some affirmative action by defendant to intervene or to control its employee, THOMAS' mere reporting for work could not unilaterally transfer to or create on the part of his employer responsibility for a wrongful act done prior to such reporting and there was no duty owed by defendant to this plaintiff to accept such responsibility. The Court notes that while at least one jurisdiction has apparently analogized Section 319 in a fashion as to impose a duty running from an employer to the public at large in circumstances similar to those at bar, [...] no authority has been cited, nor can any be found by this Court, which would suggest that this jurisdiction has judicially recognized such an expansion of an employer's vicarious liability for the acts of his employee when committed outside the scope of employment.

The Court therefore finds no basis upon which to predicate a cause of action against defendant for the injuries alleged to have been sustained by plaintiff. Accordingly, the complaint is dismissed.

Beyond the Scope of Employment

To determine whether an employee has deviated from the **scope of employment**, the courts will consider such a range of factors (see Table 14-3).

Table 14-3 Factors Courts Consider When Analyzing If There Was Deviation from the Scope of Employment

Factors	Analysis
Time	whether the agent was within the normal work hours
Duration	the length of time of the departure, frolic, or detour
Distance	the remoteness of the deviation
Motive	interests of the employer measured against the purely personal interests of the agent
Principal's business	whether the acts of the agent had any relationship to furtherance of the principal's business

Scope of Employment Distinct from Frolic and Detour

Whether an agent has acted in the scope of employment or was on a frolic or a detour that will affect whether the principal will be liable for the actions of the agent.

Because these determinations depend so heavily on specific facts, it may prove difficult to establish when an agent has exceeded the scope of employment or has gone on a frolic or on a detour. In the following case, the court examines the law surrounding these issues to determine whether a city should be liable for a parking meter ticketing agent's crash into a friend with a motorized scooter (see Case in Point 14-4).

CASE IN POINT 14-4

Karangelen v. Snyder

40 Md. App. 393 (1978)

We are here concerned with the extent to which a policeman is entitled to the defense of governmental immunity. [...] The facts, as related by appellee, showed that he was on duty at the date and time in question, and that his assignment was to check parking meters and issue citations in a certain section of Baltimore County. His means of transportation was a police vehicle described as a Cushman Truckster which is a small motorized vehicle not much larger than a motor scooter but with a semi-enclosed area where the operator is seated. Being unfamiliar with the handling of the scooter, and desiring to avoid making a U-turn, the appellee pulled into a service station lot with the intention of crossing to an adjacent street onto which he could turn safely and proceed in the desired direction. The appellant [footnote omitted] and appellee were personally acquainted with each other and while appellee was on the service station lot he observed the appellant motioning for him to come over. From appellee's police report it appears that the appellant's purpose was to get a look at the vehicle which appellee was operating, although it is not clear what purpose appellee had in responding. While driving toward appellant, appellee "misjudged the distance due to [his] inability...to see the full length of the Cushman through the curtain provided for a door." A collision ensued in which the appellant suffered the injuries for which he now seeks compensation.

The only issue is whether the appellee is entitled to the protection of governmental immunity.

[...]

We have been unable to locate any cases addressing the question of whether a deviation from the strict course of his duties will take a public official outside the protection of governmental immunity. It may be that the lack of such cases is due to the prevailing rule that police officers and similar officials will be held liable, under most circumstances, for the consequences of their negligence when performing routine functions, such as operating motor vehicles. (citation omitted). Maryland, however, has made no such distinction, conditioning a public official's immunity on the absence of malice and action within the scope of his authority. (citation omitted). In *Duncan v. Koustenis* [...], the Court acknowledged that in some states the rule is not to extend immunity to government employees when acting negligently on the theory that negligent acts fall outside their governmental authority, but, as we have said, Maryland does not follow this rule under the cases heretofore cited.

In the present case the contention is not that the appellee exceeded the scope of his authority in the jurisdictional sense; nor is it argued that mere negligence took his acts outside the realm of his governmental authority. Rather, the argument is that the appellee was not performing his assigned police duties at the time of the accident. Appellant contends that by deviating from his planned course appellee embarked upon a purely personal mission of his own and temporarily suspended the performance of his role as a policeman. In the absence of any case law on the precise question it may be helpful to turn to the authorities dealing with the somewhat analogous problem of when an employee is acting within the scope of his employment for purposes of applying the doctrine of *respondeat superior*. That doctrine holds that an employer may be held liable for damages negligently caused by his employee while the employee was acting within the scope of his employment. (citation omitted). Ordinarily, the question of whether a servant has acted within the scope of his employment is for the finder of fact, (citation omitted), but "[w]here there is no conflict in the evidence relating to the question and but one inference can be drawn therefrom, the question is one of law for the court. (citation omitted).

In determining whether a servant's acts are within the scope of employment the courts also have attempted to draw a line between "detours" and "frolics." The former being treated as within the scope of employment and the latter being considered a complete abandonment of it. [footnote omitted] (citation omitted). A variety of factors have been cited as bearing on the determination of whether a particular deviation amounts to a detour or a frolic.

"These factors include the time and place of the deviation, its extent with relation to the prescribed route, whether its motivation is in part to serve the master, and whether it is the usual sort of deviation for servants on such a job." (citation omitted).

In *Carroll v. Hillendale Golf Club* [...], the Court of Appeals adopted the following statement [...]:

"When the servant's deviation from the strict course of his employment or duty is slight and not unusual, the court may determine as a matter of law that he is still executing the master's business, and if the deviation is very marked and unusual it may determine the contrary."

In *Ritchie*, a servant on his return from picking up a load of manure for his master took a slight detour to a shoemaker's shop for his own purposes. While at the shoemaker's his master's team ran away causing damage to the plaintiff. The Court held that at a minimum this case presented a question of fact on the scope of employment issue; but it went on to say that, even as a matter of law, the slight deviation from the strict course of his master's business was insufficient to take the servant's action outside the scope of employment. (citation omitted).

> In *Marquardt v. United States* [...] a federal employee was traveling in his own automobile to an official work assignment while at the same time traveling to a personal destination en route. The facts were stipulated and the United States District judge presiding over the case held that the employee was acting within the scope of his employment, applying the following rule:
>
> "'...where the servant is combining his own business with that of his master, or attending to both at substantially the same time, no nice inquiry will be made as to which business the servant was actually engaged in when a third person was injured; but the master will be held responsible, unless it clearly appears that the servant could not have been directly or indirectly serving his master.'" (citation omitted).
>
> The facts in the present case are susceptible of the inference that appellee deviated from the direct course of his duties in order to answer the call of appellant. [footnote omitted] This deviation was so slight that under the principles in the cases mentioned above it may be held as a matter of law to be insufficient to constitute a "frolic" which would take the appellee outside the scope of his employment as a police officer. While we recognize the differences between determining scope of authority for the purpose of fixing liability on an employer and for the purpose of determining whether a policeman is entitled to governmental immunity, we think the problems are sufficiently close that the analogy is proper.
>
> *Judgment affirmed.*

Not only did the court find that the police officer was acting within the scope of the employment, but it agreed with the trial court that whatever deviation from the officer's fulfilling an obligation, it was so slight as not to be an issue.

Intentional Torts

Previously, U.S. courts refused to hold the principal liable for the willful tortious conduct of the agent. That view has softened if the intentional tort may be within the scope of the employment. The general rule is that the principal will be held liable for the intentional torts of the agent when the agent is acting wholly or in part to further the principal's business (see box below).

> ### INTENTIONAL TORTS
>
> Thus he will be held liable where his bus driver crowds a competitor's bus into a ditch, or assaults a trespasser to eject him from the bus, or a salesman makes fraudulent statements about the products he is selling, or defames a competitor or disparages his product, or where the servant resorts to false imprisonment or malicious prosecution for a like purpose. Thus a railway ticket agent who assaults, arrests or slanders a passenger, in the belief that he has been given a counterfeit bill for a ticket is within the scope of his employment.
>
> W. Page Keeton et. al., *Prosser & Keeton on the Law of Torts* §70 at 506 (5th ed. 1984)

Yet if the agent acts for entirely personal motives unconnected to the employer's interests, he or she has deviated from the scope of the employment. So if an agent follows a pre-established route to visit clients, the principal generally will not be liable when the agent also robs ATMs along the way.

The court in the *Webb* case, analyzing the agent's motives and the interests of the principal, found that the agent's sexual assault on a customer was not in furtherance of the principal's interests (see Case in Point 14-5).

CASE IN POINT 14-5

Webb v. Jewel Companies, Inc.

137 Ill. App. 3d 1004 (1st Dist. 1985)

This is an appeal from the dismissal, for failure to state a cause of action, of the second amended Count I of a complaint filed on behalf of the minor plaintiff against defendants, Charles Hiley and Jewel Companies, Inc. (Jewel) for damages because of injuries she suffered as a result of a sexual assault allegedly committed by Hiley while he was employed as a security guard for Jewel. The sole issue presented for review is the propriety of the dismissal.

In Count I, as amended, plaintiff alleged in substance that she was a customer in a Jewel supermarket located in Chicago; that she had just purchased an item when Hiley, acting in his capacity as a security guard, stopped her and then led her to an enclosed office for the purpose of searching her; and that in the course of that search, he sexually molested her. The trial court granted Jewel's motion to dismiss Count I with prejudice, and this appeal followed [....]

Plaintiff contends that the allegations in Count I are sufficient to state a cause of action against Jewel on the theory of respondeat superior. It is Jewel's position, however, that Count I is both legally and factually deficient and that dismissal was, therefore, proper.

Under the doctrine of *respondeat superior*, an employer may be liable for the negligent, wilful, malicious or even criminal acts of its employees when such acts are committed in the course of employment and in furtherance of the business of the employer; however, the employer is not liable to an injured third party where the acts complained of thereby were committed solely for the benefit of the employee. [...]

In the instant case, plaintiff asserts that the trial court erred in ruling, as a matter of law, that Hiley was not acting within the scope of his employment, but rather acted solely for his own benefit in molesting her. [...] [S]he argues that this was a question of fact which should have been left to a jury for determination. We disagree. [...]

[T]he fact remains that the sexual molestation of a young girl by a security guard is nonetheless a deviation having no relation to the business of Jewel or the furtherance thereof. Thus, we find that the trial court properly dismissed the second amended Count I of plaintiff's complaint for failing to state a cause of action.

Dangerous Instrumentality

Some jurisdictions impose liability on a principal when an agent, under the grant of authority, uses a **dangerous instrumentality**—that is, an instrument or material that is inherently dangerous. For example, the courts could find vicarious liability in the use of dynamite or the sale of poisonous gases. A finding of liability will apply only when the agent acts within the scope of the grant of authority and legal control over the instrumentality. The rejection of a finding of vicarious liability against a principal may be due more to a principal's strict liability rather than to any change in philosophy regarding vicarious liability (see Chapter 12).

Yet courts are open to the possibility that the principal may be vicariously liable where the agent used an inherently dangerous instrumentality. In Case in Point 14-6, a boat repair business subcontracted some of the work of refurbishing a vessel. When a passenger suffers injury, the principal might be liable.

CASE IN POINT 14-6

Fisherman's Paradise, Inc. v. Greenfield
417 So.2d 306 (Fla. Dist. Ct. App. 3d Dist. 1982)

Appellee Melvin Greenfield took his ten-year-old boat to Fisherman's Paradise for refurbishing. Fisherman's Paradise subcontracted part of the work, including replacement of the refrigerator, to Endeavor Marine. During a boating trip, the refrigerator broke loose from its mounting and injured Mrs. Greenfield. The Greenfields sued both Fisherman's Paradise and Endeavor Marine. They alleged that Fisherman's Paradise was responsible for the negligent installation and included a claim predicated upon strict liability. They also charged Endeavor Marine with negligently installing the refrigerator. Upon motion, the trial court entered summary judgment against both Fisherman's Paradise and Endeavor Marine, denying the motion for summary judgment filed by Fisherman's Paradise. In this appeal, Fisherman's Paradise contends it should not be held liable for negligent acts of Endeavor Marine, because it operated as an independent contractor. Finding that genuine issues of material fact remain to be decided, we reverse the summary judgment.

According to the general rule, an employer is not liable for the negligent acts of an independent contractor because he lacks control over the manner in which the work is performed [....] One of the many exceptions to the general rule, however, occurs when the employer's liability arises from the contractor's negligent performance of inherently dangerous tasks [....] Furthermore, an employer may not escape liability for the creation of an inherently dangerous condition (at least on premises where public use is invited) unless it was not discoverable on reasonable inspection [....]

Whether Fisherman's Paradise may be held liable for Endeavor's negligent conduct under the foregoing principles is subject to a factual determination. We find no merit in the arguments presented in support of liability on other grounds. We therefore reverse the summary judgment and remand for further proceedings.

If a principal could discover an inherently dangerous condition through reasonable inspection, the principal may be vicariously liable.

■ INDEPENDENT CONTRACTOR

Under the common law, an employer will generally not experience vicarious liability for the tortious actions of an **independent contractor** (see box below).

INDEPENDENT CONTRACTORS
[T]he employer of an independent contractor is not liable for physical harm caused to another by an act or omission of the contractor or his servants.

Restatement (Second) of Torts §409 (1956)

When a Worker Is an Independent Contractor

When employers need someone with a specific set of skills or experience to do a particular task, they often hire an independent contractor. No fixed definition exists for when someone works as an independent contractor, as Professor Dobbs notes:

DEFINITION OF AN INDEPENDENT CONTRACTOR

Independent contractors are usually persons who are perceived to be operating their own business and hence not subject to the employer's right of control over the manner, means, and details of the work. [footnote omitted]

Dobbs, *The Law of Torts* §336, (2000)

Neither the employer nor the independent contractor expects the employment arrangement to last beyond completing the task. The employer exerts no specific control over the independent contractor, but specifies only what needs to be done so that the independent contractor can decide the methods needed to complete the assignment. An employer usually does not pay an independent contractor hourly wages, instead paying a flat fee to get the job done, does not pay taxes on the independent contractor's wages nor provides benefits such as unemployment compensation or medical insurance coverage. Because of the distinct nature of each task, no set standards exist for determining whether a worker is an employee or an independent contractor (see table below).

What a Court Might Consider to Determine Whether a Worker Is an Independent Contractor
• Degree of control over the methods the worker uses to fulfill employer's wishes
• Whether the work receives a flat fee or an hourly wage
• That the employer has provided benefits such as unemployment compensation or health insurance coverage
• If the employer contributed to the payment of taxes on an worker's wages

Not Vicariously Liable

If the employer has no control over the performance of the work and the work is to be regarded as the independent contractor's own, the courts often have concluded that only the contractor faces responsibility for a tortious act. On the other hand, if the employer could control the contractor's performance of the work, the employer could be found vicariously liable for the contractor's tortious conduct.

For instance, assume that Danforth asked his neighbor, Johnson, to cut his lawn while he was away on vacation. In the course of cutting the lawn the following week and unaware of Danforth's exact property line, Johnson mowed over Mrs. Goodhart's prize lilies. Johnson would be considered an independent contractor hired only to perform a specific task and not subject to Danforth's control. Any harm caused by tortious conduct on Johnson's part would not be Danforth's responsibility. Mrs. Goodhart's action would be directed at Johnson.

Some courts recently have applied the rationale of vicarious liability when an employer–independent contractor relationship exists. If the employer benefits from the relationship, the employer should expect to face liability for tortious conduct that occurred while the independent contractor fulfilled the terms of the employment contract. The employer selected the contractor, may recoup the funds paid out in damages from the independent contractor, and would be best able to spread the risk of an award in damages to customers as a cost of doing business. Paralegal students should survey the law periodically as some courts may continue to reject this argument.

Exceptions to the Rule

Under the general rule, principals don't bear responsibility for torts caused by an independent contractor. Exceptions to the rule fall into three categories (see table below).

Exceptions to the Rule That a Principal Is Not Vicariously Liable for the Actions of an Independent Contractor
• Negligence of the principal in directing the independent contractor's work • Where the principal attempts to have the independent contractor engage in a non-delegable duty • When the independent contractor engages in an inherently dangerous activity on behalf of the principal

Negligence of the Principal

An employer's liability for the conduct of an independent contractor may be based on a failure to exercise reasonable care. The following list outlines ways an employer could fail in this duty (see table below).

Ways in Which an Employer Has Failed to Exercise Reasonable Care Regarding an Independent Contractor
• in giving orders or directions on how the work is to be done, • to employ a competent independent contractor, • to take precautions in advance to allow the work to be done safely, • in performance of his or her own work, or • in supervising equipment and tools.

For example, a principal owes a duty of reasonable care when selecting an independent contractor to complete a task. If a principal failed to check the contractor's credentials (for example, an individual who claimed to be licensed to do a particular job), the principal would be liable for any resulting injuries. When a principal hires an independent contractor to rewire an electrical fuse box but did not check to see whether the individual was licensed, the principal would be liable for damages from the fire sparked by a short circuit in the rewired fuse box.

When the employer is negligent in failing to exercise reasonable care in the direction of the work, he or she may be found liable (see box below).

> **EMPLOYER'S NEGLIGENCE**
>
> The employer of an independent contractor is subject to the same liability for physical harm caused by an act or omission committed by the contractor pursuant to order or directions negligently given by the employer, as though the act or omission were that of the employer himself.
>
> *Restatement (Second) of Torts* §410 (1965)

A fundamental principle of negligence law states that when one negligently directs another, that person will face liability for the consequences of failing to give sufficient direction to a worker. An employer negligently directs the work of an independent contractor when the employer knew (or should have known) that the work involved an unreasonable risk of harm to another. This rule often applies in construction cases where the employer has supplied a contractor with defective plans or specifications. In such a case, the employer is liable for the acts or omissions of the contractor.

Non-Delegable Duty

Another exception to the general rule that an employer can avoid liability for torts caused by an independent contractor involves a **non-delegable duty.** An employer may have a duty, arising under contract or by law, that cannot be delegated to another. For example, if a famous surgeon assigned a new medical student to do a complicated surgery, the surgeon would be liable for any injuries caused by the student.

Examples of a Non-Delegable Duty
• Those providing transportation services must transport passengers safely;   • Rail lines must properly fence its right of way;   • Communities must maintain sidewalks to remain safe; or   • A business owner must keep the premises in a safe condition for its business visitors.

Paralegal student should consult state statutes and case law to determine which duties may be considered non-delegable.

Inherently Dangerous Activities

The third exception involves the independent contractor engaging in inherently dangerous activities on behalf of the principal. The principal, not the independent contractor, will be held responsible for damages occurring in the performance of a principal's inherently dangerous work. These activities include keeping vicious animals and handling electrical wires, dynamite, or fireworks. The principal generally remains responsible for any highly risky work.

Collateral Negligence

A principal generally will not face liability for the collateral negligence of the independent contractor. **Collateral negligence** involves negligence that is secondary to the inherent risks of the work that the principal has the independent contractor perform. A principal may face liability for risks inherent in fulfilling the work, such as building a dam. Yet the principal will not face liability when the independent contractor negligently fails to control some detail of the work. For example, if the independent contractor fails to check if the concrete has properly set and a leak spouts shortly after the dam is completed, a court likely will not hold the principal liable for damages caused by the leak. If the negligence of an independent contractor significantly falls outside the risk for which the employer is responsible, the independent contractor remains liable.

Case in Point 14-7 considers the *Wilton* case, in which dynamite subsequently exploded and caused injury after an independent contractor left it under a sidewalk.

CASE IN POINT 14-7

Wilton v. City of Spokane
73 Wash. 619 (1913)

The respondent brought this action against the city of Spokane, Foster & Hindle, a copartnership, and the Washington Water Power Company, a corporation, to recover for personal injuries. Before issue was joined on the complaint, the action was dismissed as to the Washington Water Power Company. Afterwards it was prosecuted to a judgment against the other defendants, both of whom appeal. The facts of the case are not complicated, nor seriously in dispute. The city of Spokane let a contract to Foster & Hindle for the improvement of one of its streets. The work included the grading of a roadway along the center of the street and the construction of a parking strip and a sidewalk on each side thereof. By the terms of the contract Foster & Hindle were made independent contractors, responsible to the city for the result of the work only, not as to the manner in which it was to be performed. In grading the street to its proper level, a ledge of rock was encountered which the contractors removed by blasting; the explosive used being dynamite. In the course of the work a blast put in near the bottom of the required grade failed to explode, and the contractors, instead of removing it, covered it up and constructed the surface of the street over it. Afterwards the city accepted the work as in compliance with the contract without knowledge of the unexploded blast. Some months later the Washington Water Power Company applied for and was granted permission to erect a line of poles along the margin of the improved street on which to string electric wires for lighting purposes. The holes in which to set the poles had to be dug somewhat deeper than the street was cut down in the performance of the improvement work, and where the ledge of rock was encountered the rock necessary to be removed was broken up by blasting. While the employees of the Washington Water Power Company, among whom was the respondent, were drilling for the purpose of putting in a blast in one of such holes, the drill encountered the unexploded blast left in the rock by Foster & Hindle, causing it to explode. The explosion put out one of the respondent's eyes and otherwise seriously injured him, and he brought the present action, with the result before stated.

The record does not make clear the grounds on which the judgment against the city was rested. Several grounds on which it is thought it may rest, however, are suggested in the argument, and these we will notice briefly in their order. It is first said that the work was of such a character that it could not be let to independent contractors, and that the city could not escape liability for the negligent performance by endeavoring to so let it. The particular contention is that the work of blasting rock in an inhabited portion of a city is so inherently dangerous in itself that public policy forbids that the city be permitted to let the work to an independent contractor. But if this be the general rule, we do not think the present case falls within it. The leaving of an unexploded blast of dynamite in the rock below the surface of a street is not an incident to the work of blasting rock to make a grade for a street. Such an action is negligence and nothing else, and the city is liable for the act only in the same way, and to the same extent, that it would have been liable had the contractors left the dynamite on the surface of the street in the traveled part of the roadway on leaving the work; it is liable for injuries resulting therefrom only in the case it knew of its being so left, or by the exercise of reasonable diligence could have known of it. But the employer is not liable where the obstruction or defect in the street causing the injury is wholly collateral to the contract work, and entirely the result of the negligence or wrongful acts of the contractor, subcontractor, or his servants. In such a case the immediate author of the injury is alone liable [....] There is no evidence that the city had knowledge of the existence of this unexploded blast, and, of course, there was no sort of diligence that it could have exercised which would have made it acquainted with the fact.

A second reason suggested for sustaining the judgment against the city is that the relation of master and servant existed between the city and the respondent. But it is manifest that the respondent was not in the employ of the city. He was a mere licensee upon the street, and while the city owed him the duty to refrain from doing him willful injury, and from setting snares for him, it owed no duty to provide him with a safe place in which to work.

Again, it is said that the city is responsible for the condition of its streets, and hence liable for any injury arising from defects therein, no matter by whom the defect may have been caused. But the rule is not so broad as this. The city is liable only for those defects in its streets of which it has knowledge, or by the exercise of reasonable diligence could have obtained knowledge. It is not a guarantor of the safe condition of its streets for all purposes and at all times. Its full duty is performed when it exercises reasonable diligence in keeping its streets in repair. We think therefore that the court erred in holding the city liable for the injury.

The appellants Foster & Hindle make the contention that the evidence is insufficient to justify the verdict against them. They argue that when they completed the contract and turned the street over to the city, and the city accepted the work as in compliance with the contract, their liability to third persons for the negligent performance of the work ceased, and from thence-forth the city alone was responsible for any such negligent performance. This argument is perhaps sound in so far as it relates to defects in the street arising from a mere negligent performance of the work, but we think it has no application to an act of the nature here charged against the contractors. The leaving of the unexploded charge of dynamite in the rock beneath the surface of the street was not a matter connected with the contract work. It was a matter wholly collateral thereto, and was, as we have said, of itself a negligent and wrongful act, rendering the persons wrongfully leaving it there liable to any one who in the lawful pursuit of his own business should be injured thereby. The liability of the contractors for the injury arising from the explosion rests on the same principle it would have rested had they knowingly or negligently left the explosive on the surface of the street and a traveler on the street had come into contact therewith and received an injury; it rests on the wrongful and negligent nature of the act itself. There is a distinction between an act of negligence imminently dangerous to the lives of others and one that is not so. In the former case the party guilty of the negligence is liable to the party injured, whether there be a contract between them or not; in the latter, the negligent party is liable only to the party with whom he contracted, and on the ground that negligence is a breach of the contract [....] We conclude therefore that the trial judge was right in refusing to sustain the challenge of the appellants Foster & Hindle.

The judgment will be reversed and remanded, with instructions to dismiss as to the appellant city of Spokane, but will stand affirmed as to the other appellants.

Since the city of Spokane had no control over the placement of the dynamite, the court would not hold it liable in damages for the subsequent injuries.

■ JOINT ENTERPRISE

In a **joint enterprise,** a group—with an equal say in the direction of the work— joins to accomplish a particular goal. To determine the nature of vicarious liability for members of a joint enterprise, a court would need first to determine whether a joint enterprise exists. Professor Dobbs defines the joint enterprise as follows:

> ### THE NATURE OF A JOINT ENTERPRISE
> A joint venture is a species of partnership. It characteristically involves a sharing of profits and losses by those who undertake it, but is usually limited in time and devoted to a single purpose. A special version of the joint venture in turn is the joint enterprise, which does not necessarily involve a profit and loss sharing arrangement. The joint enterprise is found to exist when two or more persons tacitly or expressly undertake an activity together—usually an automobile trip—with common purpose, community of interest and an equal right to a voice in the control.
>
> Dobbs, *The Law of Torts* §340, (2000)

A joint enterprise, occasionally called a *common enterprise*, has these four essential elements:

Elements That Need to Exist for the Creation of a Joint Enterprise
• an agreement among the associates • a common purpose to be carried out by the group • a community of monetary interest • an equal voice in the control and direction of the enterprise which includes an equal right of control

Each of the people in a joint enterprise are vicariously responsible for the others' conduct for torts committed within the scope of the enterprise. So, each group member acts as an agent to the joint enterprise.

Joint Enterprise as Less Formal Business Association

Unlike a typical joint venture or partnership, the joint enterprise can include less formal associations dedicated to limited goals. A joint enterprise might involve the construction of a church, where a few specific members of the congregation have assumed responsibility for its construction.

Paralegals should carefully review state law for any changes regarding the vicarious liability of a joint enterprise.

■ AUTOMOBILE ACCIDENTS

Consider two situations involving automobile accidents that raise an issue of vicarious liability.

Joint Enterprise

Assume that a passenger and a driver are traveling for the purposes of advancing the business interests of a joint enterprise. If the driver's negligence results in an accident and injuries to the passenger, the passenger will not receive damages for the injuries suffered since the driver and passenger are part of the same joint enterprise. Instead, the passenger could recover damages from the driver personally—even though both driver and passenger traveled on behalf of their joint enterprise (see box below).

JOINT ENTERPRISE

1. Any one of several persons engaged in a joint enterprise, such as to make each member of the group responsible for physical harm to other persons caused by the negligence of any member, is barred from recovery against such other persons by the negligence of any member of the group.
2. Any person engaged in such a joint enterprise is not barred from recovery against the member of the group who is negligent, but is barred from recovery against any other member of the group.

Restatement (Second) of Torts §491(1956)

Assume that Freeley and Bairley decide to invest in a race horse and go shopping. They decide to travel by pickup truck with a horse trailer to the Bluegrass region of their state. Rounding a sharp curve on a steep hill, Freeley loses control of the vehicle and strikes a tree, injuring Bairley. Bairley's cause of action against Freeley is barred by the law of vicarious liability as it applies to joint enterprises. Bairley can sue Freeley as an individual, however.

Where No Joint Enterprise Exists

A court will not likely view a group of friends traveling together in an automobile as a joint enterprise. Therefore, if the driver gets into an accident, injured passengers will not be barred from filing suit against the theory of vicarious liability.

Look at the *Galliher* case in Case in Point 14-8, which involves the injury of one passenger in a group going to look at used cars.

 ## CASE IN POINT 14-8

Galliher v. Holloway
130 Ill. App. 3d 628 (5th Dist. 1985)

Appeal is taken from a judgment of the circuit court of Madison County, awarding plaintiff $30,000 for personal injuries. On the evening of January 4, 1981, Melissa Galliher (plaintiff) was riding as a passenger in her automobile when it collided with a vehicle owned by James Holloway (defendant). Plaintiff's vehicle was driven by Kevin Hay (third-party defendant). Paul Edmundston and Stephen Jones were also passengers in plaintiff's automobile. Mr. Edmundston was interested in purchasing an automobile, and the four had journeyed to several locations in order to observe used vehicles.

Defendant's vehicle had stalled on Illinois Route 143. Defendant testified that he had his lights on as he attempted to restart the engine. Plaintiff, third-party defendant, and Stephen Jones testified that they did not observe lights on defendant's automobile. Defendant admitted that his emergency flashers were not activated. The front end of plaintiff's vehicle collided with the rear end of defendant's vehicle, and plaintiff, who was seated in the front passenger seat, was jolted forward into the windshield. Plaintiff sustained injuries to her forehead and mouth. Third-party defendant estimated his speed immediately before the collision at 45 miles per hour. Additional testimony established that defendant occasionally had trouble starting his automobile; however, the vehicle had received substantial repairs two days prior to the accident. [...]

Defendant maintains that, as a matter of law, he was not negligent, and that the trial court erred in submitting the issue for resolution by the jury. Defendant contends that he was confronted with a "sudden mechanical failure." This failure, defendant argues, was the result of a defective condition in defendant's automobile of which defendant had no knowledge; moreover, the defect could not have been discovered by defendant's reasonable inspection of the vehicle. Even if this factual assertion were not subject to dispute, the allegations of defendant's negligent conduct extend to defendant's purported behavior after the mechanical failure occurred. Plaintiff alleged that defendant failed to exercise proper care by defendant's failure to keep his lights on as well as defendant's failure to pull his vehicle off the road. Defendant admitted that, even without the use of his vehicle's power steering, it would have been possible for defendant to remove his vehicle from the highway. Defendant further admitted that he failed to turn on his emergency flashers. These facts, together with the conflicting testimony regarding whether defendant even had his lights activated at the time of the accident, provided factual questions bearing directly on the issue of defendant's negligence. The question was properly submitted to the jury for resolution [....]

Defendant also contends that the trial court erred in denying defendant's motions for a directed verdict and for judgment notwithstanding the verdict. Defendant's allegation of error rests upon the compound premise that (1) the negligence of third-party defendant, the driver of the vehicle in which plaintiff was a passenger, was the proximate cause of plaintiff's injuries, and (2) that third-party defendant's negligence should be imputed to plaintiff because plaintiff and third-party defendant were engaged in a "joint venture." A joint venture, by virtue of which negligence may be imputed from the driver to occupants of an automobile, exists where driver and occupant are engaged in a journey which is part of a business enterprise in which the parties have a mutual interest [....] Defendant argues that a common interest of plaintiff and third-party defendant in helping their friend shop for an automobile, together with third-party defendant's act of purchasing gasoline for plaintiff's vehicle, established the requisite business enterprise. The mere sharing of incidental expenses incurred during the journey does not, however, constitute the business purpose essential to a joint venture; neither may the endeavor of aiding a friend in shopping for an automobile reasonably be considered as such [....] The negligence of third-party defendant was not, therefore, imputable to plaintiff under this theory [....]

For the foregoing reasons, the judgment of the circuit court is affirmed.

In this case, the court ruled that something more than sharing the gas expenses must occur for a joint enterprise to exist, so that the third-party defendant's negligence was not imputed to the passenger.

A Distinction of No Difference Involving the Availability of Insurance

The idea of imputing the negligence of a motorist to the passenger on business for a joint enterprise, and not in situations involving only social trips, defies rational explanation. A passenger traveling on business for a joint enterprise would have as much right to control the direction of the vehicle, since they were both part of the joint enterprise—something in fact that's not realistically possible. The right of control is a fiction imposed by law, and does not in fact exist in most cases when the passenger realistically has little or no control over the vehicle (see box below).

CRITIQUE

One must seriously doubt the logic and fairness of imposing vicarious responsibility, whether as plaintiff or as defendant, upon the passenger who is engaged in a "joint enterprise," for the negligence of his driver. The contractual agreement by which he is said to enter into such an arrangement is all too obviously a fiction in situations where the parties have merely gotten together for the ride; and upon this there is erected a second fiction, that the passenger shares a "right of control" of the operation of the vehicle; and on this is erected in turn a third fiction, that the driver is his agent or servant. This top heavy structure tends to fall of its own weight.

W. Page Keeton et. al., *Prosser & Keeton on the Law of Torts* § 72 at 522 (5th ed. 1984)

What seems to have happened is that legal scholars, courts, and legislatures have taken to shifting financial responsibility to the party best able to afford insurance coverage. By creating a duty of reasonable care owed to all passengers by a driver, the courts can be spared denying coverage to a passenger who was on business for the joint enterprise when a collision happened.

Automobile Consent Statutes

In most states, an **automobile consent statute** imposes vicarious liability on the owner of an automobile for the negligence of those driving the vehicle. The owner does not face absolute liability, only for injuries that arose within the scope of the consent to use the vehicle. An owner can escape liability for the actions of a driver who has used the vehicle beyond the scope of permission. The clear purpose of such legislation is to protect injured persons from the financial irresponsibility of drivers. But a driver who goes beyond the scope of the consent to use may likely have no insurance coverage—hence, the need to borrow the car—so that no one would be financially liable. Courts, then, might stretch an interpretation of what constitutes the scope of consent to include the owner, as the owner often will have insurance coverage.

Family Purpose Doctrine

Under the **family purpose doctrine** (or *family car doctrine*), the owner becomes the principal and the family member, the agent. The agent has to have permission to drive the vehicle and be a member of the owner's household. Most states have abandoned this doctrine through the enactment of automobile consent statutes. Paralegal students should carefully review individual state legislation to determine the status of the consent statute.

◼ DRAM SHOP LIABILITY

The concept of vicarious liability may provide the rationale, in some states, to hold sellers of alcoholic beverages liable for damages that arose from the sale of liquor. Under a **dram shop act** (also known as a *civil liability act)*, the seller of alcoholic beverages knew or should have known that the sale of alcohol led to a level of intoxication that foreseeably led to an accident. Liability could depend upon several factors (see box below).

FACTORS A COURT MAY CONSIDER WHEN DETERMINING DRAM SHOP LIABILITY

- a theory of negligence by creating an unreasonable risk of injury
- sale of liquor to a minor
- the intoxication of the buyer

Liability may arise upon a *sale* of the liquor and for just *furnishing* liquor to an intoxicated person. For instance, assume that the Wards invited several close friends to their home to see a video of their recent trip to Qingdao. The Wards served a special Chinese punch with an extremely high alcohol content to the guests as they watched the show. Assume further that one of the guests, Sotto, was intoxicated when he arrived. Failing to appreciate what he was viewing, Sotto became even more intoxicated. Upon leaving the party, he negligently backed his automobile into the Wards' neighbor, causing severe injury. Depending upon the jurisdiction, the Wards could face dram shop liability to their neighbor for the injuries caused by Sotto.

Consider the Florida Supreme Court's discussion of the history of the development of dram shop liability in the *Ellis* case (see Case in Point 14-9).

 ## CASE IN POINT 14-9

Ellis v. N.G.N. of Tampa, Inc.
586 So.2d 1042 (Fla. 1991)

[...] This case concerns the liability of a vendor of alcoholic beverages for sales to a habitual drunkard. It commenced when Mary Evelyn Ellis filed a complaint alleging that her son, Gilbert Ellis, an alleged habitual drunkard, consumed approximately twenty alcoholic drinks served to him at a bar owned by the respondent N.G.N. of Tampa, Inc. (N.G.N.), and operated by the respondent Norbert G. Nissen. The complaint alleged that, after consuming the drinks, an intoxicated Gilbert Ellis drove his car in a manner that caused it to overturn and crash; that he sustained severe injuries, including permanent brain damage; that he has since been declared incompetent, and his mother, the complainant and petitioner, Mary Evelyn Ellis, is his legal guardian. The complaint against N.G.N. and Nissen seeks compensatory and punitive damages on the grounds that N.G.N. and Nissen served Gilbert Ellis "knowing that [he] was a person addicted to the use of any or all alcoholic beverages."

[...] To resolve this issue, it is first necessary to review the legal history of the duty placed on a vendor of alcoholic beverages. Prior to 1959, the common law established that a commercial vendor of alcoholic beverages could not be liable for the negligent sale of those beverages when either the purchaser or third persons were injured as a result of their consumption. This common law principle was based on the conclusion that the proximate cause of the injury was the consumption of the intoxicating beverage by the person, rather than the sale of intoxicating beverages to the person and, consequently, there could be no valid claim against a vendor for damages.

A change in this common law principle first occurred in 1959 when the Supreme Court of New Jersey, in *Rappaport v. Nichols* […], modified this consumption–sale distinction in the common law and, in the words of one commentator, "took upon itself to fill a judicially-perceived vacuum of restraint on commercial vendors of alcoholic beverages." […] In *Rappaport*, a tavern owner sold alcoholic beverages to a minor under circumstances in which the vendor knew the purchaser to be a minor. After consuming the alcohol, the minor became intoxicated and killed a third party while driving an automobile. In holding the vendor liable to the deceased's estate, the Supreme Court of New Jersey held:

[W]e are convinced that recognition of the plaintiff's claim will afford a fairer measure of justice to innocent third parties whose injuries are brought about by the unlawful and negligent sale of alcoholic beverages to minors and intoxicated persons, will strengthen and give greater force to the enlightened statutory and regulatory precautions against such sales and their frightening consequences, and will not place any unjustifiable burdens upon defendants who can always discharge their civil responsibilities by the exercise of due care.

[…] [T]hese cases emphasize, a major change had occurred in the legal principles governing an alcohol vendor's liability. Under the original doctrine, the vendor was absolved of liability because consumption of the alcohol was considered to be the cause of the conduct and the resulting damages, for which the vendor had no control. After *Rappaport* […] the critical fact was not consumption but whether, under the circumstances, it was foreseeable that injury or damage would occur after a sale, particularly when sales were made to persons who lacked the ability to make a responsible decision in the consumption of alcohol.

As a result of this judicial trend to extend liability towards vendors of alcoholic beverages, the legislature enacted section 562.51, now section 768.125, Florida Statutes (1989) [….] The statute effectively codified the original common law rule absolving vendors from liability for sales but provided exceptions for sales to those who were not of a lawful drinking age or to a person habitually addicted to alcoholic beverage use. […]

In summary […] although limited by the provisions of section 768.125, there is a cause of action against a vendor for the negligent sale of alcoholic beverages to a minor that results in the injury to or death of the minor or a third party. While we have not expressly addressed a case involving a habitual drunkard, we find that the same law applies because: (1) it is an express exception to the statute limiting a vendor's liability, and (2) it is also a sale of alcohol to a class of persons who lack the ability to make a responsible decision in the consumption of alcohol.

So as a policy matter, statutes have changed the common-law rule that denied liability and now impose liability on the sellers of alcoholic beverages for sales to intoxicated patrons.

States without a dram shop act have seen courts also reverse the common-law rule against liability, as Professor Dobbs explains:

NEW COMMON LAW CREATING LIABILITY FOR PROVIDERS OF ALCOHOL

Most courts without a Dram Shop statute now recognize a common law duty of reasonable care and impose liability when the licensed seller of alcohol negligently sells to a minor or intoxicated person who, as a result, causes injury to the plaintiff. If the harm is foreseeable, liability is not to be avoided merely because the provider furnished alcohol to a minor indirectly.

The new common law regime is not one of strict liability; the plaintiff must prove negligence. This ordinarily takes the form of evidence that, in violation of liquor regulations, the defendant negligently provided alcohol to a person whom the seller should have recognized as being a minor or intoxicated. The plaintiff must also prove proximate cause as in other negligence cases. The negligent provider who supplies alcohol to teenagers or intoxicated persons enhances the risk that the drinker will drive dangerously, but he does not necessarily create a risk that the drinker will set a house afire or commit rape and murder. But the proximate cause issue, as in other negligence cases, is for the jury where reasonable people could differ.

Dobbs, *The Law of Torts* §332, (2000)

KEY TERMS

SUMMARY

The law of vicarious liability is based on the relationship between the tortfeasor—the agent—and the person on whose behalf the agent is acting—the principal. Also referred to as the doctrine of *respondeat superior*, the principal faces liability for an agent's torts when the agent is acting within the scope of the principal–agent relationship. Vicarious liability imposes liability upon the party best able to bear the loss.

In some instances, even if the agent is an independent contractor, the principal may face tort liability. When people have formed a joint enterprise, each is an agent of the group so that the members of the joint enterprise share liability.

Vicarious liability may arise outside of a principal–agent relationship, such as with automobile consent statutes, where the owner of the car has granted permission to the driver to use the car, without regard to the driver's advancing the interests of the owner. This logic underlies dram shop acts, which impose liability upon an establishment that provides alcoholic beverages to an already intoxicated person.

CONCEPT REVIEW QUESTIONS

1. What is the doctrine of vicarious liability?
2. Discuss the various theories that support the doctrine of *respondeat superior*.
3. What is the principle of the allocation of risk?
4. List the criteria used in most states to determine the existence of a principal–agent relationship.
5. Describe the general rule for intentional torts as applied to the doctrine of vicarious liability.
6. Discuss the concept of an independent contractor.
7. What is the employer's liability for non-delegable duties?
8. List the four elements common to a joint enterprise.
9. What is a dram shop act?

CRITICAL THINKING APPLICATIONS

1. At a physician's office, an assistant reviews a patient's chart and discovers a chart entry, made in error, referring to a disease the patient has. The patient is a classmate of the assistant's child. The assistant warns her child to use caution when around the patient; soon, everyone is avoiding the patient. If the patient sues the physician for having disclosed confidential information and so, held the patient up to ridicule, would the physician win on a motion to dismiss the claim because the actions of the assistant were completely undertaken by the assistant and the physician had no role in the disclosure of the information?
2. Thorvald drives a paper route for the morning delivery. He uses his own car to get around. One morning, his brakes fail and he hits someone out walking a dog. The injured party sues Thorvald's employer, who raises as a defense the fact that Thorvald and not the employer had primary responsibility for the care and maintenance of the vehicle. Will this injured party prevail in court in getting damages from the employer? Why or why not?
3. Willy is a door-to-door salesman. He gets paid only if he makes a sale. Willy is given a sample case of the products to carry around. The provider of the sample case does not tell Willy when to start or to stop work but asks that Willy work only on the north side of the big city. One hot, long, frustrating day, Willy travels to the south side of town and on a highway overpass, flings the sample case onto a highway. A car hits the sample case on the roadway

and its driver is injured. In response to a suit brought by the injured driver against the provider of the samples case, the provider files a motion for summary judgment, on the grounds that as a matter of law, Willy was on a frolic and detour. In the alternative, the provider says that Willy was an independent contractor. Would a court grant summary judgment for the provider on either defense? Why or why not?

4. Jenna drives a truck. She has painted on the side of the vehicle, "Hammers on Wheels" because she occasionally responds to work requests from a business named "Hammers on Wheels." In the course of doing a repair job, Jenna accidentally causes injury to the person who has placed the request for the repair. That injured party sues "Hammers on Wheels," which claims as a defense that Jenna is an independent contractor and so, it wasn't liable for any damages caused by her. In your opinion, will this defense free "Hammers on Wheels" from any liability claim brought by the injured party? Explain your answer.

5. Plato volunteers to be a leader to a small group of boys in their early teens. This group is part of a large nonprofit organization that encourages the formation of such groups to teach boys about the wilderness and developing survival skills and a sense of consequence and responsibility for one's actions. On a camping trip, one boy stabs another out of anger, and the victim dies. The victim's family sues the large nonprofit organization because Plato was serving its interests at the time of the stabbing and so, should be liable for any damages that happened on a camping trip. Make a case why the large nonprofit organization will prevail at trial. Then offer up an explanation, consistent with the material in this course, to explain why the large nonprofit organization should bear some of the financial responsibility for the death of the boy.

6. Don works as a peanut vendor at a minor league baseball stadium. When a customer in an aisle calls out for a bag, Don makes an underhanded pitch that hits an adjacent patron. That person sues the business that provides Don with the peanuts. The provider of the peanuts argues that Don is an independent contractor and should therefore not be liable for his inability to pitch a packet of peanuts. Should this provider be vicariously liable for the injuries caused by Don's errant pitch?

7. Nia was looking for a passenger to share the cost of gas when driving home for winter break from college. Taylor learned of this and agreed to travel with Nia, splitting the cost of gasoline. During the trip home, an accident happens and Nia's car hits a pedestrian. Could the pedestrian sue Taylor as well as Nia, because they were on a joint enterprise? Why or why not?

8. Otto gets referrals to do house painting jobs. When he gets one, he goes to visit the house, works out a contract with the homeowner to get the building painted, and then does the painting. When Otto secures a contract for work, the referral agency gets 10% of what he gets paid. During one job, Otto accidentally knocks a bucket of paint onto the owner's tiny, expensive dog. The dog is drenched and needs very elaborate grooming to get the paint removed. The owner of the property sues the referral agency. Will the agency prevail on a motion to dismiss for the cost in damages to cleaning up the dog? Why or why not?

SKILL-BUILDING APPLICATION

Learned Hands, Inc., a temp agency that hired only those who had a master's degree or higher, provided the services of Jan Phillips to Arvinda Suresh, who was putting the final touches to a manuscript for a new textbook on employment law for paralegals. During the week that Jan worked for Arvinda, Jan copyedited the entire manuscript to make it gender neutral. Arvinda discovers this on a Friday, with the final and completed manuscript due the next Monday. At great expense, Arvinda gets the manuscript back into its original form by Wednesday and turns it in. Arvinda's publisher assesses a penalty for late delivery of the manuscript. If Arvinda wants to recover damages, who should Arvinda sue, in light of the materials in this chapter? Why? Does that determination change if Learned Hands, Inc. only refers people like Jan for work that someone like Arvinda needed to have done? If so, how?

42 U.S.C. §1983 A tort alleging that an official acted so as to deprive the civil rights of the plaintiff.

abatement In the context of the tort of nuisance, permission for a plaintiff to enter a defendant's land and use reasonable force, so as to end the nuisance. Most jurisdictions require the plaintiff to provide notice before entering a defendant's property.

abnormally dangerous activity In strict liability, the determination that a high degree of risk exists that harm will occur; the chance that harm will be great; and that reasonable care cannot eliminate this risk.

abuse of process A tort involving the misuse of the legal process, specifically, the civil process beyond its intended purpose.

act The process of doing something.

Act of God A sudden, unexpected, and extraordinary demonstration of the force of nature from which humans cannot protect themselves.

ad damnum clause The section of a complaint that specifies the damages award a plaintiff seeks from the court.

affirmed An appellate court's upholding of a ruling by a lower court.

alternates People selected to serve as jurors if one of the jurors cannot continue to serve.

alternative dispute resolution (ADR) A method of resolving a legal problem without going to trial; for example, arbitration or mediation.

answer A legal document filed in response to a plaintiff's filed complaint; usually contains statements by the defendant regarding allegations made by the plaintiff in the complaint.

appeal The process of reviewing decisions made during a trial by a court judge, including but not limited to the decision about whether the defendant was liable for the damages the plaintiff sustained.

arbitrator An unbiased third party who presides over the resolution of a legal problem between two parties. Such proceedings usually conclude much more quickly than a trial, since in arbitration proceedings, court procedures do not have to be followed.

assault Intent to cause apprehension of physical harm; an act creating such apprehension; and that harm is imminent.

assumption of risk A defense to a claim of negligence in cases where the plaintiff knowingly exposes himself or herself to danger and assumes responsibility for any harm.

attractive nuisance A doctrine stating that a landholder can be liable if an artificial condition on the property tempts children to trespass on the property to investigate further.

automobile consent statute A law that imposes vicarious liability on the owner of an automobile for the negligence of those driving the vehicle; also known as a *motor vehicle consent statute*.

avoidable consequences A doctrine that holds a plaintiff responsible for minimizing injuries due to his or her own actions.

bad faith breach of contract A tort in which the breaching party may have entered into an agreement simply with the intent to cheat the non-breaching party.

bar to action Circumstances that deny a plaintiff any chance of recovery under tort law.

battery A tort that involves the intent to cause physical harm; contact; done without permission.

breach An element of the tort of negligence; a failure to perform a legal obligation or duty.

burden of proof The obligation of a plaintiff, as the party who started the lawsuit, to provide sufficient evidence to establish each element of a tort.

business visitors Persons invited onto the premises for the purpose of conducting business.

"but-for" rule The concept of a defendant's liability stating that harm would not have otherwise come to a plaintiff without — "but for"—the conduct of the defendant.

case law Court decisions; rulings of courts that establish a point of law, which is supposed to be respected and followed by courts who consider the issue again in the future.

castle doctrine In the context of the use of force, the concept that a defendant does not have to retreat from his or her home when confronted with a threat that could be avoided by retreating safely before using force.

cause An act or omission that produces an effect, a result, or a consequence.

cause in fact As a matter of fact, a defendant's conduct was the cause of the plaintiff's injury.

cause of action A basis for filing a civil lawsuit.

caveat emptor An original rule of law regarding the purchase of goods, that a buyer has a duty to inspect goods before purchasing them; in Latin, means "Let the buyer beware."

challenge During the jury selection process, a strategy that legal counsel can use to seek the removal of individuals as possible jurors.

chattel An archaic term, meaning personal property.

citizen's arrest The ability of a private individual to arrest another individual for an offense.

civil suit A lawsuit designed to compensate an injured person for damages caused by the actions or inactions of another; the plaintiff need only show, by a preponderance of the evidence, that the defendant caused the plaintiff's injury and that the plaintiff should receive compensation in the form of damages.

class action suit A type of legal action in which the plaintiff files suit on behalf of those who experienced a loss like the plaintiff's, because of the defendant's conduct.

closing statement The statement made by legal counsel at the end of a trial; summarizes what the court and jury have seen during the trial and attempts to reinforce why that attorney's client must prevail.

code In the context of law, a collection of laws; for example, the complete body of federal laws is known as the *United States Code*.

collateral negligence Negligence that is secondary to the inherent risks of the work that a principal engages an independent contractor to perform.

collateral source rule A rule stating that a defendant may not benefit, through a reduction in an award of damages, from the fact that the plaintiff has received compensation for his or her injuries from some other source.

commercial disparagement A type of tortious interference with economic relations; involves injurious falsehoods made about aspects of another's business.

common law Law recognized by courts as commonly accepted; for example, killing with malice aforethought is commonly regarded as murder. Also known as *case law* or *judge-made law*.

comparative contribution A system of apportioning damages between defendants based upon their respective fault; involves an assessment by the trier of fact of the degree of fault of each defendant.

comparative fault Under strict liability, the practice of awarding damages by an amount proportional to the degree to which the plaintiff brought about the injury.

compensatory damages In negligence actions, the award intended to compensate the plaintiff for actual loss or injury.

complaint The document an injured party files to initiate a lawsuit; must contain information sufficient to notify the defendant about the nature of the dispute.

consent A defense; agreeing to participate; waiving the right to pursue an action in tort.

constitution The central document of authority for a government. Often describes the nature of government, the authority of different branches of government, and the relationship between individuals and the government.

constitutional tort An action in tort for the violation of a right described in the U.S. Constitution. For example, §1983 of Title 43 of the United States Code provides a civil tort action remedy for any person who has been deprived of his or her civil rights.

consumer protection laws Statutes intended to protect consumers from wrongful or deceptive business practices.

contract A legally valid and binding agreement.

contribution A situation under which a defendant against whom a judgment has been entered can recoup a proportionate share of the judgment from any other tortfeasors who contributed to the injury.

contributory negligence A situation in which a plaintiff's acts or omissions involved a breach of a duty to care for one's own safety, thus negating the possibility of recovery by the plaintiff.

control In vicarious liability, the principal's ability to dictate how the agent can serve the principal's interests best when exercising the authority granted from the principal.

conversion A tort in which a defendant takes possession of personal property so that an owner or possessor may not use it.

counterclaim A legal document filed by a defendant in response to a plaintiff's complaint. It contains defendant's claim for recovery due to the harm that arose out of the event(s) that caused plaintiff to file suit.

court reporters Books that contain court rulings; usually, a multivolume series of publications, categorized by the nature of the court, such as trial court rulings in the federal legal system or trial court rulings in a particular state.

criminal proceeding A type of lawsuit, filed only by a government, on the grounds that a defendant's actions or inactions disrupted the peace and safety of society. To win, the government must provide evidence, beyond a reasonable doubt, that the defendant committed the crime and should receive punishment,

which could include a fine, incarceration, or, in very rare circumstances, the death penalty.

cross-claim A legal document, filed by a defendant, to bring a third party into the proceeding. For example, a defendant might have driven a car that hit a plaintiff. The defendant could file a cross-claim against the mechanic who negligently repaired the brakes of the defendant's automobile, because the mechanic's actions actually created liability for the damages the plaintiff incurred.

damages A monetary award given to an injured party once that party has shown, by a preponderance of the evidence, that the defendant committed the tort that caused the injured party's injuries; sometimes known as *compensatory damages*.

dangerous instrumentality A principle in strict liability suits, referring to the use of a material or instrument that is inherently dangerous; for example, a mining company's use of dynamite in operating its business.

defamation A class of torts; disclosure of information with the intent to cause harm to the plaintiff.

defamatory statement Information whose release damages a plaintiff's reputation in the eyes of the community.

defective design A theory of product liability, based in strict liability; determined through the use of the consumer expectation test or the risk-utility test.

defendant The party who, according to the plaintiff, caused the plaintiff's injuries and should compensate the plaintiff for sustaining such damages.

deposition A type of discovery; involves asking someone a series of open-ended questions, often conducted in a law office.

deterrence One of the goals of criminal punishment. By imposing a sentence on a convicted defendant, society hopes to discourage such behavior (by the defendant or society) in the future.

detour A short or limited deviation from completing an assignment, then returning to complete the assignment. An issue might arise when determining if a principal should be liable for the acts of an agent, when the agent made a detour and a tort occurred.

discovery   A pre-trial process for un-covering all information that could prove relevant and material to resolving a question of law.

discovery rule   In the context of the defense of statute of limitations, the requirement that time is to be measured from when the tort is discovered, not from when it actually happened.

disparagement of business   False or misleading statements about a plaintiff's business.

disparagement of goods   False or mis-leading statements about a competitor's personal property.

disparagement of services   False or misleading statements about the services of a competitor.

disparagement of title   False or mis-leading statements about the ownership of property.

domesticated animals   Animals, like dogs or cats, which do relatively minor harm and provide great social benefit; owners may avoid a claim in strict liability since imposing that burden would be too much where so small a risk of injury exists.

dram shop act   Law that imposes liability upon a seller of alcoholic beverages who knew (or should have known) that selling alcohol to an intox-icated person would have foreseeably led to an accident. Also known as a *civil liability act*.

duty   An obligation requiring an indi-vidual to do or refrain from doing some-thing to protect others from harm.

duty of reasonable care   In the tort of negligence, the standard of conduct expected of everyone. In a claim for negligence, the plaintiff must show that the defendant owed this duty to the plaintiff and failed to meet this duty.

elements   Components of a tort that a plaintiff must prove, by a preponderance of the evidence, in order to win the suit.

Eleventh Amendment to the United States Constitution   The amendment that prevents citizens from using federal trial courts as a forum for suing a state.

eminent domain   The principle under which governments may take real or personal property if doing so would advance a public good. Under eminent domain, governments must pay the owner for the loss of the property.

employer–employee   A relationship that might give rise to vicarious liability, because an employer may be responsible for the conduct of an employee.

English common law   These court decisions, in England, over the cen-turies, served as the foundation of tort law in America.

equality rule   The notion that if a part-nership is found liable in damages for a plaintiff's injuries, each partner will pay an equal portion of the damages.

evidence   Information that the court has determined will help in resolving a dispute; information must be relevant and material before it can be admitted into evidence.

execution   A court order that allows a plaintiff to demand payment from a de-fendant for the damages set forth in the judgment.

fact   In a legal proceeding, an actual occurrence or event as determined by the evidence presented.

failure to warn   Under a claim of product liability, the defendant did not provide the plaintiff with information about a product's potential for danger-ousness and that failure contributed to the plaintiff's injuries.

false imprisonment   A tort, committed with the intent to restrain a plaintiff and performed without lawful authority.

family purpose doctrine   In the context of liability, the notion that if a family member is authorized to drive the family car and is operating the car for the benefit of the family when an acci-dent occurs; the owner of the family car may be liable even if the owner wasn't driving at the time of the accident. Also known as the *family car doctrine*.

Federal Rules of Civil Procedure (FRCP)   Rules of procedure used by the federal courts to conduct civil trials.

Federal Rules of Evidence   Rules regarding the admissibility and use of evidence.

Federal Tort Claims Act (FTCA)   Law that allows injured parties to sue the federal government as if it is a private individual.

fiduciary duty   A duty that requires exercising great care in offering service, since the person seeking the service likely would not detect any inaccuracy.

foreseeability   In the context of a claim in negligence, the reasonable an-ticipation that harm will occur from an act or omission.

fraud   A tort involving the intentional misrepresentation of information that causes harm to a plaintiff.

frolic   A material deviation from the grant of authority, such as when an agent makes a side-trip from a prescribed route to engage in personal business.

general verdict   A statement returned by the jury, declaring whether the plain-tiff has successfully made a valid claim for damages.

guest passenger statute   A law provid-ing that the driver of an automobile is liable to a gratuitous guest (as opposed to a paying customer) only for gross negligence or aggravated misconduct; also known as an *automobile guest statute*.

hornbook   A treatise used by law students or lawyers to study well-settled principles found in an area of law; for example, *Dobbs on the Law of Torts*.

immunity   A defense concept that protects individuals or governments from tort liability when fulfilling their official obligations.

implied warranty of fitness for a particular use   A promise made by a manufacturer and/or seller that the goods can be used in the manner intended for.

implied warranty of merchantability   A promise made by a manufacturer and/or seller that the goods are in good condition, for purposes of a sale; applies only to personal property.

imputed negligence   One person's negligence being legally transferred to another.

in loco parentis   The notion that adults with temporary care and custody over a child may use force to discipline that child, if allowed by statute; in Latin, literally "in place of a parent."

indemnification   Full reimbursement of a party who has paid a judgment to a plaintiff.

independent contractor   A worker with a specific set of skills or experience hired to do a particular task; usually receives no benefits; could be an agent.

injunction   A court order compelling action or inaction. Disobedience of an injunction can lead to prosecution for the crime of contempt of court.

intent   A desire to cause certain consequences.

intentional infliction of emotional distress   The deliberate act of causing psychological harm to a plaintiff by engaging in outrageous conduct.

intentional tort   An area of tort law in which a party faces civil liability for having sought to cause an injury to another.

interference with a contractual relationship   A type of tortious behavior in which a defendant deliberately seeks to damage economic relations by obstructing the completion of a contract.

interference with economic relations   A class of torts typically associated with the operation of a business.

interference with prospective economic advantage   A type of tortious behavior that damages economic relations, in which a defendant sabotages a plaintiff's efforts to acquire new business.

interplead   In a lawsuit, the joining of all parties to a lawsuit to determine who might share liability.

interrogatories   A type of discovery; involves sending a limited number of written questions to another party.

intervening cause   The act of a third person or some other force that produces injury to the plaintiff *after* the negligent conduct.

invasion of privacy   A class of torts; recognizes that individuals may wish to keep confidential those things to which the public should not freely have access. There are four versions.

invasion of privacy—appropriation   Using a plaintiff's name or likeness to gain economic advantage, without the plaintiff's authorization.

invasion of privacy—false light   A form of invasion of privacy in which a defendant makes material misrepresentations to the public about a plaintiff.

invasion of privacy—public disclosure of private facts   A type of invasion of privacy in which personal information is deliberately and offensively released without a plaintiff's permission and for which no legitimate public interest exists.

invasion of privacy—unreasonable intrusion   A type of invasion of privacy in which a defendant violates a plaintiff's solitude and seclusion.

invitation   Conduct on the part of the landholder that justifies the visitor's belief that his or her entry is welcomed.

invitee   A member of the public or a business visitor on public land.

joinder   A request by a party to add claims or parties to an existing lawsuit, so that all matters are resolved in one legal proceeding.

joint and several liability   The sharing of responsibility among defendants for an award in damages, with each having individual responsibility for the entire amount in damages or where damages are apportioned according to the degree of fault among the defendants.

joint enterprise   A group of individuals banding together to accomplish a particular goal, each with equal say in the direction of the work.

joint liability   The liability of two or more parties together.

judge-made law   The practice of using earlier court rulings to recognize what a society regards as illegal or what should be illegal; also known as *common law* or *case law*.

judgment   A determination, made by the judge, about a plaintiff's claim for liability, based upon what the jury has determined.

judicial review   The process by which a court properly gains authority to review a dispute of law; sometimes, narrowly, the process by which courts examine newly enacted statutes to determine their validity in light of what a constitution says.

jurisdiction   The authority of a court, government, or agency over an issue or problem; often related to location.

jury instructions   At the end of trial, statements made by the judge about the law that the jury should refer to when evaluating the evidence presented during the trial.

knowledge   Awareness or understanding gained through experience or study.

landholder   An owner or possessor of land or property.

landowner   An owner of land, whose claim of control is legally superior to any other such claim of control.

last clear chance   A legal doctrine that allows a plaintiff in a negligence action to recover damages regardless of his or her own negligence if the defendant had the last clear chance to avoid the injury.

law reviews   Periodicals, often published by law schools, that contain scholarly articles on the law.

lessee   The tenant, who gains a possessory interest in property.

lessor   A landholder who owns or manages property; also known as the *landlord*.

liability   A determination of financial responsibility for the injuries caused to another.

libel   A written defamatory statement communicated to a third person.

licensee   In the context of premises liability, one who is granted access to land. For example, someone having received authority to extract minerals from the land.

licensor   In the context of premises liability, one who grants access to land.

livestock   In determining strict liability, animals that are not defined as domesticated or wild. Livestock are generally kept for commercial purposes and their owners are responsible for preventing them from intruding on the property of others.

loss of consortium   An action in tort law seeking compensation from a relative of an injured party for the loss of companionship of that injured party.

malicious prosecution   Tort involving the misuse of the legal process, specifically, using the criminal process to harm another.

master–servant   Archaic usage for concept of principal–agent relationship. The "master" (principal) is responsible for the conduct of his or her "servant" (agent).

mediation   A method of dispute resolution in which an unbiased third party helps the disputing parties arrive at a result that best serves each of their interests.

mini-trial A method of dispute resolution in which a judge or other individual conducts a proceeding similar to a trial but typically speedier. In a mini-trial, there is little if any emphasis on court procedure. The result is not binding as a matter of law.

ministerial function When a government, as an organization, fulfills obligations uniquely reserved to the government, then it is exercising ministerial authority.

misfeasance An act of misconduct that may form the basis of liability for negligence if it results in harm to another and fails to meet the reasonable person standard.

misrepresentation A class of torts in which a defendant provides inaccurate information upon which a plaintiff reasonably relies.

mistake A defense; usually applies to a fact and may be sufficient to negate intent.

misuse of legal procedure A class of torts that involves the intentional use of legal process or procedure to cause harm.

motion A request made by any of the parties to the judge to make a ruling on a particular issue of law related to the litigation.

motion for additur A request by the plaintiff that the court increase the amount of damages awarded by a jury.

motion for directed verdict A defendant's request that the court end the litigation. Such a motion is made after the plaintiff's counsel has presented all evidence and is made on the grounds that the plaintiff has failed to present enough evidence to win.

motion for judgment notwithstanding the verdict A request, made after the jury has reached a verdict, that the court set aside the verdict on the grounds that the jury lacked sufficient evidence to arrive at its verdict.

motion for judgment on the pleadings A request that the court grant a judgment on the grounds that, accepting all that the plaintiff alleges in the complaint as true, the court should issue a final ruling about the case.

motion for a new trial A request that the court restart the litigation on the grounds that some defect in the original trial rendered any verdict invalid as a matter of law.

motion for remittur A defendant's request that the court decrease the amount of damages awarded by a jury.

motion for a summary judgment A request that the court render a judgment, often before the trial begins. This motion is typically made on the grounds that, if all that the plaintiff alleges in the complaint and supporting documentation is true, under no circumstances could the plaintiff prevail at a trial as a matter of law.

motion *in limine* A request by a party to the litigation whether certain information should be accepted for use as evidence.

motion to compel discovery A pre-trial request that the court compel a party to respond to a request for discovery.

motion to dismiss A request, usually made by the defendant, that the court end the litigation. This motion is often made before the trial on the grounds that the plaintiff's claim suffers from so great a defect at law that under no circumstances could the plaintiff prevail at a trial.

natural conditions The state of land unaltered by human action.

necessity A defense in which a defendant acknowledges having caused harm but claims that doing so avoided an immediate threat that would have resulted in greater injury.

negligence An area of tort law in which someone who owed a duty of care to another and failed to uphold that duty and that failure caused injury to another.

negligence *per se* Violation of a statutorily created tort of negligence.

negligent infliction of emotional distress A defendant's failure to execute a duty of care to another and in breaching that duty, caused psychological harm.

negligent interference with prospective economic advantage A type of tortious obstruction of economic relations in which a defendant has breached a duty of care regarding a plaintiff's economic advantage.

negligent misrepresentation A tort in which a defendant breaches a duty to provide a plaintiff with accurate information, thus misleading the plaintiff and causing economic harm to the plaintiff.

nominal damages The court's award to a plaintiff that recognizes the plaintiff's symbolic loss rather than any actual loss or harm. As this is symbolic, the award is usually for one dollar.

non-delegable duty A duty, arising under contract or by law, that cannot be passed to another person to fulfill.

nuisance Substantial or unreasonable interference with another's use and enjoyment of property.

omission The failure to do something.

opening statement A declaration at the beginning of a trial by lawyers of both parties, describing what the court and jury will see as counsel presents evidence during the trial about why a particular party should prevail.

opinion (1.) What a person thinks or believes as a conclusion drawn from facts. (2.) Court's written ruling that explains the judgment for a party.

personal jurisdiction The authority of a court, government, or agency over an individual, for purposes of resolving a dispute involving that person or organization.

personal property Any possession that is not land.

plaintiff The party that starts a lawsuit by filing a complaint.

precedent Prior court decisions. Relating to the principle of *stare decisis*, as a matter of the common law, the courts must rule consistent with prior judicial rulings so as to reinforce a sense of consistency and stability.

premises All attached buildings, grounds, facilities, structures, all other things, such as crops, attached to the land.

premises liability Liability that may arise for a landholder regarding the use of real property.

preponderance of the evidence The amount of evidence a plaintiff must present to win at a civil trial.

presumption An assumption at law made in all litigation, which can be disproved on a case-by-case basis.

pre-trial conference A meeting held with the parties and the court to address issues related to the case. A pre-trial conference may provide an opportunity for the parties to settle the dispute before it goes to trial.

prima facie **case** A situation in which the plaintiff has shown, by a preponderance of the evidence, that the defendant committed the tort.

primary authority A statement of law that must be obeyed within a particular jurisdiction; typically, embodied in a statute or the common law.

principal–agent relationship A principal authorizes an agent to act on behalf of the principal so that the principal becomes liable for torts committed by the agent when exercising the principal's grant of authority.

private necessity A defense that involves a violation of tort law to avoid a greater harm to a specific individual or property.

private nuisance Interference with an landholder's interest in the use and enjoyment of that landholder's land.

private trial A method of dispute resolution in which the parties go through the trial process although the result is not binding as it would be for a court-based trial.

privilege (1.) A defense; arises on a case-by-case basis, where holding the defendant liable would work contrary to social policy. (2.) In the discovery process, grounds for not complying with a request for discovery; for example, because the law wants to protect the confidential nature of communications between a physician and a patient regarding the nature of the patient's injuries.

privity of contract A principle stating that a buyer of a product, and only that buyer, can sue a seller if the product was defective in some way.

production of documents A type of discovery; involves seeking any documents related to the underlying legal dispute.

proportionality of force A privilege to use force against an alleged assailant that must not exceed the force applied against the defendant.

proximate An act or omission that is closely related in space, time, or logical order.

proximate cause An element of the tort of negligence; the link between the defendant's breach of a duty of care and the plaintiff's injury.

public invitees Individuals who are lawfully allowed to enter property to conduct business unrelated to a landholder's business.

public necessity A defense that involves a violation of tort law to avoid a greater harm to a broader public interest.

public nuisance Interference with the use and enjoyment all have in (usually public) land.

publication Communication of a defamatory statement to a third person.

punitive damages A monetary award intended to discourage a civil defendant and others from engaging in future tortious conduct; sometimes called *exemplary damages*.

questions of fact Issues that the factfinder (a judge or jury) must resolve to determine liability.

reasonable force standard In the exercise of the privilege to use force in self-defense or defense of another, it is the amount of force needed to end an unlawful intereference.

recapture of chattels The right of an individual to reclaim possession of personal property.

remand An order by an appellate court, returning the case to the trial court with instructions on how to avoid the mistake that was the basis for the appellate court's reversal of the trial court's judgment regarding a claim.

request for admission A type of discovery that involves submitting written questions to an opponent, that the opponent must admit or reject as true, where possible.

res ipsa loquitur A legal doctrine that permits an inference of negligence only when the instrumentality that caused the injury is under the defendant's control, and when in the ordinary course of things the injury would not have occurred had the defendant used proper care. Under *res ipsa loquitur*, it is implied that the injury arose from the defendant's lack of care.

respondeat superior Latin phrase, relating to vicarious liability. For example, a principal may be liable for the torts of an agent who commited those torts when exercising the principal's grant of authority.

Restatement (Second) of Torts **§402A** The second edition of a book that contains the views of scholars and others in the law as to the ideal statement of tort law. §402A sets forth the general rules of liability, followed in virtually every state today, for determining whether the product was unreasonably dangerous.

restatements Published by the American Legal Institute, books that constitute the thinking in a particular area of the law. For example, the *Restatement (Second) of Torts* contains the generally accepted views on tort law; however, the *Restatement (Third) of Torts* offers a different view on issues such as product liability.

reverse A ruling by an appellate court that the trial court made an incorrect conclusion on an issue or the judgment.

rules of evidence Rules used in every jurisdiction to determine whether information is relevant and material to the underlying issue of law.

rules of procedure Rules that courts follow when conducting litigation; these apply to all disputes, regardless of the issue in dispute.

sanctions Penalties assessed by a court, such as when a party has failed to comply with a request for discovery. It could be an award of damages or even granting judgment for the party making the request for discovery

scope of employment In vicarious liability, the parameters of a work situation within which torts can be said to be committed by an agent on behalf of a principal.

secondary authority Statements about the law that a court does not have to obey; they may present an explanation, analysis, or criticism of the law or may be court rulings from other jurisdictions, which might set forth a rule that a court wants to consider for adoption.

service of process Steps that must be taken to notify a defendant about the initiation of litigation; a neutral third party delivers a copy of the complaint, and a summons, to the defendant.

site visit A type of discovery; involves inspecting a location relevant to the lawsuit.

slander An oral defamatory statement communicated to a third person. To recover for an action for slander, plaintiff must have suffered actual damages.

slander *per se* Exceptions to a requirement that the plaintiff show actual damages caused by slander. For example, slandering someone by calling them a criminal does not require a showing of actual damages for a plaintiff to recover in tort for the slander.

social guests Individuals who have been invited as licensees onto the premises of another; not considered invitees.

sovereign immunity The doctrine that exempts from liability any government entity and those who work for it or act on its behalf.

special verdict A statement or statements returned by the jury, regarding whether a plaintiff has successfully presented evidence to establish an aspect or aspects of the underlying claim.

stare decisis A judicial rule requiring courts, where feasible, to resolve a legal dispute consistent with courts' earlier rulings. Although courts are expected to follow *stare decisis*, they do not always do so.

statute A law created by a legislature.

statute of limitations A defense, arising by statutes, that limits the amount of time a plaintiff has in which to file suit.

strict liability An area of tort law, in which a party faces civil liability for just engaging in certain behavior, such as creating a dam that could breach and flood the surrounding area, or using certain dangerous items such as dynamite.

subject matter jurisdiction The authority of a court over a specific type of legal problem. For example, a housing court would deal primarily with landlord/tenant disputes.

substantial In the context of the tort of nuisance, the requirement that a plaintiff's injuries must be more than trivial.

substantial factor rule The requirement that, for proximate cause to exist, a defendant's conduct must have been significant in bringing about the plaintiff's injury.

summons A legal document that informs the recipient of the need to do something, as a matter of law; for example, when served to the defendant along with the complaint, the summons describes how much time exists to file an answer, and where to do that.

survival statutes Laws that allow for a negligence action to continue to exist after the death of either party to the case.

tolling A delay in measuring time, for determining whether a statute of limitations has elapsed.

tort A civil wrong; an injury to a person, business, or government that serves as a basis for recovery for damages in a court of law.

tortfeasor One who causes an injury to another person sufficient to form the basis of recovery in a civil lawsuit.

tortious conduct Behavior that causes harm sufficient to form the basis of a lawsuit that seeks recovery of damages.

treatise A book that examines, in great depth, a specific area of law. For example, the *Restatement (Second) of Tort* is a treatise on tort law.

trespass A tort; an intentional interference with another's possessory or ownership interest in real or personal property.

trespass on the case Historically in tort law, any kind of civil violation against an individual; no longer the way of describing a tort.

trespass to chattels Any intentional interference with another's possessory or ownership interest in personal property.

trespass to land A tort; the intentional interference of another's possessory or ownership interest in real property.

trespass to regain chattels The lawful trespass of an owner or possessor of property onto the property of a wrongdoer to regain the owner's or possessor's possession.

trespasser One who enters the land of another without permission, privilege, or consent.

unavoidable accident A legal doctrine pertaining to an accident that was not proximately caused by the act or omission of the defendant.

unforeseeability The absence of reasonable anticipation that harm will occur from an act or omission.

Uniform Commercial Code (U.C.C.) Standard business laws, adopted by every state, that facilitate selling goods throughout the country.

unreasonable In the context of the tort of nuisance, interference that goes beyond what many people consider appropriate for the use and enjoyment of property.

"unreasonably dangerous" In the context of *Restatement (Second) of Torts* §402A, the standard of liability that asks, did the defendant expose the plaintiff to a defective product that carried an unreasonable risk of harm?

use and enjoyment In the context of the tort of nuisance, the physical condition, convenience or comfort enjoyed by a possessor or owner of property.

use of force A privilege, force used to defend oneself, another person, or property in response to a threat; must be proportional to the force arising from the threat.

vendee The buyer.

vendor The seller.

venue The location of the courthouse. In criminal proceedings, counsel for the defendant may ask for a *change of venue* to a different court to minimize the risk that pre-trial publicity may jeopardize the defendant's opportunity to get an unbiased jury.

vicarious liability Holding someone liable for the actions of another. Typically, an issue where an agent, exercising a principal's grant of authority, has engaged in tortious conduct, potentially making the principal liable for damages.

voir dire During trial, the process of questioning a prospective group of jurors to determine whether they are free from bias and/or prejudice when evaluating evidence presented at trial.

warrantless arrest An arrest made without first obtaining legal permission, in a warrant, to make such an arrest.

warranty Usually offered by a manufacturer and/or seller of goods; a promise regarding the quality of some aspect of the product, and that buyer reasonably can rely upon the truthfulness of that statement.

willful, wanton, and reckless conduct Terms often used interchangeably to describe a form of highly unreasonable behavior that goes far beyond ordinary negligence.

"work product" doctrine A policy that applies to a request for discovery, which exempts from disclosure any of the strategies, in any form, that counsel has considered on behalf of the client's legal position.

writs Formal legal documents; would indicate a request for some legal action; has fallen out of use in many jurisdictions.

wrongful civil proceedings A type of tort involving the misuse of the legal process; provides a remedy for malicious civil claims.

wrongful death statutes Laws that allow for the right of recovery from a deceased plaintiff, to the benefit of the plaintiff's heirs.

wrongful discharge A tort that involves an employer's termination of an employee in violation of certain laws designed to advance a social policy.

APPENDIX 1

TABLE OF CASES CITED

Abrams Centre National Bank v. Farmer, Fuqua & Huff, P.C., 225 S.W.3d 171 (Tex. App. El Paso 2005).

Adkins v. Thomas Solvent Company, 440 Mich. 293 (1992).

Alves v. Hometown Newspapers, Inc., 857 A.2d 743 (R.I. 2004).

Ambriz v. Kress, 148 Cal. App. 3d 963 (Cal. App. 2d Dist. 1983).

Anesthesiology Critical Care & Pain Management Consultants, P.A. v. Kretzer, 802 So. 2d 346 (Fla. Dist. Ct. App. 4th Dist. 2001).

Arbegast v. Board of Education, 65 N.Y.2d 161 (1985).

Armstrong v. Sundance Entertainment, Inc., 179 Ga. App. 635 (1986).

B & W Management, Inc. v. Tasea Investment Co., 451 A.2d 879 (D.C. 1982).

Baird v. Sickler, 69 Ohio St. 2d 652 (1982).

Baldwin v. McClendon, 292 Ala. 43 (1974).

Barnhizer v. Paradise Valley Unified School District, 123 Ariz. 253 (1979).

Barton-Barnes Inc. v. State of New York, 180 A.D.2d 4 (3d Dep't 1992).

Bazley v. Tortorich, 397 So. 2d 475 (La. 1981).

Bed, Bath & Beyond, Inc. v. Urista, 211 S.W.3d 753 (Tex. 2006).

Bogle v. Duke Power Company, 27 N.C. App. 318 (1975)

Bower v. Corbell, 408 P.2d 307 (Okla. 1965).

Bradley v. American Smelting and Refining Company, 104 Wn.2d 677 (1985).

Broad-Bussel Family LP v. Bayou Group LLC (In re Bayou Hedge Funds Inv. Litig.), 472 F. Supp. 2d 528 (S.D.N.Y. 2007)

Brown v. Glade and Grove Supply, Inc., 647 So.2d 1033 (Fla. Dist. Ct. App. 4th Dist. 1994).

Brown v. Piggly-Wiggly, 454 So.2d 1370 (Ala. 1984).

Burrow v. K-Mart Corporation, 166 Ga. App. 284 (1983).

Cacciola v. Nellhaus, 49 Mass. App. Ct. 746 (2000).

Carniol v. Carniol, 288 A.D.2d 421 (N.Y. App. Div. 2d Dep't 2001).

Castro v. NYT TV, 370 N.J. Super. 282 (App. Div. 2004).

Cowin v. Huntington Hospital, 130 Misc. 2d 267 (Sup. Ct. 1985)

Creasy v. Rusk, 730 N.E.2d 659 (Ind. 2000).

Cunningham v. Quintanilla, 2004 Tex. App. 1077 (Tex. App. Tyler Feb. 4, 2004).

Dalehite v. United States, 346 U.S. 15 (1953).

Davis v. Wood, 61 Cal. App. 2d 788 (1943).

Dessauer v. Memorial General Hospital, 96 N.M. 92 (N.M. Ct. App. 1981).

Doe v. Cahill, 884 A.2d 451 (Del. 2005).

Doe v. Maskell, 342 Md. 684 (1996).

Ellis v. N.G.N. of Tampa, Inc., 586 So.2d 1042 (Fla. 1991)

Estate of Gordon-Couture v. Brown, 152 N.H. 265 (2005).

Evans v. General Explosives Company, 293 Mo. 364 (1922).

Farmers and Mechanics Mutual Insurance Company of West Virginia v. Cook, 210 W. Va. 394 (2001).

Fisher v. Carrousel Motor Hotel, Inc., 11 Tex. Sup. J. 143 (Tex. 1967).

Fisherman's Paradise, Inc. v. Greenfield, 417 So.2d 306 (Fla. Dist. Ct. App. 3d Dist. 1982)

Fraser v. County of Maui, 855 F. Supp. 1167 (D. Haw. 1994).

Freeman v. Busch Jewelry Co., Inc., 98 F. Supp. 963 (D. Ga. 1951).

Galliher v. Holloway, 130 Ill. App. 3d 628 (5th Dist. 1985).

Garreans v. City of Omaha, 216 Neb. 487 (1984).

Goines v. James, 189 W. Va. 634 (1993).

Goodson v. American Standard Insurance Company of Wisconsin, 89 P.3d 409 (Colo. 2004).

Gorman v. McMahon, 792 So. 2d 307 (Miss. Ct. App. 2001).

Gortarez v. Smitty's Super Valu, Inc., 140 Ariz. 97 (1984).

Greenman v. Yuba Power Products, Inc., 59 Cal. 2d 57 (1963).

Greenwald v. Hooe, 2006 Mich. App. 3651 (Mich. Ct. App. Dec. 19, 2006).

Greer v. Del Mar Fairgrounds, 1999 U.S. Dist. 12429 (E.D. Mich. July 31, 1999).

Griswold v. Hollywod Turf Club, 106 Cal. App. 2d 578 (1951).

Hake v. George Wiedemann Brewing Co., 23 Ohio St.2d 65 (1970).

Halliday v. Sturm, Ruger & Company, Inc., 368 Md. 186 (2002).

Hampshire v. Ford Motor Company, 155 Mich. App. 143 (1986).

Hickman v. Taylor, 329 U.S. 495 (1947).

Hildreth v. Rogers, 2006 Ohio 5151 (Ohio Ct. App., Hardin County Oct. 2, 2006)

Hohlenkamp v. Rheem Manufacturing Company, 134 Ariz. 208 (Ct. App. 1982).

Humphrey v. Diamant Boart, 556 F. Supp. 2d 167 (E.D.N.Y. 2008)

Hundt v. LaCrosse Grain Co., 425 N.E.2d 687 (Ind. Ct. App. 1981).

Hundt v. LaCrosse Grain Co., 446 N.E.2d 327 (Ind. 1983).

In the matter of Sloan, 84 Misc. 2d 306 (1975).

Intel Corp. v. Hamidi, 30 Cal. 4th 1342 (2003).

Jackson v. Ryder Truck Rental, Inc., 16 Cal. App. 4th 1830 (3d Dist. 1993).

Jagger v. Mohawk Mountain Ski Area, Inc., 269 Conn. 672 (2004).

Jakubiec v. Hasty, 337 Mich. 205(1953).

Johnson v. Colt Industries Operating Corporation, 797 F.2d 1530 (10 Cir. Kan.1986).

Jolley v. Powell, 299 So.2d 647 (Fla. Dist. Ct. App. 2d Dist. 1974).

Karangelen v. Snyder, 40 Md. App. 393 (1978).

Katko v. Briney, 183 N.W.2d 657 (Iowa 1971).

King v. Blue Mountain Forest Association, 100 N.H. 212 (1956).

Knoetig v. Hernandez Realty Co., Inc., 255 N.J. Super. 34 (App. Div. 1992).

LaFrentz v. Gallagher, 105 Ariz. 255 (1969).

Larsen v. Vic Tanny International, 130 Ill. App. 3d 574 (1984).

Letellier v. Small, 400 A.2d 371 (Me. 1979).

Leverton v. Curtis Pub. Co., 192 F.2d 974 (3d Cir. Pa. 1951).

Ly v. State of Louisiana, 633 So. 2d 197 (La.App. 1 Cir. 1993).

MacPherson v. Buick Motor Company, 217 N.Y. 382 (1916).

Madrid v. Fifth Judicial District Court, 312 Mont. 517 (2002).

Maloney v. Washington, 690 F. Supp. 687 (N.D. Ill. 1988).

Marbury v. Madison, 5 U.S. (1 Cranch) 137 (1803).

Marcus v. Liebman, 59 Ill. App. 3d 337 (1st Dist. 1978).

Marcuso v. University of Cincinnati, 150 Ohio App. 3d 69 (Franklin County 2002).

Martin v. Union Pacific Railroad Company, 256 Ore. 563 (1970).

Massey v. Scripter, 401 Mich. 385 (1977).

Matkovich v. Penn Central, 69 Ohio St.2d 210 (1982).

Mazetti v. Armour & Co., 75 Wash. 622 (1913).

McGarr v. United States, 736 F.2d 912 (3d Cir. Pa. 1984).

McGee v. Feege, Hayes & Feege, P.C., 517 Pa. 247 (1987).

McKean v. Alliance Land Company, 200 Cal. 396 (1927).

McLean v. Colf, 179 Cal. 237 (1918).

Meier v. Ma-Do Bars, Inc., 106 A.D.2d 143 (N.Y. App. Div. 3d Dep't 1985) 484.

Merriweather v. E. W. Bliss Company, 636 F.2d 42(3rd Cir. Pa. 1980).

Micari v. Mann, 481 126 Misc. 2d 422 (Sup. Ct. 1984)

Minch v. Department of the California Highway Patrol, 140 Cal. App. 4th 895 (2006).

Morris v. Platt, 32 Conn. 75 (1864).

Mueller v. Brunn, 105 Wis.2d 171 (1982).

National Front Page, LLC v. State ex rel. Pryor, 350 Ark. 286 (2002).

Newsome v. Brown, 2005 U.S. Dist. 4088 (S.D.N.Y. 2005).

North American Chemical Company v. The Superior Court of Los Angeles County, 59 Cal. App. 4th 764 (2d Dist. 1997).

Nzongda v. The United States, 77 Fed. Cl. 64 (2007).

Ouellette v. Blanchard, 116 N.H. 552 (1976).

Padilla v. Lawrence, 101 N.M. 556 (Ct. App. 1984)

Paducah Coca-Cola Bottling Company v. Harris, 316 S.W.2d 128 (Ky. 1958).

Page County Appliance Center, Inc. v. Honeywell, Inc., 347 N.W.2d 171 (Iowa 1984).

Palsgraf v. Long Island R. Co., 248 N.Y. 339 (1928).

Parrott v. United States of America, 181 F. Supp. 425 (S.D. Cal. 1960).

Patel v. Soriano and Irvington General Hospital, 369 N.J. Super. 192 (App.Div. 2004).

Penn Harris Madison School Corporation v. Howard, 861 N.E.2d 1190 (Ind. 2007).

Poplar v. Bourjois, Inc., 272 A.D. 74 (N.Y. App. Div. 1947).

Portman v. Clementina Company, 147 Cal. App. 2d 651 (Cal. App. 1st Dist. 1957).

Preston v. Goldman, 42 Cal.3d 108 (1986).

Protectus Alpha Navigation Co. v. North Pacific Grain Growers, Inc., 585 F. Supp. 1062 (D. Or. 1984).

Reed v. Dekalb County, 264 Ga. App. 83 (2003).

Reed v. House of Decor, Inc., 468 So.2d 1159 (La.1985)

Joseph Resnick Co., Inc. v. Nippon Yusen Kaisha, 39 Misc. 2d 513 (N.Y. Civ. Ct. 1963).

Richter v. Limax International, Inc., 45 F.3d 1464 (10th Cir. Kan. 1995).

Roberie v. VonBokern, 2006 Ky. 186 (Ky. Aug. 24, 2006).

Roberson v. Kunzli, Gott, LLC, 2006 Conn. Super. 377 (Conn. Super. Ct. Feb. 9, 2006)

Rodrigue v. Copeland, 475 So.2d 1071 (La. 1985).

Ross v. Allstate Insurance Co., 40 Va. Cir. 537 (1996).

Ross v. Consumers Power Company, 420 Mich. 567 (1985).

Rylands v. Fletcher, L.R. 3 H.L. 330 (1868).

Scheuerman v. Scharfenberg, 163 Ala. 337 (1909).

Scofield v. Critical Air Medicine, Inc., 45 Cal. App. 4th 990 (Cal. App. 2d Dist. 1996).

Silva v. Melville, 12 Mass. L. Rep. 611(Super. Ct. 2001).

Strunk v. Zoltanski, 479 N.Y.S.2d 175 (1984).

T.B. Proprietary Corp. v. Sposato Builders, Inc., 1996 U.S. Dist. 17335 (E.D. Pa. 1996)

Thompson v. United States Department of Housing and Urban Development, 219 F.R.D. 93 (D. Md. 2003).

Triano v. Fitzpatrick, 2000 Conn. Super. 508 (Conn. Super. Ct. Feb. 17, 2000).

United Educational Distributors, LLC v. Educational Testing Service, 350 S.C. 7 (Ct. App. 2002).

United States v. Shearer, 473 U.S. 52 (1985).

Vento v. Strongsville Bd. of Edn., 2007 Ohio 4172 (Ohio Ct. App., Cuyahoga County 2007).

Walker v. Brown, 501 So. 2d 358 (Miss. 1987).

Waller v. First Savings & Trust Co., 103 Fla. 1025 (1931).

Weast v. Budd, 186 Kan. 249 (1960).

Webb v. Jewel Companies, Inc., 137 Ill. App. 3d 1004 (1st Dist. 1985).

Westerman v. Oregon Automobile Credit Corporation, 168 Ore. 216 (1942).

Williams v. White Mountain Construction Company, Inc., 749 P.2d 423 (Colo. 1988).

Wilton v. City of Spokane, 73 Wash. 619 (1913).

Wood v. Fineberg Management, Inc., 24 Mass. L. Rep. 140 (Mass. Super. Ct. 2008).

Young v. Darter, 363 P.2d 829 (Okla. 1961).

APPENDIX 2

TABLE OF RESTATEMENT CITATIONS

Restatement (Third), Agency §7.03, §7.07

Restatement (Second), Contracts §1

Restatement (Second), Torts: §8A, §21, §35, §36, §46, §63, §65, §106, §119, §147, §150, §222A, §282, §282, comment d, §283, 283B, §289, §329, §332, §333, §334, §339, §343, §353, §388, §395, §402A, §410, §431, §433 B, §435, §440, §463, §479, §480, §491, §500, §504, §506, Reporter's Comment, §507, §515, §519, §523, §524, §549, §552, §558, §568, §652A, §766C, §821A, §821B, §821F, §830, comment c, §870, §892C, §895B, §895C, §895D

The table of contents for the *Restatement (Third) Torts: Product Liability*

INDEX